THE INFORMED CITIZEN

Argument and Analysis

THE INFORMED CITIZEN

Argument and Analysis

Wanda Schindley

Northeast Texas Community College

Harcourt Brace College Publishers

Fort Worth Philadelphia San Diego New York Orlando Austin San Antonio

Toronto Montreal London Sydney Tokyo

Publisher	Christopher P. Klein
Acquisitions Editor	John Meyers
Developmental Editor	Sarah Helyar Smith
Project Editor	Pam Hatley
Production Manager	Serena Barnett Manning
Art Director	Gary Harman
Photo Researcher	Susan Holtz
Permissions	Aimé Merizon

Cover image: "March on Washington" from the Ollie Atkins Photographic Collection, Special Collections and Archives, George Mason University, Fairfax, Virginia.

Harcourt Brace may provide complimentary instructional aids and supplements or supplement packages to those adopters qualified under our adoption policy. Please contact your sales representative for more information. If as an adopter or potential user you receive supplements you do not need, please return them to your sales representative or send them to: Attn: Returns Department, Troy Warehouse, 465 South Lincoln Drive, Troy, MO 63379.

Requests for permission to make copies of any part of the work should be mailed to: Permissions Department, Harcourt Brace & Company, 6277 Sea Harbor Drive, Orlando, Florida 32887-6777.

Address for Editorial Correspondence: Harcourt Brace College Publishers, 301 Commerce Street, Suite 3700, Fort Worth, TX 76102.

Address for Orders: Harcourt Brace & Company, 6277 Sea Harbor Drive, Orlando, FL 32887-6777. 1-800-782-4479, or 1-800-433-0001 (in Florida).

Printed in the United States of America

ISBN: 0-15-503785-4

Library of Congress Catalog Card Number: 96-77232

8 9 0 1 2 3 4 5   016   9 8 7 6 5 4 3

PREFACE

When my search for a text that would engage, inspire, enlighten, and incite the passions of today's students failed, I began building my own course. The response from students of all ages was electrifying; the rewards were the "ah-ha's" of discovery, the passion in discussion, the demonstrated growth in skills, and the obvious maturing of thinking processes and perspectives. This argument rhetoric and reader is the product of that course.

The Informed Citizen is about interacting in communities that reach from the classroom to cyberspace to explore today's issues and develop informed opinions, effective arguments, and polished writing. The text is founded on classical rhetoric, the schema that seems most accessible to students. Fundamental, also, are the ideas that English class does not have to be dull; that everyone has something to say; that argument permeates discourse; that building skills is not only important but also exciting; and that thinking is the most important tool for writing, relating, living, and contributing.

FEATURES

The text has ten parts. Each of the ten parts contains numerous readings based on a central theme, with exercises and stylistic activities specific to that theme, and concludes with a detailed writing challenge and model student paper. The seventy practice activities, which encourage students to synthesize ideas and evaluate concepts, can be explored as a class, in small groups, or as prompts for out-of-class writing. The thirty power of style features help students explore stylistic options or examine stylistic elements in others' writings. The text is rich with resources, topics, and activities for instructors to choose from, expanding or limiting the focus of any of the parts. The writing and discussion questions, practice activities, and writing challenges provide more than one hundred opportunities to write arguments.

ORGANIZATION

Part One gives students an opportunity to explore self as related to *ethos* in writing, the development of skill, credibility, and style. Underlying is the idea that self-esteem comes through pride in a job well done—growing, honing skills, and communicating effectively. Part Two focuses on developing the necessary understanding of audience, of those who share personal circles and of those who are separated by beliefs, experience, or borders but who still share those qualities that make us all human. The writing challenges in Parts One and Two require introspection (telling how an opinion evolved) and empathy (exploring the why of diverse views). Part Three addresses *logos*, asking students to create arguments and address opposing views.

The remaining parts incorporate the elements of persuasion introduced in Part One through Part Three. Part Four shows how to detect and avoid informal fallacies and familiarizes students with common propaganda devices. Part Five and Part Six ask students to substantiate their own evaluations of articles, advertisements, and political discourse, with Part Five addressing the influence of the media and advertising in shaping opinions and Part Six demonstrating how language is used in politics and courtrooms to sway opinion. Part Seven asks readers to analyze the visceral power of music, literature, and art and Part Eight asks students to create arguments using the power of satire. Part Nine includes both substantiation and evaluation in proposals by engaging students in problem-solving activities on reforming education, allocating medical resources, creating the federal budget, and reforming welfare; and Part Ten asks students to use outside sources to substantiate an argument.

My appreciation goes to students, who have shared their perspectives and journeys of discovery. My gratitude goes to Richard Fulkerson at Texas A&M, Commerce, from whom I have learned a wealth of schemas, strategies, and activities. Thanks also to Edith Wynne for sharing activities and, for sharing their knowledge and inspiration, to Richard Tuerk and JoAnn Cocklereas, also at Texas A&M, Commerce.

For critiques and support, I thank the following colleagues at Northeast Texas Community College and elsewhere: Patricia Archer, Don Ownsby, Chris Williams, Jim Swann, Lisa LeMole, and Charlene Rodgers.

I thank Michael Rosenberg at Harcourt Brace for recognizing the promise in *The Informed Citizen* and John Meyers for being an enlightened and enthusiastic editor. Finally, I thank my husband Ken for his loving support and personal sacrifices for this project and the late Diane Dodson Hudson who inspired colleagues and students alike (in the words of novelist Tom Robbins) "to enlarge the soul, liberate the spirit, and light up the brain."

Brief Table of Contents

DETAILED TABLE OF CONTENTS

PART THREE
Creating Arguments   103

Chapter 9 WRITING CHALLENGE   161

PART FOUR

Lies, Damned Lies, and Statistics: Detecting and Avoiding Informal Fallacies   176

Chapter 10 ARGUMENTS AWRY   177

You as Writer: Identity and *Ethos*

Everyday People
Sly Stone [Sylvester Stewart]

Sometimes I'm right, but I can be wrong.
My own beliefs are in my song.
A preacher, a banker, a drummer and then—
Makes no difference what group I'm in.
5 I am everyday people.
There is a blue one who can't accept the green one
For living with the fat one, trying to be a skinny one.
Different strokes for different folks,
And so on and so on.
10 We got to live together.
I am no better, and neither are you.
We are the same whatever we do.
You love me; you hate me; you know me and then—
You can't figure out the bag I'm in.
15 I am everyday people.
There is a long hair that doesn't like the short hair
For being such a rich one that will not help the poor one.
Different strokes for different folks.
And so on and so on.
20 We got to live together.
There is a yellow one that won't accept the black one

That won't accept the rich one that won't accept the white
one.
Different strokes for different folks,
25 And so on and so on.
I am everyday people.

For Writing and Discussion

1.   *In my opinion the most significant lyrics ever written were in the song*
"Everyday People." They address such "revolutionary" concepts as equal-
ity, tolerance and the necessity of people working for the common good
of mankind. . . . In light of the hatred that is resurfacing in the United
States, Sly's message is more important now than it was in 1969.

John Walker in a letter to *Rolling Stone* magazine

The song argues that the healing power of music even encompasses
curing rifts among races and classes.

Dave Marsh, *The Heart of Rock and Soul*

Do you agree with Walker and Marsh that music can have the power
to persuade, to heal, to make a difference? Why or why not? What are other
socially conscious songs? What is the message in each? In what way might
the messages make a difference in individual lives? Think of a specific
example of how music brings people together by identifying a song that has
special meaning for many people. Explain the song's significance.

2. The expression "different strokes for different folks" has become a part
of the American vernacular, or everyday language. People who have never
heard the song may use the expression. What thoughts or feelings might
people be expressing when they use the phrase?

3. "Everyday" people are divided by differences in race, gender, age, occupation, environment, and experience. Despite these differences, what do
people have in common? What qualities are fundamental to human existence?

You, the Writer

Part One focuses on you, the writer, and on individual differences, experiences,
and skills that work together to create *ethos*. The readings in Chapter 1 deal first
with gender differences in a cartoon (a picture worth a thousand words), a
poem, and an essay. In the second pair of readings, writers discuss racial experience in a poem and an essay.

In Chapter 2, a poem, two essays, and a letter first relate the experience of life to identity, followed by two pieces by writers who go beyond
group affiliation and experience to focus on things we share as humans. As

you read each piece, think about the aspects of being and the experiences that are reflected in the writings.

The Writing Challenge in Chapter 3 offers two assignments. The first assignment asks you to take a close look at yourself as you write in a journal: Who are you? What are your many roles, values, beliefs, goals? How did you become who you are? Journal writing is an effective way to develop fluency (the ability to move thoughts freely from brain to paper), and to explore ideas privately before you make them public in your papers. You will probably want to continue writing in a journal, intermittently at least, throughout your life.

The second assignment asks you to say something to others—to explain why you hold an opinion, what people and experiences influenced that belief, and what the opinion reflects about you. As you work through the Guide to Writing, you will take an inward look that will help you present a knowledgeable and confident *ethos* as you write.

R E M I N D E R

Good writers read good writing. Just as you learn your dialect and speech patterns through listening to and assimilating the language of others, when you read good writing, your brain assimilates structures and concepts that become a part of your thinking and your ability to write well.

Chapter 1

IDENTITY

CREDIBILITY AND STYLE

YOU →

Share with others

↓

- Rights •Duties •Goals •Skills
- Values •Talents •Preferences
- Style •Experiences •Dreams
- Choices •Priorities •Beliefs
- Knowledge •Heritage •Morals
- Hobbies •Education

HUMAN CHARACTERISTICS
Ability to communicate, to reason, feel emotions, have beliefs

GROUP AFFILIATIONS
Gender, racial, ethnic, political, communal, national

ENVIRONMENTS
Families, neighborhoods, communities, cities, states

If you are now asking yourself, "What does who I am have to do with 'everyday people' and argument and analysis?" you are on the way to mastering this course. You are thinking, reasoning. You have considered Stone's lyrics (page 1) that suggest both individuality and community—individuals interacting with others who are similar in some ways but who have their own beliefs, experiences, preferences, goals, and so forth. You have probably also looked at some of the words listed under the word *you* and reflected on how they apply to you—how your experiences contribute to your identity, for instance. And now, you are trying to pull this together and make some sense of it.

Your next question may be, "What does *ethos* mean, anyway?" We could use other words instead. We could say "the character (characteristics, attitudes, and so on) a writer (sender of messages) presents to an audience that makes the audience want to believe the writer when the character presented shows the writer to be *credible*." But now that you know the meaning, you will probably agree that using the word *ethos* is more economical.

Developing a Credible *Ethos*

A credible *ethos* is one of the fundamental elements of persuasion. Writers who demonstrate to their readers that they are trustworthy have a chance of fulfilling their purpose for writing, whether the purpose is to persuade readers to believe something, to take some kind of action, or to consider seriously an idea.

In some areas, you may be known by your actions. You may have been told at some point in your life, "Words are cheap. Let's see what you can *do*." When writing, however, words are not cheap. Words are the vehicle through which a reader *knows* a writer. The writer exposes the self through words, and the reader has only words from which to form an opinion about a writer's credibility.

WHAT MAKES A WRITER CREDIBLE?

A credible writer is believed by the audience to be trustworthy. Since our "truths," or opinions, are shaped and limited by our own knowledge, experiences, and interpretations, writers are challenged to broaden their perspectives—to examine opinions, to seek out new information, to become credible authorities and critics. To maintain credibility with readers, writers must interpret and present information from other sources accurately. A credible writer understands and respects readers and does not attempt to deceive, manipulate, belittle, or patronize them. A credible writer understands the power of the pen and uses it wisely.

The pen is mightier than the sword.

Common thought at least as far back as Shakespeare's time

A credible writer knows and uses the conventions of written language.   Would you trust the writer of the paragraph above? Did you first notice the nice transition or the mechanical errors and incoherency? How credible is the author? Would anyone take this argument seriously, regardless of any merit it might have? Even if the argument itself held together, the mechanical errors alone would make most readers ask, "If the writer does not care enough to correct mechanical errors, how can I trust the writer to give me accurate information?"

Aristotle noted that a credible *ethos* involved good sense, good moral character, and good will toward the audience. The table below contains some embellishment of those three qualities, characteristics that will be explored throughout this text:

CREDIBLE ETHOS

GOOD SENSE	GOOD MORAL CHARACTER	GOOD WILL
Is knowledgeable about the subject	Is honest (not a liar)	Is aware of and understanding of the audience's concerns and feelings
Knows how to reason well	Does not unfairly manipulate the audience's emotions	
Writes with a pleasing style	Understands duties to community	Is free of bias (or acknowledges and explains)
Knows and uses the conventions of Edited American English		Is free from special interests
		Gives audience credit— does not belabor the obvious, talk down to them, or tell them directly what to think or feel

A Matter of Style

Writing with a pleasing style is one of the ways you entice your reader to keep on reading. **Style** involves level of language, structure and rhythm of sentences, kinds of figurative language, tone, and point of view.

You can learn to manipulate words in sentences by practicing—by combining your own sentences and by imitating the sentence patterns of others. The style you develop, however, will be your own. Throughout the text you will be given opportunities to perfect your style of writing. Below are a few elements of style to begin examining in the writing of others and developing in your writing.

DICTION

> *The difference between the right word and the almost right word is the difference between lightning and the lightning bug.*

> Mark Twain in a letter dated October 15, 1888

Your choice of words when writing can make the difference between dull and mediocre or inspired and brilliant writing. Your choices include formal language, slang words, emotive words, inflammatory words, descriptive words, ten-dollar words, and vivid verbs. A dictionary or thesaurus will provide options, but synonyms can vary slightly in meaning and should be used with care. If you are writing a paper on euthanasia, for instance, and want another word for *die,* your options are limited. The word *lapse* is listed as a synonym for *die,* but when you try substituting the former for the latter, you will probably find that it doesn't work in this context.

> Because of society's refusal to address the problem of the prolonged death provided through medical technology, many people are denied the right to l̶a̶p̶s̶e̶. die

Still, you have made a choice of words in using the word *die* instead of a slang expression such as *kick the bucket* or *croak* or a euphemism such as *pass away.*

FIGURATIVE LANGUAGE

Your options go beyond choosing synonyms. You can use words figuratively (in a nonliteral or unusual sense). You can manipulate the words to achieve effective, masterful sentences. The possibilities include structures and orders and omissions with names such as *antimetabole* and *epanalepsis.* However, you don't have to identify them by name to use them in your writing, just as you don't have to identify *gerunds* or *infinitives* to use them in speech and in writing. This paragraph contains an example of *polysyndeton,* the use of conjunctions to separate each item in a series: "structures and orders and omissions" instead of the usual "structures, orders, and omissions." Activities throughout the text will provide opportunities to enrich your word choices.

TYPES OF SENTENCES

Sentences can be varied for their rhythm, emphasis, and order of ideas in addition to varying the simple, compound, and complex structures. Sentences can have their main subjects and verbs early on, or they may have either the subject or verb or both delayed.

> *But sometimes (like right now), as I sit in the cool, green-draped parlor, the grindstone begins to turn, and time with all its changes is ground away—and I remember Doodle.*

> James Hurst, "The Scarlet Ibis"

Hurst could simply have written, "Sometimes, I remember Doodle." Instead, he delayed the main clause in the sentence and used the metaphor of the grindstone and the setting of the parlor to create an image and an atmosphere of reflection.

TONE

Tone is a writer's attitude toward the subject as reflected in writing. It may be serious, humorous, even sarcastic at times, but it should be consistent. When writing in a serious tone, for instance, a humorous or sarcastic twist is likely to confuse the reader. The readings in this text provide examples of serious, humorous, and irreverent tones. Although most of your writing (because of the nature of academic writing) will require a serious tone, Chapter 24 provides an opportunity to write satire.

POINT OF VIEW

You probably remember the basic options in point of view from high school: first-person, third-person limited, and third-person omniscient. Writers usually are discouraged from using first-person pronouns in academic writing. However, the writer is always the *I* behind the page, whether or not first-person pronouns are used.

Point of view is one way a writer reduces the distance between writer and reader. Some writers even use second-person pronouns to speak directly to the reader.

Should your political opinions be at extreme variance with those of your parents, keep in mind that while it is indeed your constitutional right to express these sentiments verbally, it is unseemly to do so with your mouth full—particularly when it is full of the oppressor's standing rib roast.

Fran Lebowitz, "Tips for Teens" in *Social Studies*

Elements of style are some of the tools a writer uses to create pleasing, effective prose. After you read each selection in this chapter, reflect a moment on the writer's style. Was it pleasing? What elements of style were particularly effective and why?

"Maxine" Comix © Marian Henley. Reprinted by permission of the artist.

GENDER AND IDENTITY

Barbie doll
Marge Piercy

This girlchild was born as usual
and presented dolls that did pee-pee
and miniature GE stoves and irons
and wee lipsticks the color of cherry candy.
5 Then in the magic of puberty, a classmate said:
You have a great big nose and fat legs.
She was healthy, tested intelligent,

possessed strong arms and back,
abundant sexual drive and manual dexterity.
10 She went to and fro apologizing.
Everyone saw a fat nose on thick legs.

She was advised to play coy,
exhorted to come on hearty,
exercise, diet, smile and wheedle.
15 Her good nature wore out
like a fan belt.
So she cut off her nose and her legs
and offered them up.

In the casket displayed on satin she lay
20 with the undertaker's cosmetics painted on,
a turned-up putty nose,
dressed in a pink and white nightie.
Doesn't she look pretty? everyone said.
Consummation at last.
25 To every woman a happy ending.

THE POWER OF STYLE: POETRY

Which of the following most represents poetry?

(continued)

(continued from previous page)

If you chose 1, you are correct. The poet uses few words to say many things and chooses each word for its power. In "Barbie doll," Piercy tells the story of the life of a woman who is defined by others' expectations of physical appearance. But the woman represents not a single person but a gender, or at least all women who surrender self-identity and allow themselves to be defined by others who see only "a fat nose on thick legs" instead of a complex person.
Poets express the common experiences, values, beliefs—the character—of a culture. From the poetry of a time and place, we can understand the dreams, the fears, and the perceptions of a people.

A poem is the very image of life.

Percy Bysshe Shelley, *A Defence of Poetry*

Practice: Owning a Poem

When people quote lines from a poem, the lines have become theirs in a sense. They have brought their own understanding and experience to the lines and are using the lines to create meaning in a new context.

Poems are often so rich with meaning that they cannot be understood fully with a single reading. The following strategies for reading poetry will help you to own a poem, to develop your own understanding of meaning through the window of your own experience. Keep in mind the strategies as you reread "Barbie doll."

1.   Read a poem several times. You will probably find new meanings with each reading.

2.   Read through to a punctuation mark. Line endings may indicate thought groupings or form structures, but look for punctuation marks to end complete thoughts. You may want to paraphrase difficult passages.

3.   Listen for the sounds of poetry. Poets often choose words for their sounds as well as their meanings.

4.   Explore the meanings of figurative language, and try to visualize in your mind's eye the images created with figurative language. Words also have the power to elicit sensory reactions. For instance, seeing the word *lemon* and focusing on the meaning can cause salivation. Allow yourself to experience the poem.

(For more help with the study of poetry, see The Power of Style: Poetry and The Language of Poetry in Chapter 20.)

A Time for Men to Pull Together
Andrew Kimbrell

1   Men are hurting—badly. Despite rumors to the contrary, men as a gender are being devastated physically and psychically by our socioeconomic system. As American society continues to empower a small percentage of men—and a smaller but increasing percentage of women—it is causing significant confusion and anguish for the majority of men.

2   In recent years, there have been many impressive analyses documenting the exploitation of women in our culture. Unfortunately, little attention has been given to the massive disruption and destruction that our economic and political institutions have wrought on men. In fact, far too often, men as a gender have been thought of as synonymous with the power elite.

3   But thinking on this subject is beginning to change. Over the last decade, men have begun to realize that we cannot properly relate to one another, or understand how some of us in turn exploit others, until we have begun to appreciate the extent and nature of our dispossessed predicament. In a variety of ways, men across the country are beginning to mourn their losses and seek solutions.

4   This new sense of loss among men comes from the deterioration of men's traditional roles as protectors of family and the earth (although not the sole protectors)—what psychologist Robert Mannis calls the *generative* potential of men. And much of this mourning also focuses on how men's energy is often channeled in the direction of destruction—both of the earth and its inhabitants.

5   The mission of many men today—both those involved in the men's movement and others outside it—is to find new ways that allow men to celebrate the generative potential and reverse the cycle of destruction that characterizes men's collective behavior today. These calls to action are not abstract or hypothetical. The oppression of men, especially in the last several decades, can be easily seen in a disturbing upward spiral of male self-destruction, addiction, hopelessness, and homelessness.

6   While suicide rates for women have been stable over the last 20 years, among men—especially white male teenagers—they have increased rapidly. Currently, male teenagers are five times more likely to take their own lives than females. Overall, men are committing suicide at four times the rate of women.

America's young men are also being ravaged by alcohol and drug abuse. Men between the ages of 18 and 29 suffer alcohol dependency at three times the rate of women of the same age group. More than two-thirds of all alcoholics are men, and 50 percent more men are regular users of illicit drugs than women. Men account for more than 90 percent of arrests for alcohol and drug abuse violations.

7   A sense of hopelessness among America's young men is not surprising. Real wages for men under 25 have actually declined over the last 20 years, and 60 percent of all high school dropouts are males. These statistics, added to the fact that more than 400,000 farmers have lost their land in the last decade, account in part for the increasing rate of unemployment among men, and for the fact that more than 80 percent of America's homeless are men.

8   The stress on men is taking its toll. Men's life expectancy is 10 percent shorter than women's, and the incidence of stress-related illnesses such as heart disease and certain cancers remains inordinately high among men.

9   And the situation for minority men is even worse. One out of four black men between the ages of 20 and 29 is either in jail, on probation, or on parole—ten times the proportion for black women in the same age range. More black men are in jail than in college, and there are 40 percent more black women than black men studying in our nation's colleges and universities. Homicide is the leading cause of death among black males ages 15 to 24. Black males have the lowest life expectancy of any segment of the American population. Statistics for Native American and Hispanic men are also grim.

10   Men are also a large part of the growing crisis in the American family. Studies report that parents today spend 40 percent less time with their children than did parents in 1965, and men are increasingly isolated from their families by the pressures of work and the circumstances of divorce. In a recent poll, 72 percent of employed male respondents agreed that they are "torn by conflict" between their jobs and the desire to be with their families. Yet the average divorced American man spends less than two days a month with his children. Well over half of black male children are raised without fathers. While the trauma of separation and divorce affects all members of a family, it is especially poignant for sons: Researchers generally agree that boys at all ages are hardest hit by divorce.

THE ENCLOSURE OF MEN

11   The current crisis for men, which goes far beyond statistics, is nothing new. We have faced a legacy of loss, especially since the start of the mechanical age. From the Enclosure Acts, which forced families off the land in Tudor England, to the ongoing destruction of indigenous communities throughout the Third World, the demands of the industrial era have forced men off the land, out of the family and community, and into the factory and office. The male as steward of family and soil, craftsman, woodsman, native hunter, and fisherman has all but vanished.

12   As men became the primary cog in industrial production, they lost touch with the earth and the parts of themselves that needed the earth to

survive. Men by the millions—who long prided themselves on their husbandry of family, community, and land—were forced into a system whose ultimate goal was to turn one man against another in the competitive "jungle" of industrialized society. As the industrial revolution advanced, men lost not only their independence and dignity, but also the sense of personal creativity and responsibility associated with individual crafts and small-scale farming. . . .

13   The factory wrenched the father from the home, and he often became a virtual nonentity in the household. By separating a man's work from his family, industrial society caused the permanent alienation of father from son. Even when the modern father returns to the house, he is often too tired and too irritable from the tensions and tedium of work in the factory or corporation to pay close attention to his children. As Robert Bly, in his best-selling book *Iron John* (1990, Addison-Wesley), has pointed out, "When a father, absent during the day, returns home at six, his children receive only his temperament, and not his teaching." The family, and especially sons, lose the presence of the father, uncle, and other male role models. It is difficult to calculate the full impact that this pattern of paternal absence has had on family and society over the last several generations.

14   While the loss of fathers is now beginning to be discussed, men have yet to fully come to terms with the terrible loss of sons during the mechanized wars of this century. World War I, World War II, Korea, and Vietnam were what the poet Robert Graves called "holocausts of young men." In the battlefields of this century, hundreds of millions of men were killed or injured. In World Wars I and II—in which more than 100 million soldiers were casualties—most of the victims were teenage boys, the average age being 18.5 years.

15   Given this obvious evidence of our exploitation, it is remarkable that so few men have acknowledged the genocide on their gender over the last century—much less turned against those responsible for this vast victimization. Women have increasingly identified their oppression in society; men have not. Thankfully, some men are now working to create a movement or community that focuses on awareness and understanding of men's loss and pain as well as the potential for healing. Because men's oppression is deeply rooted in the political and economic institutions of modern society, it is critical that awareness of these issues must be followed by action: Men today need a comprehensive political program that points the way toward liberation.

LOST IN THE MALE MYSTIQUE

16   Instead of grieving over and acting on our loss of independence and generativity, modern men have often engaged in denial—a denial that is linked to the existence of a "male mystique." This defective mythology of the modern age has created a "new man." The male mystique recasts what anthropologists have identified as the traditional male role throughout history—a man, whether hunter-gatherer or farmer, who is steeped in a creative and sustaining relationship with his extended family and the earth household. In

the place of this long-enduring, rooted masculine role, the male mystique has fostered a new image of men: autonomous, efficient, intensely self-interested, and disconnected from community and the earth.

17   The male mystique was spawned in the early days of the modern age. It combines Francis Bacon's idea that "knowledge is power" and Adam Smith's view that the highest good is "the individual exerting himself to his own advantage." This power-oriented, individualistic ideology was further solidified by the concepts of the survival of the fittest and the ethic of efficiency. The ideal man was no longer the wise farmer, but rather the most successful man-eater in the Darwinian corporate jungle.

18   The most tragic aspect of all this for us is that as the male mystique created the modern power elite, it destroyed male friendship and bonding. The male mystique teaches that the successful man is competitive, uncaring, unloving. It celebrates the ethic of isolation—it turns men permanently against each other in the tooth and claw world of making a living. As the Ivan Boesky-type character in the movie *Wall Street* tells his young apprentice, "If you need a friend, get a dog."

19   The male mystique also destroys men's ties to the earth. It embodies the view of 17th century British philosopher John Locke that "[l]and that is left wholly to nature is called, as indeed it is, waste." A sustainable relationship with the earth is sacrificed to material progress and conspicuous consumption.

20   Ironically, men's own sense of loss has fed the male mystique. As men become more and more powerless in their own lives, they are given more and more media images of excessive, caricatured masculinity with which to identify. Men look to manufactured macho characters from the Wild West, working-class America, and modern war in the hope of gaining some sense of what it means to be a man. The primary symbols of the male mystique are almost never caring fathers, stewards of the land, or community organizers. Instead, over several decades these aggressively masculine figures have evolved from the Western independent man (John Wayne, Gary Cooper) to the blue-collar macho man (Sly Stallone and Robert DeNiro), and finally to a variety of military and police figures concluding with the violent revelry of *Robocop*.

21   Modern men are entranced by this simulated masculinity—they experience danger, independence, success, sexuality, idealism, and adventure as voyeurs. Meanwhile, in real life most men lead powerless, subservient lives in the factory or office—frightened of losing their jobs, mortgaged to the gills, and still feeling responsible for supporting their families. Their lauded independence—as well as most of their basic rights—disappear the minute they report for work. The disparity between their real lives and the macho images of masculinity perpetrated by the media confuses and confounds many men. . . .

22   Men can no longer afford to lose themselves in denial. We need to experience grief and anger over our losses and not buy into the pseudo-male stereotypes propagated by the male mystique. We are not, after all, what we are told we are.

23   At the same time, while recognizing the pervasive victimization of women, we must resist the view of some feminists that maleness itself, and not the current systems of social control and production, is primarily responsible for the exploitation of women. For men who are sensitive to feminist thinking, this view of masculinity creates a confusing and debilitating double bind: We view ourselves as oppressors yet experience victimization on the personal and social level. Instead of blaming maleness, we must challenge the defective mythology of the male mystique. Neither the male mystique nor the denigration of maleness offers hope for the future.

24   Fortunately, we may be on the verge of a historic shift in male consciousness. Recently, there has been a rediscovery of masculinity as a primal creative and generative force equal to that of the recently recognized creative and nurturing power of the feminine. A number of thinkers and activists are urging men to substitute empathy for efficiency, stewardship for exploitation, generosity for the competitiveness of the marketplace. . . .

A MAN COULD STAND UP

25   The current generation of men face a unique moment in history. Though often still trapped by economic coercion and psychological co-option, we are beginning to see that there is a profound choice ahead. Will we choose to remain subservient tools of social and environmental destruction or to fight for rediscovery of the male as a full partner and participant in family, community, and the earth? Will we remain mesmerized by the male mystique, or will we reclaim the true meaning of our masculinity?

26   There is a world to gain. The male mystique, in which many of today's men—especially the most politically powerful—are trapped, is threatening the family and the planet with irreversible destruction. A men's movement based on the recovery of masculinity could renew much of the world we have lost. By changing types of work and work hours, we could break our subordination to corporate managers and return much of our work and lives to the household. We could once again be teaching, nurturing presences to our children. By devoting ourselves to meaningful work with appropriate technology, we could recover independence in our work and our spirit. By caring for each other, we could recover the dignity of our gender and heal the wounds of addiction and self-destruction. By becoming husbands to the earth, we could protect the wild and recover our creative connection with the forces and rhythms of nature.

27   Ultimately we must help fashion a world without the daily frustration and sorrow of having to view each other as a collection of competitors instead of a community of friends. We must celebrate the essence and rituals of our masculinity. We can no longer passively submit to the destruction of the household, the demise of self-employment, the disintegration of family and community, and the desecration of our earth.

For Writing and Discussion

1. In "A Time for Men to Pull Together," Andrew Kimbrell portrays men as victimized by changing roles. How does Kimbrell propose to reverse "the cycle of destruction" that results from men's losses? Do you agree that the reversal is needed? Do you agree with the causes of the male crisis? Why or why not?

2. What factors of the socioeconomic system does Kimbrell point to as contributing to the current male crisis? Which factors might also relate to working women?

3. In the *Maxine!* cartoon, is the man's response to the claim that women "occupy a position of inferiority" emotional or rational? Describe characteristics and experiences that might contribute to his response.

4. After you have reread the poem "Barbie doll," by Marge Piercy, explain how a second reading helped to increase your understanding of the poem. In what phrases or passages did you find additional meaning after the second reading? How does the poem relate to your experience or experiences you have observed?

5. Explain the irony of the final line of the poem "Barbie doll."

6. List three or four social issues (gun control, abortion, and so forth), and tell how your opinions on each might be affected by your experiences as a male or a female.

Practice: Applying a Concept

After rereading Piercy's poem "Barbie doll," brainstorm for ideas to use in a similar poem about boys and men. You may want to present the ideas about how boys might be pushed into stereotypical roles in prose form or in a poem, working either individually or with a small group of classmates.

RACE AND IDENTITY

Looking Out
Mitsuye Yamada

It must be odd
to be a minority
he was saying.
I looked around

and didn't see any.
5 So I said
Yeah
it must be.

THE POWER OF STYLE: WORD ORDER

Inversions of word order are used to emphasize important words by placing them at the beginning or end of sentences. In poetry, placing an important word at the end of a line has the same effect. In Yamada's poem "Looking Out," the words *odd* and *minority* are placed at the ends of lines. The first sentence might be written, "He was saying, 'Being a minority must be odd,'" but the words *he was saying* are moved to the end of the sentence to provide emphasis on *what* he was saying. e. e. cummings uses a double inversion in "i thank You God for most this amazing day." The word *most* might be reverted to the left (i thank You God most for this . . .) or to the right (i thank You God for this most amazing day).

In prose, the usual subject-verb order is often inverted. Max Schulman begins the story "Love is a Fallacy" (page 210) with a sentence in which the subject comes after the verb: "Cool was I and logical." William A. Henry III uses subject-verb inversion to introduce a quotation in "Upside Down in the Groves of Academe" (page 127): "Warns Diane Ravitch, adjunct professor of history and education at Columbia: 'If we teach kids to connect themselves to one group defined by race or language or religion, then we have no basis for public education.'"

Practice: Word Order

Write two or three sentences about your gender or your racial or ethnic identity. Arrange the sentences into a poem, using inversions of normal word order for emphasis.

from **The Content of Our Character**
Shelby Steele

Steele's book Content of Our Character *drew both acclaim and criticism. In this excerpt, Steele argues for what Yamada expresses in "Looking Out," that race is an element, not a definition, of identity.*

1   There are many profound problems facing black America today: a swelling black underclass; a black middle class that declined slightly in size during the Eighties; a declining number of black college students; an epidemic of teenage pregnancy, drug use, and gang violence; continuing chronic unemployment; astoundingly high college and high school dropout rates; an increasing number of single-parent families; a disproportionately high infant mortality rate; and so on. Against this despair it might seem almost esoteric for me to talk about the importance of individual identity and possibility. Yet I have come to believe that despite the existing racism in today's America, opportunity is the single most constant but unexploited aspect of the black condition. The only way we will see the advancement of black people in this country is for us to focus on developing ourselves as individuals and embracing opportunity.

2   I have come to this conclusion over time. In the late Sixties, I was caught up in the new spirit of black power and pride that swept over black America like one of those storms that change the landscape. I will always believe this storm was inevitable and, therefore, positive in many ways. What I gained from it was the power to be racially unapologetic, no mean benefit considering the long trial of patience that blacks were subjected to during the civil rights movement. But after a while, by the early Seventies, it became clear that black power did not offer much of a blueprint for how to move my life forward; it told me virtually nothing about who I was as an individual or how I might live in the world as myself. Of course, it was my mistake to think it could. But in the late Sixties, "blackness" was an invasive form of collective identity that cut so deeply into one's individual space that it seemed also to *be* an individual identity. It came as something of a disappointment to realize that the two were not the same, that being "black" in no way spared me the necessity of being myself.

3   In the early Seventies, without realizing it, I made a sort of bargain with the prevailing black identity—I subscribed in a general way to its point of view so that I could be free to get on with my life. Many blacks I knew did the same.

4   And what were we subscribing to? Generally, I think it was a form of black identity grounded in the spirit of black power. It carried a righteous anger at and mistrust of American society; it believed that blacks continued to be the victims of institutional racism, that we would have to maintain an adversarial stance toward society, and that a right racial unity was necessary both for

survival and advancement. This identity was, and is, predicated on the notion that those who burned you once will burn you again, and it presupposes a deep racist reflex in American life that will forever try to limit black possibility.

5   I think it was the space I cleared for myself by loosely subscribing to this identity that ultimately put me in conflict with it. It is in the day-to-day struggle of living on the floor of a society, so to speak, that one gains a measure of what is possible in that society. And by simply living as an individual in America—with my racial-identity struggle suspended temporarily—I discovered that American society offered me, and blacks in general, a remarkable range of opportunity if we were willing to pursue it.

6   In my daily life I continue to experience racial indignities and slights: This morning I was told that blacks had too much musical feeling (soul, I suppose) to be good classical musicians; yesterday I passed two houses with gnomish black lawn jockeys on their front porches; my children have been called "nigger," as have I; I wear a tie and carry a briefcase so that my students on the first day of class will know I'm the professor; and so on. I also know that actual racial discrimination persists in many areas of American life. I have been the victor in one housing-discrimination suit, as were my parents before me. My life is not immune to any of this, and I will never endure it with élan. Yet I have also come to realize that, in this same society, I have been more in charge of my fate than I ever wanted to believe and that though I have been limited by many things, my race was not foremost among them.

7   The point is that both realities exist simultaneously. There is still racial insensitivity and some racial discrimination against blacks in this society, but there is also much opportunity. What brought me into conflict with the prevailing black identity was that it was almost entirely preoccupied with the former to the exclusion of the latter. The black identity I was subscribing to in the Seventies—and that still prevails today—was essentially a "wartime" identity shaped in the confrontational Sixties. It saw blacks as victims even as new possibilities for advancement opened all around.

8   Why do we cling to an adversarial, victim-focused identity and remain preoccupied with white racism? Part of the reason, I think, is that we carry an inferiority anxiety—an unconscious fear that the notion that we are inferior may, in fact, be true—that makes the seizing of opportunity more risky for us, since setbacks and failures may seem to confirm our worst fears. To avoid this risk we hold a victim-focused identity that tells us there is less opportunity than there actually is. And, in fact, our victimization itself has been our primary source of power in society—the basis of our demands for redress. The paradoxical result of relying on this source of power is that it rewards us for continuing to see ourselves as victims of a racist society and implies that opportunity itself is something to be given instead of taken.

9   This leaves us with an identity that is at war with our own best interests, that magnifies our oppression and diminishes our sense of possibility. I think this identity is a burden for blacks, because it is built around our collective insecurity rather than a faith in our human capacity to seize opportunity as

individuals. It amounts to a self-protective collectivism that focuses on black unity instead of individual initiative. To be "black" in this identity, one need only manifest the symbols, postures, and rhetoric of black unity. Not only is personal initiative unnecessary for being "black," but the successful exercise of initiative—working one's way into the middle class, becoming well-off, gaining an important position—may, in fact, jeopardize one's "blackness," make one somehow less black.

10   This sort of identity is never effective and never translates into the actual uplift of black people. Though it espouses black pride, it is actually a repressive identity that generates a victimized self-image, curbs individualism and initiative, diminishes our sense of possibility, and contributes to our demoralization and inertia. Uplift can only come when many millions of blacks seize the possibilities inside the sphere of their personal lives and use them to move themselves forward. Collectively we can resist oppression, but racial development will always be, as Ralph Ellison once put it, "the gift" of individuals.

11   There have been numerous government attempts at remedying the list of problems I mentioned earlier. Here and there a program has worked; many more have been failures. Clearly, we should find the ones that do work and have more of them. But my deepest feeling is that, in a society of increasingly limited resources, there will never be enough programs to meet the need. We black Americans will never be saved or even assisted terribly much by others, never be repaid for our suffering, and never find that symmetrical, historical justice that we cannot help but long for.

12   As Jean-Paul Sartre once said, we are the true "existential people." We have always had to create ourselves out of whole cloth and find our own means for survival. I believe that black leadership must recognize the importance of this individual initiative. They must preach it, tell it, sell it, and demand it. Our leadership has looked at government and white society very critically. Now they must help us look at ourselves. We need our real problems named and explained, otherwise we have no chance to overcome them. The impulse of our leaders is to be "political," to keep the society at large on edge, to keep them feeling as though they have not done enough for blacks. And, clearly, they have not. But the price these leaders pay for this form of "politics" is to keep blacks focused on an illusion of deliverance by others, and no illusion weakens us more. Our leaders must take a risk. They must tell us the truth, tell us of the freedom and opportunity they have discovered in their own lives. They must tell us what they tell their own children when they go home at night: to study hard, to pursue their dreams with discipline and effort, to be responsible for themselves, to have concern for others, to cherish their race and at the same time build their own lives as Americans. When our leaders put a spotlight on our victimization and seize upon our suffering to gain us ineffectual concessions, they inadvertently turn themselves into enemies of the truth, not to mention enemies of their own people.

13   I believe that black Americans are freer today than ever before. This is not a hope; this is a reality. Racial hatred has not yet left the American landscape.

Who knows how or when this will occur. And yet the American black, supported by a massive body of law and, for the most part, the goodwill of his fellow citizens, is basically as free as he or she wants to be. For every white I have met who is a racist, I have met twenty more who have seen me as an individual. This, I am not ashamed to say, has been my experience. I believe it is time for blacks to begin the shift from a wartime to a peacetime identity, from fighting for opportunity to seizing it. The immutable fact of late-twentieth-century American life is that it *is* there for blacks to seize. Martin Luther King did not live to experience this. But then, of course, on the night before he died, he seemed to know that he would not. From the mountaintop he had looked over and seen the promised land, but he said, "I may not get there with you. . . ." I won't say we are snuggled deep in the promised valley he saw beyond the mountain; everyday things remind me that we are not. But I also know we have it better than our greatest leader. We are on the other side of his mountaintop, on the downward slope toward the valley he saw. This is something we ought to know. But what we must know even more clearly is that nothing on this earth can be promised except a chance. The promised land guarantees nothing. It is only an opportunity, not a deliverance.

For Writing and Discussion

1. List types of victims and relate them to Steele's argument that overcoming victimization must start with personal initiative. How does Steele's argument relate to the poem "Barbie doll"? In what way does the speaker in Mitsuye Yamada's poem express what Shelby Steele advocates?

2. Steele argues that the time has come to move "from fighting for opportunity to seizing it." How might this argument be applied to education? to the women's movement? to people in general?

3. Steele's critics advocate black unity and separatism rather than assimilation and playing the "capitalist game." They believe that more can be achieved through a united force, people working together for a common goal. Consider ideas for a compromise solution that would help advance the cause of any racial or ethnic group.

CHAPTER SUMMARY

This chapter introduced *ethos* and the importance of credibility. Elements of style were presented as a writer's tools with which to fashion pleasing prose.

The readings focused on gender and race as a part of identity. The next chapter deals with experience and how it contributes to identity.

Chapter 2

EXPERIENCE

Nick Ut/AP/Wide World

EXPERIENCE OF LIFE

Song of Napalm
Bruce Weigl

For My Wife

After the storm, after the rain stopped pounding,
We stood in the doorway watching horses
Walk off lazily across the pasture's hill.
We stared through the black screen,
5 Our vision altered by the distance
So I thought I saw a mist
Kicked up around their hooves when they faded
Like cut-out horses
Away from us.
10 The grass was never more blue in that light, more
Scarlet; beyond the pasture
Trees scraped their voices in the wind, branches
Criss-crossed the sky like barbed-wire
But you said they were only branches.

15 Okay. The storm stopped pounding.
I am trying to say this straight: for once
I was sane enough to pause and breathe
Outside my wild plans and after the hard rain
I turned my back on the old curses, I believed
20 They swung finally away from me . . .

But still the branches are wire
And thunder is the pounding mortar,
Still I close my eyes and see the girl
Running from her village, napalm
25 Stuck to her dress like jelly,
Her hands reaching for the no one
Who waits in waves of heat before her.

So I can keep on living,
So I can stay here beside you,
30 I try to imagine she runs down the road and wings
Beat inside her until she rises
Above the stinking jungle and her pain

Eases, and your pain, and mine.
But the lie swings back again.
35   The lie works only as long as it takes to speak
And the girl runs only so far
As the napalm allows
Until her burning tendons and crackling
Muscles draw her up
40   Into that final position
Burning bodies so perfectly assume. Nothing
Can change that; she is burned behind my eyes
And not your good love and not the rain-swept air
And not the jungle green
45   Pasture unfolding before us can deny it.

THE POWER OF STYLE:
CREATING IMAGES

The speaker in "Song of Napalm" uses words to create powerful visual images of the present that he sees with his eyes and of nightmares, "the old curses," of the past that are "behind [his] eyes."

Practice: Seeing with the Mind's Eye

Read "Song of Napalm" several times until you can visualize in your mind's eye the images from the present and from the past. How are the images related? What elements of the present images merge with images from the past?

In what way does the speaker's experience affect his present life? His relationship with his wife? How does the speaker indicate that he is struggling to overcome the nightmare of the experience?

Visualize one of your past experiences, and think about how it affected your identity.

© 1993 by Jeff Reid. Reprinted by permission of the artist.

from **All I Really Need to Know I Learned in Kindergarten**

Robert L. Fulghum

1   **E**ach spring, for many years, I have set myself the task of writing a personal statement of belief: a Credo. When I was younger, the statement ran for many pages, trying to cover every base, with no loose ends. It sounded like a Supreme Court brief, as if words could resolve all conflicts about the meaning of existence.

2   The Credo has grown shorter in recent years—sometimes cynical, some-times comical, sometimes bland—but I keep working at it. Recently I set out to get a statement of personal belief down to one page in simple terms, fully understanding the naive idealism that implied. . . .

3   I realized then that I already know most of what's necessary to live a meaningful life—that it isn't all that complicated. *I know it.* And have known it for a long, long time. Living it—well, that's another matter, yes? Here's my Credo:

4   All I really need to know about how to live and what to do and how to
be I learned in kindergarten. Wisdom was not at the top of the graduate-school
mountain, but there in the sandpile at Sunday School. These are the things I
learned:

>   Share everything.
>   Play fair.
>   Don't hit people.
>   Put things back where you found them.
>   Clean up your own mess.
>   Don't take things that aren't yours.
>   Say you're sorry when you hurt somebody.
>   Wash your hands before you eat.
>   Flush.
>   Warm cookies and cold milk are good for you.
>   Live a balanced life—learn some and think some and draw and paint and
>   sing and dance and play and work every day some.
>   Take a nap every afternoon.
>   When you go out into the world, watch out for traffic, hold hands, and
>   stick together.
>   Be aware of wonder. Remember the little seed in the Styrofoam cup: The
>   roots go down and the plant goes up and nobody really knows how or why,
>   but we are all like that.
>   Goldfish and hamsters and white mice and even the little seed in the Sty-
>   rofoam cup—they all die. So do we.
>   And then remember the Dick-and-Jane books and the first word you
>   learned—the biggest word of all—LOOK.

5   Everything you need to know is in there somewhere. The Golden Rule
and love and basic sanitation. Ecology and politics and equality and sane living.

6   Take any one of those items and extrapolate it into sophisticated adult
terms and apply it to your family life or your work or your government or your
world and it holds true and clear and firm. Think what a better world it would
be if we all—the whole world—had cookies and milk about three o'clock every
afternoon and then lay down with our blankies for a nap. Or if all governments
had as a basic policy to always put things back where they found them and to
clean up their own mess.

7   And it is still true, no matter how old you are—when you go out into the
world, it is best to hold hands and stick together.

Practice: Writing a Creed

Write a creed, or statement of beliefs, about religion, ethics, virtues, the meaning of success, rights and responsibilities, or another topic. Has the experience
of thinking about the readings and learning about the feelings of other writers
increased reflection on your own beliefs?

Confessions of a Law-and-Order Liberal
Lynnell Mickelsen

1   I remember the moment I knew I was no longer the same non-violent girl from the Midwest, the nice liberal who believed most criminals are disadvantaged types who need a good social worker. I had lived in Detroit for three years, working as a reporter for the *Detroit Free Press,* when an incident happened only a few blocks from my house.

2   An old man in his 80s was riding a city bus when a young thug knocked him down, robbed him, and kicked him in the face. Somehow the bus continued on its route and the old man, dazed and bleeding, got off at his stop.

3   He stood on the street for a moment. Then, suddenly, he jumped back on the bus, pulled out a handgun, and began to fire. His aim wasn't great, but he eventually managed to kill his tormentor, much to the relief of his fellow commuters, who were flattened on the floor.

4   Killings in Detroit were so commonplace we tended to cover them the way other newspapers cover traffic accidents—brief roundups, no more. But this was sort of a new angle—an old man in his 80s pulling a Clint Eastwood— so reporters descended on the scene, as did the chief of homicide.

5   Did he have any comment on the latest killing? the reporters asked.

6   "Yeah," said the chief. "I'm always happy when assholes and bullets meet."

7   That quote flew through the newsroom and people repeated it so often it became almost a mantra. *I'm always happy when assholes and bullets meet. * Me? I laughed. I *loved* it. So what if the chief of homicide was endorsing citizen vigilantes? Ethically, it was insane. But if you lived in Detroit, it made perfect emotional sense. Forget the courts. Forget justice. Why pay for more prisons? Just blow the stupid [expletive] away and be done with it.

8   They say a conservative is a liberal who's been mugged. I've been mugged. Twice. (I prefer *robbed,* since *mugged* sounds too quick and painless. I was knocked down once and had a knife to my throat the next time and I never got better at it. I peed in my pants each time.) I'm still a liberal-Democrat, antimilitary, pro-gun-control feminist. But I've learned why liberals have a problem with crime.

9   Either we don't experience enough of it personally or we don't tell the truth about what crime does to us psychologically, spiritually, and morally. We talk from our cool heads about justice and mercy. We ignore our angry hearts that want revenge.

10   We don't *have* to choose between hearts and heads, but we need to acknowledge both. Until we do, all our non-violent and rehabilitative solutions to crime fall on hostile, deaf ears. People in neighborhoods besieged by drugs and guns often hate liberals because they assume we don't "get it." And much of the time they are right.

11   A woman in a recent discussion group talked blithely about decriminalizing prostitution and drugs. I moved away from Detroit six years ago and I still wanted to kill her. Obviously, she's never run out of her house with shoe in hand to beat on a car roof because she was tired of hookers giving blow jobs in front of her house, I thought hatefully. And she's never had crack addicts control all her movements.

12   When I lived in Detroit in the mid-80s, violent crime affected nearly every decision I made every day. Where I lived. Where I tried to park my car. What time I left a party. When I would grocery shop. Whether I took the garbage out that night or waited till morning when the alley was safer.

13   I wasn't alone. One by one, almost everyone I knew in Detroit became a crime victim. I'm not talking about burglary or car theft—that had become so routine it was almost like getting a parking ticket. No, these were the scarier, more personal encounters with crime. A colleague got stuck while he was driving to work in a snowstorm. Two men pushed him out and when he got out to thank them, one of them pulled a gun.

14   Our minister was robbed of his wallet and wedding ring in his driveway. He remembers the gunman's shaky hands and the revolver trembling on his temples as he struggled to remove the ring. An elderly friend was held up in the elevator of his apartment building. He quietly handed over his wallet and was beaten into unconsciousness. A middle-aged advertising executive was brutally raped by a stranger who broke into the house at 2 a.m.

15   "Sara" was the fifth or sixth woman attacked in my neighborhood within a few months, apparently by the same guy, and the cops were extremely frustrated. The night Sara got raped, the cops found a man creeping around in a nearby yard. The guy had just been paroled after being convicted of a string of burglaries in the neighborhood. "He wasn't the rapist," an officer said, "But we were so pissed off we beat the hell out of him anyway. At least he's out of commission for a while."

16   Here I have a police officer admitting to beating someone because he can't find the right suspect. I'm a supposed pacifist, a reporter with a natural mistrust for cops and authority. Was I angry? Was I shocked? Hell, no. I was *grateful.* Thank God for the cops, I thought. At least they're trying.

17   You see, that's what happens. Daily violence wears on your ideals almost like HIV on your immune system. Slowly, imperceptibly, you change. But you don't notice until all of a sudden, faced with another incident, you realize your moral system has been altered.

18   Eric was a hairdresser who owned a nearby salon. He drove a white Corvette, which in Detroit was sort of like asking for it ("I'm bad enough to buy it. Are you bad enough to take it?"). He was driving away from work one evening when a man jumped in his car at a stop sign (neighborhood commentary: "Why the hell was his passenger door unlocked?") and demanded the keys.

19   Eric reached into his boot, pulled out his gun, and killed the guy. Splattered his blood all over the new upholstery. The cops questioned Eric briefly.

He had used deadly force and it wasn't as though his life was threatened, but no charges were filed. Why bother? You could never find 12 people in Detroit who'd convict him. In fact, most juries would rather dig up the would-be car thief and shoot him again.

20   And on my street, this is how my fastidious neighbor and I talked:

21   "He should have just let the guy take the car and collect on the insurance. I mean right now the car is wrecked."

22   "He'll never get the bloodstains out of those leather seats. It's just *gross.*"

23   That's when I knew I eventually had to leave Detroit—I was morally and spiritually eroding. Someone was shot to death over a car and I was talking about it like some character from a Joan Didion story.

24   It was also when I realized non-violence is an easy principle when your neighborhood is safe. When you're surrounded by brutality, non-violence is the province of the few who are strong and spiritually centered—saints, I guess. And even they find it hard. . . .

For Writing and Discussion

1. What contradictions between what she believes and what she feels does Mickelsen express in her essay?

2. How might the increasing fear of violence in America affect the justice system? How might fear affect the neighborhoods and communities of the future?

3. Contrast Mickelsen's portrayal of the affect of experience on feelings and beliefs with the idealistic philosophy expressed in Robert Fulghum's piece.

THE POWER OF STYLE: "MINOR" SENTENCES

Both Fulghum and Mickelsen include sentence fragments in their essays. Fulghum treats two series of nouns as sentences (par. 5), and Mickelsen omits "violent crime affected" in five parallel fragments that contain only adverbial clauses (par. 12). Purposeful sentence fragments have been named "English minor sentences" by Kline and Memering.[1] Although these minor sentences permeate modern prose, they are usually considered unacceptable sentence fragments in academic writing.

[1] Kline, Charles R., Jr., and W. Dean Memering. "Formal Fragments: English Minor Sentences." *Research in the Teaching of English* 11 (1977): 97–110.

An Open Letter to the Class of 1996 UNCW
Charlie Daniels

After country star Charlie Daniels was asked to speak at the University of North Carolina (Wilmington) graduation, two writers objected in the school newspaper. The writers called Daniels a "one-hit wonder" ("The Devil Went Down to Georgia") and a "goober brained red neck" and suggested that Daniels was unworthy of addressing graduating seniors. Daniels responded with the following letter.

1   I would like to clear up a few points about my addressing your class at commencement exercises, points which I feel have been distorted by a few overzealous, uninformed pseudo journalists.

2   I will not address the "one hit wonder," "goober brained redneck" aspect of these pieces, and one letter published in *The Seahawk* I will not address at all except to say that the racial overtones it contained were totally unfounded and offensive beyond description.

3   My professional life is a matter of documented public record and easily obtainable. No need to discuss that.

4   First of all, this is not the first time I have been invited to speak to a graduating class at UNCW. I have been approached for the past couple of years, but due to prearranged commitments I have been unable to accept.

5   Having been born in Wilmington, I consider it an honor to be asked to speak to you on one of the biggest days of your lives, and I accepted the honor with gratitude and humility. I cannot speak to you of lofty academic ideals nor scholarly pursuits because I have neither entree nor credential for that world.

6   The truth is I come to you from the street, from reality, the very same place you're all headed if you plan to make a living in this ever-changing, difficult, show-me world, and when your college days are just a memory and your diploma hangs beneath dusty glass or some office wall, you will still have to deal with that world on its own terms every working day of your lives.

Let me tell you why I thought I was invited to speak to your graduating class. My career spans almost 40 years and you don't go through 40 years of hard work and unrelenting competition without learning a few things.

8   My qualifications are humble, but extensive and diverse. I've stood at the 38th Parallel and looked across into the hostile eyes of the North Korean border guards. I've been catapulted from the deck of an aircraft carrier in the middle of the Adriatic Sea and ridden across the frozen wastes of Greenland on an Eskimo dog sled. I've taken a hammer and chisel to the Berlin Wall and performed with symphony orchestras. I've had conversations with Presidents and walked the halls of Congress lobbying for legislation in which I believe. I've flown on the Concorde and acted in motion pictures. I've seen the royal palaces of Europe and the hovels of Hong Kong.

9   I've seen the Mona Lisa and stared in awe at the timeless works of Vincent van Gogh. I've gathered cattle in the Big Bend country of Texas and met some of the wisest people I know at campfires in the middle of nowhere. I was privileged to have conversations with Alex Hailey and Louis L'Amour. I've appeared with The Rolling Stones, worked in the recording studio with Bob Dylan and two of The Beatles. I've been married to the same woman for over thirty years and raised a son who did, by the way, go to college. I've kept 20 people gainfully and steadily employed for over 20 years.

10   I am not a man of letters; I readily admit that. But is being a man of letters the only thing which qualifies one to speak to a group of men and women who are about to enter the real world? My world.

11   My address will not be delivered in the beautiful strains of poetry of a Maya Angelou or with the technical expertise of a Tom Clancy, but I can tell you where some of the land mines are hidden, the shortest path to the top of the mountain and the quickest way down. Been there, done that.

Thank you and God bless the Class of '96.

Practice: Writing a Letter of Qualifications

Write a letter in which you explain how your experiences qualify you to enter college, a certain profession, or a new role (marriage, parenthood, or so forth) or to speak to or assist others who are younger, who have a particular illness or disability, or who face special challenges in life.

EXPERIENCE OF SPIRIT

Desiderata
Max Ehrmann

1   **G**o placidly amid the noise and haste, and remember what peace there may be in silence. As far as possible without surrender be on good terms with all persons. Speak your truth quietly and clearly; and listen to others, even the dull and ignorant; they too have their story.

2   Avoid loud and aggressive persons, they are vexatious to the spirit. If you compare yourself with others, you may become vain or bitter, for always there will be greater and lesser persons than yourself. Enjoy your achievements as well as your plans.

3   Keep interested in your own career, however humble; it is a real possession in the changing fortunes of time.

4   Exercise caution in your business affairs; for the world is full of trickery. But let not this blind you to what virtue there is; many persons strive for high ideals; and everywhere life is full of heroism.

5   Be yourself. Especially, do not feign affection. Neither be cynical about love; for in the face of all aridity and disenchantment it is as perennial as the grass.

6   Take kindly the counsel of the years, gracefully surrendering the things of youth. Nurture strength of spirit to shield you in sudden misfortune. But do not distress yourself with dark imaginings. Many fears are born of fatigue and loneliness. Beyond a wholesome discipline, be gentle with yourself.

7   You are a child of the universe, no less than the trees and the stars; you have a right to be here. And whether or not it is clear to you, no doubt the universe is unfolding as it should.

8   Therefore be at peace with God, whatever you conceive Him to be, and whatever your labors and aspirations, in the noisy confusion of life keep peace in your soul. With all its sham, drudgery and broken dreams, it is still a beautiful world. Be cheerful. Strive to be happy.

THE POWER OF STYLE: DICTION

"Desiderata" has often been published with the inscription "found in Old Saint Paul's Church, Baltimore; dated 1692." In fact, many people believe it to be an authentic relic from the past (even though at least some of the language used in the piece would be *anachronistic,* or out of place for 1692). However, Indiana poet Max Ehrmann copyrighted the piece in 1927, and whoever added the inscription was *borrowing authority.* The borrowed authority probably played some part in the popularity the piece achieved during the 1970s. "Desiderata" appeared on posters and as lyrics to a pop song.

Practice: Paraphrasing

Paraphrase "Desiderata," using words you would normally use in conversation. After you have finished, share your rendition with at least one classmate.

The Cult of "I"
Margaret Halsey

1   The cult of "I" has taken hold with the strength and impetus of a new religion. But the joker in the pack is that it is all based on a false idea. The false idea is that inside every human being, however unprepossessing, there is a glorious, talented and overwhelmingly attractive personality. This personality—so runs the erroneous belief—will be revealed in all its splendor if the individual just forgets about courtesy, cooperativeness and consideration for others and proceeds to do exactly what he or she feels like doing.

2   Nonsense.

3   Inside each of us is a mess of unruly primitive impulses, and these can sometimes, under the strenuous self-discipline and dedication of art, result in notable creativity. But there is no such thing as a pure, crystalline and well-organized "native" personality, though a host of trendy human-potential groups trade on the mistaken assumption that there is. And backing up the human-potential industry is the advertising profession, which also encourages the idea of an Inner Wonderfulness that will be unveiled to a suddenly respectful world upon the purchase of this or that commodity.

4   However, an individual does not exist in a vacuum. A human being is not an isolated, independent thing-in-itself, but inevitably reflects the existence of others. The young adults of the "me" generation would never have lived to grow up if a great many parents, doctors, nurses, farmers, factory workers, teachers, policemen, firemen and legions of others had not ignored their human potential and made themselves do jobs they did not perhaps feel like doing in order to support the health and growth of children.

5   And yet, despite the indulgence of uninhibited expression, the "self" in self-awareness seems to cause many new narcissists a lot of trouble. This trouble emerges in talk about "identity." We hear about the search for identity and a kind of distress called an identity crisis.

6   "I don't know who I am." How many bartenders and psychiatrists have stifled yawns on hearing that popular threnody for the thousandth time!

7   But this sentence has no meaning unless spoken by an amnesia victim, because many of the people who say they do not know who they are, actually *do* know. What such people really mean is that they are not satisfied with who they are. They feel themselves to be timid and colorless or to be in some way or other fault-ridden, but they have soaked up enough advertising and enough catchpenny ideas of self-improvement to believe in universal Inner Wonderfulness. So they turn their backs on their honest knowledge of themselves—which with patience and courage could start them on the road to genuine development—and embark on a quest for a will-o'-the-wisp called "identity."

8   But a *search* for identity is predestined to fail. Identity is not found the way Pharaoh's daughter found Moses in the bulrushes. Identity is built. It is built every day and every minute throughout the day. The myriad choices, small and large, that human beings make all the time determine identity. The fatal weakness of the currently fashionable approach to personality is that the "self" of the self-awareness addicts, the self of Inner Wonderfulness, is static. Being perfect, it does not need to change. But genuine identity changes as one matures. If it does not, if the 40-year-old has an identity that was set in concrete at the age of 18, he or she is in trouble.

9   The idea of a universal Inner Wonderfulness that will be apparent to all beholders after a six-week course in self-expression is fantasy. But how did this fantasy gain wide popular acceptance as a realizable fact?

10   Every society tries to produce a prevalent psychological type that will best serve its ends, and that type is always prone to certain emotional malfunctions. In early capitalism, which was a producing society, the ideal type was acquisitive, fanatically devoted to hard work and fiercely repressive of sex. The emotional malfunctions to which this type was liable were hysteria and obsession. Later capitalism, today's capitalism, is a consuming society, and the psychological type it strives to create, in order to build up the largest possible markets, is shallow, easily swayed and characterized much more by self-infatuation than self-respect. The emotional malfunction of this type is narcissism.

11   It will be argued that the cult of "I" has done some individuals a lot of good. But at whose expense? What about the people to whom these "healthy" egotists are rude or even abusive? What about the people over whom they ride roughshod? What about the people they manipulate and exploit? And—the most important question of all—how good a preparation for inevitable old age and death is a deliberately cultivated self-love? The psychologists say that the full-blown classic narcissists lose all dignity and go mad with fright as they approach their final dissolution. . . .

12   A long time ago, in a book called "Civilization and Its Discontents," Freud pointed out that there is an unresolvable conflict between the human being's selfish, primitive, infantile impulses and the restraint he or she must impose on those impulses if a stable society is to be maintained. The "self" is not a handsome god or goddess waiting coyly to be revealed. On the contrary, its complexity, confusion and mystery have proved so difficult that throughout the ages men and women have talked gratefully about *losing* themselves. They *lose* the self in contemplating a great work of art, or in nature, or in scientific research, or in writing poetry, or in fashioning things with their hands or in projects that will benefit others rather than themselves.

13   The current glorification of self-love will turn out in the end to be a no-win proposition, because in questions of personality or "identity," what counts is not who you are, but what you do. "By their fruits, ye shall know them." And by their fruits, they shall know themselves.

For Writing and Discussion

1. Evaluate Halsey's *ethos*. In your opinion, how does her use of language, choice of examples, and use of logic (reasoning) affect her credibility? Give specific examples.

2. Halsey wrote her piece in 1978 about the generation still referred to as the "me" generation. Is it true, as some argue, that "me-ism" is more alive today than ever? What is the relationship between today's materialism and individualism and yesterday's "me" generation? Is there a relationship between "me-ism" and what some people call today's "nation of crybabies" in which so many people claim victimhood of one kind or another. Support your opinion with your own reasons and examples.

3. Some isolated tribes in South America have no concept of ambition, cruelty, or ownership for the sake of owning something. Relate Halsey's use of the Freudian idea of "unresolvable conflict between the human being's selfish, primitive, infantile impulses and the restraint he or she must impose on those impulses" to primitive people who seem to exist without the Freudian conflict. Do you think the conflict is a product of nature (innate feelings or genetic traits) or nurture (feelings created by environment)?

4. Relate Halsey's statements about self-centeredness to the idea that the quickest way to beat the blues is to do something to make someone else happy. Is it possible to be both happy and self-centered? Why or why not?

5. *Self-esteem comes from doing things well, from discovering how to tell a truth from a lie and from finding out what unites us as well as what separates us.*

Robert Hughes, "The Fraying of America." *Time* 2 Feb. 1992

Explain how you think a healthy self-esteem can be balanced against an unselfish concern for others. How does the idea expressed in the quotation relate to those expressed in "Desiderata"?

Practice: Analyzing Generation X

Young adults of the 1990s have been tagged as Generation X. Caught between media that encourage them to "just do it" and platitudes that urge them to "just say no," young adults cope with a present and a future that is different from that of other generations.

In a brief essay, describe some of the influences on today's youth and explain how those influences require coping skills that are different from those of other generations.

CHAPTER SUMMARY

As the lyrics that introduced Part One noted, we may be affiliated with this or that group and divided by experience and environment, yet we are united by our humanity. Others may define us, but, ultimately, who we are depends on our choices, beliefs, preferences, perspectives—things that others cannot see. The next chapter offers an opportunity to examine those elements of "self."

Chapter 3

WRITING CHALLENGE

THE PROCESS OF WRITING

A couple of decades ago, a thunderbolt hit the researchers studying professional and student writers. They decided, "Wait a minute. Writing is not magic. Masterpieces are not produced by simply sitting down and putting pen to paper. There is a process through which writers work to develop finished prose."

Although it was clear that not all writers worked in the same way and that the stages, or steps, in the process were not linear but were recursive (repeated, returned to), researchers were sure that thinking about writing as a process could help beginning writers. Of course, educators needed time to catch up with research, but by the mid-1980s, teaching writing as process was in; it was the thing to do.

Mrs. Grundy, however, was not so quick to adopt the new-fangled ideas that accompanied the writing-as-process movement—ideas such as teaching correctness through the students' own writing instead of having them diagram and parse sentences. And at the other end of the spectrum, teachers known in some circles as the "radical romantics" stopped worrying about teaching correctness altogether and focused instead on helping students develop fluency, contending that students would develop correctness, if it really mattered, in the same way they develop fluency—with practice.

Still there is some disagreement about the best way to teach writing, but the general consensus is that both fluency and correctness must be taught, that there is a time and place for both. Students must be given opportunities to express thoughts without fear of red failure marks in journal writing and on first drafts, but they must also learn to organize their writing and avoid embarrassing mistakes by learning the rules and applying them as they edit and proofread final drafts.

So, a Mrs. Grundy may have left her mark on you. She may have rapped your knuckles for staring out the window when you were supposed to be writing. She may have covered your masterpiece in red ink before she tossed it back to you. She may have convinced you that writing is simply too painful, too risky, to put your soul into. And now you're in this writing class, perhaps wishing you were somewhere else, but *they* made you take it. You can probably think of many reasons *not* to write, not to expose yourself, and only one reason *to* write—to pass this course.

Well, take heart. There are *many* more reasons to write. You have something to say about yourself, about others, and to others. Writing is the vehicle for expression, for passing on knowledge, and for persuading others in our personal lives, in our communities, and in our professions.

You will find that not only is writing a functional, necessary skill but also challenging and fun. And you will find that learning correctness, the conventions of written English, does not have to be painful either. You will work through the stages in the writing process—planning, prewriting, drafting, revising, editing, proofreading—to produce writing that you are not only willing to share with others, but that you *want* to share with others.

R E M I N D E R

1. Good writers *practice* writing. Like anything else you do in life, you become a better writer through practice. You have something to say. You teach your brain to spill your ideas through your fingers to paper with practice. And since your brain works faster than your fingers, ideas usually don't translate to perfect prose. A single paper might involve several revisions—much practice.
2. Good writers *read.* When you read, you absorb sentence patterns, vocabulary, ideas that become a part of your knowledge, a part of you.
3. Good writers *proofread.* You already know most of the conventions of the English language. You have had them drilled into your head all your life. If you haven't already memorized, for instance, the comma rules, you should. This is information you will be using the rest of your life, tools to keep in the back pocket of your mind. That knowledge does not always reveal itself when you are writing a first draft. Your mind is preoccupied with ideas—as it should be. But after you have written your final revision, proofread.

GUIDE TO JOURNAL WRITING

Keep a personal journal in which you record responses, feelings, attitudes, evaluations, and opinions related to experiences, people, and events. Write at least three pages per week. Your instructor may ask you to write more and, perhaps, include brief essays in response to the For Writing and Discussion questions.

WHAT IS A JOURNAL?

A journal is a book, a notebook, or a collection of loose pages that contains the personal reflections of the writer. A journal differs from a diary in that a diary usually contains a straightforward accounting of facts or events. Journals, however, contain much more. A diary entry might read, "Went to the movies with Ted," but a journal entry might have specific details of the evening and responses, feelings, and opinions related to the experience.

A PRIVATE MATTER

Because journals are the private expressions of the author, writers sometimes go to great lengths to make sure their writing is not read. That may involve keeping the journal in a safe place or disguising it in a notebook entitled Biology Notes. Colonist William Byrd kept two journals—one written in longhand that contained noninflammatory details and responses and another written in a shorthand code that contained accounts of his escapades with his girlfriend's maid, and so forth. (Byrd's secret shorthand journals were not safe from historians, however.)

In journal writing the writer is free from concerns about audience. Because there is no reader standing over his shoulder, the writer doesn't have to worry about the mechanics of writing, such as organization or correct spelling, usage, and punctuation. The writer is free to record his or her thoughts without worrying about the judgments or evaluations of others.

WHY WRITE IN A JOURNAL?

1. *To develop fluency as a writer.* Research tells us that fluency, the ability to get ideas from brain to paper easily, is developed with frequent writing in a nonthreatening situation. Like any other skill, writing well takes practice. You will find that the more you write in your journal, the better you will become at expressing yourself on paper.

2. *To discover feelings, opinions, and prior knowledge.* E. M. Forster said, "How do I know what I think until I see what I say." Joan Didion explained her discovery process as, "I write entirely to find out what I'm thinking, what I'm looking at, what I see, and what it means." Many writers find that they make important discoveries about themselves and about their beliefs as they write. You might relate the idea of discovery through writing to the ideas you blurt out during a discussion that you hadn't really put into words before.

3. *To explore feelings.* Journal writing can serve as a kind of therapy— and it's free. One student calls her journal her "bitch (gripe) book"; when she is angry or frustrated, she writes out her emotion and afterward is better able to deal with the situation rationally.

A journal can be used to record reflections. The following journal entry was written by Brad Price toward the end of his first college English course as he recalled his feelings on the first day of class:

> The classroom was cold and quiet at first. I picked out a seat in the back. School--the thought of it made my hands shake and stomach turn. The walls were yellow and dull. There weren't any desks--just three rows of tables with about five tables to a row. No one said a word, and --damn, I thought I was going to freeze.
>
> The teacher walked in. She looked like my third-grade teacher Mrs. Peerbody. Great! What a wonderful way to start a new life. I didn't know anyone. It was cold, and the same teacher who told me I was going to grow up and live on skid row was here.
>
> However, I eventually met everyone; the classroom became warmer; and the teacher wasn't my third-grade teacher. (I found out later that Mrs. Peerbody died in a motorcycle accident when her Harley slammed into an El Dorado.) With the way everything turned out, my English class became one of my favorites.

4. *To get ideas for writing other kinds of compositions.* Journal writing can be used as a prewriting activity for major assignments or even for creative writing (stories and poems). You can write out what you know about a topic, what you think about the topic, and questions that you need to answer about the topic. Or you may use your journal as a source of topics for writing. A comment in your journal describing a movie you saw about the Special Olympics might result in an idea for a paper arguing for wider public support for the games.

GETTING STARTED

Your first thought might be "What do I write about?" For journal writing, the choice is yours. You might want to start with *freewriting,* writing down anything that comes to mind without stopping, even if you have to write "I don't know what to write. I don't know what to write" until you begin to have other thoughts. *Focused freewriting* is about a particular topic, but still you write quickly and without concern for correctness. As you practice journal writing, you will find that you have plenty to write about and that every experience, emotion, or interaction with another person is a potential journal topic.

WRITER'S BLOCK

Writing is easy. All you do is stare at a blank sheet of paper until drops of blood form on your forehead.

Attributed to Gene Fowler

The two main causes of writer's block, a kind of paralysis of pen, are (1) fear that what you write will not be perfect and (2) lack of knowledge about the topic. To take care of the first possible cause, you might make a big scribble on that clean, white sheet of paper—defile it so it can no longer intimidate you. You are now committed to revising. Knowing that your first draft will not be displayed in the Smithsonian or be turned in for others to read and knowing that anything you write on the paper will be an improvement over that scribble, frees you from perfectionism.

Another cause of writer's block can be dispensed with just as easily because you are completely free to choose your own topic, and you know *something* about *something*. As a matter of fact, you know a lot of things about a lot of things. Furthermore, you don't even have to write about "things"; you can write about feelings or your response to, say, writing in your journal.

A third cause of writer's block is the idea that the writer must be inspired—that when the right time comes, brilliant prose will flow from the fingers. That kind of inspiration is rare for most people. One great writer noted that writing is ninety percent perspiration and ten percent inspiration.

R E M I N D E R

When writing in a journal, you don't have to worry about organization or about staying with the same topic throughout. A journal entry may involve several different topics.

TOPICS FOR JOURNAL WRITING: THE PERSONAL INVENTORY

The following questions can be used to prompt ideas for journal writing.

1. What are your roots?
2. What are you doing now?
3. What are your goals for the future?
4. How do your past and present relate to your goals for the future?
5. What do you believe regarding religion? politics? education? laws? family life? censorship? your rights as a citizen? your duties and responsibilities as a citizen? the influence of media on culture?

6. What makes you a winner? determination? luck? some combination of both?

7. Who or what has influenced your opinions, attitudes, style, language (parents, teachers, friends, media, environment, heredity)? In what way?

8. What do you believe in strongly enough to defend in an argument? to write a letter about? to support or protest by walking in the rain with a sign? to make other kinds of personal sacrifices for?

9. In what way do your beliefs reflect your past experiences?

10. What kinds of books do you read? escape fiction? interpretive fiction? nonfiction?

11. What kinds of movies or television programs do you enjoy? the kind with happy endings? fiction that reflects the realities of life? documentaries and biographies?

12. Are you a romanticist? Do you like musicals, fairy tales, happy endings, escape reading? Or are you a realist? Do you prefer nonfiction, realistic fiction, documentaries, and biographies?

13. Are you a planner or a dreamer?

14. Are you a liberal? a conservative? an independent? a libertarian? a UTP (Unclassifiable Thinking Person)?

15. Who are your heroes? What does that say about you?

16. What are your rights? your responsibilities?

17. What are your answers to the *big questions*—the questions that continue to serve as an itch in the collective brains of humankind:

    Where did we come from?

    Why are we here?

    Where are we going?

18. Adage: A conservative is a liberal who has been mugged.
    Adage: When you are young and liberal, you have no brains; when you're old and conservative, you have no heart.
    Explain the truth or fallacy of one of these adages as it relates to your experience. For example, do you take a tough, conservative stand on crime because you have witnessed or been a victim of crime? Do you expect to become more conservative as you get older?

19. Ask yourself: Do I want my children to do all of the things I do? Explain why or why not.

20. Rate yourself on a scale of 1 to 10, with 1 representing *gullible* and 10 representing *cynical*. Explain your choice.

21. Mark Twain said that the conscience is the sum total of all our parents' teachings. Explain the truth or fallacy of this statement. Illustrate with examples from your own experience.

22. The word *unexamined* has become a euphemism for the words *ignorant, shallow,* and *unreflective*. Describe a person who lives an "examined" life and illustrate with examples from your own experience.

23. Chinese proverb:
> He who knows not and knows that he knows not is a child: Teach him.
>
> He who knows not and knows not that he knows not is a fool: Shun him.
>
> He who knows and knows that he knows is wise: Follow him.

Explain the truth or fallacy of this proverb and illustrate with examples from your own experience.

24. Explain how you see yourself and speculate about how others might see you in terms of the classical notions of virtues, sins, and values listed below:

Cardinal Virtues	Deadly Sins	Human Values
Prudence	Avarice	Power
Justice	Pride	Respect
Temperance	Anger	Wealth
Fortitude	Lust	Enlightenment
Faith	Envy	Skill
Hope	Gluttony	Well-being
Charity	Sloth	Rectitude
		Affection

THE WRITING CHALLENGE

Write an essay in which you state an opinion about an issue and describe the influences (parents, media, an event or experience, and so forth) on your thinking about the issue. Choose an issue that you feel passionately enough about to take action (join a group, walk a picket line in the rain, donate money, and so on). Although you may mention reasons why your position is best or relate causes and effects, the main purpose of your essay is to explain *why* you have *taken* the position, to tell the story of how you came to feel strongly about the issue, not why your opinion is right. (You may want to use the same position as a springboard for the assignment in Chapter 6 in which you explore why other people might feel differently and for the assignment in Chapter 9 when you develop an argument.)

The student papers on pages 54–57 show two possible approaches to the assignment, although these examples are not intended to serve as a recipe or pattern or to stifle your creativity. There are many ways of addressing the assignment. Your audience will be your classmates.

Note: You will probably want to explore ideas in your personal journal before deciding which ones you want to make public in your paper.

GUIDE TO WRITING

Planning and Prewriting

Your prewriting might include exploring your thoughts and feelings about a particular issue in journal writing or reviewing some of your earlier writings. You might also discuss the issue with a friend, relative, or someone who is particularly knowledgeable about the issue and make notes during or soon after the discussion. Reading about your topic is another prewriting activity that will help you focus your thoughts.

As you begin planning your paper, use listing to explore ideas. Below is an example list for a paper about influences that affected an opinion on the use of medical technology on the terminally ill.

Issue: the use of medical technology to prolong life (death)

Position: I do not believe that medical technology should be used to prolong the life of the terminally ill.

Influences: experience: the prolonged death of my grandmother
parents: the guilt they feel over insisting on pointless surgeries
media: debate over the cost of health care

Related emotions and opinions: compassion: I felt sympathy for my grandmother's physical pain and my parent's emotional pain because of the use of medical technology to prolong life.
prudence: As a practical matter, I believe that the cost of medical technology to prolong the life of the terminally ill can bankrupt the government and take services away from those who could benefit most.

Summary statement: My experiences and feelings during and after my grandmother's death resulted in my opinion that medical technology should not be used to prolong the life of the terminally ill.

Organizing and Drafting

The organization of your paper should follow some logical order. In fact, each paragraph has its own organization. The organization of a paragraph or paper may be closely related to the topic or may be used for its effect. Common methods of organization are described below.

POSSIBLE METHODS OF ORGANIZATION

Spatial: Focuses the reader's attention on one scene, person, object, or part of a whole, relating it to other scenes, people, and so on.

Chronological: Events are related in the order of their occurrence in time.

Specific to general: Evidence is given to support a final conclusion.

General to specific: A generalization is given, followed by evidence to support it.

Climactic: Events are ordered from the least important or dramatic to the most important or dramatic.

Simplest to most complex: The reader is guided to an understanding of complex ideas by first presenting simple ideas.

Most familiar to least familiar: The reader is reminded of a familiar concept before he is introduced to new ideas.

R E M I N D E R

Do not worry about correctness when you write a first draft. You should feel free to make errors when getting your ideas from brain to paper. If the blank page seems intimidating, defile it by scribbling on the top of the paper. The scribbling may serve two purposes: It overcomes writer's block caused by the fear of writing something imperfect and it guarantees a revision; you won't even be tempted to try to make that first draft your last.

INTRODUCTIONS

The introduction of your paper offers an opportunity to make a good impression on your reader. You will begin revealing your character, or *ethos,* as a writer. Begin establishing your credibility by presenting thoughtful ideas with coherency and correctness. The introduction will also establish the tone of your paper as serious, humorous, sarcastic, and so forth.

In addition, your introduction assists your readers by telling them what the paper is about; it introduces the subject to the readers. Perhaps most important, it catches the interest of your readers, enticing them to continue reading.

POSSIBLE WAYS TO START A PAPER

Effective introductions can be structured in a variety of ways.

Example:

1. Question: *Would you want to be kept alive by medical technology only to suffer horrible pain and degradation?* Most people would not, yet my grandmother was subjected to three painful surgeries during the last four months of her life, surgeries that filled each of her days

with tubes and probes and pain. My experiences and feelings during and after my grandmother's death resulted in my opinion that medical technology should not be used to prolong the life of the terminally ill.

2. Relevant anecdote: For the example topic, a narrative about the grand-mother's pain as observed by the writer is a possibility.
3. Quotation: For the example topic, a quotation about what makes life worth living is a possibility.
4. Definition: For the example topic, a definition of *life,* followed by illustration of the opposite state of some terminally ill people is a possibility.
5. Startling facts or statistics: For the example topic, statistics related to the use of medical technology, perhaps comparing the length of the death process without medical technology to the length of the process with it.

Example:

6. Opposing point of view: *Many people believe that medical science owes each person the longest life possible.* This view, however, considers only the quantity of life, not the quality. In the end, it is death that is prolonged, not life. My experiences and feelings during and after my grandmother's prolonged death resulted in my opinion that medical technology should not be used to prolong the life of the terminally ill.

R E M I N D E R

The way you choose to begin your paper is related to your own personal style of writing and reveals something about your *ethos,* or character as a writer. Take care in planning your introduction. First impressions are important. You may want to rewrite your introduction after you have finished your drafting.

Evaluating and Revising

After you have written a draft, you can focus your energies on perfecting your paper. Before you offer your paper to a partner for evaluation and suggestions, reread your draft with the following questions in mind:

1. Have I focused on explaining why I hold an opinion rather than why my opinion is right? (You will have opportunities to tell why your opinion is right in papers for other assignments.)
2. Have I included information that does not support the main point of my paper? (Cutting is a painful, but necessary, process.)
3. Are the divisions of my paper logical? Is each paragraph united by a main idea, or topic sentence?

UNITY

Good paragraphs, the building blocks of good compositions, must have unity. To achieve unity in a paragraph, you must have somewhere (beginning, middle, or end) a topic sentence, either directly stated or implied, around which to focus the details, examples, and reasons in the paragraph. Sentences in the paragraph may clarify the topic by further explaining or defining it or limit it by defining its boundaries, but every sentence should be directly related to the topic sentence. To check your paragraphs, turn the topic sentence into a question and determine whether each supporting sentence in some way answers the question.

COHERENCE

Coherence is what makes a piece of writing flow smoothly. Logical organization plays an important part in coherency, yet a piece of writing may be well organized and still be difficult to read and understand. The following elements help achieve coherency:

1. **Consistency in tense, number, and person:** Errors in verb tense and agreement and in pronoun reference and agreement may confuse the reader.
2. **Synonyms and recurring terms:** Repetitions may be included for emphasis. At other times, synonyms should be used to keep the paper from becoming irritating and monotonous.
3. **Transitions:** Connective words and phrases serve as a map to help the reader understand the relationship between ideas and paragraphs.
4. **Parallelism:** Using like structures for similar elements or ideas helps writing flow smoothly.

PARTNER EVALUATION

Because writers are so close to their own work and are inclined to read what they intended to say rather than what they actually said, it is good to work with a partner to evaluate drafts. After you are satisfied that you have written a good paper, trade with a partner. The following guide will help you as you evaluate your partner's essay.

- Read your partner's essay through to get a general impression. Jot down your initial response to the essay. Was it interesting? Did you learn something from reading it? Was it logically organized?
- Read the essay again, this time slowly, evaluating each of the following questions as you read:

  1. Does the paper address the assignment? If not, what changes are needed?

  2. Is the introduction clearly written? Does it make you want to read more? How can the introduction be improved?

  3. Does each paragraph contain a clear focus? Do any of the paragraphs contain information or ideas that are unrelated to the rest of the paragraph? If so, which paragraphs?

  4. Are transitions provided to guide the reader through the analysis? If not, where are transitions needed?

  5. Do you have questions about any of the ideas or information? Do any of the ideas need clarifying? If so, note where your partner might add information.

  6. What information or ideas are especially interesting? Note the positive aspects of the paper.

  7. Are any of the sentences unclear or awkward? (Put brackets around sentences that might be improved.) Did your partner use a variety of sentence structures?

  8. Does the ending adequately conclude the essay, or does the essay just stop? How might the ending be improved?

  9. What other ideas for improving the paper can you suggest?

REVISING

To begin revising, reread your paper, jotting down additional ideas and marking sentences that interrupt the logical order. Read your partner's evaluation of your paper, carefully considering each suggested change. Decide what revisions you want to make and mark your draft to include the changes.

THE POWER OF STYLE: SENTENCE VARIETY

Writers often want to emphasize an idea or draw the reader's attention to an act or deed. Since writers cannot scream or use gestures to get their readers' attention, the temptation is to use capital letters

(continued)

(continued from previous page)

Just as I was wondering whether the man would pull the trigger, HE FIRED THE GUN.

or underlining

Just as I was wondering whether the man would pull the trigger, he fired the gun.

or exclamation points.

Just as I was wondering whether the man would pull the trigger, he fired the gun!!!

Instead, try using **sentence variety.** For example, a very short sentence that follows a longer one stops the reader momentarily and adds drama.

For a moment, I wondered whether the man would pull the trigger. He did.

R E M I N D E R

Use a variety of short, medium, and long sentences. This variation happens naturally when you include details and show the relationships of ideas in simple, compound, and complex sentences.

Practice: Sentence Modeling

Sentence modeling provides an opportunity to practice using new structures and styles to communicate effectively. Imitate the structure of the following quotations from literature. Keep the underlined parts exactly the same. For other words, substitute similar kinds of words or groups of words.

1. It <u>was in</u> this apartment, <u>also, that there</u> stood <u>against the</u> western wall <u>a</u> gigantic clock <u>of</u> ebony.

Edgar Allan Poe, "The Masque of the Red Death"

2. <u>Having</u> deposit<u>ed our</u> mournful burden <u>upon</u> trestles <u>within</u> this region <u>of</u> horror, <u>we</u> partially turned aside the yet unscrewed lid of the coffin <u>and</u> looked <u>upon the</u> face <u>of the</u> tenant.

Edgar Allan Poe, "The Fall of the House of Usher"

3. <u>The</u> dog <u>is</u> unmoving, <u>his</u> tail <u>not</u> wagging, <u>his</u> eyes <u>like</u> marbles.

Robert Cormier, *I Am the Cheese*

4. <u>Away went</u> Tom Walker, dashing <u>down the</u> streets, <u>his</u> white cap bobb<u>ing</u> up and down, <u>his</u> morning gown flutter<u>ing in the</u> wind, <u>and his</u> steed strik<u>ing</u> fire out of the pavement at every bound.

Washington Irving, "The Devil and Tom Walker"

Editing and Proofreading

R E M I N D E R

For this assignment, you will be writing from a first-person point of view. Be careful to avoid the second-person pronoun *you* unless you really intend to address the reader directly. Writers sometimes make the mistake of using *you* when they really mean *I*:

You don't know how you will feel when you finally see her.

instead of

I didn't know how I would feel when I finally saw her.

The following checklist will guide your editing and proofreading.

1. Can any groups of sentences be combined? Can awkward or over-loaded sentences be separated into clear, concise sentences?
2. Should any words or phrases be replaced with words that describe more accurately or vividly? (Look at verbs and common nouns.)
3. Are all pronoun references clear, and do they agree in number with their antecedents?
4. Are first-person pronouns limited and relevant when used? (Phrases such as "I think" and "In my opinion" can be deleted. All opinions and judgments should be yours unless clearly noted.)
5. Do all verbs agree with their subjects in number?
6. Should any passive constructions be changed to active? (Look for forms of *be*.)
7. Are direct quotations correctly introduced? Are they enclosed in quotation marks?

8. Are all words spelled correctly? (Word processor spell checkers do not detect certain kinds of spelling errors. When in doubt, look up the word in a dictionary.)
9. Is each sentence punctuated correctly? Are there sentence fragments or run-on sentences?
10. Is your final draft neat and in manuscript form? (See Part Ten.)

You might want to designate the back page of your journal to record kinds of errors that are noted on your returned papers. When you are editing, look over your list to remind yourself to check for the same kinds of errors.

An effective proofreading trick is to read each sentence, starting from the end of the essay and working up, while moving the lips or saying the words aloud. This method helps the writer to read exactly what he or she wrote instead of reading what he or she intended to write. The method is also good for detecting faulty sentences because each sentence is read in isolation.

R E M I N D E R

If you haven't already memorized basic comma rules, now is a good time to do so. The investment of time and mental energy will pay off for the rest of your life. Use a comma
1. between independent clauses separated with a coordinating conjunction (and, or, but, yet, so, for, nor);
2. after a long introductory clause or phrase;
3. to separate words, phrases, or clauses in a series (including two or more adjectives that modify the same noun);
4. to separate a parenthetical comment, a nonessential clause or phrase (modifier that can be eliminated without changing the meaning of the sentence), or a contrasting phrase; and
5. after salutations and closings in letters, and to separate items in dates (except when only the month and year are given or when the day is before the month) and addresses.
Common errors: Inserting commas between subjects and verbs, verbs and objects, and compound subjects, verbs, or objects.

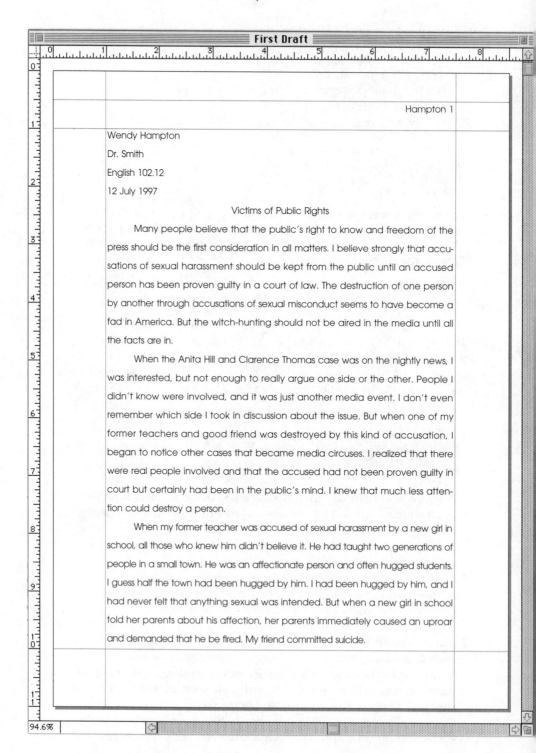

First Draft

Hampton 1

Wendy Hampton

Dr. Smith

English 102.12

12 July 1997

Victims of Public Rights

Many people believe that the public's right to know and freedom of the press should be the first consideration in all matters. I believe strongly that accusations of sexual harassment should be kept from the public until an accused person has been proven guilty in a court of law. The destruction of one person by another through accusations of sexual misconduct seems to have become a fad in America. But the witch-hunting should not be aired in the media until all the facts are in.

When the Anita Hill and Clarence Thomas case was on the nightly news, I was interested, but not enough to really argue one side or the other. People I didn't know were involved, and it was just another media event. I don't even remember which side I took in discussion about the issue. But when one of my former teachers and good friend was destroyed by this kind of accusation, I began to notice other cases that became media circuses. I realized that there were real people involved and that the accused had not been proven guilty in court but certainly had been in the public's mind. I knew that much less attention could destroy a person.

When my former teacher was accused of sexual harassment by a new girl in school, all those who knew him didn't believe it. He had taught two generations of people in a small town. He was an affectionate person and often hugged students. I guess half the town had been hugged by him. I had been hugged by him, and I had never felt that anything sexual was intended. But when a new girl in school told her parents about his affection, her parents immediately caused an uproar and demanded that he be fired. My friend committed suicide.

94.6%

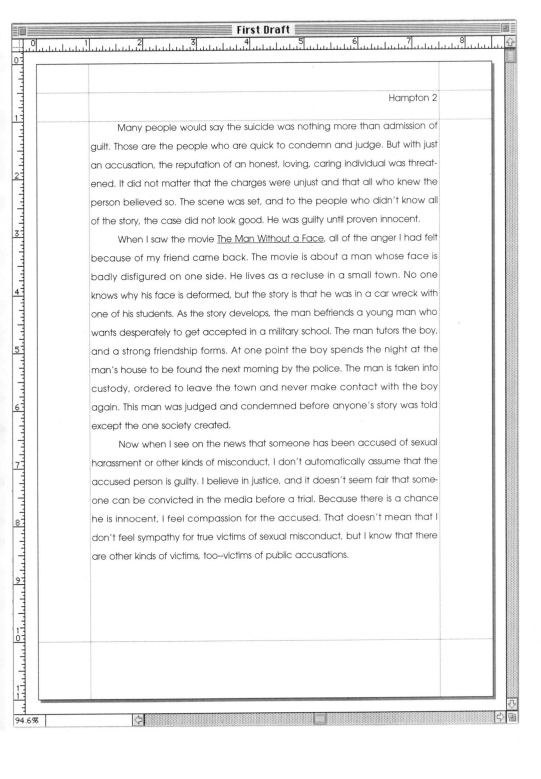

Hampton 2

  Many people would say the suicide was nothing more than admission of guilt. Those are the people who are quick to condemn and judge. But with just an accusation, the reputation of an honest, loving, caring individual was threatened. It did not matter that the charges were unjust and that all who knew the person believed so. The scene was set, and to the people who didn't know all of the story, the case did not look good. He was guilty until proven innocent.

  When I saw the movie <u>The Man Without a Face</u>, all of the anger I had felt because of my friend came back. The movie is about a man whose face is badly disfigured on one side. He lives as a recluse in a small town. No one knows why his face is deformed, but the story is that he was in a car wreck with one of his students. As the story develops, the man befriends a young man who wants desperately to get accepted in a military school. The man tutors the boy, and a strong friendship forms. At one point the boy spends the night at the man's house to be found the next morning by the police. The man is taken into custody, ordered to leave the town and never make contact with the boy again. This man was judged and condemned before anyone's story was told except the one society created.

  Now when I see on the news that someone has been accused of sexual harassment or other kinds of misconduct, I don't automatically assume that the accused person is guilty. I believe in justice, and it doesn't seem fair that someone can be convicted in the media before a trial. Because there is a chance he is innocent, I feel compassion for the accused. That doesn't mean that I don't feel sympathy for true victims of sexual misconduct, but I know that there are other kinds of victims, too--victims of public accusations.

94.6%

Norris 1

Bonnie Norris

Professor Lynch

English 102.09

20 Jan. 1996

Alcohol, Automobiles, and the Road Ahead

"Look both ways before crossing the street." "Would you jump off a cliff if your friends did?" I remember thinking as a child that my parents were telling and asking me these things just to be mean or to control me. I thought that nothing would happen to me and that they were wasting their breath. I had to suffer the consequences of giving in to peer pressure, or <u>doing</u> prior to <u>thinking</u>, to really understand what these overused clichés meant. Similarly, I had to lose some very important people in my life to understand how ultimately devastating drinking and driving can be. I know now that no amount of advertising, preaching, or even begging can make a person who is hell-bent on driving under the influence decide against it when they are intoxicated. The only way to deter someone is to make the threat of jail or heavy fines more eminent by creating tougher legislation (and strict enforcement of that legislation) against drunk driving. Those who are considering driving under the influence do not understand, in that altered state of consciousness, that they are capable of killing themselves and others. What they do understand is that they may get caught by police officers and suffer the legal consequences of their actions. These consequences must be certain and severe.

As a kindergartner, I did not understand how dangerous talking to a stranger can be; however, I understood that if Mom caught me, I would be spanked or have my toys taken away. As a teenager, I believed in the "it won't happen to me" theory, a concept I like to refer to as the "invincibility principle." I cannot remember how many times I have thought that,with a blood alcohol level ten times the legal limit, I was capable of guiding a big

94.6%

First Draft

hunk of metal to safety. No matter how many lectures I heard from teenage alcoholics or people convicted of vehicular homicide while under the influence, I, the invincibility poster girl, was immune to the effects of alcohol. The only thing that I feared was getting caught. Rather ironically, I was more concerned about my parents taking my car away than their having to pay for my funeral. This bizarre mode of thinking involves a combination of ignorance, adolescence, and intoxication (the latter has the ability to increase the effects of the former).

My philosophy did not change until I was literally faced with the tragedy that drunk driving reaps. That face is one that I will not soon forget. It was the face of a friend of mine that I will never see again because of a decision he will never make again. Jonathan was a twenty-year-old college student who opted to ride in the car of a drunk friend. His friend had convinced everyone, including himself, that he was a better driver when drunk than he was when sober. Of the three passengers and the driver, Jonathan was the only one who did not live to regret stepping foot in that car. The driver, as later revealed, had been convicted of drunk driving before, but because of the financial abilities of his family, the convictions were taken very lightly. In order to avoid the annoyance of getting caught once again, he chose to drive on a rarely traveled country road. Once again, the only worry was getting caught, not getting killed.

Jonathan's death inspired a change in my attitude about drunk driving. Since then, I have been known to, in the company of a number of my peers, wrestle someone to the ground to get his keys and prevent him from driving drunk. At that moment, popularity and invincibility did not even cross my mind. My only concern was being sure that my friend lived to complain about his hangover the next morning.

94.6%

Interactions: Knowing Your Audience

The art of argument is the art of living. Argument is the af-
firmation of our being. It is the principal instrument of human
interaction. . . .

    Argument is not the process by which we seek to destroy the
Other. *Argument is a tool with which we can achieve an end, ful-*
fill a desire. It is the incomparable art by which we connect and
interact successfully with the Other. *Thus successful argument can*
never be a verbal bludgeon with which we beat the Other *to sur-*
render. Winning is getting what we want, which often includes
assisting others in getting what they want.

    If I were required to choose the single most essential skill from
the many that make up the art of argument, it would be the ability
to listen. Listening is the ability to hear what people are saying, or
not saying, as distinguished from the words they enunciate.

Gerry Spence

Humans learn and practice communication skills first with parents or other caretakers in interactions related to basic needs and desires. As very young children, humans are egocentric—they have little awareness of others except as
others are related to themselves; others function only to fulfill the child's
needs or as obstacles to immediate wishes. Others give latitude to children
because they understand necessary developmental processes. When a two-year-

old is on a search and destroy mission in a public place, and the parents are the only onlookers smiling through unclenched teeth, the toddler is excused: How could Little Susie know that hitting someone in the shins with a baseball bat actually hurts? She's never had the experience.

But as children get older, the tolerance level for egocentric behavior shrinks and expectations of socially acceptable behavior grows inside the family as well as outside. Eventually, children's awareness of others increases, and they learn to interact in other kinds of relationships.

Part One dealt with individuality and the part *ethos* plays in writing; Part Two deals with understanding the role of emotion in communication and *pathos,* consideration of and appeals to the feelings of the audience. Part Two focuses on life's relationships and moves from interactions between parents and children in Chapter 3 to interactions with friends and lovers in Chapter 4 and then to interactions within the larger community in Chapter 5.

The Role of Emotions in Communication

Seeing is believing, but feeling is knowing.

Adage

Aristotle taught that "putting the audience in a certain right frame of mind" is one of the three necessary elements in effective communication with speech or writing. "Emotions are all those feelings that so change men as to affect their judgements, and that are also attended by pain or pleasure," he claimed more than two thousand years ago. He further noted that it is the responsibility of the effective communicator, or good writer, to "understand the emotions—that is, to name them and describe them, to know their causes and the way in which they are excited." Although many things have changed in two thousands years, human emotions have not. Below are Aristotle's descriptions of human emotions and his analysis of anger. Discover for yourself the depth of Aristotle's understanding.

ARISTOTLE'S CATALOG OF EMOTIONS

Anger: Impulse, accompanied by pain, to a conspicuous revenge for a conspicuous slight directed without justification toward what concerns oneself or one's friends (directed at individuals).

Calm: Settling down or quieting of anger; when people are amusing themselves or laughing or feasting; when they are feeling prosperous or successful or satisfied; when they are enjoying freedom from pain or inoffensive pleasure or justifiable hope.

Friendship: (includes comradeship, kinship, and intimacy, or romantic love) Feeling toward any one as wishing for him what you believe to be good things, not for your own sake but for his, and being inclined, so far as you can, to bring these things about. [Translation of the word friendship might be to be a friend, to like, to love—Aristotle doesn't distinguish between love and friendship here.]

Happiness: One or all of the following: prosperity combined with virtue; independence of life; the secure enjoyment of the maximum pleasure; a good condition of property and body, together with the power of guarding one's property and body and making use of them (excellences of the soul; excellences of the body).

Unhappiness: Opposed to happiness (sadness).

Hatred/Enmity: Feeling produced by anger, spite, or calumny, but may arise without offense; not a wish for suffering for an enemy, but rather a desire to see the enemy cease to exist; directed more at classes, even unknown people; cannot be cured with time; hatred or enmity may arise without offense.

Fear: Pain or disturbance due to a mental picture of some destructive or painful evil in the future.

Shame: Pain or disturbance in regard to bad things, whether present, past, or future, which seem likely to involve us in discredit.

Shamelessness: Contempt or indifference in regard to these same bad things.

Kindness: Helpfulness toward someone in need, not in return for anything, nor for the advantage of the helper himself, but for that of the person helped. (Social sciences use the term altruism.)

Unkindness: Opposed to kindness. Lack of kindness.

Pity: Feeling of pain caused by the sight of some evil, destructive or painful, which befalls one who does not deserve it, and which we might expect to befall ourselves or some friend of ours, and moreover to befall us soon.

Indignation: Opposed to pity. Pain at unmerited good fortune.

Envy: Pain at the sight of others' good fortune.

Emulation: Pain caused by seeing the presence in persons whose nature is like our own, of good things that are highly valued and are possible for ourselves to acquire; but it is felt not because others have these goods, but because we have not got them ourselves.

In appealing to an audience's anger, the writer will use language that causes readers to *feel* that something is very wrong and that it can and should be corrected, to *sense* the urgency of a problem and take action. The writer wants the audience to *experience vicariously* the harm that someone else is experiencing, to *feel pity* for the suffering, and to *fear* that they or others close to them may experience the harm in the future.

ARISTOTLE'S ANALYSIS OF ANGER

STATE OF MIND	WHO IS LIKELY TO CAUSE	GROUNDS
Impulse accompanied by • Feeling of pain • Concern for self or friends • Images of revenge Accompanying emotions • Shame • Sense of being "dumped on" • Sense of deprivation	People who • Laugh, mock, or jeer at us • Speak ill of us or maltreat us • Show contempt for us • Take what we feel is rightfully ours • Do not perceive our needs (when we expect them to) • Rejoice at our misfortunes or keep cheerful in the midst of our pain • Are indifferent to the pain they give us • Listen to stories about us or keep on looking at our weaknesses Classes of people who arouse our anger: • Our rivals • Those whom we admire • Those whom we wish to admire us • Those for whom we feel reverence • Those who feel reverence for us	Slight of • Contempt • Spite • Insolence People who are afflicted by sickness, poverty, love, thirst, or other unsatisfied desires are easily aroused. Seasons, times, conditions, and periods of life can affect arousal to anger.

Of course, anger is only one of the many emotions effective writers arouse in their audiences. A writer who is asking the community to donate food and clothing for a family whose home has burned might use specific examples of the hardship caused by the fire to move the audience to act. A writer who wants the public to support legislation to increase the penalty for drunk driving might use examples of the harm that has been caused by drunk drivers. But appeals to the emotions become *slimy* when the audience is manipulated through purely emotional appeals, and they become *sappy* when the audience is told what to feel with emotive language: *The poor little girl had no shoes on her little, bony feet.* (See Part Four for more on unfair emotional appeals.)

Appeal to anger

Consider the following campaign aid:

Congress is squandering your hard-earned tax dollars to study fruit flies and buy $600 toilet seats. My opponent voted to spend more money. This is *your* money. Vote for (Politician A).

The desired response from the audience is anger—a "throw the bums out" mentality and a belief that Politician A will clean up the mess (when, in fact, he could probably do very little). The ad appeals solely to the emotions. Of course, voters who are struggling to buy food, clothing, shelter, transportation, and health insurance are not thrilled with the idea that the money appropriated by Uncle Sam is squandered on $600 toilet seats. In fact, it could be hazardous to be in the same room with a taxpayer who thinks of that $600 as the money deducted from recent paychecks and who has a critical need for $600.

But the purpose of the ad is to make the audience angry enough *not* to think rationally or ask the obvious questions. No information is given on Politician A's qualifications, for instance, or on the situation in which the opponent voted to spend more money. The audience is not given enough information to make an *informed* choice between Politician A and his opponent.

R E M I N D E R

A credible writer demonstrates to the audience good sense, good moral character, and good will. All three involve understanding human emotions and using *pathos* (emotional appeals) both effectively and ethically. *Understanding human emotions is one of the necessary components of good communication.*

Chapter 4

INTERACTIONS WITH SIGNIFICANT OTHERS

PARENTS AND CHILDREN

On Children
Kahlil Gibran

And a woman who held a babe against
her bosom said, Speak to us of Children.
    And he said:
    Your children are not your children.
5   They are the sons and daughter of Life's longing for
      itself.
    They come through you but not from you,
    And though they are with you yet they belong not to
      you.
    You may give them your love but not your thoughts,
    For they have their own thoughts.
10   You may house their bodies but not their souls,
    For their souls dwell in the house of tomorrow,
      which you cannot visit, not even in your dreams.
    You may strive to be like them, but seek not to make
      them like you.
    For life goes not backward nor tarries with yesterday.
    You are the bows from which your children as living
      arrows are sent forth.
15   The archer sees the mark upon the path of the
      infinite, and He bends you with His might that His
      arrows may go swift and far.
    Let your bending in the archer's hand be for gladness;
    For even as He loves the arrow that flies, so He loves
      also the bow that is stable.

I Go Back to May 1937
Sharon Olds

I see them standing at the formal gates of their colleges,
I see my father strolling out
under the ochre sandstone arch, the
red tiles glinting like bent
5 plates of blood behind his head, I
see my mother with a few light books at her hip
standing at the pillar made of tiny bricks with the
wrought-iron gate still open behind her, its
sword-tips black in the May air,
10 they are about to graduate, they are about to get married,
they are kids, they are dumb, all they know is they are
innocent, they would never hurt anybody.
I want to go up to them and say Stop,
don't do it—she's the wrong woman,
15 he's the wrong man, you are going to do things
you cannot imagine you would ever do,
you are going to do bad things to children,
you are going to suffer in ways you never heard of,
you are going to want to die. I want to go
20 up to them there in late May sunlight and say it,
her hungry pretty blank face turning to me,
her pitiful beautiful untouched body,
his arrogant handsome blind face turning to me,
his pitiful beautiful untouched body,
25 but I don't do it. I want to live. I
take them up like the male and female
paper dolls and bang them together
at the hips like chips of flint as if
to strike sparks from them, I say
30 Do what you are going to do, and I will tell about it.

The Living Years
BA Robertson and Mike Rutherford

Every generation blames the one before
And all of their frustrations come beating on your door.
I know that I'm a prisoner to all my Father held so dear.
I know that I'm a hostage to all his hopes and fears.
5   I just wish I could have told him in the living years.
Crumpled bits of paper filled with imperfect thought
Stilted conversations. I'm afraid that's all we've got.
You say you just don't see it. He says it's perfect sense.
You just can't get agreement in this present tense.
10   We all talk a different language; talking in defense.
Say it loud, say it clear. You can listen as well as you hear.
It's too late when we die to admit we don't see eye to eye.
So we open up a quarrel between the present and the past.
We only sacrifice the future; It's the bitterness that lasts.
15   So don't yield to the fortunes you sometimes see as fate.
It may have a new perspective on a different day.
And if you don't give up, and don't give in
You may just be O.K.
Say it loud, say it clear: You can listen as well as you hear.
20   It's too late when we die to admit we don't see eye to eye.
I wasn't there that morning when my Father passed away.
I didn't get to tell him all the things I had to say.
I think I caught his spirit later that same year.
I'm sure I heard his echo in my baby's newborn tears.
25   I just wish I could have told him in the living years.
Say it loud, say it clear: You can listen as well as you hear.
It's too late when we die to admit we don't see eye to eye.

For Writing and Discussion

1. Paraphrase the speaker's message in "On Children." Tell whether you agree or disagree and why.

2. Sharon Olds said, "Poets are like steam valves, where the ordinary feelings of ordinary people can escape and be shown." In what way does her poem "I Go Back to May 1937" reflect "ordinary" feelings? In what way does the speaker in the poem put a new twist on the unpleasant events of childhood wrought by parents who are "wrong" for each other?

3. Describe a common problem of communication between parents and adolescents and how it might be resolved. Identify the emotions that are likely to be felt by both parties, and tell how each could contribute to a resolution.

4. Explain lines 3 and 4 in "The Living Years" and illustrate with examples of possible "hopes and fears."

5. Literature that has meaning for or can be related to by many people has the quality of *universality*. Everyone has a biological father, but not everyone has a relationship with that father or even knows his or her biological father. What theme in "The Living Years" includes more than just relationships between fathers and sons? What other relationships might be substituted for the father-son relationship in the lyrics?

The Art of Listening

In "The Living Years," the speaker suggests that there is a difference in listening and hearing words clearly without understanding their full meaning. Imagine hearing someone speak in a language you do not know. You might hear words, but you would not understand the meaning of the words. In line 10 ("We all talk a different language"), the speaker implies that two people can be so far apart in understanding each other that they may as well be speaking foreign languages.

Hearing is something most people are able to do without conscious effort; however, listening is a learned art. When people listen, they often indicate that they are understanding the speaker through body language, such as making eye contact, nodding, smiling, and moving closer.

THE POWER OF STYLE:
PARAPHRASING AND CLARIFYING

An active listener cares about what the other person is saying and wants to understand the intended meaning of the speaker. A good listener uses phrases such as "I'm not sure I understand" instead of "You're not making yourself clear." A good listener tries to understand the speaker's point of view and respond to the speaker's needs. To ensure that he or she has correctly understood, an active listener may ask for clarification or paraphrase the speaker's words.

SPEAKER:	I'm tired of school. I want to do something else with my time.
LISTENER:	Do you mean that you are quitting college?
SPEAKER:	No. I'm just taking a break from studying tonight to see a movie.
LISTENER:	Oh. You need a break from the study routine?

In contrast, a poor listener short-circuits communication when he or she

- criticizes the speaker,
- becomes defensive,
- starts making excuses,
- shows impatience,
- puts words in the speaker's mouth,
- loses control of emotions,
- forces a win-lose situation,
- rolls eyeballs, folds arms, or moves away, or
- takes an offensive position that puts the speaker on the defensive.

When we listen to and develop understanding of those around us, it becomes easier to think of an audience as made up of real people. The relationship between speaker and listener and writer and reader is based on understanding those human qualities we all share. And the relationship between speaker and listener is reciprocal—it works both ways. You are both speaker and listener, reader and writer. The skills you develop as a listener will help you when reading the writing of others. When you are writing, listening skills will also help you hear the answers to the mental questions you ask when reflecting on how your audience might react.

What a writer asks of his reader is not so much to like *as to* listen.

Henry Wadsworth Longfellow

R E M I N D E R

Active listening is similar to active reading. When you are reading, search out underlying assumptions and look for subtle clues that might help you understand the author's full meaning.

Practice: Listening between the Lines

The following dialogue is between a father and his eighteen-year-old son who is at home from college for the holidays. The son has been out with friends and has come in at 3 a.m. Read the dialogue or listen as classmates act out the scene. Next, read the dialogue again and fill in "between the lines" with the fuller message you think is intended with each line of dialogue.

FATHER: (Sounding angry) Where have you been? It's 3 o'clock in the morning, and the weather is terrible!

SON: What's wrong? I just walked through the door.

FATHER: What's wrong? I'll tell you what's wrong. Your mother has been walking the floor. That's what's wrong.

SON: You treat me like a baby.

FATHER: Have you ever heard of telephones?

SON: Look. I was with other people. Okay?

FATHER: Maybe that's the problem. You are hanging around with the wrong kind of friends.

SON: You're trying to ruin my life! (Goes in room and slams the door.)

Write another dialogue, using the same situation, in which both father and son listen to each other and understand the other's feelings.

FRIENDS AND LOVERS

Letter to Sarah
Sullivan Balou

A week before Balou was killed at the first battle of Bull Run, he wrote this letter to his beloved.

July 14, 1861
Camp Clark, Washington

My very dear Sarah:

1   The indications are very strong that we shall move in a few days—perhaps tomorrow. Lest I should not be able to write again, I feel impelled to write a few lines that may fall under your eye when I shall be no more. . . .

2   I have no misgivings about, or lack of confidence in the cause in which I am engaged, and my courage does not halt or falter. I know how strongly American Civilization now leans on the triumph of the Government, and how great a debt we owe to those who went before us through the blood and sufferings of the Revolution. And I am willing—perfectly willing—to lay down all my joys in this life to help maintain this Government, and to pay that debt. . . .

3   Sarah my love for you is deathless, it seems to bind me with mighty cables that nothing but Omnipotence could break; and yet my love of Country comes over me like a strong wind and bears me unresistibly on with all these chains to the battlefield.

4   The memories of the blissful moments I have spent with you come creeping over me, and I feel most gratified to God and to you that I have enjoyed them so long. And hard it is for me to give them up and burn to ashes the hopes of future years, when, God willing, we might still have lived and loved together, and seen our sons grown up to honorable manhood, around us. I have, I know, but few and small claims upon Divine Providence, but something whispers to me—perhaps it is the wafted prayer of my little Edgar, that I shall return to my loved ones unharmed. If I do not my dear Sarah, never forget how much I love you, and when my last breath escapes me on the battlefield, it will whisper your name. Forgive my many faults, and the many pains I have caused you. How thoughtless and foolish I have often times been! How gladly would I wash out with my tears every little spot upon your happiness. . . .

5   But, O Sarah! if the dead can come back to this earth and flit unseen around those they loved, I shall always be near you; in the gladdest days and in the darkest nights . . . *always, always,* and if there be a soft breeze upon your cheek, it shall be my breath, as the cool air fans your throbbing temple, it shall be my spirit passing by. Sarah do not mourn me dead; think I am gone and wait for thee, for we shall meet again. . . .

The friend
Marge Piercy

We sat across the table.
he said, cut off your hands.
they are always poking at things.
they might touch me.
5   I said yes.

Food grew cold on the table.
he said, burn your body.
it is not clean and smells like sex.
it rubs my mind sore.
10   I said yes.

I love you, I said.
That's very nice, he said
I like to be loved,
that makes me happy.
15   Have you cut off your hands yet?

For Writing and Discussion

1. In the letter Sullivan Balou wrote shortly before his death, he reveals understanding of the grieving process his wife will go through at his death and tries to comfort her. There is no indication of self-pity or fear in the letter—just selfless love. Reread Aristotle's definition of love (included under Friendship, pages 59–60), and write your own definition of love. Illustrate your definition with examples.

2. "The friend" suggests a relationship in which "he" is extremely egocentric and the other is willing to do anything to please. Discuss how hyperbole, or exaggeration, is used in the poem to characterize an all-too-common kind of relationship. Translate the hyperbole into characterization of a relationship in which one person (of either gender) ignores another's needs and makes selfish demands, and explain the role the abused person's self-esteem (or lack of self-esteem) might play.

3. Contrast "The friend" and "Letter to Sarah" in terms of realism and romanticism. Discuss the tone (attitude toward the subject) and style (especially the choice of words) of each.

4. B. K. Eakman, in "When Sex Conquers Love" (*Chronicles,* June 1994), writes that in today's society, romantic love has taken a back seat to sex. Eakman concedes that sex "may be the strongest *animal* drive after hunger" but argues that sex "is not the strongest *human* drive. Love is. Love is what separates animals from humans. Animals may exhibit loyalty, trust, and affection, but these are not the equivalents of compassion and commitment, which comprise the key elements of what we know as romantic love." Is romance dead or alive? Illustrate your answer with examples from contemporary culture.

5. One reason that has been cited for today's high divorce rate is "unrealistic expectations." Couples see each other on their best behavior before marriage; after marriage they wake up and say, "Is that really your breath I smell?" Reality sets in, and disillusionment can lead to apathy, anger, and even violence. Change in a relationship is inevitable. Explain why you think some relationships last while others fail.

R E M I N D E R

When incorporating quotations from the works of others into your own writing, remember to use quotation marks around direct quotations and reproduce the quotations exactly as written. When quoting two or more lines of poetry, use a slash (/) with spaces on either side to separate the lines.

RESPONSES TO A SLIGHT (MAJOR OR MINOR)

FOCUS ON YOUR OWN FEELINGS	FOCUS ON 'THE OTHER'S' FEELINGS
• Go ballistic (become visibly and audibly angry)	• Stay calm
• Exaggerate the slight	• Ask yourself what motivates *the other's* words or actions
• Strike back with sarcasm	• Consider *the other's* fears, etc. (What does *the other* have to lose or gain?)
• Strike back with a "below the belt" comment—a personal attack (You know the other's soft spots.)	• Respond appropriately
	• Suggest a compromise
• Retreat behind a slammed door	• Think about how to get *the other* to understand your feelings (The responses in the left-hand column are counterproductive.)

Resolving Conflicts (Fair Fighting)

Conflict, or at least disagreement, is a part of any relationship. On a rational level, we know that people are different; it's easy to accept the concept of "different strokes for different folks" when those "different folks" don't live in the same house as we do. Those "folks" are remote; our significant others are near, perhaps even in our faces at times. Emotions are fueled during disagreements, often unnecessarily.

We might say hurtful things to those who are closest to us, people we love, that we wouldn't think of saying to a stranger or even one of those vague people we might think of as enemies. And those hurtful things are usually said in response to a "slight" as Aristotle calls it. (Slights can be *very* serious.)

SAMPLE RESPONSES TO POTENTIAL CONFLICT

The responses below illustrate two ways of responding to a statement that might provoke conflict.

THE OTHER: I didn't like the movie you chose. What kind of person would enjoy watching blood and guts every half-second?

Response that may defuse the conflict:

YOU: I'm sorry you didn't like it. It was pretty bloody, but I thought the story was good. Next time, you pick one you think you'll like.

Response that may make the other become defensive and the conflict escalate:

YOU: You never like anything I like. You're just a whimp. Everyone in the world liked that movie except you. You are totally out of touch with reality!

Practice: Responding to Conflict

Write two responses (one to defuse a conflict and one to escale a conflict) for each of the following statements:

1. Your mother doesn't like me. She's so stuck-up. I know she thinks I'm not good enough for you. Who does she think she is, anyway?

2. You are such a tightwad! What is life for if you can't enjoy spending the money you earn? I won't spend my whole life saving every dime for the future!

3. Does clumsiness run in your family? You stepped on my foot again! I need full body armor to be close to you.

4. I told your boss that you said he's a jerk. I guess it just slipped out. Oh well, someone needs to tell him.

5. You care more about your friends than you do me. You might as well sleep with them! It's obvious you enjoy their company more than you do mine.

Practice: Walking in Another Person's Shoes

In this chapter you have read about and discussed friend and family relationships. Try writing about a family or friendship crisis in which you assume the persona, or mask, of another person who was involved in the crisis. Use first-person to tell the story as the other person and present tense as though it were happening right now. Use specific details to create the scene and reveal the emotions involved in the crisis. After you have finished telling the story as the other person, change to your own voice and tell what insights you gained from writing as the other person.

Practice: Firsthand Information

According to statistics, about one-half of the people who marry will end up in divorce court. In many families, the only people who have not been divorced at least once are grandparents or even great-grandparents.

Interview at least three people who have long-lasting relationships and ask them the secret, the key, to making a relationship last. You might want to ask them about romantic notions of love as opposed to the realism of long-term relationships. You might also ask them what kinds of things they do to keep love alive and what their response is to the idea that relationships change as people change. How does a successful relationship accommodate change?

After you have completed your interviews, write a summary of what you have learned from the people you interviewed.

CHAPTER SUMMARY

In this chapter, you have explored emotions involved in relationships to understand better yourself and others. Recall the importance Aristotle placed on understanding human emotions when speaking or writing. In order to make ethical emotional appeals, a writer must understand and consider the audience. Chapter 5 deals with communities made up of people with a myriad of differences and perspectives who all share the common experience of being human.

Chapter 5

INTERACTIONS IN COMMUNITIES

Theme for English B
Langston Hughes

1 The instructor said,

> *Go home and write*
> *a page tonight.*
> *And let that page come out of you—*
> 5 *Then, it will be true.*

I wonder if it's that simple?
I am twenty-two, colored, born in Winston-Salem.
I went to school there, then Durham, then here
to this college on the hill above Harlem.
10 I am the only colored student in my class.
The steps from the hill lead down into Harlem,
through a park, then I cross St. Nicholas,
Eighth Avenue, Seventh, and I come to the Y,
the Harlem Branch Y, where I take the elevator
15 up to my room, sit down, and write this page:

It's not easy to know what is true for you or me
at twenty-two, my age. But I guess I'm what
I feel and see and hear, Harlem, I hear you:
hear you, hear me—we two—you, me, talk on this page.
20 (I hear New York, too.) Me—who?
Well, I like to eat, sleep, drink, and be in love.
I like to work, read, learn, and understand life.
I like a pipe for a Christmas present,
or records—Bessie, bop, or Bach.
25 I guess being colored doesn't make me *not* like
the same things other folks like who are other races.

So will my page be colored that I write?
Being me, it will not be white.
But it will be
30   a part of you, instructor.
You are white—
yet a part of me, as I am a part of you.

That's American.
Sometimes perhaps you don't want to be a part of me.
35   Nor do I often want to be a part of you.
But we are, that's true!
As I learn from you,
I guess you learn from me—
although you're older—and white—
40   and somewhat more free.

This is my page for English B.

For Writing and Discussion

1. In what way is the speaker in "Theme for English B" struggling to find the truth that is in him? How is his page shaded by racial experience?

2. What truth does the speaker discover that surpasses race and age?

March 6, 1989
Beatrice High

Red fog dances in the black sky,
pirouetting east, then west,
bouncing, sweeping over humming lines—
"Do you see? Do you see?"

5   Sweet and ominous to the faithful,
it heralds the Second Coming. "I told you so;
let the weeping and wailing begin."
"The Messiah has come!" They rejoice, then fear.

"Ah ha!" says the Left. "It's proof.
10   The Establishment mesmerizes with its poison;

it sucks our will. For Chris' sake, don't breathe!"
"Take arms!" cries the Right. "The commies come
from within. Shoot the ether—no, don't."

"Wow, man. It's like an encounter
15   of the fourth kind."
"Is it magic?" asks the child.

They watch; they quake—
too human to enjoy the one time in a life
wonder of aurora borealis south of the
thirty-third.

Practice: Hearing Voices

Explain the perceptions of each of the voices in the poem "March 6, 1989,"
and tell how their perceptions are related to their experiences and beliefs.
You might also want to relate the poem to the myths and legends of ancient
cultures and how they attempted to explain natural phenomena.

from Gang Bang Bang
P. J. O'Rourke

As the foreign affairs correspondent for Rolling Stone, *O'Rourke traveled to the
former Yugoslavia during the civil war. He found a lesson to be learned from
"the land of a thousand grievances."*

1   You mustn't ever ask the Yugoslavs why they're fighting. They'll tell you. And
there's no straightening it out. If you look at a geographical map of the Balkans,
you see nothing that would serve as a natural boundary and no area—no plain,
valley, coastline or mountain fastness—coherent or extensive enough to put a
boundary around. It was a confused region before nations or even people
existed—not big enough to be a subcontinent, too big to be a peninsula, wrin-
kled, creased, puckered, the cellulite thigh of Europe.

2   To this bad hash of terrain came a worse omelet of population. The
Balkans separate Asia from the West, divide the steppes from the Mediter-
ranean, lie athwart the road from Baltic ice and snow to Adriatic topless
beaches. Most of the roving bands, nomadic tribes, pillaging hordes and migrat-
ing populations of history have passed through the Balkans. Every time they

did, they'd tell their most objectionable members to go camp around the corner. Then the band, tribe, horde or population would sneak off.

3   The Christians hate the Muslims because Christians were peons under the Ottomans. The Muslims hate the Christians because Muslims were pissants under the Communists. The Croats hate the Serbs for collaborating with the Communists the same way the Serbs hate the Croats for collaborating with the Nazis; now the Bosnians hate the Montenegrins for collaborating with the Serbs. The Serbs hate the Albanians for coming to Yugoslavia. The Macedonians hate Yugoslavia and want to go to Greece. Everybody hates the Serbs because there are more of them than anyone else to hate and because, when Yugoslavia was created in 1918 (with the help of know-it-all U.S. president Woodrow Wilson), the Serbs grabbed control of the government and army and haven't let go yet. And everybody hates the Slovenes, too, for getting out of this civil war after only ten days.

4   It's hard to come back from the Balkans and not sound like a Pete Seeger song. Even those of us who are savagely opposed to pacifism are tempted to grab the Yugoslavs by their fashionably padded shoulders and give them nonviolent what for: "Even if you win, you assholes, all you've got is *Yugoslavia!* It's not like you're invading France or something."

5   Yugoslavia's ethnic wounds are also, unfortunately, infected with idealism. There's a surplus of intellectuals in the region. Yugoslavia, like the rest of Eastern Europe, has more artists, writers and teachers than it has art, literature or schools. In the resultant mental unemployment, idealism flourishes.

6   Idealism is based on big ideas. And as anybody who has ever been asked, "What's the big idea?" knows, most big ideas are bad ones. Particularly in Yugoslavia. First there is the bad idea of nationalism, the notion that every little group of human twerps with its own slang, haircut and pet name for God should have a country. Then there's the bad idea of what the government of that country is supposed to do—kill everybody whose hair looks different. And finally there is the worst idea of all—a belief common to the benighted people in underdeveloped areas everywhere from the Bosnian hills to the Clinton White House—that nationhood is a zero-sum business. The thing that makes Croatia rich makes Serbia poor. But Britain and Japan are powerful without natural resources. Singapore and Hong Kong are important without physical territory. And Luxembourg and the Cayman Islands wield enormous influence and barely have people. Modern nations do not triumph by conquering territory or dominating strangers. War doesn't work anymore. Rape and slaughter may get Serbia on the evening news, but from the point of view of becoming major players upon the international stage, Serbs would be better off selling Yugos.

7   Between Zagreb and Belgrade, the Serbs and the Croats fought their war on the freeway. It's an ordinary-looking toll road with guardrails, median strips, service plazas and long, straight lanes of pavement. The guardrails have been crushed by tanks, the median strips dug up for trenches, the service plazas reduced to ruins and the pavement gashed with shell holes. The Croats still

give out toll tickets at one end of the road, but the tollbooths at the other have been blown to pieces. Ed Gorman and I drove ninety miles east on this thoroughfare to Slavonski Brod. There was no other traffic, just an occasional UN blue hat or Serbian Chetnik waving us over to check our papers. The highway runs toward the Danube through the flat, open country of the Sava River valley. The scenery—except for the tile roofs and Lombardy poplars—is exactly Midwestern. It made me feel at home to be driving on an American-style road through an American-style landscape and then see war damage as good as the set for any Hollywood movie.

8   Someday, no doubt, the various constituent parts of America will become "empowered" the way Serbia and Croatia are. Someday Aryan Nation, NOW, the VFW, ACT UP, the AARP, Native Americans, right-to-life fetuses, people with Hispanic surnames, the blind, the deaf, the rest of the differently abled, Pat Buchanan, Robert Bly and Spike Lee will have their dreams come true. The great thing about making the drive to Slavonski Brod is that now I know what America will look like when it happens. . . .

For Writing and Discussion

1. Consider O'Rourke's analogy between what he saw during the drive to Slavonski Brod and the future America. Do you see a danger in a divided America? Why or why not? What makes it possible for people with diverse views to live together in harmony?

2. Robert Hughes, in "The Fraying of America," argues that "America is a construction of mind, not of race or inherited class or ancestral territory . . . a collective act of the imagination whose making never ends, and once that sense of collectivity and mutual respect is broken, the possibilities of American-ness begin to unravel" (*Time,* 3 Feb. 1992). What is your definition of *American-ness?* How do the different factions with grievances fit into American-ness?

3. In the civil war in the Balkans, everyone wanted to win. Who lost? Why?

4. O'Rourke injects humor in his writing about serious subjects. Recall the stylistic elements that O'Rourke uses to create humor. How does the humor affect the tone of the piece? Cite specific examples.

The Healing Powers of Community
Carolyn R. Shaffer and Kristen Anundsen

*Shaffer and Anundsen argue that interpersonal relationships serve a vital func-
tion to humans.*

1   In the early 1960s, a small town in Pennsylvania became the focus of attention
for scores of medical researchers. The community of Roseto appeared unre-
markable in every way except one: Its inhabitants were among the healthiest
people in the United States. The rate at which they died of heart disease was
significantly lower than the national average, and they exhibited greater resistance to peptic ulcers and senility than other Americans.

2   When researchers searched for clues to the Rosetans' health and longevity
among the usual array of factors, they came up empty-handed. The folks in
Roseto smoked as much, exercised as little, and faced the same stressful situations as other Americans. The residents of this closely knit Italian-American
community practiced no better health habits than their neighbors. So why were
they so healthy?

3   The answer surprised the researchers. After extensive testing, they learned
that the Rosetans' remarkable health was linked to their strong sense of community and camaraderie. The town was not so ordinary after all. "More than that of
any other town we studied, Roseto's social structure reflected old-world values
and traditions," says Dr. Steward Wolf in a booklet summarizing the study that
he directed. "There was a remarkable cohesiveness and sense of unconditional
support within the community. Family ties were very strong."

4   Developments since the initial study underscored this conclusion. As
young Rosetans began to marry outside the clan, move away from the town's
traditions, and sever emotion and physical ties with the community, the healthy
edge Roseto held over neighboring towns began to lessen until, by the mid-
1970s, its mortality rates had climbed as high as the national average.

5   While you cannot, and for many reasons would not want to, recreate the
patriarchal, religion-bound, old-world traditions that helped keep Rosetans
healthy, you can discern the positive qualities of social interaction that contributed to their health and take steps to nourish these qualities in various areas
of your life.

6   An important reason to seek functional or conscious community, even
protocommunity, is that it can keep you healthier in many respects. The Roseto
findings are far from unique. Contemporary medical, psychological, and sociological literature overflows with studies that point to the life-prolonging, even
life-saving qualities of interpersonal support. For example:

7   • Dr. Dean Ornish, a California specialist in coronary heart disease, developed a treatment program with support groups that surprised even him and his

colleagues with its positive results: Chest pains diminished or went away entirely, severe blockages in coronary arteries reversed, and patients became more energetic. In Ornish's study, which was partially funded by the National Institutes of Health, patients lived together for a week in a retreat, then met two evenings every week for four hours.

8   "At first," Ornish writes in *Dr. Dean Ornish's Program for Reversing Heart Disease,* "I viewed our support groups simply as a way to motivate patients to stay on the other aspects of the program that I considered most important: the diet, exercise, stress management training, stopping smoking, and so on. Over time, I began to realize that the group support itself was one of the most powerful interventions, as it addressed what I am beginning to believe is the more fundamental cause of why we feel stressed and, in turn, why we get illnesses like heart disease: the perception of isolation.

9   "In short, anything that promotes a sense of isolation leads to chronic stress and, often, to illnesses like heart disease. Conversely, anything that leads to real intimacy and feelings of connection can be healing in the real sense of the word: to bring together, to make whole. The ability to be intimate has long been seen as a key to emotional health; I believe it is essential to the health of our hearts as well."

10   • The University of Michigan's Dr. James House and two fellow sociologists concluded, from their own studies and those of others, that there is a clear link between poor social relationships and poor health. "It's the 10 to 20 percent of people who say they have nobody with whom they can share their private feelings, or who have close contact with others less than once a week, who are most at risk," the researchers declared. This risk extends to life itself. In fact, House reports, the people with the weakest social ties have significantly higher death rates—100 percent to 300 percent for men, 50 percent to 150 percent for women—than their counterparts who are more socially integrated in terms of marital and family status, contacts with friends, church memberships, and other group affiliations.

11   • A study at St. Luke's-Roosevelt Hospital and Columbia University in New York City revealed that, for people with heart disease, living alone is a major independent risk factor comparable to such factors as previous heart damage and heart rhythm disturbances. The data indicate that heart attack patients living alone are twice as likely as others to suffer another heart attack, and more likely to die of an attack, within six months.

12   "What's particularly significant is the magnitude of the effect," said clinical psychologist Nan Case, co-author of the study. "We know that emotions and [social] integration have an effect, but we never knew it could come close to the physiological factors in heart disease."

13   • A team of Stanford Medical School psychiatrists, led by Dr. David Spiegel, found that metastatic breast cancer patients who joined support groups lived nearly twice as long as those receiving only medical care.

14   • At Ohio State University, psychologist Janice Kiecolt-Glaser and her colleagues discovered, in comparing thirty-eight married women with thirty-eight

separated or divorced women, that the married women had better immune functions than the unmarried women.

15   Several studies suggest that it is not the number of personal contacts that affects people's health, but the degree to which people perceive that they have someone they can turn to. Social networks do not always feel like community. Unhappy marriages, alcoholic families, and other dysfunctional relationships can actually damage a person's health. Psychologists at the University of Washington concluded that even supportive actions and words do not necessarily translate into perceived support. "It all depends on whether your social support comes from someone you believe truly loves, values, and respects you," concluded one of the researchers, Dr. Gregory Pierce.

16   Psychologist Robert Ornstein and physician David Sobel believe that human beings evolved as social animals, and that our brains are programmed to connect us with others in order to improve our chances of survival. When the brain detects signals of isolation or emotional imbalance, it transmits these signals to other parts of the body. The way you interact with family members, co-workers, and others in your social sphere is translated by brain mechanisms into changes in hormone levels and in neurotransmitters.

17   "People need people," the researchers conclude in *The Healing Brain*. "Not only for the practical benefits which derive from group life, but for our very health and survival. Somehow interaction with the larger social world of others draws our attention outside of ourselves, enlarges our focus, enhances our ability to cope, and seems to make the brain reactions more stable and the person less vulnerable to disease."

Reprinted by permission: Tribune Media Services

The Virtual Community
Howard Rheingold

Computer networking can help bring community back to the center of modern life.

1   In the summer of 1986, my then-2-year-old daughter picked up a tick. There was this blood-bloated *thing* sucking on our baby's scalp, and we weren't quite sure how to go about getting it off. My wife, Judy, called the pediatrician. It was 11 o'clock in the evening. I logged onto the WELL, the big Bay Area infonet, and contacted the Parenting conference (a conference is an on-line conversation about a specific subject). I got my answer on-line within minutes from a fellow with the improbable but genuine name of Flash Gordon, M.D. I had removed the tick by the time Judy got the callback from the pediatrician's office.

2   What amazed me wasn't just the speed with which we obtained precisely the information we needed to know, right when we needed to know it. It was also the immense inner sense of security that comes with discovering that real people—most of them parents, some of them nurses, doctors, and midwives— are available, around the clock, if you need them. There is a magic protective circle around the atmosphere of the Parenting conference. We're talking about our sons and daughters in this forum, not about our computers or our opinions about philosophy, and many of us feel that this tacit understanding sanctifies the virtual space.

3   The atmosphere of this particular conference—the attitudes people exhibit to each other in the tone of what they say in public—is part of what continues to attract me. People who never have much to contribute in political debate, technical argument, or intellectual gamesmanship turn out to have a lot to say about raising children. People you knew as fierce, even nasty, intellectual opponents in other contexts give you emotional support on a deeper level, parent to parent, within the boundaries of this small but warmly human corner of cyberspace.

4   In most cases, people who talk about a shared interest don't disclose enough about themselves as whole individuals on-line to inspire real trust in others. But in the case of the subcommunity called the Parenting conference, a few dozen of us, scattered across the country, few of whom rarely if ever saw the others face to face, have a few years of minor crises to knit us together and prepare us for a serious business when it comes our way. Another several dozen read the conference regularly but contribute only when they have something important to add. Hundreds more read the conference every week without comment, except when something extraordinary happens.

5   Jay Allison and his family live in Massachusetts. He and his wife are public-radio producers. I've never met them face to face, although I feel I know

something powerful and intimate about the Allisons and have strong emotional ties to them. What follows are some of Jay's postings on the WELL:

6   *"Woods Hole. Midnight. I am sitting in the dark of my daughter's room. Her monitor lights blink at me. The lights used to blink too brightly so I covered them with bits of bandage adhesive and now they flash faintly underneath, a persistent red and green, Lillie's heart and lungs.*

7   *"Above the monitor is her portable suction unit. In the glow of the flashlight I'm writing by, it looks like the plastic guts of a science-class human model, the tubes coiled around the power supply, the reservoir, the pump.*

8   *"Tina is upstairs trying to get some sleep. A baby monitor links our bedroom to Lillie's. It links our sleep to Lillie's too, and because our souls are linked to hers, we do not sleep well.*

9   *"I am naked. My stomach is full of beer. The flashlight rests on it, and the beam rises and falls with my breath. My daughter breathes through a white plastic tube inserted into a hole in her throat. She's 14 months old."*

10   Sitting in front of our computers with our hearts racing and tears in our eyes, in Tokyo and Sacramento and Austin, we read about Lillie's croup, her tracheostomy, the days and nights at Massachusetts General Hospital, and now the vigil over Lillie's breathing and the watchful attention to the mechanical apparatus that kept her alive. It went on for days. Weeks. Lillie recovered, and relieved our anxieties about her vocal capabilities after all that time with a hole in her throat by saying the most extraordinary things, duly reported on-line by Jay.

11   Later, writing in *Whole Earth Review,* Jay described the experience:

12   *"Before this time, my computer screen had never been a place to go for solace. Far from it. But there it was. Those nights sitting up late with my daughter, I'd go to my computer, dial up the WELL, and ramble. I wrote about what was happening that night or that year. I didn't know anyone I was "talking" to. I had never laid eyes on them. At 3:00 a.m. my "real" friends were asleep, so I turned to this foreign, invisible community for support. The WELL was always awake.*

13   *"Any difficulty is harder to bear in isolation. There is nothing to measure against, to lean against. Typing out my journal entries into the computer and over the phone lines, I found fellowship and comfort in this unlikely medium."*

14   Many people are alarmed by the very idea of a virtual community, fearing that it is another step in the wrong direction, substituting more technological ersatz for yet another natural resource or human freedom. These critics often voice their sadness at what people have been reduced to doing in a civilization that worships technology, decrying the circumstances that lead some people into such pathetically disconnected lives that they prefer to find their companions on the other side of a computer screen. There is a seed of truth in this fear, for communities at some point require more than words on a screen if they are to be other than ersatz.

15   Yet some people—many people—who don't do well in spontaneous spoken interaction turn out to have valuable contributions to make in a conversation in which they have time to think about what to say. These people, who might constitute a significant proportion of the population, can find written communication more authentic than the face-to-face kind. Who is to say that this preference for informal written text is somehow less authentically human than opting for audible speech? Those who critique computer-mediated communication because some people use it obsessively hit an important target, but miss a great deal more when they don't take into consideration people who use the medium for genuine human interaction. Those who find virtual communities cold places point at the limits of the technology, its most dangerous pitfalls, and we need to pay attention to those boundaries. But these critiques don't tell us how the Allisons, my own family, and many others could have found the community of support and information we found in the WELL when we needed it. And those of us who do find communication in cyberspace might do well to pay attention to the way the medium we love can be abused.

16   Although dramatic incidents are what bring people together and stick in their memories, most of what goes on in the Parenting conference and most virtual communities is informal conversation and downright chitchat. The model of the WELL and other social clusters in cyberspace as "places" emerges naturally whenever people who use this medium discuss its nature. In 1987, Stewart Brand quoted me in his book *The Media Lab* about what tempted me to log onto the WELL as often as I did: "There's always another mind there. It's like having the corner bar, complete with old buddies and delightful newcomers and new tools waiting to take home and fresh graffiti and letters, except instead of putting on my coat, shutting down the computer, and walking down to the corner, I just invoke my telecom program and there they are. It's a place."

17   I've changed my mind about a lot of aspects of the WELL over the years, but the sense of place is still as strong as ever. As Ray Oldenburg proposes in his 1989 book *The Great Good Place,* there are three essential places in people's lives: the place we live, the place we work, and the place we gather for conviviality. Although the casual conversation that takes place in cafés, beauty shops, pubs, and town squares is universally considered to be trivial, idle talk, Oldenburg makes the case that such places are where communities can come into being and continue to hold together. These are the unacknowledged agoras of modern life. When the automobilecentric, suburban, fast-food, shopping-mall way of life eliminated many of these "third places" from traditional towns and cities around the world, the social fabric of existing communities started shredding.

18   . . . Perhaps cyberspace is one of the informal public places where people can rebuild the aspects of community that were lost when the malt shop became a mall. Or perhaps cyberspace is precisely the *wrong* place to look for the rebirth of community, offering not a tool for conviviality but a life-denying simulacrum of real passion and true commitment to one another. In either case, we need to find out soon.

19   Because we cannot see one another in cyberspace, gender, age, national origin, and physical appearance are not apparent unless a person wants to make such characteristics public. People whose physical handicaps make it difficult to form new friendships find that virtual communities treat them as they always wanted to be treated—as thinkers and transmitters of ideas and feeling beings, not carnal vessels with a certain appearance and way of walking and talking (or not walking and not talking).

20   One of the few things that enthusiastic members of virtual communities in places like Japan, England, France, and the United States all agree on is that expanding their circle of friends is one of the most important advantages of computer conferencing. It is a way to *meet* people, whether or not you feel the need to affiliate with them on a community level. It's a way of both making contact with and maintaining a distance from others. The way you meet people in cyberspace puts a different spin on affiliation: In traditional kinds of communities, we are accustomed to meeting people, then getting to know them; in virtual communities, you can get to know people and *then* choose to meet them. Affiliation also can be far more ephemeral in cyberspace because you can get to know people you might never meet on the physical plane.

21   How does anybody find friends? In the traditional community, we search through our pool of neighbors and professional colleagues, of acquaintances and acquaintances of acquaintances, in order to find people who share our values and interests. We then exchange information about one another, disclose and discuss our mutual interests, and sometimes we become friends. In a virtual community we can go directly to the place where our favorite subjects are being discussed, then get acquainted with people who share our passions or who use words in a way we find attractive. In this sense, the topic is the address: You can't simple pick up a phone and ask to be connected with someone who wants to talk about Islamic art or California wine, or someone with a 3-year-old daughter or a 40-year-old Hudson; you can, however, join a computer conference on any of those topics, then open a public or private correspondence with the previously unknown people you find there. Your chances of making friends are increased by several orders of magnitude over the old methods of finding a peer group.

22   You can be fooled about people in cyberspace, behind the cloak of words. But that can be said about telephones or face-to-face communication as well; computer-medicated communications provide new ways to fool people, and the most obvious identity swindles will die out only when enough people learn to use the medium critically. In some ways, the medium will, by its nature, be forever biased toward certain kinds of obfuscation. It will also be a place where people often end up revealing themselves far more intimately than they would be inclined to do without the intermediation of screens and pseudonyms.

23   Point of view, along with identity, is one of the great variables in cyberspace. Different people in cyberspace look at their virtual communities through differently shaped keyholes. In traditional communities, people have a strongly shared mental model of the sense of place—the room or village or city

where their interactions occur. In virtual communities, the sense of place requires an individual act of imagination. The different mental models people have of the electronic agora complicate the question of why people seem to want to build societies mediated by computer screens. A question like that leads inexorably to the old fundamental questions of what forces hold any society together. The roots of these questions extend farther than the social upheavals triggered by modern communications technologies.

24   When we say "society," we usually mean citizens of cities in entities known as nations. We take those categories for granted. But the mass-psychological transition we made to thinking of ourselves as part of modern society and nation-states is historically recent. Could people make the transition from the close collective social groups, the villages and small towns of premodern and precapitalist Europe, to a new form of social solidarity known as society that transcended and encompassed all previous kinds of human association? Ferdinand Tönnies, one of the founders of sociology, called the premodern kind of social group *gemeinschaft,* which is closer to the English word *community,* and the new kind of social group he called *gesellschaft,* which can be translated roughly as *society.* All the questions about community in cyberspace point to a similar kind of transition, for which we have no technical names, that might be taking place now.

25   Sociology student Marc Smith, who has been using the WELL and the Net as the laboratory for his fieldwork, pointed me to Benedict Anderson's *Imagined Communities,* a study of nation-building that focuses on the ideological labor involved. Anderson points out that nations and, by extension, communities are imagined in the sense that a given nation exists by virtue of a common acceptance in the minds of the population that it exists. Nations must exist in the minds of their citizens in order to exist at all. "Virtual communities require an act of imagination," Smith points out, extending Anderson's line of thinking to cyberspace, "and what must be imagined is the idea of the community itself."

For Writing and Discussion

I fear that calling a network a community leads people to complacency and delusion, to accepting an inadequate substitute because they've never experienced the real thing and they don't know what they're missing.

                                                                Eric Utne

1. Recall from "The Healing Powers of Community" the evidence that people need supportive relationships to maintain physical as well as mental health. Evaluate the possible effects on physical and mental health of the computer age in which many children and adults interact in isolation via computers. What is the affect on the development and maintenance of social skills?

2. What are the advantages and disadvantages of virtual communities? Do you believe that virtual communities will replace other kinds of social relationships?

3. Recall the "Shoe" cartoon on page 81. Are people more susceptible to misrepresentation and fraud on-line? Does it matter? Why or why not? How might "information warfare"—breaking into and using information from corporate, military, banking, and even personal data banks—affect individuals and communities of the future?

Communicating in Groups

When communicating in groups, each group member must be willing to accept certain responsibilities. He or she must take an active role in discussion and in accomplishing the group task. The task may be to share ideas, to solve problems, or to make evaluations and decisions. The group can appoint a leader, or chairperson, who keeps the discussion moving and on the topic. A volunteer may act as reporter, taking notes on the discussion to distribute to the group later.

Each group member must be considerate of others' feelings. Remember that whatever uncertainties one member feels are probably felt by others in the group. Focusing on making the situation better for others will decrease personal concerns. Also, each member should listen patiently to others, pay compliments when they are due, and express appreciation for the good will of others.

In group settings, conflict is inevitable and can be productive. When members are responding to criticism, they should make sure you understand the criticism. Instead of agreeing or disagreeing immediately, they can ask for clarification. If the criticism is warranted or if the other person has a good point, agreement will be reached; otherwise, the one being criticized can calmly restate his or her ideas.

Practice: Communicating in Groups

1. Work with a group to develop definitions and specific examples for each of the pro-social and antisocial behaviors listed in the chart below. Provide at least one more example of each type of behavior to define and illustrate with examples.

Pro-social Behavior	Antisocial Behavior
Leadership	Rudeness
Altruism	Cruelty
Courtesy	Misanthropy
Philanthropy	Breaking laws

2. Americans have been accused of achieving victim status by blaming someone else for their behaviors or failures. Parents are often the objects of blame. While the perfect parents of the world could probably fit in a hot tub, parents learn to be parents by practicing on their children—and mistakes are a part of practice. Discuss why so many people blame their parents for present conditions, and why other people become more understanding of their parents' imperfections as they become older. Note characteristics and emotions that might contribute to each group's attitude toward their parents.

3. Contrast Aristotle's definition of *anger* with his definition of *hatred*. Relate each emotion to prejudice toward a group of people and then in one-on-one interactions with a member of a group.

4. Social philosophers often blame the need for "instant gratification" for many of society's ills: A fifteen-year-old boy kills another teen for his trendy jacket or expensive shoes. A couple of teens kill two other teens for a $2000 stereo they want to sell for $200.

   Is it true that past generations were more willing to delay pleasure and work toward long-range goals? Did the era of "instant gratification" begin with buying on credit? To what do you attribute today's preoccupation with material things? What might turn the situation around?

5. Discuss the implications of the following passage from *Shadows of Forgotten Ancestors* by Carl Sagan and Ann Druyan:

> In the annals of primate ethics, there are some accounts that have the ring of parable. In a laboratory setting, macaques [a kind of monkey] were fed if they were willing to pull a chain and electrically shock an unrelated macaque whose agony was in plain view through a one-way mirror. Otherwise, they starved. After learning the ropes, the monkeys frequently refused to pull the chain; in one experiment, only 13 percent would do so—87 percent preferred to go hungry. One macaque went without food for nearly two weeks rather than hurt his fellow. Macaques who had themselves been shocked in previous experiments were even less willing to pull the chain. The relative social status or gender of the macaques had little bearing on their reluctance to hurt others.
>
> If asked to choose between the human experimenters offering the macaques this Faustian bargain and the macaques themselves—suffering from real hunger rather than causing pain to others—our own moral sympathies do not lie with the scientists. But their experiments permit us to glimpse in non-humans a saintly willingness to make sacrifices in order to save others—even those who are not close kin. By conventional human standards, these macaques—who have never gone to Sunday school and never squirmed through a junior high school civics lesson—seem exemplary in their moral grounding and their courageous resistance to evil. Among the macaques, at least in this case, heroism is the norm. If the circumstances were reversed, and captive humans were offered the same deal by macaque scientists, would we do as well?

6. Environmental activist and author Kirkpatrick Sale made the following comment in response to the questions "Where is the darkness? Where is the light?"

> The darkness is all around us; it is called industrial civilization. And it is leading the world to the verge of ecocide, the final extinction of surface life as we know it. The darkness has been fashioned for us by an industrialization that is, in effect, declaring war on the biosphere. And in that war, the war of technology against nature, technology—modern, cybermad technology—is winning.

Discuss the effects of technology on the natural world and on humankind and what can save them from the "cybermad technology" Sales describes.

CHAPTER SUMMARY

The readings in this chapter focused on the different perspectives within the community and the function that communities serve. Ralph Waldo Emerson cited the fable of One Man from which humans were split off in order to better serve each other and Self in their various functions as members of the community. But modern society, Emerson notes, "is one in which the members have suffered amputation from the trunk, and strut about like so many walking monsters—a good finger, a neck, a stomach, an elbow, but never a man." In the next chapter, you will have an opportunity to reflect on the various "parts," or voices, of the national community.

Chapter 6

WRITING CHALLENGE

Imagine that an important decision or change in law about an issue that directly or indirectly affects all Americans is being discussed. You have been given the task of briefing the President of the United States or another leader about how people are likely to respond to the change. Choose an issue (perhaps the one you addressed in Chapter 1) about which you have strong feelings. The important decision will be to do things as you think they should be done or change the law as you think it should be changed.

Write a memorandum to the president in which you describe how at least three different groups or factions of people who either support or oppose the decision might feel about the change and why. Further advise the president how he or she might address the concerns and feelings of each group or faction when announcing the change. The sample paper on page 100 is one possible approach.

JOURNAL TOPIC SUGGESTIONS

- The role of parenthood
- The importance of a specific relationship—what you give, what you get
- What a "psychic vampire" does to a relationship
- Abuse of power in a relationship
- The story of a lasting relationship and its apparent elements
- Effects of changing traditions (social, political, economic, or cultural) on relationships
- Predictions about how technology will change everyday living for individuals or communities
- People who care about the world that future generations will inhabit
- The difference in a world view and a view of the world that ends at the tip of one's nose

GUIDE TO WRITING

Planning and Prewriting

For this assignment, you will need an issue that has many different sides. To test your issue, or topic, use a graphic organizer similar to the one below to organize your ideas. If you cannot think of at least three possible positions on the issue, you can choose another issue or use the questions under the heading Exploring a System to explore the issue further.

ISSUE: CAPITAL PUNISHMENT

FACTION	POSSIBLE VIEWS
Criminal sentenced to death	Killing is wrong. The state is no better than the murderer when it executes a human being. Every human has a right to life. Emotion: fear
Criminal's family	He/she might be innocent. At any rate, he/she is really a good person who made a mistake but who can be rehabilitated. He/she has a right to life. The death penalty punishes the family of the criminal more than the criminal. Emotions: love, grief, and fear for criminal; anger at state
Victim's family	He/she deserves the same fate as the victim. He/she surrendered all rights with the taking of another's rights (life). He/she can be rehabilitated in the after-life. They are better equipped to do it there. Emotions: grief; anger (anticipation of vengeance)
Liberal taxpayer	There is hope for every person. Everyone deserves a second chance. Society created the monster that committed the crime, and society should pay, too.
Conservative taxpayer	The death penalty serves to deter others who would commit murder and thereby saves lives. Why feed him/her? It's not practical.
Lawyers	He/she may be innocent. It was my responsibility to prove it.

To brainstorm about possible points of view, write questions about your topic such as those in the examples below:

Exploring a system: health care

- Who benefits from it or uses its services? How might they feel about it and why?
- Who works in it and has responsibility for it? How might they feel about it and why?

- Who pays for it? How might they feel about it and why?
- Who makes sacrifices for it? How might they feel about it and why?
- What ethical or moral aspects are involved? Who makes the decisions regarding ethics?

Organizing and Drafting

Make an informal outline or organizational list to guide your thinking as you draft your paper. For each faction or group of people, include

1. a description of experiences, characteristics, and so forth, that members of the group have in common,
2. emotions that the group has in common,
3. possible views that most members of the group share, and
4. reasons for the shared view.

You may want to begin drafting your paper by exploring thoroughly possible views of each faction and what kinds of emotions are involved. After you have completed the body of your paper, you can then work on your introduction and conclusion.

THE POWER OF STYLE: TONE

A writer's persona is the "I," either spoken or unspoken, in a piece of writing. A newspaper reporter might present an objective and impersonal tone, to subdue the "I" and let others speak:

> Statistics reveal that almost one-third of today's babies are born to unwed mothers. Studies show that these babies are likely to live in poverty and to have a greater chance of becoming involved in crime than babies born in two-parent families.

The same content might be presented with a more involved and passionate tone:

> The almost one-third of babies born to unwed mothers are usually handicapped by poverty. These babies, lacking the advantage of a two-parent family, will often become involved in crime rather than making the hard climb out of the dire circumstances of their heritage.

(continued)

(continued from previous page)

In the second paragraph, the writer's "I" is still unspoken. Yet, the phrases "handicapped by poverty," "hard climb," and "dire circumstances of their heritage" reveal the writer's attitude toward the subject, or tone. From the writer's choice of words, the reader learns that the writer has sympathy for babies born into poverty and understands something about the obstacles the babies will face. The writer uses words to appeal to the reader's emotions, to persuade the reader to understand and sympathize with poor children.

Another writer might use an ironic tone, or use words that mean the opposite of what they say:

> Everyone knows that the one-third of babies born to unwed mothers will have a life of luxury. At most, they only have one parent who believes that to spare the rod is to spoil the child. And if mom happens to be more interested in smoking crack or entertaining boyfriends, these babies have freedom to grow and bloom without the terrible restrictiveness of family life.

The writer's choice of tone depends on the purpose of the writing, the audience, and how the writer can best create a credible ethos.

Purpose What do I hope to accomplish with my words?

Audience Who is my audience?
What are they likely to know or believe before they read?
How do I want them to feel as they read?

Ethos How can I show my audience that I am knowledgeable, trustworthy, and benevolent?

Practice: Changing Tone

A writer uses diction, sentence structure, active or passive voice, and even punctuation to help create tone. Choose a sentence from an earlier paper or from a journal entry and identify the tone as amusing, serious, objective, ironic, or so forth. Rewrite the sentence with two additional tones, and analyze the elements of each sentence that contribute to the tone.

R E M I N D E R

Your introduction will put the reader in the "right frame of mind." Before you write yours, you may want to review the information on introductions in Chapter 3, pages 47–48.

CONCLUSIONS

With your introduction, you hooked the reader; you enticed the reader into joining you in a journey. Now that the journey is over, you must give your reader a sense of completion. Your conclusion should reinforce your thesis statement in some way. Below are different types of conclusions that may be effectively used in paragraphs or developed for concluding paragraphs in longer compositions. General information on types of conclusions and brief examples are included here, and you may find that some types will be suitable for the different assignments in later chapters.

1. *Restatement of Main Idea or Thesis*   If the main idea or thesis is restated, be sure to vary the wording. A reader may easily accept the repetition of a concept; however, a reader who recognizes the same wording might think that the writer is "talking down" or is, at best, redundant.

> Thesis:
>
> International terrorists should be dealt with in a way that serves as a deterrent to future terrorism against American citizens.
>
> Conclusion:
>
> So that American citizens do not have to travel in fear when they go abroad, the United States should take a strong stand against international terrorism.

2. *Summary*   The thesis statement and important supporting details may be summarized in the conclusion, especially in longer compositions.

> Thesis:
>
> Today's society exemplifies the concept of *quid pro quo*, the exchange theory in which interpersonal relationships are based on mutual needs and reciprocity.
>
> Conclusion:
>
> The exchange theory sees human beings as pleasure-seeking, pain-avoiding creatures whose goals are to fulfill their needs at the least cost to themselves. They weigh their actions on a reward/cost basis, marketing their assets for the assets that others have to offer.

3. *General Impression*   For a review, an evaluative or descriptive paper, or a stylistic or character analysis, an effective ending might consist of a statement of the dominant impression of the subject.

Thesis:

George Orwell's *1984* was a prophetic work at the time of its creation in 1949, a work that must have read at the time as the most imaginative and improbable kind of science fiction.

Conclusion:

For today's reader, *1984* offers a life-altering experience, a mirror of contemporary society in many ways and an omen in others that challenges the reader to take a closer look and rethink the concept of "one nation under television."

4. *Recommendation* If your paper is about a controversial issue or your purpose is to persuade your audience (as it will be for many of the assignments in this textbook), you might conclude with a call for action on the part of the reader.

Thesis:

The problem of street crime is not being solved, and in fact may be exacerbated, by a lackadaisical criminal justice system.

Conclusion:

Citizens should take an active part in stopping crime by letting their political representatives know they are tired of an ineffective, "hand-slapping" court system.

5. *Prediction or Evaluation* A prediction or an evaluation should be supported by the points in the paper, or a reasonable inference drawn from the arguments already presented.

Thesis:

Today's children have become lost in a world of situation comedies and hour-long adventure stories.

Conclusion:

If the present trend continues, children may someday only experience the joys of wandering through woods or riding bicycles vicariously as they sit in front of television sets.

Remember, the primary function of a conclusion is to give your reader a sense of closure. The following suggestions can help you do so smoothly and logically.

1. Transition words such as *consequently, as a result,* and *therefore* are useful to indicate to your reader that you are ending your paper. However, phrases such as *in conclusion, in summary,* or *as I have attempted to show* are redundant and will insult or bore your reader.
2. Do not introduce new topics or details. If you find you must add something that is grand and wonderful, go back and look for an appropriate place in the body of the paper. The conclusion is not a place to "stick in" what you forgot to say earlier.
3. Be careful not to contradict yourself. If you have taken a firm stand in your paper, a contradiction will leave your reader confused and wondering how sincere you were about everything you wrote.
4. Avoid one-sentence conclusions. Even if you think you have said all that can be said, you can play around with different approaches until you find a conclusion that enriches your paper rather than merely stops it.
5. Avoid clichés such as "You can't judge a book by looking at the cover." Metaphors and other figurative language may be used effectively in conclusions, but they must be fresh and new. (Quotations may also be used effectively in conclusions.)
6. Make the tone (straightforward, witty, serious, humorous, and so forth) of the conclusion match the overall tone of the paper. A switch in tone can confuse the reader about the purpose of the paper.

Evaluating and Revising

AUDIENCE AWARENESS

Consider your reader, the president or another important leader who needs the information you are providing. You will need to explain the role emotions and experiences play in developing opinions about a particular issue. You will also want to take care to treat the descriptions of groups with care and avoid unwarranted stereotyping.

Before you prepare a draft for a partner to read, review your paper with the following questions in mind:

1. Have I written anything that might be interpreted by my reader as biased or belittling?
2. Have I demonstrated an understanding of the experiences and emotions of each group?
3. Have I included irrelevant information to increase the length of (pad) my paper?
4. Do the ideas in my paper flow smoothly, or should I add transitions?
5. Does each paragraph have unity and coherence? (See page 49.)

PARTNER EVALUATION

Your partner expects the same kind of help you want from a partner—thoughtful and honest feedback. As you read your partner's paper, think of questions you can ask your partner that will lead to greater exploration of the topic. After you have read the paper once, write three or four questions to ask your partner later. Then read the essay again, responding to the following questions on a separate sheet of paper:

1. Is the tone and level of language appropriate for the audience?
2. Does information about each faction or group reveal an understanding of that group's emotions and experiences?
3. What information is especially insightful or interesting?
4. What did I learn from this paper?
5. What are two ways that the paper might be improved?

Discuss both papers with your partner, starting with the positive aspects of each and then moving to what might improve the paper. Make notes as your partner reviews your paper.

After rereading your paper, evaluate your partner's feedback. Rewrite your paper with your partner's questions and comments in mind.

Editing and Proofreading

THE POWER OF STYLE: ACTIVE AND PASSIVE VOICE

When discussing sentence style, the word *voice* refers to a verb form showing the relation of the subject to the action. Active sentences feature the doer of the action; the subject performs the action.

> The supervisor asked the employees to work overtime.

Passive sentences feature the receiver of the action; the subject receives the action.

> The employees were asked by the supervisor to work overtime.

(continued)

(continued from previous page)

As a general rule, use active sentences. Active sentences require fewer words, are more direct, and are easier to understand.

WHEN PASSIVE VOICE IS APPROPRIATE

Passive sentences are used deliberately in the following circumstances:

1. When the actor, or doer of the action, is understood from the context.

> Employees are offered health insurance.

(The context makes it clear that the employer offers the health insurance to the employees.)

2. When it is appropriate for the actor to remain anonymous to avoid blame, embarrassment, or danger.

> The supervisor was told about the employees' behavior.

(We don't want to divulge the informant's name.)

3. When the actor is unknown.

> The supervisor was told about the problem last week.

(We don't know who told the supervisor about the problem.)

4. When the actor is unimportant.

> The contracts were delivered yesterday morning.

(We don't care who delivered the contracts.)

Take care not to mix active and passive clauses in the same sentences:

Awkward:

> American companies lost some markets to foreign competitors in the 1980s; new markets are being explored in the 1990s.

(continued)

(continued from previous page)

Better:

American companies lost some markets to foreign competitors in the 1980s; consequently, the companies are exploring
new markets in the 1990s.

Note: When editing, look for passive sentences that might be more
effective if written in active voice.

Clues: forms of *be* (*is, are, am, was, were, been*), *by* phrases (*by
the supervisor*), past participles, and past tense verbs (verbs
ending in *-ed, -en,* or irregular forms such as *gone,* and
swept)

Practice: Changing Voice

From your paper, take the first sentence in each paragraph and change voice.
Note the effect on the emphasis, on the level of language, on the "sound,"
and on the tone and mood of each sentence.

EDITING CHECKLIST

1. Can any groups of sentences be combined? Are there awkward or
   overloaded sentences that can be separated into clear, concise sentences?
2. Is the emphasis in each sentence as I intended?
3. Does each sentence have correct subject/verb and pronoun/antecedent
   agreement?
4. Should any passive constructions be changed to active voice? or active
   to passive (for one of the reasons above)?

PROOFREADING

Proofread your final draft from the bottom up to check for errors in spelling,
usage, and punctuation. If your instructor allows, make neat corrections; if
not, rewrite the paper to eliminate errors.

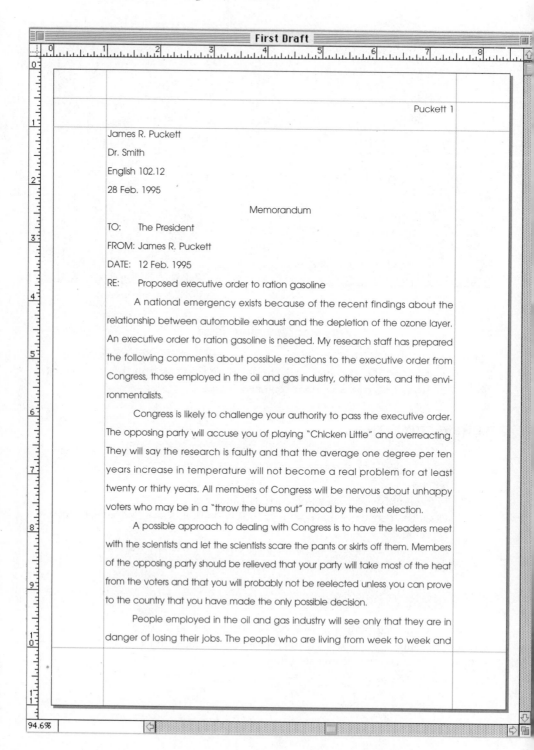

First Draft

Puckett 1

James R. Puckett

Dr. Smith

English 102.12

28 Feb. 1995

Memorandum

TO: The President

FROM: James R. Puckett

DATE: 12 Feb. 1995

RE: Proposed executive order to ration gasoline

A national emergency exists because of the recent findings about the relationship between automobile exhaust and the depletion of the ozone layer. An executive order to ration gasoline is needed. My research staff has prepared the following comments about possible reactions to the executive order from Congress, those employed in the oil and gas industry, other voters, and the environmentalists.

Congress is likely to challenge your authority to pass the executive order. The opposing party will accuse you of playing "Chicken Little" and overreacting. They will say the research is faulty and that the average one degree per ten years increase in temperature will not become a real problem for at least twenty or thirty years. All members of Congress will be nervous about unhappy voters who may be in a "throw the bums out" mood by the next election.

A possible approach to dealing with Congress is to have the leaders meet with the scientists and let the scientists scare the pants or skirts off them. Members of the opposing party should be relieved that your party will take most of the heat from the voters and that you will probably not be reelected unless you can prove to the country that you have made the only possible decision.

People employed in the oil and gas industry will see only that they are in danger of losing their jobs. The people who are living from week to week and

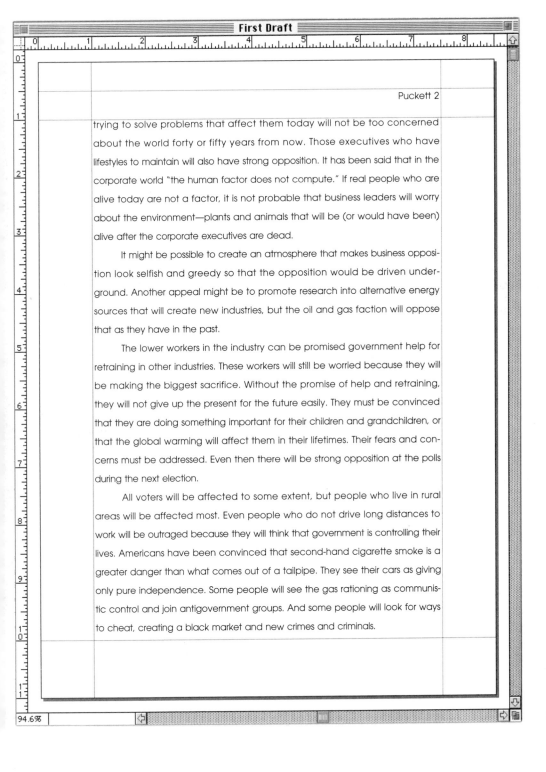

First Draft

Puckett 2

trying to solve problems that affect them today will not be too concerned about the world forty or fifty years from now. Those executives who have lifestyles to maintain will also have strong opposition. It has been said that in the corporate world "the human factor does not compute." If real people who are alive today are not a factor, it is not probable that business leaders will worry about the environment—plants and animals that will be (or would have been) alive after the corporate executives are dead.

It might be possible to create an atmosphere that makes business opposition look selfish and greedy so that the opposition would be driven underground. Another appeal might be to promote research into alternative energy sources that will create new industries, but the oil and gas faction will oppose that as they have in the past.

The lower workers in the industry can be promised government help for retraining in other industries. These workers will still be worried because they will be making the biggest sacrifice. Without the promise of help and retraining, they will not give up the present for the future easily. They must be convinced that they are doing something important for their children and grandchildren, or that the global warming will affect them in their lifetimes. Their fears and concerns must be addressed. Even then there will be strong opposition at the polls during the next election.

All voters will be affected to some extent, but people who live in rural areas will be affected most. Even people who do not drive long distances to work will be outraged because they will think that government is controlling their lives. Americans have been convinced that second-hand cigarette smoke is a greater danger than what comes out of a tailpipe. They see their cars as giving only pure independence. Some people will see the gas rationing as communistic control and join antigovernment groups. And some people will look for ways to cheat, creating a black market and new crimes and criminals.

94.6%

Puckett 3

One appeal to citizens is to promise more mass transportation in cities and towns. The government could help pay for construction that could begin immediately. Another appeal is to paint a dire picture of the consequences of not acting immediately.

The environmentalists should be pleased with the executive order to ration gasoline. However, Mr. President, we can not count on their support at this time since it is easier to ask other people to make sacrifices than to make them personally. The environmentalists will be inconvenienced, too, so we can expect some grumbling at least. In addition, strong support from the environmentalist movement may be a drawback. Some factions will accuse you of giving in to protesters and troublemakers.

The country must be made to understand that there is no real choice in this matter. All citizens must know that now is the time to pay for the luxuries and excesses of the past or there will be no future.

94.6%

P A R T   T H R E E

Creating Arguments

Of the modes of persuasion furnished by the spoken [or written] word, there are three kinds. The first kind depends on the personal character of the speaker [or writer]; the second on putting the audience into a certain frame of mind; the third on the proof, or apparent proof, provided by the words of the speech itself. Persuasion is achieved by the speaker's personal character when the speech is so spoken as to make us think him credible. We believe good men more fully and more readily than others: this is true generally whatever the question is, and absolutely true where exact certainty is impossible and opinions are divided. This kind of persuasion, like the others, should be achieved by what the speaker says, not by what people think of his character before he begins to speak. . . .

Secondly, persuasion may come through the hearers, when the speech stirs their emotions. Our judgements when we are pleased and friendly are not the same as when we are pained and hostile. . . .

Thirdly, persuasion is effected through the speech itself when we have proved a truth or an apparent truth by means of the persuasive arguments suitable to the case in question. . . . A statement is persuasive and credible either because it is directly self-evident or because it appears to be proved from other statements that are so.

Aristotle, *The Rhetoric*

Chapter 7

ARGUMENTS

Objection to the Child Labor Amendment
Manufacturers Record

Efforts to pass federal legislation to outlaw child labor were declared uncon-
stitutional by the Supreme Court in rulings in 1918 and in 1922. The
National League of Women Voters was among groups that lobbied for the pas-
sage of a constitutional amendment to deal with the problem of child labor.
The Manufacturers Record *printed this view opposing the amendment on*
September 4, 1924.

1   Because the Child Labor Amendment in reality is not legislation in the interest of children but legislation which would mean the destruction of manhood
and womanhood through the destruction of the boys and girls of the country,
the *Manufacturers Record* has been giving much attention to the discussion
of the subject, and will continue to do so.

2   In this week's issue, Mrs. Margaret C. Robinson, president of the Massachusetts Public Interests League, Boston, a woman's organization, presents
very strongly the reasons why the men and women of this country should
awaken to the seriousness of this proposition.

3   It is an interesting fact that Massachusetts, which was for so many years
noted for its work in behalf of eliminating child workers from factory life, is
now aggressively fighting the proposed amendment, realizing that it would
endanger the very existence of this government.

4   Last week we published a strong letter from Mr. Felix Rackemann, a
leading attorney of Boston, long known for his humanitarian activities, and
now Mrs. Robinson and her associates in the Massachusetts Public Interests
League are carrying on an active campaign in many directions to prevent this
amendment becoming a part of our Constitution.

5   [The following is Mrs. Robinson's letter.]

6   This proposed amendment is fathered by Socialists, Communists, and
Bolshevists. They are the active workers in its favor. They look forward to its
adoption as giving them the power to nationalize the children of the land and

bring about in this country the exact conditions which prevail in Russia. These people are the active workers back of this undertaking, but many patriotic men and women, without at all realizing the seriousness of this proposition, thinking only of it as an effort to lessen child labor in factories, are giving countenance to it.

7   If adopted, this amendment would be the greatest thing ever done in America in behalf of the activities of hell. It would make millions of young people under eighteen years of age idlers in brain and body, and thus make them the devil's best workshop. It would destroy the initiative and self-reliance and manhood and womanhood of all the coming generations.

8   A solemn responsibility to this country and to all future generations rests upon every man and woman who understands this situation to fight, and fight unceasingly, to make the facts known to their acquaintances everywhere. Aggressive work is needed. It would be worse than folly for people who realize the danger of this situation to rest content under the belief that the amendment cannot become a part of our Constitution. The only thing that can prevent its adoption will be active, untiring work on the part of every man and woman who appreciates its destructive power and who wants to save the young people of all future generations from moral and physical decay under the domination of the devil himself.

For Writing and Discussion

1. The *Manufacturers Record*, representing the views of manufacturers who benefited from cheap child labor, had to overcome the perception that any opinion the magazine presented was self-serving. What did the magazine do, as represented in this piece, to build *ethos?*

2. How does the piece (introduction and letter) use *pathos to* appeal to the audience's emotions?

3. Summarize the main points in the piece. Explain how a contemporary audience might react to the piece and why.

WHAT IS AN ARGUMENT?

Chapter 1 focused on *ethos,* the writer's role in convincing the audience. Chapter 2 dealt with *pathos,* appeals to the audience's emotions. You now understand two of the elements of persuasive writing, and soon you will understand the third—*logos,* the use of reasoning and evidence (support) in persuasion. Whether you attempt to persuade others to believe something, to take a particular action, or just to give an idea serious consideration, you will need *logos.* But first, we will explore the meanings associated with the term *argument.*

The word *argument* is often used to mean *dispute, quarrel, disagreement,* or even *verbal fight.* Here we will use the word *argument* to mean **at least two statements** (claims, propositions, assertions) **in which one statement is offered as support** (premise/evidence/backing) **for the other** (conclusion). Later we will use the word *argument* to refer to a kind of writing that includes many statements/claims offered as support for one or more conclusions.

R E M I N D E R

Don't confuse the word *conclusion* as we use it here (argumentative conclusion) with the way it is used to identify the part of a piece of writing that comes last. An argumentative conclusion may come first in a piece of writing, but the conclusion as one of the three parts of a piece of writing (introduction, body, conclusion) always comes last.

A conclusion might be offered as a premise, or supporting claim, for another conclusion. And often a premise is not stated directly because the writer (or speaker) assumes that the audience understands and agrees with the unstated premise.

PERSON ONE: This is a wonderful day (conclusion) because the weather is perfect. (premise)
[Perfect weather makes a wonderful day.] (unstated premise)

PERSON TWO: Are you kidding? The sky is overcast, (premise) so my solar panels aren't working. (conclusion/premise for major conclusion)
[Solar panels don't work without sunshine.] (unstated premise)
Because there is no sunshine, (premise) I am depressed—winter light syndrome. (conclusion/ premise for major conclusion)
[Lack of sunlight causes winter syndrome/depression.] (unstated premise)
This is a terrible day. (major conclusion)

PERSON ONE: Well, let me clarify my definition of the word *perfect.* I say the weather is perfect (conclusion) because the temperature is just right, (premise) not too hot and not too cold. (premise)

PERSON TWO: I'll give you that. [You are right.] (conclusion/premises affirmed)

As indicated above the words *assertion, proposition,* and *claim* can be used to identify either the support or the conclusion. The words *support, premise,* and *evidence* can also be used synonymously. To simplify, we will use the word ***claim*** in instances when we are determining whether a statement is used as a supporting statement or conclusion, ***premise*** to identify a supporting statement (premise is shorter), ***support*** in a more general sense to identify evidence, and ***conclusion*** to identify an argumentative conclusion.

WHAT IS A CLAIM?

Questions are not claims. Commands are not claims. To test a statement to determine whether it is a claim, follow it with the words *"I disagree."* If someone might (sensibly) disagree with the statement, the statement is a claim.

> Statement: I like pizza.

(It makes no sense for someone to disagree with that statement.)

> Statement: Pizza is a healthy food.

(Saying "I disagree" makes sense.)

To determine which of two related claims is the premise and which is the conclusion, test each of the claims by putting the word *since* in front of them. The one that can reasonably include the word *since* is the premise. Words such as *since* and *because* indicate that a claim is a premise; words such as *therefore, consequently,* and *so* indicate a claim is a conclusion.

Inductive and Deductive Reasoning

You may remember seeing the terms *inductive* and *deductive* in high school English textbooks. And you may have read something like "induction moves from the specific to the general, and deduction moves from the general to the specific." You may have been taught that if you start with a thesis statement and then support it, you are using deduction, but if you start with support and end with your thesis, you are using induction. These terms are easily confused with the order in which an argument is presented, but the order of the premise and conclusion do not determine the type of argument. You still have a horse and a cart, no matter which comes first.

In formal logic, the term *deduction* actually has to do with degree of proof and the validity of a syllogism (a three-statement argument, or structured deduction). And whether a syllogism is valid or invalid has to do with its form—not with whether it is "true" or even in the realm of possibility.

The second syllogism below is as valid as the first classic representation of the categorical syllogism:

All Greeks are mortal.
Socrates was a Greek.
Therefore, Socrates was mortal.
All pigs are flying animals.
Porky is a pig.
Therefore, Porky is a flying animal.

Representing a syllogism symbolically helps uncover a faulty, or invalid, structure.

All Greeks are mortal.

Major premise: States that all members of a specific category (Greeks) are included in a larger category (mortals).

A = B

Socrates was a mortal.

Minor premise: Identifies a particular case (Socrates) as a member of the specific category (mortals).

C = A

Therefore, Socrates was mortal.

Conclusion: Says that what is true of all members must be true of one member of the larger category.

C = B

You can quickly check the validity, or structure, of a categorical syllogism by making sure it contains the A=B, C=A, C=B formula and making sure it adheres to certain rules.

Rule 1. The major premise (contains the "all" category) must be stated in clear and precise language.

Rule 2. There must be only three terms and each must appear twice:
Major term—predicate noun of the major premise and the conclusion (mortals/B)
Minor term—subject of the minor premise and conclusion (Socrates/C)
Middle term—term that appears in both premises (Greeks/A)

Rule 3. Only one term can be negative, and one negative term forces a negative conclusion.

Rule 4. The relationship among the terms must force only one possible conclusion.

The syllogism can also be represented with a diagram:

Note: This is a simplified treatment of a complex subject. There are 256 forms of syllogisms. We have discussed only one, and that discussion has been for a limited purpose and not comprehensive.

Although we may not often put our deductions into syllogistic form, the structure of the categorical syllogism underlies much of our thinking. We go through life using the powers of deduction and induction, beginning at an early age. Pretend, for instance, that you are seven years old and believe that there is a real Santa Claus who lives at the North Pole and delivers gifts to children all over the world on Christmas Eve. You believe it is true because some very credible people told you so. Your parents told you elaborate stories about Santa and his elves. You read about him in books. You saw him with your own eyes in a department store and sat in his lap while someone took a picture. Santa was even on television. Your teacher helped you write a letter to Santa, and your mother put a real stamp on it and mailed it at the post office. You even heard on the police scanner officers talking on Christmas Eve about a strange flying object that turned out to be Santa's sleigh. Teachers, ministers, and firemen asked you what Santa was bringing you for Christmas.

So, you use deductive reasoning in the form of an *enthymeme*—a shortened argument that contains unspoken assumptions. The unstated or

unthought major premise of the argument is that *all things spoken about by adults are real*. As a categorical syllogism, the argument looks like this:

> All things spoken about by adults are real.
> Santa is spoken about by adults.
> Therefore, Santa is real.

In a categorical syllogism, what is true of all things in a category (things spoken about by adults) *must* be true of one thing (Santa). In other words, if everything said by adults is true, then what adults say about Santa must also be true.

And then one day, your "truth" is shattered. With no warning, a playmate tells you that Santa isn't real and, furthermore, neither is the tooth fairy or the Easter bunny. You feel angry and challenge your playmate. "Santa *is* real. My parents wouldn't lie to me. I *know* Santa is real." You are prepared to fight for what you believe is true.

But in the back of your mind, there are doubts. You begin using inductive reasoning: "I saw Mom lay a big kiss on Santa. It's funny that Santa's favorite cookies are the same as Dad's. And why did Santa give my friend, who everyone knows was *bad*, everything on his list, when I, who was *good* all year, didn't get even half the things on my list? And what do all those reindeer eat at the frozen North Pole? And why did we take that broken toy Santa gave me back to Wal-Mart to exchange it?" You accepted flimsy explanations for each incident before, but now you are pulling it all together and your doubts are growing. You run home and tell your mother what your playmate said. She stammers, looks as though she has been caught in a lie, and remembers that she has to make a phone call. You vow not to go to sleep that night until you get to the bottom of the thing. You want the truth.

So you begin an investigation. You refuse to accept the flimsy explanations you were given in the past and put your own puzzle pieces together to reach the conclusion that Santa probably isn't real. You are using inductive reasoning. You observe:

1. Santa isn't really an unknown person. (Evidence: I saw Mom kiss Santa. She only kisses members of the family.)
2. Santa doesn't really bring presents based on whether or not children are good. (Evidence: My friend was bad and received everything on the list; I was good and didn't get everything I wanted.)
3. Santa's elves don't really make all those toys at the North Pole. (Evidence: We exchanged at Wal-Mart the toy Santa's elves supposedly made.)

Then you connect your observations and make an inductive leap, or educated guess to reach a probable conclusion: The things I have heard about Santa are probably not true. Santa probably isn't real.

Most of our reasoning is inductive. We draw probable conclusions or make generalizations from the limited examples and samples we collect. We don't have to see all the dogs in the world, for instance, to conclude that probably all dogs walk on four legs. We often draw inferences about what causes something by observing the effect and quickly eliminating all but the most probable cause. If we turn on the television in the middle of a newscast and see crumbled houses and buildings, we might conclude that the destruction was caused by either war or an earthquake. But when we see that the location of the ruined buildings is somewhere in Mexico, we determine that the ruin was probably caused by an earthquake.

We also use comparisons, or analogies, to make inferences: If we determine that two things of different types are alike in some ways, we might conclude that the two things may be alike in other ways. An artichoke, for example, is not the same type vegetable as lettuce. But because it is the flower head of an edible plant, we might conclude that it contains vitamins and is high in fiber like lettuce.

When we use deductive reasoning, we conclude from a "law" (of the natural world, for instance), that something is absolutely true. At one time it was a "law" that humans were the only animals capable of using tools. From that universal, we could conclude that dogs do not use tools and that elephants do not use tools and that monkeys do not use tools. But then researchers find that monkeys do, in fact, use tools. So, the universal law is no longer true.

We often make statements that include unspoken assumptions of universal laws, or truths.

John must be a fast runner. He plays football, you know.

Inherent in this enthymeme is the major premise that *all football players are fast runners*. Putting the argument in syllogistic form allows us quickly to see that the factual content is faulty.

All football players are fast runners.
John is a football player.
Therefore, John is a fast runner.

To point out the fault in this argument, we identify one football player who is not a fast runner. That all football players are fast runners is not a universal truth. As you might imagine, there are few universal truths, and examining our own arguments and the arguments of others to find unstated assumptions is an important reasoning process in daily life. Prejudices and stereotypes, for instance, are built on faulty assumptions. Once the faulty assumption is uncovered, the argument falls apart.

ARGUMENT AS A TYPE OF WRITING

We have discussed a simple form of argument containing one or two premises and one conclusion. However, arguments may contain several premises and one conclusion or several premises and several conclusions. And the main argumentative conclusion of a piece of writing is the **thesis.** Here we broaden the definition of the word *argument* to "any piece of writing that has a thesis."

The traditional classification of writing as Descriptive, Expository, Argumentative, or Narrative (DEAN) has fallen from favor because it assumes that arguments are not involved in the other three kinds of writing. Not so. Any type of writing may include an argument, and certainly an argument might include a description, narration, and exposition.

> The room was a mess. Clothes were scattered around the floor and bed and draped over an overturned chair. Dirty dishes were on every flat service in the room. An empty spaghetti can was on the nightstand, and sauce was smeared on the lamp. The floor was stained with puddles of spilled coffee, coke, and apple juice (we hope).

Several premises support the conclusion that the room was a mess. The premises are all descriptive and, in fact, define the word *mess*. A piece of expository prose (writing that explains) is argumentative if it contains a thesis. And a story (narrative) that is told to make the point, for instance, that children should do as they are told by their parents, is an argument. (We will limit our discussion to nonfiction writing.)

Types of Arguments

A useful way to classify arguments is by the type of claim made in the argument or the purpose for making the claim. Three major divisions are substantiation, evaluation, and policy recommendation.

Substantiation (something) is true.

Evaluation (something) is good or bad, right or wrong, effective or ineffective, and so on.

Policy recommendation (something) should be done.

Many kinds of supporting arguments, or evidence, can be used in each, and for each of the types of argument, we can list criteria for support and questions that beg to be answered. In addition, the three types of argument have a natural progression. Substantiation arguments are used in evaluation arguments, and policy arguments include both substantiation and evaluation. In this and the next two chapters, we will focus on substantiation arguments. (For information on evaluation arguments, see Chapters 22 and 24; for information on policy arguments, see Chapter 26.)

SUBSTANTIATION ARGUMENTS

Before we discuss substantiation as a type of argument, let's deal with the word itself. The word *substantiate* is from the word *substance* (the real or essential part of anything). To **substantiate** something, then, is to **show to be true or real by giving evidence.** So, a substantiation argument is, for our purposes, an attempt by someone (you, the writer) to persuade some-one (the audience) that something is true by offering evidence. We are expanding our definition of argument somewhat to include the three ele-ments of persuasion: *ethos, pathos,* and *logos.*

KINDS OF SUPPORT

Definition

A definition explains the components of the topic or a major element in the argument. Definitions are essential for establishing a starting point. Even a topic that has a common definition requires a limiting of the scope of your use of the topic in your paper. The word *crime*, for instance, is understood to mean "the breaking of laws." But will you be addressing white-collar crime, juvenile crime, computer crime, or street crime? And what does *street crime* mean? A crime committed in the street? drug-related crime? crime that happens in cities? any assaultive crime? Can the assault be against property, or only against people?

The word *censorship* has different meanings for different people regarding different situations. Some possible meanings include

- Marking *damns* and *hells* out of school library books
- Setting standards of acceptability for school books by committee
- Rating movies and music
- Restricting grants to artists on the basis of a standard for the art to be produced
- Restricting the sale of pornography to minors
- Prohibiting the sale or distribution of certain books, movies, music, or paintings
- Burning books, movies, music, or paintings
- Preventing publication of books or the production of movies, music, or paintings

Certainly an argument advocating that it is in the best interest of children for school textbooks to be censored should include a definition of *censorship.* In fact, an entire paper might be written to define a concept such as censor-ship, and the paper would be an argument—an attempt to persuade the audience that the definition presented is true. Definitions both identify and limit the meaning of a term.

Definition by substitution   Definitions may include the substitution of synonyms or phrases and may be either negative or positive. You might, for instance, use synonyms with positive connotations to identify your subject—courage is bravery, determination, and spirit. You could also use antonyms or phrases that includes the word *not,* to limit your definition—courage is not greed or lust. A definition that includes the substitution of a dictionary meaning uses the authority of the dictionary's publisher as support and is fairly simple; however, some definitions require more support or explanation.

Definition by example   Definitions may include examples to illustrate the point: A great football player is someone like Emmit Smith. Examples may be extended and may include comparisons and contrasts to clarify further. Words that may have different meanings for different people may include a comparison that requires additional support. For instance, if you define the word *time* with something like "time is money," you will need to explain the definition.

Definition by function or structure   Definition by function or structure explains how something works or what it does. For instance, you might define *wafer board* by telling how it is made and what it is used for:

> Wafer board is used instead of plywood in some construction. It is made of wood chips that are held together with glue. Because the glue surrounds and coats each piece of wood, the board is more water resistant than plywood.

Analytical definitions   Analytical definitions are especially helpful in limiting a topic. An analytical definition includes calling forth an image of a class and then focusing on one subtype of the class, differentiating the subtype from other subtypes in the class. For instance, *censorship* may be defined broadly as the control of access to something. Then the censorship of textbooks by modifying works of literature may be contrasted with other kinds of censorship that involve ratings or labels on record albums or restricting the sale of pornographic literature to minors.

FACTS

A fact is a statement that can be verified. A supporting argument of fact requires its own support. In other words, a fact is presented as a conclusion and must have verification. One way of verifying a fact is through definition. Other ways include citing an authority or expert, using historical data, or citing the result of an experiment.

Citing an authority or expert   When factual evidence is used as support, a normal response from the audience is to question the source or authority on which the information is founded.

Statement of fact: One-third of babies born in the United States are born to unwed mothers.
Question from audience: Who says?
Answer to audience: According to the Census Bureau, one-third of the babies born in the United States are born to unwed mothers.
Statement of fact: Today, conflict between nations raises the possibility of the destruction of civilization as we know it.
Question from audience? Who says?
Answer to audience: When asked about the weapons that might be used in a third world war, Albert Einstein replied that he didn't know what World War III would be fought with, but that World War IV would be fought with sticks and stones.

We can use the acronym STAR to recall questions to use in checking the reliability of information from authorities or experts:[1]

Are the credentials of the authorities **Sufficient?**

Are the experts **Typical** of other experts in the field?

Is the information from the experts cited **Accurately?**

Is information from the experts **Relevant** to the conclusion drawn?

Using historical data Historical data might be used to support a statement of fact. In the following example, the conflict in East Timor (a historical fact) is used to support the assertion that "There has [not] been world peace [since the end of World War II]."

> There has been no world war since the end of World War II in 1945. That does not mean, however, that there has been world peace. At any given time, there may be as many as fifty regional conflicts. For instance, in 1975, Indonesian troops invaded East Timor, a place most Americans have never heard of. Resistance to Indonesian rule still persists.

Citing data from experiments Information from experiments might be used to support a statement of fact. In the following example, the assertion "Hair, bodily fluids, and flesh all contain DNA" has been verified through scientific experiments.

> DNA is now used as a kind of genetic fingerprint to identify a person. Hair, bodily fluids, and flesh all contain DNA.

The audience trusts the writer who has established a credible *ethos* to make sure the facts used as support are recent, reliable, and relevant.

---

[1]Acronym from Richard Fulkerson's *Teaching the Argument in Writing.* (In press, NCTE.)

R E M I N D E R

Failure to interpret facts correctly or to cite facts accurately can destroy a writer's credibility. To maintain a credible *ethos*, check facts carefully and eliminate factual information that is irrelevant.

GENERALIZATIONS

Generalizing is reasoning from example or observation or experience, using the inductive reasoning process we discussed earlier. We make generalizations constantly and make decisions based on them. For example, if you buy popcorn at a movie and the first couple of pieces taste stale, you probably will generalize that the whole bag is stale because all the popcorn in the bag came from the same place.

Public opinion surveys make predictions and television producers cancel shows based on information from a relatively small sample. What pollsters and ratings folks assume is that the sample they have chosen is representative of the millions of other people they represent. Sometimes they are wrong.

From polling information prior to the 1948 election, pollsters decided that Republican Thomas Dewey would win the election over Democrat Harry Truman. Based on the polling information, newspapers carried the headline that Dewey had won before the election results were in. From the sample of the electorate polled, the generalization that Dewey would win was probable. Some people believed it to be certain. However, the polling was done of a subgroup that was not **representative** of the entire electorate. The polling was done by telephone, and at the time, only the relatively well-to-do (who tended to vote Republican) in urban areas had telephones. The people in rural areas who didn't have telephones had a vote, and they voted for Truman.

Had the pollsters also included people in the survey who didn't have telephones and the results turned out the same, the reason might have been that the sample was **insufficient,** or too small. Had the pollsters surveyed only people in a certain area of the country and drawn the same incorrect conclusion, the reason might have also involved a **faulty analysis** of the sample data. Perhaps a correct inference could be drawn that people in that area or even that state would vote for Dewey, not that voters in the entire country would vote for Dewey.

Types of generalizations   Generalizations that apply to an entire population and are based on careful scientific study and experiment are **universal generalizations.** They become laws. From these generalizations, we can make deductions.

FROM INDUCTION   TO   DEDUCTION

Every object I have dropped in the past falls to the earth.

All objects that are dropped fall to the earth.

Therefore, it is probably true that

all objects that are dropped fall to the earth.

Therefore, it is absolutely true that the object that I am about to drop will fall to the earth.

A **qualified generalization** claims that certain characteristics are common to a described and specific population. If we claim, for instance, that cats like to play in boxes, we must limit our generalization to domestic house cats unless we have observed the same characteristic in bobcats, cheetahs, leopards, lions, and tigers in the wild. A **statistical generalization** identifies certain characteristics of a subgroup and expresses it in a ratio: Almost one out of five (or one-fifth or 20%) of the people who voted in the 1992 election voted for Ross Perot.

The STAR acronym used to organize questions regarding authorities can be used to evaluate generalizations as well.

Is the sample **Sufficient?**

Is the sample **Typical?**

Is information about the sample **Accurate?**

Is the information about the sample **Relevant** to the conclusion?

R E M I N D E R

A conclusion drawn from insufficient data, a nonrepresentative sample, or an incorrect analysis of the data is called a hasty generalization and is one of the material fallacies discussed in Part Four.

CAUSAL RELATIONSHIPS

A generalization about the cause of an observable condition or situation involves inductive reasoning. For an argument involving a causal relationship, the relationship between a cause and a certain condition must be demonstrated or reasonably assumed. If, for instance, you fell off a ladder and broke your arm, the relationship between the fall and the broken arm can be reasonably assumed. But what if you argue that flu shots *give* the flu instead of prevent it because you took a flu shot one year and immediately became ill? Because you took the flu shot before you became ill is not sufficient to show a causal relationship.

Ways of determining a probable causal relationship   One way to determine if a relationship is causal is to look for **agreement among factors** of the situation. Suppose twenty people ate at the same restaurant, and eight of them became ill a few hours later. Health investigators determined that each of the eight people who became ill ate raw oysters; the twelve people who did not become ill ate other items from the menu. None of the twelve who did not become ill ate raw oysters. If other factors, such as sauces and side dishes are eliminated through the same process, a conclusion with a high degree of probability can be drawn that the raw oysters caused the eight people to become ill. Each case shared a common factor.

Another way to identify a causal connection is to determine **differences among factors.** Scientists are studying the relationship between genetic markers and a newly discovered type of cancer. Suppose in a study of patients who had this type of cancer, the following factors were observed:

15% of the patients were vegetarians

30% of the patients held high-stress jobs

100% of the patients had genetic markers on the same chromosome

40% of the patients ate high-fiber diets

30% of the patients drank coffee

20% of the patients smoked cigarettes

Because the patients all shared factors related to heredity, a qualified generalization could be drawn that genetic factors caused the new type of cancer. However, the generalization would be premature until researchers looked for the same factors among those who did not have the cancer. Perhaps everyone had the particular genetic marker.

Researchers then studied the same factors in people who were at least 70 years of age and who did not have the cancer. They eliminated the factors that were observed in people who did not have or had never had the type of cancer. The remaining factor was a particular genetic marker. At this point, a legitimate conclusion could be drawn.

When analyzing causal relationships, the following questions can be helpful guidelines:

What factors do all cases of a condition or situation have in common?

What factors can be eliminated because they occur in cases where the condition is not observed?

Are there variations in the condition that can be related to variations in a particular cause?

R E M I N D E R

Reasoning that because X happened before Y, X must have caused Y is referred to as a *post hoc*, or false cause, argument— a special kind of *hasty generalization*. (See more about this in Part Four.)

ANALOGIES

Arguments from analogy use similarities between two things and apply what is commonly known about one to the other. In other words, two things that are similar in some ways are asserted to be similar in other ways. An argument from analogy includes support for the premise (stated or unstated) that the two things are similar enough in some ways to make inferences about other similarities.

Mark Twain uses the analogy of a machine, fabricated from raw ore, to illustrate characteristics of humans in "What is Man?" In a dialogue between a young man and an old man, Twain argues that humans are born as what psychologists later called "blank slates" with certain "inborn heredities" (compared to the properties of ore). Training and education turn the savage (compared to the original rock from which the engine was eventually made) into civilized man (the steel engine). Twain uses analogy to address a question that has perplexed humans for hundreds of years: Is nature (heredity) or nurture (training, environment) the primary influence on individuals?

Practice: Creating Arguments

Write brief arguments that illustrate the following types of supporting arguments: description, fact, generalization, authority, causal relationship. Each argument should contain one or two premises and one conclusion. For ideas for topics, you may want to refer to your journal or to a newspaper or magazine.

Diagramming Arguments

Stripping a piece of writing of repetitions, transitions, and digressions to find the premise(s) and conclusion can be useful in evaluating the arguments of others and checking your own or a peer's to make sure they are sound, thorough, and forceful. Below is a part of Mrs. Robinson's letter from the "Objection to the Child Labor Movement" that introduced this chapter. Each statement is numbered and arranged in list form.

1. This proposed amendment is fathered by Socialists, Communists, and Bolshevists.
2. They are the active workers in its favor.
3. [They look forward to] its adoption as giving them the power to nationalize the children of the land and . . .
4. [Its adoption will] bring about in this country the exact conditions which prevail in Russia.
5. These people are the active workers back of this undertaking, . . .

   If we look at the argument closely, we see that three of the statements say the same thing—that the people behind the Child Labor Amendment are "Socialists, Communists, and Bolshevists." And these people are supporting the amendment for the purpose of "nationalizing the children" and making this country like Russia. So the main conclusion of the passage is that the amendment will result in socialism in America, and the proof is in the fact that the amendment is supported by socialists.

   One way of diagramming the argument is to write the number of the conclusion at the bottom and put a circle around it. In this case, statements 3 and 4 work together to form the conclusion. They are joined with a plus sign and bracketed. Each of the other statements are premises that support the conclusion, so we write those numbers and draw arrows to the conclusion to indicate the relationship.

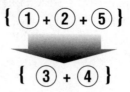

Premise: Socialists support the Child Labor Amendment.

Conclusion: [therefore] The Child Labor Amendment will result in nationalizing children and making America like Russia.

Note: An unstated premise can be represented with a letter instead of a number. Use an arrow to point from a minor conclusion that is then used as support for the main conclusion.

Practice: Diagramming an Argument

Diagram the second paragraph (printed below) of Mrs. Robinson's letter, using the diagram above as an example. Keep in mind that arguments are sometimes interpreted differently and premises and conclusions might be represented differently on a diagram. (You might find it helpful to paraphrase each sentence before analyzing it.)

1. [If adopted,] this amendment would be the greatest thing ever done in America in behalf of the activities of hell.
2. It would make millions of young people under eighteen years of age idlers in brain and body, and
3. thus make them the devil's best workshop.
4. It would destroy the initiative and self-reliance and manhood and womanhood of all the coming generations.

A CLOSER LOOK

Trudy Govier, in "Are There Two Sides to Every Question?" points out that an argument is balanced and objective when it meets all or most of the following criteria:

1. The language used is relatively neutral. (Example: a speaker opposing religion in public schools refers to religious people as believers or adherents, not as bigots or fanatics.)
2. Facts that would tend to support an interpretation or evaluation different from that of the speaker or writer are acknowledged. Their apparent impact is either recognized or argued against and accounted for. (Example: A speaker defending religion as making a contribution to human progress acknowledges wars in Ireland and Lebanon as an apparent counterexample to his thesis. But the speaker contends that broader economic and political issues exist behind these conflicts so that, appearances notwithstanding, they are not fundamentally religious conflicts.)
3. The point is acknowledged where expert opinion is cited and the relevant experts differ from each other. Either the case developed does not depend entirely on citing expert opinion or good reasons for selecting particular experts are given. Those experts whose views are not accepted are not attacked on irrelevant personal grounds.
4. Controversial interpretations of events or texts, explanations for which there are plausible alternatives, disputable predictions, estimations, or value judgments are acknowledged as such. Reasons for them are given and, where appropriate, the impact on the analysis of making another such judgment is recognized.
5. The speakers or writers do not insidiously introduce their own special point of view as being the one the audience would naturally

adopt. (Example: If a feminist is speaking in favor of equal pay for work of equal value, the speaker does not refer to the audience as "we in the feminist movement.")

6. Sources are indicated and, where practically feasible, quoted so that they may be checked in contexts where this is sufficiently important.

7. Arguments are careful and well reasoned, not fallacious.

8. Where time and space permit, alternative positions are stated, explained, and considered. Reasons are given as to why these positions are seen to be less satisfactory than the one advocated. Alternative positions are fairly and accurately represented and described in nonprejudicial language. People holding them are described accurately, politely, and respectfully.

9. The point is acknowledged where evidence and reasons offered are less than rationally compelling. An explanation is given as to why the position taken nevertheless seems the most nearly correct or appropriate in the context.

As you read the following argument for reforming immigration laws, evaluate it in terms of Govier's criteria.

Take a Number:
A New Way to Let Immigrants In
Peter D. Salinas

1   The trouble with the recent immigration debate is that much of it is simply unreal. Intellectuals have been arguing over abstractions, while the insecurities of ordinary Americans have been inflamed by prejudice and misinformation. Those both for and against immigration behave as if it were politically conceivable that the United States might drastically cut immigration again, as we did in the 1920s, and as if our borders could be effectively sealed if we chose to do so. In spite of resurgent nativism, any proposal to sharply curtail legal immigration would meet massive resistance across the political spectrum—from liberals who see open immigration as a basic ingredient of the universalist American idea to conservatives attached to free markets and open international borders. If it came to a vote in Congress, a bipartisan pro-immigration alliance would emerge, even stronger than the one that backed NAFTA, using the same arguments (long-term economic benefits outweigh short-term stresses, the politics of fear versus the politics of hope, etc.). Buttressing the argument would

be our proven inability to stem illegal immigration, because any reduction in the quota of legal immigrants almost certainly would be offset by an increase in illegal immigration—an unsettling prospect for most Americans, but especially for the nativists.

2   So rather than contest the volume of immigrants, we might re-examine how we actually allocate immigration in a world in which the number of potential immigrants vastly exceeds the most generous quota we could tolerate, and how we treat immigrants once they get here. But first, a few facts to reassure ourselves about the benign nature of immigration. To begin with, America is not being inundated with immigrants. While the volume has risen steadily since the national origins quota system was scrapped in 1965, the rate of immigration relative to the nation's base population is far below historic levels. Due in large part to the amnesty of 1.5 million illegal immigrants as part of the Immigration Reform and Control Act of 1986, the average rate of legal immigration between 1981 and 1990 reached a post-Depression high of 3.1 per 1,000 U.S. residents. This rate is below that of every decade from 1830 to 1930, and is about the same as the long-term immigration rate since American independence. Moreover, the percentage of foreign-born people in the U.S. population has fallen from 8.8 in 1940 to 6.8 today.

3   As important as volume is geography. Most immigrants remain near America's gateways, at the perimeters of the country. The greatest number, nearly 40 percent of the total since 1987, live in Southern California; other large cohorts are in New York City, south Florida, Texas, and Chicago. Most of the rest can be found in a handful of urban areas on the east and west coasts. Most Americans do not live near immigrants. This suggests either that the new nativism is confined to the peripheral immigrant bastions or that some nativists don't need to meet immigrants to dislike them.

4   Another critical fact: Immigrants have been moving to—and staying in—America's cities, filling a vacuum left by the flight to the suburbs over the past 40 years. Until a new surge of immigration into New York in the 1980s, the city had been losing population—nearly a million between 1970 and 1980. New York is the only city east of the Mississippi to gain population since 1980. Wherever they have settled, immigrants have reclaimed decayed inner-city neighborhoods.

5   In spite of their growing presence in American cities, immigrants have not displaced the native minority poor in the labor force. Hypothetically, the low-wage, low-skill work done by the least skilled immigrants in these ethnic enclaves might overwise have been done by native workers would have spurned them if they had. In fact, recent studies show that unemployment rates among blacks living in or near immigrant enclaves actually fell following the immigrant influx. Nor does immigrant labor appreciably lower native workers' wages. One study estimates that when immigrant participation in a local labor market doubles, the wages of young blacks in general may fall by 4 percent or less, and those of other minorities are unaffected.

6   How about the indirect economic impact of immigration on state and local government budgets that California's Governor Pete Wilson is so concerned about? All these immigrant children require an education and, at $5,000 per child—thousands more than their parents' local contribution— they have filled up the inner-city schools. Here too, the burden looks greater in the abstract than in reality. These inner-city school systems—in New York, Chicago, Miami, Los Angeles—were dying before the immigrants came. In spite of declining populations, the districts still absorbed a large amount of public funds, without much to show for them. The immigrants rescued the schools not only from bankruptcy, but also from irrelevance.

7   The truth is, the immigration scare does not reflect a genuine problem, it reflects a genuine panic. The panic is brought on by economic dislocation, which is all too easily laid at the door of immigrants. This is not to say there should not be an immigration debate. On the contrary, it is long overdue. The debate should be not about how many, but rather who should be let into the country, and how. Categorical preferences built into the current immigration policy exacerbate both the geographic and ethnic concentration of immigrants, adding to the burden of their assimilation and pouring fuel on the nativists fires. It's time for an overhaul.

8   The liberalization of immigration legislation in 1965 was supposed to end the northern European bias of the nativist-inspired national origins quota system of 1925. The reforms certainly succeeded in that respect, redirecting immigration from northern Europe to Latin America and Asia. But, at the same time, the preference categories of the current law have perpetuated the root bias of a national origins system, only with a new set of favored nationalities. The largest preference categories favored under present immigration policy promote "family reunification." This means that once a nationality gains a significant demographic foothold in the United States, it has a vested claim on the immigration quota roughly in proportion to its share of the foreign-born population: exactly the concept that animated the old national origins system. Indeed, family preference was written into the 1965 law primarily to reassure the nativists that the national origins idea was not being scrapped entirely. Since the new law's inception, around 70 percent of all legal immigrants have been admitted under one or another family reunification preference category. And with the amnesty provision of the 1986 law, the preference has been effectively extended to millions of illegal immigrants as well.

9   The primary beneficiaries of the family reunification tilt have been Mexicans. Since 1981 more than 30 percent of all legal immigrants to the United States have come from Mexico. The fact that Mexicans account for only 18 percent of all legal immigration since 1965 proves that the national origins bias of family reunification increases over time. Family preferences have also ensured that what remains of the pool of legal entrants is dominated by other Latin Americans and Asians from just a few countries: the Philippines, China,

Korea, and India. The 1986 amnesty of 2.5 million illegals, the vast majority of them Mexicans, has further intensified the nationality biases of family reunification and has been a major factor in provoking a nativist backlash.

10   The other favored foreigners are those admitted under refugee and asylum preferences; they account for 15 percent of all immigrants during the past decade. Refugee and asylum preferences have a solid justification, given all the repressive regimes in the world, but they have been seriously compromised by our foreign policy biases. When both Nicaragua and El Salvador were in turmoil during the 1980s, Nicaraguans fleeing a communist dictatorship were accepted as refugees, while Salvadorans fleeing right-wing death squads were not. Likewise, Cubans were admitted as refugees from the time Castro took power, while no dictator is bloody enough for Haitians to be welcomed. And since most Third World autocracies are also poor, every case involves a judgment call about motivation: Is it economic or political?

11   There are good reasons to change the preference system. How to do it? Some advocate favoring high levels of skill or education, as Canada does. But "designer immigration" is not only unfair—vesting the privilege of immigration in precisely those who have been the most privileged in their native lands—it is not even especially helpful to the American economy. Our real labor needs—popular perceptions and high unemployment rates among unskilled natives notwithstanding—are at the bottom of the labor market, mainly in services. The labor market's demand for skilled professionals is amply met by the large number of foreign students who stay and work here after graduation and by immigrants admitted on other than skill preferences.

12   Why not, instead of unfair family rules and unnecessary skills rules, adopt a first-come, first-served policy? Of the roughly 700,000 legal (non-amnesty) immigration slots we make available in a typical year, perhaps 150,000 could be reserved for the spouses or minor children of U.S. residents—a much reduced preference for the reunification of nuclear families—and 75,000 for refugees. The other 475,000 would be available to applicants from any nation on earth. Subject to an annual global cap, applications for immigration would be reviewed in the order they were received at designated centers in each country. To avoid the immigrant pool's being swamped by applicants from the most populous countries (with 40 percent of the world's population, China and India might dominate such a system), perhaps no country's annual quota should exceed some percentage of the total. However it were fleshed out, a first-come, first-served system would offer immigration to the most highly motivated candidates, from maximally diverse backgrounds, selected by the fairest and most objective procedures.

13   The United States has not made a mistake by admitting millions of immigrants since the law was changed in 1965. Indeed, America's liberal immigration policy is one of our proudest public accomplishments. Let's not turn our backs on one of the most successful American ideas. Let's get it right.

For Writing and Discussion

1. Does Salinas use neutral language when he addresses opponents to immigration? Give specific examples.

2. Does Salinas provide facts and statistics that might be used to support an anti-immigration position? Can you think of additional information that should have been addressed?

3. Does Salinas provide information from experts who might be challenged by other experts or authorities? If so, what information might be challenged and by whom?

4. Does Salinas assume that his audience agrees with him on any specific points or issues that should be explained and supported?

5. Does Salinas provide sources for factual information and statistical data? Is information sufficient for the reader to find and evaluate the source of such information? Give specific examples.

6. What is Salinas's thesis? What kinds of support does he offer? Is the support sufficient? Why or why not?

7. An element of classical rhetoric is *refutation,* or acknowledgment and rebuttal of opposing views. What opposing views does Salinas address? Does he provide sufficient reasons to reject each opposing view? Can you think of additional arguments that an opponent of immigration might make?

8. Evaluate Salinas's interpretation of opposing views. Can you think of alternative interpretations of any of the information Salinas cited and evaluated?

9. Wanda Coleman, writing in *The Nation,* claims that minority workers are affected by immigrants in Los Angeles, that immigrants "pushed blacks out of the marketplace altogether." Does Salinas offer adequate proof to refute the claim that immigrants displace native workers?

10. According to Jeremy Rifkin (see pages 150–155), there will be a reduction in low-skilled jobs in the future. How does Salinas address the future needs for low-skilled labor?

11. Discuss Salinas's use of *ethos, pathos,* and *logos* in his argument. Illustrate with specific examples.

Chapter 8

OPPOSING VIEWS

Upside Down in the Groves of Academe
William A. Henry III

1   **I**magine places where it is considered racist to speak of the rights of the individual when they conflict with the community's prevailing opinion. Where it is taboo to debate the moral fitness of homosexuals as parents, and sexist to order a Domino's pizza because the chain's chairman donates money to an antiabortion group. Imagine institutions that insist they absolutely defend free speech but punish the airing of distasteful views by labeling them unacceptable "behavior" instead of words—and then expel the perpetrators.

2   Imagine a literature class that equates Shakespeare and the novelist Alice Walker, not as artists but as fragments of sociology. Shakespeare is deemed to represent the outlook of a racist, sexist and classist 16th century England, while Walker allegedly embodies a better but still oppressive 20th century America. Finally, imagine a society in which some of the teachers reject the very ideas of rationality, logic and dialogue as the cornerstone assumptions of learning—even when discussing science.

3   Where is this upside-down world? According to an increasing number of concerned academics, administrators and students, it is to be found on many U.S. college campuses. And it is expanding into elementary and secondary school classrooms.

4   For most of American history, the educational system has reflected and reinforced bedrock beliefs of the larger society. Now a troubling number of teachers at all levels regard the bulk of American history and heritage as racist, sexist and classist and believe their purpose is to bring about social change—or, on many campuses, to enforce social changes already achieved.

5   This new thinking is not found everywhere, to be sure, but in many places professors contend it is becoming dominant. While American universities and colleges have always been centers for the critical examination of Western assumptions and beliefs, the examination has taken a harsh and strident turn. At times it amounts to a mirror-image reversal of basic assumptions held by the nation's majority.

6   To the dismay of many civil libertarians, the new turns of thought are fostering a decline in tolerance and a rise in intellectual intimidation. Says Leon Botstein, president of New York's liberal Bard College: "Nobody wants to listen to the other side. On many campuses, you really have a culture of forbidden questions."

7   Obfuscatory course titles and eccentric reading lists frequently are wedded to a combative political agenda or outlandish views of the nation's culture and values. At Duke University in North Carolina, an English-department course uses plays and films to pursue the theme that organized crime "is a metaphor for American business as usual." Another Duke offering condemns a heterosexual bias in traditional Western literature; its professor has written about such topics as "Jane Austen and the masturbating girl."

8   A University of Texas professor of American studies has constructed a course on 19th century writers to alternate between famous white men one week and obscure women the next, in part to illuminate "the prison house of gender." A woman who has been visiting professor at both the University of Hawaii and the University of Texas describes traditional liberal arts as prone to "a fetishized respect for culture as a stagnant secular religion." Mary Louise Pratt, a Stanford professor of comparative literature, has objected to "the West's relentless imperial expansion" and its "monumentalist cultural hierarchy that is historically as well as morally distortive."

9   Although most students at most colleges continue to take courses bearing at least some resemblance to what their predecessors studied, even the traditional curriculum is often read in new ways. Valerie Babb, an assistant professor of English at Georgetown, is teaching a course this semester called White Male Writers. Among them: Hawthorne, Melville and Faulkner. The title reflects one of the course's chief assertions: that just as women or black writers are studied as a class that shares a particular sensibility, so too should these white male artists be. However great their works might be, they speak merely as "one element of the large and diversified body of literature."

10   The flowering of new and at times exotic theory is in keeping with the great tradition of liberal-arts education. But many of the new critics have a hostile view of traditional scholarship and seem to judge ideas by their "political correctness" (abbreviated as P.C.)—that is, on the basis of whom they might offend.

11   The University of Delaware barred Linda Gottfredson from accepting money for her educational research from the controversial Pioneer Fund because it had financed unrelated studies into possible hereditary differences in intelligence among the races. The review committee judged that by underwriting such studies, Pioneer had exhibited "a pattern of activities incompatible with the university's mission." The University of Michigan student newspaper condemned sociologist Reynolds Farley for, as he phrases is, "lack of ideological perspective, for not directly attacking gender and racial differences in wages." A male philosophy professor at Pomona College in California has been fighting a lonely and losing battle to get a course critical of feminist

theory listed among women's studies. Several schools have punished students for expressing religious objections to homosexuality or, as at the University of Washington, questioning a professor's assertion that lesbians make the best mothers.

12   Taboos on fields of inquiry are increasingly accompanied by bans on language. According to a growing number of academic theorists, the First Amendment guarantee of freedom of speech can be legitimately laid aside for worthy reasons. Chief among them is if it interferes with what is billed as a new and nonconstitutional right: the right to avoid having one's feelings hurt, or what Botstein calls a "subjective interpretation of harm." Thus dozens of universities have introduced tough new codes prohibiting speech that leads to, among other things, a "demeaning atmosphere," and some of them have suspended students for using epithets toward blacks, homosexuals or other minorities, not only in classrooms but also in dormitories, in intramural sports and even off campus altogether.

13   "Freedom of expression is no more sacred than freedom from intolerance or bigotry," says John Jeffries, a black who is associate dean of the graduate school of management and urban policy at New York's New School for Social Research. But on some campuses, hostility to white males is more or less condoned. The University of Wisconsin at Parkside suspended one student for addressing another as "Shaka Zulu"; yet the university's Madison campus held that the term "red-neck" was not discriminatory. At some schools, professors teach that white males can never be victims of racism, because racism is a form of repressive political power—and white males already hold the power in Western society.

14   At Brown University, President Vartan Gregorian redefined the racist, wee-hours tirade of a drunken student as unacceptable behavior rather than as protected free speech and, having thereby finessed First Amendment concerns, expelled the offender. Although Gregorian insists he was responding to the whole set of circumstances, his explanation is widely disputed. Says *Village Voice* columnist Nat Hentoff, a First Amendment activist: "Gregorian is engaged, unwittingly I suppose, in classic Orwellian speech."

15   In an unlikely tactical alliance to ban such activities, Representative Henry Hyde of Illinois, a conservative Republican, this month introduced a bill with the backing of the American Civil Liberties Union. The measure is designed to discourage private colleges from disciplining students "solely on the basis of conduct that is speech or other communication." It is given a good chance of passage.

16   In the nation's elementary and secondary schools, the polarization is not yet so extreme. But increasingly curriculums are being written to satisfy the political demands of parents and community activists. In some cases, expediency counts for more than facts. New York State officials, for example, have responded to pressure from Nation American leaders by revamping the state high school curriculum to include the shaky assertion that the U.S.

Constitution was based on the political system of the Iroquois Confederacy. In Berkeley, chicana activist Martha Acevedo, who is vice chairman of the school board, has blocked adoption of new textbooks despite state approval for their multicultural approach. According to her, the books lack "positive role models." She cites the depiction of a 19th century Hispanic Robin Hood-style figure who is shown in one text on a wanted poster.

17   Perhaps the most problematic development is the emergence in dozens of cities of "Afrocentric" curriculums. All of them legitimately seek to bolster black children's confidence in their ability to achieve and to debunk the patronizing notion that black American history and culture began with the Emancipation Proclamation. When pursued with intellectual discipline, the Afrocentric idea can be inspirational. Says Franklyn Jenifer, president of Howard University, in recalling his own education at that historically black school: "Every course I took was infused with some sense of our destiny or my personal destiny and the possibility of my achieving it."

18   But through zealotry or inadequate research, too many of these courses have expanded their claims far beyond the generally accepted list of black attainments. Among the most controversial assertions: that ancient Greece derived—no, stole—its culture from black Africa; that black Africans invented science and mathematics; that the Egypt of the pharaohs was a black culture; and that a racist white Establishment has systematically hidden these and other black achievements. The hazard of such courses is that they may instill less pride than resentment.

19   Ethnic material increasingly is taught to children of all races; conventional history increasingly is not. In education-minded Brookline, Mass., where 79% of high school graduates go on to college, parents have had to fight to restore a European history course that was canceled as Eurocentric and elitist. Meanwhile, students have been enticed into fringe electives with such sales pitches as "Have you ever wondered what goes on in the mind of a voodoo doctor?"

20   Why are Western cultural and social values so out of favor in the classroom when so much of the rest of the world has moved, during the past couple of years, to embrace them? Richard Kimball, conservative author of *Tenured Radicals,* a book harshly critical of the trend, blames the coming of age of the academic generation shaped by the struggles of the '60s. Its members, he says, vowed back then to transform campuses into engines of ongoing social change; now they are in a position to impose their will. A much less conspiratorial interpretation is that American schools and colleges are dealing with a demographic change that will take another couple of decades to grip society as a whole—the shift, because of higher birth and immigration rates among nonwhite and Hispanic people, from a majority-white to a truly multiracial society. These nonwhite and Hispanic students want a curriculum that gives them more dignity. So do women and gays—and faculty from all those groups. Says the Rev. Clarence Glover Jr., who teaches a course about the sins of "the European-American male" at Southern Methodist University in Dallas: "People of color have always been a majority in the world and are

now becoming a majority in America. The issue becomes, How do we begin to share power?"

21   Courses that explore these questions are increasingly popular among students in general, but the primary audience for minority-oriented curriculums is usually the minorities themselves. Typically, they seek courses that reassure as much as instruct them. At San Francisco State College and also in that city's two-year City College, students can minor in gay and lesbian studies, with such offerings as Gay Male Relationships and Sexual Well-Being. The City College department was founded in 1989, says chairman Jack Collins, because "it will raise the self-esteem of lesbian and gay students who will realize that they are complete people, that we do have recognizable and describable cultures."

22   The chief risk in any ideologically based curriculum is that it can promote tribalism and downplay the value of discovering common cultural ground. The very idea of the melting pot, of assimilation, indeed of a common American identity, is under fire in some academic circles. Warns Diane Ravitch, adjunct professor of history and education at Columbia: "If we teach kids to connect themselves to one group defined by race or language or religion, then we have no basis for public education. We need to retain a sense of the common venture."

23   Colleges are as subject to fad and fashion as the rest of society—perhaps more, for the client base of students turns over quickly. But few scholars believe the current intellectual battles will end soon—particularly as the confrontation permeates other levels of education. In the process, the American tradition of tolerance in diversity, an uneven tradition at best, may be strained as rarely before. (Reported by Anne Hopkins and Daniel S. Levy/New York, with other bureaus.)

Teach Diversity—With a Smile
Barbara Ehrenreich

1   Something had to replace the threat of communism, and at last a workable substitute is at hand. "Multiculturalism," as the new menace is known, has been denounced in the media recently as the new McCarthyism, the new fundamentalism, even the new totalitarianism—take your choice. According to its critics, who include a flock of tenured conservative scholars, multiculturalism aims to toss out what it sees as the Eurocentric bias in education and replace Plato with Ntozake Shange and traditional math with the Yoruba

number system. And that's just the beginning. The Jacobins of the multiculturalist movement, who are described derisively as P.C., or politically correct,
are said to have launched a campus reign of terror against those who slip
and innocently say "freshman" instead of "freshperson," "Indian" instead of
"Native American" or, may the Goddess forgive them, "disabled" instead of
"differently abled."

2   So you can see what is at stake here: freedom of speech, freedom of
thought, Western civilization and a great many professorial egos. But before
we get carried away by the mounting backlash against multiculturalism, we
ought to reflect for a moment on the system that the P.C. people aim to
replace. I know all about it; in fact it's just about all I *do* know, since I—along
with so many educated white people of my generation—was a victim of
monoculturalism.

3   American history, as it was taught to us, began with Columbus' "discovery" of an apparently unnamed, unpeopled America, and moved on to the Pil-
grims serving pumpkin pie to a handful of grateful red-skinned folks. College
expanded our horizons with courses called Humanities or sometimes Civ,
which introduced us to a line of thought that started with Homer, worked its
way through Rabelais and reached a poignant climax in the pensées of
Matthew Arnold. Graduate students wrote dissertations on what long-dead
men had thought of Chaucer's verse or Shakespeare's dramas; foreign languages meant French or German. If there had been high technology in ancient China, kingdoms in black Africa, or women anywhere, at any time,
doing anything worth noticing, we did not know it, nor did anyone think to
tell us.

4   Our families and neighborhoods reinforced the dogma of monoculturalism. In our heads, most of us '50s teenagers carried around a social map that
was about as useful as the chart that guided Columbus to the "Indies." There
were "Negroes," "whites" and "Orientals," the latter meaning Chinese and
"Japs." Of religions, only three were known—Protestant, Catholic and Jew-
ish—and not much was known about the last two types. The only remaining
human categories were husbands and wives, and that was all the diversity the
monocultural world could handle. Gays, lesbians, Buddhists, Muslims,
Malaysians, Mormons, etc. were simply off the map.

5   So I applaud—with one hand, anyway—the multiculturalist goal of
preparing us all for a wider world. The other hand is tapping its finger impatiently because the critics are right about one thing: when advocates of multiculturalism adopt the haughty stance of political correctness, they quickly
descend to silliness or worse. It's obnoxious, for example, to rely on university administrations to enforce P.C. standards of verbal inoffensiveness. Racist,
sexist and homophobic thoughts cannot, alas, be abolished by fiat but only by
the time-honored methods of persuasion, education and exposure to the other
guy's—or, excuse me, woman's—point of view.

6   And it's silly to mistake verbal purification for genuine social reform.
Even after all women are "Ms." and all people are "he or she," women will

still earn only 65¢ for every dollar earned by men. Minorities by any other name, such as "people of color," will still bear a hugely disproportionate burden of poverty and discrimination. Disabilities are not just "different abilities" when there are not enough ramps for wheelchairs, signers for the deaf or special classes for the "specially" endowed. With all due respect for the new politesse, actions still speak louder than fashionable phrases.

7   But the worst thing about the P.C. people is that they are such poor advocates for the multicultural cause. No one was ever won over to a broader, more inclusive view of life by being bullied or relentlessly "corrected." Tell a 19-year-old white male that he can't say "girl" when he means "teen-age woman," and he will most likely snicker. This may be the reason why, despite the conservative alarms, P.C.-ness remains a relatively tiny trend. Most campuses have more serious and ancient problems: faculties still top-heavy with white males of the monocultural persuasion; fraternities that harass minorities and women; date rape; alcohol abuse; and tuition that excludes all but the upper fringe of the middle class.

8   So both sides would be well advised to lighten up. The conservatives ought to realize that criticisms of the great books approach to learning do not amount to totalitarianism. And the advocates of multiculturalism need to regain the sense of humor that enabled their predecessors in the struggle to coin the term P.C. years ago—not in arrogance but in self-mockery.

9   Beyond that, both sides should realize that the beneficiaries of multiculturalism are not only the "oppressed peoples" on the standard P.C. list (minorities, gays, etc.). The "unenlightened"—the victims of monoculturalism—are oppressed too, or at least deprived. Our educations, whether at Yale or at State U, were narrow and parochial and left us ill-equipped to navigate a society that truly is multicultural and is becoming more so every day. The culture that we studied was, in fact, *one* culture and, from a world perspective, all too limited and ingrown. Diversity is challenging, but those of us who have seen the alternative know it is also richer, livelier and ultimately more fun.

For Writing and Discussion

1. Summarize Henry's main argument in "Upside Down in the Groves of Academe," and evaluate his use of *logos* in the piece. Did you notice emotional appeals in Henry's essay? If so, explain his use of *pathos*. Relate the quotation from Diane Ravitch (par. 22) to the end of the excerpt from "Gang Bang Bang" on page 78. Is the fear of a future divided America justified? How might opponents of assimilation respond to the fears?

2. Ehrenreich maintains that requiring politically correct speech, or "verbal purification," is ineffective. What does she advocate instead? What is Ehrenreich's main argument for multicultural education? What support does she cite? Evaluate her use of *logos, pathos,* and *ethos.*

3. A student wrote in a letter to *Harper's* magazine:

> *To be a liberal arts student with progressive politics today is at once to be at the center of a raging national debate and to be completely on the sidelines, watching others far from campus describe you and use you for their own ends.*
>
> Rosa Ehrenreich, December 1991

Has your experience been similar or different? Do you feel personally involved in or affected by the debate? From your experience, is the debate over real or imagined problems?

4.   *Those who believe don't need to be convinced; those who don't believe* can't *be convinced.*

Adage regarding the miracle of the weeping statue at Lourdes, France

Positions on some issues are based on faith or moral beliefs. Relate the quotation above to the controversy over abortion. Is a compromise that would please both abortion opponents and choice advocates possible? Why or why not?

Practice: Exploring Issues

Trudy Govier notes in "Are There Two Sides to Every Question?" that there are many sides to most issues. She provides some possible sides to the issue of religion in school, noting that although the example is "moral and political," purely intellectual issues also have many possible positions.

1. Religion has no place in public schools.
2. Religion has no place in public schools except in programs about world religions (descriptive comparative religion) or about the history of some major religions.
3. Religion may occupy a minor place in education in public schools, but parents should be able to remove children from any classes on religion in a way that will not embarrass them.
4. Religion has a large role in education. In a pluralistic society, public monies should be given to a variety of religious groups so that each can sponsor its own educational system within which religion will have what that group sees as its proper educational role.
5. Religion has a large role to play in education. Only the religion of the majority can and should be taught in public schools. Minority religions can opt for private systems to teach their own religion in schools.
6. Religion has a large role to play in education. There is only one true religion, and it is that religion that should be taught in public schools.

Identify a current issue, and list four or five positions that might be taken on the single issue. Explain how you might use *logos* to appeal to adherents of each position. Then tell how might you use *pathos* fairly in an attempt to persuade each faction that another position was better. Be prepared to tell which appeal you think might be most effective for each position and why.

Honey, I Warped the Kids
Carl M. Cannon

1   . . . This is Hollywood's last line of defense for why it shows murder and mayhem on the big screen and the little one, in prime time and early in the morning, to children, adolescents, and adults:

2   We don't cause violence, we just report it.

3   Four years ago, I joined the legion of writers, researchers, and parents who have tried to force Hollywood to confront the more disturbing truth. I wrote a series of newspaper articles on the massive body of evidence that establishes a direct cause-and-effect relationship between violence on television and violence in society.

4   The orchestrated response from the industry—a series of letters seeking to discredit me—was something to behold.

5   Because the fact is, on the one issue over which they have power, the liberals in Hollywood don't act like progressive thinkers; they act like, say, the National Rifle Association:

Guns don't kill people, people kill people.

We don't cause violence in the world, we just reflect it.

6   The first congressional hearings into the effects of television violence took place in 1954. Although television was still relatively new, its extraordinary marketing power was already evident. The tube was teaching Americans what to buy and how to act, not only in advertisements, but in dramatic shows, too.

7   Everybody from Hollywood producers to Madison Avenue ad men would boast about this power—and seek to utilize it on dual tracks: to make money and to remake society along better lines.

8   Because it seemed ludicrous to assert that there was only one area—the depiction of violence—where television did not influence behavior, the television industry came up with this theory: Watching violence is cathartic. A violent person might be sated by watching a murder.

9   The notion intrigued social scientists, and by 1956 they were studying it in earnest. Unfortunately, watching violence turned out to be anything but cathartic.

10   In the 1956 study, one dozen four-year-olds watched a "Woody Woodpecker" cartoon that was full of violent images. Twelve other preschoolers watched "Little Red Hen," a peaceful cartoon. Then the children were observed. The children who watched "Woody Woodpecker" were more likely to hit other children, verbally accost their classmates, break toys, be disruptive, and engage in destructive behavior during free play.

11   For the next thirty years, researchers in all walks of the social sciences studies the question of whether television causes violence. The results have been stunningly conclusive.

12   "There is more published research on this topic than on almost any other social issue of our time," University of Kansas Professor Aletha C. Huston, chairwoman of the American Psychological Association's Task Force on Television and Society, told Congress in 1988. "Virtually all independent scholars agree that there is evidence that television can cause aggressive behavior."

13   There have been some three thousand studies of this issue—eighty-five of them major research efforts—and they all say the same thing. Of the eighty-five major studies, the only one that failed to find a causal relationship between television violence and actual violence was paid for by NBC. When the study was subsequently reviewed by three independent social scientists, all three concluded that it actually did demonstrate a causal relationship.

14   Some highlights from the history of TV violence research:

15   • In 1973, when a town in mountainous western Canada was wired for television signals, University of British Columbia researchers observed first- and second-graders. Within two years, the incidence of hitting, biting, and shoving increased 160 percent in those classes.

16   • Two Chicago doctors, Leonard Eron and Rowell Huesmann, followed the viewing habits of a group of children for twenty-two years. They found that watching violence on television is the single best predictor of violent or aggressive behavior later in life, ahead of such commonly accepted factors as parents' behavior, poverty, and race.

17   "Television violence effects youngsters of all ages, of both genders, at all socioeconomic levels and all levels of intelligence," they told Congress in 1992. "The effect is not limited to children who are already disposed to being aggressive and is not restricted to this country."

18   • Fascinated by an explosion of murder rates in the United States and Canada that began in 1955, after a generation of North Americans had come of age on television violence, University of Washington Professor Brandon Centerwall decided to see if the same phenomenon could be observed in South Africa, where the Afrikaner-dominated regime had banned television until 1975.

19   He found that eight years after TV was introduced—showing mostly Hollywood-produced fare—South Africa's murder rate skyrocketed. His most

telling finding was that the crime rate increased first in the white communities. This mirrors U.S. crime statistics in the 1950s and especially points the finger at television because whites were the first to get it in both countries.

20   Bolder than most researchers, Centerwall argues flatly that without violent television programming, there might be as many as ten thousand fewer murders in the United States each year.

21   • In 1983, University of California, San Diego, researcher David P. Phillips wanted to see if there was a correlation between televised boxing matches and violence in the streets of America.

22   Looking at crime rates after every televised heavyweight championship fight from 1973 to 1978, Phillips found that the homicide rate in the United States rose by an average of 11 percent for approximately one week. Phillips also found that the killers were likely to focus their aggression on victims similar to the losing fighter: if he was white, the increased number of victims were mostly white. The converse was true if the losing fighter was black.

23   • In 1988, researchers Daniel G. Linz and Edward Donnerstein of the University of California, Santa Barbara, and Steven Penrod of the University of Wisconsin studied the effects on young men of horror movies and "slasher" films.

24   They found that depictions of violence, not sex, are what desensitizes people.

25   They divided male students into four groups. One group watched no movies, a second watched nonviolent, X-rated movies, a third watched teenage sexual-innuendo movies, and a fourth watched the slasher films *Texas Chainsaw Massacre, Friday the 13ᵗʰ Part 2, Maniac,* and *Toolbox Murders.*

26   All the young men were placed on a mock jury panel and asked a series of questions designed to measure their empathy for an alleged female rape victim. Those in the fourth group measured lowest in empathy for the specific victim in the experiment—and for rape victims in general.

27   The anecdotal evidence is often more compelling than the scientific studies. Ask any homicide cop from London to Los Angeles to Bangkok if television violence induces real-life violence and listen carefully to the cynical, knowing laugh.

28   Ask David McCarthy, police chief in Greenfield, Massachusetts, why nineteen-year-old Mark Branch killed himself after stabbing an eighteen-year-old female college student to death. When cops searched his room they found ninety horror movies, as well as a machete and a goalie mask like those used by Jason, the grisly star of *Friday the 13ᵗʰ.*

29   Ask the families of thirty-five young men who committed suicide by playing Russian roulette after seeing the movie *The Deer Hunter.*

30   Ask George Gavito, a lieutenant in the Cameron County, Texas, sheriff's department, about a cult that sacrificed at least thirteen people on a ranch west of Matamoros, Mexico. The suspects kept mentioning a 1986 movie, *The Believers,* about rich families who engage in ritual sacrifice. "They talk about it like that had something to do with changing them," Gavito recalled later.

31   Ask LAPD lieutenant Mike Melton about Angel Regino of Los Angeles, who was picked up after a series of robberies and a murder in which he wore a blue bandanna and fedora identical to those worn by Freddy, the sadistic anti-hero of *Nightmare on Elm Street.* In case anybody missed the significance of his disguise, Regino told his victims that they would never forget him because he was another Freddy Krueger.

32   Ask Britain Home Secretary Douglas Hurd, who called for further restrictions on U.S.-produced films after Michael Ryan of Hungerford committed Britain's worst mass murder in imitation of *Rambo,* massacring sixteen people while wearing a U.S. combat jacket and a bandoleer of ammunition.

33   Ask Sergeant John O'Malley of the New York Police Department about a nine-year-old boy who sprayed a Bronx office building with gunfire. The boy explained to the astonished sergeant how he learned to load his Uzi-like firearm: "I watch a lot of TV."

34   Or ask Manteca, California, police detective Jeff Boyd about thirteen-year-old Juan Valdez, who, with another teenager, went to a man's home, kicked him, stabbed him, beat him with a fireplace poker, and then choked him to death with a dog chain.

35   Why, Boyd wanted to know, had the boys poured salt in the victim's wounds?

36   "Oh, I don't know," the youth replied with a shrug. "I just seen it on TV." . . .

37   But all of the scientific studies and reports, all of the wisdom of cops and grief of parents have run up against Congress's quite proper fear of censorship. For years, Democratic Congressman Peter Rodino of New Jersey chaired the House Judiciary Committee and looked at calls for some form of censorship with a jaundiced eye. At a hearing five years ago, Rodino told witnesses that Congress must be a "protector of commerce."

Civil Liberties Watch
Barbara Dority

PROFILE OF A CENSOR

This cleaning up of our culture must extend to nearly all domains. Theater, art, literature, movies, the press, posters, and window displays must be cleaned of the symptoms of a rotting world and put into the service of a moral idea of state and culture. Public life must be freed from the suffocating perfume of modern eroticism. . . . It is

the affair of the state . . . to prevent a people from being driven into
the arms of spiritual lunacy.

Adolf Hitler, *Mein Kampf*

1   Throughout the 1980s, as the lengthening tentacles of censorship crept down alleys and under back doors, civil libertarians did not sleep well. We became increasingly alarmed by the relentless erosion of our intellectual and personal freedoms. We had collective nightmares about Ronald Reagan, George Bush, Ed Meese, and Jesse Helms.

2   Many of us tried to sound an alarm. "Wake up!" we cried. "We're losing our liberties bit by bit. Look there! The monster is creeping upon us, shrouded in the fog. Can't you see it?"

3   Most people thought we were alarmists—until recently. Feeding on its many "small" successes, the insidious monster has grown bold and confident, revealing itself for all to see.

4   No medium is safe. Individuals and groups seeking to restrict the flow of information, images, and ideas are targeting public libraries, school classrooms, and resource centers. Motion pictures and television programs are policed by such groups as the American Family Association. Librarians, educators, school boards, publishers, bookstores, theaters, video stores, artists, musicians, and the electronic media are under persistent and organized attack. Under threats of legal action and boycott, many are capitulating to pressure tactics. America's marketplace of ideas is shrinking on a daily basis.

5   Artists, previously unconcerned, have been rudely awakened. They no longer believe that censorship only happens to other people. With the visual and performing arts under fire, the National Endowment for the Arts has been forced to implement funding restrictions on "offensive" works. Musicians and music distributors have been arrested and charged with violation of obscenity laws. Record companies have been pressured into censorship and labeling. The government restricts foreign educational films and speakers. The Supreme Court expands the definition of libel. The Freedom of Information Act slowly continues to erode.

6   Sexually explicit publications and information about sexuality are subject to severe restrictions. Magazines such as *Playboy* and *Penthouse* have been pulled from many retail shelves. Public school health and sex education books are being challenged and, all too often, banned. In many school districts, opponents of sex education have succeeded in implementing programs based solely upon abstinence—programs which contain no information on prevention of pregnancy or sexually transmitted diseases.

7   In short, our public schools are under siege and held hostage by those who would impose a narrow view of life on all our children. Orchestrated censorship campaigns by highly organized and well-funded conservative groups are successful in over one-third of reported cases.

8   As a result of this hysterical climate, many are engaging in self-censorship. Librarians don't order "possibly controversial" books, school administrators

censor student publications, and textbook publishers remove "controversial" materials from reading and science texts.

9   Liberty is like good health: we take it for granted until we lose it. During the past year, scores of "ordinary Americans" have seen the face of the monster. Bred with a sense of personal autonomy and rebellion and accustomed to a good measure of freedom, they have realized that alarm is the only appropriate response to this epidemic of censorship. They know that we can't sit around the kitchen table agreeing that censorship is wrong and waiting for someone else to do something about it. We can no longer afford to say we support freedom of expression while maintaining serious reservations about the Larry Flynts and the neo-Nazi skinheads.

10   It is our responsibility to organize and instruct these newly activated individuals. What we do not understand, we cannot effectively combat. Thus, it is essential that we possess and pass on an understanding of the pro-censorship mindset. In my experience, the following profile has remained consistent whether the would-be censor is male or female or from the left or right of the political spectrum. Without an understanding of this profile, defenders of intellectual freedom are at a considerable disadvantage.

11   The pro-censorship mindset has remained the same throughout the history of civilization. The censors always aim at protecting us from the perceived harmful effects of what we read, see, and hear. Historically, they did this to protect our souls from blasphemy (the ultimate victimless crime) or to protect society from alien political, social, or economic ideas. Today, it is more commonly done to protect us from explicit sexual imagery and words and to "protect" children from learning about the real world, as well as how to think critically. The justification, however, remains the same: it is best for us and best for society, and it will help bring about the realization of our noble aims.

12   The censor's most visible and striking characteristic is a flagrantly displayed belief in his or her own moral and spiritual superiority. Self-appointed moralists are never concerned about the welfare and protection of their *own* souls; they are concerned about yours and mine. They are never worried about their own ability to differentiate between fantasy and reality, to resist being seized by uncontrollable urges to commit violent or immoral acts, or to remain decent, law-abiding human beings who do not wish to hurt or degrade others. But they are *very* worried about *your* ability to do so.

13   Opponents of sexual information and sexually explicit materials display this trait more obviously than do opponents of other types of material. They often maintain extensive collections of the materials they pronounce to be a deadly peril to the human psyche. They frequently announce this fact, followed by detailed descriptions of what they have learned from their hours of intensive study. They describe in horrifying detail some of the crimes and degradation inevitably committed by ordinary people after viewing this material. They and their colleagues, of course, remain totally unaffected.

14   This superior, moralistic attitude often enrages supporters of intellectual freedom, thus diminishing our effectiveness. If we are to avoid engaging in counterproductive, knee-jerk reactions to this self-righteousness, we must delve further into the censorship mindset and truly understand its source.

15   At the root of the compulsion to censor lies a powerful and dangerous force: *fear.* We live in a rapidly changing and imperiled world in which many people never feel safe. Worse yet, they don't feel at home in their own bodies. They are often traumatized survivors from abusive backgrounds who are genuinely terrified of the sexuality of others. They are even more terrified of *their own* sexuality and live with a nearly overwhelming feeling of profound anxiety as they frantically try to control the world around them.

16   Unfortunately, in their desperate grasp for some measure of safety and control, they often turn to religion. There they are presented with a simplistic interpretation of good and evil. Their fears are fed and directed into efforts to force the complexities of the real world into simple black-and-white order—to make all human beings, including themselves, behave in ways which do not threaten their fragile security. If the chosen religion is the fundamentalist variety, such frightened people become particularly dangerous. When God is on your side and your aims are holy, the ends justify any and all means.

17   These pro-censorship forces have a stranglehold on many elected officials—not because they are in the majority but because they are well-organized, well-funded, extremely vocal, and full of missionary zeal. Legislators are afraid to speak out against censorship because they know they will be accused of supporting smut and perversion and of contributing to the destruction of the moral fiber of America.

18   It is up to us to tell our elected representatives—from the smallest local school boards to the most powerful U.S. senators—that we will support them in efforts to halt the erosion of our civil rights and that any steps they take to restrict free speech and press will be met appropriately at the ballot box.

19   Restriction of free thought and speech is the ultimate un-American act. Those of us who support the diversity and freedom of a pluralistic society have much to do. If you haven't already joined us, the time to do so is now.

For Writing and Discussion

1. Summarize Cannon's main argument in "Honey, I Warped the Kids." What kind of support does he use? Evaluate the sufficiency of his support.

2. Following the excerpt included here, Cannon goes on to discuss efforts that have been made to curb media violence. What, if anything, do you believe should be done? In the absence of any real reform, what would you suggest to parents?

3. Some people who argue that television and movie violence does no harm claim that television and movies *reflect* a violent society rather than help create it. Others say that viewing violence actually invokes catharsis, a relieving of the emotions, and serves a positive function for the audience. Respond to each of the views with your own brief argument that supports or rebuts the views.

4. Summarize Dority's argument in "Civil Liberties Watch." What support does she use? How does she refute opposing views? Of *pathos, logos,* and *ethos,* which appeal does she use most effectively?

5. How does Dority address the idea that viewing violence can increase violent behavior? Do you agree or disagree with her refutation? Why or why not?

6. Where do you think Cannon would stand on the issues of rights of the individual vs. rights of society as a whole? Why? Where would Dority stand? Why?

7. What is your response to the idea that "Hollywood is only giving people what they want" in producing violent movies? How do you account for the popularity of violent movies?

Practice: Taking a Stand

Write a brief essay in which you take a stand on the issue of media violence versus the first amendment right of freedom of speech. Include answers to the following questions in your essay: How and when do the two come in opposition? Which should prevail and why? How does the issue correspond to the general issue of the rights of the individual versus the rights of the larger society? Which should prevail and why?

Should You Own a Gun?
Gordon Witkin

The answer may depend on which of the two seminal researchers you believe. They have reached sharply different conclusions.

1   In a nation gripped by fear of crime, it has become an essential question: Should you buy a gun to protect yourself? More and more people are answering in the affirmative. As many as 216 million firearms are in private hands nationwide, more than double the total in 1970, and a new *U.S. News* poll reveals that fully 45 percent of gun owners, asked why they have guns, cite self-protection as one of the main reasons.

2   While the violent-crime rate has declined a bit over the past couple of years, it remains at historically high levels. But what has truly shaken people is the seeming randomness of crime: Carjackings, drive-by shootings and abductions in even the quietest suburbs have created the impression that everyone is vulnerable and that police cannot protect us.

3   The arguments for and against buying a gun for self-defense are shrill and confusing. Gun control advocates say having a gun at home represents a real danger and a false hope of safety; the National Rifle Association says a gun at home may be your last line of protection.

4   Each side has horror stories to support its claims. Gun opponents cite the case of Sonya Barnes of Conyers, Ga., whose ex-husband—frequently out of town—had bought her a .357 Magnum for self-defense. Early last year, her 2-year-old son found the gun and accidentally fired it into the back of his 14-month-old brother, leaving the younger sibling a paraplegic. Sonya got rid of the gun and now says, "I'd rather have the hell beat out of me than take another chance."

5   **The other side.** Gun proponents cite Suzanna Gratia. She was eating lunch with her parents at Luby's cafeteria in Kileen, Texas, on Oct. 16, 1991, when a deranged man drove a truck through the front window and began shooting people. Gratia reached into her purse for her .38 revolver—then remembered she'd decided to stop carrying it, fearing she was in violation of the state's concealed weapons law. Before the incident was over, 23 people were dead, including Gratia's parents. "If I'd had my weapon, I could have made a difference," she says.

6   But sweep away the horror stories and the quarrel over guns for self-defense boils down to the seminal researchers on the subject. Gary Kleck, a Florida State University criminology professor, says his evidence shows that millions of times each year, people use guns successfully to defend themselves. Arthur Kellermann, director of the Center for Injury Control at Emory University's School of Public Health in Atlanta, says his studies show guns in the home are 43 times more likely to kill a family member or friend than an intruder. The two men are quoted endlessly in the press and congressional testimony. Understanding their work is essential to trying to make the right choice about a deadly serious matter.

7   **Gary Kleck:** *The reluctant poster child for the National Rifle Association*

8   Gary Kleck seems to enjoy defying stereotypes. A native of the Chicago suburbs, he occasionally played with toy guns while growing up but otherwise has no shooting background, though he is a bit of an archery enthusiast.

9   Now 43, Kleck earned a Ph.D. in sociology from the University of Illinois and has been at Florida State since 1978. He lectures in jeans, pacing back and forth as he teaches courses in criminology and research methods. On his office door are stickers from Greenpeace, the Nature Conservancy, the Sierra Club and the Defenders of Wildlife; he freely labels himself a "tree hugger." He is also a member of Common Cause and the American Civil Liberties

Union, and describes his political bent as orthodox liberal, "which means I basically think the way to reduce crime is to reduce poverty." Kleck voted for Bill Clinton, though he calls the president's positions on crime "absolutely awful." He says he has never used a gun defensively but won't say whether he owns a firearm.

10   **The numbers.** Kleck got into gun research in the late 1970s because "it was an absolutely open field—somebody could really make a contribution." He produced a series of estimates on successful use of guns in self-defense. In his earlier work, Kleck extrapolated from nine surveys made between 1976 and 1990. He relied heavily on a 1981 poll of 1,228 registered voters by Peter Hart Research Associated and concluded that, excluding police and military uses, guns were used defensively against persons between 606,000 and 960,000 times per year.

11   In 1993, trying to refine the numbers and respond to criticism, Kleck and a colleague commissioned their own phone survey of 4,977 randomly selected households. They clarified that each defensive gun use was against a person in connection with a crime and that an actual confrontation had occurred. Extrapolating, Kleck concluded that guns were used in self-defense between 800,000 and 2.45 million times a year. He says the higher figure represents the respondents' most recent and reliable recollections. Rarely is anyone shot in these incidents, Kleck says; in fact, the defender fires in fewer than 1 in 4 cases. In most instances, the mere display of a weapon is sufficient to scare off the intruder.

12   Kleck thinks the findings have several important implications. The first is that Americans probably use guns in self-defense more often than they use guns to commit violent crimes. The Bureau of Justice Statistics estimates that about 1.1 million violent crimes were committed with guns in 1992; that is dwarfed by Kleck's estimate of up to 2.45 million defensive uses. "Gun ownership among prospective victims may well have as large a crime-*inhibiting* effect as the crime-*generating* effects of gun possession among prospective criminals," Kleck concludes in his book, *Point Blank.*

13   In addition, 1 of 6 survey respondents who had used a gun defensively was almost certain a life would have been lost without it—implying some 400,000 cases of guns saving lives. If even one tenth of those people were right, says Kleck, the number of lives saved by guns would exceed the 38,000 annually lost to guns.

14   Kleck also contends that people who defend themselves with a gun are more likely to successfully resist the crime and less likely to be hurt. Indeed, an analysis from the annual National Crime Survey for 1979–87 showed that criminals are successful in only 14 percent of burglary attempts at occupied residents in which folks defend their property with guns—compared with a success rate of 33 percent overall. And a new study from the Bureau of Justice Statistics reveals that only 1 in 5 crime victims defending themselves with a firearm suffered injury, compared with almost half of those who defended themselves with another weapon or no weapon at all.

15   **Fearful felons.** Kleck suspects gun ownership also has some deterrent effect. A 1986 survey of 1,900 incarcerated felons by sociologists James Wright and Peter Rossi found that 40 percent had at some time decided not to commit a crime because they believed the intended victim was armed. Three-fifths of the felons said criminals are more worried about meeting an armed victim than they are about the police. Kleck also notes that countries with far lower rates of gun ownership than the United States—like Great Britain and the Netherlands—have far higher rates of burglaries of *occupied* residences. The reason, he argues, is that the thieves have little to fear from unarmed occupants.

16   If all this is true, Kleck reasons, measures that reduce public gun ownership may be counterproductive. "If you take guns away from people who could have used them defensively, you are depriving them of something that would have allowed them in some cases to save lives or prevent injury," he says. He also argues that most gun control restrictions have no net effect on violence.

17   While other experts generally respect Kleck, several disagree sharply with the survey numbers that support his conclusions. They cite the Census Bureau's annual National Crime Victimization Survey, considered the broadest and most accurate measure of crime. Data from that survey indicate that only about 800,000 crime victims per year use firearms to defend themselves (compared with Kleck's high of 2.45 million). If that number is correct, the use of guns to commit crime would outnumber the use of guns in self-defense by about 14 to 1.

18   Kleck contends that the victimization survey is a poor measure of self-defense gun usage, largely because it is a nonanonymous survey conducted by the federal government. Respondents, he said, are unlikely to talk about defensive gun use in the context of intensely personal crimes like domestic violence or rape. And since carrying a gun in public may be technically illegal, that, too, is not the kind of thing someone is going to admit to the feds. He notes that a total of 10 private, anonymous surveys, including his own, all show upwards of a million self-defense uses of guns a year.

19   Kleck's critics admit that the victimization survey undercounts sexual assault and domestic violence. But they note that it is conducted by highly trained interviewers who return to the same households seven times over a three-year period and guarantee confidentiality. The survey, in the field for 20 years, "reflects the best thinking on how to get reliable answers to sensitive questions about crime," says Duke University public policy Prof. Philip Cook, a respected gun scholar. "I don't understand why people would be so much more forthcoming with Kleck's survey callers than with the government's. I find that absurd."

20   Another complaint is that Kleck's conclusions rest on the respondent's own, perhaps ambiguous, definition of self-defense. A report by the National Academy of Sciences' National Research Council says it may refer "to homeowners with a generalized fear of burglary . . . and even to criminals in the course of their crimes." Kleck admits this was a problem in earlier polls but

says his most recent survey painstakingly fleshed out exactly what happened in each "self-defense" confrontation.

21   Finally, survey experts believe Kleck's work may be susceptible to "telescoping," in which memorable events are brought forward in a respondent's memory and reported as having occurred more recently than they actually did. These authorities say the national victimization survey is much less likely to suffer from telescoping problems because interviews are conducted every six months over a three-year period. Kleck accepts the point but says the telescoping would have to be massive indeed to significantly alter his conclusions.

22   These arguments aren't likely to be resolved anytime soon. The National Academy of Sciences panel, which conducted perhaps the most exhaustive review of the data, essentially threw up its hands and called for more research. Kleck doubts that is necessary. "Show me the evidence that I've ignored. People don't do that. They just keep speculating," he says. "But you know, an ounce of evidence outweighs a ton of maybes."

23   **Arthur Kellermann:** *The long-gun shooter who thinks guns are a menace*

24   Unlike Kleck, Arthur Kellermann grew up with guns. There were two shotguns and a .22-caliber rifle in a rack in the kitchen in South Pittsburg, Tenn., and his father taught Kellermann to shoot. Most of his shooting was plinking and skeet, but he also did some target practice at a YMCA summer camp. "I was familiar with long guns," he says. "We were not a handgun family."

25   Kellermann has not had guns in his own home for years, in part because he has a small child—a son, now 6. But he notes that somehow the boy has developed a fascination with guns. "Anything longer than it is wide, he'll point and make gun sounds," sighs Kellermann.

26   Trained as an emergency physician, Kellermann got interested in the gun issue during a two-year fellowship in public health. The pivotal event was the fatal shooting in 1984 of rhythm-and-blues singer Marvin Gaye by his father. "My response was, 'This is crazy,'" he says. "All these guns are in people's homes, and most of the deaths that occur there apparently involve domestic disputes. Surely somebody has examined the relationship between having a gun in the home and family victimization." But he found very little research on the subject.

27   **Greater danger?** Kellermann set out to fill that void and is best known for three studies that have appeared in the *New England Journal of Medicine*. In the first study, published in 1986, Kellermann and a colleague reviewed six years' worth of gunshot deaths in Seattle. About half occurred in the home where the weapon was kept. The researchers found that "for every case of self-protection homicide involving a firearm kept in the home, there were 1.3 accidental deaths, 4.6 criminal homicides and 37 suicides involving firearms"—an overall ratio of almost 43 to 1. "It may reasonably be asked," they wrote, "whether keeping firearms in the home increases a family's protection or places it in greater danger."

28   In 1988, Kellermann was one of nine doctors responsible for a seven-year comparison of burglaries, robberies, assaults and homicides in Seattle and in Vancouver, British Columbia, which had adopted far more restrictions on handguns. The authors found similar overall rates of crime but discovered that the risk of homicide was far greater in Seattle. "Virtually all of this excess risk," they said, "was explained by a 4.8-fold higher risk of being murdered with a handgun in Seattle." They concluded that "restricting access to handguns may reduce the rate of homicide in a community."

29   The most recent study was published last fall. This time, Kellermann and company studied homicides in the home in Memphis, Cleveland and Seattle over a five-year period. These households were compared with households that were not the scene of a killing but included individuals demographically similar to the victims; the idea was to identify factors affecting a family's risk of homicide in the home. Homes that contained guns were almost three times more likely to be the scene of a homicide than comparable homes without guns. "The greatest threat to the lives of household members appears to come from within," says Kellermann. He adds that the study also was capable of demonstrating a protective effect from guns but did not.

30   For Kellermann, the implications couldn't be clearer. The first is that a gun almost automatically makes any altercation potentially more lethal. Second, he says, "The risks of having a gun in the home substantially outweigh the benefits." His most recent study concludes that "people should be strongly discouraged from keeping guns in their homes."

31   Kellermann's critics argue that using death as the sole criterion for measuring the risks of gun ownership is inappropriate: The huge majority of defensive firearm uses—99 percent, critics say—involve no more than wounding, missing the target or brandishing the gun. Kellermann, they say, passes off his work as a risk-benefit analysis even though it measures risks alone. "The benefit of defensive gun ownership that would be parallel to innocent lives *lost* to guns would be innocent lives *saved* by guns," argues Kleck—conceding that "it is impossible to count the latter." In his 1986 study, Kellermann seems to admit the problem: "Studies such as ours do not include cases in which intruders are wounded or frightened away by the use or display of a firearm. A complete determination of firearm risks versus benefits would require that these figures be known."

32   Doubters also think Kellermann has underplayed the possibility that it may not be the guns causing the violence but the violence causing the guns. "In places where there is more violence, people will get guns for self-protection," argues Kleck. "But is it because the violence brought about gun ownership? Or is it the gun ownership that helped bring about the violence?"

33   Kellermann allows that the questions have some merit. But he says he made statistical adjustments to take into account a history of household violence and notes that reverse causation would have to be "enormous" to completely explain the difference in homicide rates among gun-owning households. He says, too, that if a violent atmosphere were the cause of all that

gunfire, he might have found a higher risk of homicide by other means in those homes—but he didn't.

34   **Common ground:** *Points on which the disputing researchers agree*

35   It comes as something of a surprise that Kleck and Kellermann actually agree on a few things—including certain gun control measures. Both, for instance, support the kind of background checks mandated by the Brady law. Such screening, says Kleck, "appears to reduce homicide and suicide."

36   Both men also see benefit in stricter regulation of federal firearms dealer's licenses, which require $30 and a cursory background check in many states. The number of licensees has grown 67 percent since 1975— to 245,000—outstripping the Bureau of Alcohol, Tobacco and Firearms' ability to regulate them. Only about 1 in 4 is actually a storefront business; the rest are "kitchen table" dealers who sometimes operate in violation of local laws. Proposals before Congress would hike the license fee and allow for more meaningful oversight. "It's difficult for me to imagine that society's interest is served by someone selling guns across their kitchen table," says Kellermann.

37   In addition, both men would bar those convicted of violent misdemeanors from buying or owning guns (current law applies only to convicted felons). Kleck points out that nearly all criminal convictions are obtained from plea bargains, which often reduce felony charges to misdemeanor versions of the same crime.

38   Finally, Kellermann and Kleck agree that harsher sentencing will never be the total answer to America's gun violence. "A long series of get-tough strategies have been tried, carefully evaluated and found to be either ineffective . . . or hopelessly expensive," writes Kleck.

39   **Last word.** And what about the big question: Should I buy a gun for protection? Here's Kellermann's answer: "It's natural to want to do everything possible to defend yourself and your family. It's also natural to want to seek cover under the nearest tree in a thunderstorm. That doesn't make it a good idea." Kleck says he avoids giving advice. But in *Point Blank,* he writes: "Possession of a gun gives its owner an additional option for dealing with danger. If other sources of security are adequate, the gun does not have to be used; but where other sources fail, it can preserve bodily safety and property in at least some situations."

40   Even so, Kleck says, each person must evaluate other circumstances, such as the presence of children in the home or of anyone who's chronically depressed, aggressive or alcoholic. And people must consider their neighborhood's real danger; the higher the crime rate, he says, the more need for a firearm. Still, says Kleck, for most Americans, "there's little or no need for a gun for self-protection because there's so little risk of crime. People don't believe it, but it's true. You just can't convince most Americans they're not at serious risk."

For Writing and Discussion

1. Summarize the main arguments for owning a gun and the main arguments against it. In what way did how you already felt about the issue color your perceptions of the arguments?

2. How does the argument over whether citizens should own guns relate to the larger issue of gun control? What effect do you think the passage in several states of concealed weapon laws will have on the issue of gun control?

3. List statistics used by Gary Kleck in support of citizens' rights to own a gun, then list statistics used by Arthur Kellermann in his case for curbing that right. Are any of the statistics overlapping? How might each respond to the other's argument from statistics?

4. Evaluate Witkin's account of the debate using Trudy Govier's criteria for a fair and balanced account (pages 121–122).

5. Archie Bunker, of the *All in the Family* television series, responds to his daughter's statistics on the percentage of victims who were killed with guns by asking, "Would it make you feel any better, Little Girl, if they was pushed outta windows?"

A news analyst commenting on a rash of urban arsons that were attributed to warring drug factions noted that it was easier to get matches to kill a building full of people than to get a gun to kill one person. What is the underlying argument from the fictional television show and from the news analyst's comment?

6. Josh Sugarmann and Kristen Rand in *Rolling Stone* (March 10, 1994) propose a framework for regulating firearms that includes "Reduce[ing] the availability of specific categories of weapons shown to pose an unreasonable risk of injury," and "Place[ing] controls on an industry that today is free to manufacture and sell firearms or related products without any consideration of the consequences to the public's health and safety." How do you think the pro-gun control advocates would respond to these suggestions? The anti-gun control advocates?

7. Explain the fact that the argument involving *constitutional rights* is used by liberals in arguments against censorship and by conservatives in arguments against gun control.

Practice: Using *Ethos, Pathos,* and *Logos* to Compromise

Write a brief essay in which you offer a compromise to start to bring *pro* and *con* gun control factions together. After you have finished the essay, explain how you used *ethos, pathos,* and *logos* to persuade the two sides.

Vanishing Jobs
Jeremy Rifkin

Some business leaders are concerned, but politicians seem strangely deaf to what is likely to be the most explosive issue of the decade.

1   "Will there be a job for me in the new Information Age?" This is the question that most worries American voters—and the question that American politicians seem most determined to sidestep. President Bill Clinton warns workers that they will have to be retrained six or seven times during their work lives to match the dizzying speed of technological change. Speaker of the House Newt Gingrich talks about the "end of the traditional job" and advises every American worker to become his or her own independent contractor.

2   But does the president really think 124 million Americans can reinvent themselves every five years to keep up with a high-tech marketplace? Does Gingrich honestly believe every American can become a freelance entrepreneur, continually hustling contracts for short-term work assignments?

3   Buffeted by these unrealistic employment expectations, American workers are increasingly sullen and pessimistic. Most Americans have yet to recover from the recovery of 1993–1995, which was essentially a "jobless" recovery. While corporate profits are heading through the roof, average families struggle to keep a roof over their heads. More than one-fifth of the workforce is trapped in temporary assignments or works only part time. Millions of others have slipped quietly out of the economy and into an underclass no longer counted in the permanent employment figures. A staggering 15 percent of the population now lives below the official poverty line.

4   Both Clinton and Gingrich have asked American workers to remain patient. They explain that declining incomes represent only short-term adjustments. Democrats and Republicans alike beseech the faithful to place their trust in the high-tech future—to journey with them into cyberspace and become pioneers on the new electronic frontier. Their enthusiasm for technological marvels has an almost camp ring to it. If you didn't know better, you might suspect Mickey and Pluto were taking you on a guided tour through the Epcot Center.

5   Jittery and genuinely confused over the yawning gap between the official optimism of the politicians and their own personal plight, middle- and working-class American families seem to be holding on to a tiny thread of hope that the vast productivity gains of the high-tech revolution will somehow "trickle down" to them in the form of better jobs, wages, and benefits. That thread is likely to break by election time if, as I anticipate, the economy skids right by the soft landing predicted by the Federal Reserve Board and crashes headlong into a deep recession.

6   The Labor Department reported that payrolls sank by 101,000 workers in May alone—the largest drop in payrolls since April 1991, when the U.S. economy was deep in a recession. In June, overall unemployment remained virtually unchanged, but manufacturing jobs declined by an additional 40,000. At the same time, inventories are up and consumer spending and confidence are down—sure signs of bad economic times ahead.

7   The psychological impact of a serious downturn coming so quickly upon the heels of the last one would be devastating. It is likely to set the framework for a politically wild roller-coaster ride for the rest of the decade, opening the door not only to new parties but to extralegal forms of politics.

8   Meanwhile, few politicians and economists are paying attention to the underlying causes of—dare we say it?—the new "malaise" gripping the country. Throughout the current welfare reform debate, for example, members of both parties have trotted onto the House and Senate floors to urge an end to welfare and demand that all able-bodied men and women find jobs. Maverick Sen. Paul Simon (D-Ill.) has been virtually alone in raising the troubling question: "What jobs?"

9   The hard reality is that the global economy is in the midst of a transformation as significant as the Industrial Revolution. We are in the early stages of a shift from "mass labor" to highly skilled "elite labor," accompanied by increasing automation in the production of goods and the delivery of services. Sophisticated computers, robots, telecommunications, and other Information Age technologies are replacing human beings in nearly every sector. Factory workers, secretaries, receptionists, clerical workers, salesclerks, bank tellers, telephone operators, librarians, wholesalers, and middle managers are just a few of the many occupations destined for virtual extinction. In the United States alone, as many as 90 million jobs in a labor force of 124 million are potentially vulnerable to displacement by automation.

10   A few mainstream economists pin their hopes on increasing job opportunities in the knowledge sector. Secretary of Labor Robert Reich, for example, talks incessantly of the need for more highly skilled technicians, computer programmers, engineers, and professional workers. He barnstorms the country urging workers to retrain, retool, and reinvent themselves in time to gain a coveted place on the high-tech express.

11   The secretary ought to know better. Even if the entire workforce could be retrained for very skilled, high-tech jobs—which, of course, it can't—there will never be enough positions in the elite knowledge sector to absorb the millions let go as automation penetrates into every aspect of the production process.

12   It's not as if this a revelation. For years the Tofflers and the Naisbitts of the world have lectured the rest of us that the end of the industrial age also means the end of "mass production" and "mass labor." What they never mention is what "the masses" should do after they become redundant.

13   Laura D'Andrea Tyson, who now heads the National Economic Council, argues that the Information Age will bring a plethora of new technologies and products that we can't as yet even anticipate, and therefore it will create many new kinds of jobs. After a debate with me on CNN, Tyson noted that when the automobile replaced the horse and buggy, some people lost their jobs in the buggy trade but many more found work on the assembly line. Tyson believes that the same operating rules will govern the information era.

14   Tyson's argument is compelling. Still, I can't help but think that she may be wrong. Even if thousands of new products come along, they are likely to be manufactured in near-workerless factories and marketed by near-virtual companies requiring ever-smaller, more highly skilled workforces.

15   This steady decline of mass labor threatens to undermine the very foundations of the modern American state. For nearly 200 years, the heart of the social contract and the measure of individual human worth have centered on the value of each person's labor. How does society even begin to adjust to a new era in which labor is devalued or even rendered worthless?

16   This is not the first time the issue of devalued human labor has arisen in the history of the United States. The first group of Americans to be marginalized

by the automation revolution was black men, more than 40 years ago. Their story is a bellwether.

17   In the mid-1950s, automation began to take a toll on the nation's factories. Hardest hit were unskilled jobs in the industries where black workers concentrated. Between 1953 and 1962, 1.6 million blue-collar manufacturing jobs were lost. In an essay, "Problems of the Negro Movement," published in 1964, civil rights activist Tom Kahn quipped, "It's as if racism, having put the Negro in his economic place, stepped aside to watch technology destroy that 'place.'"

18   Millions of African-American workers and their families became part of a perpetually unemployed "underclass" whose unskilled labor was no longer required in the mainstream economy. Vanquished and forgotten, many urban blacks vented their frustration and anger by taking to the streets. The rioting began in Watts in 1965 and spread east to Detroit and other Northern industrial cities.

19   Today, the same technological and economic forces are beginning to affect large numbers of white male workers. Many of the disaffected white men who make up ultraright-wing organizations are high school or community college graduates with limited skills who are forced to compete for a diminishing number of agricultural, manufacturing, and service jobs. While they blame affirmative action programs, immigrant groups, and illegal aliens for their woes, these men miss the real cause of their plight—technological innovations that devalue their labor. Like African-American men in the 1960s, the new militants view the government and law enforcement agencies as the enemy. They see a grand conspiracy to deny them their basic freedoms and constitutional rights. And they are arming themselves for a revolution.

20   The Information Age may present difficulties for the captains of industry as well. By replacing more and more workers with machines, employers will eventually come up against the two economic Achilles' heels of the Information Age. The first is a simple problem of supply and demand: If mass numbers of people are underemployed or unemployed, who's going to buy the flood of products and services being churned out?

21   The second Achilles' heel for business—and one never talked about—is the effect on capital accumulation when vast numbers of employees are let go or hired on a temporary basis so that employers can avoid paying out benefits—especially pension fund benefits. As it turns out, pension funds, now worth more than $5 trillion in the United States alone, keep much of the capitalist system afloat. For nearly 25 years, the pension funds of millions of workers have served as a forced savings pool that has financed capital investments.

22   Pension funds account for 74 percent of new individual savings, more than one-third of all corporate equities, and nearly 40 percent of all corporate bonds. Pension assets exceed the assets of commercial banks and make up nearly one-third of the total financial assets of the U.S. economy. In 1993 alone, pension funds made new investments of between $1 trillion and $1.5 trillion.

23   If too many workers are let go or marginalized into jobs without pension benefits, the capitalist system is likely to collapse slowly in on itself as employers drain it of the workers' funds necessary for new capital investments. In the final analysis, sharing the vast productivity gains of the Information Age is absolutely essential to guarantee the well-being of management, stockholders, labor, and the economy as a whole.

24   Sadly, while our politicians gush over the great technological breakthroughs that lie ahead in cyberspace, not a single elected official, in either political party, is raising the critical question of how we can ensure that the productivity gains of the Information Age are shared equitably.

25   In the past, when new technology increased productivity—such as in the 1920s when oil and electricity replaced coal- and steam-powered plants—American workers organized collectively to demand a shorter workweek and better pay and benefits. Today, employers are shortening not the workweek, but the workforce—effectively preventing millions of American workers from enjoying the benefits of the technology revolution.

26   Organized labor has been weakened by 40 years of automation, a decline in union membership, and a growing temp workforce that is difficult to organize. In meetings with union officials, I have found that they are universally reluctant to deal with the notion that mass labor—the very basis of trade unionism—will continue to decline and may even disappear altogether. Several union leaders confided to me off the record that the labor movement is in survival mode and trying desperately to prevent a rollback of legislation governing basic rights to organize. Union leaders cannot conceive that they may have to rethink their mission in order to accommodate a fundamental change in the nature of work. But the unions' continued reluctance to grapple with a technology revolution that might eliminate mass labor could spell their own elimination from American life over the next three or four decades.

27   Working women may hold the key to whether organized labor can reinvent itself in time to survive the Information Age. Women now make up about half of the U.S. workforce, and a majority of employed women provide half or more of their household's income.

28   In addition to holding down a 40-hour job, working women often manage the household as well. Significantly, nearly 44 percent of all employed women say they would prefer more time with their family to more money.

29   This is one reason many progressive labor leaders believe the rebirth of the American labor movement hinges on organizing women workers. The call for a 30-hour workweek is a powerful rallying cry that could unite trade unions, women's groups, parenting organizations, churches, and synagogues. Unfortunately, the voice of trade union women is not often heard inside the inner sanctum of the AFL-CIO executive council. Of the 83 unions in the AFL-CIO, only one is headed by a woman.

30   The women's movement, trapped in struggles over abortion, discriminatory employment practices, and sexual harassment, has also failed to grasp

the enormous opportunity brought on by the Information Age. Betty Friedan, the venerable founder of the modern women's movement and someone always a step or two ahead of the crowd, is convinced that the reduction of work hours offers a way to revitalize the women's movement, and take women's interests to the center of public policy discourse.

31   Of course, employers will argue that shortening the workweek is too costly and would threaten their ability to compete both domestically and abroad. That need not be so. Companies like Hewlett-Packard in France and BMW in Germany have reduced their workweek while continuing to pay workers at the same weekly rate. In return, the workers have agreed to work shifts. Management executives reason that, if they can operate the new high-tech plants on a 24-hour basis, they can double or triple productivity and thus afford to pay workers the same.

32   In France, government officials are playing with the idea of forgiving the payroll taxes for employers who voluntarily reduce their workweek. While the government will lose tax revenue, economists argue that fewer people will be on welfare, and the new workers will be taxpayers with purchasing power. Employers, workers, the economy, and the government all benefit.

33   In this country, generous tax credits could be extended to any company willing both to reduce its workweek voluntarily and implement a profit-sharing plan so that its employees will benefit directly from productivity gains.

34   The biggest surprise I've encountered in the fledgling debate over rethinking work has been the response of some business leaders. I have found genuine concern among a small but growing number of business executives over the critical question of what to do with the millions of people whose labor will be needed less, or not at all, in an increasingly automated age. Many executives have close friends who have been re-engineered out of a job—replaced by the new technologies of the Information Age. Others have had to take part in the painful process of letting employees go in order to optimize the bottom line. Some tell me they worry whether their own children will be able to find a job when they enter the high-tech labor market in a few years.

35   To be sure, I hear moans and groans from some corporate executives when I zero in on possible solutions—although there are also more than a few nods of agreement. But still, they are willing—even eager—to talk about these critical questions. They are hungry for engagement—the kind that has been absent in the public policy arena. Until now, politicians and economists have steadfastly refused to entertain a discussion of how we prepare for a new economic era characterized by the diminishing need for mass human labor. Until we have that conversation, the fear, anger, and frustration of millions of Americans are going to grow in intensity and become manifest through increasingly hostile and extreme social and political venues. . . .

The Future of Work
Robert Reich

This essay was adapted from "On Planning a Career," a memorandum Robert B. Reich circulated to his undergraduate students at Harvard University. Reich was appointed Secretary of Labor in 1992.

1   It's easy to predict what jobs you *shouldn't* prepare for. Thanks to the wonders of fluoride, America, in the future, will need fewer dentists. Nor is there much of a future in farming. The federal government probably won't provide long-term employment unless you aspire to work in the Pentagon or the Veterans Administration (the only two departments accounting for new federal jobs in the last decade). And think twice before plunging into higher education. The real wages of university professors have been declining for some time, the hours are bad, and all you get are complaints.

2   Moreover, as the American economy merges with the rest of the world's, anyone doing relatively unskilled work that could be done more cheaply elsewhere is unlikely to prosper for long. Imports and exports now constitute 25 percent of our gross national produce (up from 9 percent in 1950), and barring a new round of protectionism, the portion will move steadily upward. Meanwhile, 10,000 people are added to the world's population every hour, most of whom, eventually, will happily work for a small fraction of today's average American wage.

3   This is good news for most of you, because it means that you'll be able to buy all sorts of things far more cheaply than you could if they were made here (provided, of course, that what your generation does instead produces even more value). The resulting benefits from trade will help offset the drain on your income resulting from paying the interest on the nation's foreign debt and financing the retirement of aging baby boomers like me. The bad news, at least for some of you, is that most of America's traditional, routinized manufacturing jobs will disappear. So will routinized service jobs that can be done from remote locations, like keypunching of data transmitted by satellite. Instead, you will be engaged in one of two broad categories of work: either complex services, some of which will be sold to the rest of the world to pay for whatever Americans want to buy from the rest of the world, or person-to-person services, which foreigners can't provide for us because (apart from new immigrants and illegal aliens) they aren't here to provide them.

4   Complex services involve the manipulation of data and abstract symbols. Included in this category are insurance, engineering, law, finance, computer programming, and advertising. Such activities now account for almost 25 percent of our GNP, up from 13 percent in 1950. They already have surpassed

manufacturing (down to about 20 percent of GNP). Even *within* the manufacturing sector, executive, managerial, and engineering positions are increasing at a rate almost three times that of total manufacturing employment. Most of these jobs, too, involve manipulating symbols.

5   Such endeavors will constitute America's major contribution to the rest of the world in the decades ahead. You and your classmates will be exploring engineering designs, financial services, advertising and communications advice, statistical analyses, musical scores and film scripts, and other creative and problem-solving products. How many of you undertake these sorts of jobs, and how well you do at them, will determine what goods and services America can summon from the rest of the world in return, and thus—to some extent—your generation's standard of living.

6   You say you plan to become an investment banker? A lawyer? I grant you that these vocations have been among the fastest growing and most lucrative during the past decade. The securities industry in particular has burgeoned. Between 1977 and 1987, securities-industry employment nearly doubled, rising 10 percent a year, compared with the average yearly job growth of 1.9 percent in the rest of the economy. The crash of October 1987 temporarily stemmed the growth, but by mid-1988 happy days were here again. Nor have securities workers had particular difficulty making ends meet. Their average income grew 21 percent over the decade, compared with a 1 percent rise in the income of everyone else. (But be careful with these numbers; relatively few securities workers enjoyed such majestic compensation. The high average is partly due to the audacity of people such as Henry Kravis and George Roberts, each of whom takes home a tidy $70 million per year.)

7   Work involving securities and corporate law has been claiming one-quarter of all new private sector jobs in New York City and more than a third of all the new office space in that industrious town. Other major cities are not too far behind. A simple extrapolation of the present trend suggests that by 2020 one out of every three American college graduates will be an investment banker or a lawyer. Of course, this is unlikely. Long before that milestone could be achieved, the nation's economy will have dried up like a raisin, as financiers and lawyers squeeze out every ounce of creative, productive juice. Thus my advice: Even if you could bear spending your life in such meaningless but lucrative work, at least consider the fate of the nation before deciding to do so.

8   Person-to-person services will claim everyone else. Many of these jobs will not require much skill, as is true of their forerunners today. Among the fastest growing in recent years: custodians and security guards, restaurant and retail workers, day-care providers. Secretaries and clerical workers will be as numerous as now, but they'll spend more of their time behind and around electronic machines (imported from Asia) and have fancier titles, such as "paratechnical assistant" and "executive paralegal operations manager."

9   Teachers will be needed (we'll be losing more than a third of our entire corps of elementary- and high-school teachers through attrition over the next

seven years), but don't expect their real pay to rise very much. Years of pub-lic breast-beating about the quality of American education notwithstanding, the average teacher today earns $28,000—only 3.4 percent more, in constant dollars, than he or she earned fifteen years ago.

10   Count on many jobs catering to Americans at play—hotel workers, recreation directors, television and film technicians, aerobics instructors (or whatever their twenty-first-century equivalents will call themselves). But note that Americans will have less leisure time to enjoy these pursuits. The average American's free time has been shrinking for more than fifteen years, as women move into the work force (and so spend more of their free time doing household chores) and as all wage earners are forced to work harder just to maintain their standard of living. Expect the trend to continue.

11   The most interesting and important person-to-person jobs will be in what is now unpretentiously dubbed "sales." Decades from now most sales-people won't be just filling orders. Salespeople will be helping customers define their needs, then working with design and production engineers to customize products and services in order to address those needs. This is because standardized (you can have it in any color as long as it's black) prod-ucts will be long gone. Flexible manufacturing and the new information tech-nologies will allow a more tailored fit—whether it's a car, machine tool, insurance policy, or even a college education. Those of you who will be deal-ing directly with customers will thus play a pivotal role in the innovation pro-cess, and your wages and prestige will rise accordingly.

12   But the largest number of personal-service jobs will involve health care, which already consumes about 12 percent of our GNP, and that portion is ris-ing. Because every new medical technology with the potential to extend lives is infinitely valuable to those whose lives might be extended—even for a few months or weeks—society is paying huge sums to stave off death. By the sec-ond decade of the next century, when my generation of baby boomers will have begun to decay, the bill will be much higher. Millions of corroding bodies will need doctors, nurses, nursing-home operators, hospital administrators, technicians who operate and maintain all the fancy machines that will measure and temporarily halt the deterioration, hospice directors, home-care specialists, directors of outpatient clinics, and euthanasia specialists, among many others.

13   Most of these jobs won't pay very much because they don't require much skill. Right now the fastest growing job categories in the health sector are nurse's aides, orderlies, and attendants, which compose about 40 percent of the health-care work force. The majority are women; a large percentage are minorities. But even doctors' real earnings show signs of slipping. As malprac-tice insurance rates skyrocket, many doctors go on salary in investor-owned hospitals, and their duties are gradually taken over by physician "extenders" such as nurse-practitioners and midwives.

14   What's the best preparation for one of these careers?

15   Advice here is simple: You won't be embarking on a career, at least as we currently define the term, because few of the activities I've mentioned

will proceed along well-defined paths to progressively higher levels of responsibility. As the economy evolves toward services tailored to the particular needs of clients and customers, hands-on experience will count for more than formal rank. As technologies and markets rapidly evolve, moreover, the best preparation will be through cumulative learning on the job rather than formal training completed years before.

16   This means that academic degrees and professional credentials will count for less; on-the-job training, for more. American students have it backwards. The courses to which you now gravitate—finance, law, accounting, management, and other practical arts—may be helpful to understand how a particular job is *now* done (or, more accurately, how your instructors did it years ago when they held such jobs or studied the people who held them), but irrelevant to how such a job *will* be done. The intellectual equipment needed for the job of the future is an ability to define problems, quickly assimilate relevant data, conceptualize and reorganize the information, make deductive and inductive leaps with it, ask hard questions about it, discuss findings with colleagues, work collaboratively to find solutions, and then convince others. And *these* sorts of skills can't be learned in career-training courses. To the extent they can be found in universities at all, they're more likely to be found in subjects such as history, literature, philosophy, and anthropology—in which students can witness how others have grappled for centuries with the challenge of living good and productive lives. Tolstoy and Thucydides are far more relevant to the management jobs of the future, for example, than are Hersey and Blanchard.

For Writing and Discussion

1. What does the cartoonist argue in "This Modern World"?

2. Summarize both Rifkin's and Reich's conclusions about the future of work. What do they have in common? How do they differ? How does Rifkin's argument relate to the argument in the "This Modern World" cartoon? How does Reich's relate?

3. What issues for debate might be sparked by Reich's predictions for the future work world? Which of Rifkin's predictions do you believe should be addressed and how?

4. As Secretary of Labor, Reich supported trade treaties such as NAFTA, assuming that they would ultimately increase the number of jobs available in the U.S. How do you think Rifkin would respond to Reich's assumption? Could they both be right? Why or why not?

5. Is Reich's style formal or informal? To whom does he speak? What is the effect of Reich's use of the second-person pronoun *you* to address his audience?

6.   *In times of change, learners inherit the earth, while the learned find themselves beautifully equipped to deal with a world that no longer exists.*

Eric Hoffer

What does the quotation suggest young people should be taught to prepare them to deal with and lead the future world? What does Reich recommend that his students do to prepare themselves for the future world?

7.   *Human history becomes more and more a race between education and catastrophe.*

H. G. Wells

Do you believe that Wells' assertion is accurate? Why or why not?

8. What did you read in either or both articles that caused you to reflect on your own future? What advice would you propose to high school students who do not plan to go to college?

Practice: Search and Evaluate

Many people believe that the class structure of the future will be based not on gender, race, or ethnic group but on education: The educated will be the "haves"; the uneducated will be the "have nots"; and the middle class will continue to shrink and be absorbed in the upper or lower classes. Using on-line or traditional library sources, find data on earning trends for education levels over the past 30 years. Also find data on the cost-of-living trends over the same period. Evaluate the data and summarize your conclusions in a brief argument for or against the claim that the American class structure is changing.

CHAPTER SUMMARY

In this chapter, you have had the opportunity to explore many sides to many different issues in the writing of others, probably drawing your own conclusions on most of them. You know how the use of *ethos* and *pathos* come into play when you are trying to persuade others to listen to and consider your opinions, and you know that the backbone of argumentative writing is *logos*. In the next chapter, you will have an opportunity to write your own argument, to take a stand on an issue that is important to you.

Chapter 9

WRITING CHALLENGE

Choose a topic from the list below or another source, or use an issue you mentioned in Chapter 3 or Chapter 6. Write an essay in which you support a personal opinion. Your audience is a general audience who is concerned about not only the present but also the future world that the next generation will inherit. Use information from at least two outside sources in your paper. The Guide to Writing will help you develop your essay. The student paper on page 173 illustrates a possible approach to the assignment.

Topic Suggestions

The death penalty

Gun control

Street crime

Parole and probation

An environmental issue

The Balanced Budget Amendment

School prayer

AIDS education

National health care

Euthanasia

The drug war

The global marketplace

Drug legalization

Welfare reform

Assisted suicide for the terminally ill

Medical ethics

Trade treaties

Journal Topic Suggestions

- Your goals for the future and how to get there
- What you are gaining from college

- How you can make your voice heard
- Ways you will be a learner for the rest of your life
- The benefits of knowing how to persuade others
- What you can do with the tools you have learned

GUIDE TO WRITING

Planning and Prewriting

CHOOSING AN ARGUABLE ISSUE

Choose a topic that is both important to you and for which there is an arguable issue. Although many people write better about a topic that is important to them, that fact alone does not make a good topic for a persuasive paper. A paper about child abuse, for example, would work for merely spouting an opinion. A ninth-grade student voiced a strong opinion when she wrote, "I think we should kill all the rapists and have somebody rape them." There is passion in that statement, but clearly it is not a well developed idea. In the first place, who is going to rape the rapists? Are we going to use people who are already rapists or create new rapists by ordering them to rape? And are the rapists already dead when they receive the eye-for-an-eye punishment?

In the same way, the topic of child abuse lends itself to passionate statements and emotional appeals, yet it is not necessarily a good topic for an argumentative paper. Yes, it is an important problem; it is abhorrent. Child abuse damages those who are most innocent and most vulnerable in our society. It is abhorrent. We can scream "Boo, child abuse!" until our lungs collapse, but to what end? What worthy opponent is going to say, "Yea, child abuse"?

But still the topic may be a start for a good paper after brainstorming about related issues that are arguable:

What can be done to prevent child abuse? (Can you argue for a controversial prevention program?)

What is the proper punishment for a child abuser?

What laws might be enacted to help prevent child abuse?

Does a law that prohibits the release of a person, even after serving a complete sentence, who can be expected to repeat his or her crime unjustly infringe on the rights of the perpetrator? Is that infringement justified to protect the innocent?

Is chemical castration an appropriate punishment or deterrent for a sex offender?

Now we are getting somewhere. Clearly, chemical castration is a debat-able topic, as is a law that prohibits parole of some violent offenders. There are arguments for at least two opposing opinions.

DEBRIEFING

After you have chosen a topic that interests you, write out what you already know about the topic, perhaps in your journal. As you write, ask yourself the following questions:

- What is my definition of the topic?
- What facts do I know about my topic?
- What arguable issues are related to the topic?
- What is my stance on related issues?
- Who or what influenced my opinion?
- Is my opinion secondhand, or do I have personal experiences that contribute to my feelings about the topic?

EXPLORING THE TOPIC

To explore the topic further, make lists of related issues and possible sources of information.

- List three or more issues related to the topic.
- List three questions related to the topic. (What do I need to know about my topic?)
- List possible sources of information. What information do you want from the sources? (Where can I find the most current information? Do I know someone who has an expert opinion or information on the topic? What questions would I ask that person in an interview?)

SEARCHING FOR ANSWERS AND IDEAS

After you have decided on a direction for your search, use an on-line search or traditional library sources to find books or articles about your topic for general reading. Make notes about important ideas and answers to your questions, placing quotation marks around information that is taken directly from the source. Documenting your notes with complete information about the source (see Part Ten) will save time later.

PRIMARY AND SECONDARY SOURCES

Your instructor will tell you how many sources to include in your paper and whether or not you must include primary research. *Primary research* involves firsthand observation or study, including interviews or surveys, and analysis of the findings. It can also be the study of a historical document; analysis of a work of literature, art, or music; evaluation of statistical data; and so forth. *Primary sources* are the actual statistical data, historical documents, works of literature, art, or music. For example, if you use the *Statistical Abstract of the United States* to find information on the numbers of juvenile arrests during 1960 and 1990 and the juvenile population in those years to determine whether there has been an increase in juvenile crime per capita, you are doing primary research and using a primary source. If, however, you find an article in which someone else has studied the data and drawn inferences, the article would be a *secondary source.*

Much of academic research involves secondary sources. However, the secondary sources are vehicles that take us to new places. We don't merely patch the ideas of others together and leave it at that. We use secondary sources to support our own conclusions and to make leaps toward new ideas or new ways of seeing the world.

WRITING A THESIS STATEMENT

After you have "primed your brain" with the thoughts and ideas in the readings, you probably know what argumentative conclusion you want to support. Your argumentative conclusion, or thesis statement, will be an assertion that you will support with logical reasons. Although a purpose statement is not the same as a thesis statement, a purpose statement can be used in prewriting to develop a thesis statement.

> *The purpose of my paper is to convince my audience that* so-called "chemical castration" with depo provera is a safe and effective method of ensuring that certain types of sex offenders will not create additional victims.

After you have formulated a purpose statement, discard the first part of the sentence; the independent clause that follows the word *that* will be your thesis statement. To check your thesis statement, turn it into a question:

> Why is depo provera a safe and effective method for ensuring that certain types of sex offenders will not create additional victims?

Every reason should answer some part of that question: It is safe because . . . . It is effective because . . . . It is appropriate for sex offenders who . . . because . . . . And every reason will, in turn, be supported with evidence from examples, facts, anecdotes, authorities, and so forth.

THINKING ABOUT AUDIENCE

Before deciding exactly what kind of *logos* you will use to support your thesis, consider your audience and what kind of supporting arguments will serve best to persuade your readers. Think of your readers as a general audience made up of people who hold different views. Respond to the following questions to analyze your audience:

- What do my readers already know?
- What information do my readers need?
- What kinds of support will be necessary to convince my audience?
- How do others feel about my topic?
- What emotions and experiences might be related to opposing viewpoints?
- How can I use *pathos* in an ethical way?

DEVELOPING A PERSUASIVE ETHOS

Recall that credibility and a pleasing style are two essential elements of a persuasive *ethos* that reveals good sense, good will, and good moral character.

- How can I establish credibility with my audience?
- How can I establish an objective tone for my argument?
- Do I have examples from my own experiences to share?
- What authorities or experts can I cite to support my stance?
- What kinds of statistical data will make powerful support?
- What kind of introduction will hook my readers?

Organizing and Drafting

You probably will want to make at least an informal outline of your material to make your work easier when you begin drafting. Although many writers write their final introductions after they have finished the first draft of a paper, one part of the introduction, the thesis statement, deserves careful study now.

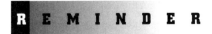

R E M I N D E R

Before writing your introduction, you may want to look back at the section titled "Possible Ways to Start a Paper" on pages 47–48.

ASSUMPTIONS AND DEFINITIONS

Reread your thesis statement, looking for unstated assumptions and words that must be defined. For instance, a thesis that contains a position that abortion is morally wrong because it involves the taking of human life assumes that all readers will agree that a fetus, at any point after conception, is a human being. The position also includes the assumption that the taking of human life for any reason is morally wrong, when we know that the state can take the life of a capitol offender and soldiers are taught to take the lives of the enemy in times of war. So, any unstated assumption that might not be held by any reasonable person must be clarified. An assumption that seems obvious to you might require support to convince someone else. In fact, whole papers, perhaps even whole books, might be written to persuade that what some people assume to be true is logically so.

Also, look for words and concepts that need to be defined. The word *euthanasia,* for instance, to some people means using an overt method to cause death; to others, the term includes withdrawing life support devices. Whole papers might be written to argue for one or another definition of a concept, using various kinds of support. For other definitions, your support may simply be *Webster's* dictionary.

SUPPORTING ARGUMENTS

In addition to defining words and concepts and clarifying unstated assumptions, you will need to decide what kinds of support will be most effective and organize the order of presentation. For instance, you may decide to start with an example or anecdote, followed by statistical information and a causal relationship. You can note on your outline the kind of information and the sources that will be used in each section.

As you organize your material, check the strength of the *logos,* the logic, of your support. Remember that *logos* is appeal through logical reasons or persuading by demonstrating that something is true.

USING FACTS AS SUPPORT

Facts make compelling support. Because most people accept factual information as truth, at least as it is known at a given time, the writer has an ethical obligation to be especially careful when using facts. The same facts or statistical data might be used legitimately in a number of ways or twisted and misrepresented unethically. And a careless error in copying can become a lie, though unintentionally. When using facts and statistics, ask yourself the following questions:

- Are the facts accurately represented?
- Are the facts recent enough to draw conclusions from today?
- Are the facts from a reliable source?
- Are the facts or statistical information relevant to my argument?

GENERALIZING FROM EXAMPLE OR SAMPLE

When using an anecdote—an example experience or observation—you are reasoning from generalization, just as when you are using a small sample or a public opinion poll, to support the idea most people believe this or prefer that. Inherent in the "preference" argument is the argument that the people sampled are representative of other people.

From a limited sample, you are arguing that what happened in a particular incident is representative of what happens often or usually. To check your anecdote or sample, ask yourself:

- Is the anecdote or sample relevant to my thesis?
- Is the anecdote or sample typical of what usually or often happens, or is it an aberration (a deviation from the norm)?
- Is the anecdote or sample sufficient for making a generalization?
- Is my representation accurate of the information and conclusions drawn from it?

USING SUPPORT FROM AUTHORITIES OR EXPERTS

When using an authority or expert in a supporting argument, ask yourself:

- What are the credentials of the authority or expert?
- Is the opinion or research findings of the expert or authority typical of others in his field? (If the opinion or research deviates substantially from that of others in the field, support will be needed for why the expert was chosen.)
- Is the information and any quoted material from the authority or expert represented accurately?
- Is the information from or opinion of the authority or expert relevant as support for my thesis?

USING CAUSAL RELATIONSHIPS AS SUPPORT

An argument that decreasing the incidence of poverty is a way to solve the problem of street crime contains an unstated argument that poverty causes, or at least is one cause of, crime. An argument based on causes of a particular situation or condition, unless the relationship would be obvious to reasonable people, needs further support. Entire books have been written on the relationship between poverty and crime, yet proving that poverty causes crime involves more than proving that the rate of crime is higher among the poor. When arguing that one thing causes another or when using a causal relationship as support for an argument, ask yourself:

- Is the "cause" the only factor involved in producing the condition or situation?
- Does the particular cause always produce a specific condition or situation?
- Can the condition or situation be produced by other causes?

If the answer to the questions are anything other than "yes, yes, and no," you will need to determine what kind of proof is necessary to demonstrate a causal relationship.

ARGUING FROM ANALOGY

When arguing from analogy, you are comparing one thing or situation to another and drawing the same conclusion about both. An argument from analogy assumes that the two things or situations are similar in fundamental ways and argues that, because of that fundamental likeness, certain conclusions can be drawn about other characteristics. (Recall Twain's analogy of the characteristics of a machine to demonstrate certain characteristics of humankind, page 119.)

When arguing from analogy, you must determine in what ways the two things or situations are alike, and whether they differ in significant ways. Then decide if the similarities are sufficient to draw one conclusion about both things or situations.

DRAFTING

After you have analyzed and organized your support, you are ready to begin drafting your paper. Since you are using information from sources outside yourself, you will need to give credit for any idea or information that originated somewhere other than in your own head. Your instructor may tell you to either identify your sources in the text of your paper and, perhaps, turn in copies of the material you used with your paper, or you may be asked to identify sources in parenthetical citations and prepare a Works Cited page. (See Part Ten for help with parenthetical citations and preparing a Works Cited page.)

Incorporating Information from Sources into Your Writing

The following examples show how to incorporate sources smoothly into your paper.

> Neil Postman, in the preface to *Conscientious Objections,* identifies the three dramatic upheavals in Western education as the change in the fifth century from the oral tradition to the alphabet and writing, the invention of the printing press, and the technology revolution of this century (xv).

Note: The page number is in parenthesis before the period. If the passage had ended with a word or words in quotation marks, the marks would have come inside the period, an exception to the rule that quotations always follow periods and commas.

> Data from *The Statistical Abstract of the United States* show a dramatic increase in violent crime in the U.S. over the past twenty years. In 1974, for instance, there were 26,888 rapes; in 1994 there were 191,315 rapes reported (205). Some of the increase might be attributed to the increased attention to sexual crimes and the resulting increase in reporting and record-keeping.

Note: Because the title of the source is given in the sentence, it need not be repeated in parentheses.

> Although misanthropes by definition hate and distrust people, Florence King claims that Rousseau was actually a "misanthrope of the naked intellect" and "the true friend of mankind" (*With Charity toward None* 63).

Note: When the source title is not given in the sentence, it must be stated with the page number in parentheses.

> Neil Postman, in the preface to *Conscientious Objections,* emphasizes the relevance of television to education and to culture:
>
> > By my reckoning, the three most traumatic conflicts in Western education occurred, first, in the fifth century B.C., when Athens was undergoing a change from an oral culture to an alphabet-writing culture; second, the sixteenth century A.D., when Europe underwent a radical transformation as a result of the printing press; and third, now, in the late twentieth century, as a result of the electronic revolution, particularly the invention of television. (xv)

Note: When using a direct quotation of more than three lines, the quotation is indented one inch or ten spaces and the page number is in parentheses. In this case, the end parenthesis follows the period.

R E M I N D E R

When using direct quotations, the sentence surrounding the quoted material must make sense and be grammatically correct. The quotation itself must retain the original punctuation, spelling, and capitalization.

Remember to limit the use of long quotations when drafting your paper. Instead, summarize the information, using your own words and giving credit to the original source.

Evaluating and Revising

After you have written your first draft, you will probably want to check the logic of your support again, using the questions you used when organizing your supporting arguments. Before you exchange papers with a partner, reread your paper several times, and write as many drafts as necessary to make sure your paper is well organized.

R E M I N D E R

A strong conclusion to your essay will include summarization of your main points and strong restatement of your thesis. (Qualifiers such as "In my opinion" or "I believe very strongly" weaken your assertions.) Also, recall the rule about not introducing new information in your conclusion.

PARTNER EVALUATION

As you read your partner's paper the first time, jot down notes about things you do not understand or that you would like to know more about. The following questions will guide you as you evaluate your partner's paper.

1.   Does the essay center on a well-defined, controversial issue? Check to see how the writer presents the issue. Is it clearly arguable? How well defined is it?

2.   Is the writer's position on the issue stated clearly and appropriately qualified? Indicate at what point in the essay you think the thesis is most explicitly stated. Tell the writer if you think the thesis is clear and appropriately qualified.

3.   Study the kinds of supporting arguments given. Indicate which support you find most convincing and which is least convincing. Point to any reasons that need more development or support.

4.   Focus on the evidence supporting the reasons. Note whether any of the evidence seems unbelievable or irrelevant. Also indicate where you think more evidence is needed.

5.   Look for any reference to opposing points of view. Is the opposition represented fairly?

6.   Focus on passages in which counterarguments are refuted. Tell the writer what is most and least convincing in the refutation. If you have any suggestions on how to strengthen the argument, offer them.

7.   If the writer defines any terms in the essay, indicate whether or not you accept the definitions. Point out any terms that you think need to be defined.

8.   Look for unstated assumptions in the arguments. Are the assumptions shared by most reasonable people? If not, ask for clarification and support for the assumptions.

9.   Reread the introduction and the conclusion of the essay. Explain why you think they are or are not effective. Suggest improvements for weak introductions or conclusions.

10. Skim the essay, paying special attention to the tone the writer adopts. Think of some adjectives to describe the tone. Indicate how you respond to the essay's tone.

Editing and Proofreading

Look carefully at the structure of each sentence in your paper. Make sure each sentence is complete, not a fragment or run-on sentence. Pay special attention to sentences containing direct quotations. Even though a direct quotation might be a complete sentence, the sentence surrounding the quotation must make sense and be a complete sentence also.

Example of incomplete sentence containing a quotation

Mark Twain, who wrote in the margin of a book " . . . what a man sees in the human race is merely himself in the deep and honest privacy of his own heart."

To check a sentence, read the sentence without the quotation, perhaps substituting the word *something* for the quotation. Note that an ellipsis (three periods with space on either side of each period) is used to replace part of Twain's original sentence.

THE POWER OF STYLE: PARALLEL STRUCTURE

Parallel structure involves using like forms in like structures. Parallel structure makes writing flow smoothly.

Nonparallel example

Teaching kindergarten requires limitless patience, a nurturing personality, and controlling the emotions.

The last descriptor is not parallel with the first two. The words *limitless* and *nurturing* are used as adjectives; the word *controlling* is used as a verb form. The last phrase must be changed to include a modifier and noun.

Parallel

Teaching kindergarten requires limitless patience, a nurturing personality, and emotional control.

Practice: Parallel Structure

Combine the following sentences to make one sentence with parallel structure. You will need to change the form of some words.

In our time millions of people viewed wars and natural disasters as they happen.

In our time people are sitting in their living rooms and sending messages around the world in seconds.

In our time satellites beam the same communication signal to all parts of the world.

PROOFREADING

Remember to look for elements of MLA style when you proofread. A common error is to put a comma between an author or work and the page number in a parenthetical citation. MLA style uses only a space. Also, recall that most instructors prefer underlining of titles of books to the hard-to-read italics of some printers. Additional items to check are:

- Periods after parenthetical citations except when following an indented quotation.
- Beginning and ending quotation marks around direct quotations.
- Alphabetical order of entries on a Works Cited page.
- Indentation of the second line of entries on a Works Cited page (five spaces for typed manuscripts and one-half inch for word-processed manuscripts).

R E M I N D E R

Semicolons replace commas to avoid confusion when separating items in a series that contains commas within items. Otherwise, use semicolons to join independent clauses that are related and have equal weight when a coordinating conjunction is not used.

R E M I N D E R

Being a poor speller is neither a sin nor a handicap in itself. Not knowing how to use a dictionary to avoid embarrassing errors is a handicap, and not caring enough to use a dictionary is sloth.

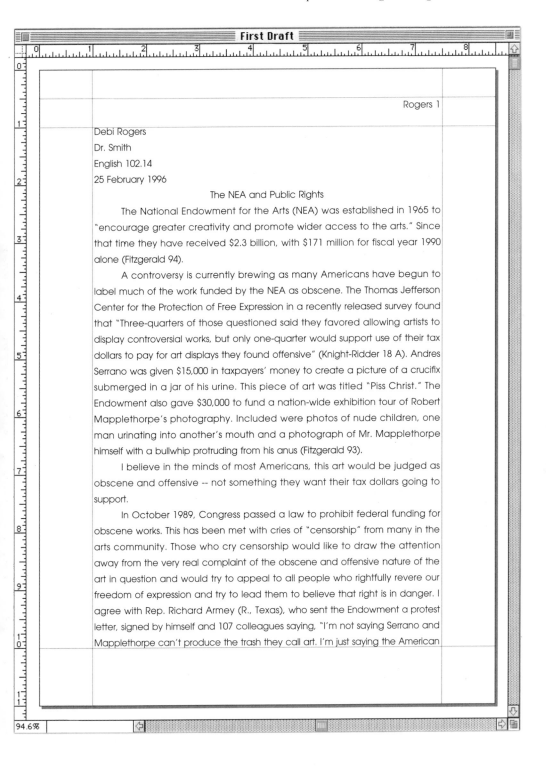

Rogers 1

Debi Rogers
Dr. Smith
English 102.14
25 February 1996

The NEA and Public Rights

The National Endowment for the Arts (NEA) was established in 1965 to "encourage greater creativity and promote wider access to the arts." Since that time they have received $2.3 billion, with $171 million for fiscal year 1990 alone (Fitzgerald 94).

A controversy is currently brewing as many Americans have begun to label much of the work funded by the NEA as obscene. The Thomas Jefferson Center for the Protection of Free Expression in a recently released survey found that "Three-quarters of those questioned said they favored allowing artists to display controversial works, but only one-quarter would support use of their tax dollars to pay for art displays they found offensive" (Knight-Ridder 18 A). Andres Serrano was given $15,000 in taxpayers' money to create a picture of a crucifix submerged in a jar of his urine. This piece of art was titled "Piss Christ." The Endowment also gave $30,000 to fund a nation-wide exhibition tour of Robert Mapplethorpe's photography. Included were photos of nude children, one man urinating into another's mouth and a photograph of Mr. Mapplethorpe himself with a bullwhip protruding from his anus (Fitzgerald 93).

I believe in the minds of most Americans, this art would be judged as obscene and offensive -- not something they want their tax dollars going to support.

In October 1989, Congress passed a law to prohibit federal funding for obscene works. This has been met with cries of "censorship" from many in the arts community. Those who cry censorship would like to draw the attention away from the very real complaint of the obscene and offensive nature of the art in question and would try to appeal to all people who rightfully revere our freedom of expression and try to lead them to believe that right is in danger. I agree with Rep. Richard Armey (R., Texas), who sent the Endowment a protest letter, signed by himself and 107 colleagues saying, "I'm not saying Serrano and Mapplethorpe can't produce the trash they call art. I'm just saying the American

94.6%

First Draft

taxpayer should not be forced to pay for it" (qtd. in Fitzgerald: 95). To state that refusal of funds to these artists is censorship is to say that a refusal to provide flags to protesters desiring to burn them denies their freedom of speech. If the artists are motivated by a burning desire to create this kind of work, they have the freedom to do so whether they receive federal funding or not. If it truly is a valid form of art, the art-loving segment of our society will recognize that, there will be a demand for it, and it will be self-sustaining. If that does not happen, then the American public has spoken. True art shouldn't need the endorsement, promotion or funding of the NEA to succeed or survive.

There are many legitimate forms of art that most everyone would agree are worthy and deserving of federal support. The NEA should focus it's energy and sources on this common middle-ground and stay away from controversy.

According to Paul Hasse, a former special assistant to the Endowment Chairman, "You're regarded as a philistine if you ask whether the public would approve of how its money is being spent on particular grants. The Endowment is extremely uncomfortable with public scrutiny" (qtd. in Fitzgerald: 94).

I think the NEA needs to remember where its money comes from and needs to seek harder to represent the general consensus of the American people, or the very merit of the NEA's existence may be called into question. More taxpayers may decide they cannot trust the Endowment and choose to exercise their freedom of expression and speech to their lawmakers by demanding that the NEA be abolished the next time they're looking for areas to trim the "fat" out of an already strained budget. If that happens many legitimate and deserving artists and projects will suffer due to the extremes of a few and the poor judgment of those given the responsibility of disbursing funds properly.

94.6%

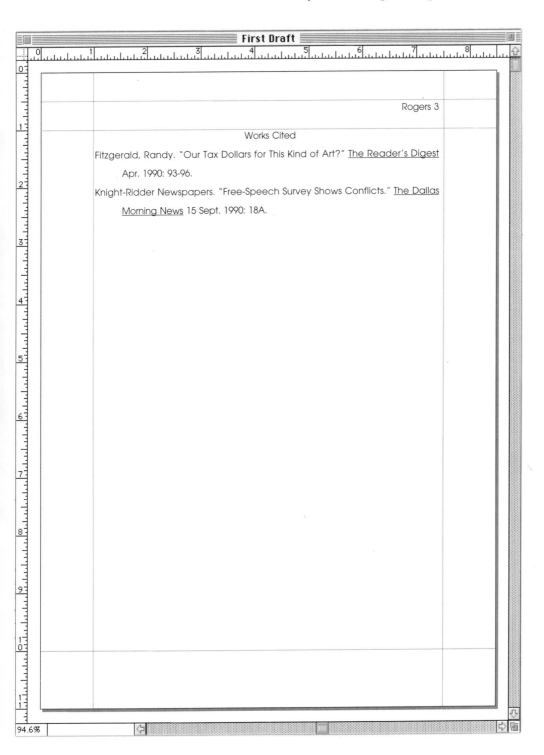

First Draft

Rogers 3

Works Cited

Fitzgerald, Randy. "Our Tax Dollars for This Kind of Art?" <u>The Reader's Digest</u>
Apr. 1990: 93-96.

Knight-Ridder Newspapers. "Free-Speech Survey Shows Conflicts." <u>The Dallas</u>
<u>Morning News</u> 15 Sept. 1990: 18A.

94.6%

Lies, Damned Lies, and Statistics:[1] Detecting and Avoiding Informal Fallacies

I'm a doctor;
I'm a lawyer;
I'm a movie star.
I'm an astronaut,
And I own this bar.
And I'd lie to you for your love.
I'd lie to you for your love.
I'd lie to you for your love,
And that's the truth.

from "I'd Lie to You for Your Love," Frankie Miller and Jeff Barry

---

[1]"There are three kinds of lies: lies, damned lies, and statistics" attributed to Benjamin Disraeli, British statesman and author, in Mark Twain's *Autobiography*.

Chapter 10

ARGUMENTS AWRY

In Part One and Part Two you explored the role in the writing process of *ethos*—appeal based on the writer's competence, trustworthiness, and benevolence—and *pathos*—appeals to the emotions and predispositions of the audience. Part Three dealt with *logos*—the use of reasoned argument to persuade—and the form of arguments. You learned that an argument contains at least two claims (statements, or assertions)—one offered as premise, or support, and one offered as conclusion. You also learned that a good argument must be based on sufficient evidence (examples, facts, authority, and so forth). This chapter deals primarily with arguments that are defective because of the content of the premises or conclusions—arguments that contain irrelevant information that masquerades as pertinent support, arguments that omit relevant information, arguments that contain falsehoods—in other words, arguments that lie.

A lie is a proposition that is intended to deceive. A teenager who has a 12 o'clock curfew and tells his parents he met that curfew but who actually arrived home at 3 o'clock in the morning is using his statement in an argument.

Unstated Major Premise: Teenagers who are at home by midnight are (according to my parents) good, thoughtful, and obedient.

Minor Premise: I was home by midnight.

Unstated Conclusion: Therefore, (according to my parents) I am good, thoughtful, and obedient.

The problem is that one of the premises is a lie, intended to mislead. The purpose is to persuade others (parents) to believe something (I am obedient, and so forth) in order to escape punishment (disapproval, grounding) or to gain reward (approval, trust).

In Part Four, we will explore the many faces of lies—from deliberate manipulation of facts to omission of relevant evidence. You will learn about the devices commonly used in deceptive propaganda so you can detect them in the arguments of others and avoid them in your own.

CAN YOU BELIEVE YOUR EYES?

At one time, photographs could be used as reliable evidence in court. Today, even experts can be fooled. Look at the photograph of the dinner party on page 179. If we accept that the dinner party took place during the time of Reagan's presidency (1981–1989), the photograph might be used as evidence to support the conclusion that Elvis did not die in 1977. But the photograph is a lie.

When Photographs Lie
Jonathan Alter

1   **A**dvances in "electronic imaging" are assaulting the meaning of the picture.

2   If the Empire State Building hadn't been moved, it would have stuck out of the sportscaster's head. So Gil Cowley, former art director for New York's WCBS-TV, had the landmark building shifted four blocks uptown on the huge skyline backdrop photo he built for his anchor set. His tool was a Quantel Graphic Paintbox, just one of several computer technologies that are changing the face of photography. "It's just so easy to manipulate images and objects for the effect you want," Cowley says. That's wonderful for art and advertising. But with more than 700 companies now possessing advanced electronic-imaging systems, the implications for photojournalism are scary.

3   Deceptive photography dates back all the way to the 1840s. The "histories" of entire nations, like Stalin's Soviet Union, have been revised by scissors and glue. In the 1950s, allies of Sen. Joseph McCarthy doctored a photo to make it seem as if a senator was talking to a communist. In the 1980s, an official White House photo of President Ronald Reagan in the hospital had the intravenous tube cropped out so that the public would not see how sick he was. For generations, armies of pimples have been magically airbrushed away. Even last year's famous case of Oprah Winfrey's head being placed on Ann-Margret's body in *TV Guide* could have been done years ago. It's actually a realistic drawing copied from pictures, not a photograph.

4   But if "the camera doesn't lie" was always a fallacy, it's now both easier to change the essence of photographs and harder to detect the process. Simple alterations, such as removing a diet Coke can from a picture of a Pulitzer Prize winner (which the St. Louis Post-Dispatch did last year), can be accomplished with a series of key strokes on the widely available Scitex Response system. The process involves giving "pixels"—electronic squares—a binary code that makes them easy to adjust. Layout design, cropping, sizing and other changes are made quicker, cheaper and infinitely more flexible.

From *Newsweek,* July 30, 1990 © Newsweek Inc. All Rights Reserved. Reprinted by permission.

5   More complicated matching of resolution and color, which once required a technically trained artist, now merely entails more elaborate digitized systems. R/Greenberg Associates was hired by *Newsweek* to assemble the strange cast of characters pictured [above]. The graphic artist, Robert Bowen, spent about eight hours with Pixar and Sun systems hooked up to an Apple Macintosh to create a lifelike composite color photo impossible only a couple of years ago. Within a few more years, some form of electronic imaging will be inexpensive enough for wide use with personal computers.

6   The potential for abuse is obvious. "You have to be like a hawk to keep the technology from taking advantage of you," says M.C. Marden, picture editor of *People* magazine. But the long-term effect may be more insidious. For 150 years, the photographic image has been viewed as more persuasive than written accounts as a form of "evidence." Now this authenticity is breaking down under the assault of technology. In an absorbing new book, *In Our Own Image: The Coming Revolution in Photography* (158 pages. Aperture. $15.95), Fred Ritchin, a former photo editor of the *New York Times Magazine,* asks: "What would happen if the photograph appeared to be a straightforward recording of physical reality, but could no longer be relied upon to depict actual people and events?"

7   **No "proof":** Ritchin's answer is frightening. Take China's leaders, who last year tried to bar photographers from exposing their lies about the Beijing massacre. In the future, the Chinese or others with something to hide wouldn't even worry about photographers. With "electronic photography they could deny the veracity of the newly malleable image," Ritchin says. In other words, pictures, like words, would be "proof" of little. Imagine how this would have affected, say, the Kurt Waldheim case. The Austrian president consistently denied his Nazi past until presented with the photographic proof in 1986, at which point he admitted that the picture was real. Future Waldheims could plausibly claim they had been placed in compromising positions by computer. While the old cut-and-paste method was easily detectable, especially on color photos, electronic re-imaging is not.

8   Photo editors first confronted this brave new world in 1982, when *National Geographic* came under fire for moving two Egyptian pyramids closer together so that they would fit on a vertical cover. *Time* magazine apologized in 1987 when a story about espionage at the American Embassy in Moscow was illustrated with a studio shot of a Marine, wrongly implying that the picture was taken at the embassy. Last year *Newsweek* regretted making it seem, in photo, that *Rain Man* costars Tom Cruise and Dustin Hoffman were posing together when, in fact, one was in Hawaii and the other in New York. Ben Blank, art director for ABC News, says he routinely altered still images (for example, straightening jacket wrinkles) until a "recreation" of accused spy Felix Bloch passing a briefcase made the network re-examine its practices.

9   Unfortunately, news organizations have few guidelines for use of the new technology. A famous 1984 picture of marathoner Mary Decker falling down was marred slightly by an antenna in the frame. The antenna was left in the picture in *Life* and was removed in *Time,* according to Michele Stephenson, *Time*'s picture editor. Newspapers are generally stricter. A car antenna that distracted from a picture of Marion Barry's wife was consciously left in a picture that ran in *USA Today*. Says Larry Nylund, deputy managing editor: "We don't alter photographs."

10   But *USA Today* uses other little-examined new photographic technologies, such as "frame grabbing," where the picture is taken off TV (always with a credit, Nylund says), and "still video cameras." The latter eliminates the need for film processing on late-breaking stories like the Oscars or World Series and allows pictures to get into the paper in as little as 10 minutes. While video stills won't soon replace 35-mm film (which is also dramatically improving), they may soon be easier to fake: there's no negative to prove what the original shot looked like.

11   Beyond technological change, the deeper problem is a continual blurring of lines between commercialism and journalism. "Zipper heads" (star's face, model's body) that are acceptable in the artificial world of movie posters and display advertising take on another meaning in editorial pages—even as jokes (e.g. *Atlanta* magazine's cover spoofing the Rob Lowe sex-tape scandal, which many readers believed was the actor himself). So do lesser alterations, like

extending backgrounds or keying up colors. "As feature magazines do it more and more, it will be harder to hold the line," says *Time*'s Stephenson. Tina Brown, editor of *Vanity Fair,* who last year authorized the creation of a blue-sky background for a Melanie Griffith cover, speaks for many editors when she draws a distinction between feature and news pictures. "I would never do it on a journalism piece," she says, referring to a recent political profile.

12   Unfortunately, this common distinction degrades the whole notion of journalism; it implies that the integrity of images applies only to some narrowly defined notion of "news." Editors need not opt for unflattering pictures to agree that fakery—even on the food page—pollutes the whole publication. Like athletes on steroids, enhanced photographs may perform better, but at bottom they are liars.

For Writing and Discussion

1. If it is okay to alter photographs for some purposes, perhaps for a book jacket that some would argue is actually an advertisement, when is it not okay to alter photographs? Support your argument with examples that illustrate the harm that might result from the altering of photographs. (Recall *Time*'s alteration of a cover photo of O. J. Simpson prior to his trial.)

2. Photographer John Long says, "If the public thinks we're lying, even in a small way, how can they know we're not lying in a big way?" You are "the public." How does it make you feel to know that you can't always trust photographs to be unaltered? Why?

3. Would you suggest legislation to control the altering of photographs? If so, what kind of legislation? Write out the law you would propose.

CAN NUMBERS LIE?

"You can prove anything with numbers" has become a common defense against statistical information. The readings in this section are provided to help you defend yourself against statistical manipulation and to determine how to use statistics correctly in your own writing.

If the word *recommended,* instead of *recommend,* had been used, we might be more inclined to believe that only four doctors had been questioned and that three of them had recommended Pain-eze. We still would not know whether the four doctors were researchers for, or otherwise employed by, the Pain-eze company, and we don't know what kinds of incentives were offered to the doctors for their responses.

The present tense verb *recommend* implies an on-going recommendation. The advertiser would like us to infer that three-fourths of all the doctors in the world did, do, and will continue to recommend Pain-eze. However, the "fact" may be that three doctors on the Pain-eze payroll recommended Pain-eze and will continue to recommend it as long as they work for the company.

The Numbers Game
Stephen Budiansky

1   **S**tatistics are an American obsession. Politicians burnish their positions with them, advertisers bombard us with them, corporations make multimillion dollar decisions based on them. The Bureau of the Census used to count just people; now it tabulates everything from envelopes and shoes to dolls and caskets.

2   "Numbers suggest understanding," says Peter Reuter, an economist at the RAND Corporation. Adds Michael Jay Robinson, a consultant to the Gallup-Times Mirror survey, "Numbers are safe: when you use them, you can't be accused of ideological or political bias."

3   But rarely is the truth behind the numbers questioned—and all too easily are numbers manipulated. Whatever your position, a statistic is available to back it up. Crime? It's going down—unless you're a law-enforcement official pleading for a higher budget. Then crime is going up. The crisis in education? School superintendents can prove that students' test scores are above the national norm—*everywhere.*

4   Sometimes numbers concocted to support a position are just guesses—but once in the public record, they take on a life of their own. Take the figure of $140 billion—given as the size of the illegal-drug-trafficking industry. This figure has been cited in the press and most prominently this year by Rep. Charles Rangel (D., N.Y.), chairman of the House Select Committee on Narcotics Abuse and Control, in his push for an expanded war on drugs. The number's seeming precision—140, not 100 or 150—implies real knowledge. But where does it come from?

5   The figure seems to have originated in 1978, when the National Narcotics Intelligence Consumers Committee (NNICC) put the drug trade at $50 billion in 1980. After much criticism, NNICC quietly dropped the estimate. But the cause was then taken up by Rangel's committee. John Cusack, the committee's former chief of staff, figured that since the NNICC estimate had risen $30 billion within three years, "adding $10 billion a year seemed to make sense"—and that's what the committee has done ever since. The figure "is not scientifically accurate," he admits.

6   The case of all test scores being above average is a classic example of statistical manipulation. In 1987 virtually every state reported that its students scored above the national norm on reading, writing and math tests. Obviously, if the norm really had been a norm, some states would be below it. It turned out that the norms for the tests had not been revised for up to ten years. There are over a dozen tests to choose from, and schools were selecting those that best matched their curriculums. Teachers then tailored lessons to conform to these tests.

7   Fiddling with the sample group is one of the most common ways to tease a desired result out of statistics. That's how partisans on each side of the 65-m.p.h.-speed-limit debate used the same data to prove their cases. Depending on how states are grouped in the sample, you can prove that a higher speed limit has caused more traffic fatalities—or fewer.

8   Why are we so impressed by numbers? "Human judgment and intuition are fallible," says Prof. Amos Tversky, a Stanford University psychologist. Some of our errors in interpreting statistics fall into definable patterns.

9   One rule is that losses loom larger than gains. People are more willing to support a public-health program when told how many lives will be lost without it—as opposed to lives saved by it. Psychologists have also found that people rarely question the contest of numbers—as in accepting that a detergent is "35 percent better" without asking, "35 percent better than what?" But most important, numbers have taken on the role of compelling anecdote—the story that people repeat without ever asking where it came from.

10   John Walsh campaigned for missing children after the disappearance of his son. He came up with an estimate of 50,000 abductions per year after speaking with missing-children organizations around the country. Parents were alarmed, the faces of missing children appeared on milk cartons, and the Justice Department created a National Center for Missing and Exploited Children. The center no longer gives estimates. In its four years of operation, it has received only 471 confirmed reports of kidnappings by strangers.

11   Another number with a strange history is the "three million homeless Americans." In 1980 Mitch Snyder, an advocate for the homeless, asked 100 agencies and organizations to estimate the fraction of homeless people in 25 cities and states. The numbers ranged from a few hundredths of a percent to one percent. In 1982 he repeated the survey and came up with the same figures. He then began claiming that "one percent of the population, or 2.2

million people, lacked shelter." He added that the number "could" reach three million in 1983. That number was widely quoted.

12   Other studies have found the number to be much too large. Even Snyder subsequently told a Congressional hearing: "These numbers are meaningless. We have tried to satisfy your gnawing curiosity for a number because Americans have to quantify everything in sight."

13   Number blindness even besets the experts. The October 1987 stock market crash was triggered in part by government figures showing a trade deficit approximately $1.5 billion greater than Wall Street expected. Never mind that trade figures are notoriously unreliable because of the difficulty of tracking our own exports and capital. It was a number from the government—and that was enough basis for experts to make financial decisions worth billions. That market-crashing figure has since been revised downward—by $600 million.

14   "There's an overreliance on numbers," says Bruce Meyers, director of research services for the BBDO advertising agency. "Any research should be an aid to judgment, not a replacement for it." But here's one number that shows what American business thinks of that advice: the survey-research industry now earns more than $2 billion a year—and is growing at an annual rate of 15 percent.

The Doublespeak of Graphs
William Lutz

1   Just as polls seem to present concrete, specific evidence, so do graphs and charts present information visually in a way that appears unambiguous and dramatically clear. But, just as polls leave a lot of necessary information out, so can graphs and charts, resulting in doublespeak. You have to ask a lot of questions if you really want to understand a graph or chart.

2   In 1981 President Reagan went on television to argue that citizens would be paying a lot more in taxes under a Democratic bill than under his bill. To prove his point, he used a chart that appeared to show a dramatic and very big difference between the results of each bill (see Figure 1). But the president's chart was doublespeak, because it was deliberately designed to be misleading. Pointing to his chart, President Reagan said, "This red space between the two lines is the tax money that will remain in your pockets if our bill passes, and it's the amount that will leave your pockets if their bill is passed. On the one hand, you see a genuine and lasting commitment to the future of working Americans. On the other, just another empty promise."

Figure 1
*President Reagan's misleading and biased chart, compared
with a neutral presentation regarding the same tax proposals.*

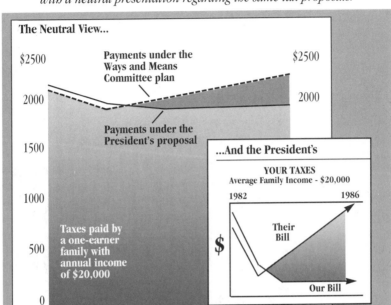

That was a pretty dramatic statement, considering that the maximum difference between the two bills, after five years, would have been $217.

3   The president's chart showed a deceptively dramatic difference because
his chart had no figures on the dollar scale and no numbers for years except
1982 and 1986. The difference in tax payments was exaggerated in the president's chart by "squashing" or tightening the time scale as much as possible,
while stretching the dollar scale, starting with an oddly unrounded $2,150
and winding up at $2,400. Thus, the chart had no perspective. Using the
proper method for constructing a chart would have meant starting at $0 and
going up to the first round number after the highest point in the chart, as
done in the "neutral view" in Figure 1. Using that method, the $217 seems
rather small in a total tax bill of $2,385.

4   What happened to the numbers on the president's chart? "The chart
we sent over to the White House had all the numbers on it," said Marlin
Fitzwater, then a press officer in the Treasury Department. Senior White
House spokesperson David Gergen said, "We took them off. We were trying
to get a point across, not the absolute numbers." So much for honesty.

Figure 2
*Misleading graph from the Department of Education,
showing school spending relative to SAT scores.*

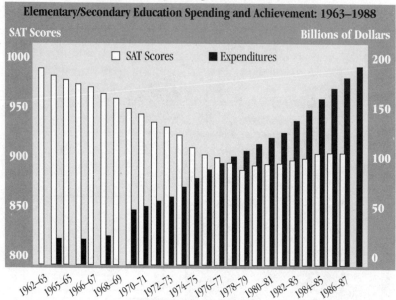

5   In 1988 the Department of Education issued a graph that seemed to prove that there was a direct connection between the rise in elementary and secondary school spending and the decline in scores on the Scholastic Aptitude Test (see Figure 2). The Reagan Administration had been arguing that spending more money doesn't improve education and may even make it worse. But the chart was doublespeak. First, it used current dollars rather than constant dollars, adjusted for inflation. Because each year it takes more money to buy the same things, charts are supposed to adjust for that increase so the measure of dollars remains constant over the years illustrated in the chart. If the Department of Education had figured in inflation over the years on the chart, it would have shown that the amount of constant dollars spent on education had increased modestly from 1970 to 1986, as Figure 3 shows.

6   Second, scores on the Scholastic Aptitude Test go from 400 to 1,600, yet the graph used by the Education Department (Figure 2) used a score range of only 800 to 1,000. By limiting the range of scores on its graph, the department showed what appeared to be a severe decline in scores. A properly prepared graph, shown in Figure 4, shows a much more gradual decline.

7   The Department of Education's presentation is a good example of diagrammatic doublespeak. Without all the information you need in order to understand the chart, you can be easily misled, which of course was the purpose of the chart. You should always be skeptical whenever you see a graph or chart being used to present information, because these things are nothing

Figure 3
Elementary/secondary education spending in constant dollars (billions).

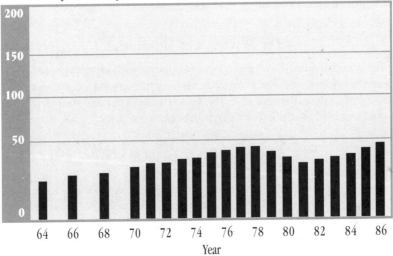

Figure 4
SAT scores, 1963–1986.

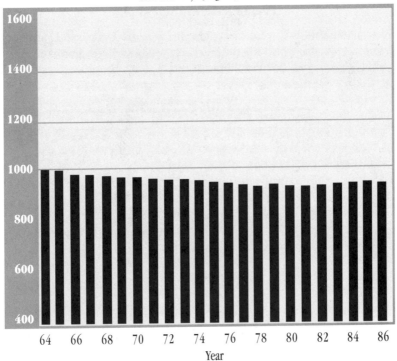

more than the visual presentation of statistical information. And as for statistics, remember what Benjamin Disraeli is supposed to have said: "There are three kinds of lies—lies, damn lies, and statistics."

For Writing and Discussion

1. Had you already heard any of the statistics profiled in "The Numbers Racket" (3 million homeless, 50,000 children kidnapped every year, and so forth)? How did you respond to the figure when you first heard it? How did you respond to Budiansky's analysis of the statistics?

2. The wording on survey questions can determine specific responses as well as a reader's perception of the question. For instance, a question such as "How many homeless people do you know?" might be perceived as meaning either "How many people do you know who live on the street?" or "How many people do you know who don't own their own homes and live in an apartment or in another person's home?" What are questions we might ask of any survey results?

3. Why do you think using charts to represent statistics is so common today? Do you more easily interpret information you read in a paragraph or information you see on a chart?

Practice: Creating Graphs

From statistics below, create two graphs, one that accurately reflects the data and one that is skewed. Be prepared to show your graphs to the class and explain how the skewed graph distorts the truth.

World Population

TIME	POPULATION
40,000 B.C.	3 million
8,000 B.C.	5 million
Time of Christ	200 million
1650 A.D.	500 million
1850	1.3 billion
1945	2.3 billion
1980	4.4 billion
1994	5.6 billion
2020	8.2 billion (projected)

THE POWER OF STYLE: ELLIPSIS

During President Reagan's 1981 discussion of two tax bills that were being considered (see page 184), he compares the two bills:

"On the one hand, you see a genuine and lasting commitment to the future of working Americans. On the other, just another empty promise."

The second sentence contains two ellipted (understood, but not written) parts. This is how the sentences would read with the ellipted words included:

"On the one hand, you see a genuine and lasting commitment to the future of working Americans. On the other (hand), (you see) just another empty promise."

The elliptical construction retains the comparison but eliminates unnecessary repetition, adding conciseness and drama.

Practice: Testing Statistics

The following "tests" will help you evaluate the statistical information you read or hear.

1. When presented with an average, ask what kind of average (mean, median, mode)[2] and consider deviation.

Otherwise you are like the man choosing a camp site from a report of mean temperature alone. One place in California with a mean annual temperature of 61 is San Nicolas Island on the south coast, where it always stays in the comfortable range between 47 and 87. Another with a mean of 61 is in the inland desert, where the thermometer hops around from 15 to 104. The deviation from the mean marks the difference, and you can freeze or roast if you ignore it.

Darrell Huff, "How to Lie with Statistics"

2. When presented with research information, question the source.

Does the source have something to gain? Although a study done by the tobacco industry that shows tobacco smoke ranks below air pollution and

---

[2]*Mean* is the arithmetic average of a group of numbers; *median* is the number in the middle if all numbers were listed in a row; *mode* is the most common of a group of numbers.

radon gas in causing lung cancer might be both valid and reliable, we are justified in asking for an independent study before accepting the information.

3. When presented with public opinion polls, again, question the source. Even reputable polling firms can make mistakes, but to stay "reputable," they must make every effort to make sure their samples are representative of the general population and their survey questions are well prepared.

4. Is the level of accuracy reasonable? We are also justified in questioning statistics that show unrealistic levels of accuracy (average sleep of working women: 7.352 hours per night).

Practice: Survey Questions

[American psychologist Gordon Allport] tells of two priests who were engaged in a dispute on whether or not it is permissible to pray and smoke at the same time. One believed that it is, the other that it is not, and so each decided to write to the Pope for a definitive answer. After doing so, they met again to share their results and were astonished to discover that the Pope had agreed with both of them. "How did you pose the question?" the first asked. The other replied, "I asked if it is permissible to smoke while praying. His Holiness said that it is not, since praying is a very serious business. And how did you phrase the question?" The first replied, "I asked if it is permissible to pray while smoking, and His Holiness said that it is, since it is always appropriate to pray."

The point of this story, of course, is that the form in which we ask our questions will determine the answers we get. To put it more broadly: all the knowledge we ever have is a result of questions. Indeed, it is a commonplace among scientists that they do not see nature as it is, but only through the questions they put to it. I should go further: we do not see anything as it is except through the questions we put to it. And there is a larger point even than this: since questions are the most important intellectual tool we have, is it not incredible that the art and science of question-asking is not systematically taught?

Neil Postman, *Conscientious Objections* 25–26

For the fictitious survey results below, write at least two different ways that a question might have been worded to elicit the responses. Be prepared to tell how the wording on each question could affect the response.

1. Two-thirds of women prefer men who are emotionally sensitive to those who are emotionally strong.

2. Three out of four people believe that it is okay for department stores to insert subliminal messages in store music.

3. Sixty-five percent of Americans believe that the criminal justice system needs drastic reform.

Examples

Survey results: Only one-fifth of taxpayers would pay $5 more per year in taxes to finance political campaigns.

Question 1: Would you pay $5 more per year in taxes to finance the campaigns of professional politicians?

Question 2: Would you pay $5 more per year in taxes to have your voice heard above the special interests who now finance political campaigns?

Survey results: Nine out of ten people would rather call a plumber than repair a leaky faucet themselves.

Question 1: If money were not a factor, would you fix a leaky faucet yourself or call a plumber?

Question 2: Would you prefer to save money and fix a leaky faucet yourself, or would you call a plumber for even a simple repair?

DISINFORMATION

The word *disinformation* applies to intentional fabrications released by government agencies or private organizations for the purpose of persuading. Since most of us depend on the information released through the media to form opinions and make decisions, then receiving the truth, or correct information, is important. Sometimes the truth (or parts of the truth) surfaces years after disinformation has been released. At that time, the public is faced with reevaluating a situation and, perhaps, feeling they have been duped.

Portions of the Gulf War Were Brought to You By . . . the Folks at Hill and Knowlton
Morgan Strong

1 By now, it is well known that some portions of the Persian Gulf war effort were stage-managed in an effort to rally public opinion for military action against Iraq. The two leading television newsmagazines, ABC's *20/20* and CBS's *60 Minutes,* devoted segments last month to the fact that an emotional

appeal in 1990 before a Congressional caucus hearing, supposedly by an anonymous Kuwaiti refugee girl called Nayirah, was, in fact, delivered by the daughter of Kuwait's ambassador to the U.S. Both stories followed a *New York Times* op-ed piece that exposed Nayirah's true identity, by John R. MacArthur, publisher of *Harper's Magazine.*

2   Further, it was revealed that the public-relations firm of Hill and Knowlton, headed at the time by Craig Fuller, former chief of staff to George Bush when he was Vice President, helped to package and rehearse the young woman's appearance on behalf of their client, Citizens for a Free Kuwait, an exile organization primarily funded by the Emir of Kuwait. Nayirah's testimony was that Iraqi soldiers had stormed hospitals and torn newborn babies from their incubators, leaving them to die. Her story, which received wide network coverage—and was invoked on numerous occasions by President Bush—had, in fact, been rehearsed before video cameras by Hill and Knowlton. But according to Kuwaiti doctors interviewed by *20/20* and *60 Minutes,* no such incident had occurred.

3   If this had been the only occurrence of packaged war reporting broadcast in the heat of war hysteria, it might be excusable. But what I found during my long stint in Saudi Arabia (I was a consultant for both PBS's *Frontline* and England's *Thames Television*) was a far more systematic manipulation of news by the PR firm than is generally known:

4   • Following the August 1990 invasion of Kuwait by Iraq, refugees with stories about conditions in their country were selected and coached by Hill and Knowlton. Those with the most compelling tales—and the ones most in keeping with the agenda of Hill and Knowlton's client—were made available to news organizations, thus limiting journalists' ability to independently assess claims of brutalities. Indeed, the PR firm's operatives were given free rein to travel unescorted throughout Saudi Arabia, while journalists were severely restricted.

5   • Hill and Knowlton also was the source for a large number of the amateur videos shot inside Kuwait and smuggled out. The videos were collected, screened and edited at the PR firm's TV studios in the Saudi capital, Riyadh, and in the coastal city of Dharan. The packaged videotapes were then distributed free of charge to the networks, ostensibly by Citizens for a Free Kuwait. In the U.S., Hill and Knowlton also distributed the tapes to affiliated and independent stations.

6   • A second woman who was identified as simply another Kuwaiti refugee, and who made an appearance before a widely televised session of the UN Security Council on Nov. 27, 1990, turned out to be a close relative of a senior Kuwaiti official. The woman, Fatima Fahed, came before the world body as it was debating the use of force to oust the Iraqis from Kuwait. She gave harrowing details of Iraqi atrocities inside her country.

7   What was not reported is that Fahed was, in fact, the wife of Sulaiman Al-Mutawa, Kuwait's minister of planning, and herself a well-known TV person-

ality in Kuwait. Surprised that a high-profile Kuwaiti could be labeled, and accepted, as just another "refugee," I asked one of the leaders of Citizens for a Free Kuwait, Fawzi Al-Sultan, why Fahed had been chosen to speak to the UN. "Because of her professional experience," he said, "she is more believable."

8   But, like the story related by Nayirah, Fahed's testimony was not necessarily true. In testifying to the UN, she implied that her information was first-hand. "Such stories . . . I personally have experienced," she said. But when I had interviewed her in Jedda, Saudi Arabia, *before* her UN appearance, she told me that she had *no* firsthand knowledge of the events she was describing. Some weeks later, in advance of her UN testimony, she and other witnesses were coached—including rehearsals, wardrobe and prepared scripts—extensively by employees of Hill and Knowlton.

9   • A tape from inside Kuwait, supplied to journalists by the PR firm before the U.S.-led invasion, purported to show peaceful Kuwaiti demonstrators being fired upon by the occupying Iraqi troops.

10   But, on the ground in Saudi Arabia, I managed to interview a Kuwaiti refugee present at the demonstration whose story was quite different. The man, a Kuwaiti policeman, said that no demonstrators were injured, and that gunshots captured on tape were, in fact, those of Iraqi troops firing on nearby resistance fighters, who had fired first at the Iraqis. When I asked him to appear on camera and tell the true story, he refused. "I do not want to harm the resistance," he said.

11   None of this is to suggest that the Iraqis did not perpetrate atrocities while occupying Kuwait, nor does it underestimate the difficulties facing the media in obtaining original material under censorship conditions. However, these examples are but a few of the incidents of outright misinformation that found their way onto the network news. It is an inescapable fact that much of what Americans saw on their news broadcasts, especially leading up to the Allied offensive against Iraqi-occupied Kuwait, was in large measure the contrivance of a public-relations firm.

12   In 1968, American soldiers were fighting and dying in the jungles of Southeast Asia. But the Vietnam war didn't start this way. It started secretly, off the books, like so many of these ventures that have ended disastrously.

13   The CIA got there early, soon after the Vietnamese won their independence from the French in 1954. Eisenhower warned that the nations of Southeast Asia would fall like dominoes if the communists, led by Ho Chi Minh, took over all Vietnam. To hold the line, we installed a puppet regime in Saigon under Ngo Dinh Diem. American-trained commandoes were used to sabotage bus and rail lines and contaminate North Vietnam's oil supplies. The situation kept getting worse.

14   President Kennedy sent the Green Berets to Vietnam and turned to full-scale counterinsurgency. As a senator, he had once said Vietnam was "the ultimate test of our will to stem the tide of world communism." As president,

he sent 15,000 Americans to be "advisers" there. The secret war was leading to deeper involvement and more deception.

> PRES. LYNDON B. JOHNSON (August 4, 1964):
> It is my duty to the American people to report that renewed hostile actions against United States ships on the high seas in the Gulf of Tonkin have today required me to order the military forces of the United States to take action in reply.

This president was not telling the truth, either. The action in the Gulf of Tonkin was not unprovoked. South Vietnam had been conducting secret raids in the area against the North, and the American destroyer ordered into the battle zone had advance warning it could be attacked. But Johnson seized the incident to stampede Congress into passing the Gulf of Tonkin Resolution, which he then used as a blank check for the massive buildup of American forces.

Bill Moyers, The Secret Government

For Writing and Discussion

1. To what extent do you think contrived testimonies and misinformation influenced the president's and Congress's attitude toward the pending Gulf War? How much do you think the testimony influenced the American people in general to support the Gulf War?

2. What role do you think public relations firms should have in swaying public opinion on political matters? Consider that political candidates hire public relations firms to "polish" them, make them acceptable to the public. How can the public determine how much of a candidate is "polish" and how much represents the beliefs and attitudes of the candidate?

3. You witnessed President Bush's confrontation with Congress over the Gulf War. As it turned out, Congress did support the president's actions; however, the president made it clear that he was prepared to act without the approval of Congress. Explain why his stance was or was not appropriate.

4. What does President Johnson's use of disinformation prior to the Vietnam war have in common with what was done to gain public support prior to the Gulf War?

5. Describe possible situations in which a government might release disinformation because of a responsibility to protect citizens and public interests.

LIES OF OMISSION

Grief and Mourning for the Night
Mark Twain

After Spain gave the United States rights to the Philippine Islands at the end of the Spanish-American War in 1899, rebel groups continued to fight for Philippine independence. In 1906 U.S. troops massacred a rebel tribe of 600 Moro men, women, and children. The horrid details that surfaced were released by press correspondents, not by government officials. Even today, the incident is ignored in history textbooks. Mark Twain wrote about the incident in "Grief and Mourning for the Night."

1   This incident burst upon the world last Friday in an official cablegram from the commander of our forces in the Philippines to our Government at Washington. The substance of it was as follows:

2   A tribe of Moros, dark skinned savages, had fortified themselves in the bowl of an extinct crater not many miles from Jolo; and as they were hostiles, and bitter against us because we have been trying for eight years to take their liberties away from them, their presence in that position was a menace. Our commander, General Leonard Wood, ordered a reconnaissance. It was found that the Moros numbered six hundred, counting women and children; that their crater bowl was in the summit of a peak or mountain twenty-two hundred feet above sea level, and very difficult of access for Christian troops and artillery. Then General Wood ordered a surprise, and went along himself to see the order carried out. Our troops climbed the heights by devious and difficult trails, and even took some artillery with them. The kind of artillery is not specified, but in one place it was hoisted up a sharp acclivity by tackle a distance of some three-hundred feet. Arrived at the rim of the crater, the battle began. Our soldiers numbered five hundred and forty. They were assisted by auxiliaries consisting of a detachment of native constabulary in our pay—the numbers not given—and by a naval detachment, whose numbers are not stated. But apparently the contending parties were about equal as to number—six hundred men on our side, on the edge of the bowl; six hundred men, women and children in the bottom of the bowl. Depth of the bowl, 50 feet.

3   General Wood's order was "Kill or capture the six hundred."

4   The battle began—it is officially called by that name—our forces firing down into the crater with their artillery and their deadly small arms of precision; the savages furiously returning the fire, probably with brickbats— though this is merely a surmise of mine, as the weapons used by the savages are not nominated in the cablegram. Heretofore the Moros have used knives and clubs mainly; also ineffectual trade-muskets when they had any.

5   The official report stated that the battle was fought with prodigious energy on both sides during a day and a half, and that it ended with a complete victory for the American arms. The completeness of the victory is established by this fact: that of the six hundred Moros not one was left alive. The brilliancy of the victory is established by this other fact, to wit: that of our six hundred heroes only fifteen lost their lives.

6   General Wood was present and looking on. His order had been "Kill *or* capture those savages." Apparently our little army considered that the "or" left them authorized to kill *or* capture according to taste, and that their taste had remained what it has been for eight years, in our army out there—the taste of Christian butchers.

7   The official report quite properly extolled and magnified the "heroism" and "gallantry" of our troops; lamented the loss of the fifteen who perished, and elaborated the wounds of thirty-two of our men who suffered injury, and even minutely and faithfully described the nature of the wounds, in the interest of future historians of the United States. It mentioned that a private had one of his elbows scraped by a missile, and the private's name was mentioned. Another private had the end of his nose scraped by a missile. His name was also mentioned—by cable, at one dollar and fifty cents a word.

8   Next day's news confirmed the previous day's report and named our fifteen killed and thirty-two wounded *again,* and once more described the wounds and gilded them with the right adjectives.

9   Let us now consider two or three details of our military history. In one of the great battles of the civil war ten percent of the forces engaged on the two sides were killed or wounded. At Waterloo, where four hundred thousand men were present on the two sides, fifty thousand fell, killed and wounded, in five hours, leaving three hundred and fifty thousand sound and all right for further adventures. Eight years ago, when the pathetic comedy called the Cuban war was played, we summoned two hundred and fifty thousand men. We fought a number of showy battles, and when the war was over we had lost two hundred and sixty-eight men out of our two hundred and fifty thousand, in killed and wounded in the field, and just *fourteen times as many* by the gallantry of the army doctors in the hospitals and camps. We did not exterminate the Spaniards—far from it. In each engagement we left an average of *two percent* of the enemy killed or crippled on the field.

10   Contrast these things with the great statistics which have arrived from that Moro crater! There, with six hundred engaged on each side, we lost fifteen men killed outright, and we had thirty-two wounded—counting that nose and that elbow. The enemy numbered six hundred—including women and children—and we abolished them utterly, leaving not even a baby alive to cry for its dead mother. *This is incomparably the greatest victory that was ever achieved by the Christian soldiers of the United States.*

11   Now then, how has it been received? The splendid news appeared with splendid display-heads in every newspaper in this city of four million and thirteen thousand inhabitants, on Friday morning. But there was not a single

reference to it in the editorial columns of any one of those newspapers. The news appeared again in all the evening papers of Friday, and again those papers were editorially silent upon our vast achievement. Next day's additional statistics and particulars appeared in all the morning papers, and still without a line of editorial rejoicing or a mention of the matter in any way. These additions appeared in the evening papers of that same day (Saturday) and again without a word of comment. In the columns devoted to correspondence, in the morning and evening papers of Friday and Saturday, nobody said a word about the "battle." Ordinarily those columns are teeming with the passions of the citizens; he lets no incident go by, whether it be large or small, without pouring out his praise or blame, his joy or his indignation about the matter in the correspondence column. But, as I have said, during those two days he was as silent as the editors themselves. So far as I can find out, there was only one person among our eighty millions who allowed himself the privilege of a public remark on this great occasion—that was the President of the United States. All day Friday he was as studiously silent as the rest. But on Saturday he recognized that his duty required him to say something, and he took his pen and performed that duty. If I know President Roosevelt—and I am sure I do—this utterance cost him more pain and shame than any other that ever issued from his pen or his mouth. I am far from blaming him. If I had been in his place my official duty would have compelled me to say what he said. It was a convention, an old tradition, and he had to be loyal to it. There was no help for it. This is what he said:

> *Washington, March 10*
>   Wood, *Manila:*—
>   I congratulate you and the officers and men of your command upon the brilliant feat of arms wherein you and they so well upheld the honor of the American flag.
>   (Signed) THEODORE ROOSEVELT

12   His whole utterance is merely a convention. Not a word of what he said came from his heart. He knew perfectly well that to pen six hundred helpless and weaponless savages in a hole like rats in a trap and massacre them in detail during a stretch of a day and a half, from a safe position on the heights above, was no brilliant feat of arms—and would not have been a brilliant feat of arms even if Christian America represented by its salaried soldiers, had shot them down with Bibles and the Golden Rule instead of bullets. He knew perfectly well that our uniformed assassins had *not* upheld the honor of the American flag, but had done as they have been doing continuously for eight years in the Philippines—that is to say, they had dishonored it.

13   The next day, Sunday,—which was yesterday—the cable brought us additional news—still more splendid news—still more honor for the flag. The first display-head shouts this information at us in stentorian capitals: "WOMEN SLAIN IN MORO SLAUGHTER."

14   "Slaughter" is a good word. Certainly there is not a better one in the Unabridged Dictionary for this occasion.

15   The next display line says:

16   *"With Children They Mixed in Mob in Crater, and All Died Together."*

17   They were mere naked savages, and yet there is a sort of pathos about it when the word children falls under your eye, for it always brings before us our perfectest symbol of innocence and helplessness; and by help of its deathless eloquence color, creed and nationality vanish away and we see only that they are children—merely children. And if they are frightened and crying and in trouble, our pity goes out to them by natural impulse. We see a picture. We see the small forms. We see the terrified faces. We see the tears. We see the small hands clinging in supplication to the mother; but we do not see those children that we are speaking about. We see in their places the little creatures whom we know and love.

18   The next heading blazes with American and Christian glory like to the sun in the zenith:

19   *"Death List is Now 900."*

20   I was never so enthusiastically proud of the flag till now!

21   The next heading explains how safely our daring soldiers were located. It says:

22   *"Impossible to Tell Sexes Apart in Fierce Battle on Top of Mount Dajo."*

23   The naked savages were so far away, down in the bottom of that trap, that our soldiers could not tell the breasts of a woman from the rudimentary paps of a man—so far away that they couldn't tell a toddling little child from a black six-footer. *This was by all odds the least dangerous battle that Christian soldiers of any nationality were ever engaged in.*

24   The next heading says:

25   *"Fighting for Four Days."*

26   So our men were at it four days instead of a day and a half. It was a long and happy picnic with nothing to do but sit in comfort and fire the Golden Rule into those people down there and imagine letters to write home to the admiring families, and pile glory upon glory. Those savages fighting for their liberties had the four days too, but it must have been a sorrowful time for them. Every day they saw two hundred and twenty-five of their number slain, and this provided them grief and mourning for the night—and doubtless without even the relief and consolation of knowing that in the meantime they had slain four of their enemies and wounded some more on the elbow and the nose.

27   The closing heading says:

28   *"Lieutenant Johnson Blown from Parapet by Exploding Artillery Gallantly Leading Charge."*

29   . . . Johnson was wounded in the shoulder with a slug. The slug was in a shell—for the account says the damage was caused by an exploding shell which blew Johnson off the rim. The people down in the hole had no artillery; therefore it was our artillery that blew Johnson off the rim. And so it is now a matter of historical record that the only officer of ours who acquired

a wound of advertising dimensions got it at our hands, not the enemy's. It seems more than probable that if we had placed our soldiers out of the way of our own weapons, we should have come out of the most extraordinary battle in all history without a scratch. . . .

30   The ominous paralysis continues. There has been a slight sprinkle—an exceedingly slight sprinkle—in the correspondence columns, of angry rebukes of the President for calling this cowardly massacre a "brilliant feat of arms" and for praising our butchers for "holding up the honor of the flag" in that singular way; but there is hardly a ghost of a whisper about the feat of arms in the editorial columns of the papers.

31   I hope that this silence will continue. It is about as eloquent and as damaging and effective as the most indignant words could be, I think. When a man is sleeping in a noise, his sleep goes placidly on; but if the noise stops, the stillness wakes him. This silence has continued five days now. Surely it must be waking the drowsy nation. Surely the nation must be wondering what it means. A five-day silence following a world-astonishing event has not happened on this planet since the daily newspaper was invented.

32   At a luncheon party of men convened yesterday to God-speed George Harvey, who is leaving to-day for a vacation in Europe, all the talk was about the brilliant feat of arms; and no one had anything to say about it that either the President or Major General Dr. Wood or the damaged Johnson would regard as complimentary, or as proper comment to put into our histories. Harvey said he believed that the shock and shame of this episode would eat down deeper and deeper into the hearts of the nation and fester there and produce results. He believed it would destroy the Republican party and President Roosevelt. I cannot believe that the prediction will come true, for the reason that prophecies which promise valuable things, desirable things, good things, worthy things, never come true. Prophecies of this kind are like wars fought in a good cause—they are so rare that they don't count.

Number One with a Bullet
Harper's Magazine

1   [**T**he following is from] "Gulf Discs," a list of sixty-seven songs "with lyrics that need thought in scheduling," sent on January 17 by the Radio Training Department of the British Broadcasting Corporation to music programmers at the BBC's local radio stations. The department advised that broadcasting these songs might be "inappropriate or hurtful" in light of the war in the Persian Gulf; the decision whether or not to exclude them from playlists, however, was left to the local programmers.

Artist	**Song**
Abba	Under Attack
The Alarm	68 Guns
The Animals	We Gotta Get Out of This Place
Joan Baez	The Night They Drove Old Dixie Down
Bangles	Walk Like an Egyptian
Pat Benatar	Love Is a Battlefield
Big Country	Fields of Fire
Blondie	Atomic
Kate Bush	Army Dreamers
Cher	Bang Bang (My Baby Shot Me Down)
Eric Clapton	I Shot the Sheriff
Phil Collins	In the Air Tonight
Elvis Costello	Oliver's Army
Cutting Crew	I Just Died in Your Arms Tonight
Desmond Dekker	Israelites
Dire Straits	Brothers in Arms
Duran Duran	View to a Kill
José Feliciano	Light My Fire
First Choice	Armed and Extremely Dangerous
Roberta Flack	Killing Me Softly
Elton John	Saturday Night's Alright for Fighting
John Lennon	Give Peace a Chance
	Imagine
Bob Marley	Buffalo Soldier
Billy Ocean	When the Going Gets Tough
Donny Osmond	Soldier of Love
Paper Lace	Billy Don't Be a Hero
Queen	Killer Queen
	Flash
Tom Robinson	War Baby
The Specials	Ghost Town
Bruce Springsteen	I'm on Fire
Edwin Starr	War
Status Quo	In the Army Now
Cat Stevens	I'm Gonna Get Me a Gun
Tears for Fears	Everybody Wants to Rule the World
10cc	Rubber Bullets
Stevie Wonder	Heaven Help Us All

For Writing and Discussion

1. In what way does Twain begin to inject his opinions in the relaying of the official report at the beginning of the essay? Give specific examples.

2. How does Twain use *pathos* in the essay? How is *logos* used? In 1906 Twain had long been a public figure whose name carried *ethos*. In what way does Twain add *ethos*? How is *ethos* related to *pathos* in this essay?

3. Compare the account of the Moro massacre with incidents such as the Panama invasion and the Gulf War. How quick was the government to release information about civilian casualties during the capture of Noreiga? To release information about friendly fire deaths during the Gulf War?

4. Governments often make decisions based on information that is not available to the public. How can we as citizens assess such actions? Should we even try to evaluate the rightness or wrongness, the ethics, of our government? Why or why not?

5. Choose one of the songs listed by the BBC and speculate on why the song might be "inappropriate or hurtful" during the Gulf War. (What do the lyrics suggest? To whom might the lyrics be "inappropriate or hurtful"? Is it unpatriotic to listen to the song or to think about the message of the song?)

Practice: Project Censored

Project Censored at Sonoma State University (California) publishes a yearly list of the ten most under-reported stories. Using on-line or traditional print sources, find the latest list in the *Newsletter on Intellectual Freedom,* the *Utne Reader,* or another publication. List reasons that two of the stories might not have received adequate news coverage.

THE POWER OF STYLE: REPETITION

Repetition in writing can be boring and irritating, or it can be powerfully persuasive. Martin Luther King's "Letter from a Birmingham Jail," for instance, contains a 356-word sentence that consists of a series of similarly constructed clauses. The repetition of the structure in the sentence builds drama for the powerful end of the sentence. In "Grief and Mourning for the Night," Twain uses repetition to create *pathos* through a visual image of the dying Moro children:

(continued)

(continued from previous page)

And if they are frightened and crying and in trouble, our pity goes out to them by natural impulse. We see a picture. We see the small forms. We see the terrified faces. We see the tears. We see the small hands clinging in supplication to the mother; but we do not see those children that we are speaking about. We see in their places the little creatures whom we know and love.

By repeating "We see" instead of using a series separated by commas, Twain creates an image that the reader cannot ignore.

SHADOWS OF TRUTH

The word *propaganda* has acquired a negative connotation, suggesting deception or distortion. Yet, technically it refers to any deliberate indoctrination, any promotion of particular ideas. Pope Gregory in 1622 used the term when he founded the Sacred Congregation of Propaganda, a committee to spread the doctrines of Christianity. One might argue that all education involves propaganda; a systematic attempt to teach others involves a selection of facts and focuses that inherently began with someone's or society's biases. High school history books until recently didn't mention the Japanese

© Associated Features, Inc.

internment camps in the United States, but they certainly discussed the fact that America was drawn into World War II when the Japanese bombed Pearl Harbor. And Japanese children, until recently, were not told that their country attacked the American naval base at Pearl Harbor.

Both propaganda and education want your mind—your attention, your loyalty, your support. In general, though, we can draw some distinctions between propaganda and education at its finest. Propaganda seeks to teach *what* to think; education (at its best, remember) seeks to teach students *how* to think. Similarly, propaganda presents only one side of the story. Education seeks to present diverse viewpoints so that students may arrive at "truths" or make informed judgments, or, better yet, helps students collect facts themselves and explore various possibilities before reaching conclusions. Propaganda seeks quick results *(Believe this and vote for me* or *Believe this and buy my product)*; education seeks to teach skills and strategies that are transferable to situations outside the classroom. Ultimately, propaganda seeks to control your thinking; the goal of education (again, at its best) is to *develop* your mind. The next chapter focuses on propaganda "devices," informal fallacies that are used to persuade.

Chapter 11

Common Propaganda Devices

Discussion of propaganda often involves mention of informal fallacies, or material fallacies—so-called because the deceit or distortion is in content rather than in a breach of the rules of argumentation. A common definition of *fallacy* is "error in argument," a definition that suggests a mistake was made unintentionally. Informal fallacies sometimes do contain unintentional errors in reasoning, but often there is something more sinister going on—a deliberate attempt to mislead.

Many of the ways of lying we have discussed so far are commonly used in propaganda. Here we will deal with those devices that are used intentionally, that are carefully considered (often highly paid for) attempts to persuade through manipulating or omitting what may reasonably be considered truths and distorting the content of an argument rather than violating the rules of logic.

Keep in mind that, while we point the finger of blame at politicians and advertisers who want our support and our money, we have all been guilty of short-circuiting the reasoning process: "Mom, please let me go. Everybody else is going." (Sound familiar?)

But here we will focus on informal, or material, fallacies as they are used in propaganda, organized efforts to persuade, rather than on those that are used by individuals. (See Chapter 14 for more discussion of fallacies related to advertising.)

Wrenching from Context

Taking quotations out of their full context for use as support is acceptable and even necessary. The deception occurs when isolated quotations are used to create or imply a meaning different from the original intended meaning. Direct quotations can be used to carry meaning opposite from the original intention, and with spoken statements it is easier than with written statements because of the paralanguage, variations in volume, pitch, and rate of speech that are used to help relay meaning.

"You're *such* a nice person" can be spoken with a sarcastic tone and given a meaning exactly opposite the literal meaning of the words. It can mean, "You're slimy" or "You have the morals of an alley cat" or "You're Atilla the Hun made over."

The following example from fiction illustrates an attempt to use something that was said ironically as an admission of guilt. In Scott Turow's *Presumed Innocent,* Prosecutor Molto accuses fellow prosecutor Rusty Sabich of murder, "You killed her. You're the guy." Sabich responds sarcastically with, "Yeah, you're right."

In court, the defense challenges Molto's status as prosecutor and as witness for the prosecution. Prosecutor Nico Della Guardia wants the right to use Molto as a witness to Sabich's "confession," claiming "the man admitted the crime." Judge Lyttle's response points out the error of **wrenching from context:**

> "Oh, Mr. Delay Guardia," says Judge Lyttle. "Really! You see, that is my point. You tell a man he's engaged in wrongdoing and he says, 'Yeah, you're right.' Everyone recognizes that's facetious. We all are familiar with that. Now, in my neighborhood, had Mr. Sabich come from those parts, he would have said, 'Yo' momma.' . . . But you know, in Mr. Sabich's part of town, I would think people say, 'Yeah, you're right,' and what they mean is 'You are wrong.'"

R E M I N D E R

Wrenching meaning from context or quoting out of context can be done unintentionally if a reader or listener doesn't understand the speaker or writer's original meaning. For that reason, be especially careful when repeating another's words. Also, properly documenting original sources allows your audience to go to the original source and determine whether you have used the information accurately.

OVERSIMPLIFICATION

HASTY GENERALIZATION

Hasty generalizations, conclusions based on insufficient evidence, are often used in propaganda. Stereotyping is one kind of hasty generalization: "Teenage mothers don't know anything about nutrition. Tina feeds her baby potato chips and marshmallows."

FALSE DILEMMA

A false dilemma gives the audience only two choices when actually many more exist. Asking the public to choose between a "Pay or Play" (businesses pay employee insurance or pay into an insurance fund) health insurance plan or a national tax credit for insurance gives the impression that these are the only options for finding ways to insure more people. In fact, more options exist, and many other countries have programs that don't involve insurance companies at all.

BEGGING THE QUESTION

Begging the question is a term used to identify faulty reasoning that occurs when a conclusion is based on an unsupported assumption. A conclusion that people should stop eating beef because chicken is more nutritious begs the questions, "In what way is chicken more nutritious than beef?" and "Is beef inherently unhealthy?"

FALSE ANALOGY

A false analogy compares two things and assumes that because they are alike in some ways, they are alike in all respects. ABC's *Nightline* used a chart to compare the direct investment in the U.S. of Japan ($80 billion) and that of all of Europe ($220 billion). Japan is a country; Europe is a continent made up of more than 30 countries.

STRAW MAN

The straw man fallacy involves misrepresenting an opponent's views in order to refute, or argue against, them. (Example: "My opponent claims he wants to put America first. What that means is simple protectionism, the first step to a socialist society.")

USING IRRELEVANT EVIDENCE
OR SKIRTING THE TRUTH

RED HERRING

When irrelevant information is used to divert attention from the real issue, the information is called a red herring after the smelly fish that can throw off a trailing bloodhound. Red herrings may be in the form of personal attacks, but there are many other ways that irrelevant information may be used to distract from the real issue. Emotional appeals are often used to substitute for logical argument in courtrooms, in political campaigns, and in advertising. The prosecution in the O. J. Simpson trial accused the defense of using a red herring in bringing in the Fuhrman tapes. Prosecutors contended that the tapes were a distraction from the real issue of the guilt or innocence of Simpson.

FALSE USE OF EVIDENCE

Using evidence, no matter how sound, that is not related to the claim can fool a careless audience.

> If you can't prove that your nostrum cures colds, publish a sworn laboratory report that the stuff killed 31,108 germs in a test tube in eleven seconds. There may be no connection at all between assorted germs in a test tube and the whatever-it-is that produces colds, but people aren't going to reason that sharply, especially while sniffling.
>
> Darrell Huff, *How to Lie with Statistics*

FALSE CAUSE

Establishing that one event happened before another is not sufficient evidence to show a relationship between the two incidents or to claim that the first event caused the second. If a black cat crosses a person's path right before an accident, blaming the accident on the cat might be tempting. However, the real cause might be found in the answers to these questions: Was the driver looking where he or she was going? Was he or she paying attention or thinking of something other than the task at hand? Was the person reasonably cautious?

PERSONAL ATTACKS

Mudslinging, smear, and innuendo are common campaign tactics in which an opponent's personal life, lifestyle, personality, or past history is attacked. Whether or not allegations are true, they may have nothing to do with the person's ability to perform the duties required in the elected office. (Example: "My opponent has been seen in a gay bar.")

Mudslinging may also serve as a red herring to divert attention from real issues. Attacking a person's ideas or opinions might involve devices such as "wrenching from context," but there are other ways to do what Aristotle called *argumentum ad hominen.*

SCAPEGOATING

Scapegoating, blaming someone for the mistakes of another, can be used to attack a person or group of people. An individual might be blamed for offenses of other members of his group, or a group might be blamed for the ills of a whole society. (Example: "Immigrant workers are to blame for high unemployment and low wages in our country.")

BORROWING OF PRESTIGE

Borrowing of prestige involves building a connection between something that is widely accepted as positive and something or someone who would like to be widely accepted as positive. For instance, a politician who arranges to be photographed with the president or even with a movie star attempts to borrow some of the popularity and prestige from the other person. **Transfer** is a related term which indicates that the good associated with one person, thing, or idea is transferred to another. For instance, an advertisement might try to build a connection between a product and patriotism, good health, or happiness. An athlete might give an endorsement, or **testimonial** for a brand of athletic shoes. A television preacher might assure you that you will receive your "seed money" back ten-fold if you give your money to God—through that preacher's hands. Different cultures have similar appeals: The Unification Church in Japan has been accused of soliciting donations by telling people that their "ancestors are suffering in hell, and if you really care about your father, you will give money" (CNN interview with Japanese witness, Sept. 15, 1995).

CARD STACKING

Card stacking involves giving only the information that is helpful to make a point and eliminating other relevant information. For instance, a politician might accuse an opponent of not having a plan to solve a particular problem and fail to mention that he doesn't have a plan himself.

APPEALS TO POPULARITY

When the World War II government propaganda machine attempted to persuade those at home to buy organ meats so that other cuts could be used in rations for soldiers, the **bandwagon** appeal proved invaluable. Other

appeals to popularity include the **snob** appeal ("It cost more, but I'm worth it.") and the **plain folks** appeal (A politician who inherited wealth claims to have the same concerns as the middle class).

EMOTIONAL APPEALS

Although appeals to the emotions of the audience are involved in many informal fallacies, the most blatant emotional appeals include appeals to **pity** ("If you sent this man to jail, his four children will not have a father"), to gender, race, or class **identities** ("A real man needs a strong deodorant"), to **physical well-being** ("This toothpaste makes you feel sexy, peppy, and happy!"), and to **emotional health** ("Acme insurance gives you peace of mind").

GLOSSING THE TRUTH WITH LANGUAGE

GLITTERING GENERALITIES

In glittering generalities positive words are used with little real meaning. Words or phrases such as *freedom, brotherly love, decent standard of living,* and *honorable* are used to conjure up positive images, but without real definition as they apply to the situation. Glittering generalities are also used as diversions and are closely related to **borrowing prestige or authority.** For example, "If you elect me, I promise to work toward ensuring that every American enjoys a decent standard of living" makes no real promise for which the candidate could be held accountable.

DOUBLESPEAK

There are many kinds of doublespeak, but one common type is using euphemisms to soften the impact of unpleasantries. For instance, a company that is firing or laying off workers might say that it is "downsizing" because of "negative growth" or "eliminating redundancies in the human resource area"; it is simply "dehiring," "nonretaining," or "selecting out" employees. A proposal to tax Social Security benefits was referred to as a "spending cut" because it would mean that less money would be spent to pay retirees.

For Writing and Discussion

1. A claim, based on five examples, that the children of ministers always become wild as teenagers involves what kind of faulty reasoning? What would it take to make the claim sound? What kind of modification would make the claim more acceptable?

2. If a woman claimed that eating broccoli three days in a row cured her backache, what faulty reasoning seems likely? What questions would you ask to determine the relationship between the broccoli and the backache?

3. A member of Congress is accused of writing 893 bad checks to the House bank in thirteen months. He responds by accusing the president of failing to cooperate with Congress to get a middle-class tax cut. What propaganda ploy is he using?

4. Many of the logical fallacies mentioned in Chapter 7 were included in this chapter because of their frequent use as propaganda techniques. Explain the difference between an error in reasoning and a material fallacy.

5. Describe three examples of emotional appeals—one used in advertising, one used in politics, and one in family or social life.

6. List two examples of doublespeak that have become a part of our daily language.

Practice: Writing a Crank Letter

Write a crank letter to the editor that includes at least two informal fallacies. After you have finished, trade letters with a partner and identify the fallacies your partner has included.

Love Is a Fallacy
Max Schulman

1   Cool was I and logical. Keen, calculating, perspicacious, acute and astute—I was all of these. My brain was as powerful as a dynamo, as precise as a chemist's scales, as penetrating as a scalpel. And—think of it!—I was only eighteen.

2   It is not often that one so young has such a giant intellect. Take, for example, Petey Bellows, my roommate at the university. Same age, same background, but dumb as an ox. A nice enough fellow, you understand, but nothing upstairs. Emotional type. Unstable. Impressionable. Worst of all, a faddist. Fads, I submit, are the very negation of reason. To be swept up in every new craze that comes along, to surrender yourself to idiocy just because everybody else is doing it—this, to me, is the acme of mindlessness. Not, however, to Petey.

3   One afternoon I found Petey lying on his bed with an expression of such distress on his face that I immediately diagnosed appendicitis. "Don't move," I said. "Don't take a laxative. I'll get a doctor."

4   "Raccoon," he mumbled thickly.

5   "Raccoon?" I said, pausing in my flight.

6   "I want a raccoon coat," he wailed.

7   I perceived that his trouble was not physical, but mental. "Why do you want a raccoon coat?"

8   "I should have known it," he cried, pounding his temples. "I should have known they'd come back when the Charleston came back. Like a fool I spent all my money for textbooks, and now I can't get a raccoon coat."

9   "Can you mean," I said incredulously, "that people are actually wearing raccoon coats again?"

10   "All the Big Men on Campus are wearing them. Where've you been?"

11   "In the library," I said, naming a place not frequented by Big Men on Campus.

12   He leaped from the bed and paced the room. "I've got to have a raccoon coat," he said passionately. "I've got to!"

13   "Petey, why? Look at it rationally. Raccoon coats are unsanitary. They shed. They smell bad. They weigh too much. They're unsightly. They—"

14   "You don't understand," he interrupted impatiently. "It's the thing to do. Don't you want to be in the swim?"

15   "No," I said truthfully.

16   "Well, I do," he declared. "I'd give anything for a raccoon coat. Anything!"

17   My brain, that precision instrument, slipped into high gear. "Anything?" I asked, looking at him narrowly.

18   "Anything," he affirmed in ringing tones.

19   I stroked my chin thoughtfully. It so happened that I knew where to get my hands on a raccoon coat. My father had had one in his undergraduate days; it lay now in a trunk in the attic back home. It also happened that Petey had something I wanted. He didn't have it exactly, but at least he had first rights on it. I refer to his girl, Polly Espy.

20   I had long coveted Polly Espy. Let me emphasize that my desire for this young woman was not emotional in nature. She was, to be sure, a girl who excited the emotions, but I was not one to let my heart rule my head. I wanted Polly for a shrewdly calculated, entirely cerebral reason.

21   I was a freshman in law school. In a few years I would be out in practice. I was well aware of the importance of the right kind of wife in furthering a lawyer's career. The successful lawyers I had observed were, almost without exception, married to beautiful, gracious, intelligent women. With one omission, Polly fitted these specifications perfectly.

22   Beautiful she was. She was not yet of pin-up proportions, but I felt sure that time would supply the lack. She already had the makings.

Gracious she was. By gracious I mean full of graces. She had an erectness of carriage, an ease of bearing, a poise that clearly indicated the best of breeding. At table her manners were exquisite. I had seen her at the Kozy Kampus Korner eating the specialty of the house—a sandwich that contained scraps of pot roast, gravy, chopped nuts, and a dipper of sauerkraut—without even getting her fingers moist.

23   Intelligent she was not. In fact, she veered in the opposite direction. But I believed that under my guidance she would smarten up. At any rate, it was worth a try. It is, after all, easier to make a beautiful dumb girl smart than to make an ugly smart girl beautiful.

24   "Petey," I said, "are you in love with Polly Espy?"

25   "I think she's a keen kid," he replied, "but I don't know if you'd call it love. Why?"

26   "Do you," I asked, "have any kind of formal arrangement with her? I mean are you going steady or anything like that?"

27   "No. We see each other quite a bit, but we both have other dates. Why?"

28   "Is there," I asked, "any other man for whom she has a particular fondness?"

29   "Not that I know of. Why?"

30   I nodded with satisfaction. "In other words, if you were out of the picture, the field would be open. Is that right?"

31   "I guess so. What are you getting at?"

32   "Nothing, nothing," I said innocently, and took my suitcase out of the closet.

33   "Where you going?" asked Petey.

34   "Home for the weekend." I threw a few things into the bag.

35   "Listen," he said, clutching my arm eagerly, "while you're home, you couldn't get some money from your old man, could you, and lend it to me so I can buy a raccoon coat?"

36   "I may do better than that," I said with a mysterious wink and closed my bag and left.

37   "Look," I said to Petey when I got back Monday morning. I threw open the suitcase and revealed the huge, hairy, gamy object that my father had worn in his Stutz Bearcat in 1925.

38   "Holy Toledo!" said Petey reverently. He plunged his hands into the raccoon coat and then his face. "Holy Toledo!" he repeated fifteen or twenty times.

39   "Would you like it?" I asked.

40   "Oh yes!" he cried, clutching the greasy pelt to him. Then a canny look came into his eyes. "What do you want for it?"

41   "Your girl," I said, mincing no words.

42   "Polly?" he said in a horrified whisper. "You want Polly?"

43   "That's right."

44   He flung the coat from him. "Never," he said stoutly.

45   I shrugged. "Okay. If you don't want to be in the swim, I guess it's your business."

46   I sat down in a chair and pretended to read a book, but out of the corner of my eye I kept watching Petey. He was a torn man. First he looked at the coat with the expression of a waif at a bakery window. Then he turned away and set his jaw resolutely. Then he looked back at the coat, with even more longing in his face. Then he turned away, but with not so much resolution this time. Back and forth his head swiveled, desire waxing, resolution waning. Finally he didn't turn away at all; he just stood and stared with mad lust at the coat.

47   "It isn't as though I was in love with Polly," he said thickly. "Or going steady or anything like that."

48   "That's right," I murmured.

49   "What's Polly to me, or me to Polly?"

50   "Not a thing," said I.

51   "It's just been a casual kick—just a few laughs, that's all."

52   "Try on the coat," said I.

53   He complied. The coat bunched high over his ears and dropped all the way down to his shoe tops. He looked like a mound of dead raccoons. "Fits fine," he said happily.

54   I rose from my chair. "Is it a deal?" I asked, extending my hand.

55   He swallowed. "It's a deal," he said and shook my hand.

56   I had my first date with Polly the following evening. This was in the nature of a survey; I wanted to find out just how much work I had to do to get her mind up to the standard I required. I took her first to dinner. "Gee, that was a delish dinner," she said as we left the restaurant. Then I took her to a movie. "Gee, that was a marvy movie," she said as we left the theater. And then I took her home. "Gee, I had a sensaysh time," she said as she bade me good night.

57   I went back to my room with a heavy heart. I had gravely underestimated the size of my task. The girl's lack of information was terrifying. Nor would it be enough merely to supply her with information. First she had to be taught to think. This loomed a project of no small dimensions, and at first I was tempted to give her back to Petey. But then I got to thinking about her abundant physical charms and about the way she entered a room and the way she handled a knife and fork, and I decided to make an effort.

58   I went about it, as in all things, systematically. I gave her a course in logic. It happened that I, as a law student, was taking a course in logic myself, so I had all the facts at my finger tips. "Polly," I said to her when I picked her up on our next date, "tonight we are going over to the Knoll and talk."

59   "Oo, terrif," she replied. One thing I will say for this girl: you would go far to find another so agreeable.

60   We went to the Knoll, the campus trysting place, and we sat down under an old oak, and she looked at me expectantly. "What are we going to talk about?" she asked.

61   "Logic."

62   She thought this over for a minute and decided she liked it. "Magnif," she said.

63   "Logic," I said, clearing my throat, "is the science of thinking. Before we can think correctly, we must first learn to recognize the common fallacies of logic. These we will take up tonight."

64   "Wow-dow!" she cried, clapping her hands delightedly.

65   I winced, but went bravely on. "First let us examine the fallacy called Dicto Simpliciter."

66   "By all means," she urged, batting her lashes eagerly.

67   "Dicto Simpliciter means an argument based on an unqualified generalization. For example: Exercise is good. Therefore everybody should exercise."

68   "I agree," said Polly earnestly. "I mean exercise is wonderful. I mean it builds the body and everything."

69   "Polly," I said gently, "the argument is a fallacy. Exercise is good is an unqualified generalization. For instance, if you have heart disease, exercise is bad, not good. Many people are ordered by their doctors not to exercise. You must qualify the generalization. You must say exercise is usually good, or exercise is good for most people. Otherwise you have committed a Dicto Simpliciter. Do you see?"

70   "No," she confessed. "But this is marvy. Do more! Do more!"

71   "It will be better if you stop tugging at my sleeve," I told her, and when she desisted, I continued. "Next, we take up a fallacy called Hasty Generalization. Listen carefully: You can't speak French. I can't speak French. Petey Bellows can't speak French. I must therefore conclude that nobody at the University of Minnesota can speak French."

72   "Really?" said Polly, amazed. "Nobody?"

73   I hid my exasperation. "Polly, it's a fallacy. The generalization is reached too hastily. There are too few instances to support such a conclusion."

74   "Know any more fallacies?" she asked breathlessly. "This is more fun than dancing even."

75   I fought off a wave of despair. I was getting nowhere with this girl, absolutely nowhere. Still, I am nothing if not persistent. I continued. "Next comes Post Hoc. Listen to this: Let's not take Bill on our picnic. Every time we take him out with us, it rains."

76   "I know somebody just like that," she exclaimed. "A girl back home—Eula Becker, her name is. It never fails. Every single time we take her on a picni—"

77   "Polly," I said sharply, "it's a fallacy. Eula Becker doesn't cause the rain. She has no connection with the rain. You are guilty of Post Hoc if you blame Eula Becker."

78   "I'll never do it again," she promised contritely, "Are you mad at me?"

79   I sighed. "No, Polly, I'm not mad."

80   "Then tell me some more fallacies."

81   "All right. Let's try Contradictory Premises."

82   "Yes, let's," she chirped, blinking her eyes happily.

83   I frowned, but plunged ahead. "Here's an example of Contradictory Premises: if God can do anything, can He make a stone so heavy that He won't be able to lift it?"

84   "Of course," she replied promptly.

85   "But if He can do anything, He can lift the stone," I pointed out.

86   "Yeah," she said thoughtfully. "Well, then I guess He can't make the stone."

87   "But He can do anything," I reminded her.

88   She scratched her pretty, empty head. "I'm all confused," she admitted.

89   "Of course you are. Because when the premises of an argument contradict each other, there can be no argument. If there is an irresistible force, there can be no immovable object. If there is an immovable object, there can be no irresistible force. Get it?"

90   "Tell me some more of this keen stuff," she said eagerly.

91   I consulted my watch. "I think we'd better call it a night. I'll take you home now, and you go over all the things you've learned. We'll have another session tomorrow night."

92   I deposited her at the girls' dormitory, where she assured me that she had had a perfectly terrif evening, and I went glumly home to my room. Petey lay snoring in his bed, the raccoon coat huddled like a great hairy beast at his feet. For a moment I considered waking him and telling him that he could have his girl back. It seemed clear that my project was doomed to failure. The girl simply had a logic-proof head.

93   But then I reconsidered. I had wasted one evening; I might as well waste another. Who knew? Maybe somewhere in the extinct crater of her mind a few embers still smoldered. Maybe somehow I could fan them into flame. Admittedly it was not a prospect fraught with hope, but I decided to give it one more try.

94   Seated under the oak the next evening I said, "Our first fallacy tonight is called Ad Misericordiam."

95   She quivered with delight.

96   "Listen closely," I said. "A man applies for a job. When the boss asks him what his qualifications are, he replies that he has a wife and six children at home, the wife is a helpless cripple, the children have nothing to eat, no clothes to wear, no shoes on their feet, there are no beds in the house, no coal in the cellar, and winter is coming."

97   A tear rolled down each of Polly's pink cheeks. "Oh, this is awful, awful," she sobbed.

98   "Yes, it's awful," I agreed, "but it's no argument. The man never answered the boss's question about his qualifications. Instead he appealed to the boss's sympathy. He committed the fallacy of Ad Misericordiam. Do you understand?"

99   "Have you got a handkerchief?" she blubbered.

100   I handed her a handkerchief and tried to keep from screaming while she wiped her eyes. "Next," I said in a carefully controlled tone, "we will discuss False Analogy. Here is an example: Students should be allowed to look at their textbooks during examinations. After all, surgeons have X rays to guide them during an operation, lawyers have briefs to guide them during a trial, carpenters have blueprints to guide them when they are building a house. Why, then, shouldn't students be allowed to look at their textbooks during an examination?"

101   "There now," she said enthusiastically, "is the most marvy idea I've heard in years."

102   "Polly," I said testily, "the argument is all wrong. Doctors, lawyers, and carpenters aren't taking a test to see how much they have learned, but students are. The situations are altogether different, and you can't make an analogy between them."

103   "I still think it's a good idea," said Polly.

104   "Nuts," I muttered. Doggedly I pressed on. "Next we'll try Hypothesis Contrary to Fact."

105   "Sounds yummy," was Polly's reaction.

106   "Listen: if Madame Curie had not happened to leave a photographic plate in a drawer with a chunk of pitchblende, the world today would not know about radium."

107   "True, true," said Polly, nodding her head. "Did you see the movie? Oh, it just knocked me out. That Walter Pidgeon is so dreamy. I mean he fractures me."

108   "If you can forget Mr. Pidgeon for a moment," I said coldly, "I would like to point out that the statement is a fallacy. Maybe Madame Curie would have discovered radium at some later date. Maybe somebody else would have discovered it. Maybe any number of things would have happened. You can't start with a hypothesis that is not true and then draw any supportable conclusions from it."

109   "They ought to put Walter Pidgeon in more pictures," said Polly. "I hardly ever see him any more."

110   One more chance, I decided. But just one more. There is a limit to what flesh and blood can bear. "The next fallacy is called Poisoning the Well."

111   "How cute!" she gurgled.

112   "Two men are having a debate. The first one gets up and says, 'My opponent is a notorious liar. You can't believe a word that he is going to say.' . . . Now, Polly, think. Think hard. What's wrong?"

113   I watched her closely as she knit her creamy brow in concentration. Suddenly a glimmer of intelligence—the first I had seen—came into her eyes. "It's not fair," she said with indignation. "It's not a bit fair. What chance has the second man got if the first man calls him a liar before he even begins talking?"

114   "Right!" I cried exultantly. "One hundred per cent right. It's not fair. The first man has poisoned the well before anybody could drink from it. He

has hamstrung his opponent before he could even start. . . . Polly, I'm proud of you."

115   "Pshaw," she murmured, blushing with pleasure.

116   "You see, my dear, these things aren't so hard. All you have to do is concentrate. Think—examine—evaluate. Come now, let's review everything we have learned."

117   "Fire away," she said with an airy wave of her hand.

118   Heartened by the knowledge that Polly was not altogether a cretin, I began a long, patient review of all I had told her. Over and over and over again I cited instances, pointed out flaws, kept hammering away without letup. It was like digging a tunnel. At first everything was work, sweat, and darkness. I had no idea when I would reach the light, or even if I would. But I persisted. I pounded and clawed and scraped, and finally I was rewarded. I saw a chink of light. And then the chink got bigger and the sun came pouring in and all was bright.

119   Five grueling nights this took, but it was worth it. I had made a logician out of Polly; I had taught her to think. My job was done. She was worthy of me at last. She was a fit wife for me, a proper hostess for my many mansions, a suitable mother for my well-heeled children.

120   It must not be thought that I was without love for this girl. Quite the contrary. Just as Pygmalion loved the perfect woman he had fashioned, so I loved mine. I decided to acquaint her with my feelings at our very next meeting. The time had come to change our relationship from academic to romantic.

121   "Polly," I said when next we sat beneath our oak, "tonight we will not discuss fallacies."

122   "Aw, gee," she said, disappointed.

123   "My dear," I said, favoring her with a smile, "we have now spent five evenings together. We have gotten along splendidly. It is clear that we are well matched."

124   "Hasty Generalization," said Polly brightly.

125   "I beg your pardon," said I.

126   "Hasty Generalization," she repeated. "How can you say that we are well matched on the basis of only five dates?"

127   I chuckled with amusement. The dear child had learned her lessons well. "My dear," I said, patting her hand in a tolerant manner, "five dates is plenty. After all, you don't have to eat a whole cake to know that it's good."

128   "False Analogy," said Polly promptly. "I'm not a cake. I'm a girl."

129   I chuckled with somewhat less amusement. The dear child had learned her lessons perhaps too well. I decided to change tactics. Obviously the best approach was a simple, strong, direct declaration of love. I paused for a moment while my massive brain chose the proper words. Then I began:

130   "Polly, I love you. You are the whole world to me, and the moon and the stars and the constellations of outer space. Please, my darling, say that you will go steady with me, for if you will not, life will be meaningless. I will

languish. I will refuse my meals. I will wander the face of the earth, a sham-
bling, hollow-eyed hulk."

131   There, I thought, folding my arms, that ought to do it.

132   "Ad Misericordiam," said Polly.

133   I ground my teeth. I was not Pygmalion; I was Frankenstein, and my
monster had me by the throat. Frantically I fought back the tide of panic surg-
ing through me. At all costs I had to keep cool.

134   "Well, Polly," I said, forcing a smile, "you certainly have learned your
fallacies."

135   "You're darn right," she said with a vigorous nod.

136   "And who taught them to you, Polly?"

137   "You did."

137   "That's right. So you do owe me something, don't you, my dear? If I
hadn't come along you never would have learned about fallacies."

139   "Hypothesis Contrary to Fact," she said instantly.

140   I dashed perspiration from my brow. "Polly," I croaked, "you mustn't
take all these things so literally. I mean this is just classroom stuff. You know
that the things you learn in school don't have anything to do with life."

141   "Dicto Simpliciter," she said, wagging her finger at me playfully.

142   That did it. I leaped to my feet, bellowing like a bull. "Will you or will
you not go steady with me?"

143   "I will not," she replied.

144   "Why not?" I demanded.

145   "Because this afternoon I promised Petey Bellows that I would go steady
with him."

146   I reeled back, overcome with the infamy of it. After he promised, after
he made a deal, after he shook my hand! "The rat!" I shrieked, kicking up
great chunks of turf. "You can't go with him, Polly. He's a liar. He's a cheat.
He's a rat.

147   "Poisoning the Well," said Polly, "and stop shouting. I think shouting
must be a fallacy too."

148   With an immense effort of will, I modulated my voice. "All right," I said.
"You're a logician. Let's look at this thing logically. How could you choose
Petey Bellows over me? Look at me—a brilliant student, a tremendous intellectual, a man with an assured future. Look at Petey—a knothead, a jitterbug, a
guy who'll never know where his next meal is coming from. Can you give me
one logical reason why you should go steady with Petey Bellows?"

149   "I certainly can," declared Polly. "He's got a raccoon coat."

For Writing and Discussion

1. What is the author's tone? Evaluate the effectiveness of the tone and use
of dialogue in the story.

2. What is the effect of the author's use of a first-person narrator?

3. Explain the irony of the ending of the story, and relate it to the title of the story. Which character does the speaker seem to be mocking? The narrator? Polly? Petey?

4. In what way were the gender roles in the story stereotypical, at least for past decades? Do remnants of the stereotypes persist? If so, in what ways?

Practice: Relating Fallacies

Relate the fallacies identified in "Love Is a Fallacy" to those explained on pages 204–209. Define the fallacies in your own words and provide an example of each.

R E M I N D E R

Fallacies are sometimes distinguished by whether the flaw is with the logic, the reasoning, or the substance of the argument. Arguments that have flawed premises or that fail to include relevant information are informal, or material, fallacies. Arguments that are defective because of violation of a rule of formal logic are called logical fallacies. The most common fallacies and the ones that most concern writers, readers, speakers, and listeners are material fallacies.

THE POWER OF STYLE: USING SLANG IN FICTION

Slang is the language of subcultures. It is sometimes like a password, or code, admitting members who understand its meaning to groups. Although teenagers have made outstanding use of slang, its use did not begin with them. The word *slang* was first used to describe the jargon of British criminals in the 1800s. Early dictionaries described slang as "vulgar" and "of the lower classes." Newer dictionaries, however, describe slang in more flattering terms, referring to it as "colorful" and "vivid" language.

(continued)

(continued from previous page)

The history of teen slang is one of change and recycling. Generally, once the slang of a subculture is picked up by the larger population, the word is discarded and replaced with a new term. Probably another reason teen slang changes is that often it is misunderstood and perverted by adults. The teen expression "hang it up," for instance, might be translated by an adult to "put it in the closet."

Often, the same word might be recycled by different generations of teens but with new meanings. For instance, the word *foxy* meant "clever" or "sly" to one generation, but to another it describes someone who is especially good-looking or who looks "sexy."

Although slang is rarely acceptable in academic writing, it is often used in literature to create realistic characters. Max Schulman's teenage characters in "Love Is a Fallacy" would be stiff and unnatural without the use of slang in the dialogue and in the words of the teenage narrator. Schulman uses slang to help create a "talking" style: he is telling the story to the reader through the persona.

Practice: Analyzing Slang

"Love is a Fallacy" was written in the 1950s. Since that time, many slang words have acquired new meaning or have been discarded and replaced. Identify several of the slang words in "Love is a Fallacy," and tell whether the meaning has changed or whether the word has been replaced with another term.

CHAPTER SUMMARY

In this chapter, you examined some of the many faces of lies and learned how to detect informal fallacies and specious appeals in propaganda. You looked at *ethos, pathos,* and *logos* in their perverted, but all too common, forms. Although even informed citizens can sometimes be pulled in by dubious propaganda, you will be armed with the questions to ask and the skills to navigate through the smoke of lies and shadows of truth.

Chapter 12

WRITING CHALLENGE

Assume you have been assigned by a major magazine to write and report on some aspect of media ethics. The magazine has a general readership, but you have the freedom to take a position and argue that position, using specific examples and support from other sources. Choose one of the following general topics, or ask your instructor to approve another topic that is related to the content of this chapter. Limit the topic by focusing on one or more specific areas or issues. Research your topic using on-line or print sources, and write an argumentative report that includes your findings and your conclusions. Your audience will be a general public who needs to be informed about these issues but who has other immediate concerns. Your challenge will be to make the information both interesting and relevant to a general audience.

Topic Suggestions

Government or industry disinformation

Wartime propaganda

Censorship (textbooks, music, news releases, etc.)

Fake photographs/computer imaging

Special-interest lobbyist

Political doublespeak

Statistical manipulation

Political or marketing polls

An aspect of advertising

Media coverage of an event

Journal Topic Suggestions

- Your response to one of the readings in this chapter
- What you remember about formal and informal fallacies
- When you felt "duped" and why
- What you once believed but now do not

- How to look at the world through an informed, rather than a jaundiced, eye

GUIDE TO WRITING

Planning and Prewriting

CHOOSING A TOPIC

Reports are written summaries of knowledge or experience. The purpose of writing an argumentative report is to inform an audience about a particular topic and persuade that your position is the best position. Reports are based on facts, so you will want to choose a topic that has been researched and discussed in lay and/or professional publications. Any broad topic includes a multitude of smaller, more specific topics.

General Topic	Specific Topic	Even More Specific
Censorship	Wartime censorship	The Office of War Information censorship during World War II

In choosing your topic, you may want to explore a number of topics related to a general topic. You might find ideas by listening for current topics in news reports (the changing role of the press in Russia), watching for related topics in newspapers and magazines (conflicting reports about the Panama invasion), and thinking about things in your own experience (something believed to be true before you learned the facts). If possible, use an on-line search to find articles related to a general topic. (See Part Ten.) Then you can choose a specific topic that interests you.

The following questions will help you decide if the topic you have chosen is appropriate for a report.

1. **Can you find facts about your topic?** Facts are bits of information that can be verified either through observation or through the processes of science. Yes, some "facts" have changed over time with new knowledge; therefore, you want to use up-to-date sources. Since you have limited time, however, you will probably have to rely on publications that, because of time required for the publishing process, are slightly dated, especially in areas of prolific research where knowledge and facts can change daily.

2. **Can the topic be treated in-depth in a short paper?** If your topic is too general, you cannot do justice to the topic and give your reader specific information.

3. **Is your topic interesting to you?** Do you care enough about the subject to take a position on it? Your interest in the topic will encourage you to do the necessary research and make the discovery and writing process more fun. You will have more information about your topic than anyone else in your class, and sharing that information with other students will be fun.

USING SOURCES

The obvious reason to collect information is that we don't know everything there is to know. We might be able to express our feelings or opinions about a number of topics, but when it comes to hard data, we need help, and for that help, we must give credit—we must document sources.

THREE REASONS TO DOCUMENT SOURCES

1. Not giving credit to sources implies the information is original, that you wrote it. If you did not, omitting your source constitutes *plagiarism,* a serious offense. You already know that putting your name on someone else's work is plagiarism; however, borrowing or buying a paper is not the only form of plagiarism.
2. Using properly documented sources lends *credibility* to your paper. No, you are not an expert, but you know how to find information from experts.
3. Documentation provides your reader with the information necessary to do *further research.*

PLAGIARISM

Plagiarism—passing off someone else's work as your own—is serious, and unintentional plagiarism can carry the same consequences. Consequences can include public embarrassment and shame, failure of a course, or expulsion from school. The following constitute plagiarism:

- Padding a bibliography by including entries that are not cited in the paper. (A *Works Consulted* heading includes works that are consulted but not cited.)
- Quoting from a secondary source without identifying it as such.
- Using exact phrases and sentences from the original source under the guise of paraphrasing.
- Failing to document a summary or paraphrase of someone else's ideas.
- Omitting quotation marks around directly quoted material.

(For help incorporating the words of others into your report, see The Power of Style: Using Paraphrases, Summaries, and Quotations on page 230.)

R E M I N D E R

In report writing, the focus is on the information, not the writer. The personal pronouns *I*, *me*, and *mine* are rarely used. However, you will find exceptions in some excellent reports in which the writer includes a relevant personal experience.

GATHERING INFORMATION

Part Ten provides information on using the references in the library. Pay special attention to the activity that will prepare you to use on-line sources. Use discretion when selecting sources from the CD-ROM or on-line magazine banks and the *Reader's Guide*. Although the sources contain many reliable publications that will be credible sources for your report, some publications will have a slanted view or brief and unsupported articles. (See Chapter 13 for information on bias in reporting.)

R E M I N D E R

Copying title and copyright pages from books and writing down publication information for magazines and journals will save time when you start to prepare your Works Cited page.

INTERVIEWING EXPERTS

If you ask an expert for interview time, be sure to have your questions prepared in advance. To avoid getting yes or no answers, ask questions that begin with Who, What, When, Where, Why, and How. Put each question at the top of a separate sheet of paper to allow plenty of room for recording answers. If you plan to use a direct quotation, read it back to the expert, and make corrections if necessary. In addition to getting information from experts in particular fields, you can also get leads on additional good sources during an interview. Ask the expert to recommend books or articles on your topic, and write down title and author information, including spelling of the author's name if necessary.

R E M I N D E R

Write down the names and titles of your experts as well as dates of the interviews for your Works Cited page.

TELEVISION NEWS

If you hear information about your topic on a news broadcast, listen carefully and try to paraphrase the information accurately in quick notes. If the broadcast will be aired at a later time, watch again to verify your notes. If the information is about a research study, you may find the same information with more in-depth coverage in a newspaper—either a past issue or the next day's issue, depending on the kind of story. Some stories are reported first on television; others are taken from newspaper reports for television commentary.

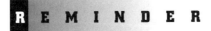

R E M I N D E R

Write down the name of the commentator, date and time, station, and network for your Works Cited page.

FORMULATING QUESTIONS

To prepare yourself for your reading, freewrite your knowledge about and feelings and attitudes toward your topic, and write down questions to answer during your research. A writer preparing a paper on music censorship, for instance, might include questions similar to these:

1. Does censorship include rating tapes and CDs? Putting them behind the counter? Making minors show IDs to buy them?
2. Do other countries censor music? Do they censor performing artists?
3. What is the definition of *pornography* as related to music?
4. What are the effects of music on kids? On adults? *Are* there measurable effects of music, or is all the hub-bub simply psychobabble?
5. How does the First Amendment apply to music?

5W-HOW QUESTIONS

From the questions *Who? What? Where? When? Why?* and *How?*, answer those questions that apply to your report.

What?	Censorship of some music
Who?	Courts, mad mothers, and the religious right
Where?	In music stores and at concerts
When?	Contemporary, during the past year
Why?	Some groups claim that music can influence kids to commit suicide, homicide, etc.

How?   Groups advocate X-ratings for records and age limits for
             concerts

READING AND NOTETAKING

If you are required to keep a journal for this or another class, you may
want to do some of your prewriting as a journal entry.

AUDIENCE AWARENESS

Consider your audience as you collect information for your report. Ask
yourself these questions:

1. How can I make my audience care about this issue?
2. What information will interest my readers?
3. What information do my readers need?
4. What do my readers already know? (The only reason to include
   information that is common knowledge is to emphasize a point.)
5. Do I need to define any terms?
6. How can I hold my reader's attention?

T I P

**If you have a stack of copies to read from books and periodicals,
you may want to make a master list of codes or colors to use as
you read to help with organization later. For instance, you might
use different-colored highlighters to mark information and quotations as you read that are related to aspects of your paper
(green for recent cases of music censorship; orange for reasons
cited to support censorship, and so on). You might also make a
code list for each source. When you begin work on each section
of your first draft, reread the highlighted areas, and include the
information, source code, and page number. Using copies of
your source material as you work prevents the need to write out
notes and the risk of miscopying and misquoting information. It
saves time.**

If you prefer the traditional method of using notecards, see Part Ten.

ORGANIZING AND DRAFTING

DEVELOPING A THESIS

A thesis will be an assertion, and you will provide information to support that assertion. To develop a thesis statement, write on your scrap paper:

> The purpose of my report is to convince my readers that <u>the American people were given incorrect information about the Panama invasion.</u>

Discard the first part of the sentence. You can use the independent clause after the word *that* as your thesis statement. (There is some distinction between a purpose and a thesis. A purpose may be to inform readers about sexist language in advertising; a thesis may be to demonstrate that sexist language has decreased during the past ten years in most kinds of advertising.)

R E M I N D E R

Developing a thesis, a main claim of the report early on, will guide you in knowing which information to include and how to organize your report. However, your thesis may change as you read more and begin writing.

LISTING AND OUTLINING

Keep in mind your thesis statement as you develop an outline. A helpful outline may begin as a simple list of main points for a more structured outline. If you do take the time to write a fairly complete, though informal, outline, your report will be much easier to write. The following rough outline on sexist language in advertising would make the drafting part of the writing process move smoothly.

Introduction--grab the reader
        include definition of "sexist language"
        include general information about findings
        give clue to findings
Body--inform the reader
        Part I   sexist language in ads directed at men
                1. television ads
                      include data on average viewing
                      include examples
                      compare and contrast ads for different kinds of products

2. magazine ads
   include data on audience--lay or professional
   compare and contrast examples of each
   give facts on change from 1980s to '90s

Part II   sexist language in ads directed at women
   1. television ads
      include data on average viewing
      include examples
      compare and contrast ads for different kinds of
      products
   2. magazine ads
      include data on audience--lay or professional
      compare and contrast examples of each
      give facts on change from 1980s to '90s

Part III sexist language in ads directed at children
   1. television ads
      include data on average viewing
      include examples
      compare and contrast ads for different kinds of
      products
   2. ads on toys and cereal boxes
      include examples
      include facts on change from 1980s to '90s

Conclusion--summarize findings
   relate to introduction/thesis
   include trend analysis from data

R E M I N D E R

Organization for reports may be chronological, spatial, classification, least-to-most-important order, or most-to-least-important order, depending on the kinds of details and supporting information (see page 46). See page 47 for help with introductions and page 94 for help with conclusions.

WAYS TO DEVELOP AN ARGUMENTATIVE REPORT

How you develop your report depends on the kind of information you have and how you plan to use it to increase your reader's understanding of your subject. You may use several of the following developmental strategies.

Definition Definition is especially important in report writing. Even simple terms may need to be defined, especially the key term in your report.

For instance, the word *censorship* is familiar to most people, yet censorship can mean *banning, restricting,* or *rating.* Make sure your reader understands how you are using the word in your paper.

Narration   You may include anecdotes, or brief stories, in your report as examples. If so, you will probably organize the story in time order, and you will probably precede the story with a statement that ties the story to your report.

Description and Illustration   You may find it necessary to describe something or someone for your reader. Illustration is simply an extended description, a word picture in which examples, facts, and anecdotes are used to help the reader "see" what the writer sees.

Classification   Separating details and supporting ideas into categories based on similar aspects is a good way to begin organization. In the outline (pages 227–228), details are classified according to gender and age of the audience (ads directed at men, ads directed at women, ads directed at children). Categorizing is necessary if you plan to compare and contrast things, people, or ideas.

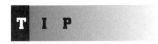

If you are using a word processor, you can develop a code list for your sources and use your search-and-replace feature to speed up documentation. Example: Code 1A = Shaughnessy, Mina. *Errors and Expectations.* New York: Oxford UP, 1977. Type the code 1A 3 (3 = the page number on which the information is located) in your draft; replace 1A with *Shaughnessy.*

USING HEADINGS AND LISTS

Your instructor may prefer that you do not include headings in your final report. However, you can use headings and lists to help organize your draft as you write. As you revise your draft, eliminate the headings, replacing them with transitional sentences. Any lists that you included in your rough draft can be rewritten in sentence form.

Business writing differs from academic writing in that you will use headings, lists, and white space to help your busy reader find information fast. Managers and executives write reports on everything from proposed budgets for multi-million dollar projects to daily production on the assembly line; police officers write reports on everything from crime scenes to traffic accidents; social workers write case reviews—the list goes on.

Regardless of the field you enter, you will be required to write many different kinds of reports as a professional, and clear presentation becomes part of your *ethos*.

R E M I N D E R

Avoid "blocking" (writing by logical order all of the information from Source A, then from Source B, and so on) by skipping lines in each section to remind yourself to insert material you may need to obtain from other sources.

THE POWER OF STYLE: USING PARAPHRASES, SUMMARIES, AND QUOTATIONS

Use only direct quotations that are especially interesting, authoritative, or so technical that you are afraid you might make a mistake in paraphrasing. Even so, use quotations sparingly and keep them short.

The differences among summaries, paraphrases, and quotations can be confusing. The following exercise is designed to help you determine when to use each of these methods of citing sources, how to write each one, and how to incorporate these passages into the body of your essay. The following example shows you some of the possibilities.

Original passage from the source
For [grunge music's] primary audience, white male teens, [the idea of] damage offers a defense against the claims of gangsta rappers and punk rock feminists. It's a great equalizer at a time when multiculturism seems to have devolved into competing schools of victimization. Grunge appeals to white kids because it tells them that they're not responsible for the evils of racism and injustices, that they are victims too.

Ferguson, Sarah. "The Comfort of Being Sad." *Utne Reader* July-Aug. 1994: 60.

Summary

Grunge music provides a defense for white male teens by validating the harm done to them and providing them equal victim status, thereby absolving them of the blame of the country's sins (Ferguson 60).

Paraphrase

Grunge music's main audience of white teenaged males finds a defense in the music against radical rappers and feminists rockers who claim victim status. The message of grunge music equalizes the claim. The message is that white males are also victims who should not be accountable for racism and injustice (Ferguson 60).

Direct quotation

"For grunge's primary audience, white male teens, damage offers a defense against the claims of gangsta rappers and punk rock feminists" and "appeals to white kids because it tells them that they're not responsible for the evils of racism and injustices, that they are victims too" (Ferguson 60).

Paraphrase with quoted material

Grunge music's main audience of white teenaged males finds a defense in the music against "gangsta rappers and punk rock feminists" who claim victim status. The message of grunge music equalizes the claim. The message is that white males are also victims who are "not responsible for the evils of racism and injustices" (Ferguson 60).

Quotation with ellipsis

"For (grunge music's) primary audience, white male teens, damage offers a defense against the claims of gangsta rappers and punk rock feminists. . . . Grunge appeals to white kids because it tells them that they're not responsible for the evils of racism and injustices, that they are victims too." (Ferguson 60)

R E M I N D E R

Do not overuse direct quotations in brief reports. Including more than five or six lines of directly quoted material in a three- or four-page report is excessive. The report should be in your words; use the words of others sparingly. Quoted passages of more than four lines are indented ten spaces from the left margin, and the documentation is placed outside the period.

Practice: Examining a Summary, Paraphrase, and Quotation

Carefully study the passages above, and answer the questions according to what you have observed.

Summary

1. How many words are used in the original source?
2. How many words are used in the summary?
3. Is the order of words and sentences changed from the original source in the summary?
4. Are any words or phrases taken directly from the original source? If so, list them.
5. What is the main value in writing a summary?

Paraphrase

1. Is the word or sentence order changed from the original source?
2. How does a paraphrase differ from a summary?
3. What are the advantages of a paraphrase?

Direct quotation

1. Does a direct quotation differ in *any way* from the original?
2. Why use a direct quotation?

Paraphrase with quoted material

1. Why are the two sections enclosed in quotation marks?
2. Why quote some phrases from the original?
3. What is the difference between a complete paraphrase and a paraphrase with quoted material?

Quotation with ellipsis

1. What words or phrases from the original are omitted by the *first* ellipsis?
2. What words or phrases from the original are omitted by the *second* ellipsis?

3. Why does the second ellipsis consist of four spaced periods instead of three?

4. Why is the phrase "grunge music's" placed in brackets?

Practice: Writing a Summary, Paraphrase, and Quotation

Based on the following original passage from page 19 of *Mediaspeak*, by Donna Woolfolk Cross, write (1) a summary, (2) a paraphrase, (3) a direct quotation, (4) a paraphrase with quoted material, and (5) a quotation with ellipsis.

> Corporate America is continually inventing new ailments in order to create a demand for their manufactured ministrations. The rate at which our human frailty is advancing is truly alarming. We are afflicted by "underarm wetness," "dandruff shoulders," and "feminine itching"— not to mention "that occasional discomfort."

R E M I N D E R

Include parenthetical documentation as you go, even if in an abbreviated form. Especially important is including the page number on which you read information. Backtracking is no fun. See Part Ten for information on using parenthetical documentation and on preparing a Works Cited page.

THE POWER OF STYLE: USING TRANSITIONS

Transitions serve as pointers to guide your reader from one idea to the next and from one major division in your paper to the next. When properly used, transitions also clarify and add sophistication to your writing.

Without transition: The two graduates applied for the same job. Only one was qualified for the position.

With transition: The two graduates applied for the same job; however, only one was qualified for the position.

Evaluating and Revising

You have already finished the most time-consuming part of your writing process. You have gathered information, and you have written a draft that includes selected information to support a thesis. Now you can focus your energies on perfecting your paper. Before you offer your paper to a partner for evaluation and suggestions, read your draft over with the following questions in mind:

1. Have I maintained a focus on my thesis?
2. Have I included information that does not support the main point of my paper? (Cutting is a painful, but necessary, process.)
3. Are the divisions of my paper logical? Is each paragraph united by a main idea, or topic sentence?
4. In what ways have I established my credibility?
5. What tone would work best for my topic?
6. Do the beginning and ending work together to frame the report?
7. Can I eliminate wordiness? (The following activity will give you practice in eliminating wordiness. After you have completed the activity, look through your paper for buried subjects and verbs and wordy or redundant phrases.)

Practice: Focusing on the Real Subject.

In the sentences below, the real subject is buried. *There* or *it* (expletives) becomes the grammatical subject of the sentence instead of the real subject. Revise the following sentences, eliminating the expletives and emphasizing the real subject by placing it first in the sentence.

1. It is a part of the process of writing to explore ideas through prewriting.
2. There are many prewriting techniques such as brainstorming.

In the following sentences, the real subject is buried in a prepositional phrase. Revise the sentences, placing the real subject in the lead position.

1. The idea of the brainstorming technique was developed in corporate board rooms.
2. The use of this method was found to produce exciting and innovative ideas.

Practice: Focusing on the Real Verb

Just like buried subjects, buried verbs muddy and lengthen sentences. Verbs are usually buried when they are turned into nouns and when another verb is added. Revise the following sentences to eliminate unnecessary words and make the real verb do its job. (Watch for *-tion* endings. They often indicate a verb that has been changed to a noun.)

1. An investigation of a variety of ideas is conducted during brain-storming sessions.
2. Brainstorming is a way to effect the production of creative ideas.

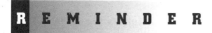

R E M I N D E R

Paragraphs help guide your reader. Each paragraph should contain only information directly related to the main idea of the paragraph.

PARTNER EVALUATION

Read your partner's paper through carefully, making check marks beside passages that are unclear or that you suspect have some other kind of problem. First, write out your initial response to the paper, noting positive aspects and possible problems. (Was it interesting? Did you learn something?) (Was any part of it confusing?) Next, respond to each of the questions below on a separate sheet of paper. Bracket on your partner's paper any sentences that are unclear or that you believe contain errors in usage or mechanics.

Evaluation checklist

1. What is the writer's main point? Was the writer's thesis clear in the introduction?
2. Did the writer include sufficient information about the subject? Is any of the information confusing? If so, ask the writer to clarify it. Do you have questions about some of the information, perhaps whether it is up-to-date or credible? If so, write your questions.
3. Is any of the information unnecessary? Suggest information that the writer might consider cutting.
4. For each body paragraph tell the main idea, the method of development (narration, description, classification, evaluation), and the kinds of support (facts, examples, reasons).
5. Is the information logically organized? Can you suggest another organization. If so, write down the change of sequence.
6. Do transitions guide you from one idea to the next and from one group of ideas (paragraph) to the next? If not, note the problem area.
7. Is the writer's attitude toward and treatment of the subject consistent? If not, point out changes in the writer's tone.

Editing and Proofreading

EDITING CHECKLIST

1. Check your manuscript for sentences that could be combined.
    Example: The news media now prints information about celebrities'
    private lives. It prints information about politicians' private lives, too.
    Combination: The news media now prints information about the
    private lives of celebrities and politicians.
2. Check your manuscript for subject/verb agreement.
    Example: The main point of the examples are to help readers
    understand the difficult theory.
    Revision: The main point of the examples *is* to help readers under-
    stand the difficult theory. (*Point* is the subject of the sentence.)

R E M I N D E R

**The verb matches the subject of a sentence in number. The sub-
ject is never found in a prepositional phrase. Singular verbs in
the present tense end in -s; plural forms don't:**

It is.	They are.
She runs.	He and she run.
He sings.	They sing.

You is treated as a plural verb: You are. You run. You sing.

3. Check your manuscript for unnecessary shifts in verb tense.
    Example: Research scientists *studied* the role of language acquisition
    in learning a foreign language. Scientists *discover* that language *is*
    difficult to learn after about age 12; however, young children *have
    learned* second languages easily.
    Note the unnecessary shift in verb tense from past (studied) to pre-
    sent (discover, is) to past participle (have learned).
4. Make sure that each comma is consistent with the comma rules
    (page 53) and that each sentence has an appropriate end mark.
5. Check homophones (words that sound alike) such as *to, two, too*
    and *there, they're, their* and use a dictionary to find the correct
    spelling of difficult words. (Word processing spell checkers are not
    useful in finding misspelled homophones.)
6. Type your final draft according to the manuscript rules in Part Ten
    or according to your instructor's directions.

PROOFREADING

Proofread your final manuscript before handing it in. You have probably read this advice before, but here it is again: Reading your paper aloud, or at least moving your mouth for every word, will help you catch sentence problems.

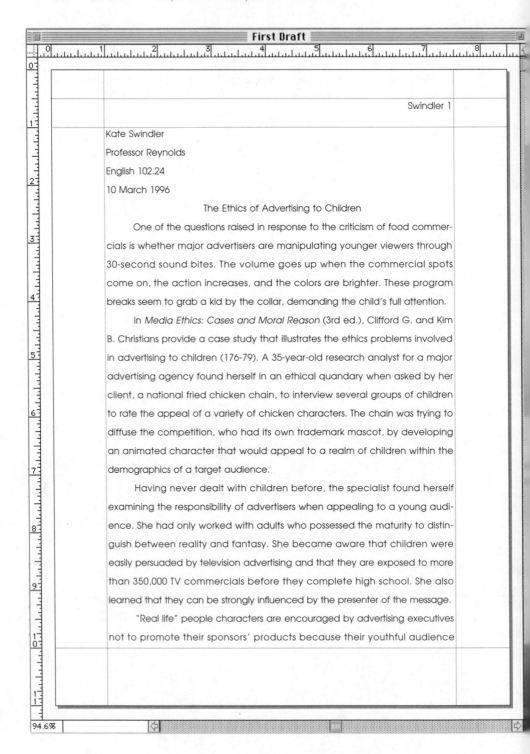

Swindler 1

Kate Swindler

Professor Reynolds

English 102.24

10 March 1996

The Ethics of Advertising to Children

One of the questions raised in response to the criticism of food commercials is whether major advertisers are manipulating younger viewers through 30-second sound bites. The volume goes up when the commercial spots come on, the action increases, and the colors are brighter. These program breaks seem to grab a kid by the collar, demanding the child's full attention.

In *Media Ethics: Cases and Moral Reason* (3rd ed.), Clifford G. and Kim B. Christians provide a case study that illustrates the ethics problems involved in advertising to children (176-79). A 35-year-old research analyst for a major advertising agency found herself in an ethical quandary when asked by her client, a national fried chicken chain, to interview several groups of children to rate the appeal of a variety of chicken characters. The chain was trying to diffuse the competition, who had its own trademark mascot, by developing an animated character that would appeal to a realm of children within the demographics of a target audience.

Having never dealt with children before, the specialist found herself examining the responsibility of advertisers when appealing to a young audience. She had only worked with adults who possessed the maturity to distinguish between reality and fantasy. She became aware that children were easily persuaded by television advertising and that they are exposed to more than 350,000 TV commercials before they complete high school. She also learned that they can be strongly influenced by the presenter of the message.

"Real life" people characters are encouraged by advertising executives not to promote their sponsors' products because their youthful audience

Swindler 2

places so much trust in them. However, animated characters are pitching wares from one network to the next, and many children find them as believable as the "real life" figures. Popeye is as real to them as Mr. Rogers.

Advertised foods are said to be related to attributes irrelevant to their inherent food value, including sweet taste of flavors, fun, adventure, hero figures and other likable characters. Children get the impression that eating such sugary, fatty products is consistent with good health, as is implied by showing happy, healthy children enjoying these products in commercials.

The specialist mentioned earlier centers her thinking on her duty to the families of the children to whom her fantasy character will be pandering. Will her fantasy character turn kids into droning little nags who drive their parents to the brink for this particular food item? She concluded that the company and the agency seemed on the right track and that nothing in the message itself or in the use of the chicken character would infringe upon any business, media, or government guidelines. She supported her opinion by supposing that the parents are adults who will make the ultimate decision whether or not to purchase the product. She continued to screen children on which costume, voice, and overall image they liked best.

When faced with the ethical paradox, the specialist overlooked the utilitarian code espoused by British philosopher John Stuart Mill. In his *Principle of Utility*, Mill claims that choosing the morally correct option constitutes the symmetry of good over evil (*Media Ethics* 15). In this approach, Mill seeks the greatest happiness for the greatest number of people. The end-all of this philosophy is happiness for everyone.

Under this doctrine, there should be a way to advertise to pique the interest of children without blasting covetous messages that transform them into an army of mindless gluttons. Utilitarianism depends on our making accurate measurements of the consequences.

94.6%

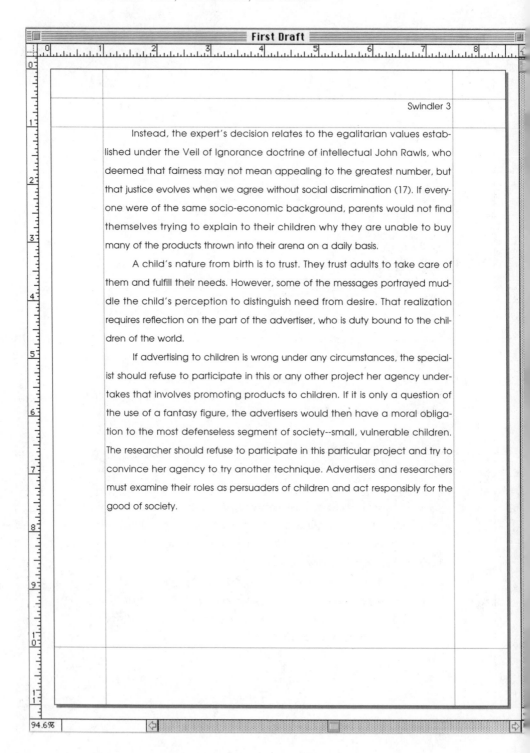

First Draft

Swindler 3

Instead, the expert's decision relates to the egalitarian values established under the Veil of Ignorance doctrine of intellectual John Rawls, who deemed that fairness may not mean appealing to the greatest number, but that justice evolves when we agree without social discrimination (17). If everyone were of the same socio-economic background, parents would not find themselves trying to explain to their children why they are unable to buy many of the products thrown into their arena on a daily basis.

A child's nature from birth is to trust. They trust adults to take care of them and fulfill their needs. However, some of the messages portrayed muddle the child's perception to distinguish need from desire. That realization requires reflection on the part of the advertiser, who is duty bound to the children of the world.

If advertising to children is wrong under any circumstances, the specialist should refuse to participate in this or any other project her agency undertakes that involves promoting products to children. If it is only a question of the use of a fantasy figure, the advertisers would then have a moral obligation to the most defenseless segment of society--small, vulnerable children. The researcher should refuse to participate in this particular project and try to convince her agency to try another technique. Advertisers and researchers must examine their roles as persuaders of children and act responsibly for the good of society.

94.6%

PART FIVE

MediaSpeak

There are two ways by which the spirit of a culture may be shriv-
eled. In the first—the Orwellian—culture becomes a prison. In the
second—the Huxleyan—culture becomes a burlesque. . . .

What Huxley teaches is that in the age of advanced technol-
ogy, spiritual devastation is more likely to come from an enemy
with a smiling face than from one whose countenance exudes sus-
picion and hate. In the Huxleyan prophecy, Big Brother does not
watch us, by his choice. We watch him, by ours. There is no need
for wardens or gates or Ministries of Truth. When a population be-
comes distracted by trivia, when cultural life is redefined as a per-
petual round of entertainments, when serious public conversation
becomes a form of baby-talk, when, in short, a people become an
audience and their public business a vaudeville act, then a nation
finds itself at risk; culture-death is a clear possibility.

Neil Postman, *Amusing Ourselves to Death*

Chapter 13

PRIME TIME AND PRIME NEWS

That much of our information comes to us via television is no surprise. It is surprising, however, that by the time an infant born today starts first grade, she will have watched 10,000 hours of television and seen 150,000 commercials. And by the time she graduates from high school, she will have watched 30,000 hours of television and seen between 350,000 and 600,000 commercials. Television, in fact, becomes another kind of feeding by which we grow: not only do we absorb information from television but also we are affected by the source itself.

After the presidential debate between John Kennedy and Richard Nixon, of those who listened to the debate on the radio, a majority thought Nixon had won. Of those who watched the debate on television, a majority thought Kennedy had won. Although Nixon was no slouch at using television to his advantage (see the "Checkers" speech, page 330), the tall and suave Kennedy was judged by viewers as superior to Nixon. Kennedy's demeanor on television influenced the viewer's perception of what he said.

Since then, the power of television has revealed itself in other ways. In *Mediaspeak: How Television Makes Up Your Mind,* Donna Woolfolk Cross illustrates the power of television to control:

> Our work, our play, our sleep, our lovemaking—all are regulated by television. So are our bathroom habits. Municipal water departments report that water pressure dips dramatically during commercials and at the end of television programs as people leave their sets to go to the bathroom. During the first TV broadcast of the movie *Airport,* the Layfayette, Louisiana, water department reported that for an entire half hour, from the moment a bomb exploded on board a plane to the moment the pilot landed safely at the end, almost nobody left the television set. Then, at the conclusion of the broadcast, twenty thousand people flushed eighty thousand gallons of water at the same time, causing a twenty-five-pound drop in water pressure! Oddly enough, this alternative to the Nielson rating has been overlooked by advertisers who want to judge how successful a television program is. (2)

And to many observers, the successful programs have created a nation of spectators who are spoon-fed an artificial reality. Sometimes that artificial reality entertains; sometimes it informs; at other times, it persuades.

In addition to the power of television itself, there are accusations that both the television and print news media are unreasonably biased. Prominent political thinker and linguist Noam Chomsky argues that the government and industrialists control the news media:

> I think it is one of the best established conclusions in the social sciences that the media serve what we may call a propaganda function—that is, that they shape perceptions, select the events, offer interpretations, and so on, in conformity with the needs of the power centers in society, which are basically the state and the corporate world. (In an interview with Rick Szykowny, *The Humanist* "Bewildering the Herd," Nov./Dec. 1990, 9)

Chomsky says the exposure of Watergate, often offered as support that the media actually play an adversarial role to government, illustrates his point: The victims in the case were powerful also; the press played their roles as championing the powerful while ignoring what Chomsky claims was a much more important story—the FBI COINTELPRO operations, which included "political assassinations, instigation of ghetto riots, a long series of burglaries and harassment against a legal political party—namely, the Socialist Workers Party, which, unlike the Democratic party, is not powerful and did not have the capacity to defend itself" (9).

Chomsky cites another example to demonstrate that the press, even when in a clearly adversarial role, glosses over important reality. He notes that during the Iran/Contra scandal, the press evaded the obvious question: "What was happening before 1985?"

> *Before 1985,* the United States was authorizing the sale of arms to Iran via Israel—exactly as it was doing *after 1985.* Now at that time, remember, there were no hostages. So what's going on? If the whole operation was supposed to be an arms-for-hostages deal, how come we were doing exactly the same thing before there were any hostages? (11)

On the other hand, many conservatives claim that news media are controlled by just such liberal academics as Chomsky himself. In *That's The Way It IsN'T,* L. Brent Boswell and Brent H. Baker cite studies using the Nexis computer system that reveal significant differences in labeling of individuals or groups as *conservative* or *liberal,* with an indication that *liberal* is mainstream and *conservative* is not. The authors also cite surveys that reveal that more journalists vote Democratic and that they most often have liberal personal opinions on major issues. And Boswell and Baker give conservative versions of statements made by what they call the liberal press. Below are two examples:

PRESS VERSION

"Once the Kremlin was the home of czars. Today it belongs to the people. . . . Atheist though the state may be, freedom to worship is enshrined in the Soviet Constitution." (From the TBS program *Portrait of the Soviet Union,* March 1988.)

CONSERVATIVE VERSION

"The Kremlin, once the home of czars, now belongs to the party elite. . . . Freedom to worship is enshrined in the Soviet Constitution, but the gulag is full of those who took that guarantee seriously." (Boswell and Baker 12)

PRESS VERSION (CONTINUED)

"Ah yes. The dreaded federal deficit, created, for the most part, by the most massive peacetime military buildup in America's history." (Reporter Jim Wooten on ABC's *Nightline,* January 29, 1990.)

CONSERVATIVE VERSION (CONTINUED)

"Ah yes. The dreaded federal deficit, created, for the most part, by the most massive federal social spending drive in America's history." (Boswell and Baker 14)

So, there you have it—or *don't* have it. Perhaps the answer to the question of control of the media lies somewhere in the middle, or perhaps there is no grand conspiracy—just a string of accidental complicities. Andrew Glass of Cox Newspapers, when questioned about the frivolous nature of some of the reporter's questions at a presidential press conference, noted that the press strives to engage serious debate, yet, "On some days we're a craft; on some days we're a trade; on other days—well, I don't even want to say" (*Crossfire,* CNN, 11 June 1992).

In this chapter you will be asked to think about the role of media and to evaluate the boundaries of that role. The readings in Chapter 13 will take you from the viewer's living room to behind the scenes in the newsroom. You will hear from journalists such as Molly Ivins, Dan Rather, Sydney Harris, and Nora Ephron, who take a reflective look at their trades. In Chapter 14, you will be asked to think about the role advertising plays in the media, and you will learn how perceptions are created by professionals.

The Make-Believe Media
Michael Parenti

Media images influence how we appraise a host of social realities.

1   *Make-believe.* The word connotes the playful games and fantasies of our childhood—a pleasant way of pretending. But in the world created by movies and television, make-believe takes on a more serious meaning. In some way or other, many people come to believe the fictional things they see on the big and little screens. The entertainment media are the make-believe media; they make us believe.

2   Today, instead of children's games, storytelling, folk tales, and fables of our own making, we have the multibillion-dollar industries of Hollywood and television to fill our minds with prefabricated images and themes. Nor are these just idle distractions, for such images often have real ideological content. Even if supposedly not political in intent, the entertainment industry has been political in its impact, discouraging critical perceptions of our social order while planting pictures in our heads that have been supportive of U.S. militarism, armed intervention abroad, phobic anti-communism, authoritarian violence, consumer acquisitiveness, racial and sexual stereotypes, vigilantism, simple-minded religiosity, and anti-working-class attitudes.

3   Remarking on the prevalence of media-induced stereotypes of African-Americans, Ellen Holly put it well: "Again and again, I have seen black actors turned down for parts because they were told that they did not look the way a black person should or sound the way a black person should. What is this business of 'should'? What kind of box are we being put into? I have seen black writers told that the black characters they put down on a page were not believable because they were too intelligent."

4   Studies show that women, too, are put in a box: portrayed mostly in subsidiary roles and depicted as less capable, effective, or interesting than the more numerous white male principals. To be sure, things have changed somewhat. Women can now be seen playing lawyers, judges, cops, executives, professionals, and sometimes even workers, but the questions of gender equality and the fight for feminist values are seldom joined. Likewise, the struggles of sleep-starved, under-paid single mothers trying to raise their children and survive in an inhospitable environment are not usually considered an appropriate theme for prime-time television or Hollywood.

5   Working people of both genders and whatever ethnic background are still underrepresented in the media. With few exceptions, such as the movie *Norma Rae,* they play minor walk-on roles as waiters, service people, gas station attendants, and the like in an affluent, upper-middle-class, media-created world. Blue-collar people are portrayed as emotional, visceral, simple-hearted

and simple-minded, and incapable of leadership or collective action against the injustices they face in their workplace and community. Their unions are depicted as doing more harm than good for them. Given the hostility that network and studio bosses have manifested toward organized labor in the entertainment industry, it is small wonder that labor unions are almost always portrayed—if at all—in an unsympathetic light.

6   Generally speaking, whether it's a movie about factory workers, cops and crime, or the invasion of galactic monsters, it is individual heroics rather than collective action that save the day. Solutions and victories are never won by ordinary good people, organizing and struggling for mutual betterment, but by the hero in self-willed combat, defying the odds and sometimes even the authorities to vanquish the menace and triumph.

7   In great supply as heroes of the make-believe media are the purveyors of violence and macho toughness: the military man, cop, counterinsurgency agent, spycatcher, private investigator, and adventurer. From Dirty Harry to Rambo, it's all helicopter gunships, screeching car chases, and endless shoot-em-ups and punch-em-outs. Check the movie ads in your newspaper and count the number of weapons displayed. Flip your television dial during prime time and count the number of guns or fistfights or other acts of violence and aggression. They are even more numerous than the commercials.

8   To be sure, iconoclastic opinions and images get through now and then. Liberal and even strongly progressive themes can be found in an occasional movie or television episode. Underdog and dissident voices are heard for rare moments. But these are the exceptions. As media critic Erik Barouw concludes: "Popular entertainment is basically propaganda for the status quo." And sociologist Hal Himmelstein believes that television has become "one of our society's principal repositories of [conventional] ideology."

9   Do these media images and themes have any real effect on us? Indeed they do. In modern mass society, people rely to a great extent upon distant image-makers for their cues about a vast world. In both entertainment and news shows, the media invent a reality much their own. Our notion of what a politician, a detective, a corporate executive, a farmer, an African, or a Mexican-American is supposed to be like; our view of what rural or inner city life should be; our anticipations about romantic experience and sexual attractiveness, crime and foreign enemies, dictators and revolutionaries, bureaucrats and protestors, police and prostitutes, workers and communists—all are heavily colored by our exposure to movies and television shows.

10   Many of us have never met an Arab, but few of us lack some picture in our minds of what an Arab is supposed to be like. If drawn largely from the mass media, this image will be a stereotype—and most likely a defamatory one. As Walter Lippmann noted almost 70 years ago, stereotypic thinking "precedes reason" and "as a form of perception [it] imposes a certain character on the data of our senses." When we respond to a real life situation with the exclamation "Just like in the movies!" we are expressing our recognition and even satisfaction that our media-created mental frames find corroboration in the real world.

11   The media images in our heads influence how we appraise a host of social realities, including our government's domestic and foreign policies. If we have "learned" from motion pictures and television series that our nation is forever threatened by hostile alien forces, then we are apt to support increased military spending and warlike interventions. If we have "learned" that inner-city denizens are violent criminals, then we are more apt to support authoritarian police measures and cuts in human services to the inner city.

12   Audiences usually do some perceptual editing, projecting something of their own viewpoint upon what they see. But this editing itself is partly conditioned by the previously internalized images fed to us by the same media we are now viewing. In other words, rather than being rationally critical of the images and ideologies of the entertainment media, our minds—after prolonged exposure to earlier programs and films—sometimes become active accomplices in our own indoctrination.

13   We are probably more affected by what we see than we realize. Jeffrey Schrank notes that 90 percent of the nation's adult viewers consider themselves to be "personally immune" from the appeals of television advertisements; yet, this same 90 percent accounts for about 90 percent of all sales of advertised products. While we might think it is always other people (less intelligent than ourselves) who are being manipulated by sales appeals and entertainment shows, the truth might be something else.

14   Media critic Jerry Mander argues that electronic images are "irresistible," since our brains absorb them regardless of how we might consciously perceive such images. Children believe that what they are seeing on television and in the movies is real; they have no innate capacity to distinguish between real and unreal images. Only as they grow older, after repeated assurances from their elders, do they begin to understand that the stories and characters on the big and little screens do not exist in real life. In other words, *their ability to reject media images as unreal has to be learned.*

15   The problem does not end there, however. Even as adults, when we consciously know that a particular media offering is fictional, we still "believe" it to some extent—that is, we still accumulate impressions that lead to beliefs about the real world. When drawing upon images in our heads, we do not keep our store of media imagery distinct and separate from our store of real-world imagery. "The mind doesn't work that way," says Mander.

16   The most pervasive effect of television—aside from its actual content—may be its very existence, its readily available, commanding, and often addictive presence in our homes, its ability to reduce hundreds of millions of citizens to passive spectators for major portions of their lives. Television minimizes interactions between persons within families and communities. One writer I know only half-jokingly claims, "I watch television mainly as a way of getting to know my husband and children." Another associate of mine, who spent years in Western agricultural regions, relates how a farmer once told her: "Folks used to get together a lot. Now with television, we see less of each other."

17   Claims made about the media's influence sometimes can be unduly alarmist. It is not all a matter of our helpless brains being electronically pickled by the sinister tube. But that is no excuse for dismissing the important impact the media do have. The more time people spend watching television and movies, the more their impressions of the world seem to resemble those of the media. Academic media critics George Gerbner and Larry Gross found that heavy television users, having been fed abundant helpings of crime and violence, are more likely to overestimate the amount of crime and violence that exists in real life. They are also more apt to overestimate the number of police in the United States, since they see so many on television. "While television may not directly cause the results that have turned up in our studies," conclude Gerbner and Gross, "it certainly can confirm or encourage certain views of the world."

18   In sum, it is not just a matter of the entertainment industry giving the people what they want but of playing an active role in creating those wants. As any advertiser knows, supply not only satisfies demand, it helps create demand, conditioning our tastes and patterning our responses. The single greatest factor in consumption is product availability. For every ounce of quality programming and quality movies made available to us, the media also give up a ton of mind rot.

19   Those who produce images for mass consumption exercise an enormous power, but they are not omnipotent. They are not entirely free from public pressure. The viewing audience is sometimes more than just a passive victim. There are times when popular agitation, advances in democratic consciousness, and changes in public taste and educational levels have forced the media to modify or discard the images that are served up. The public has to keep fighting back. We got rid of Amos 'n' Andy and Sambo; we can get rid of Dirty Harry and Rambo.

20   More important than eliminating the bad shows is demanding better ones—for our children and ourselves. Viewing movies like *Glory* and television series like "Roots" are a far better way to learn about the African-American experience than watching shows like "The Jeffersons." A movie like *Salt of the Earth* tells us more about the realities of the labor struggle and blue-collar life than the clownlike Archie Bunker on "All in the Family." A film like *Born on the Fourth of July* tells us more about the heart-wrenching realities of war than all the John Wayne and Rambo flicks put together. Better entertainment can be produced that is not only intelligent and socially significant but also capable of attracting large audiences. But at present there is not enough of it, and the little there is usually gets poorly distributed and modestly advertised—if at all.

21   There is nothing wrong with mindless relaxation in front of a viewing screen now and then. What is wrong is when it becomes a way of life, preempting our experience and taking over our brains, providing us with a prefabricated understanding of what the world is supposed to be. And this it does for too many people. A better awareness of how we are manipulated by the make-believe media might cause us to waste fewer hours of our precious lives in

front of both the big and little screens and allow us more time for reading, conversing, relating to our friends and families, criticizing social injustice, and becoming active citizens of our society and the effective agents of our own lives.

For Writing and Discussion

1. Explain what Parenti means by the term *make-believe* in his title.

2. In the second paragraph, Parenti lists "pictures" the media plant in our heads. Parenti's list includes items that those who call themselves liberals protest. What items might be on a politically and philosophically conservative list?

3. Parenti notes that many media heroes are "purveyors of violence and macho toughness" and that this violence validates militarism and authoritative toughness. Conservative critics also attack violence in movies and television programming but from a different angle. Can you cite a common conservative perspective on media violence?

4. According to Parenti, how does the media shape our perception of reality? Do you agree that media has the power to at least evoke a "willing suspension of disbelief"? What role does *pathos* play in visual media?

5. If, as Parenti notes, "Children believe that what they are seeing on television and in the movies is real; they have no innate capacity to distinguish between real and unreal images," how would you characterize television's influence on children? For instance, from what they see on television, what might children believe to be true of the American family? of the American standard of living? of morals and values in America?

6. Analyze and evaluate Parenti's use of *ethos, pathos*, and *logos* in "The Make-Believe Media."

7. Comment on the concern of some social scientists that human consciousness may be changing—that humans may be losing the ability to imagine, to create images from thought, because of the constant blitz of spoon-fed images from television and other visual media. Why is imagination important? What effect can loss of imagination have on individuals? on society?

The Boston Photographs
Nora Ephron

1   "I made all kinds of pictures because I thought it would be a good rescue shot over the ladder . . . never dreamed it would be anything else. . . . I kept having to move around because of the light set. The sky was bright and they were in deep shadow. I was making pictures with a motor drive and he, the fire fighter, was reaching up and, I don't know, everything started falling. I followed the girl down taking pictures. . . . I made three or four frames. I realized what was going on and I completely turned around, because I didn't want to see her hit."

2   You probably saw the photographs. In most newspapers, there were three of them. The first showed some people on a fire escape—a fireman, a woman and a child. The fireman had a nice strong jaw and looked very brave. The woman was holding the child. Smoke was pouring from the building behind them. A rescue ladder was approaching, just a few feet away, and the fireman had one arm around the woman and one arm reaching out toward the ladder. The second picture showed the fire escape slipping off the building. The child had fallen on the escape and seemed about to slide off the edge. The woman was grasping desperately at the legs of the fireman, who had managed to grab the ladder. The third picture showed the woman and child in midair, falling to the ground. Their arms and legs were outstretched, horribly distended. A potted plant was falling too. The caption said that the woman, Diana Bryant, nineteen, died in the fall. The child landed on the woman's body and lived.

Stanley J. Forman/Pulitzer Prize 1976

Stanley J. Forman/Pulitzer Prize 1976

3   The pictures were taken by Stanley Forman, thirty, of the *Boston Herald American.* He used a motor-driven Nikon F set at 1/250, f5.6-S. Because of the motor, the camera can click off three frames a second. More than four hundred newspapers in the United States alone carried the photographs: the tear sheets from overseas are still coming in. The *New York Times* ran them on the first page of its second section; a paper in south Georgia gave them nineteen columns; the *Chicago Tribune,* the *Washington Post* and the *Washington Star* filled almost half their front pages, the *Star* under a somewhat redundant head-line that read: SENSATIONAL PHOTOS OF RESCUE ATTEMPT THAT FAILED.

4   The photographs are indeed sensational. They are pictures of death in ac-tion, of that split second when luck runs out, and it is impossible to look at them without feeling their extraordinary impact and remembering, in an almost subconscious way, the morbid fantasy of falling, falling off a building, falling to one's death. Beyond that, the pictures are classics, old-fashioned but perfect ex-amples of photojournalism at its most spectacular. They're throwbacks, really, fire pictures, 1930s tabloid shots; at the same time they're technically superb and thoroughly modern—the sequence could not have been taken at all until the development of the motor-driven camera some sixteen years ago.

5   Most newspaper editors anticipate some reader reaction to photographs like Forman's; even so, the response around the country was enormous, and al-most all of it was negative. I have read hundreds of the letters that were printed in letters-to-the-editor sections, and they repeat the same points. "In-vading the privacy of death." "Cheap sensationalism." "I thought I was reading the *National Enquirer.*" "Assigning the agony of a human being in terror of imminent death to the status of a side-show act." "A tawdry way to sell

newspapers." The *Seattle Times* received sixty letters and calls; its managing editor even got a couple of them at home. A reader wrote the *Philadelphia Inquirer:* "*Jaws* and *Towering Inferno* are playing downtown; don't take business away from people who pay good money to advertise in your own paper." Another reader wrote the *Chicago Sun-Times:* "I shall try to hide my disappointment that Miss Bryant wasn't wearing a skirt when she fell to her death. You could have had some award-winning photographs of her underpants as her skirt billowed over her head, you voyeurs." Several newspaper editors wrote columns defending the pictures: Thomas Keevil of the *Costa Mesa* (California) *Daily Pilot* printed a ballot for readers to vote on whether they would have printed the pictures; Marshall L. Stone of Maine's *Bangor Daily News,* which refused to print the famous assassination picture of the Vietcong prisoner in Saigon, claimed that the Boston pictures showed the dangers of fire escapes and raised questions about slumlords. (The burning building was a five-story brick apartment house on Marlborough Street in the Back Bay section of Boston.)

6   For the last five years, the *Washington Post* has employed various journalists as ombudsmen, whose job is to monitor the paper on behalf of the public. The *Post*'s current ombudsman is Charles Seib, former managing editor of the *Washington Star;* the day the Boston photographs appeared, the paper received over seventy calls in protest. As Seib later wrote in a column about the pictures, it was "the largest reaction to a published item that I have experienced in eight months as the *Post*'s ombudsman. . . .

7   "In the *Post*'s newsroom, on the other hand, I found no doubts, no second thoughts . . . the question was not whether they should be printed but how they should be displayed. When I talked to editors . . . they used words like 'interesting' and 'riveting' and 'gripping' to describe them. The pictures told of something about life in the ghetto, they said (although the neighborhood where the tragedy occurred is not a ghetto, I am told). They dramatized the need to check on the safety of fire escapes. They dramatically conveyed something that had happened, and that is the business we're in. They were news. . . .

8   "Was publication of that [third] picture a bow to the same taste for the morbidly sensational that makes gold mines of disaster movies? Most papers will not print the picture of a dead body except in the most unusual circumstances. Does the fact that the final picture was taken a millisecond before the young woman died make a difference? Most papers will not print a picture of a bare female breast. Is that a more inappropriate subject for display than the picture of a human being's last agonized instant of life?" Seib offered no answers to the questions he raised, but he went on to say that although as an editor he would probably have run the pictures, as a reader he was revolted by them.

9   In conclusion, Seib wrote: "Any editor who decided to print those pictures without giving at least a moment's thought to what purpose they served and what their effect was likely to be on the reader should ask another question:

Have I become so preoccupied with manufacturing a product according to professional traditions and standards that I have forgotten about the consumer, the reader?"

10   It should be clear that the phone calls and letters and Seib's own reaction were occasioned by one factor alone: the death of the woman. Obviously, had she survived the fall, no one would have protested; the pictures would have had a completely different impact. Equally obviously, had the child died as well—or instead—Seib would undoubtedly have received ten times the phone calls he did. In each case, the pictures would have been exactly the same—only the captions, and thus the responses, would have been different.

11   But the questions Seib raises are worth discussing—though not exactly for the reasons he mentions. For it may be that the real lesson of the Boston photographs is not the danger that editors will be forgetful of reader reaction, but that they will continue to censor pictures of death precisely because of that reaction. The protests Seib fielded were really a variation on an old theme—and we saw plenty of it during the Nixon-Agnew years—the "Why doesn't the press print the good news?" argument. In this case, of course, the objections were all dressed up and cleverly disguised as righteous indignation about the privacy of death. This is a form of puritanism that is often justifiable; just as often it is merely puritanical.

12   Seib takes it for granted that the widespread though fairly recent newspaper policy against printing pictures of dead bodies is a sound one; I don't know that is makes any sense at all. I recognize that printing pictures of corpses raises all sorts of problems about taste and titillation and sensationalism; the fact is, however, that people die. Death happens to be one of life's main events. And it is irresponsible—and more than that, inaccurate—for newspapers to fail to show it, or to show it only when an astonishing set of photos comes in over the Associated Press wire. Most papers covering fatal automobile accidents will print pictures of mangled cars. But the significance of fatal automobile accidents is not that a great deal of steel is twisted but that people die. Why not show it? That's what accidents are about. Throughout the Vietnam war, editors were reluctant to print atrocity pictures. Why *not* print them? That's what that was about. Murder victims are almost never photographed; they are granted their privacy. But their relatives are relentlessly pictured on their way in and out of hospitals and morgues and funerals.

13   I'm not advocating that newspapers print these things in order to teach their readers a lesson. The *Post* editors justified their printing of the Boston pictures with several arguments in that direction; every one of them is irrelevant. The pictures don't show anything about slum life; the incident could have happened anywhere, and it did. It is extremely unlikely that anyone who saw them rushed out and had his fire escape strengthened. And the pictures were not news—at least they were not national news. It is not news in Washington, or New York, or Los Angeles that a woman was killed in a Boston fire. The only newsworthy thing about the pictures is that they were taken. They deserve to be printed because they are great pictures, breathtaking pictures of

something that happened. That they disturb readers is exactly as it should be: that's why photojournalism is often more powerful than written journalism.

For Writing and Discussion

1. Do you agree with the public reaction that publication of the Boston photographs were an "invasion of privacy," or do you agree with Ephron that the photographs warranted publication because they were outstanding photographs. Give reasons to support your opinion.

2. Where should the lines be drawn on the publication of photographs depicting tragedies? Give specific examples to support your opinion.

3. In what way is a journalist's use of *pathos* related to the *ethos* of the journalist and the magazine or newspapers that publishes the journalist's work? Consider tabloids such as the *National Inquirer* and *The Star.*

THE POWER OF STYLE: PERIODICALS

Thousands of periodicals are published to appeal to thousands of different types of people, people with different interests or different levels of interest in the same thing. The *National Inquirer* is a newspaper that publishes articles about current events and people, yet the tabloid is different from *U.S. News and World Report,* and it appeals to different audiences.

Of two periodicals on the same sport—golf, for instance—one might appeal to the weekend golfer and one might appeal to the professional golfer. Of two magazines for teenagers, one might appeal to teens who are interested in reading about their favorite celebrities, and one might appeal to teens who are interested in learning about interpersonal relationships or environmental issues or particular hobbies.

In addition to variations on content, periodicals that appeal to the same general audience vary in scope (the depth at which a topic is treated) and style (manner of expression with language and design). The scope of a periodical can be related to whether or not the subject is treated for a lay or for a professional audience. A lay person, or non-professional in a particular field, might be interested in reading
(continued)

(continued from previous page)

articles in *Prevention Magazine* about how to stay healthy and physically fit, for instance, but not be interested in reading the jargon used by doctors and researchers who publish in the *New England Journal of Medicine.* A lay person might be interested in reading articles about the way people behave and interact in *Psychology Today,* but not be interested in reading a journal for professional psychologists such as *American Psychologist.* Of the two examples, the latter treats topics in depth and in an academic style.

The style of a periodical includes the level of language (academic, formal, or informal), the use of jargon (language that is used and understood by professionals in a certain field), and the design (graphics and color or straight text). Some periodicals have a friendly style that may include humor; others are "no-nonsense" or serious.

Practice: Comparing and Evaluating Periodicals

Choose two periodicals that are similar in some way for a comparative study. Two periodicals that focus on the same hobby or vocation, two periodicals that deal with the same religious or political issues, or two that appeal to the same gender and age group would make good choices.

Another option is to compare and contrast early and contemporary issues of a particular magazine to analyze the changes. One student made some interesting discoveries when he compared World War II era *Time* magazines with contemporary issues. He found, for instance, that seventy-five percent of the advertising in the war issues was geared toward productivity, while one hundred percent of the advertising in contemporary issues was geared toward consumerism, or consumption.

Priming the Brain   Read at least one issue of each magazine from cover to cover. Make notes as you read. When you begin your analysis, start by comparing the tables of content of the two magazines. How are the formats similar? How are they different? What are the departments and regular features of each magazine?

You may want to focus your attention on several of the following elements, making lists of the characteristics of each magazine, figuring ratios of ads to text, and so forth:

Audience (lay or professional, age range, gender, affiliation, and so forth)

Appeals to the audience

Editorial stance

Features

Vocabulary

Level of language (formal or informal)

Use of jargon

Advertising (ratio of ads to text, products advertised, and so forth)

Organization Options There are two organizational formats for comparison and contrast papers: whole-to-whole and part-to-part. For whole-to-whole organization, you would deal with all the characteristics of one periodical and then deal with the same characteristics of the other periodical. For part-to-part organization, you would deal with one aspect of your study (advertising, editorial slant, or so forth) at a time, discussing both periodicals. Making an outline will make the actual writing task much easier.

Journalism and the Public Trust
Dan Rather

1   **A** public journal is a public trust. This is true whether you are talking about a newspaper or a magazine or a radio station or a television news program. I've always been fond of the maxim—slightly paraphrased here—that it's the journalist's duty to report the news and to raise hell. I was taught early on that one of the fundamentals of being a good journalist is to play no favorites, pull no punches, and—insofar as humanly possible—have no fear of the results.

2   Having said that, I'm pretty sure that, when I'm sitting in my rocker at the old folks' home or fishing my last river, among my regrets will be that I didn't raise enough hell—not that I raised too much. Believe me, there's plenty to raise hell about, and too few reporters left who believe in asking the tough questions—in raising a little hell. I do like the fact that, lately, that diminishing number of good reporters has been asking some pretty tough questions about leadership. *Time* magazine put it most bluntly last fall with a cover story asking the question: "Is Government Dead?" It went on to sum up the problem in a nutshell: "Unwilling to Lead, Politicians Are Letting America Slip into Paralysis."

3   David Broder recently expanded this discussion in the *Washington Post*. The headline to his column read: "Nation's Capitol in Eclipse as Pride and Power Slip Away." Broder laid the blame at the feet of those politicians who

are too weak, he said, to exert American influence in a time of global change. "There's a lot of talk around Washington these days . . . about an allegedly pussyfooting Congress and a President who refuses to lead from the front." (Mark well, I'm quoting.) Most recently, the *New York Times* devoted a series to the fact that leadership in government has been replaced by an obsession with public opinion polls. Michael Orkesis, the *Times* reporter, came up with some pithy quotes. From Congressman David Obey: "Is American politics so brain dead that we've been reduced to having political shysters manipulate symbols?" From Congressman Mickey Edwards: "We've tended to trivialize issues to the point where meaningful debate has become almost impossible." From Lee Atwater: "Bull permeates everything."

4   That level of frustration and cynicism from government officials is disturbing. It is also news. It's good, honest reporting—the kind of tough questioning we're supposed to do to bring important issues to the public's attention. Personally, I don't think we need to apologize when our questions turn out to be disturbing. We're supposed to be honest brokers of information; our job certainly isn't to please the people we're covering, nor is it always to make America feel good about itself.

5   But as we in journalism ask these tough questions, honesty demands that we also face some facts about ourselves. One of those facts is that, when it comes to leadership, we aren't in a very good position to be casting stones. I'm reminded of the cartoon showing a politician on the stump saying, "If it's demonstrated to me that the American public wants leadership, then, by God, I'll give them leadership." Journalists *should* denounce government by public opinion polls. But we also ought to acknowledge that our own coverage of the news is more and more driven by this same kind of market research. "What kind of news are you most interested in hearing? Are you more interested in medicine, consumer affairs, the Trumps, or Tiananmen Square?" The networks have already gotten into the habit of screening news programs for "focus groups" in order to find out which stories are the most popular. Not which stories are the most *important*—which are the most *popular.* And focus groups have long been used by many newspapers as well.

6   Market research tells us that the public isn't clamoring for more news about government. Stories about the national debt and the national trade deficit—so we're told—don't sell newspapers or attract advertisers to broadcasts. And so too many of us use that rationale to avoid covering the issues that will shape our lives and the lives of our children—indeed, the very future of our country. Market research also tells us that international news is not of paramount concern to the public; and, sure enough, the trend in coverage is *away* from foreign news stories, the incredible events of 1989 notwithstanding. Last fall, one of those fancy think-tanks in New York which seems to specialize in bashing television news (at least from my standpoint) published a study entitled "The International News Hole: An Endangered Species." This study documented how deeply 10 of our most acclaimed newspapers have slashed foreign news coverage over the past two decades. In 1971, over 10

percent of their editorial space was devoted to foreign news. In 1988, their foreign news coverage dropped to *one-quarter* of that—2.6 percent. And this is in our best newspapers: 2.6 percent of their editorial space devoted to foreign news coverage at the very time it has become indisputably clear that America's future depends upon our having a better understanding of that great big world beyond our shores. Foreign news coverage was slashed by our best newspapers at the very time when we watched our economy falter in the face of foreign competition. . . .

7   As journalism becomes more and more competitive, all of us—whether in broadcast news or in print (some may want to argue that this is true more of broadcast news, and I perhaps wouldn't want to debate that)—are falling back on the tried and true local news formulas. We have, by and large, accepted the proposition that people don't care about foreign news, don't really care much about hard news at all—that "feel-good" news, entertainment, "infotainment," features, and gossip sell better than anything serious and certainly sell better than anything too disturbing.

8   I believe that kind of talk is wrong. I believe that kind of talk is dangerous. And I know that kind of talk has nothing to do with leadership and public service. Using public opinion polls, focus groups, and other market research techniques in a limited role as *informational tools* is one thing; using them as an excuse to duck our responsibility to the public trust is quite another. And for journalists to become slaves to market research—like the politicians before us—is, I submit, most dangerous of all. Where are the publishers, editors, and reporters of grit, gumption, and guts? Where are the ones who will follow their conscience or even their "nose for news" instead of the public opinion polls? Harry Truman once said that, if Moses had taken a public opinion poll, he would never have left Egypt.

9   Of course, there is one special problem for those of us who earn our living reporting the news that others make. Leadership requires definite opinions on which course to take, what path to follow; but those of us in the mainstream media are trained to set our opinions aside as far as humanly possible. We try to keep open minds; by and large, we aren't joiners. We know (often better than we're given credit for) that we don't have any secret formulas for answering the important questions. So we can justifiably ask: "How are we to lead?" I think a lot of politicians are ducking this very question. I *know* that we in the media are. George Bernard Shaw once observed that newspapers are unable to distinguish between a bicycle accident and the collapse of civilization. Today he might say that we are unable to distinguish between the breakup of the Trump marriage and the breakup of the communist empire. For us, leadership should be the willingness to distinguish between what's merely interesting and what's vitally important. . . .

10   "Okay," you say, "so what are your answers?" Well, for one, as simple as it may sound—and I hope it sounds simple because it is something we can ac-

complish—we need to *rededicate* ourselves to original reporting and analysis by first-rate writers, journalists, and thinkers. Sometimes that will mean paying more money for reporters with better minds and giving them the chance to do what they do best. Broadcast news and newspapers are in danger of sinking into a miasma of mediocrity, with a new generation of hacks turning out clichéd images which match their clichéd writing, in formats rapidly degenerating into trite and stale formulas.

11   Make no mistake: we are in considerable danger of losing our appeal to the best and the brightest of the next generation. Journalism is now attracting more than its share of lightweights and careerists instead of writers, reporters, and dreamers. We're attracting too many people who love the limelight and too few people who love the news. Too many of us are becoming known as news *packagers,* not news gathers. Once we had the reputation of working for organizations that would pay any price, go any distance to get an important story; now we have the reputation of working for a bunch of bean counters in yet another news factory.

12   We in print and broadcasting can dish it out—and we should. Many politicians are not doing their jobs at either end of Pennsylvania Avenue nor around most state capitals nor around most city halls or courthouses. The *Time* magazine cover is dead on the money: "Unwilling to Lead, Politicians Are Letting America Slip into Paralysis." But we in journalism can't lay the blame exclusively at the feet of the politicians. There *is* such a thing as journalistic leadership. It has nothing to do with arrogance or self-righteousness, with journalists setting themselves up as some kind of shadow government. Nor does it have anything to do with ratings or circulation or bigger profits. It has to do instead with nobler ideas: with public service and caring and, yes—I don't flinch from the word—patriotism. The *Time* article talks about a "frightening inability to define and debate America's emerging problems. A *not-nowism.* Our collective short-sightedness." And it concludes that the list of missed opportunities and challenges is already much too long: "The sooner government sets about doing its job again, the better." To which I say, "Amen," but add that the sooner we in journalism set about doing *our* job again, the better.

For Writing and Discussion

1. From Rather's opinions on the responsibilities of journalists, do you think he would view the publication of the Boston photographs as a part of the "If it bleeds, it leads" mentality, or would he agree with Ephron that the photos were news in their own right? Substantiate your opinion with statements or paraphrases from Rather's article.

2. Do you agree that journalism as a field is in danger of losing "the best and the brightest . . . writers, reporters, and dreamers" to those who just want to be "stars," actors who merely read the news instead of write it? Why or why not?

3. How do you account for the appeal of the "tabloid journalism" of such shows as *Day One* and *Hard Copy*?

4. Do you think most people are more interested in three S's of journalism (sex, sin, and scandal) than in the news that affects their lives in indirect ways? Substantiate your opinion with examples and reasons.

THE POWER OF STYLE:
OBJECTIVITY VS SUBJECTIVITY

News reporting, at its best, is objective: The reporter relays to the audience the facts, the reality of a situation, without attaching personal feelings through emotive language. An anchor person reports events surrounding the Oklahoma bombing, for instance, without making blatant pleas for sympathy from the audience. But critics say the trend is for newscasts to take on the flavor of "checkbook journalism": If it bleeds, it leads. Subjective appeal, or *pathos,* is used to draw and maintain audiences.

Practice: Evaluating a Newscast

As you watch a favorite network television program, write down the stories that are mentioned when the nightly news is previewed or advertised. Then watch the nightly news and write down the kinds of stories that are featured or spotlighted. What was the lead (first) story? Was an important story saved until last to keep you watching? What were most of the stories about? Did you see any good news or human interest stories about heroism, courage, or overcoming adversity?

Killing the Messenger
Molly Ivins

1   **A** few years ago, Jules Feiffer drew an Everyman who offered, in serial panels, these observations about the state of the nation:

   1. Truth hurts.
   2. Before truth, this was a happy country.
   3. But look what truth did to us in Vietnam.
   4. Look how the truth fouled us up in the 1960s *and* the 1970s.
   5. Truth has changed us from a nation of optimists to a nation of pessimists.
   6. So when the president makes it a crime for government workers to go public with truth, I say, "Hoorah!"
   7. And when he bars the press from reporting our wars, I say, "About time!"
   8. America doesn't need any more truth.
   9. It needs to feel better.

2   Ronald Reagan, Feiffer observed elsewhere, represented "a return to innocence; a new moral, ethical, and political Victorianism. Reagan's Victorianism transcends truth. It circumvents politics. It gives America what it demands in a time of insoluble crisis: fairy tales."

3   Lately, through no initiative of its own, the American press has been debunking fairy tales and once more telling depressing, pessimistic, hurtful, unhappy truth. With predictable results. "The nation's news organizations have lost substantial public esteem and credibility as a result of the Iran-Nicaragua affair . . . according to a new Gallup Poll for the Times Mirror Company," said a front-page story in the *New York Times* on January 4 [1987].

4   What we have really lost is popularity. People don't like being roused from the rosy Reagan dream that it's morning in America, so they turn on the messenger who brings the bad news.

5   Here is a sample—a letter to the editor of my local paper, the *Austin American-Statesman:* "Like sharks circling, the news media are in a feeding frenzy. They would love to bring down a very popular President. From the beginning, President Reagan's foreign policy has been under attack. First it was Grenada, but that turned out to be a triumph; next it was the bombing of Libya. During that attack we were deluged with quotes from *Pravda* and TASS, but, alas, that too was a triumph for Reagan."

6   The letter writer, Jean Whitman, continued: "The media are delighted that irresponsible and traitorous Congressmen are leaking top-secret information to them. . . . Consider the media score: They loved Castro, hated the Shah; they champion the leaders in Zimbabwe and Angola, where tribal murder is now common; they champion the African National Congress, a communist party, in South Africa. They ignore the plight of Afghanistan. They so divided the country, making heroes out of the SDS and Jane Fonda, that the real heroes came home to hostility after fighting a horrible war in Vietnam."

7   Whitman is as serious as a stroke, and while there may not be many citizens who hold her detailed agenda of grudges, the 17 percent drop in confidence in the television news and the 23 percent drop in confidence in the

credibility of newspapers uncovered by the Times-Mirror poll do represent a kill-the-messenger response.

8   The reaction is predictable, of course, but that isn't helping the press deal with it. Like the Supreme Court, the press follows the election returns. And the press, like politicians, wants to be popular. The trouble with waking up America so rudely, after six years of letting it slumber happily in dreamland, is that we're now being greeted with all the enthusiasm reserved for a loud alarm clock that goes off much too soon. "Ah, shaddap!" "Turn it off!" "Throw it at the cat!"

9   And when the going gets tough for the press in America, the press fudges, the press jellies. That's what we're doing now. We are retreating to a fine old American press cop-out we like to call objectivity. Russell Baker once described it: "In the classic example, a refugee from Nazi Germany who appears on television saying monstrous things are happening in his homeland must be followed by a Nazi spokesman saying Adolf Hitler is the greatest boon to humanity since pasteurized milk. *Real* objectivity would require not only hard work by news people to determine which report was accurate, but also a willingness to put up with the abuse certain to follow publication of an objectively formed judgment. To escape the hard work or the abuse, if one man says Hitler is an ogre, we instantly give you another to say Hitler is a prince. A man says the rockets won't work? We give you another who says they will.

10   "The public may not learn much about these fairly sensitive matters, but neither does it get another excuse to denounce the media for unfairness and lack of objectivity. In brief, society is teeming with people who become furious if told what the score is."

11   The American press has always had a tendency to assume that the truth must lie exactly halfway between any two opposing points of view. Thus, if the press presents the man who says Hitler is an ogre and the man who says Hitler is a prince, it believes it has done the full measure of its journalistic duty.

12   This tendency has been aggravated in recent years by a noticeable trend to substitute people who speak from a right-wing ideological perspective for those who know something about a given subject. Thus we see, night after night, on *MacNeil/Lehrer* or *Nightline,* people who don't know jack-shit about Iran or Nicaragua or arms control, but who are ready to tear up the peapatch in defense of the proposition that Ronald Reagan is a Great Leader beset by comsymps. They have nothing to offer in the way of facts or insight; they are presented as a way of keeping the networks from being charged with bias by people who are themselves replete with bias and resistant to fact. The justification for putting them on the air is that "they represent a point of view."

13   The odd thing about these television discussions designed to "get all sides of the issue" is that they do not feature a spectrum of people with different views on reality: Rather, they frequently give us a face-off between those who see reality and those who have missed it entirely. In the name of objectivity, we are getting fantasyland.

For Writing and Discussion

1. Recall Aristotle's analysis of anger (page 61). Aristotle noted that we may become angry with those who bring us bad news. Relate Ivin's explanation to Aristotle's analysis of anger. Why might people become angry at the media messenger?

2. Do you agree with Jules Feiffer's ironic observation that Americans just want to feel better and would prefer being uninformed about depressing issues? If so, where would you draw the line? (What truth *must* Americans know? Can you think of a circumstance in which not knowing the truth can result in feeling worse?)

3. William Colby, former Director of the CIA, said that the American people can't know all the secrets because "then we wouldn't have *secrets*." (What kind of argument is this?) Do you think Americans want to know government secrets? What kinds of "secrets" should Americans know? What kinds of "secrets" should the CIA keep?

4. Ivins accuses the media of setting up false dichotomies in their efforts to be objective. Relate Ivins' explanation of why this happens to Trudy Govier's criteria for a fair and balanced account (pages 121–122). How far do you think the press should go to try to present two sides of an issue? What should be the criteria for determining what issues have more than one legitimate side? Who should determine whether an issue fits the criteria?

THE POWER OF STYLE: MEDIASPEAK

Euphemisms are words used to replace terms that have unpleasant or ugly connotations, such as these:

fired/laid off	non-retained
lie	inoperative statement
budget cuts	advance downward adjustments
civilian casualties	noncollateral damage
janitor	cleaning technician
sweat	nervous wetness

(continued)

(continued from previous page)

Ambiguous words or terms—terms such as *free trade, global marketplace, democracy,* and *capitalism*—may be used as catch words that seem to identify a philosophy but may carry different meanings to different people or groups.

Vague, or **weasel words,** mean nothing in their contextual settings but seem at first glance to be definitive. In "This plan is *better,*" the word *better* is used with comparative vagueness; we might ask, "Better than what?"

Jargon are words shared by a special group. Terms such as *random access memory* (electronics*), outcome-based objectives* (education), and *municipal bonds* (finance) often have the effect of excluding those outsiders who do not understand the group's language.

Words with highly charged connotations The denotation of a word is the literal, or dictionary, meaning; the connotation of a word is the indirect meaning with all the emotional baggage attached. The word *activist,* for example, is "someone who takes a direct action to achieve a political or social end." But to someone who is in disagreement with an activist's particular political or social agenda, the word has a connotation of *rabble-rouser, troublemaker,* or *hell-raiser.* Many of those who are in general agreement that something should be done still have negative feelings toward those who take action.

Words such as *murder* have widely shared, loaded connotations. When a small-town paper ran the headline "Man Murdered in Police Shoot-Out," the police department protested. The man was *killed,* they said, after he shot at police; the word *murder* implies "malicious intent."

Other words or terms may be related to specific situations or issues. President Bush used the term *naked aggression* repeatedly during the Gulf War to add emotional impact to his statements about Saddam Hussein.

Practice: Detecting MediaSpeak

As you read a news article or listen to a newscast, note examples of mediaspeak. For your examples, write down the dictionary meanings of the words or phrases, and tell how each might be used to mean different things or why the words or phrases are vague.

Media Strategy: The Path to (Ratings) War
Harper's Magazine

[The following is] from a memo sent last November [1991] to more than a hundred local television stations around the country by Frank Magid Associates, a Marion, Iowa, media consulting firm, as part of a regular advisory service to its clients. The document was obtained by Howard Kurtz, a reporter for the Washington Post.

1   The U.S. military is gearing up for war. A quarter of a million troops and billions of dollars in money and equipment have been committed to the Middle East. Tension is rising; our troops say they're ready to go. Are you? When/if war breaks out, it could be the biggest story in history. Imagine if a hurricane hit the entire country and no one knew how long it would last. A war will command that kind of attention. Again: Are you ready?

2   Covering the home front of a war is not a game in which it's easy to play catch-up. You have to get out and OWN that story in the first twenty-four hours. Do that and the viewers are yours to lose. Make them believe that you are on this story like no station has ever covered a story in your market. Some specifics to talk about and work on:

- Decide NOW who'll be handling your coverage. If war breaks out at 2:00 a.m., should one of your primary anchors be brought in? What about Saturday afternoon? Should you stagger your anchors, or work them together?
- You'll want a review of which local troops are stationed in the Gulf, and what their roles are. Reactions from family members of soldiers are a must. Sure you want to get those quickly, but what if it's 2:00 a.m.? Are you going to wait until 9:00 a.m.? Or do you wake them up and break the news to them? Have your own battle plans that include flexibility to allow for time of day.
- Compile a catalogue entry for every serviceman from your area, including not only family members but other biographical information: What local high school did he or she attend? When did he or she graduate? Is he or she married? Kids? Try to have a photo of every soldier from your area who is now in the Middle East. Compiling the info now will be a whole lot easier than having to ask the family for it when casualty reports start arriving.
- Americans do not accept death well. An entire nation can be made distraught by a tornado that kills five, or a random shooting that kills three, or a plane crash that kills fifty. How will we handle it if reports start coming in that thousands of America's young people are dying?

- Have a list of experts ready to go. Get some of them to agree to come down to the station as soon as war breaks out to help you analyze what's going on. Of course, Middle East experts are necessary, and a military strategist could be interesting.
- Work now on setting up props and graphics. Remember that great map Peter Jennings had in the ABC special *A Line in the Sand*?
- Be ready to contact your senators and representatives. Catch them as fast as you can so you can get a reaction from the heart, not the prepared statement they'll come up with a few hours later. And make sure you ask them, Why are we fighting this war?
- Know, as well as you can, who the war protesters in your area are likely to be. Is there a vocal "peace activist"? Be ready to get a comment from him or her as soon as fighting breaks out.
- Get in touch with all the military contacts you've made in the past six months. Let them know—confidentially—that you intend to commit everything you have to help them communicate with the people of your region, and that you're willing to provide all the help the military needs, and that you'd sure appreciate any help the military units can give you to keep those families and taxpayers informed.
- Set guidelines so everybody knows how to handle different situations. If word of a local soldier's death reaches your studio, do you break into programming?
- Plan now for what kind of on-air promotion you'll have. You want to tell viewers you're there when they need you, not remind them that you brought them the bad news first. You might want to make sure you have somebody from your promotion department involved in coverage and planning discussions.
- When/if war comes, network schedules will change. Uncle Buck will not air if we have bombers over Baghdad. Your sales department needs a battle plan almost as much as your news department. Set up stationwide procedures so there won't be mass confusion when every schedule you're familiar with is blown up.

For Writing and Discussion

1. What was your first response to the "Media Strategy" piece? Comment on the use of *ethos, pathos*, and *logos* in the memo.

2. Did the Gulf War deliver the "promise" of the consulting firm that issued this memo? Why or why not?

3. According to *TV Guide*, "When Kuwait was invaded, it was a public-relations firm and its camera crews—not news organizations—that distributed much of the news and film about atrocities in the occupied country and whipped up war fever." Do you think the public reaction might have been different if people had known they were being manipulated by consultants who were being paid by the Emir of Kuwait and others?

4. Public relations firms prepare Video News Releases (VNRs) that they distribute to be aired during newscasts. The editors of *TV Guide* made this recommendation: When a TV news organization includes film or tape prepared by an outside source in a broadcast, the label "Video supplied by [company or group name]" should be visible for as long as the material is on-screen. What groups might oppose such a regulation and why? What effect do you think this label might have on the viewers?

One Person's Facts Are Another's Fiction
Sydney J. Harris

1   Journalism, like history, is supposed to rely on "facts." But what are facts? They are just the building-blocks of truth, and since no one has the time or space to use *all* the blocks, we have to select those we think most important. That's where the rub comes in.

2   Suppose I were an early American historian, recording the career of one of our Founding Fathers. Here is what I might say:

3   "He early opposed the Stamp Act and other British restrictions. When his ship, *Liberty,* was confiscated and burned, he became a martyr and was elected to the Massachusetts legislature. He was a member and president of the Continental Congress. His name appears first on the Declaration of Independence. After the Revolution, he was elected governor of Massachusetts."

4   Now let's suppose I were a British historian, recording the same career.

5   This is what I might say:

6   "Son of a poor clergyman whose father died when he was nine, he was favored by a rich uncle who sent him to Harvard. When he was still in his 20s, his uncle died and without working a day he inherited the greatest fortune ever amassed in New England.

7   "He wore lavender suits and rode in bright yellow coaches. He loved dancing, card parties, wine and all festivities. He was lazy and unpunctual. John Adams called him a 'leaky vessel,' who betrayed state secrets. He was the greatest smuggler on the continent, who yearned to be Commander in Chief of the continental Army, and was mortified when George Washington was nominated."

8   Of course you have recognized the eminent name of John Hancock. Everything said about him in both these versions is perfectly true and factual. But

history, and much more journalism, must condense these facts. Which shall be left in, and which left out? What balance shall be struck? How much of the positive facts are "veneration"; how much of the negative facts are "depreciation"?

9   What is said about Hancock depends, in large part, upon the historian's bias, perspective, and sense of values. He cannot put everything in (unless he is writing a full biography of the man), and anything he leaves out inevitably distorts the total portrait. Everything that is written is "selective."

10   Ponder on this the next time you demand that a story be "objective." All we have a right to ask is that the historian—or journalist—tries to be as honest as he can, and does not deliberately distort. Beyond this, one man's patriot is all too often another man's smuggler.

For Writing and Discussion

1. Make a list of facts you might use to persuade people from other countries to visit America. Now, make a list of facts that might have appeared in a negative story in the now-defunct Soviet newspaper *Pravda*. Would the two lists accurately represent America? Why or why not?

2. Newsman Tom Brokaw said in an interview on *Larry King Live,* "We try to tell you the facts as best we can determine them—the truth is somewhat more illusive" (March 16, 1992). Illustrate Brokaw's statement with an example of how facts may not accurately represent the truth.

3. As suggested in "One Person's Facts are Another's Fiction," what questions might readers pose as they read a news story or article?

Practice: Search and Evaluate

Using on-line or printed library sources, find original research studies, perhaps in one of the areas listed below. Prepare a written or an oral report on your findings, including the conclusions of each study and your evaluation of the use of facts in each study. (See Part Ten for information on finding, using, and documenting sources.)

> Original research on Gulf War Syndrome conducted by the government and another research study conducted by private physicians
>
> Original research funded by the American Tobacco Institute and another independent research study on the addictive quality of nicotine
>
> Research funded by a television network and another independent research study on effects of television violence
>
> Research funded by breast implant makers and an independent research study on possible effects of silicon implants

Practice: Writing a News Article

Use the facts you listed for the first question under For Writing and Discussion to write a news article about America for publication in another country.

CHAPTER SUMMARY

The readings in this chapter examined media that feeds your brain daily. Although you may now have a different attitude toward what you read and see in the media, the goal here was not to have you look at a generally competent and ethical media through a jaundiced, or diseased and bitter, eye but through a critical eye. An informed citizen is equipped with the skills needed to evaluate media and make informed judgments.

Chapter 14

ADVERTISING

The Hard Sell
Deborah Baldwin

1   Consider a day in the life of one semi-fictional American household—let's call them the Urbanes. The Urbane family awakens to the strains of National Public radio—"non-commercial" radio brought to us this morning by "REI, Recreational Equipment Inc., providing outdoor gear and clothing." Mom grabs her Liz Claiborne signature purse, stuffs her Fila sweats into a Bloomies shopping bag and heads downstairs. Let's eat! Pass the Teenage Mutant Ninja Turtle cereal to the kids. Front page of the newspaper looks grim, but not the ad for Petites Week at Macy's or the article by the 15-Minute Gourmet on the back of the Safeway ad in yesterday's Food section.

2   Snatches of conversation about world affairs emanate from *Good Morning America* between plugs for Tylenol and Toyota. Dad reminds the kids to

take their Flintstone vitamins. And for the third time, put on your Reeboks! They pile into the car with the She-Ra lunchboxes and Lands' End backpacks, drive past the bus-stop billboard advertising those bright Benetton clothes, turn on the oldies station and sing along with the Connie Francis remake that's now an ad for the local mall—"Where the Stores Are."

3   Five o'clock and time to go home! The country music station is playing a song from Barbara Mandrell's album "No Nonsense"—as in No Nonsense Panty-hose, which the singer is under contract to promote. Flipping through the mail, Mom finds three fund-raising appeals, a glossy from Hecht's department store announcing unbelievable sales, four catalogs, and a *New Yorker* with an attractive 10-page spread on the glories of the Caribbean, which turns out to be not colorized John McPhee but a paid "advertorial."

4   After the Urbanes wrest their kids away from the TV, they tuck them into their Little Mermaid sheets and catch the tail end of *Washington Week in Review,* made possible by a generous grant from Ford Motor Co., whose high-powered Crown Victoria sedan fills the screen. Checking the time on tomorrow's theater tickets, they notice a plug for USAir. Dad spends a few absorbing moments with the J. Crew catalog, then admires the way car ads during the 11 o'clock news are always photographed on empty mountaintops.

5   Bedtime already?

6   Welcome to Real Life, circa 1991. While our forefathers and mothers rose with the sun to labor in the fields, we rise with the radio and TV, immersed every waking hour in non-stop nudges from corporate America to Just Say Yes.

7   Round-the-clock commercialism has crept up on us, evolving from 19th-century pitches for products like Lydia Pinkham's medicinal pick-me-up into a sophisticated art form that pops up everywhere we are—from the brand-name labels that turn consumers into walking billboards to the corporate-sponsored informational posters that hang in classrooms.

8   Few things, it seems, are sacred: *Advertising Age* says there's a firm that sells space at the bottom of golf cups, reasoning that nothing concentrates the mind amid all that green like a word from a sponsor. Some advertisers have been known to put their messages in public restrooms—one of the few places most people think of as a commercial-free zone.

9   Despite such incursions, many people might nonetheless wonder: With all the problems besetting the world, why lie awake at night worrying about commercialism? Besides, what can one person do to beat back the media equivalent of a 20-foot snowstorm?

10   Enter the brave little Center for the Study of Commercialism. Just over a year old, it is headed by nutrition activist Michael Jacobson of the Center for Science in the Public Interest. Jacobson hopes to do the same thing to ad glut that he has done to greasy food: make the public realize that too much of this stuff can make a person sick.

11   Armed with a board of advisers whose professional lives are dedicated to the study of the commercial culture, the Washington-based center wants to raise awareness of commercialism's costs and counteract the gimmees with a

vision of a "less selfish, more civic-minded" lifestyle. As Jacobson and co-founder Ronald Collins wrote in one manifesto, "Omnipresent commercialism is wrecking America. Our cultural resources are dwindling. Value alternatives beyond those of the marketplace are disappearing. The very idea of *citizen* has become synonymous with *consumer.*"

12   Fighting commercialism, of course, is like wrestling your way out of a spider web. Indeed the commercial and non-commercial often blend together so seamlessly, says critic Mark Crispin Miller, an adviser to the center and author of *Boxed In: The Culture of TV,* that life can be lived as "a theme park experience."

13   He points to the way the war in the Persian Gulf was turned into a spectacle—partly thanks to the networks' presentation of this dramatic conflict in the best mini-series tradition. While advertisers initially were reluctant to sponsor war footage, before long they rushed to associate their products with patriotic good feelings, donating goods to the troops and incorporating the red white and blue in their ad campaigns.

14   Miller sees sharp parallels between the way the war was presented to the public and the way the 1988 presidential campaign unfolded on TV. Both involved simplistic plots, with beginnings, middles, and ends, and both made heavy use of emotional images and sound bites.

15   Sort of like ads.

16   Advertising has long oiled the machinery of our economy and probably always will. All told, corporations spent an unbelievable $130 billion on it last year—the equivalent of $6 a week for every man, woman, and child in the United States, according to the *Wall Street Journal.* That's 50 percent more per capita than is spent in any other nation. Essayist Pico Iyer once calculated that by age 40 we've seen one million ads, with incalculable effects on the way we view the world—never mind our capacity to absorb information of a more profound nature. And conventional ads are only the flotsam in the flood tide: Every day the average American is bombarded by hundreds of marketing messages, many of them adroitly woven into the content of the print and electronic media we depend on for information and entertainment.

17   The post office delivered 63 billion pieces of junk mail last year, much of it aimed at selling something. Product manufacturers stuck ads on videotapes and in movie theaters, and they spent millions to plant their products in Hollywood movies. Automatic dialing systems delivered canned messages at a rate of seven million a day, according to a congressional study, and that's nothing—coming soon to a store near you will be grocery carts outfitted with TV monitors that sense which aisle you're strolling down and advertise the relevant name-brand products.

18   The big brains on Madison Avenue are coming up with such innovations at a time when the public suffers, in the words of the *Wall Street Journal,* from "ad nauseum." The ads on TV come so thick that many advertisers overcompensate, stepping up the volume and intensity in order to be heard over the clutter. Or they act as seductively entertaining as the sitcoms and melodramas

they make possible. Try zapping through the Taster's Choice campaign that basically consists of 45-second episodes from an ongoing soap opera, complete with romantic leads.

19   "It's no longer enough to show the product and tell what's good about it," says one marketing executive at a personal-care products company that is among the nation's top advertisers. "You have to be as entertaining as the regular programs."

20   Ads once celebrated the pleasures of society and the senses, says Miller, but today they're more likely to celebrate personal empowerment. Kids' candy ads, for example, used to suggest that having some would make you popular. Now such ads are more likely to revolve around the "story" of having it when someone else wants it.

21   Some of the most sophisticated ads—the so-called post-modernist genre—poke fun at the art form itself, which becomes a kind of shared joke. But this appealing self-parody doesn't mean audiences are so savvy that they know they're being manipulated. "Everybody's sophisticated," Miller says, "in a superficial kind of way. But a kind of knowingness, the fact of growing up with TV, does not imbue you with an understanding of how images work." And even when a specific ad fails to sell a certain product, adds Pat Aufderheide, a communications professor at American University who writes about popular culture for *In These Times,* it contributes to the ceaseless message that "you can solve life problems with commodities."

22   Corporations use various strategies to reach the various segments of the market. To move the consumer spirit of opinion leaders, they buy time on public broadcasting, where $250,000 will yield two mentions on National Public Radio six days a week for a year. Private art galleries and museums have become so dependent on corporate money in recent years they hardly mind when it comes with name-brand banners and posters attached.

23   To reach middle America, advertisers are turning to cable TV, which has greatly eroded the networks' hegemony because it divides the market into easily targeted segments. Low-cost time during sports events on cable, for example, is a big draw for the makers of shaving cream.

24   When companies aren't hawking their goods during halftime, they're hanging their logos everywhere the eye or camera can see, plugging beer and cigarettes to armchair athletes with no apparent irony. Sports sponsorship is a booming business, reports the *Wall Street Journal,* with 4,200 companies pouring nearly $3 billion into special events ranging from the Olympics to the Virginia Slims tennis tournament. Nike invested $7 million last year on basketball-related promotional efforts alone, including contracts with college coaches to put their teams in name-brand hightops, a *Washington Post* investigation revealed.

25   One of the fastest growing target audiences is America's youth. Companies spent about $500 million last year to reach children age 2 to 12—five times what they spent in the early '80s—according to James McNeal, a marketing professor at Texas A&M University.

26   As many beleaguered parents may suspect, advertisers are drawn to children because children have more influence over the household pocketbook than ever before. According to Consumers Union, children age 4 to 12 spend $8 billion annually and indirectly influence household expenditures of $1 billion *a week*. Bombarded by slick ads for fast-food joints, junky breakfast cereals, and—a recent phenomenon—shoes and clothes, children have learned to speak up at the mall.

27   Corporations long ago infiltrated the schools, emblazoning their logos on educational materials and offering rewards like free computers and pizza in exchange for brand-name recognition among the next generation of consumers. Whittle Communications, which is credited with some of the most innovative marketing practices of the '80s, beams Channel One, a 12-minute TV news show that includes two minutes of ads, free to more than 8,900 high schools. To sweeten the deal, Whittle gives the schools satellite dishes, VCRs, and TVs as well; all the teachers have to do is round up the kids to watch the spots for Burger King, etc.

28   Unfortunately, many of us aren't even aware of the extent to which we are immersed in messages that say "buy, buy, buy," says George Gerbner, former dean of the Annenberg School for Communication and a member of the commercialism study center's board of advisors. "It's like saying, 'Is the average fish aware it's swimming in salt water?'" The average consumer literally can't imagine life without commercials, not to mention life without the many possessions commercials so effectively sell.

29   "My interest is the kind of culture we have created and in which our children are being raised," says Gerbner, a longtime critic of commercial TV who is trying to launch what he calls a cultural environment movement. "The mainstream of our culture is television, which is on an average of seven hours a day. It's not a product of the home, family, community, or even the native country for some, but transnational corporations with something to sell." He adds ominously, "Entertainment is the main source of information for most people . . . and whoever tells all the stories will guide what we think and do as a civilization."

30   If Gerbner seems most concerned about the impact of commercialism on the littlest consumers, it's because preschoolers spend more time watching TV than doing anything else except sleeping and are perceived as especially vulnerable to Madison Avenue's unsavory ways. As Neil Postman, an adviser to the center, argues in his book *The Disappearance of Childhood*, TV reduces literacy and distorts the learning process. Children also age quickly from exposure to violence, ineptitude, and other adult themes on TV.

31   If the ceaseless barrage of hyped-up, MTV-style plugs for toys and junk food during Saturday-morning cartoon shows strikes adults as manipulative and almost cynically deceptive, so are the ads targeted at the rest of society. "The thing I hear most often is, 'I don't even look at ads, I don't pay any attention to them,'" Jean Kilbourne, a lecturer and adviser to the center, said in her film

Killing Us Softly: Advertising's Image of Women. Yet "advertising is one of the most powerful socializing forces in the culture. And the effects are as inescapable as the effects of pollution in the air. . . . Ads sell more than products. They sell images, values, goals, concepts of who we are and who we should be. . . . They shape our attitudes, and our attitudes shape our behavior."

32   When we aren't buying self-images, we are "turning time into entertainment and connecting entertainment to buying," says Tom Engelhardt, who writes about advertising and children's TV. Tackling kidvid alone won't do much as long as kids keep getting the message that buying stuff is the ultimate fun. Adds Engelhardt, a father himself, "You can barely head into a museum without stumbling into seven gift shops. . . . Take the family on a visit to a historic site, and everything boils down to, yes or no, do we buy the Liberty Bell earrings?"

33   Once upon a time, Pat Aufderheide observes, children and adults alike could seek refuge from the commercial world at school—not to mention at home. Now the average busy household is itself a target of new products—such as kids' microwavable TV dinners—emanating from the outside world. The only sanctuary left, she says, is inside a church.

34   What's got the critics upset is not just marketing's encouragement of the human urge to own, which has done so much damage to the environment and eaten away so thoroughly at our sense of values. It's the changing nature of commercialism, its gradual intrusion into the privacy of our homes, the fabric of our cultural lives, and the sanctity of our public places.

35   The corporate invasion is taking place at a time when public institutions are particularly vulnerable to economic pressure—one legacy of the Reagan era, when taxes declined and so did the resources available for public libraries, schools, museums, and other institutions. Robbed of government support, these institutions "now have to appreciate the crumbs they get from corporations," says the Center for the Study of Commercialism's Michael Jacobson. "Instead of giving these companies tax deductions for their contributions," he adds, "the government ought to raise corporate income taxes."

36   That seems unlikely, given the tax-loathing politics of the '90s. Indeed, one elements of President Bush's ballyhooed education initiative would be greater corporate involvement in the classroom, not less. This is the same administration, incidentally, that asked the Beer Institute to sponsor a safe-driving campaign for the National Highway Traffic Safety Administration.

37   Because corporate America feels strapped—thanks partly to the merger mania of the '80s—it is becoming more demanding of the media. In the magazine world, advertisers have become shameless in seeking special treatment from editors, a practice that has long plagued women's magazines. "It's not just a matter of individual advertisers influencing editorial content," says a former *Self* magazine editor. "The whole point of the magazine is to promote products, so the advertiser doesn't even have to ask." Once unique to beauty and fashion rags, this concept is spreading throughout the magazine world.

38   Moviemakers have long been open to the notion of incorporating paid ads into their works, but in the '80s the practice became institutionalized, says Mark Crispin Miller, as professional brokers set up business in Hollywood to negotiate ever more lucrative deals. According to one tally, the creative minds behind *Die Hard 2* found room for 19 paid ads. When one company, Black & Decker, discovered "its" scene on the cutting room floor, it sued for $150,000.

39   Feeding into the product placement phenomenon is the sheer cost of producing movie blockbusters, TV series, new magazines, and even books. While the practice is hardly commonplace—at least not yet—the *New York Times* uncovered one instance of literary encroachment in a novel featuring a Maserati whose "V-6 engine had two turbochargers, 185 horsepower, and got up to 60 in under seven seconds." Turns out the author had cut a deal with Maserati that landed her $15,000 worth of book promotion in exchange for the mention. The publisher meanwhile was thrilled to have the help.

40   So symbiotic are commercial and creative interests that well-known actors, producers, and filmmakers frequently "cross over," lending their talents to Madison Avenue and further blurring the line between merchandising and the arts.

41   In his book *Boxed In,* Miller quotes Bill Cosby as saying his popularity stems not from his role as the quintessential TV dad, but from his appealing ads for Jell-O and the like. Thirty-second commercials, he confided, "can cause people to love you and see more of you than in a full 30-minute show." Along with sheer entertainment, there's an intensity in these spots, a one-on-one connection that few can resist. Such intimacy helps explain why kids not only stick around when the commercials come on during those tiresome Saturday-morning cartoon shows, but pay special attention. "Don't turn it down!" my 9-year-old daughter exclaimed when I wandered by the TV during one particularly colorful, fast-cut spot. "This is the best part!"

For Writing and Discussion

1. What would advertisers argue are the positive effects of advertising in society? What would society not have without advertising? How do benefits weigh against other effects of advertising on society?

2. Some people have called for elimination of funds for PBS (Public Broadcasting Station), which is not supported by advertising. Do you think funding should or should not be cut?

3. What are the possible results of the increased focus on advertising that reaches two- to twelve-year-old children? What are your feelings about the Channel One ads that are aired in classrooms? Do you think the benefits of the channel justifies having children exposed to advertising in school? Why or why not?

4. If we assume there is at least some truth in George Gerbner's statement, "Entertainment is the main source of information for most people . . . and whoever tells all the stories will guide what we think and do as a civilization," what are the responsibilities of those who tell the stories? What possibilities can you imagine as both the negative and positive extremes?

5. How is it that ads might, as Jean Kilbourne notes, "sell more than products. They sell images, values, goals, concepts of who we are and who we should be. . . . They shape our attitudes, and our attitudes shape our behavior"?

6. Some critics say that advertising is responsible for materialism and an individual's attachment of self-worth to products that results in such things as children killing other children for tennis shoes or jackets. Others say advertising is a necessary but really not-so-effective function of capitalism, and that it is the citizen's responsibility to sift through advertising and make rational decisions. What is your position?

7. How does Baldwin use *ethos* and *logos* in "The Hard Sell"?

8. Baldwin quotes Pico Iyer as noting that advertising effects "the way we view the world." What is the difference between "the way we view the world" and a "world view"?

The Language of Advertising
Jeffrey Schrank

1   **H**igh school students, and many teachers, are notorious believers in their immunity to advertising. These naive inhabitants of consumerland believe that advertising is childish, dumb, a bunch of lies, and influences only the vast hordes of the less sophisticated. Their own purchases are made purely on the basis of value and desire, with advertising playing only a minor supporting role. They know about Vance Packard and his "hidden persuaders" and the adwriter's psychosell and bag of persuasive magic. They are not impressed.

2   Advertisers know better. Although few people admit to being greatly influenced by ads, surveys and sales figures show that a well-designed advertising campaign has dramatic effects. A logical conclusion is that advertising works below the level of conscious awareness and it works even on those who claim immunity to its message. Ads are designed to have an effect while being laughed at, belittled, and all but ignored.

3   A person unaware of advertising's claim on him or her is precisely the one most defenseless against the adwriter's attack. Advertisers delight in an audience which believes ads to be harmless nonsense, for such an audience is rendered

defenseless by its belief that there is no attack taking place. The purpose of a classroom study of advertising is to raise the level of awareness about the persuasive techniques used in ads. One way to do this is to analyze ads in microscopic detail. Ads can be studied to detect their psychological hooks, they can be used to gauge values and hidden desires of the common person, they can be studied for their use of symbols, color, and imagery. But perhaps the simplest and most direct way to study ads is through an analysis of the language of the advertising claim. The "claim" is the verbal or print part of an ad that makes some claim of superiority for the product being advertised. After studying claims, students should be able to recognize those that are misleading and accept as useful information those that are true. A few of these claims are downright lies, some are honest statements about a truly superior product, but most fit into the category of neither bold lies nor helpful consumer information. They balance on the narrow line between truth and falsehood by a careful choice of words.

4   The reason so many ad claims fall into this category of pseudo-information is that they are applied to parity products, products in which all or most of the brands available are nearly identical. Since no one superior product exists, advertising is used to create the illusion of superiority. The largest advertising budgets are devoted to parity products such as gasoline, cigarettes, beer and soft drinks, soaps, and various headache and cold remedies.

5   The first rule of parity involves the Alice in Wonderlandish use of the words "better" and "best." In parity claims, "better" means "best" and "best" means "equal to." If all the brands are identical, they must all be equally good, the legal minds have decided. So "best" means that the product is as good as the other superior products in its category. When Bing Crosby declares Minute Maid Orange Juice "the best there is" he means it is as good as the other orange juices you can buy.

6   The word "better" has been legally interpreted to be a comparative and therefore becomes a clear claim of superiority. Bing could not have said that Minute Maid is "better than any orange juice." "Better" is a claim of superiority. The only time "better" can be used is when a product does indeed have superiority over other products in its category or when the "better" is used to compare the product with something other than competing brands. An orange juice could therefore claim to be "better than a vitamin pill," or even "the better breakfast drink."

7   The second rule of advertising claim analysis is simply that if any product is truly superior, the ad will say so very clearly and will offer some kind of convincing evidence of the superiority. If an ad hedges the least bit about a product's advantage over the competition you can strongly suspect it is not superior—maybe equal to but not better. You will never hear a gasoline company say, "We will give you four miles per gallon more in your car than any other brand." They would love to make such a claim, but it would not be true. Gasoline is a parity product, and, in spite of some very clever to deceptive ads of a few years ago, no one has yet claimed one brand of gasoline better than any other brand.

8   To create the necessary illusion of superiority, advertisers usually resort to one or more of the following ten basic techniques. Each is common and easy to identify.

1. THE WEASEL CLAIM

9   A weasel word is a modifier that practically negates the claim that follows. The expression "weasel word" is aptly named after the egg-eating habits of weasels. A weasel will suck out the inside of an egg, leaving it appear intact to the casual observer. Upon examination, the egg is discovered to be hollow. Words or claims that appear substantial upon firstlook but disintegrate into hollow meaninglessness on analysis are weasels. Commonly used weasel words include "helps" (the champion weasel); "like" (used in a comparative sense); "virtual" or "virtually"; "acts" or "works"; "can be"; "up to"; "as much as"; "refreshes"; "comforts"; "tackles"; "fights"; "come on"; "the feel of"; "the look of"; "looks like"; "fortified"; "enriched"; and "strengthened."

SAMPLES OF WEASEL CLAIMS

"Helps control dandruff *symptoms* with *regular use."* The weasels include "helps control," and possibly even "symptoms" and "regular use." The claim is not "stops dandruff."

"Leaves dishes *virtually* spotless." We have seen so many ad claims that we have learned to tune out weasels. You are supposed to think "spotless," rather than "virtually" spotless.

"Only half the price of *many* color sets." "Many" is the weasel. The claim is supposed to give the impression that the set is inexpensive.

"Tests confirm one mouthwash *best* against mouth odor." "Hot Nestles' cocoa is the very *best."* Remember the "best" and "better" routine.

"Listerine *fights* bad breath." "Fights" not "stops."

"Lots of things have changed, but Hershey's *goodness* hasn't." This claim does not say that Hershey's chocolate hasn't changed. "Bacos, the crispy garnish that tastes just *like* its name."

2. THE UNFINISHED CLAIM

10   The unfinished claim is one in which the ad claims the product is better, or has more of something, but does not finish the comparison.

SAMPLES OF UNFINISHED CLAIMS

"Magnavox gives you more." More what?

"Anacin: Twice as much of the pain reliever doctors recommend most." This claim fits in a number of categories but it does not say twice as much of what pain reliever.

"Supergloss does it with more color, more shine, more sizzle, more!"

"Coffee-mate gives coffee more body, more flavor." Also note that "body" and "flavor" are weasels.

"You can be sure if it's Westinghouse." Sure of what?

"Scott makes it better for you."

"Ford LTD—700% quieter." When the FTC asked Ford to substantiate this claim, Ford revealed that they meant the inside of the Ford was 700% quieter than the outside.

3. THE "WE'RE DIFFERENT AND UNIQUE" CLAIM

11　This kind of claim states that there is nothing else quite like the product advertised. For example, if Schlitz would add pink food coloring to its beer they could say "There's nothing like new pink Schlitz." The uniqueness claim is supposed to be interpreted by readers as a claim to superiority.

SAMPLES OF "WE'RE DIFFERENT AND UNIQUE" CLAIM

"There's no other mascara like it."

"Only Doral has this unique filter system."

"Cougar is like nobody else's car."

"Either way, liquid or spray, there's nothing else like it."

"If it doesn't say Goodyear, it can't be polyglas." "Polyglas" is a trade name copyrighted by Goodyear. Goodrich or Firestone could make a tire exactly identical to the Goodyear one and yet couldn't call it "polyglas"—a name for fiberglass belts.

"Only Zenith has chromacolor." Same as the "polyglas" gambit. Admiral has solarcolor and RCA has accucolor.

4. THE "WATER IS WET" CLAIM

12　"Water is wet" claims say something about the product that is true for any brand in that product category, (e.g., "Schrank's water is really wet.") The claim is usually a statement of fact, but not a real advantage over the competition.

SAMPLES OF "WATER IS WET" CLAIM

"Mobil: the Detergent Gasoline." Any gasoline acts as a cleaning agent.

"Great Lash greatly increases the diameter of every lash."

"Rheingold, the natural beer." Made from grains and water as are other beers.

"SKIN smells differently on everyone." As do many perfumes.

5. THE "SO WHAT" CLAIM

13　This is the kind of claim to which the careful reader will react by saying "So what?" A claim is made which is true but which gives no real advantage to the product. This is similar to the "water is wet" claim except that it claims an advantage which is not shared by most of the other brands in the product category.

SAMPLES OF THE "SO WHAT" CLAIM

"Geritol has more than twice the iron of ordinary supplements." But is twice as much beneficial to the body?

"Campbell's gives you tasty pieces of chicken and not one but two chicken stocks." Does the presence of two stocks improve the taste?

"Strong enough for man but made for a woman." This deodorant claim says only that the product is aimed at the female market.

6. THE VAGUE CLAIM

14 The vague claim is simply not clear. This category often overlaps with others. The key to the vague claim is the use of words that are colorful but meaningless, as well as the use of subjective and emotional opinions that defy verification. Most contain weasels.

SAMPLES OF THE VAGUE CLAIM

"Lips have never looked so luscious." Can you imagine trying to either prove or disprove such a claim?

"Lipsavers are fun—they taste good, smell good and feel good."

"Its deep rich lather makes hair feel good again."

"For skin like peaches and cream."

"The end of meatloaf boredom."

"Take a bite and you'll think you're eating on the Champs Elysées."

"Winston tastes good like a cigarette should."

"The perfect little portable for all around viewing with all the features of higher priced sets."

"Fleishman's makes sensible eating delicious."

7. THE ENDORSEMENT OR TESTIMONIAL

15 A celebrity or authority appears in an ad to lend his or her stellar qualities to the product. Sometimes the people will actually claim to use the product, but very often they don't. There are agencies surviving on providing products with testimonials.

SAMPLES OF ENDORSEMENTS OR TESTIMONIALS

"Joan Fontaine throws a shot-in-the-dark party and her friends learn a thing or two."

"Darling, have you discovered Masterpiece? The most exciting men I know are smoking it." (Eva Gabor)

"Vega is the best handling car in the U.S." This claim was challenged by the FTC, but GM answered that the claim is only a direct quote from *Road and Track* magazine.

8. THE SCIENTIFIC OR STATISTICAL CLAIM

16   This kind of ad uses some sort of scientific proof or experiment, very specific numbers, or an impressive sounding mystery ingredient.

SAMPLES OF SCIENTIFIC OR STATISTICAL CLAIMS

"Wonder Bread helps build strong bodies 12 ways." Even the weasel "helps" did not prevent the FTC from demanding this ad be withdrawn. But note that the use of the number 12 makes the claim far more believable than if it were taken out.

"Easy-Off has 33% more cleaning power than another popular brand." "Another popular brand" often translates as some other kind of oven cleaner sold somewhere. Also the claim does not say Easy-Off works 33% better.

"Special Morning—33% more nutrition." Also an unfinished claim.

"Certs contains a sparkling drop of Retsyn."

"ESSO with HTA."

"Sinarest. Created by a research scientist who actually gets sinus headaches."

9. THE "COMPLIMENT THE CONSUMER" CLAIM

17   This kind of claim butters up the consumer by some form of flattery.

SAMPLES OF "COMPLIMENT THE CONSUMER" CLAIM

"We think a cigar smoker is someone special."

"If what you do is right for you, no matter what others do, then RC Cola is right for you."

"You pride yourself on your good home cooking. . . ."

"The lady has taste."

"You've come a long way, baby."

10. THE RHETORICAL QUESTION

18   This technique demands a response from the audience. A question is asked and the viewer or listener is supposed to answer in such a way as to affirm the product's goodness.

SAMPLES OF THE RHETORICAL QUESTION

"Plymouth—isn't that the kind of car America wants?"

"Shouldn't your family be drinking Hawaiian Punch?"

"What do you want most from coffee? That's what you get most from Hills."

"Touch of Sweden: could your hands use a small miracle?"

For Writing and Discussion

1. Schrank notes, "Ads are designed to have an effect while being laughed at, belittled, and all but ignored." What makes it possible for ads to have an effect when they are "all but ignored"?

2. Have you seen an ad that promoted a new product that you really needed but didn't know existed? What kinds of information did the ad provide? Have you bought a name-brand product because you liked the ads? Were you pleased or disappointed with the product?

3. Although some of Schrank's examples are still being used after many years, other examples are dated. Cite an additional current example for each of the ten categories of claims.

4. Does Schrank appeal to the reader mainly through *ethos, pathos,* or *logos?*

THE POWER OF STYLE: SOPHISTICATED APPEAL

Contemporary ads reflect the visual blitz and special effects of the technology culture. Often words play a secondary role as advertisers use affective, or emotional, appeals through visuals. In an ad for the Union Bank of Sweden, an actor recites Frost's "Stopping by Woods on a Snowy Evening" before the advertiser's name appears briefly on the screen. One may ponder about the message or association the advertiser intended, but the viewer is seduced by the dramatic recitation to stop a moment and watch.

At other times, humor or wit is used without a "hard sell." Consider the IBM "Solutions for a small planet" ads in which a nun talks about "surfing the Internet" and elderly men discuss what a "bummer" it is to have a "maxed out" hard drive.

Practice: The Good, the Bad, and the Ugly

Terrible ads can be effective—even ads we hate. Extremely corny ads can become memorable because they are so terrible—like a catchy song or jingle that comes to mind uninvited. Think of an ad you enjoyed because it was witty or visually appealing. Analyze what you liked about the ad. Then think of an ad you thought was disgusting or corny. Which of the two do you recall most vividly?

Bryan Wilson Key has written several books on subliminals, hidden objects or words, in advertisements. He points them out in ads, while advertisers claim they don't exist, that Key's imagination is working overtime. Try to find a magazine ad that contains what could be a subliminal and decide whether you think it was created intentionally or was merely a design accident.

Self-Defense against the Pitch
Hugh Rank

HOW TO ANALYZE ADS

Based on *The Pitch* © 1982 by Hugh Rank   (Teachers may photocopy for classroom use.)

Recognize that a 30-second-spot TV ad is a **synthesis**, the end product of a complex process in which scores of people (writers, researchers, psychologists, artists, actors, camera crews, etc.) may have spent months putting together the details. TV commercials are often the best *compositions* of our age, skillful combinations of purposeful words and images. Be patient and systematic: **analysis** takes time to sort out all of the things going on at once. We perceive these things *simultaneously*, but we must discuss them *sequentially*. Use this 1-2-3-4-5 pattern of "the pitch" as a sequence to start your analysis.

Recognize "surface variations". In 30 seconds, a TV spot may have 40 quick-cut scenes of "good times" (happy people, sports fun, drinking cola); or 1 slow "tracking" scene of an old-fashioned sleighride through the woods, ending at "home" with "Season's Greetings" from an aerospace corporation; or a three-scene drama: a problem suffered by some "friend," a product/solution recommended by a trusted "authority," and a final grateful smile from the relieved sufferer. But, the structure underneath is basically the same.

Recognize our own involvement in a mutual transaction. Persuaders are *benefit-promisers*, but we are *benefit-seekers*. Most ads relate to simple "trade-offs" of mutual benefits: consumers get a pleasure, producers get a profit. However, investigate issues relating to any non-consumer ad; these are paid presentations of only one side of an issue, often involving more than a simple purchase transaction.

Understand that advertising is basically persuasion, not information nor education, *and not coercion!* Many important moral and ethical issues (concerning intent and consequences, priorities, individual and social effects, truth and deception, legal and regulatory problems) are related. The more we know about the basic techniques of persuasion, the better able we are not only to cope with the multiple persuaders in our society, but also to consider these ethical issues.

Observe. Understand. Judge. (In *that* sequence!) We "jump to conclusions" too often: we judge before we really understand, or even know what we're talking about. Observe closely what is explicitly said and shown; consider carefully what may be implied, suggested either by verbal or nonverbal means.

Anticipate incoming information. Have some way to sort, some place to store. If you know common patterns, you can pick up cues from bits and fragments, recognize the situation, know the probable options, infer the rest, and even note the omissions. Some persuaders use these techniques (and some observers analyze them) consciously and systematically; others, intuitively and haphazardly.

Categorize, but don't "pigeonhole." Things may be in many categories at the same time. "Clusters" and "mixes" are common. Observers often disagree.

Seek "dominant impressions," but relate them to the whole. You can't analyze *everything*. Focus on what seems (*to you*) the most *noticeable, interesting,* or *significant* elements (e.g. an intense "urgency" appeal, a very strong "authority" figure). By relating these to the whole context of "the pitch," your analysis can be *systematic, yet flexible,* appropriate to the situation.

Translate "indirect" messages. Much communication is *indirect,* through metaphoric language, allusions, rhetorical questions, irony, nonverbals (gestures, facial expressions, tone of voice), etc. Millions of specific concrete ways of communicating something can be grouped in the general abstract categories listed here as "product claims" (3c) and "common needs" (3d). Visuals imply. We complete the connection: e.g. very few "sex" words used, but many *images.*

Train yourself by first analyzing those ads which explicitly use the full sequence of "the pitch," including "urgency-stressing" and a specific "response-seeking." Always check for this full sequence; when it does not appear, consider what may have been omitted: *assumed* or *implied.* "Soft sell" ads and corporate "image-building" ads are harder to analyze: *less is said, more is implied.*

Practice. Analysis is a skill which can be learned, but needs to be practiced. Take notes. Use print ads. Videotape, if possible; replay in slow motion. No one can "see" or "understand" everything during the actual 30 seconds while watching a TV spot. At best, we pick up a few impressions. Use the pattern of "the pitch" to organize your analysis and aid your memory. Such organization helps to avoid randomness and simple subjectivity ("that's swell . . . I liked that!"). "**The 30-Second-Spot quiz**" provides a lot of specific information, but even after you lose that paper, you should be able to remember the basic structure.

Read more. *The Pitch* gives details (word lists, examples) of this way to analyze ads. Use the **Intensify/Downplay** schema for a more comprehensive analysis, especially as a systematic way to examine omissions. Libraries have many other books available about advertising: gossip, anecdotes, gee-whiz statistics, nuts-and-bolts about the business and economic aspects. (See also: *rhetoric, persuasion, propaganda.*) For current information, see the weekly trade magazine, *Advertising Age.*

Are ads worth all of this attention? Ads may not be, but *your mind is* . If we can better learn how to analyze things, to recognize patterns, to sort out incoming information, to see the parts, the processes, the structure, the relationships within things so common in our everyday environment, then it's worth the effort.

Professor Hugh Rank   Governors State University   University Park, Illinois

THE 30-SECOND SPOT QUIZ

Use this 1-2-3-4-5 sequence of questions, based on the pattern of "the pitch" to focus on the skeleton underneath the surface variations of radio and TV commercials, newspaper and magazine ads.

1. What ATTENTION-GETTING techniques are used?

Anything unusual? Unexpected? Noticeable? Interesting? Related to:

senses: motions, colors, lights, sounds, music, visuals (e.g. computer graphics, slow motion)

emotions: any pleasant associations suggested? (e.g. sex, scenery, exciting action, fun, family, pets)

thought: news, lists, displays, claims, advice, questions, stories, demonstrations, contests. (Popular TV **programs** function as attention-getters to "deliver the audience" to advertisers.)

2. What CONFIDENCE-BUILDING techniques are used?

Do you **recognize**, know (from earlier repetition) the brand name? company? symbol? package?

Do you **already know, like, or trust** the presenters: the endorsers, actors, models?

Are these presenters **authority figures** (expert, wise, protective, caring)? Or, are they **friend figures** (someone you like, or like to be, "on your side" — including "cute" cartoons)?

What key **words** are used? (trust, sincere, etc.) **Nonverbals?** (smiles, voice tones, sincere look)

In mail ads, are computer-written "personalized" touches used? On telephones: tapes? scripts?

3. What DESIRE-STIMULATING techniques are used?

Main part of ad: consider **(a) "target audience"** as **(b) benefit-seeking;** and persuaders benefit-promising strategies as focused on **(c) product claims,** or **(d) "added values"** associated with the product.

a. Who is the "target audience"? Are you? (If not, as part of the unintended audience, are you uninterested or hostile toward the ad?)

b. What's the primary motive of that audience's benefit-seeking?

Use this chart. Most ads are simple **acquisition** (lower left). Often several motives co-exist, but one may be dominant. Ads which intensify a problem (that is, a "bad" already hated or feared; the opposite or absence of "goods") and then offer the product as a solution are here called '**scare-and-sell**' ads.

To keep a "good" (protection)	To get rid of a "bad" (relief)
To get a "good" (acquisition)	To avoid a "bad" (prevention)

c. What kinds of product claims are emphasized?

What key words? Images? Any measurable claims? Or are they subjective opinions, generalized praise words, "puffery"? Use these 12 general categories:

Superiority ("best")	Scarcity ("rare")	Simplicity ("easy")
Quantity ("most")	Novelty ("new")	Utility ("practical")
Efficiency ("really works")	Stability ("classic")	Rapidity ("fast")
Beauty ("lovely")	Reliability ("solid")	Safety ("safe")

d. Are any "added values" implied or suggested?

Are there words or images which associate the product with some "good" already loved or desired by the intended audience? With such common human needs/wants/desires as in these 24 categories:

"Basic" needs:
Food ("tasty")
Activity ("exciting")
Surroundings ("comfort")
Sex ("alluring")
Health ("healthy")
Security ("protect")
Economy ("save money")

"Certitude" needs:
Religion ("right")
Science ("research")
Best People ("elite")
Most People ("popular")
Average People ("typical")

"Territory" needs:
Neighborhood ("hometown")
Nation ("country")
Nature ("earth")

"Love & Belonging" needs:
Intimacy ("lover")
Family ("Mom," "kids")
Groups ("teamwork")

"Growth" needs:
Esteem ("respected")
Play ("fun")
Generosity ("gift")
Creativity ("creative")
Curiosity ("discover")
Completion ("success")

4. Are there URGENCY-STRESSING techniques used?
(Not in all ads, but always check.)

If an urgency appeal: what **words** are used? (e.g. hurry, rush, now, deadline, sale, offer expires)

If **no** urgency: is this a "**soft sell**" — part of a repetitive long-term ad campaign for a standard item?

5. What RESPONSE-SEEKING techniques are used?

Are there specific **triggering words** used? (e.g. buy, get, do, act, join, smoke, drink, taste, call 800).

If **not**, is it **conditioning** ("public relations" or "image building") to make us **feel good** about the company, to get favorable public opinion on its side (against government regulations, taxes)?

Persuaders always seek some kind of response.

INTENSIFY/DOWNPLAY SCHEMA

INTENSIFY

REPETITION

Intensifying by repetition is an easy, simple, and effective way to persuade. People are comfortable with the known, the familiar. As children, we love to hear the same stories repeated; later, we have "favorite" songs, TV programs, etc. All cultures have prayers, chants, rituals, and dances based on repetition. Advertising slogans, brand names, logos, and signs are common. Much education, training, and indoctrination is based on repetition to imprint on the memory of the receiver to recognize and respond.

ASSOCIATION

Intensifying by association links the (1) the idea or product with (2) something already loved/desired by — or hated/feared by — (3) the intended audience. Thus, there is the need for audience analysis: surveys, polls, "market research," "consumer behavior," psychological and sociological studies to find out what the target audience likes and dislikes. Association can be done by direct assertions or indirect ways (metaphoric language, allusions, backgrounds, contexts, etc.). Some "good" things often linked with products are those common human needs/wants/desires for "basics," "certitude," "intimacy," "space," and "growth."

COMPOSITION

Intensifying by composition uses design, patterns and arrangements, variations in sequence and in proportion, to add to the force of words, images, movements, and so on. How we put the parts together, or compose, is important. For example, in verbal communication, we choose the words, their level of abstraction, their patterns within sentences, and the strategies of longer messages. Our framework of logic, inductive and deductive, puts ideas together systematically. Non-verbal composition choices relate to visuals (color, shape, size); sounds and music, movements, gestures, and facial expressions, and even mathematics (quantities, relationships), and time and space patterns.

DOWNPLAY

OMISSION

Downplaying by omission is common since the basic selection/ omission process necessarily omits more than can be presented. All communication is limited, is edited, is slanted or biased to include and exclude items. But omission can also be used as a deliberate way of concealing, hiding. Half-truths, quotes out of context, etc. are very hard to detect or find. Political examples include cover-ups, censorship, bookburning, managed news, and secret police activities. Receivers too can omit, can "filter out" or be closed-minded and prejudiced.

DIVERSION

Downplaying by diversion is common by distracting focus or diverting attention away from key issues or important things, usually by intensifying the side-issues, the non-related, the trivial. Common variations include diversionary tactics called "hair-splitting," "nit-picking," "attacking a straw man," and "red herring." Diversions also relate to emotional attacks and appeals (ad hominem, ad populum), plus things which drain the energy of others: "busy work," legal harassment, and so on. Humor and entertainment ("bread and circuses") are used as pleasant ways to divert attention from major issues.

CONFUSION

Downplaying by confusion occurs when issues are made so complex or so chaotic, that people get weary, feel overloaded, and "give up" or "drop out." This is dangerous when people are unable to understand, comprehend, or make reasonable decisions. Chaos can be the accidental result of a disorganized mind, or the deliberate flim-flam of a con man or a political demagogue who then offers a "simple solution" to the confused. Confusion can result from faulty logic, equivocation, circumlocution, contradictions, multiple diversions, inconsistencies, jargon, or anything which blurs clarity or understanding.

From *The Pitch* © 1982 by Hugh Rank (Teachers may photocopy for classroom use.) Published by the Counter-Propaganda Press, Box 365, Park Forest, Illinois, 60466.

Practice: Creating an Advertisement

Create an advertisement to sell a bogus product. Present the ad to your class, and tell what devices (pages 285–289) you used in the ad and why. You may want to refer to Tips to Curtail Stagefright (page 347) before you present your ad.

CHAPTER SUMMARY

The readings in this chapter examined the role advertising plays in our culture. You have acquired the skills needed to take a closer look at advertisements and television commercials. An informed citizen is equipped with the skills needed to evaluate advertising, resist the onslaught of "the pitch," and make choices based on reason rather than emotion.

Chapter 15

WRITING CHALLENGE

Analyzing a News Report or an Editorial

From a newspaper or a magazine, choose a news story or magazine article that is rich in emotional language, biased selection of facts, opinions, and propaganda techniques. Analyze the target article for use of loaded language, unsubstantiated or fallacious arguments, and inappropriate uses of statistics (see Part Four).

Analyzing an Advertisement

Analyze an advertisement, using Hugh Rank's information on pages 285–289. Write an essay in which you report your findings, and present the ad and your findings to your class. You may choose either to read your essay or speak from notes, while showing your ad to the class.

The class will be your audience. You are giving them information about a particular advertisement. Keep in mind that the class shares your knowledge of Rank's terms and tools for analysis.

The Guide to Writing will help you with your analysis and reporting. You may want to review the information in Tips to Curtail Stagefright (page 347) before presenting your analysis to the class.

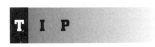

You can use the word *art* to identify pictures and graphics in the article or ad, and the word *copy* to identify blocks of text.

Journal Topic Suggestions

- What you watched on television last night and what you learned from watching it
- What a particular movie made you think about
- The educational merit of television
- Why you do or don't want to know (about certain event or issue)

- Why you read certain magazines
- Why you watch certain television programs
- Your future relationship with the media
- How home computers can be used to stay informed

GUIDE TO WRITING

Evaluation Arguments

Three kinds of argumentative writing were mentioned in Chapter 7: substantiation (which you have already written several times), evaluation (which is the assignment for this chapter), and policy recommendation or proposal (which will be addressed in Chapter 26).

Evaluation arguments generally address three questions:

1. What is the purpose of (something)?
2. How well does (something) fulfill its purpose?
3. Is the purpose worth fulfilling?

Open evaluations attempt to establish a standard. They are devoted to answering such questions as, "What makes a good news story?" or "What makes a good magazine article about a controversial issue?" or "Why is a particular advertisement good or (from the advertiser's point of view) effective?" Then substantiation arguments are created to establish the relevance of each element in that standard to a piece of writing or advertising.

Closed evaluations apply previously established standards to a given example. You already know, for instance, that a good news story is well written, informative, and objective. You know that magazine accounts and commentaries about controversial subjects contain adequate support, are well argued, and address opposing points of view. To evaluate a news story or a magazine article, examine each trait of the example in light of the standard and make a judgement about how well the example "measures up." A good advertisement is not offensive to any group of people. It uses ethical means and provides information to an audience about a product. The elements described in Hugh Rank's "Self-Defense against the Pitch" will help you in evaluating an advertisement. You are the critic.

Planning and Prewriting

EXPLORING THE ASSIGNMENTS

News Story or Article   Before you begin searching for an article, you may want to read the sample analysis on page 300 to get a general idea of what is expected for this assignment. You may also want to refer to Trudy Govier's criteria for a balanced account on p. 121.

Advertisement   Before you begin searching for an advertisement to analyze, read Hugh Rank's tools for analyzing an ad (pages 287–289) and the sample ad analysis that is based on "Rank's Intensify/Downplay Schema" (pages 288–289).

CHOOSING AN ARTICLE

Although many people argue that there is no unbiased reporting, most journalists try to be as objective as possible in their reporting. You may want to look for a story about a controversial subject. Many newspapers have an editorial *slant,* or position, which may involve supporting either liberal or conservative points of view.

If you choose a magazine account, you will also want to find out whether the publication has a political or philosophical slant. Magazines such as *The New Republic* and *The Nation,* for instance, have a liberal slant, while magazines such as *National Review* and *Chronicles* are conservative. An account on the conflict in Bosnia in *The New Republic,* for instance, might contain different kinds of information and a different approach to the same information found in an article in *National Review.* Magazines such as *Time* and *Newsweek* strive for balanced reporting but contain essays that may be good targets for analysis if your instructor approves. The *Newsweek* essay is titled "My Turn"; the *Time* essay is titled "Essay."

CHOOSING AN ADVERTISEMENT

Look at the ads in one or several publications and write down the most striking features—the things you notice first about the ads. What elements are most appealing to you? Which ads made you want to know more about the product?

ANALYZING YOUR ARTICLE

Before you begin writing your analysis, read your target article several times. First, read the article to determine whether you are interested in the topic and whether the article is rich enough in bias for your purposes. If you decide the article is both interesting and appropriate, begin the process of analysis by rereading the article several times, looking for a different stylistic or rhetorical element each time and listing those elements under headings (i.e., Emotional Language).

Answering the following questions will help you start your analysis:

1. What is the targeted audience of the publication in which the article or essay appeared? Most magazines have a fairly clear intended audience. For example, *George,* the magazine started by John Kennedy Jr. and a partner, is aimed at a relatively young adult audience who has some interest in politics but who is also very interested in celebrities. Other

magazines might be aimed at an audience with particular political or religious views or leisure or professional interests. Newspaper audiences might be more general, but still, you will find audience bias in editorials. The section in which you find the article or editorial will be a clue (sports, the arts, business, and so forth).

2. What is the organization? Newspaper items are often arranged as inverted pyramids: What the writer considers most important comes first and least important last. Therefore, if your article begins with attention to, say, the criminals on death row, rather than the victims of the criminals on death row, you can see a developing slant.

3. What words or phrases are used? Look for loaded connotations, buzz words, clichés, slang, jargon, and figurative language. Pay special attention to descriptive words and verbs.

4. Are there any discrepancies in the "facts"? You may need to read one or several more articles on the topic to get a better perspective about how the "facts" were selected and used.

5. Does the reporter use eyewitness accounts, interviews with concerned parties, or quotations from experts? Who is quoted in the article? What is quoted? Why? Look for inaccuracies and for selectivity.

6. Does the article contain sensationalism that may substitute for reasoned argument? Is the item written, for example, to emphasize gory details or mud-slinging gossip? How does the writer make it clear which side he or she has taken? How does the writer hook you into reading further?

7. What is the writer's tone (attitude toward the subject)? What is your assessment of the writer's style? What characteristics most clearly define the writer's style? Does the writer have special qualifications for writing the piece?

8. Study the headline or title carefully. Does the impression given by the title match the conclusion one might draw from the details in the article? Is there ambiguity or vagueness? Is the headline sensational? What tone is set by the headline? If pictures or illustrations are included, what is the significance?

9. What is the purpose of the article or essay? How well does it fulfill its purpose?

T I P

To save time, make several copies of your article and write an element for analysis at the top of each copy. For instance, one copy might be titled *Supporting Statements,* another *Emotional Language: Verbs,* and another *Emotional Language: Modifiers.* Use a highlighter to mark each example of the element indicated by the title on each copy.

ANALYZING YOUR ADVERTISEMENT

Answer the questions asked in Hugh Rank's "The 30-Second Spot Quiz" (pages 287–287), and address the elements under "How to Analyze Ads." You may want to focus your analysis on the language of the ad, or you may choose to address mainly the elements of the Intensify/Downplay Schema. Remember to include an analysis of color, white space, and artistic design. (If you are permitted to analyze a television ad, you will want to include an analysis of the way music and motion are used in the ad.)

Organizing and Drafting

After you have listed or highlighted the various elements in your target article or advertisement, choose the most outstanding aspects, categorize them, and organize them into a logical sequence.

In the introduction include relevant information about the article and about the magazine or newspaper in which you found the article. Include a unifying statement that gives your readers a clue about your findings.

The body should contain topic sentences for each major aspect of your analysis. Support your findings with examples (summaries, paraphrases, and direct quotations) from the article.

To conclude, summarize your findings with statements about what the specific examples indicate or prove.

As you write your analysis, you will make a decision about whether to summarize, paraphrase, or directly quote each of the examples you use from the article. The following guidelines will help you decide:

1. Summarize large blocks of material containing general ideas or philosophies, but use summary with care. Your objective in writing this analysis is to explain to your reader how the writer of the article made his or her points rather than merely telling your reader what the writer said.

2. Paraphrase ideas that may be confusing to readers who are unfamiliar with the topic.

3. Directly quote, punctuating with quotation marks, words or terms that illustrate the writer's use of loaded language, and make clear to your reader the context in which the word or term was used.

R E M I N D E R

Ask your instructor whether you should include parenthetical citations that tell the paragraph in which information can be found in the article. If you include that information, abbreviate the word *paragraph* (par.) and put ending periods *after* the closing parenthesis.

Use your informal outline to guide your writing. Remember, your objectives are to (a) point out the elements of the advertisement and (b) explain the intended effects of the art and copy.

R E M I N D E R

Include your ad and Hugh Rank's pieces on a Works Cited page. The ad may be treated as an article, with the name of the product used as a title. (See Part Ten for more information on citing sources.)

Evaluating and Revising

PARTNER EVALUATION

Read your partner's paper through carefully, making check marks beside passages that are unclear or that you suspect have some other kind of problem. Then write out your initial response to the paper, noting positive aspects (Was the analysis thorough? Did you learn something?) and possible problems (Did you understand which thoughts were your partner's and which were from the article?) Finally, respond to each of the questions below on a separate sheet of paper. Bracket on your partner's paper any sentences that you think contain mechanical errors.

EVALUATION CHECKLIST: ARTICLE

1. Does the introduction make you want to read on? Why? If not, how might the introduction be changed?
2. Are the findings in the paper well-organized? What is the organizational pattern (categorization, sequential order, etc.)?
3. Has your partner clearly distinguished between her or his ideas and comments and those of the writer of the article? If not, note the problem area.
4. Is sufficient support given for each claim made about the article's style and argument?
5. Do transitions guide the reader from one idea to the next and from one group of ideas (paragraph) to the next? If not, note the problem area.
6. Does your partner introduce any new bias in her or his interpretation of the article? If so, how?
7. Are your partner's conclusions about the article clear and well supported?

EVALUATION CHECKLIST: ADVERTISEMENT

1. Does the introduction make you want to read on? Why? If not, how might the introduction be changed?
2. Does the writer identify the advertiser and source in which the ad appeared?
3. Are the findings in the paper well-organized? What is the organizational pattern (categorization, sequential order, etc.)? Do all paragraphs contain a clear focus? If not, list problem paragraphs.
4. Are direct quotations from the ad punctuated correctly?
5. Do transitions guide the reader from one idea to the next and from one group of ideas (paragraph) to the next? If not, note the problem area.
6. Are your partner's conclusions about the advertisement clear and well supported?
7. What is your overall impression of the ad analysis? How might the final draft of the paper be improved?

THE POWER OF STYLE: WAYS TO BEGIN SENTENCES

Using a variety of sentence beginnings helps keep writing interesting and readers alert. Below are fifteen ways to begin sentences.

1. Subject alone	McGovern wrote the article.	
2. Article and subject	The report is biased.	
3. Adjective and subject	Limited support was offered for the conclusion.	
4. Adverb before subject	He sarcastically noted the discrepancy.	
5. Adjective phrase	From the class, only two attended the meeting.	
6. Participle-present	Taking the offensive, the team scored points early.	
7. Infinitive	To win was his main objective.	
8. Gerund	Debating was his forte.	
9. Adverbial clause	When the convention was over, the party had developed a platform.	

(continued)

(continued from previous page)

10. Noun clause	That the delegates had no part in the process was disheartening.
11. Verb first inversion	There are the people who drafted the legislation.
12. Object first	A prominent position the chairman demanded.
13. Interjection	Well, it did not happen.
14. Transitional word	In fact, the proclamation was ignored.
15. Predicate adjective	Calm was the atmosphere.

Practice: Varying Sentence Beginnings

Write your own example for each of the sentence patterns above.

Editing and Proofreading

Read over your paper, looking for sentence variety and clarity of meaning. Did you include a variety of simple, compound, complex, and compound-complex constructions? Do your sentences have a variety of beginnings? Can you improve your paper by including some of the sentence beginnings above? Are there sentences that should be combined? Can you eliminate wordiness in some sentences? Can you use more descriptive modifiers and vivid verbs to make your writing more exciting to read?

Proofread your paper aloud (or move your lips silently) before you submit your final draft. In addition to finding omitted words, you will probably also find any faulty sentence structures, unnecessary repetition, and punctuation errors.

Tennessee Man Convicted in Killing

Markle Gets 25 Years

Father Says Good-Bye

By HUDSON OLD
The Record

Guilty.

His reaction was slow; the judge had dismissed the jury, which retired to the jury room after delivering its verdict. His wife walked in the second-floor court, three state lines from home, their 15-month-old son riding what there is of the hip of a straight-figured girl.

He saw his wife and moved from the defendant's table to the front row of the gallery where she stood; they touched for a moment. The white tail of this shirt hung beneath an ill-fitting suit jacket.

Parting Touch   DONALD MARKLE, convicted in the October, 1982 killing of a 3-week-old infant, stops outside the courtroom for a moment with his wife and son while awaiting sentencing following his conviction. He got 25 years.

Tennessee aiming for jobs in inadmissable by virtue of being Texas. When they reached the immaterial under the rules of eastern part of the state, car

By Sherry Lee
The Record

A five-man, seven-woman jury found Donald Gene Markle guilty of brutally murdering 3-week-old John Anthony Goodin and sentenced him to 25 years confinement in the Texas Department of Correction Friday.

Markle continued to maintain a placid composure even when the infant's father, Jeff Goodin entered the courtroom.

Goodin, who had not attended the first two days of the

Foster asked if the parents had been read their rights, which they had and also found out that they had been living in a camp at the KOA Campground.

"They weren't going to be allowed to just leave," Foster said when asked if the Goodins and Markle were arrested in connection with the baby's death.

Before Markle made his formal statement he

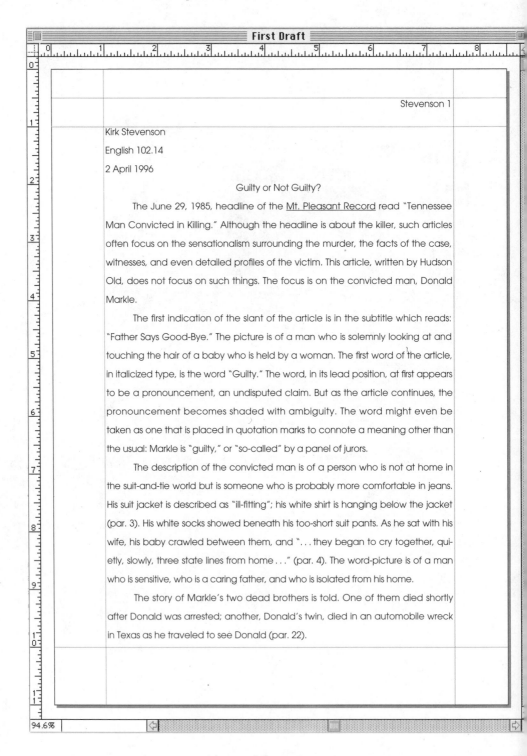

First Draft

Stevenson 1

Kirk Stevenson

English 102.14

2 April 1996

Guilty or Not Guilty?

The June 29, 1985, headline of the Mt. Pleasant Record read "Tennessee Man Convicted in Killing." Although the headline is about the killer, such articles often focus on the sensationalism surrounding the murder, the facts of the case, witnesses, and even detailed profiles of the victim. This article, written by Hudson Old, does not focus on such things. The focus is on the convicted man, Donald Markle.

The first indication of the slant of the article is in the subtitle which reads: "Father Says Good-Bye." The picture is of a man who is solemnly looking at and touching the hair of a baby who is held by a woman. The first word of the article, in italicized type, is the word "Guilty." The word, in its lead position, at first appears to be a pronouncement, an undisputed claim. But as the article continues, the pronouncement becomes shaded with ambiguity. The word might even be taken as one that is placed in quotation marks to connote a meaning other than the usual: Markle is "guilty," or "so-called" by a panel of jurors.

The description of the convicted man is of a person who is not at home in the suit-and-tie world but is someone who is probably more comfortable in jeans. His suit jacket is described as "ill-fitting"; his white shirt is hanging below the jacket (par. 3). His white socks showed beneath his too-short suit pants. As he sat with his wife, his baby crawled between them, and "... they began to cry together, quietly, slowly, three state lines from home ..." (par. 4). The word-picture is of a man who is sensitive, who is a caring father, and who is isolated from his home.

The story of Markle's two dead brothers is told. One of them died shortly after Donald was arrested; another, Donald's twin, died in an automobile wreck in Texas as he traveled to see Donald (par. 22).

94.6%

First Draft

Stevenson 2

The slides of the victim, a three-week-old baby, are mentioned as sensational, but the details of the injuries are not given. The testimony is called "unspectacular" (par. 5). The word "unspectacular" might be taken to mean "lacking concrete evidence." A horrible crime was committed, but the article cites little in the way of evidence that was presented in the courtroom. A statement is mentioned. The writer used quotation marks around the word "confession" to show his doubt about a statement in which the accused said "he might have killed John Anthony Goodin because he couldn't remember if he had or if he hadn't" (par. 13).

The writer proceeds to do what could not be done in the courtroom: point the finger of guilt at another possible suspect, the father of the baby. A comparison is drawn between Markle and the baby's father, Jeff Goodin. Markle is described by police officers in his home town as "a peaceful, law-abiding citizen (par. 20). Leon Rushing, Assistant Police Chief, said all four Markle brothers "were pretty straight characters," but Donald "might have squealed a tire here and there as a teenager" (par. 21). This quotation seems to put Markle in the "average" or "normal" category. A reader might associate with this kind of harmless prank as he remembers his own escapades as a teenager. Squealing tires as a teenager does not mean that a person will become a brutal killer. No indication of brutality is given in the profile of Donald Markle.

On the other hand, Jeff Goodin is described by Tennessee police as one who was "continuously in and out of trouble with the law" and who had a "history of violence involving police and his family" (par. 17). The writer points out that these statements were not given to the jurors, as they were "ruled inadmissible by virtue of being immaterial under the rules of evidence" (par. 19). The writer also tells how Goodin and his wife refused subpoenas to testify in the trial. Goodin was brought here by police and placed under $50,000 bond during the trial (par. 8). Goodin's wife, the mother of the baby, didn't come at all.

94.6%

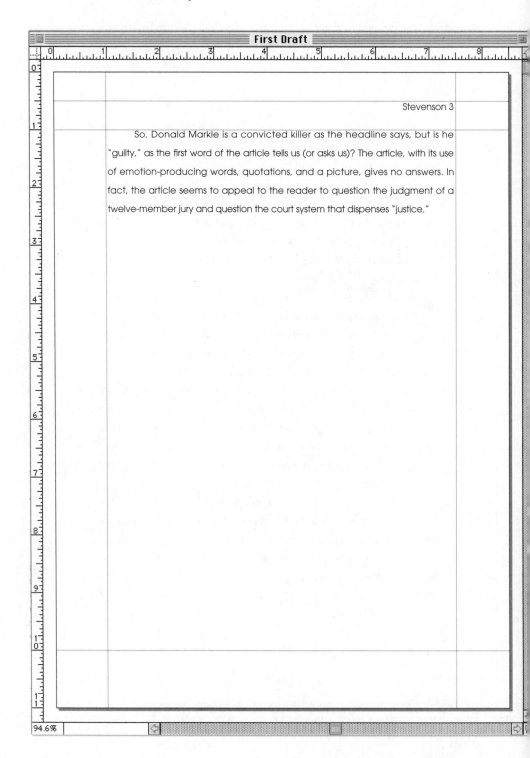

First Draft

Stevenson 3

So, Donald Markle is a convicted killer as the headline says, but is he "guilty," as the first word of the article tells us (or asks us)? The article, with its use of emotion-producing words, quotations, and a picture, gives no answers. In fact, the article seems to appeal to the reader to question the judgment of a twelve-member jury and question the court system that dispenses "justice."

94.6%

═══
First Draft
═══

Worth 1

Sharon K. Worth

English 102.14

3 March 1996

Taking a Second Look at a Magazine Ad

A towering white mansion looms in the background; old family retainers stand waiting to satisfy your every whim. Your polo ponies patiently await your attention. You exude grace, beauty, breeding, taste, and money. These are the things dreams are made of--dreams and advertisements. By fulfilling our fantasies, catering to our yearnings, and taking advantage of our dreams, advertisers are able to manipulate us into buying a product, often without mentioning the product itself.

Revlon's "Meanwhile, back at the ranch" ad appeared in the January, 1983, issue of <u>McCalls</u>. This ad is directed exclusively toward women and tries to interest as many types of women as possible. Close examination of this advertisement by applying Hugh Rank's Intensify/Downplay schema, reveals evidence of repetition, association, omission, and diversion.

The Revlon ad intensifies through repetition, firmly fixing the brand name in all but the most feeble reader's mind. "Revlon" is seen five times—twice in the copy and three times on nail polish bottles in the art. Another form of repetition is the use of the words "rich," "influential," "private," "big deal" and "dynasty." All of these words convey the same impression--an impression of affluence and influence.

Another way of intensifying is to associate the product with things the consumer is fond of or already desires: wealth, beauty, status, sex, glamour, and even a favorite television program. Housewives, career women, and those influenced by the sexual revolution might be attracted to the product by the color names: "Private Stock Brandy," "Strike-it-Rich Ruby," and "Big Deal Blackberry."

Revlon's ad takes advantage of the time of publication, January, by associating the product with our wish to make a new start, to begin the new year by

94.6%

First Draft

Worth 2

making changes and resolutions. The phrase "New Year, New You, New Colors" prompts us to change our image and resolve to buy the product. More adventurous women might even identify with the "good-girl-gone-bad (but not too bad)" image.

The phrase "Meanwhile, back at the ranch" once brought to mind the unsophisticated, Saturday morning world of television westerns. The word "ranch" is now associated with wealth. Southfork, from the hit program <u>Dallas</u>, is familiar to most television viewers. The Revlon color "Wine Dynasty" could be associated with the show <u>Dynasty</u>. Even daytime soap opera fans are included in this ploy; the copy "and for all the days of your lives" is easily translated into <u>Days of Our Lives</u>.

Meanwhile, back at the ranch, our advertisers have totally failed to mention the product itself. Rank's schema helps us to understand how the downplay tactics of diversion and omission have been applied. While diverting us from the product with the daydream presented in the art and copy, the ad omits some important points and leaves us with a few questions. The nail polish, lipstick, and eye makeup have catchy names, but what else is there to recommend them? Will the user's fingernails fall off? Will her lips become chapped? Will her eyes water? Is the product safe for women with allergies? The advertiser also fails to explain that a shriveled up octogenarian isn't going to acquire all this wealth, grace, and beauty by the application of their product.

By allowing us to view the greener pastures of the other side of the economic fence, exploiting our dreams, repeating the brand name often enough for us to remember it, and associating it with those things we already care about or desire, advertisers create a longing within us to be a part of the environment they have already created. By diverting us with the beautiful art and clever copy, they keep us from questioning product quality. Revlon's ad campaign dangles the carrot of glamour before us and we (predictably) follow it to our local stores and buy, buy, buy.

94.6%

The Rhetoric of Courtrooms and Coliseums

There are two kinds of crimes: those committed by people who are caught and convicted, and those committed by people who are not. Which category a particular crime falls into is directly related to the wealth, power, and prestige of the criminal. The former category includes such crimes as purse snatching, mugging, armed robbery, and breaking and entering. The latter category includes war atrocities, embezzlement, most political actions, and budget appropriations.

Dick Gregory, *Dick Gregory's Political Primer* (1972)

The word rhetoric meant "the art of persuasion" in classical times. Today, however, the word has taken on additional meaning and includes the language used to achieve a desired effect in the audience. Part Six explores the rhetoric of the courtroom and politics in America. First, we go behind the scenes of the court system in search of answers to these questions: Why do people commit crimes? How do decisions in the courtroom affect real people? Why do lawyers defend guilty clients? How are juries influenced? What is the role of psychology in the courtroom?

In Chapter 17 we look at the rhetoric of the coliseum, the "large stadium" of American politics. We examine the arguments of Margaret Chase Smith as she denounces government actions during the McCarthy era, of

Richard Nixon's historical "Checkers" speech, and of Sojourner Truth as she pleads for women's suffrage. Additional readings point out elements of election rhetoric and offer solutions for change.

You will have opportunities to explore your own ideas about justice and public discourse as you read the words of others. Finally, the Writing Challenge asks you to analyze a persuasive speech from the text or from another source. The Guide to Writing will help you work through the process.

Chapter 16

THE COURTROOM

Why People Commit Crimes
Aristotle

Many aspects of civilization have changed in two thousand years, but human nature has not.

1   There are three things we must ascertain—first, the nature and number of the incentives to wrongdoing; second, the state of mind of wrongdoers; third, the kind of persons who are wronged, and their condition. We will deal with these questions in order. But before that let us define the act of "wrong-doing."

2   We may describe "wrong-doing" as injury voluntarily inflicted contrary to law. "Law" is either special or general. By special law I mean that written law which regulates the life of a particular community; by general law, all those unwritten principles which are supposed to be acknowledged everywhere. We do things "voluntarily" when we do them consciously and without constraint. (Not all voluntary acts are deliberate, but all deliberate acts are conscious—no one is ignorant of what he deliberately intends.) The causes of our deliberately intending harmful and wicked acts contrary to law are (1) vice, (2) lack of self-control. For the wrongs a man does to others will correspond to the bad quality or qualities that he himself possesses. Thus it is the mean man who will wrong others about money, the profligate in matters of physical pleasure, the effeminate in matters of comfort, and the coward where danger is concerned—his terror makes him abandon those who are involved in the same danger. The ambitious man does wrong for the sake of honour, the quick-tempered from anger, the lover of victory for the sake of victory, the embittered man for the sake of revenge, the stupid man because he has misguided notions of right and wrong, the shameless man because he does not mind what people think of him; and so with the rest—any wrong that any one does to others corresponds to his particular faults of character. . . .

3   Thus every action must be due to one or other of seven causes: chance, nature, compulsion, habit, reasoning, anger, or appetite. It is superfluous further to distinguish actions according to the doers' ages, moral states, or the like;

307

it is of course true that, for instance, young men do have hot tempers and strong appetites; still, it is not through youth that they act accordingly, but through anger or appetite. Nor, again, is action due to wealth or poverty; it is of course true that poor men, being short of money, do have an appetite for it, and that rich men, being able to command needless pleasures, do have an appetite for such pleasures: but here, again, their actions will be *due* not to wealth or poverty but to appetite. . . .

4   The things that happen by chance are all those whose cause cannot be determined, that have no purpose, and that happen neither always nor usually nor in any fixed way. . . . Those things happen through compulsion which take place contrary to the desire or reason of the doer, yet through his own agency. Acts are done from habit which men do because they have often done them before. Actions are due to reasoning when, in view of any of the goods already mentioned, they appear useful either as ends or as means to an end, and are performed for that reason: "for that reason," since even licentious persons perform a certain number of useful actions, but because they are pleasant and not because they are useful. To passion and anger are due all acts of revenge. Revenge and punishment are different things. Punishment is inflicted for the sake of the person punished; revenge for that of the punisher, to satisfy his feelings . . . Appetite is the cause of all actions that appear pleasant. . . .

5   We may lay it down that Pleasure is a movement, a movement by which the soul as a whole is consciously brought into its normal state of being; and that Pain is the opposite. If this is what pleasure is, it is clear that the pleasant is what tends to produce this condition, while that which tends to destroy it, or to cause the soul to be brought into the opposite state, is painful. . . . [Explanation of the relationship between actions and pleasure.]

6   The above are the motives that make men do wrong to others; we are next to consider the states of mind in which they do it, and the persons to whom they do it.

7   They must themselves suppose that the thing can be done, and done by them: either that they can do it without being found out, or that if they are found out they can escape being punished, or that if they are punished the disadvantage will be less than the gain for themselves or those they care for. The general subject of apparent possibility and impossibility will be handled later on, since it is relevant not only to forensic but to all kinds of speaking. But it may here be said that people think that they can themselves most easily do wrong to others without being punished for it if they possess eloquence, or practical ability, or much legal experience, or a large body of friends, or a great deal of money. Their confidence is greatest if they personally possess the advantages mentioned: but even without them they are satisfied if they have friends or supporters or partners who do possess them: they can thus both commit their crimes and escape being found out and punished for committing them.

8   They are also safe, they think, if they are on good terms with their victims or with the judges who try them. Their victims will in that case not be on their

guard against being wronged, and will make some arrangement with them instead of prosecuting; while their judges will favour them because they like them, either letting them off altogether or imposing light sentences. They are not likely to be found out if their appearance contradicts the charges that might be brought against them: for instance, a weakling is unlikely to be charged with violent assault, or a poor and ugly man with adultery.

9   Public and open injuries are the easiest to do, because nobody could at all suppose them possible, and therefore no precautions are taken. The same is true of crimes so great and terrible that no man living could be suspected of them: here too no precautions are taken. For all men guard against ordinary offenses, just as they guard against ordinary diseases; but no one takes precautions against a disease that nobody has ever had.

10   You feel safe, too, if you have either no enemies or a great many; if you have none, you expect not to be watched and therefore not to be detected; if you have a great many, you will be watched, and therefore people will think you can never risk an attempt on them, and you can defend your innocence by pointing out that you could never have taken such a risk. You may also trust to hide your crime by the way you do it or the place you do it in, or by some convenient means of disposal.

11   You may feel that even if you are found out you can stave off a trial, or have it postponed, or corrupt your judges; or that even if you are sentenced you can avoid paying damages, or can at least postpone doing so for a long time; or that you are so badly off that you will have nothing to lose.

12   You may feel that the gain to be got by wrong-doing is great or certain or immediate, and that the penalty is small or uncertain or distant. It may be that the advantage to be gained is greater than any possible retribution: as in the case of despotic power, according to the popular view. You may consider your crimes as bringing you solid profit, while their punishment is nothing more than being called bad names. Or the opposite argument may appeal to you: your crimes may bring you some credit (thus you may, incidentally, be avenging your father or mother, like Zeno), whereas the punishment may amount to a fine, or banishment, or something of that sort. People may be led on to wrong others by either of these motives or feelings; but no man by both—they will affect people of quite opposite characters.

13   You may be encouraged by having often escaped detection or punishment already; or by having often tried and failed; for in crime, as in war, there are men who will always refuse to give up the struggle.

14   You may get your pleasure on the spot and the pain later, or the gain on the spot and the loss later. That is what appeals to weak-willed persons—and weakness of will may be shown with regard to all the objects of desire. It may on the contrary appeal to you—as it does appeal to self-controlled and sensible people—that the pain and loss are immediate, while the pleasure and profit come later and last longer. You may feel able to make it appear that your crime was due to chance, or to necessity, or to natural causes, or to habit: in fact, to put it generally, as if you had failed to do right rather than actually done wrong.

You may be able to trust other people to judge you equitably. You may be stimulated by being in want: which may mean that you want necessaries, as poor people do, or that you want luxuries, as rich people do. You may be encouraged by having a particularly good reputation, because that will save you from being suspected: or by having a particularly bad one, because nothing you are likely to do will make it worse.

15   The above, then, are the various states of mind in which a man sets about doing wrong to others. The kind of people to whom he does wrong, and the ways in which he does it, must be considered next. The people to whom he does it are those who have what he wants himself, whether this means necessities or luxuries and materials for enjoyment. His victims may be far off or near at hand. If they are near, he gets his profit quickly; if they are far off, vengeance is slow, as those think who plunder the Carthaginians. They may be those who are trustful instead of being cautious and watchful, since all such people are easy to elude. Or those who are too easy-going to have enough energy to prosecute an offender. Or sensitive people, who are not apt to show fight over questions of money. Or those who have been wronged already by many people, and yet have not prosecuted; such men must surely be the proverbial "Mysian prey." Or those who have either never or often been wronged before; in neither case will they take precautions; if they have never been wronged they think they never will, and if they have often been wronged they feel that surely it cannot happen again. Or those whose character has been attacked in the past, or is exposed to attack in the future: they will be too much frightened of the judges to make up their minds to prosecute, nor can they win their case if they do: this is true of those who are hated or unpopular.

Another likely class of victim is those who their injurer can pretend have, themselves or through their ancestors or friends, treated badly, or intended to treat badly, the man himself, or his ancestors, or those he cares for; as the proverb says, "wickedness needs but a pretext." . . .

For Writing and Discussion

1. Summarize Aristotle's key points about why people commit crimes. Can you think of other motivations for committing crimes?

2. Relate Aristotle's motivations and causes for wrongdoing to crimes such as street crimes, embezzlement and stock-market manipulation, and crimes of passion.

3. What does Aristotle say about who criminals victimize? Illustrate Aristotle's assessment of who becomes victims with contemporary examples.

To Judge Faolain,
Dead Long Enough:
A Summons

Linda McCarriston

Your Honor, when my mother stood
before you, with her routine
domestic plea, after weeks
of waiting for speech to return
5 to her body, with her homemade
forties hairdo, her face purple still
under pancake, her jaw off just a little,
her *holy of holies* healing,
her breasts wrung, her heart
10 the bursting heart of someone
snagged among rocks deep
in a sharkpool—no, not "someone,"

but a woman there, snagged
with her babies, *by* them,
15 in one of hope's pedestrian
brutal turns—when, in the tones
of parlors overlooking the harbor,
you admonished that, for the sake
of the family, the wife
20 must take the husband back to her bed,
what you willed not to see before you
was a woman risen clean to the surface,
a woman who, with one arm flailing,
held up with the other her actual

25 burdens of flesh. When you clamped
to her leg the chain of *justice,*
you ferried us back down to *the law,*
the black ice eye, the maw, the mako
that circles the kitchen table nightly.
30 What did you make of the words
she told you, not to have heard her,
not to have seen her there? Almost-
forgiveable ignorance, you were not
the fist, the boot, or the blade,

35   but the jaded, corrective ear and eye
     at the limits of her world. Now

     I will you to see her as she was, to ride
     your own words back into light: I call
     your spirit home again, divesting you
40   of robe and bench, the fine white hand
     and half-lit Irish eye. Tonight, put on
     a body in the trailer down the road
     where your father, when he can't
     get it up, makes love to your mother
45   with a rifle. Let your name be
     Eva-Mary. Let your hour of birth
     be dawn. Let your life be long
     and common, and your flesh endure.

For Writing and Discussion

1. What curse does the speaker "will" on Judge Faolain? Why does she want him to be "common," or powerless?

2. How is the image of a drowning woman created in the poem?

3. Linda McCarriston's poem about domestic violence is reflective of her own childhood when her father was "the law," and "the church, the state, the schools, the doctor, the lawyer" all subscribed to the idea that a man could do what he wanted in his home, "his castle." How much has that attitude changed over the past few years? Can you think of groups or institutions in which that attitude, or remnants of that attitude, still persist?

4. How are the appeals of *ethos, pathos,* and *logos* present in the poem?

5. Seymour Wishman writes in *Confessions of a Criminal Lawyer:*

> My own capacity for outrage [at human suffering], genuine outrage, had long ago been traded for cynicism. What had once been a shield of self-protection separating me from a psychologically threatening criminal world had assumed the pretension of a personal philosophy.

To what extent do you think cynicism pervades the criminal justice system? Can you think of a way that professionals might protect themselves from this loss of sensitivity?

Why I Stand to Defend Guilty Clients
Barry Winston

1   Let me tell you a story. A true story, although the names and some details have been changed to protect my client's privacy. It's over four years ago. I'm sitting in my office when I get a call from a lawyer I hardly know. Tax lawyer. Some kid is in trouble, and would I be interested in helping him? He's charged with manslaughter—a felony—and driving under the influence. I tell him sure, have the kid call me.

2   So the kid makes an appointment. He's a nice guy, fresh out of college, and he's been spending some time with his older sister, who's in med school. One day she tells him they're invited to a cookout. She's going directly from class, and he's going to take her car and meet her there. He arrives before she does, introduces himself around and pops a beer. She shows up after a while, and he pops another beer. Then he eats a hamburger and drinks a third beer. At some point, his sister says, "Well, it's time to go," and they head for the car.

3   And, the kid tells me, the next thing he remembers, he's waking up in a hospital room, bandages and casts all over him, and somebody is telling him he's charged with manslaughter and driving under the influence because he wrecked his sister's car, killed her in the process, and had a blood-alcohol content of .14. I ask him what he means by the next thing he remembers, and he looks me straight in the eye and says he can't remember anything from the time they leave the cookout until he wakes up in the hospital. He tells me the doctors say he has post-retrograde amnesia. I say of course I believe him, but I'm worried about finding a judge who will.

4   I agree to represent him and get the wreck report. It says there are four witnesses: a couple in a car going the other way who passed the kid and his sister just before the car ran off the road, a guy who heard the crash from his backyard and drove to the accident, and the trooper who investigated. I call the guy who drove to the scene from his house. He isn't home. I leave word. Later he calls me back, and I introduce myself, tell him I'm representing the kid and need to talk to him. He hems and haws, and I figure he thinks it's against the law to talk to a defense lawyers. I say the D.A. will tell him it's okay to talk to me, but he doesn't have to. I give him the name and number of the D.A., and he says he'll call me back.

5   Then I go out and hunt up the trooper. He tells me the whole story. The kid and his sister are coming into town on a curvy, rural road where the speed limit is 45. The Thornes—the couple—are driving out of town. They say this car passes them, going the other way, heading into a bad turn, going at least 65 or 70. Halfway into the curve, it runs off the road on the right, whips back onto the road, spins, runs off on the left, and disappears with an enormous crash.

6   In a very short time, Trooper Johnson says, the guy who heard the crash from his backyard arrives on the scene. Holloway, that's his name. He gives the trooper this account: the car flipped over, and when a couple of other people run up, they pull the boy, who is seat-belted in, from the driver's side of the car. Then they extricate the girl from the other side. She is still breathing but later dies in the hospital.

7   And that, says Trooper Johnson, is that. Not only was the kid's blood-alcohol content high, but he was going way too fast, and the girl is dead. He had to charge him. It's a shame, he seems a nice kid, it was his own sister and all, but what else can he do?

8   In view of Holloway's statement, things are not looking so hot for my client, and I'm thinking it's about time to have a little chat with the D.A. But Holloway still hasn't called me back, so I call him. Not home. Leave word. I wait a couple days and call again. Finally I get him. He's very agitated, and won't talk to me except to say that he doesn't have to talk to me.

9   I know I better look for a deal, so I go to the D.A. He's very sympathetic— but . . . a young woman is dead, promising career cut short, all because somebody has too much to drink and drives. The kid has to pay. Not, the D.A. says, with jail time. But he's got to plead guilty to two misdemeanors: death by vehicle and driving under the influence. That means probation, a big fine. Several thousand dollars. Still, it's hard for me to criticize the D.A. After all, he's probably going to be criticized for reducing the felony to a misdemeanor.

10   On the day of the trial, I get to court early. There is Trooper Johnson, and three people I assume are the Thornes and Holloway. Sure enough, when Holloway sees me, he comes over and introduces himself and starts right in: "I just want you to know how serious all this drinking and driving really is," he says. "If those young people hadn't been drinking and driving that night, that poor young girl would be alive today."

11   Now, as I'm trying to hold my temper, I spot the D.A. I bolt across the room, grab him by the arm and say, "We gotta talk. Why the hell have you got all these people here? That jerk Holloway! Surely you're not going to call him as a witness. This is a guilty plea! My client's parents are sitting out there. You don't need to put them through a dog-and-pony show."

12   The D.A. looks at me and says, "Man, I'm sorry, but in a case like this, I gotta put on witnesses. Weird Wally is on the bench. If I try to go without witnesses, he might throw me out."

13   The D.A. calls Trooper Johnson first. After he finishes, the judge looks at me. "No questions," I say. Then the D.A. calls Holloway. He describes going to the scene, the upside down car, helping to pull my client out of the window on the left side of the car, and then going around to the other side to help with the girl.

14   The D.A. says, "No further questions, Your Honor." The judge looks at me. I shake my head, and he says to Holloway, "You may step down."

15   But Holloway doesn't move. He looks at me, and at the D.A., and then at the judge. "Can I say something else, Your Honor?"

16   All my bells are ringing at once. My gut is screaming at me, "Object! Object!" I'm trying to decide in three-quarters of a second whether it'll be worse to listen to a lecture on the evils of drink from Holloway or tick off the judge by objecting. But all I say is, "No objections, Your Honor." The judge smiles at me, then at Holloway, and says, "Very well, Mr. Holloway."

17   It all comes out in a rush. "Well, you see, Your Honor," Holloway says, "it all happened so fast. I heard the noise, and it was night, and I was excited, and the next morning, when I had a chance to think about it, I figured out what had happened. We did pull that boy out of the left-hand side of the car, but don't you see, the car was upside-down, and if you turned it over on its wheels like it's supposed to be, the left-hand side is really on the right-hand side. Your Honor, that boy wasn't driving that car at all. It was the girl who was driving, and when I had a chance to think about it the next morning, I realized that I'd told Trooper Johnson wrong, and I was scared and I didn't know what to do, and that's why"— and now he's looking right at me—"why I wouldn't talk to you."

18   Naturally, the defendant is allowed to withdraw his guilty pleas. The charges are dismissed and the kid and his parents and I go into one of the back rooms and sit there looking at one another for a while. Finally, we recover enough to mutter some Oh my Gods and Thank yous and You're welcomes. And that's why I can stand to represent somebody when I know he's guilty.

For Writing and Discussion

1. Relate the crime of which Barry Winston's client was accused in "Why I Stand to Defend Guilty Clients" to Aristotle's categories. Do Aristotle's motivations to commit crimes apply? Why or why not?

2. Do you accept Winston's use of the case as a valid reason for representing "guilty" people? Why or why not?

3. Seymour Wishman writes in "A Lawyer's Guilty Secrets":

> It is a fundamental principle of our system of justice that every criminal defendant is entitled to a lawyer, but too much of what I've done in the courtroom is beyond justifying by that abstract principle. I've humiliated pathetic victims of crimes by making liars out of them to gain the acquittal of criminals; I've struggled to win for clients who would go out and commit new outrages. This is not what I had in mind when I entered law school.
>
> One of the reasons I became a criminal lawyer was to defend the innocent, but I haven't had much opportunity to do that. Instead, I find myself facing a difficult question: why have I fought so hard for the interests of the guilty?

How far should a lawyer go in being an advocate for a client? Does an "adequate defense" require an attorney to use any legal tactic that might help a client? Why or why not?

Exhibit A: Language
Lori B. Andrews

A lawyer examines the language of the courtroom and finds that justice may hinge not only on words but also on the manner in which words are spoken.

1   **M**ore than two centuries ago, Jonathan Swift satirized lawyers, describing them as "a society of men among us, bred up from their youth in the art of proving by words multiplied for that purpose that *white* is *black* and *black* is *white.*"

2   Perhaps today's lawyer does not deserve so scathing a criticism, but at its heart is one undeniable fact: Far from being a straightforward fact-finding mission, a trial is a labyrinth of language, with the words of the judge, lawyers and witnesses creating numerous obstacles that prevent juries from making accurate decisions.

3   Since at least 1975, social scientists have fervently studied our trials, approaching the courtroom interchanges with the careful scholarship previously saved for studies of rare languages in distant lands. They have found the psychology of language in the courtroom to be more intricate and influential than they had ever imagined.

4   During a trial, the judge, attorneys, plaintiffs, defendants and witnesses may all be using different styles of speech, each with its own psychological force. Some of the effects of the language used are intentional, while others are inadvertent.

5   The judge refers to himself in the third person in order to underscore his authority. He turns himself from mere human to neutral decision-maker by using phrases like "approach the bench" instead of "Come up here and talk to me."

6   The language used by attorneys is also chosen for its influence. In rape cases, prosecutors may refer to the incident in language that accentuates force and aggression, while defense attorneys may use terms suggesting romance to subtly convey the victim's consent to and responsibility for the alleged rape.

7   A lawyer's linguistic style can mean the difference between winning and losing a case. One study of 38 criminal cases found that the prosecutors who won cases made significantly different use of language than those who lost them. Winning prosecutors asked more questions referring to the witness, spoke longer and made more assertive statements than did losing prosecutors.

8   Successful defense attorneys also had a distinct speech pattern. They used more abstract language, more legal jargon and more ambiguous words than losers did. Another key tactic of good defense attorneys was to distance the accused from the crime by using confusing or abstract terms so that the jurors would not focus clearly on what activities had taken place.

9   Brenda Danet, a Hebrew University sociologist, studied the contrasting language used by the prosecution and defense in the trial of Kenneth Edelin, a Boston physician accused of manslaughter in connection with a late abortion. She found that the defense used passive verbs and nominalization (using verb forms as nouns) to distance Edelin from the incident (for example, "after two unsuccessful attempts"), while the prosecutor employed the active tense with identifying nouns and pronouns ("They tried twice. . . . They were unsuccessful") to focus blame on the defendant.

10   In that same trial, the semantics of referring to the abortus—either as fetus or baby—was so psychologically powerful that negotiation between prosecution and defense was necessary to agree on neutral terms. Defense counsel William Homans submitted a motion to prevent the prosecutor from using the terms "baby boy" and "human being" to refer to the fetus and "suffocate," "smother" and "murder" to refer to Edelin's actions. Homans argued that "certain words have connotations above and beyond their meaning when they are used in the presence of laymen, especially in a case in which there are undoubtedly emotional considerations." The judge agreed to censor the courtroom language, forbidding the use of "baby boy," as well as "smother" and "murder."

11   The term "fetus," according to Danet, "mitigates the connotation of aliveness for the 'baby/fetus' in question, thereby distancing the defendant from wrongdoing."

12   "Although the Edelin case was the only one in which I filed a formal motion about the language," Homans says, "I've frequently asked judges during the course of a trial to prohibit the prosecutor from using certain terms or characterizations."

13   Beyond the words and emphasis a lawyer uses, the forms of questions he employs can shape the facts in the jury's mind, cause a witness to "remember" things that did not in fact happen, and even inadvertently reveal the lawyer's feeling about the truthfulness of his client.

14   Danet has classified typical courtroom questions according to how much they coerce or constrain an answer. The most coercive questions either tell more than they ask ("You didn't return home that night, did you?") or require yes or no answers ("Did you return home that night?") or multiple-choice responses (". . . at 9 or at 10 o'clock?"). In between are typical who-what-where-when questions ("What did you do that night?").

15   In a study of six criminal trials in Boston's Superior Court, Danet found, understandably, that coercive questions were used more often on cross-examination than on direct examination: Eighty-seven percent of the questions on cross-examination were from the most coercive category, compared to 47 percent on direct. Danet also found that the more serious the offense charged in the case, the greater the coerciveness of the prosecutor's cross-examination.

16   The importance of coercive (or "leading") questions has been demonstrated by researchers studying not the frequency of such questions but their effects. Leading questions allow lawyers to tell their versions of the facts and, for many jurors, this is the version that is remembered.

17   In a study by psychologist Elizabeth Loftus and colleagues at the University of Washington, mock jurors read transcripts from a murder trial in which the prosecutor either used questions containing words associated with violence and words intended to evoke emotion, or questions that were neutral. Witnesses' responses were identical in both styles of questioning. Jurors who read leading questions like "How much of the *fight* did you see? were more likely to find a defendant guilty than those who heard neutral versions of the same question ("How much of the *incident* did you see?").

18   Loftus also has found that when a lawyer uses an aggravating, aggressive, active manner to ask about an incident, a witness is more apt to describe it as noisier and more violent than when the lawyer uses a neutral form of questioning.

19   Even the simple choice between an indefinite and a definite article in a question can influence the witness's response. In another study, adults were shown a short film of an auto accident and later asked what they saw. When a definite article was used in the question ("Did you see *the* broken headlight?" rather than "Did you see *a* broken headlight?"), witnesses responded with more certainty—but also were twice as likely to "remember" a broken headlight even when there was none.

20   A large body of general linguistic research can also be applied to courtroom language. For example, studies have shown that people who speak rapidly or in a standard accent are perceived as more competent than people who speak slowly or with an unusual accent. Analysis of actual criminal trials in which the defendant's native tongue was not English suggests that language constraints leave the jury with an unwarranted poor impression of the defendant.

21   William O'Barr, a Duke University anthropologist, has conducted numerous studies regarding the language used by lawyers and witnesses. He concludes that "seemingly minor differences in phraseology, tempo and length of answers, by the covert messages they convey, can have a major effect on the jurors."

22   O'Barr and his colleagues taped 10 weeks of criminal trials in North Carolina to identify patterns of courtroom communication and uncover previously unstudied aspects of legal language. Listening to the tapes, O'Barr noticed that a number of the witnesses spoke in a tentative style, using hedges ("I think . . .", "It seems like . . .", "Perhaps . . ."), intensifiers (saying "very close friends," instead of "close friends" or just "friends") and rising intonation in declarative statements (such as in answer to a lawyer's question about a car's speed, "Thirty, 35?" in a questioning tone, as if seeking approval for the answer). He termed the style "powerless" language.

23   O'Barr chose a 10-minute segment of an actual trial in which a witness spoke in powerless language and rewrote the testimony, removing the hedges and rising intonations and minimizing the intensifiers. Using both scripts, he created four tapes of the testimony—of a man and a woman speaking in the powerless mode and of a man and a woman speaking in the powerful mode. The tapes were identical in substance but differed in style as does the following:

Question: What was the nature of your acquaintance with her?

Powerless answer: We were, uh, very close friends. Uh, she was even sort of like a mother to me.

Powerful answer: We were close friends. She was like a mother to me.

24   Mock jurors who listened to the tapes rated the powerful speaker—whether male or female—more convincing, competent, intelligent and trustworthy than the powerless speaker.

25   O'Barr says that speech has these effects because it provides "clues about the status, trustworthiness and believability of the speaker. Listeners may see the use of a powerful style as reflecting high status and may tend to think favorably of such individuals. In contrast, the use of hedges, like 'uh,' diminishes the significance of what the speaker says. It's interpreted as though the person was warning you not to trust him."

26   Analyzing the original trial tapes, O'Barr also discovered that some witnesses, possibly intimidated by the formality of the courtroom, tried to speak in a more grandiose style than usual. These witnesses often sounded like Alexander Haig, since their "hypercorrect" style tended to be stilted and unnatural and sometimes led to errors in word choice. As he had done in the powerless-speech experiment, O'Barr rewrote a section of hypercorrect testimony in a less formal style. In substance, the two versions were the same but differed alone the lines of the following example:

Question: Immediately after the collision, what happened to you?

Hypercorrect answer: . . . directly after the implosion, I vaguely remember being hurled in some direction. I know not where. . . .

Less formal answer: . . . directly after the collision, I vaguely remember being hurled in some direction. I don't know where. . . .

27   Mock jurors perceived witnesses who used hypercorrect speech as less convincing, competent and intelligent than those who testified in a more informal style.

28   O'Barr has also tested various beliefs that trial lawyers have about language in the courtroom. Trial tactics texts, for example, advise lawyers that a witness will be more credible on direct examination if he testifies in a narrative style, rather than in a fragmented style, interrupted by numerous questions from the lawyer. So O'Barr devised a comparison of narrative and fragmented styles, as follows:

Question: Now, calling your attention to the 21st day of November, a Saturday, what were your working hours?

Narrative answer: Well, I was working from, uh, 7 a.m. to 3 p.m. I arrived at the store at 6:30 and opened the store at 7.

Fragmented answers: Well, I was working from 7 to 3.

Q: Was that 7 a.m.?

> *A:* Yes.
> *Q:* And what time that day did you arrive at the store?
> *A:* 6:30.
> *Q:* 6:30. And did, uh, you open the store at 7 o'clock?
> *A:* Yes, it has to be opened.

29   Neither style, O'Barr found, affected listeners' evaluation of the witness as much as it did their evaluation of the questioning lawyer. When a lawyer allowed a witness to testify in a narrative, listeners believed that the lawyer thought his witness was more intelligent, more competent and more assertive, and in turn tended to judge the witness in the same way.

30   Despite the fact that lawyers' gut feelings and experience could have predicted some of O'Barr's findings, O'Barr believes that the legal system has not given sufficient consideration to the effects of language. In fact, the courts may be unwittingly encouraging linguistic biases. A typical California jury instruction advises jurors that they may determine the truthfulness of a witness's testimony based on his "demeanor while testifying and the manner in which he testifies."

31   "Sometimes these presentational effects may serve the cause of justice, as when stylistic differences are actually related to whether a witness is telling the truth, or when a juror or judge uses stylistic clues to infer credibility," O'Barr and colleagues write in the *Duke Law Journal.* "Sometimes, however, style effects may have less desirable consequences. For example, lower social-status witnesses, *by virtue of the way they speak,* may have less credibility and thus a lesser chance of a fair hearing than do higher-status witnesses. This, of course, is not congruent with the ideals of American justice."

32   Once jurors have been subjected to the semantic and stylistic eccentricities of various lawyers and witnesses, they are asked to weave these confusing stories into a tapestry of facts in order to reach a verdict. No matter how many dozens of witnesses are called or how many months jurors sit for a single trial, there are no guideposts. Notetaking is not allowed in the courtroom, and the jurors may not ask the judge, witnesses or lawyers to clarify a point.

33   In John Hinckley's trial for the attempted assassination of the President, for example, jurors seized on a particular word, poetry, as an important clue in how they should vote in the case. A defense attorney pointed to Hinckley's "bizarre poetry" as evidence of insanity, while a prosecution psychiatrist said Hinckley was a sane man whose poetry was "eccentric fiction."

34   Was all poetry fiction? If so, the prosecution witness must have been correct and Hinckley was sane. The jurors sent a note to the judge requesting a dictionary. The judge denied the request, and the jurors apparently were forced to decide the case on some other basis.

35   "The court is a strange institution," O'Barr says. "In very few other instances in life do you have people trying to make relevant decisions without asking questions."

36   Instead of explaining to jurors at the beginning of the trial what law they should apply (so that they may weigh the facts in that light), judges wait until

the end of the trial to render their instructions to the jury. And even then the language of the jury instructions is often incomprehensible.

37 According to Bruce Sales, professor of psychology and director of the Law-Psychology Program at the University of Arizona, the current method of presenting evidence and jury instructions is "psychologically suspect." He argues that jurors should be given instructions orally before the trial begins and again after all the evidence is presented and should be allowed to take a written copy of the instructions into the deliberation room.

38 "When jurors are not told the law before they begin listening to the evidence, they may not pay attention and remember the relevant facts. At the end of the trial, when the judge tells the jurors they must consider X, Y and Z, a juror may think 'I didn't think X was going to be important' and have a hard time remembering anything to do with X."

39 "It is much better if the jurors have some idea of the instructions at the beginning of the case," says Justice Charles Weltner of the Georgia Supreme Court, who experimented with giving instructions at the beginning of trials during his five-year stint as a trial judge.

40 "Jurors are picked by and large for their ignorance of legal matters, yet when it's all over, the judge tells them the law they should have understood from the beginning," he says.

41 As if the legal complexity and timing of jury instructions aren't enough, they are often presented in a hard-to-understand form. Law professor Robert Charrow and his wife, Veda Charrow, a linguist at the American Institutes for Research in Washington, D.C., used 35 prospective jurors in Prince George's County, Maryland, to show just how incomprehensible these instructions can be. The Charrows read 14 widely used California jury instructions to the jurors, asking them to paraphrase each instruction after they heard it. Overall, only 32 percent of the instructions were understood correctly.

42 Analyzing the juror's paraphrases, the Charrows were able to pinpoint some of the confusing aspects of the instructions. The phrase "as to" confounded jurors; it was correctly paraphrased only 25 percent of the time. Yet "as to's" are common in jury instructions, as in one instruction the Charrows tested: "As to any question to which an objection was sustained, you must not speculate as to what the answer might have been or as to the reason for the objection."

43 The use of multiple negatives, in phrases like "innocent misrecollection is not uncommon," produced correct paraphrases only one-quarter of the time.

44 Confusion about words also can lead jurors to apply an erroneous version of the law. For a person to be held liable for negligence, for example, his actions must have proximately (directly) caused the injury at issue. Yet, Robert Charrow says, "25 percent of the jurors thought they were being asked to determine the 'approximate' cause," a term that is conceptually the opposite of proximate cause.

45 When the Charrows rewrote the jury instructions and tested the new version on other Prince George's County jurors, they found comprehension had improved somewhat, but only to a disappointing 40 percent.

46   Sales and his colleagues analyzed another aspect of jury instructions—
their effect on the verdict. They found that in more than 40 states, judges didn't
create their own jury instructions but chose from particular standardized jury
instructions that applied to that state. Even though the instructions had been
drafted by blue-ribbon panels of lawyers and judges, they were often linguisti-
cally deficient and showed little regard for the effects of the words used.

47   When Sales and colleagues compared the effect on the verdict of the standardized instructions, no instructions and instructions that had been rewritten to
be comprehensible, they found that "Reading the standard jury instructions had
the same effect as reading no instructions at all, whereas understandable instructions led to different verdicts and, in civil cases, different awards of money.

48   "The urgent need for improvement in jury instructions cannot be over-
stated," Sales says. "Where jurors do not understand the rules they should be
applying to the evidence, they instead apply whim, sympathy or prejudice in
their decisions."

49   Even though the problems of language in the courtroom have been identified by social scientists, Justice Weltner is pessimistic about how much judges
can do to improve or even change the situation.

50   "On at least one side of each lawsuit, there's a lawyer who wants to confuse, not clarify," he says. "So even if a judge wants to try to help jurors understand, at least one side will resist the change."

51   Weltner's concerns echo those of Thomas More who, writing in the 1500s,
opined that in Utopia "they have no lawyers among them, for they consider
them as a sort of people whose profession is to disguise matters."

52   "Lawyers have always been conscious of the psychological effect of how
they address the defendant," O'Barr says, "but now some clever attorneys are
using speech by themselves and the defendants to do subliminal things."

53   Yet Danet, in an article in *Law and Society Review,* questions the ethics
of applying psycholinguistics to the courtroom. "Should social scientists be
helping lawyers win cases?" she asks. "Expertise about how to manipulate eyewitness testimony, for instance, like all other resources marshalled in the adver-
sary confrontation, is differentially distributed. . . . It is essential to ponder how

54 linguists can help to make the legal system more just and humane."
      As an anthropologist, O'Barr has studied the ways in which other societies
resolve disputes—for example, the Eskimo head-butting contests or song duels.

55   "Based on our cultural values, it seems terribly unfair that how hard your
head is or how well you sing, rather than what the facts are, determines if you
prevail in a dispute," O'Barr says. "But there may be more similarities to our system than we would like to think. Just as settling disputes on physical means
favors the physically strong and powerful, settlements based on verbal means
favor people who are most able to manipulate words."

For Writing and Discussion

1. In what ways can the language of lawyers influence jurors' perceptions of the accused? In what ways can the responses of witnesses influence the outcome of a trial? In what ways might justice be compromised by the use of language?

2. Researcher O'Barr notes that "presentational effects may serve the cause of justice, as when stylistic differences are actually related to whether a witness is telling the truth, or when a juror or judge uses stylistic clues to infer credibility." What "stylistic clues" might suggest a speaker's credibility?

3. Psychologists are often used in trials of wealthy defendants to select jurors and to create and monitor shadow juries during trials. James J. Gobert wrote in "Can Psychologists Tip the Scales of Justice":

> [A]s techniques are further refined, the results may be disastrous. In a criminal trial a jury psychologically stacked to acquit may loose a dangerous defendant on society; one predisposed to convict may send an innocent person to prison. In either case, society's interest in seeing justice done will be frustrated and confidence in the fairness of jury trials eroded.

Gobert published his essay eleven years before the O. J. Simpson trial in which the jury consultant was given a large amount of credit for the acquittal. Does the use of psychologists pervert the objective of an impartial jury and allow a different quality of justice for the rich and the poor? If so, how can the problem be resolved to maintain a fair justice system for all.

4. Both the prosecution and the defense try to find jurors who are uninformed about the case, who haven't heard or read about the case. In 1875 Mark Twain said, "We have a criminal jury system which is superior to any other in the world; and its efficiency is only marred by the difficulty of finding 12 everyday men who don't know anything and can't read." Today's media technology allows for instant visual *and* print coverage. Should the expectations, and even the desirability, of finding uninformed jurors remain? Why or why not?

5. Defense attorneys may strike potential jurors who have had advanced high school or college science courses in cases that rely on DNA or other scientific evidence. People with graduate degrees are often stricken, supposedly because they would tend to be more rational and less open to emotional appeals. Evaluate this defense strategy as it relates to the assumed purpose of a jury trial to seek justice. What role should *pathos* and *logos* play in the courtroom?

THE POWER OF STYLE: PARALANGUAGE

Paralanguage is communication through the *sound* of the voice when speaking. Variations in pitch, tone, volume, and rate of spoken words conveys much of our meaning when we are speaking. Pauses, or the temporary absence of sound, are also elements of paralanguage that can be used to reveal hesitation or to build suspense (The winner is [pause] Betty Rubble!). Words such as "um," "you know," and "well, uh" are also paralanguage that communicate, even though they are sometimes said out of habit. Paralanguage is important in everyday speech, but it takes on added significance in the courtroom.

Use paralanguage to convey the meaning of the following sentences to a partner. (You may want to vary the order of the sentences.)

- The Green house (house occupied by the Green family) is across the street.
- The greenhouse (building for growing plants) is across the street.
- The green house (green-colored house) is across the street.

- Women in the mountains can (perform a process) fish (direct object).
- Women in the mountains can (are able to) fish (noun).

- Advertisement: See our chicken strip (noun).
- Advertisement: See our chicken strip (verb).

Practice: Computers as Jurors?

Although the Solomon Project computer jury that supposedly found Mike Tyson innocent and Claus von Bülow and O. J. Simpson guilty turned out to be a hoax, many people believe that the human jury system is seriously flawed and in need of change. Disagreement with jurors in high-profile cases is only part of the reason an increasing number of people are dissatisfied with a system that seems to "bend over backward" in favor of defendants. Often verdicts hinge on evidence that is, for a variety of reasons, ruled inadmissable. Still, the "human factor" is likely to be blamed.

Argue for or against using computers as jurors. What opposition could be expected and from whom? What information could be fed in? Could a computer jury be fair? Could racial or gender bias be eliminated? Could the truth of witness statements be evaluated? How do the words *objective* and *subjective* come into play?

Practice: Observing the Real Thing

Observe a trial for two or three hours. Make notes about your observations and feelings about the proceedings, and report them to your class. You might also want to compare what you observed to your previous beliefs and impressions about trials that were based on what you had seen in fictional television shows or movies.

CHAPTER SUMMARY

This chapter invited you to take a close look at the rhetoric of the courtroom. You related the elements of persuasion—*ethos, pathos,* and *logos*—to the reality of the courtroom. You probably have many opinions about what is good about the criminal justice system and about what should be improved. As an informed citizen and a shaper of the future, you will have opportunities throughout your life to apply your knowledge.

Chapter 17

⚫

THE COLISEUM

A Declaration of Conscience
Margaret Chase Smith

What started as Joe McCarthy's campaign rhetoric ended in ruin for many people who were accused by McCarthy of spying. None of the people who were investigated and black-listed were proven to have been involved in spying, but McCarthy's tactics so terrified even his colleagues that otherwise prudent men remained silent. Margaret Chase Smith, the only woman in the Senate at the time, had the courage to speak out and to help break McCarthy's grip on a nation.

1 Mr. President, I would like to speak briefly and simply about a serous national condition. It is a national feeling of fear and frustration that could result in national suicide and the end of everything that we Americans hold dear. It is a condition that comes from the lack of effective leadership either in the legislative branch or the executive branch of our Government. That leadership is so lacking that serious and responsible proposals are being made that national advisory commissions be appointed to provide such critically needed leadership.

2 I speak as briefly as possible because too much harm has already been done with irresponsible words of bitterness and selfish political opportunism. I speak as simply as possible because the issue is too great to be obscured by eloquence. I speak simply and briefly in the hope that my words will be taken to heart.

3 Mr. President, I speak as a Republican. I speak as a woman. I speak as a United States Senator. I speak as an American.

4 The United States Senate has long enjoyed world-wide respect as the greatest deliberative body in the world. But recently that deliberative character has too often been debased to the level of a forum of hate and character assassination sheltered by the shield of congressional immunity.

5 It is ironical that we Senators can in debate in the Senate, directly or indirectly, by any form of words, impute to any American who is not a Senator any conduct or motive unworthy or unbecoming an American—and without that

non-Senator American having any legal redress against us—yet if we say the same thing in the Senate about our colleagues we can be stopped on the grounds of being out of order.

6   It is strange that we can verbally attack anyone else without restraint and with full protection, and yet we hold ourselves above the same type of criticism here on the Senate floor. Surely the United States Senate is big enough to take self-criticism and self-appraisal. Surely we should be able to take the same kind of character attacks that we "dish out" to outsiders.

7   I think that it is high time for the United States Senate and its Members to do some real soul searching and to weigh our consciences as to the manner in which we are performing our duty to the people of America and the manner in which we are using or abusing our individual powers and privileges.

8   I think it is high time that we remembered that we have sworn to uphold and defend the Constitution. I think it is high time that we remembered that the Constitution, as amended, speaks not only to the freedom of speech but also of trial by jury instead of trial by accusation.

9   Whether it be a criminal prosecution in court or a character prosecution in the Senate, there is little practical distinction when the life of a person has been ruined.

10   Those of us who shout the loudest about Americanism in making character assassinations are all too frequently those who, by our own words and acts, ignore some of the basic principles of Americanism—

The right to criticize.

The right to hold unpopular beliefs.

The right to protest.

The right of independent thought.

11   The exercise of these rights should not cost one single American citizen his reputation or his right to a livelihood nor should he be in danger of losing his reputation or livelihood merely because he happens to know someone who holds unpopular beliefs. Who of us does not? Otherwise none of us could call our souls our own. Otherwise thought control would have set in.

12   The American people are sick and tired of being afraid to speak their minds lest they be politically smeared as Communists or Fascists by their opponents. Freedom of speech is not what it used to be in America. It has been so abused by some that it is not exercised by others.

13   The American people are sick and tired of seeing innocent people smeared and guilty people whitewashed. But there have been enough proved cases, such as the Amersia case, the Hiss case, the Coplon case, the Gold case, to cause nationwide distrust and strong suspicion that there may be something to the unproved, sensational accusations.

14   As a Republican, I say to my colleagues on this side of the aisle that the Republican Party faces a challenge today that is not unlike the challenge which it faced back in Lincoln's day. The Republican Party so successfully met that

challenge that it emerged from the Civil War as the champion of a united nation—in addition to being a party which unrelentingly fought loose spending and loose programs.

15   Today our country is being psychologically divided by the confusion and the suspicions that are bred in the United States Senate to spread like cancerous tentacles of "know nothing, suspect everything" attitudes. Today we have a Democratic administration which has developed a mania for loose spending and loose programs. History is repeating itself—and the Republican Party again has the opportunity to emerge as the champion of unity and prudence.

16   The record of the present Democratic administration has provided us with sufficient campaign issues without the necessity of resorting to political smears. America is rapidly losing its position as leader of the world simply because the Democratic administration has pitifully failed to provide effective leadership.

17   The Democratic administration has completely confused the American people by its daily contradictory grave warnings and optimistic assurances, which show the people that our Democratic administration has no idea of where it is going.

18   The Democratic administration has greatly lost the confidence of the American people by its complacency to the threat of communism here at home and the leak of vital secrets to Russia through key officials of the Democratic administration. There are enough proved cases to make this point without diluting our criticism with unproved charges.

19   Surely these are sufficient reasons to make it clear to the American people that it is time for a change and that a Republican victory is necessary to the security of the country. Surely it is clear that this Nation will continue to suffer so long as it is governed by the present ineffective Democratic administration.

20   Yet to displace it with a Republican regime embracing a philosophy that lacks political integrity or intellectual honesty would prove equally disastrous to the Nation. The Nation sorely needs a Republican victory. But I do not want to see the Republican Party ride to political victory on the Four Horsemen of Calumny—fear, ignorance, bigotry, and smear.

21   I doubt if the Republican Party could do so, simply because I do not believe the American people will uphold any political party that puts political exploitation above national interest. Surely we Republicans are not so desperate for victory.

22   I do not want to see the Republican Party win that way. While it might be a fleeting victory for the Republican Party, it would be a more lasting defeat for the American people. Surely it would ultimately be suicide for the Republican Party and the two-party system that has protected our American liberties from the dictatorship of a one-party system.

23   As members of the minority party, we do not have the primary authority to formulate the policy of our Government. But we do have the responsibility of rendering constructive criticism, of clarifying issues, of allaying fears by acting as responsible citizens.

24   As a woman, I wonder how the mothers, wives, sisters, and daughters feel about the way in which members of their families have been politically mangled in Senate debate—and I use the word "debate" advisedly.

25   As a United States Senator, I am not proud of the way in which the Senate has been made a publicity platform for irresponsible sensationalism. I am not proud of the reckless abandon in which unproved charges have been hurled from this side of the aisle. I am not proud of the obviously staged, undignified countercharges which have been attempted in retaliation from the other side of the aisle.

26   I do not like the way the Senate has been made a rendezvous for vilification, for selfish political gain at the sacrifice of individual reputations and national unity. I am not proud of the way we smear outsiders from the floor of the Senate and hide behind the cloak of congressional immunity and still place ourselves beyond criticism on the floor of the Senate.

27   As an American, I am shocked at the way Republicans and Democrats alike are playing directly into the Communist design of "confuse, divide, and conquer." As an American, I do not want a Democratic administration white-wash or cover up any more than I want a Republican smear or witch hunt.

28   As an American, I condemn a Republican Fascist just as much as I condemn a Democrat Communist. I condemn a Democrat Fascist just as much as I condemn a Republican Communist. They are equally dangerous to you and me and to our country. As an American, I want to see our Nation recapture the strength and unity it once had when we fought the enemy instead of ourselves. . . .

For Writing and Discussion

1. What double-standard did Smith point out regarding the relationship between the American people and those in elected office?

2. The FBI investigated even people who were said to have been associated with a member of the Communist party or a number of other groups that were judged subversive. The investigations resulted in humiliation and, often, loss of jobs, friends, and families. How does Smith refer to the process (as opposed to jury trials)? Why do you think so many people participated in the investigations or failed to speak out against them?

3. The following is an example of notices received by employees: Your name appeared in an article in the 4 April 1946 edition of the *York Gazette and Daily* as a sponsor of a Philadelphia, Pa. mass meeting . . . sponsored by the National Committee to Win the Peace. The National Committee to Win the Peace has been cited by the Attorney General as Communist. . . . The foregoing information indicates that you have been and are a member, close affiliate, or sympathetic associate of the Communist Party. [Notice of dismissal] (qtd. in Manchester, *The Glory and the Dream* 495) In what ways does this accusation and its result violate the Constitution?

4. Evaluate the effectiveness of Smith's use of parallel structure and repetition. Cite specific examples.

Practice: Search and Evaluate

After McCarthy smeared General George Marshall, President Truman realized the threat that McCarthy posed. Still, Truman would not allow his advisors to leak to the press personal information about McCarthy that would have destroyed McCarthy's credibility early on. In view of the destruction to reputations and lives that McCarthy brought, some might view Truman's taking the "high road" a mistake and believe that sometimes the end (stopping McCarthy) justifies the means (using a dirty trick). Using on-line or traditional library sources, research the McCarthy era and speculate about how history might have been changed if Truman had approved his advisors' plan.

The "Checkers" Speech
Richard M. Nixon

In September 1952, the press discovered a slush fund for Richard Nixon that was collected from 76 prominent Californians. The fund contained $18,235 and was, according to the press, for Nixon's personal expenses. Nixon was then a California senator, but he was also running for vice president on the Republican ticket with Dwight Eisenhower. The press had called for Nixon's resignation from his Senate seat, and Eisenhower had been pressured to drop him as a running mate; Nixon's future was on the line. As a last-ditch effort to save himself, Nixon gave a speech to a radio and television audience of 60 million people. The speech is said to have changed the course of history by making it possible for Nixon to become vice president and, later, president.

1   My fellow Americans: I come before you tonight as a candidate for the Vice Presidency and as a man whose honesty and integrity have been questioned.

2   The usual political thing to do when charges are made against you is to either ignore them or to deny them without giving details.

3   I believe we've had enough of that in the United States, particularly with the present Administration in Washington, D.C. To me the office of the Vice Presidency of the United States is a great office, and I feel that the people have got to have confidence in the integrity of the men who run for that office and who might obtain it.

4   I have a theory, too, that the best and only answer to a smear or to an honest misunderstanding of the facts is to tell the truth. And that's why I'm here tonight. I want to tell you my side of the case.

5   I am sure that you have read the charge and you've heard that I, Senator Nixon, took $18,000 from a group of my supporters.

6   Now, was that wrong? And let me say that it was wrong—I'm saying, incidentally, that it was wrong and not just illegal. Because it isn't a question of whether it was legal or illegal, that isn't enough. The question is, was it morally wrong?

7   I say that it was morally wrong if any of that $18,000 went to Senator Nixon for my personal use. I say that it was morally wrong if it was secretly given and secretly handled. And I say that it was morally wrong if any of the contributors got special favors for the contributions that they made.

8   And now to answer those questions let me say this:

9   Not one cent of the $18,000 or any other money of that type ever went to me for my personal use. Every penny of it was used to pay for political expenses that I did not think should be charged to the taxpayers of the United States.

10   It was not a secret fund. As a matter of fact, when I was on "Meet the Press," some of you may have seen it last Sunday—Peter Edson came up to me after the program and he said, "Dick, what about this fund we hear about?" And I said, Well, there's no secret about it. Go out and see Dana Smith, who was the administrator of the fund. And I gave him his address, and I said that you will find that the purpose of the fund simply was to defray political expenses that I did not feel should be charged to the Government.

11   And third, let me point out, and I want to make this particularly clear, that no contributor to this fund, no contributor to any of my campaigns, has ever received any consideration that he would not have received as an ordinary constituent.

12   I just don't believe in that and I can say that never, while I have been in the Senate of the United States, as far as the people that contributed to this fund are concerned, have I made a telephone call for them to an agency, or have I gone down to an agency in their behalf. And the record will show that, the records which are in the hands of the Administration. . . .

13   And so now what I am going to do—and incidentally this is unprecedented in the history of American politics—I am going at this time to give to this television and radio audience a complete financial history; everything I've earned; everything I've spent; everything I owe. And I want you to know the facts. I'll have to start early.

14   I was born in 1913. Our family was one of modest circumstances and most of my early life was spent in a store out in East Whittier. It was a grocery store—one of those family enterprises. The only reason we were able to make it go was because my mother and dad had five boys and we all worked in the store.

15   I worked my way through college and to a great extent through law school. And then, in 1940, probably the best thing that ever happened to me happened, I married Pat—sitting over here. We had a rather difficult time after

we were married, like so many of the young couples who may be listening to us. I practiced law; she continued to teach school. I went into the service.

16   Let me say that my service record was not a particularly unusual one. I went to the South Pacific. I guess I'm entitled to a couple of battle stars. I got a couple of letters of commendation but I was just there when the bombs were falling and then I returned. I returned to the United States and in 1946 I ran for the Congress. . . .

17   [Lists of assets and debts.]

18   That's what we have and that's what we owe. It isn't very much, but Pat and I have the satisfaction that every dime we've got is honestly ours. I should say this—that Pat doesn't have a mink coat. But she does have a respectable Republican cloth coat. And I always tell her that she'd look good in anything.

19   One other thing I probably should tell you because if I don't they'll probably be saying this about me too, we did get something—a gift—after the election. A man down in Texas heard Pat on the radio mention the fact that our two youngsters would like to have a dog. And, believe it or not, the day before we left on this campaign trip we got a message from Union Station in Baltimore saying they had a package for us. We went down to get it. You know what it was?

20   It was a little cocker spaniel dog in a crate that he sent all the way from Texas. Black and white spotted. And our little girl—Trisha, the 6-year-old—named it Checkers. And you know, the kids love the dog and I just want to say this right now, that regardless of what they say about it, we're gonna keep it.

21   It isn't easy to come before a nation-wide audience and bare your life as I have done, but I want to say something before I conclude, that I think most of you will agree on.

22   Mr. Mitchell, chairman of the Democratic National Committee, made the statement that if a man couldn't afford to be in the United States Senate, he shouldn't run for the Senate. And I just want to make my position clear. I don't agree with Mr. Mitchell when he says that only a rich man should serve his government in the United States Senate or in the Congress. I don't believe that represents the thinking of the Democratic Party and I *know* that it doesn't represent the thinking of the Republican Party.

23   I believe that it's fine that a man like Gov. Stevenson,[1] who inherited a fortune from his father, can run for President, but I also feel that it's essential in this country of ours that a man of modest means can also run for President, because, you know, remember Abraham Lincoln. You remember what he said: God must have loved the common people; he made so many of them.

24   And now I'm going to suggest some courses of conduct. First of all, you have read in the papers about other funds now. Mr. Stevenson apparently had a couple, one of them in which a group of business people *paid* and helped to supplement the salaries of state employees. Here is where the money went *directly* into their pockets, and I think that what Mr. Stevenson should do

---

[1]Adlai Stevenson, governor of Illinois (1949–1953) and Democratic candidate for president in 1952 and 1956.

should be to come before the American people as I have done and give the names of the people who contributed to this fund, give the names of the people who put this money into their pockets at the same time they were receiving money from their state government and see what favors, if any, that they gave out for that. I don't condemn Mr. Stevenson for what he did, but until the facts are in, there is a doubt that will be raised.

25   And as far as Mr. Sparkman[2] is concerned, he has had his wife on the payroll. I don't condemn him for that, but I think that he should come before the American people and indicate what outside sources of income he has had. I would suggest that under the circumstances both Mr. Sparkman and Mr. Stevenson should come before the American people as I have and make a complete financial statement as to their financial history, and if they don't, it will be an admission that they have something to hide—and I think you will agree with me. Because, folks, remember, a man who is to be President of the United States, a man that's to be Vice President of the United States, must have the confidence of all the people, and that's why I'm doing what I'm doing, and that's why I suggest that Mr. Stevenson and Mr. Sparkman, since they are under attack, should do what they're doing.

26   Now, let me say this: I know that this is not the last of the smears. In spite of my explanation tonight, other smears will be made. Others have been made in the past. And the purpose of the smears is this: to silence me, to make me let up. Well, they just don't know who they're dealing with. I'm going to tell you this: I remember in the dark days of the Hiss[3] case. Some of the columnists who are attacking me now and misrepresenting my position were violently opposed to me at the time I was after Alger Hiss. But I continued to fight because I knew I was right. And I can say to this great television and radio audience that I have no apologies to the American people for my part in putting Alger Hiss where he is today. And as far as this is concerned, I intend to continue to fight.

27   Why do I feel so deeply? Why do I feel that in spite of the smears, the misunderstandings, the necessity for a man to come up here and bare his soul as I have—why is it necessary for me to continue this fight? And I want to tell you why. Because you see, I love my country, and I think my country is in danger. And I think the only man who can save American at this time is the man that is running for president on my ticket—Dwight Eisenhower. . . . [Call for people to wire or write the Republican National Committee to help them decide whether Nixon should stay on or get off the ticket and call for votes for Eisenhower.]

For Writing and Discussion

1. During the weeks after the speech, the National Republican Committee received two million letters and telegrams that were 350 to 1 in support of

---

[2]John Sparkman, vice-presidential running mate of Adlai Stevenson.

[3]Alger Hiss, accused by a communist courier of helping transfer documents to the communists. Hiss was convicted in a second trial but maintained his innocence.

Nixon. How do you account for this outpouring of support? How does the fact that television was relatively new relate to Nixon's success?

2. Nixon said in his book *Six Crises*, "I knew I had to go for broke. This broadcast must not just be good. It had to be a smash hit—one that really moved people, one that was designed not simply to explain the complicated and dull facts about the fund to the people, but one that would inspire them to enthusiastic, positive support." Speculate about how our history might have been different if Nixon had failed to achieve his purpose with the speech.

3. Do you think today's politicians are more sophisticated in their appeals, or do you think similar tactics are used in contemporary speeches? Cite examples to support your opinion.

4. Contrast the style of Nixon's speech to Margaret Chase Smith's speech ("A Declaration of Conscience"). In which speech was *logos* most apparent? In which speech was *ethos* used most? In what way was *pathos* used in each speech?

Practice: Identifying Informal Fallacies

In a brief essay, identify examples in Nixon's speech of the informal fallacies you learned in Part Four. Since the speech is so replete with examples, you will probably want to narrow your discussion to two or three types of fallacies, keeping in mind that many examples could be classified in more than one way. Remember to include quotation marks around specific examples from the speech.

Address to the Ohio Women's Rights Convention: And Ain't I a Woman?
Sojourner Truth

Sojourner Truth, born as a slave in 1797 and freed in the 1820s, was active as an abolitionist, a minister, and a feminist. She gave this speech to the Ohio Women's Rights Convention in 1851. The audience, fearing that the feminist movement would become associated with the abolitionist cause, was hostile when she rose to speak. By the time she finished, however, she had won them.

1   Well, children, where there is so much racket there must be something out of kilter. I think that 'twixt the Negroes of the South and the women at the North,

all talking about rights, the white men will be in a fix pretty soon. But what's all this here talking about?

2   That man over there says that women need to be helped into carriages, and lifted over ditches, and to have the best place everywhere. Nobody ever helps me into carriages, or over mud-puddles, or gives me any best place! And ain't I a woman? Look at me! Look at my arm. I have ploughed and planted, and gathered into barns, and no man could head me! And ain't I a woman? I could work as much and eat as much as a man—when I could get it— and bear the lash well! And ain't I a woman? I have borne thirteen children, and seen them most all sold off to slavery, and when I cried out with my mother's grief, none but Jesus heard me! And ain't I a woman?

3   Then they talk about this thing in the head; what's this they call it? (Intellect, someone whispers.) That's it, honey. What's that got to do with women's rights or Negro's rights? If my cup won't hold but a pint, and yours holds a quart, wouldn't you be mean not to let me have my little half-measure full?

4   Then that little man in black there, he says women can't have as much rights as men, 'cause Christ wasn't a woman! Where did your Christ come from? From God and a woman! Man had nothing to do with Him.

5   If the first woman God ever made was strong enough to turn the world upside down all alone, these women together ought to be able to turn it back, and get it right side up again. And now they is asking to do it, the men better let them.

6   Obliged to you for hearing me, and now old Sojourner ain't got nothing more to say.

For Writing and Discussion

1. Which of *ethos, pathos,* and *logos* is foremost in Truth's speech? Give specific examples.

2. Summarize in a list Truth's main points. What is her main argument? To whom does she allude (refer to indirectly) in the fifth paragraph? What is the significance of the allusion?

3. Identify stylistic elements such as repetition, use of figurative language, and so forth, and illustrate with examples from the speech.

A CLOSER LOOK

The readings in this section invite you to examine elements of contemporary politics and evaluate what is said, what is not said, and the empowerment of people.

How to Analyze Election Rhetoric
Hugh Rank

IMAGES & ISSUES
How to Analyze Election Rhetoric

People often complain vaguely about political language ("it's all promises ... all lies ... too confusing") or ignore it and drop out, because they don't understand some basics. Appreciate free elections: using words and images (not force and violence), persuaders seek support for themselves and their ideas.

Prepare yourself to analyze political language in a non-partisan, common sense way. We don't know in advance whether a message is true or not, beneficial or not, cogent or not; but, we do know some predictable patterns in **content** and **form**.

CONTENT. The core message of a candidate can be basically summarized as: **"I am competent and trustworthy; from me, you'll get more good and less bad."** This one sentence contains three claims (**competent, trustworthy,** and **benevolent** — as in Aristotle's ethos) and a promise of benefits.

If politicians are "always promising," remember that **we** are always **benefit-seeking**. No matter how we define "good" and "bad," we want to get and to keep the "good" and to avoid or to change the "bad." Thus:

> Expect from the Haves, a **conservative rhetoric**, stressing protection (keep the "good") and prevention (avoid the "bad").

> Expect from the Have-Nots, a **progressive rhetoric**, stressing relief (change the "bad") and acquisition (get the "good").

Persuaders often "make problems." To an audience of Haves, conservative persuaders stir up fears and anxieties of loss; to an audience of Have-Nots, progressive persuaders stir up discontent and dissatisfaction with an existing "bad," or anger and resentment for being deprived. After stirring up these fears and hatreds, persuaders often try to bond their group together, then direct and trigger their energies toward a specific action.

From *The Pitch* © 1982 by Hugh Rank (Teachers may photocopy for classroom use.) Published by the Counter-Propaganda Press, Box 365, Park Forest, Illinois 60466

FORM. The **"pitch"** and the **"pep talk"** are terms used here to describe two commonly seen patterns of persuasion, the structure underneath most messages.

The **"pitch"** is basically a five-part strategy, usually seen in commercial advertising, but also common in political ads. To focus on this pattern, **ask these questions:**

1. What attention-getting techniques are used?

Often, simple repetition for name recognition; thus, many posters, buttons, TV spots.

2. What confidence-building techniques are used?

The goal is to project the "image" of being competent, trustworthy, and benevolent. Note the smiles, handshakes, sincere looks, the endorsements, and the patriotic associations.

3. What desire-stimulating techniques are used?

Conservatives and progressives emphasize different aspects, stimulating either desires for "goods" or fears of "bads." Commercial ads focus on specific individual benefits, whereas most political ads stress general social benefits (e.g. peace, prosperity, honest and efficient government). Everyone agrees on these as general goals, but disagrees about specific means to them.

4. Are there urgency-stressing techniques used?

Common in campaigns; sometimes an intense "now-or-never, before it's too late" plea.

5. What response is sought?

Often, simply to vote for the person or party.

The "**pep talk**" seeks *committed collective action.* It's less common, but more intense, stirring emotions of fear and anger, as in party rallies, single-issue or "cause" groups, war propaganda, and in targeted direct-mail ads. The "pep talk" usually has a four-part pattern of Threat, Bonding, Cause, and Response. To focus on this pattern, **ask these questions:**

1. What is the threat feared?

The danger? The possible loss? Who are the foes? The victims? The warning-givers? What "horror stories" are told?

2. What words and nonverbals are used in bonding the group?

Sometimes meetings, rallies, marching, singing, or cheering stressing unity, loyalty, and pride ("We're Number 1 !")

3. What is the "cause" defended?

What duty words are used? (should, ought, must) What defense words? (save, protect, help) What other needs the defending? (the nation, the people, the workers, the poor, the children, the animals, the environment).

4. What response is sought?

Simply to vote? Or more? (e.g. to join, enlist, work, fight, picket, march, give, donate)

Analysis of form and content is limited. It does not examine truth or deception, accuracy or error, intent or consequences, but it's a useful start. Our ultimate goal? Knowledge, understanding, insight, tolerance, and perhaps even compassion.

Conservative rhetoric, as used here, is the rhetoric of the Haves who seek **to keep the "good"** (protection) and **to avoid the "bad"** (prevention). It is the rhetoric of the Establishment, defending the *status quo*, justifying the way things are. Generally this is the rhetoric of the current administration (whoever is in the White House, the State House, and City Hall); of corporations, organizations, and government bureaucracies; of those people who have control and power. Conservative rhetoric stresses satisfaction, contentment, appreciation, and enjoyment of the existing "goods"; pride in the group, its past history, traditions, and heroes; and in its present accomplishments and leaders. Conservative rhetoric encourages the self-image of being a defender of the society (the nation, the culture, the faith). Warnings, precautions, and anxieties are focused on the main threat: the *fear of loss* — either suddenly (by seizure, by being overwhelmed or conquered) or slowly (by decay, attrition, or infiltration). It is reasonable to expect that people who have a "good" will want to keep it, and to avoid the "bad" of losing it or having it taken away.

Progressive rhetoric, as used here, is the rhetoric of the Have-Nots who seek **to change the "bad"** (relief) and **to get the "good"** (acquisition). It is the rhetoric of dissatisfaction, discontent, and anger for not having the "good"; it is also the rhetoric of hopes, dreams, change, progress, and improvement. It not only attacks the existing evils, but also holds out hope for a better future. Generally, this is the rhetoric of the opposition, the Outs, the protesters and the picketers, the people not in power. Progressive rhetoric ranges from reformers, who want to change or fix up parts of the existing system, to revolutionaries who want to destroy it and replace it with a better one. Progressive rhetoric stresses the problems of the existing order and criticizes the caretakers, especially for corruption (intentional) or incompetence (unintentional). Progressive rhetoric encourages the self-image of being a defender of the poor (the unfortunate, the underprivileged, the victims). In addition to the specific problem involved, progressive rhetoric often suggests fears of *stasis* (being stopped, stalled, thwarted), either suddenly (banned, controlled) or slowly (exhausted, burned out). It is reasonable to expect that people who have a "bad" will want to get rid of it, and to get the "good."

Practice: Parting the Parties' Positions

If a nation expects to be ignorant and free, in a state of civilization, it expects what never was and never will be.

Thomas Jefferson

Make a list of five or six current issues, and write for each issue the positions of the Democratic and the Republican parties. If you are not sure about an issue, try reading some of the political magazines and watching C-SPAN or CNN's *Inside Politics*. Decide with which party you agree on most issues. You may also want to examine the positions of third parties.

"THE SENATOR IS OUT RIGHT NOW, BUT PERHAPS I CAN DODGE SOME OF YOUR QUESTIONS?"

© Dave Carpenter

The Art of the Dodge
Harper's magazine

1   [T]he following is] from an exchange between White House press secretary Marlin Fitzwater and reporters at a February 13 (1992) press briefing, following Richard Truly's departure as NASA administrator. Though the White House claimed that Truly left voluntarily, Truly said that he was forced to resign after repeated clashes with Vice President Quayle, the chairman of the National

Space Council, which advises the President on space policy. A transcript of the exchange appeared in the February 14 *Washington Post.*

2   **REPORTER:** What's happening to the search for a successor for Admiral Truly, and what do you say to the reports on Capitol Hill that he was forced out by the White House, which expressed regrets?

3   **MARLIN FITZWATER:** Well, we are actively searching for a successor. We would hope to have a candidate very soon. Admiral Truly has served long and well in various capacities in the government. As you all know, he is a friend of the President's, and we think that he's done an outstanding job of bringing that agency back to life following the Challenger incident.

4   Whether there are policy differences or not, from our point of view, he deserves our gratitude and our support, and we want to only herald the outstanding job that he has done there—

5   **REPORTER:** Admiral Truly says flatly that his resignation was demanded. He was told to resign and wasn't given a reason. Do you have a reason for us?

6   **FITZWATER:** I suggest you ask him, because from our point of view—

7   **REPORTER:** I'm sorry, the reason I'm asking you is because Admiral Truly says that he was not given a reason.

8   **FITZWATER:** Well, he submitted his resignation, and we have responded with the praise that we think he deserves, and we do not intend to say anything critical of his tenure here because he has done an admirable and a dedicated job of restoring confidence to that agency.

9   **REPORTER:** Forgive me, the question still remains. Why was it that his resignation was requested?

10 **FITZWATER:** His resignation was submitted, and it was—

11 **REPORTER:** But it was submitted, he says, after he was told to submit it.

12 **FITZWATER:** Well, again I refer you to him.

13 **REPORTER:** He said he met with the President here Monday night and that his resignation was demanded.

14 **FITZWATER:** We've had meetings with the admiral time and again in the last several months, and there have been any number of considerations of policy. But once again, we have only the highest regard for him, and I—we would say nothing that's critical.

15 **REPORTER:** Is his version of events not true?

16 **FITZWATER:** I'm simply saying that from our point of view he's done a great job, and we have the highest praise for him.

17 **REPORTER:** Did the administration request his resignation?

18 **FITZWATER:** The admiral submitted his resignation and we accepted it—

19 **REPORTER:** Marlin, let me put it another way. Are you denying that his resignation was forced? Are you denying that?

20 **FITZWATER:** I'm saying that he submitted his resignation, that we accepted it, but we think he's done an outstanding job in many areas and we wish him nothing but the best in the future.

21 **REPORTER:** But did he submit it upon request?

22   **FITZWATER:** Again, those are questions you have to ask him.
23   **REPORTER:** He has already said that.
24   **FITZWATER:** Well, then fine. You've got his answer, now you've got mine.

Growing Politics
in the Backyards of America
Ellen Ryan

1   **S**o many Americans steer clear of politics that it looks as though there's an organized general strike under way. Unfortunately, there isn't. Rather than a noisy, concerted effort that might enliven and transform our political process, millions of people have just quietly given up hope on politics as a way to improve society.

2   Activists concerned about this situation search for ways to motivate people to get involved in politics—as if the problem is that something is wrong with the people. Instead of assuming that people are not motivated to act, activists and others concerned about political apathy might look at it a different way—that acting motivates people. And much of the action of American political life today motivates people to stay home.

SUPERMARKET POLITICS

3   Look at what passes for political action in this country. People are asked to take positions for or against specific issues, candidates, and proposals that they have very little role in defining, selecting, or developing. This amounts to little more than mass-consumer citizenship; one votes on school bonds, political leaders, and referenda in the same way one selects laundry detergent at a supermarket. A person's individual preferences and economic circumstances determine whether to go for the cheapest one or pay a few extra cents for the lemon scent and fancy packaging.

4   This is true of local politics as well as national politics. At a recent meeting of a St. Paul community council, neighborhood residents concerned about a proposed housing development were told that they could speak in favor of or against the project. Residents who wanted to make changes in the proposal were ruled out of order. What one learns from such an experience is that you are welcome to say yes or no, but if you want to participate in working out a compromise and finding a solution, you might just as well stay at home. Given the dishes left in the sink after rushing the kids through supper, the mail left unopened, and the hundred other chores that fill an evening after a hard day's work, the choice is simple.

5   Many activist organizations, despite their dedication to the ideals of equality and democracy, operate in a similar manner. They try to enlist everyday people as supporters, but in effect involve only a small group of people in defining the goals and strategies of the organization or movement. It's little wonder that these groups wind up representing only the interests of a narrow collection of activists (or at best the activists' interpretation of what everyday people should want) rather than the public as a whole.

GOURMET SHOP POLITICS

6   At the other extreme in American politics are organizations that embrace a democratic process open to all but demand such internal consistency among their members that the only action is endless discussion. Everyone in the organization must agree on everything, and everything that is agreed upon must be consistent with what has already been agreed upon. These organizations tumble into paralysis or deteriorate into feuding factions when consensus cannot be reached. In attempting to build a perfect blueprint for the world as it might be, little action gets taken in the world as it is.

7   This is a complaint often leveled at the Green movement. While acknowledging the creative vision of the Green activists in the United States, one wonders if they will ever mount a mass-based politics. The conceptual, verbal, and group process skills required to be an active Green, not to mention the commitment of time, makes it difficult for most people to ever get involved. Unlike mass-consumer citizenship, this is citizenship for gourmets.

BOUTIQUE POLITICS

8   Much of what passes for progressive political action today is little more than exhorting people to take a position on one or more issues: abortion, affirmative action, saving the whales, the latest Supreme Court nominee, etc. There are numerous causes and organizations for environmentalists, labor unionists, farm activists, feminists, and world hunger activists to choose from depending on their particular tastes—these are the activist boutiques. Sometimes the activists talk to each other from the doorways of their little shops and form a coalition, or a one-stop shopping center for the politically correct. Meanwhile the rest of the American public, exhausted from the crazed pace of modern life, stays home. While many of these issue-focused organizations must be credited with making some real improvements in people's lives, as well as preventing some real deterioration in living conditions, they have not been very successful in reaching the politically inactive majority of the American public.

GROW-YOUR-OWN POLITICS

9   Rather than assuming that citizens are the consumers of politics, it might work better to imagine them as the producers of politics. Rather than attempting to motivate people to take positions on specific issues, it makes more sense to ask people what issues they want to take action on, what results they want to achieve, and what they are willing to do to achieve the results. This approach is

employed by many grass-roots community organizations around the country. They are called multi-issue organizations because they work on any issue the membership decides, after debate and consideration, to work on. These organizations are often dismissed by progressive organizations and leaders because they do not consistently take positions on progressive issues. But they do what many progressive organizations and leaders wish they could do: They involve thousands of people in collective, long-term action on political issues.

10   Kentuckians for the Commonwealth (KFTC), for example, a nine-year-old, 2,400-member community organization with most of its membership in the eastern Kentucky coalfields, has been consistently successful in achieving victories on state and local issues ranging from water quality to public education, from tax reform to hazardous waste management. In an eight-year battle with the coal industry, KFTC succeeded in passing a state referendum (by more than 80 percent of the vote) to stop the industry from strip-mining land over the objections of local property owners. They won despite being out-spent by the coal industry by a ratio of three to one.

11   In Baltimore, the leadership of BUILD, an inner-city community organization based in churches and neighborhood groups, took on the issue of high school dropouts. Instead of coming up with the usual demands for increased funding and creative programs in the schools, BUILD took the novel approach of asking discouraged high school students why they were dropping out. Students said that high school itself was not the problem. Instead, it was the realization that as inner-city minority kids they were unlikely to get an interview, much less a job, coupled with the fact that they had virtually no way to pay for college without a job. All this made staying in school seem meaningless. Armed with the testimony from the students and the power of a disciplined, committed membership, BUILD brought Baltimore's corporate leaders and school administrators together to hammer out an agreement that may not make much sense to education reformers, but that certainly made sense to Baltimore's high school students. All public high school graduates with good attendance records are now assured of getting at least three job interviews with local corporations or having the option to attend college if they qualify through a $25 million scholarship program funded by the city and local businesses.

12   This solution, while not a panacea, is a creative and workable alternative to the problem of the drop-out rate. More importantly, BUILD's process of involving church members, neighborhood groups, the schools, the corporate community, and the students in taking responsibility for together coming up with a solution moved the issue to the top of the political agenda in Baltimore and moved thousands of people into political life with it.

13   Like KFTC, BUILD was called upon to demonstrate its political power at the ballot box. The National Rifle Association targeted inner-city neighborhoods in Baltimore to defeat progressive handgun control legislation on Maryland's ballot last year. Pandering to fears about black-on-black crime, the NRA's well-financed campaign assumed that African-Americans would agree they needed handguns to protect themselves from one another. BUILD countered with a

low-tech, face-to-face education and get-out-the-vote effort in the neighbor-hoods, producing a record turnout in their precincts and a resounding defeat of the NRA initiative.

14   How did KFTC and BUILD win? By never defining winning solely in terms of winning the issue. They measure success in terms of the number of people they recruit into active participation in the organization and any of the many issues it works on. They measure success in terms of the number of peo-ple who develop leadership skills and move into the arena of public politics for the first time. They track their progress in terms of the number of people who learn how to chair meetings and speak in public, who bring not only them-selves but their friends and neighbors to organizational events, who make phone calls and collect dues and run fund-raising events, who directly negoti-ate agreements within the group and with the organization's opponents.

15   The members, leaders, and organizers of KFTC and BUILD are not alien-ated from politics because they refuse to be passive consumers of political mes-sages. Rather than choosing between Brand X and Brand Z, or going without, they develop their own brand of politics that works for them. Few of them ever have or ever will hold elected public office. Few would call themselves progres-sive or even liberal. A few do not read or write very well, but they are perfectly capable of analyzing and speaking out authoritatively on public issues. Groups such as these all around the country are living proof that citizens can not only practice politics effectively, but can also create political organizations on their own terms to move ideas and causes of their own making.

16   Packaging politics for supermarkets, gourmet shops, and boutiques treats citizens like consumers and discourages them from seeing their own power to shape the future of their communities. Helping people grow their own politics produces citizens who act rather than react, who can articulate their values and self-interests and project themselves into the heart of political debate.

For Writing and Discussion

1. Summarize points in Rank's "How to Analyze Election Rhetoric" that you can remember and use in a practical way when confronted with political rhetoric. What effect might Rank's advice have? Will you feel better or worse when you go to the polls to vote?

2. Although the media is often maligned for not covering important issues fairly, in some cases the press is unable to break through official roadblocks. Comment on what is learned from the reporter's attempts to break through the block in "The Art of the Dodge."

3. Ryan ("Growing Politics") notes that activist groups often represent only a faction rather than the broader interests of the public. Is it necessary that activist groups appeal to only "a narrow collection" of people who are con-cerned about a particular issue? Why or why not? How can groups appeal to a broader range of "everyday people"?

4. David Morris writes in "You Can Fight City Hall," "While a great number of Americans purport to hate politics and don't want any part of it, a good many of them still get riled up about local issues and become fervently involved in town, municipal, and county government." Why might people become involved in local politics when they are apathetic about state or national politics? Can you think of a neighborhood, city, or county problem that was solved because one person or a small group of people took some kind of action? Can you think of a local problem or issue that you would address in some way, perhaps by writing a letter to the editor of a local newspaper?

Practice: Looking at All Sides

The Green movement that Ryan mentions in "Growing Politics in the Back-yards of America" protested in a variety of ways France's underwater testing of nuclear weapons in 1995. The protests brought the tests to the attention of many who might not have known about them otherwise. Several governments, including our own, condemned the testing. In other instances, the Green movement has stiff opposition from governmental agencies. Think of an issue that involves the Green movement (or use on-line or traditional library sources to find an article about one), and discuss factors involved on at least two sides of the issue. Evaluate the moral and ethical issues involved, and tell where you stand on the issue.

Practice: Informal Group Debate

To develop research, group participation, and presentation skills, work with a group to debate an issue with another group of classmates. Two groups share the same issue, one advocating for and the other arguing against. Groups prepare 15-minute presentations that may include visuals such as charts and graphs. Group members assign or select responsibilities as researchers and presenters, and each member participates in some way in the presentation. Following presentations by each pair of groups, one member from each side presents a two-minute rebuttal in which the opposing group's sources or support may be questioned, arguments may be reinforced, and evidence may be reiterated. Remaining class members can evaluate how well the paired groups' cases were presented to determine winners.

THE POWER OF STYLE: ORATION

As with everyday communication, the *way* something is said when speaking to a group can be as important as *what* is said. The enthusiasm and conviction with which you present information will help establish a competent and trustworthy *ethos*. Establish rapport with the audience by maintaining eye contact. Try to look at each person in the room at least once, looking randomly at individuals or groups in different areas of the room.

Good posture helps create a confident image, and gestures can help emphasize a point. Remember also the importance of paralanguage in oral communication (see page 324).

TIPS TO CURTAIL STAGEFRIGHT

- Anxiety causes physical reactions such as sweaty palms, shaky legs, a squeaky voice, a dry mouth, and a sinking feeling in the stomach. To calm biological systems prior to your speech or presentation, take deep breaths, press your fingertips together, do stretching exercises as the situation allows, and think of a song or a pleasant place.
- As others give their speeches or presentations, focus on sending them positive thoughts and reactions (such as smiling and nodding).
- Remember that no one has ever died from stagefright and that what you are feeling is not as obvious to others as you probably think it is.
- If you have prepared visuals or handouts for your speech or presentation, focus on handing out the papers or setting up your visuals. The activity should reduce anxiety.
- Remember that this is an opportunity to talk about something you probably know more about than anyone else in the class. Also, you are getting valuable practice that will serve you the rest of your life. Each oral presentation you make should become easier if you are prepared.

GIVING FEEDBACK TO OTHERS

When evaluating your classmates' presentations, begin with two or three positive statements. Limit negative comments to one or two and present negative feedback as suggestions for improving the speech.

Practice: Writing a Political Speech

Write a brief political speech that addresses a controversial issue or a change in policy, keeping in mind that when you take a clear stand, many people will disagree with you. Write an analysis of different viewpoints and note possible appeals to people who hold them. If you are asked to deliver the speech, see the information on page 347 for help.

CHAPTER SUMMARY

The readings in this chapter invited you to take a close look at the rhetoric of the political arena. You have probably heard complaints about the political system in America. Many people complain and follow the complaint with a statement such as, "Well, it's still the best system around." Few would question that statement. However, it is the duty of citizens to do more than complain or admire democracy. You have the skills to seek and use information as an active participant in democracy.

Chapter 18

WRITING CHALLENGE

Choose one of the political speeches in this part or a speech from another source such as *Vital Speeches of the Day*. Analyze the speech for use of *logos,* logical argument; *ethos* of the speaker; *pathos,* emotional appeal to the audience; and use of fallacies, or propaganda techniques. Summarize your findings in a review of the speech for your classmates. (If your instructor approves, as an alternative to a speech, you might want to analyze a closing argument from the transcript of a trial.)

Journal Topic Suggestions

- How you feel about the criminal justice system
- What changes should be made to the juvenile justice system
- The experience you would bring with you if you served on a jury
- How social factors relate to street crime
- Why you should or should not be concerned about national politics
- What you would do if you were President of the United States
- Things you can do in your community to make a difference
- Finish this sentence and outline specific actions and expected results: "I may not be able to change the world, but I can make a small part of it better by _____ ."
- Your response to a city council or county commissioner's meeting

GUIDE TO WRITING

Planning and Prewriting

Read the selection several times, first to get an overall impression of the speech and then to respond to the questions that follow.

ANALYZING THE PURPOSE

Keep the speaker's purpose in mind throughout your analysis by focusing on these questions:

1. What was the speaker trying to accomplish with words?
2. What is the speaker's tone (attitude toward the subject), and what does it reveal?
3. What effect did the speaker seem to want the words to have on the audience? Is there an attempt to change beliefs or attitudes? Is there an attempt to provoke some kind of action?

ANALYZING THE SPEAKER'S AUDIENCE

Knowledge of the intended audience helps you understand why an appeal is effective. For at least one reading of the speech, try to put yourself in the intended audience's mindset. For instance, knowing that television was new to Nixon's 1952 audience and that TV was a technological wonder, a kind of "miracle box," helps you understand one of the reasons for Nixon's success. Television itself carried an appeal and credibility that we in the 1990s have outgrown.

At a minimum, you should be able to answer the following questions about the speechmaker's audience:

1. What is the age range of the audience?
2. Is the audience primarily male, female, or mixed?
3. What is the educational background of the audience?
4. What is the cultural and technological background of the audience?
5. Does the audience have a particular political mindset? religious mindset?

Organizing and Drafting

MAKING AN OUTLINE

To make the writing task easier, make an informal outline based on your responses to the questions below.

T I P

Make several copies of your speech and write a different heading at the top of each copy (i.e., Fallacies, Emotional Language). Use a highlighter to mark examples on each copy.

A.   Explain the persuasive techniques the speaker uses.
  1. *Ethos*—appeals through the speaker's own character and status.
  2. *Pathos*—appeals to the emotions of the audience.
  3. *Logos*—appeals through reasoned arguments.

B.   List the supporting reasons, evidence, or examples for each argument.
1.   Which arguments are faulty? In what way?
2.   Which of the material fallacies do you find?
3.   What unstated assumptions do you find?

C.   Analyze how the speaker uses language and rhythm.
1.   What is the author's level of language?
2.   Do you notice many words that you seldom hear in everyday conversation, or are most of the words common?
3.   Are most of the words short, containing only one or two syllables, or do many of the words contain several syllables?
4.   Are there slang words in the essay?
5.   Are there words that are not in common use today?
6.   Is there an abundance of words that have something in common—perhaps words that have emotional connotations, words that are related to a particular topic (crime, family, diet, etc.) or field (science, law, electronics, etc.)?
7.   What do you notice about the verbs in the piece? Are most of them active, or are there many state-of-being verbs (passive)? Are they mostly general (walk) or specific (sauntered)?
8.   Do most of the nouns have a concrete meaning, or are there many words dealing with abstract concepts? Are there many modifiers (adjectives and adverbs)?
9.   Do any of the words give you clues about the speaker's interests, time period, bias, or education?
10.   Does the speaker use straight description or figurative language? Create a world we can see, hear, touch?
11.   Is there a variety of sentence lengths in the speech, including very short sentences? What is the effect?
12.   Does the speaker use repetition to make points?
13.   Do you detect a certain rhythm in the speech? If so, how is it created? What is the effect?

Writing the first draft may prove to be the easiest part of the process. If you have done a thorough analysis, your brain is saturated with ideas about the piece; you have knowledge that is ready to spill onto the page.

Use your informal outline to make the writing flow smoothly. As you begin writing your analysis, remember to provide adequate support for any claims you make about the arguments, techniques, and language used in the speech. You will need to use specific examples from the speech. However, direct quotations should be limited to brief passages, so you will probably want to paraphrase or summarize some ideas and arguments. (See The Power of Style: Using Paraphrases, Summaries, and Quotations, page 230.)

As you write your paper, assume that your audience has read the speech. This assumption will help you avoid the pitfall of summarizing the essay for your reader.

Include in your introduction brief background information and a general evaluation of the target speech.

After reviewing your notes, decide which aspects of the speech you plan to focus on in the body of your paper. If your speech is long, you may need to limit the scope of your paper by focusing on only one or two aspects of the paper. The sample analysis of the "Checkers" speech, for example, focuses on analysis of propaganda techniques in the speech. The examples of different propaganda techniques might be organized by category or by the order in which they appear in the speech. For your conclusion, write a synthesis of your findings and your evaluation of the speech.

Evaluating and Revising

PARTNER EVALUATION

Read your partner's paper through to get a general impression. Jot down your initial response to the paper. Was it interesting? Did you learn something from reading it? Was it logically organized? Now read the paper again, this time slowly, responding to each of the following questions as you read:

1. Did your partner include the relevant information about the speech in the introduction? Is the introduction clearly written? Does it make you want to read more? How can the introduction be improved?
2. Is each claim about the speech supported with details and quotations? If not, what claims need more support?
3. Does each paragraph contain a clear focus? Do any of the paragraphs contain information or ideas that are unrelated to the rest of the paragraph? If so, which paragraphs?
4. Are transitions provided to guide the reader through the paper? If not, where are transitions needed?
5. Do you have questions about any of the ideas or information? Do any of the ideas need clarifying? If so, note where your partner might add information.
6. What information or ideas are especially interesting? Note the positive aspects of the paper.
7. Are any of the sentences unclear or awkward? Put brackets around sentences that might be improved. Did your partner use a variety of sentence structures?
8. Does the ending adequately conclude the essay, or does the essay just stop? How might the ending be improved?
9. What other ideas for improving the analysis can you suggest?

REVISING

Before revising, reread your paper, jotting down additional ideas and marking sentences that interrupt the logical order. Read your partner's evaluation, carefully considering each suggested change. Decide what revisions you want to make and mark your draft to include the changes.

If you are not using a word processor, you may want to use scissors and tape to cut and paste passages you want to add, delete, or rearrange.

Editing and Proofreading

The following checklist will guide your editing.

1. Can any groups of sentences be combined? Are there awkward or overloaded sentences that can be separated into clear, concise sentences?
2. Should any words or phrases be replaced with words or phrases that more accurately or vividly describe? (Look at verbs and common nouns.)
3. Are all pronoun references clear, and do they agree in number with their antecedents?
4. Do all verbs agree with their subjects in number?
5. Should any passive constructions be changed to active? (Look for forms of *be.*)
6. Can any wordy or unclear sentences be revised?
7. Are direct quotations correctly introduced?

R E M I N D E R

Quotation marks are put outside commas and ending periods and inside colons and semicolons; the placement of question marks and semicolons depends on the meaning of the sentence.

An effective proofreading trick is to read each sentence, starting from the end of the essay and working to the beginning and moving the lips or saying the words aloud. The method is good for detecting faulty sentences because each sentence is read in isolation. Read slowly to see that all words are spelled correctly, each sentence is punctuated correctly, there are no sentence fragments or run-on sentences, and direct quotations are enclosed in quotation marks. (If you are unsure at any point, consult a dictionary or handbook.)

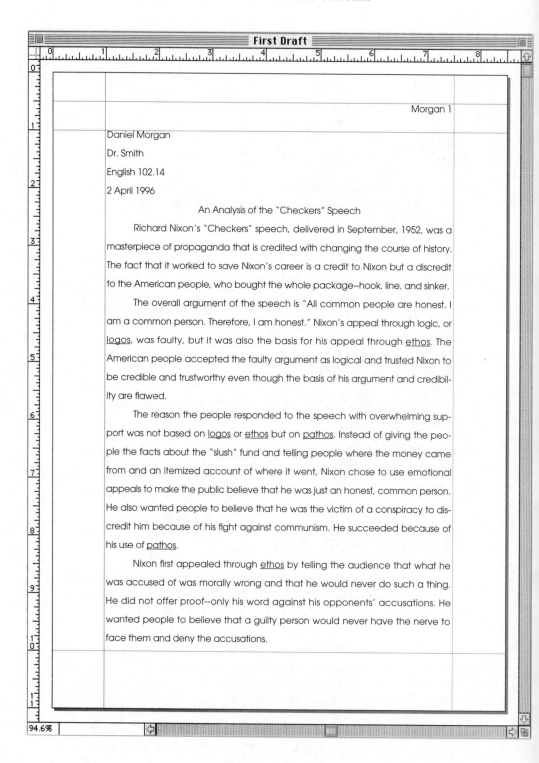

First Draft

Morgan 1

Daniel Morgan

Dr. Smith

English 102.14

2 April 1996

An Analysis of the "Checkers" Speech

Richard Nixon's "Checkers" speech, delivered in September, 1952, was a masterpiece of propaganda that is credited with changing the course of history. The fact that it worked to save Nixon's career is a credit to Nixon but a discredit to the American people, who bought the whole package--hook, line, and sinker.

The overall argument of the speech is "All common people are honest. I am a common person. Therefore, I am honest." Nixon's appeal through logic, or logos, was faulty, but it was also the basis for his appeal through ethos. The American people accepted the faulty argument as logical and trusted Nixon to be credible and trustworthy even though the basis of his argument and credibility are flawed.

The reason the people responded to the speech with overwhelming support was not based on logos or ethos but on pathos. Instead of giving the people the facts about the "slush" fund and telling people where the money came from and an itemized account of where it went, Nixon chose to use emotional appeals to make the public believe that he was just an honest, common person. He also wanted people to believe that he was the victim of a conspiracy to discredit him because of his fight against communism. He succeeded because of his use of pathos.

Nixon first appealed through ethos by telling the audience that what he was accused of was morally wrong and that he would never do such a thing. He did not offer proof--only his word against his opponents' accusations. He wanted people to believe that a guilty person would never have the nerve to face them and deny the accusations.

94.6%

Morgan 2

Nixon then moved into a series of appeals through <u>pathos</u>. He painted a picture of his family as hard-working Americans and of himself as a patriotic (but modest) war hero with "I guess I'm entitled to a couple of battle stars. I got a couple of letters of commendation but I was just there when the bombs were falling and then I returned." It is not unusual for a politician to use his military experience, but Nixon's war experiences had nothing to do with the "slush fund."

Next, Nixon shows himself and his wife to be like other common couples with debts and a little savings. He gives the public a full account of his assets and liabilities. That may have been interesting to some people, but the main purpose was to make people think that if he was straightforward enough to do that, he must be honest. His assets and liabilities had nothing to do with how the money in the "slush" fund was spent. The list of assets and liabilities is just a red herring.

Nixon then used a series of fallacies, mainly "plain folks" appeals, to create pathos. The statement that "Pat doesn't have a mink coat. But she does have a respectable Republican cloth coat" was intended to separate his wife from the wives of rich people who wore mink coats and to associate "respectability" with the Republican party. He implies that the democrats must be the rich people in the mink coats. The line that follows ("I always tell her that she'd look good in anything") was intended to make Nixon look like the thoughtful husband and hero to all the women in the audience.

The most powerful fallacy is the use of the dog Checkers to make people feel sorry for him and his family. He planted the idea that his opponents would actually rip the dog from the arms of his little girls because it was a gift. The mention of Checkers is both a plain folks appeal and a red herring that distracts attention from the real issue.

Nixon then proceeds to try to turn the tables and accuse his opponents of doing what he has been accused of doing. He attacks Sparkman for having a slush fund and sets up Stevenson as a rich person who "inherited a fortune

94.6%

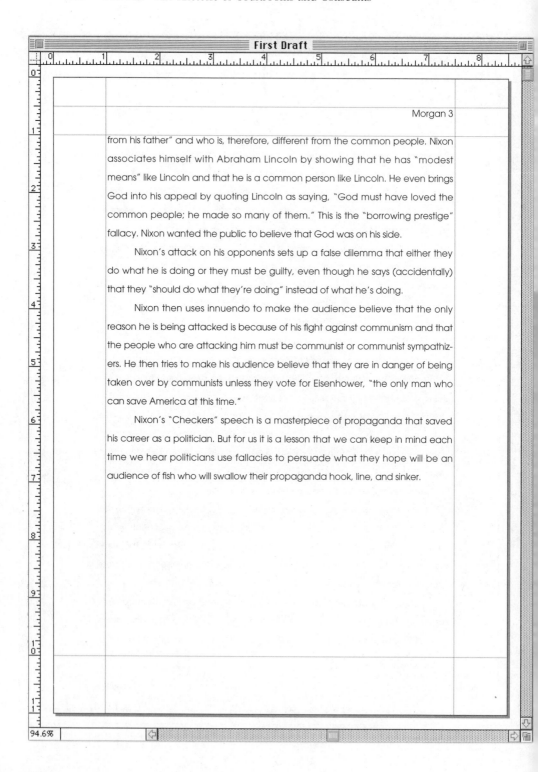

First Draft

Morgan 3

from his father" and who is, therefore, different from the common people. Nixon associates himself with Abraham Lincoln by showing that he has "modest means" like Lincoln and that he is a common person like Lincoln. He even brings God into his appeal by quoting Lincoln as saying, "God must have loved the common people; he made so many of them." This is the "borrowing prestige" fallacy. Nixon wanted the public to believe that God was on his side.

Nixon's attack on his opponents sets up a false dilemma that either they do what he is doing or they must be guilty, even though he says (accidentally) that they "should do what they're doing" instead of what he's doing.

Nixon then uses innuendo to make the audience believe that the only reason he is being attacked is because of his fight against communism and that the people who are attacking him must be communist or communist sympathizers. He then tries to make his audience believe that they are in danger of being taken over by communists unless they vote for Eisenhower, "the only man who can save America at this time."

Nixon's "Checkers" speech is a masterpiece of propaganda that saved his career as a politician. But for us it is a lesson that we can keep in mind each time we hear politicians use fallacies to persuade what they hope will be an audience of fish who will swallow their propaganda hook, line, and sinker.

94.6%

PART SEVEN

Beyond Words:
Ways of Saying

Vincent van Gogh, *Starry Night*, 1889. Oil on canvas, 29" × 36 1/4". The Museum of Modern Art, New York.
Acquired through the Lillie P. Bliss Bequest. Photograph © 1996 The Museum of Modern Art, New York.

Vincent
Don McLean

Starry, starry night. Paint your palette blue and gray,
Look out on a summer day with eyes that know the darkness in
　my soul.
Shadows on the hill, sketch the trees and daffodils,
Catch the breeze and winter chills
5　In colors on the snowy linen land.
Now I understand what you tried to say to me,
And how you suffered for your sanity, how you tried to set them
　free.
They would not listen; they did not know how.
Perhaps they'll listen now.
10　Starry, starry night. Flaming flowers that brightly blaze,
Swirling clouds in violet haze
Reflecting Vincent's eyes of china blue.
Colors changing hue, morning fields of amber grain,
Weathered faces lined in pain,
15　Are soothed beneath the artist's loving hand.
Now I understand what you tried to say to me;
And how you suffered for your sanity, how you tried to set them
　free.
They would not listen; they did not know how.
Perhaps they'll listen now.
20　For they could not love you, but still your love was true.
And when no hope was left in sight on that starry, starry night,
You took your life as lovers often do.
But I could have told you, Vincent,
This world was never meant for one as beautiful as you.
25　Starry, starry night. Portraits hung in empty halls,
Frameless heads on nameless walls
With eyes that watch the world and can't forget,
Like the strangers that you've met, the ragged men in ragged
　clothes,
The silver thorn, the bloody rose
30　Lie crushed and broken on the virgin snow.
Now I think I know what you tried to say to me,
And how you suffered for your sanity,
And how you tried to set them free.
They would not listen. They're not listening still.
35　Perhaps they never will.

For Writing and Discussion

1. What are some of the emotive words and phrases McLean uses to convey the passion of Vincent van Gogh's devotion to art? Did the words create for you a feeling of empathy for the artist?

2. Today, van Gogh's paintings sell for millions; during his lifetime (1853–90), he only sold one painting. He was supported mainly by his brother Theo and died a pauper. Relate McLean's words to the tragedy of the lack of appreciation for van Gogh's work during his lifetime.

3. In a letter to his brother, van Gogh wrote, "Instead of trying to reproduce exactly what I have before my eyes, I use color more arbitrarily so as to express myself forcibly. . . ." Look at van Gogh's painting of the night sky (page 357) and speculate on what he expresses about the universe in the painting.

Part Seven deals with the power of art to communicate and to evoke feelings. Art may be in the words of literature, the sounds of music, or the visual images of paintings or film. Art can re-create the human experience, either objectively or subjectively, or manifest dreams of the unknown and call forth images of still greater impossibilities. Everything great that has been created or built, every innovative way of doing things, every invention that we now take for granted started with the dream of a visionary, an artist. Art is the domain of the emotional and the intellectual; it may be conceived in an emotional state and created with logical precision. Its persuasive power may bring people together with its symbolism of what is best in the human experience, or it may divide people emotionally and intellectually.

The artist reaches our emotions, or uses *pathos,* to communicate and, often, to persuade. The artist often relies on the *sensory,* rather than the *sensible,* the irrational, rather than the rational, even though art may be created within guidelines and respect certain rules and may provide a means of achieving a logical end. Although art may be created purely for entertainment, it may also be created on an intellectual plane with a purposeful argument in mind and may bring about intended or accidental results. In good literature, for instance, the carefully crafted elements of fiction create a powerful force that can move one to laughter or to tears, that can inflame passions or paint pictures in the mind's eye. The mechanics of animation has been used in films such as *Bambi* and *The Lion King* to move children and adults alike to weep.

The power of art to move the human soul was regarded by Plato as being so great that it required the censorship of intellectuals. Plato believed that art could strengthen the human inclination toward good or toward evil and that tragedies depicting the base nature of humans actually strengthened that base nature in the audience.

Aristotle responded with the idea that seeing or reading about tragedy or violence provided a *katharsis* through which the emotions are aroused and then purged, leaving the audience in a calmer state of mind. Stephen King makes a similar argument in justifying his horror stories.

So, what can stir emotions to the point that our bodies react and that Plato's "parts of the soul" (reason, will, and appetite) are affected for good or ill? How does art unite us as a community? How does it divide us when some members of the community feel it is unpatriotic, sacrilegious, racially divisive, or pornographic?

Chapter 19 examines the power of music and the implications of music's effect on mind and body. The literature in Chapter 20 is related to emotions evoked with music or visual images or a mysterious box that induces euphoria, and Chapter 21 deals with the human instinct to create art and the integral part art plays in community. The Writing Challenge in Chapter 22 provides an opportunity to evaluate a work of art: a painting, a movie, an art or music movement.

Chapter 19

MUSIC

Musical Awakenings
Clayton S. Collins

1   Oliver Sacks danced to the Dead. For three solid hours. At sixty. And with "two broken knees."

2   The Oxford-educated neurologist who likes to say, with an impish grin, that he doesn't like any music after Mozart's *Magic Flute,* wasn't particularly taken by the Grateful Dead concert in Friedrich Nietzsche's mnemonic sense, he explains (as only he would), "But in a tonic and dynamic sense they were quite overwhelming. And though I had effusions for a month after, it was worth it."

3   The power of music—not just to get an aging physician with classical tastes up and rocking, but also to "bring back" individuals rendered motionless and mute by neurological damage and disorders—is what's driving Sacks these days. The shyly brilliant and best-selling author of *The Man Who Mistook His Wife for a Hat* and *Awakenings*—the latter of which was made into a 1990 film starring Robin Williams—is working on another case-study book, one that deals in part with the role of music as a stimulus to minds that have thrown up stiff sensory barriers, leaving thousands of victims of stroke, tumors, Parkinson's disease, Tourette's syndrome, Alzheimer's, and a wide range of less-publicized ailments alone, debilitated, and disoriented.

4   "One sees how robust music is neurologically," Sacks says. "You can lose all sorts of particular powers, but you don't tend to lose music and identity." His conviction regarding the role of music in helping the neurologically afflicted to become mentally "reorganized" runs deep: "Whenever I get out a book on neurology or psychology, the first thing I look up in the index is music," he says. "And if it's not there, I close the book."

5   Born in London in 1933 and a permanent resident of the United States for the past thirty-four years, Sacks is a frequent public speaker, careening from stories about great composers and poets to a report about goldfish dancing to a Strauss waltz. However, Sacks is a reluctant celebrity. The fourth son (three of them doctors) of two physicians, he preferred solitary research early in his career, far more comfortable extracting myelin from earthworms than working

with humans. But when he misplaced a vial of the white fatty substance in 1966, he was banished, in effect, to the less-prestigious realm of clinical medicine. Since then, Sacks has burrowed deep into the illnesses and the lives of persons in his care, a miner in the catacombs of the catatonic, chipping away at the walls around their neurological cores. . . .

6   Much of what he has encountered, particularly in working with patients at Beth Abraham Hospital, in the Bronx, is startling. Much of it relates to music.

7   "One saw patients who couldn't take a single step, who couldn't walk, but who could dance," he says. "There were patients who couldn't speak, but who could sing. The power of music in these patients was instantaneous . . . from a frozen Parkinsonian state to a freely flowing, moving, speaking state."

8   Sacks remembers a woman with Parkinson's who would sit perfectly still until "activated" by the music of Chopin, which she loved and knew by heart. She didn't have to hear a tune played. "It was sometimes sufficient to give her an opus number," Sacks says. "You would just say 'Opus 49,' and the F-minor *Fantasy* would start playing in her mind. And she could move."

9   Music is certainly cultural, acknowledges the doctor, but it is basically biological. "One listens to music with one's muscles," he says, quoting Nietzsche again. "The 'tonic' [the key] is mostly brainstem, an arousal response." The "dynamic"—how loud or forcefully the music is played—registers in the basal ganglia. And the "mnemonic" aspect of songs speaks to the unique memories of individuals: from tribal chant to the blare of bagpipes to Bizet. The old cliché about music's universality, he says, has merit.

10   "Deeply demented people respond to music, babies respond to music, fetuses *probably* respond to music. Various animals respond to music," Sacks says. "There is something about the animal nervous system . . . which seems to respond to music all the way down.

11   "I don't know how it is with invertebrates. I think it's a desperately needed experiment to see how squids and cuttlefish respond," he says, his grin widening.

12   In 1974, Sacks was able to apply music therapy to himself to speed an orthopedic recovery. Hospitalized after a fall while climbing in Norway, he experienced neural damage and partial paralysis and sensed that he was, as a result, losing his "motor identity"—forgetting how to walk.

13   For weeks, flat on his back, he listened to a recording of a Mendelssohn violin concerto. One morning, awakened by the familiar piece, he got up and walked across the room to turn off the tape. He found that the concerto wasn't playing, except in his head. Then he realized he'd been walking, carried along by the tune. It was, he says, "the most dynamic experience in my life.

14   "I'm not normally all that fond of Mendelssohn," he jokes.

15   "I think the notion of music as being a prosthesis in a way, for neurological dysfunctions, is very fundamental," Sacks says, citing the case of a patient with damage to the frontal lobes of his brain.

16   "When he sings, one almost has the strange feeling that [music] has given him his frontal lobes back, given him back, temporally, some function that has

been lost on an organic basis," Sacks says, adding a quote from T. S. Eliot: "You are the music, while the music lasts."

17   The key, says Sacks, is for patients to "learn to be well" again. Music can restore to them, he says, the identity that predates the illness. "There's a health to music, a life to music."

18   Those may not sound like the words of a typical clinician. But don't toss terms like "new age" and "holistic" at the good doctor. "I always tighten up a little bit when I hear the word 'holistic,'" he says, professing disdain for "Californian and Eastern" practices. For Sacks, who's been affiliated with a half-dozen neurological institutes and written dozens of seminal papers, medicine needs to be demonstrable, firmly grounded in physiology. Music's been healing for thousands of years, Sacks says. "It's just being looked at now more systematically and with these special populations."

19   So if the Grateful Dead moved Sacks to dance, it had been in the name of research. Seeking a clinical application, Sacks returned to Beth Abraham the next day and "kidnapped" one of his patients. "Greg" was an amnesiac with a brain tumor and no coherent memories of life since about 1969—but an encyclopedic memory of the years that came before, and a real love of Grateful Dead tunes.

20   Sacks took Greg to that night's show. "In the first half of the concert they were doing early music, and Greg was enchanted by everything," Sacks recalls. "I mean, he was not an amnesiac. He was completely oriented and organized and with it."

21   Between sets Sacks went backstage and introduced Greg to band member Mickey Hart, who was impressed with the depth of Greg's knowledge of the group but quite surprised when Greg asked after Pigpen. When told that the former band member had died twenty years before, "Greg was very upset," Sacks recalls. "And then thirty seconds later he asked, 'How's Pigpen?'"

22   During the second half, the band played its newer songs. And Greg's world began to fall apart. "He was bewildered and enthralled and frightened. Because the music for him—and this is an extremely musical man, who understands the idiom of the Grateful Dead—was both familiar and unfamiliar. . . . He said, 'This is like the music of the future.'"

23   Sacks tried to keep the new memories fresh. But the next day Greg had no memory of the concert. It seemed as if all had been lost. "But—and this is strange—when one played some of the new music, which he had heard for the first time at the concert, he could sing along with it and remember it."

24   It is an encouraging development. Amnesiacs have never been found capable of learning anything new. Children have been found to learn quickly lessons that are embedded in song. Sacks, the one-time quiet researcher, is invigorated by the possibilities. He wonders whether music could carry such information, to give his patient back a missing part of his life. To give Greg "some sense of what's been happening in the last twenty years, where he has no autobiography of his own."

25   That would have Sacks dancing in the aisles.

It's Not Only Rock 'n' Roll
Richard Louv

1   One of the best ways to understand how children and teenagers perceive their environment, and the need to change it, is through their music—not through the music itself, or its packaging, but through what kids say about their music.

2   At Baldi Middle School in Philadelphia I asked a class, What about all the people who say heavy metal music causes kids to take drugs?

3   One boy who listened to heavy metal said: "People who are going to take drugs are going to take drugs anyway, and if a lot of people like to blame the music—I mean, if someone says, 'Go jump off of the Empire State Building,' or 'Go jump off a bridge,' or 'Shoot your mother,' are you going to do it? The only people that are saying, 'If you play a record backwards you get a Satanic message and it's going to harm your child,' the only people who are saying that are the ones trying to find an excuse why their daughter or son did drugs, 'cause they're scared it's just going to come down to their kid had emotional problems."

4   A boy who favored rap music explained why he likes to turn his boom box up loud. He likes to create an *environment:* "Since we like it so much, we get into the illusion that a lot of people must like it, so we go around playing it loud and we have this feeling that we're bringing them the music—so we can make everybody dance, make everybody say *ho,* and it's like a symbol or power, just making you believe that you can bring the music that everybody likes to them, like you're the supplier of what they want." . . .

5   Baby boomers grew up thinking of rock 'n' roll, the music of defiance and rebellion, as their personal sound track. *Tsk, tsk,* they cluck today. Look at all the teenagers listening to all that imitation rock. No meaning, no context.

6   In fact, today's children may be the first generation since the advent of vinyl and radio to embrace its parents' music; in that sense, teenagers today are more unusual, musically, than the boomers.

7   Francis Thumm, forty, is a musician, a contributor to the albums of singer-songwriter Tom Waits, and a music teacher at Point Loma High School in San Diego. He says teenage music today is as rich and diverse as it was in the sixties.

8   "But young people today have a sense of history about the music. A kid who listens to heavy metal knows instinctively that the guitar solos he hears had roots in Jimmy Page and Eric Clapton." The Beatles are popular. (One of the Baldi girls said she liked the Beatles because "some of their music sounds like hard rock, and some of it sounds like Easy One-Oh-One music, and some of it sounds like elevator music and that's why I like it, because whatever I feel like, I can listen to.") Thumm continued: "Jimi Hendrix is a god to these kids. They don't know much about him personally. But musically, he's a symbol of fiery virtuosity."

9   Revealingly, Jim Morrison, dark prince of the Doors, is a bigger star today than he was in the sixties—bigger than the Beatles. "Kids love the gothic quality of his songs, the preoccupation with death, the sense of isolation and waywardness, and the fact that he died young." The Jim Morrison biography *No One Here Gets Out Alive* is the current teen generation's corollary to what *The Autobiography of Malcolm X* meant to baby boomers. . . .

10   In Thumm's songwriting class, students stand or sit under the light of a single lamp and sing or simply read their songs or poetry. A frequent subject of these songs is their painful home life.

11   What impresses Thumm most is how closely the kids listen to one another. "When they sing, you can hear a pin drop. Unlike most of us baby boomers at that age, these kids listen to each other with absolute respect."

12   Sometimes they write about suicide. A few years ago, one girl, "tall and stunning, like a model," killed herself. Thumm pulled one of her poems from a manila folder. It read, "The air gets warm / and thinner by the breath / when will be the mercy / of the coming of my death. . . ." The lines, written so neatly, nearly disappear on the page.

13   When Thumm showed me this poem, his face filled with pain. "I have learned over time to pay close attention to these songs and poems."

14   Despite the inherent sadness of rock 'n' roll nostalgia, many teenagers display strong survival instincts. For every sad song, there's a song of hope. Thumm is moved by his students' reverence for nature. And some things never change. "Quality music always wins," he says. "For example, they love gospel music. Just today, when I asked the members of the chorus what they wanted to sing, most of them held up 'Ave Maria,' a thirteenth-century motet. We had a school assembly that began with six students singing an a cappella rendition of Leadbelly's 'Sylvie,' a southern work song. Suddenly this chaotic auditorium became as quiet as a church. I attribute that to the surprising peer respect among these young people and to the simple, noble power of the music."

15   For teenagers, the need for approval and love from parents and peers has never changed. Teenagers are insecure and scared to death. That hasn't changed either.

16   Joan Baez has complained that youth music today has no context—no Vietnam War or civil rights movement for which to serve as sound track. But the affinity for classic rock suggests a context. And surely heavy metal and rap music have their own context. Some of this music glorifies destruction, but much of it criticizes what drugs, advertising, environmental ignorance, and divorce have done to our society. Of *course* there's hysteria in much of today's music, and *sure,* it lacks grace and joy. But the context is kids growing up with single parents trying to make ends meet, growing up with divorce, growing up with disintegration.

17   "There's a sense now, in the music, of a people about to slide over a cultural waterfall," said Thumm. "My response to Joan is, Wake up, honey, it's a different world."

For Writing and Discussion

1. What are some of the implications of the information in Collins' article about the power of music to help heal mind and body? Research in this area is new and rare. Some doctors are beginning to play patients' favorite music during surgery, claiming that people do better during and after surgery because of the joy the music brings them during the ordeal. What suggestions do you have for what researchers should investigate and how they should go about it?

2. What examples in "It's Not Only Rock 'n' Roll" illustrate the power of music to express feelings? What examples reveal music's power to move its audience?

3. Choose a kind of music (rock, folk, jazz, blues, rap, etc.) and tell how that music might be representative of a "perceived environment, and the need to change it" (Louv).

4. Aaron Copland, in "How We Listen to Music," argues that we all listen to music on three separate planes: the sensuous, the expressive, and the "sheerly musical plane." Think about a favorite song and relate your act of listening to the song to Copland's explanation of how we listen to music. Illustrate listening on the "sensuous," "expressive," and "sheerly musical planes" with examples from your own experience.

5. Many observers of contemporary culture believe that today's constant blitz of visual images results in a changed society. They believe that the children growing up today lose some of their abilities to imagine and, consequently, to create. Evaluate the possible effects of MTV on imagination. (Recall images and associations for a song that you have seen in video form and then one that you have not.)

6. What makes your heart beat faster than usual while watching a scary scene in a movie? You may not be reacting to the visuals or the dialogue. Even the words *I'll kill you* have no power without the emotion created by context. (In fact, those words are used more often in jest or to show mild irritation than to show real intent.) The scary scene will probably be accompanied by carefully selected music. Try watching a scene in a movie (perhaps one "narrated" by Eric Clapton) and writing your response to the scene. Then watch the same scene with the sound turned off, and record your response. What do your responses suggest about the power of music in film?

7. Ezra Pound said, "Music rots when it gets too far from the dance." What do you think Pound means? Do you agree? Can you relate Pound's statement to Agnes De Mille's claim, "The truest expression of a people is in its dances and its music" and to Oliver Sacks claim that "One listens to music with one's muscles"?

8. Give an example of the use of music in social commentary or activism. What statement does the song make about society, or what action does the song advocate and by whom?

9. If young people are disproportionately represented as songwriters of popular music and Ireland produces a disproportionate number of great poets and writers, how would you explain this phenomena?

Practice: Explicating Music

Listen to a favorite song several times, each time listening for a different musical element (pitch, intensity, tone, and rhythm). Describe each element as closely as you can before listening for the next element. How do the sounds of the music instruments and the singer's voice correspond? What is the most prominent musical element in the song? Sounds of instruments or vocals? What quality of the music makes it "good"? Relate Aaron Copland's ways of listening to music (sensuous, expressive, and sheerly musical planes) to your experiences as you listen.

THE POWER OF STYLE: MUSIC

Musicians are known to their fans by their style. You can probably identify the singer of a new song before you are told, especially if the singer or group is one you listen to often. Certain styles of music are favored by different cultures and subcultures, and certain instruments and renditions become national symbols and carry a message of their own.

Most people can identify sounds of "Revelie," for instance, and know immediately that the sounds mean to wake up, to move. On the other hand, the sounds of "Taps," are a solemn farewell to someone who has died. The national anthem unites people in a way at sports events and can inspire feelings of patriotism that moves many people to have a "lump in the throat," even when they are not sure why.

At other times, music divides. When Rosanne Barr parodied the national anthem, she became a member of a small minority who thought it was funny. Most of the people in the stadium immediately expressed disgust. Time/Warner finally dropped their "gangsta" rap division after much public debate about violence and pornography in lyrics.

Practice: Exploring a Genre

Explore a particular genre of music (blues, country, gospel, folk, Christian rock, hip-hop, grunge, rap, punk, and so forth). In a brief essay, identify the standards (basis for measuring quality of individual songs) for the genre, and explain the appeal of the style and message of the music and how they relate to the life experiences of musicians and fans.

Chapter 20

LITERATURE

Music in the Ghetto
Jenny Robertson

On Leszno Street a pre-war picture-house
becomes a concert hall. The Ghetto's full
of melodies which shine across each pool
of black despair. Beggars tout tunes to ease
5 their hunger. Trades, ballads disappear
as, promised bread, families volunteer
for "journeys further east"; are first to hear
the gas. Can music sweeten nightmares, fear;
do more than rabbi, cantor, psalm or God?
10 "Ave Maria, young maid full of grace . . ."
Defying censorship, a solo voice
soars clear and strong. Violins shiver, sob.
Her listeners weep, last accolade of tears.
The death camp ends her songs, her eighteen years.[1]

For Writing and Discussion

1. What is the time and place setting of the experiences referred to in the poem? What words or phrases in the poem allude to time and place setting?

2. What does the poem suggest about the power of music to lift the human spirit? What argument, or statement about the human condition, does the poem make indirectly?

---

[1]The soloist was Maria Eisenstadt. Her conductor was Szymon Pulmon. Both were rounded up in the first wave of deportations in July 1942 and are thought to have perished in Treblinka. The story is told by Janina Bauman in *Winter in the Morning*, Virago Press, 1986. (Robertson)

3. Theodore Dreiser wrote in *Life, Art and America,* "Art is the stored honey of the human soul, gathered on the wings of misery and travail." What do you believe is the relationship between human suffering and art? Why are war and death and unrequited (not returned) love common topics for poetry?

How I Learned to Sweep
Julia Alvarez

My mother never taught me sweeping. . . .
One afternoon she found me watching
TV. She eyed the dusty floor
boldly, and put a broom before
5 me, and said she'd like to be able
to eat her dinner off that table,
and nodded at my feet, then left.
I knew right off what she expected
and went at it. I stepped and swept;
10 the TV blared the news; I kept
my mind on what I had to do,
until in minutes, I was through.
Her floor was as immaculate
as a just-washed dinner plate.
15 I waited for her to return
and turned to watch the President,
live from the White House, talk of war;
in the Far East our soldiers were
landing in their helicopters
20 into jungles their propellers
swept like weeds seen underwater
while perplexing shots were fired
from those beautiful green gardens
into which these dragonflies
25 filled with little men descended.
I got up and swept again
as they fell out of the sky.
I swept all the harder when
I watched a dozen of them die . . .
30 as if their dust fell through the screen
upon the floor I had just cleaned.
She came back and turned the dial;

The screen went dark. *That's beautiful,*
she said, and ran her clean hand through
35 my hair, and on, over the window-
sill, coffee table, rocker, desk,
and held it up—I held my breath—
That's beautiful, she said, impressed,
she hadn't found a speck of death.

For Writing and Discussion

1. Visual images of a real war on television for the first time confused children in the 1960s. When a five-year-old asked his mother, "Do the Vietcong have mothers too?" he was trying make some sense of the confusion. Explain Alvarez's use of learning to sweep as a metaphor for learning about war and dealing with confusion.

2. What does Alvarez suggest by using the mundane on an objective level (concerned with the realities rather than thoughts) to illustrate the horror of war on a subjective level (thinking that results from feeling—in this case, feeling produced by a visual image)?

THE POWER OF STYLE: POETRY

What is considered "good" poetry depends on standards (characteristics for measuring quality) set by a culture or subculture, and those standards vary with time.

The first poems were spoken and heard instead of read. They were often legends that had been passed down from generation to generation in the form of ballads or epics. The oldest example of written poetry is the epic poem "Beowulf" (about 800 A.D.) about a monster named Grendel who is terrorizing a community. Beowulf, the hero in the poem, kills the monster and his horrible mother. The community is then safe.

The rhyme and repetition that serve as memory aids for the oral delivery of poetry are variable stylistic elements. During the Elizabethan Period, for instance, poetry was written mainly in rhymed couplets, often in the form of sonnets (lyric poems with fourteen lines of iambic pentameter).

(continued)

(continued from previous page)

At one time rhyme was considered essential in poetry and still is present in song lyrics. But contemporary poets favor free verse and free form. The characteristic that remains constant, however, is that poems suggest more than they say: Instead of communicating directly, poems are indirect and the words are often ambiguous (have more than one possible meaning).

A poem's power is in its ability to use language to evoke images and feelings by re-creating a facet of human experience.

THE LANGUAGE OF POETRY

Alliteration: Repetition of sounds in the initial positions of words or repetition of consonant sounds within words: *lively little lion.*

Allusion: Indirect references to current events, historical events, or to earlier works of literature or art. For an allusion to be successful, the audience must be familiar with the earlier work or event and recall a wealth of associations.

Ambiguity: Double meaning that may be accomplished by using a *pun*, words with more than one possible meaning; a *paradox*, statement which appears to be self-contradictory, yet has truth (Iron bars do not a prison make); or an *oxymoron,* association of opposite terms in an expression ("Parting is such sweet sorrow").

Assonance: Repetition of vowel sounds in words, with disregard to spellings: *EYElids that hIde mY eyes lIke blankets.*

Ballad: Short narrative poem, often handed down orally and containing refrains and incremental repetition. (Long narrative poems are called *epics.*)

Connotation: The emotional meaning or association of a word that may vary with the experience and culture of the reader or writer.

Denotation: The dictionary, or commonly agreed upon, meaning of a word.

Figures of speech: Figures of speech take words beyond their literal meaning to evoke images, comparisons, and sensory experiences and feelings.

Hyperbole: Deliberate overstatement or exaggeration for effect.

Imagery: A mental effect, created with words, that is near the effect created by stimulation of the sense organs (to see, hear, touch, taste, and smell).

(continued from previous page)

Irony: Difference in what may be expected and what actually happens (*situational irony*). *Verbal irony* uses language that appears innocent, but, for the speaker, has a different meaning.

Metaphor: Figure of speech in which one thing is said to be another; a *simile* uses the word "like" or "as" in making a comparison.

Meter: Basic pattern, or rhythmical organization, of syllables according to stresses and unstresses (marked off in units called "feet"). Iamb (Its fleece was white as snow); trochee (Starry, starry night); anapest (But we loved with a love that was more . . .); dactyl (This is the forest primeval . . .).

Metonymy: Replacing the name of a thing with a related or suggested word ("stars and stripes" to represent the American flag).

Onomatopoeia: (on o MAT o PE a) Words that imitate natural sounds: *moo, hum, clatter.*

Personification: Attributing of human qualities to animals, inanimate objects, or abstractions. (The moon danced across the sky.)

Repetition: Repetition might be used for emphasis or to create a certain rhythm. (Robert Frost claims to have not been able to think of an ending line for "Stopping by Woods on a Snowy Evening," so he just repeated "And miles to go before I sleep.") Other kinds of repetition for effect include *alliteration* (repetition of initial sounds) and *assonance* (repetition of vowel sounds).

Rhythm: Flow of words based on stresses and unstresses in a regular pattern. If you read the "The Highwayman," by Alfred Noyes, in the sixth or seventh grade, you can probably recall the power of the rhythm that created the sound of the highwayman's ride: "And the highwayman came riding— / Riding— riding— / The highwayman came riding, up to the old inn door." Note how the last six words create the sound image of the slowing down and then full stop of the horse.

Rhyme: Similarity in the sounds of words.

Scansion: Examining the kind and number of feet in a line of poetry. (Monometer, one foot; dimeter, two feet; trimeter, three feet; tetrameter, four feet; pentameter, five feet; hexameter, six feet.)

Symbol: Anything used to represent something else.

Synecdoche: Figure of speech in which a part represents the whole (*blood* to represent relatives, *uniforms* to represent police officers).

Practice: Explicating a Poem

Using an art book that contains the collected works of Vincent van Gogh, explain the allusions and other poetic elements in McLean's "Vincent" (page 358), or choose another poem that your instructor approves. The following questions will help guide your analysis:

1. Who is the speaker? What kind of person is he or she?
2. To whom is he or she speaking? What kind of person is the audience?
3. What is the occasion or situation?
4. What is the setting in time (time of day, century, season, and so on)?
5. What is the setting in place (indoors or out, city or country, nation, and so on)?
6. What is the central purpose of the poem?
7. State the central idea, or theme, of the poem in a sentence or a word.
8. Discuss the tone of the poem. How is it achieved (language, imagery, and so on)?
9. Outline the poem to show its structure and development, or summarize the poem.
10. Discuss the word choices (diction) of the poem. Point out words that create an emotional/sensory response in the reader.
11. Discuss the imagery of the poem. What kinds of images are used? What do images and figures of speech make you feel or think?
12. Point out examples of metaphor, simile, personification, and metonymy and discuss their effects.
13. Point out and explain any symbols. If the poem is allegorical, explain the allegory.
14. Point out and explain examples of paradox, overstatement, understatement, and irony. What is their function?
15. Point out and explain any allusions. What is their function?
16. Point out significant examples of sound repetition and explain their function.
17. Mark the scansion of the poem. What is the meter of the poem?
18. Discuss the adaptation of sound to sense.
19. Describe the form or pattern of the poem. (Lyric—having song-like qualities: song, ode, sonnet. Narrative—telling a story: ballad, epic.)

Practice: Search and Compare

A common theme in lyrics and poems is alienation in society. You may recall that poems such as W.H. Auden's "Unknown Citizen" and E.A. Robinson's "Richard Corey" have the same theme as Bob Seger's lyrics "Feel Like a Number." You can probably think of other songs and poems that have the same theme.

At other times, the same theme may be treated with a different tone. The war poetry of World War I, for instance, can be distinguished by whether or not the poet is in the war or safe at home. Some poets are referred to as "armchair poets," while other poets wrote from the trenches and expressed the horror rather than the glory of war.

Other poems and lyrics share the same metaphors. Paul Simon's "I Am a Rock" and Bob Seger's "Like a Rock" use the rock metaphor for different personality characteristics.

Find lyrics or poems that deal with the same theme or that contain the same metaphors and compare the elements of poetry in the lines. (If you want to practice your computer search skills, the University of Wisconsin [Parkside] has an on-line lyric bank.)

R E M I N D E R

Lines from song lyrics are treated as lines of poetry in quotations: Each line is separated by a slash (/) with a space on either side.

In a few pages a good story portrays the complexity of a life while producing the surprise and effect of knowledge—not a bad payoff.

Bernard Malamud

Marigolds
Eugenia W. Collier

1   When I think of the hometown of my youth, all that I seem to remember is dust—the brown, crumbly dust of late summer—arid, sterile dust that gets into the eyes and makes them water, gets into the throat and between the toes of bare brown feet. I don't know why I should remember only the dust. Surely there must have been lush green lawns and paved streets under leafy shade trees somewhere in town; but memory is an abstract painting—it does not present things as they are, but rather as they *feel*. And so, when I think of that time and place, I remember only the dry September of the dirt roads and grassless yards of the shantytown where I lived. And one other thing I remember, another incongruency of memory—a brilliant splash of sunny yellow against the dust—Miss Lottie's marigolds.

2   When the memory of those marigolds flashes across my mind, a strange nostalgia comes with it and remains long after the picture has faded. I feel again the chaotic emotions of adolescence, illusive as smoke, yet as real as the potted geranium before me now. Joy and rage and wild animal gladness and shame become tangled together in the multicolored skein of fourteen-going-on-fifteen as I recall that devastating moment when I was suddenly more woman than

child, years ago in Miss Lottie's yard. I think of those marigolds at the strangest times; I remember them vividly now as I desperately pass away the time. . . .

3   I suppose that futile waiting was the sorrowful background music of our impoverished little community when I was young. The Depression that gripped the nation was no new thing to us, for the black workers of rural Maryland had always been depressed. I don't know what it was that we were waiting for; certainly not for the prosperity that was "just around the corner," for those were white folks' words, which we never believed. Nor did we wait for hard work and thrift to pay off in shining success, as the American Dream promised, for we knew better than that, too. Perhaps we waited for a miracle, amorphous in concept but necessary if one were to have the grit to rise before dawn each day and labor in the white man's vineyard until after dark, or to wander about in the September dust offering one's sweat in return for some meager share of bread. But God was chary with miracles in those days, and so we waited—and waited.

4   We children, of course, were only vaguely aware of the extent of our poverty. Having no radios, few newspapers, and no magazines, we were somewhat unaware of the world outside our community. Nowadays we would be called culturally deprived and people would write books and hold conferences about us. In those days everybody we knew was just as hungry and ill clad as we were. Poverty was the cage in which we all were trapped, and our hatred of it was still the vague, undirected restlessness of the zoo-bred flamingo who knows that nature created him to fly free.

5   As I think of those days I feel most poignantly the tag end of summer, the bright, dry times when we began to have a sense of shortening days and the imminence of the cold.

6   By the time I was fourteen, my brother Joey and I were the only children left at our house, the older ones having left home for early marriage or the lure of the city, and the two babies having been sent to relatives who might care for them better than we. Joey was three years younger than I, and a boy, and therefore vastly inferior. Each morning our mother and father trudged wearily down the dirt road and around the bend, she to her domestic job, he to his daily unsuccessful quest for work. After our few chores around the tumbledown shanty, Joey and I were free to run wild in the sun with other children similarly situated.

7   For the most part, those days are ill-defined in my memory, running together and combining like a fresh watercolor painting left out in the rain. I remember squatting in the road drawing a picture in the dust, a picture which Joey gleefully erased with one sweep of his dirty foot. I remember fishing for minnows in a muddy creek and watching sadly as they eluded my cupped hands, while Joey laughed uproariously. And I remember, that year, a strange restlessness of body and of spirit, a feeling that something old and familiar was ending, and something unknown and therefore terrifying was beginning.

8   One day returns to me with special clarity for some reason, perhaps because it was the beginning of the experience that in some inexplicable way marked the end of innocence. I was loafing under the great oak tree in our yard,

deep in some reverie which I have now forgotten, except that it involved some secret, secret thoughts of one of the Harris boys across the yard. Joey and a bunch of kids were bored now with the old tire suspended from an oak limb, which had kept them entertained for a while.

9   "Hey, Lizabeth," Joey yelled. He never talked when he could yell. "Hey, Lizabeth, let's go somewhere."

10   I came reluctantly from my private world. "Where you want to go? What you want to do?"

11   The truth was that we were becoming tired of the formlessness of our summer days. The idleness whose prospect had seemed so beautiful during the busy days of spring now had degenerated to an almost desperate effort to fill up the empty midday hours.

12   "Let's go see can we find some locusts on the hill," someone suggested.

13   Joey was scornful. "Ain't no more locusts there. Y'all got 'em all while they was still green."

14   The argument that followed was brief and not really worth the effort. Hunting locust trees wasn't fun anymore by now.

15   "Tell you what," said Joey finally, his eyes sparkling. "Let's us go over to Miss Lottie's."

16   The idea caught on at once, for annoying Miss Lottie was always fun. I was still child enough to scamper along with the group over rickety fences and through bushes that tore our already raggedy clothes, back to where Miss Lottie lived. I think now that we must have made a tragi-comic spectacle, five or six kids of different ages, each of us clad in only one garment—the girls in faded dresses that were too long or too short, the boys in patchy pants, their sweaty brown chests gleaming in the hot sun. A little cloud of dust followed our thin legs and bare feet as we tramped over the barren land.

17   When Miss Lottie's house came into view we stopped, ostensibly to plan our strategy, but actually to reinforce our courage. Miss Lottie's house was of the most ramshackle of all our ramshackle homes. The sun and rain had long since faded its rickety frame siding from white to a sullen gray. The boards themselves seemed to remain upright not from being nailed together but rather from leaning together, like a house that a child might have constructed from cards. A brisk wind might have blown it down, and the fact that it was still standing implied a kind of enchantment that was stronger than the elements. There it stood and as far as I know is standing yet—a gray, rotting thing with no porch, no shutters, no steps, set on a cramped lot with no grass, not even any weeds—a monument to decay.

18   In front of the house in a squeaky rocking chair sat Miss Lottie's son, John Burke, completing the impression of decay. John Burke was what was known as queer-headed. Black and ageless, he sat rocking day in and day out in a mind-less stupor, lulled by the monotonous squeak-squawk of the chair. A battered hat atop his shaggy head shaded him from the sun. Usually John Burke was totally unaware of everything outside his quiet dream world. But if you disturbed him, if you intruded upon his fantasies, he would become enraged,

strike out at you, and curse at you in some strange enchanted language which only he could understand. We children made a game of thinking of ways to disturb John Burke and then to elude his violent retribution.

19   But our real fun and our real fear lay in Miss Lottie herself. Miss Lottie seemed to be at least a hundred years old. Her big frame still held traces of the tall, powerful woman she must have been in youth, although it was now bent and drawn. Her smooth skin was a dark reddish brown, and her face had Indian-like features and the stern stoicism that one associates with Indian faces. Miss Lottie didn't like intruders either, especially children. She never left her yard, and nobody ever visited her. We never knew how she managed those necessities which depend on human interaction—how she ate, for example, or even whether she ate. When we were tiny children, we thought Miss Lottie was a witch and we made up tales that we half believed ourselves about her exploits. We were far too sophisticated now, of course, to believe the witch nonsense. But old fears have a way of clinging like cobwebs, and so when we sighted the tumbledown shack, we had to stop to reinforce our nerves.

20   "Look, there she is," I whispered, forgetting that Miss Lottie could not possibly have heard me from that distance. "She's fooling with them crazy flowers."

21   "Yeh, look at 'er."

22   Miss Lottie's marigolds were perhaps the strangest part of the picture. Certainly they did not fit in with the crumbling decay of the rest of her yard. Beyond the dusty brown yard, in front of the sorry gray house, rose suddenly and shockingly a dazzling strip of bright blossoms, clumped together in enormous mounds, warm and passionate and sun-golden. The old black witch-woman worked on them all summer, every summer, down on her creaky knees, weeding and cultivating and arranging, while the house crumbled and John Burke rocked. For some perverse reason, we children hated those marigolds. They interfered with the perfect ugliness of the place; they were too beautiful; they said too much that we could not understand; they did not make sense. There was something in the vigor with which the old woman destroyed the weeds that intimidated us. It should have been a comical sight—the old woman with the man's hat on her cropped white head, leaning over the bright mounds, her big backside in the air—but it wasn't comical, it was something we could not name. We had to annoy her by whizzing a pebble into her flowers or by yelling a dirty word, then dancing away from her rage, reveling in our youth and mocking her age. Actually, I think it was the flowers we wanted to destroy, but nobody had the nerve to try it, not even Joey, who was usually fool enough to try anything.

23   "Y'all git some stones," commanded Joey now and was met with instant giggling obedience as everyone except me began to gather pebbles from the dusty ground. "Come on, Lizabeth."

24   I just stood there peering through the bushes, torn between wanting to join the fun and feeling that it was all a big silly.

25   "You scared, Lizabeth?"

26   I cursed and spat on the ground—my favorite gesture of phony bravado. "Y'all children get the stones, I'll show you how to use 'em."

27   I said before that we children were not consciously aware of how thick were the bars of our cage. I wonder now, though, whether we were not more aware of it than I thought. Perhaps we had some dim notion of what we were, and how little chance we had of being anything else. Otherwise, why would we have been so preoccupied with destruction? Anyway, the pebbles were collected quickly, and everybody looked at me to begin the run.

28   "Come on, y'all."

29   We crept to the edge of the bushes that bordered the narrow road in front of Miss Lottie's place. She was working placidly, kneeling over the flowers, her dark hand plunged into the golden mound. Suddenly *zing*—an expertly aimed stone cut the head off one of the blossoms.

30   "Who out there?" Miss Lottie's backside came down and her head came up as her sharp eyes searched the bushes. "You better git!"

31   We had crouched down out of sight in the bushes, where we stifled the giggles that insisted on coming. Miss Lottie gazed warily across the road for a moment, then cautiously returned to her weeding. *Zing*—Joey sent a pebble into the blooms, and another marigold was beheaded.

32   Miss Lottie was enraged now. She began struggling to her feet, leaning on a rickety cane and shouting. "Y'all git! Go on home!" Then the rest of the kids let loose with their pebbles, storming the flowers and laughing wildly and senselessly at Miss Lottie's impotent rage. She shook her stick at us and started shakily toward the road crying, "Git 'long! John Burke! John Burke, come help!"

33   Then I lost my head entirely, mad with the power of inciting such rage, and ran out of the bushes in the storm of pebbles, straight toward Miss Lottie, chanting madly, "Old witch, fell in a ditch, picked up a penny and thought she was rich!" The children screamed with delight, dropped their pebbles, and joined the crazy dance, swarming around Miss Lottie like bees and chanting, "Old lady witch!" while she screamed curses at us. The madness lasted only a moment, for John Burke, startled at last, lurched out of his chair, and we dashed for the bushes just as Miss Lottie's cane went whizzing at my head.

34   I did not join the merriment when the kids gathered again under the oak in our bare yard. Suddenly I was ashamed, and I did not like being ashamed. The child in me sulked and said it was all in fun, but the woman in me flinched at the thought of the malicious attack that I had led. The mood lasted all afternoon. When we ate the beans and rice that was supper that night, I did not notice my father's silence, for he was always silent these days, nor did I notice my mother's absence, for she always worked until well into evening. Joey and I had a particularly bitter argument after supper; his exuberance got on my nerves. Finally I stretched out upon the pallet in the room we shared and fell into a fitful doze.

35   When I awoke, somewhere in the middle of the night, my mother had returned, and I vaguely listened to the conversation that was audible through the thin walls that separated our rooms. At first I heard no words, only voices. My mother's voice was like a cool, dark room in summer—peaceful, soothing, quiet. I loved to listen to it; it made things seem all right somehow. But my father's voice cut through hers, shattering the peace.

36   "Twenty-two years, Maybelle, twenty-two years," he was saying, "and I got nothing for you, nothing, nothing."

37   "It's all right, honey, you'll get something. Everybody out of work now, you know that."

38   "It ain't right. Ain't no man ought to eat his woman's food year in and year out, and see his children running wild. Ain't nothing right about that."

39   "Honey, you took good care of us when you had it. Ain't nobody got nothing nowadays."

40   "I ain't talking about nobody else, I'm talking about *me*. God knows I try." My mother said something I could not hear, and my father cried out louder, "What must a man do, tell me that?"

41   "Look, we ain't starving. I git paid every week, and Mrs. Ellis is real nice about giving me things. She gonna let me have Mr. Ellis's old coat for you this winter—"

42   "Damn Mr. Ellis's coat! And damn his money! You think I want white folks' leavings? Damn, Maybelle"—and suddenly he sobbed, loudly and painfully, and cried helplessly and hopelessly in the dark night. I had never heard a man cry before. I did not know men ever cried. I covered my ears with my hands but could not cut off the sound of my father's harsh, painful, despairing sobs. My father was a strong man who could whisk a child upon his shoulders and go singing through the house. My father whittled toys for us, and laughed so loud that the great oak seemed to laugh with him, and taught us how to fish and hunt rabbits. How could it be that my father was crying? But the sobs went on, unstifled, finally quieting until I could hear my mother's voice, deep and rich, humming softly as she used to hum to a frightened child.

43   The world had lost its boundary lines. My mother, who was small and soft, was now the strength of the family; my father, who was the rock on which the family had been built, was sobbing like the tiniest child. Everything was suddenly out of tune, like a broken accordion. Where did I fit into this crazy picture? I do not now remember my thoughts, only a feeling of great bewilderment and fear.

44   Long after the sobbing and humming had stopped, I lay on the pallet, still as stone with my hands over my ears, wishing that I too could cry and be comforted. The night was silent now except for the sound of the crickets and of Joey's soft breathing. But the room was too crowded with fear to allow me to sleep, and finally, feeling the terrible aloneness of 4 a.m., I decided to awaken Joey.

45   "Ouch! What's the matter with you? What you want?" he demanded disagreeably when I had pinched and slapped him awake.

46   "Come on, wake up."

47   "What for? Go 'way."

48   I was lost for a reasonable reply. I could not say, "I'm scared and I don't want to be alone," so I merely said, "I'm going out. If you want to come, come on."

49   The promise of adventure awoke him. "Going out now? Where to, Lizabeth? What you going to do?"

50   I was pulling my dress over my head. Until now I had not thought of going out. "Just come on," I replied tersely.

51   I was out the window and halfway down the road before Joey caught up with me.

52   "Wait, Lizabeth, where you going?"

53   I was running as if the Furies were after me, as perhaps they were—running silently and furiously until I came to where I had half known I was headed: to Miss Lottie's yard.

54   The half-dawn light was more eerie than complete darkness, and in it the old house was like the ruin that my world had become—foul and crumbling, a grotesque caricature. It looked haunted, but I was not afraid, because I was haunted too.

55   "Lizabeth, you lost your mind?" panted Joey.

56   I had indeed lost my mind, for all the smoldering emotions of that summer swelled in me and burst—the great need for my mother who was never there, the hopelessness of our poverty and degradation, the bewilderment of being neither child nor woman and yet both at once, the fear unleashed by my father's tears. And these feelings combined in one great impulse toward destruction.

57   "Lizabeth!"

58   I leaped furiously into the mounds of marigolds and pulled madly, trampling and pulling and destroying the perfect yellow blooms. The fresh smell of early morning and of dew-soaked marigolds spurred me on as I went tearing and mangling and sobbing while Joey tugged my dress or my waist crying, "Lizabeth, stop, please stop!"

59   And then I was sitting in the ruined little garden among the uprooted and ruined flowers, crying and crying, and it was too late to undo what I had done. Joey was sitting beside me, silent and frightened, not knowing what to say. Then, "Lizabeth, look."

60   I opened my swollen eyes and saw in front of me a pair of large, calloused feet; my gaze lifted to the swollen legs, the age-distorted body clad in a tight cotton nightdress, and then the shadowed Indian face surrounded by stubby white hair. And there was no rage in the face now, now that the garden was destroyed and there was nothing any longer to be protected.

61   "M-miss Lottie!" I scrambled to my feet and just stood there and stared at her, and that was the moment when childhood faded and womanhood began. That violent, crazy act was the last act of childhood. For as I gazed at the immobile face with the sad, weary eyes, I gazed upon a kind of reality which is hidden to childhood. The witch was no longer a witch but only a broken old woman who had dared to create beauty in the midst of ugliness and sterility. She had been born in squalor and lived in it all her life. Now at the end of that life she had nothing except a falling-down hut, a wrecked body, and John Burke, the mindless son of her passion. Whatever verve there was left in her, whatever was of love and beauty and joy that had not been squeezed out by life, had been there in the marigolds she had so tenderly cared for.

62   Of course I could not express the things that I knew about Miss Lottie as I stood there awkward and ashamed. The years have put words to the things I knew in that moment, and as I look back upon it, I know that that moment marked the end of innocence. Innocence involves an unseeing acceptance of things at face value, an ignorance of the area below the surface. In that humiliating moment I looked beyond myself and into the depths of another person. This was the beginning of compassion, and one cannot have both compassion and innocence.

63   The years have taken me worlds away from that time and that place, from the dust and squalor of our lives, and from the bright thing that I destroyed in a blind, childish striking out at God knows what. Miss Lottie died long ago and many years have passed since I last saw her hut, completely barren at last, for despite my wild contrition she never planted marigolds again. Yet, there are times when the image of those passionate yellow mounds returns with a painful poignancy. For one does not have to be ignorant and poor to find that his life is as barren as the dusty yards of our town. And I too have planted marigolds.

For Writing and Discussion

1. What does the narrator suggest is the cause of the children's destructive behavior? How does she explain her own destructive behavior? Do you accept the narrator's explanations? Why or why not? What is your own explanation for children's destructive or cruel acts?

2. "Marigolds" is a "coming of age," or "initiation" story. Sociologists often attribute irresponsible youthful behaviors to the fact that in America there is no "rite of passage" from childhood to adulthood, leaving adolescents in a kind of limbo. Many other cultures have ceremonies or processes through which an adolescent obtains adult status. Do you believe that a rite of passage serves a useful function for a society? Why or why not? Can you think of an incident or achievement that served as a kind of rite of passage for you?

3. What does the narrator in "Marigolds" suggest about the power of and the need for beauty in the human psyche? The narrator recalls strongly the feelings she had many years ago, even though she cannot recall the related thoughts or words. What does the story suggest about the power of emotions such as shame and guilt? Explain the narrator's claim that "one cannot have both compassion and innocence."

4. People who see movies made from books they have read often find the movie disappointing. How do the processes of reading a story and watching a movie differ? How do the differences explain why a reader might be disappointed in a movie? Did you create your own mental "movie" as you read "Marigolds"?

5. Eugenia Collier is often asked whether "Marigolds" is autobiographical. She responds that it is not, that she grew up in a comfortable home and that she and Lizabeth are very different. Collier notes, "I am always pleased with the question, because it means that I must have done my job well—convinced my reader that the incidents in the story are actually happening." As you read, did you believe the story to be an autobiographical account of events? If so, what specific content or style elements were most convincing?

THE POWER OF STYLE: ELEMENTS OF FICTION

Length and complexity of plot distinguish short stories from novels. A short story usually presents one person or a group of people involved in the same problem or conflict, which creates the plot. Novels and novellas present greater complexity of plot and usually involve many more characters than do short stories. Novels often contain one or more subplots which serve to develop or contrast with the main plot.

Setting: Where and when does the action take place? Is the setting crucial to the story, or could it happen anywhere, anytime?

Characterization: Who is the story really about? Who is involved in a problem, conflict, new understanding? Who grows or changes? What role do the secondary and minor characters play?

The *protagonist* is the central character, often called the "hero." Today's literary/media heroes often have superhuman or supernatural qualities. The hero may be with the forces of society, such as the characters played by Arnold Schartzenegger; against the forces of society, such as the characters often played by Sylvester Stallone; or have his own code of conduct yet manage to gain our sympathy.

Plot: What happens to whom? What events, situation, mental/emotional conditions create a conflict that must be resolved?

Conflict is a clash of ideas, actions, goals, desires, and so forth, which may be between the protagonists and another character or society (human against human/society); against one of the character's own personality traits (human against self); or against the elements or environment (human against nature).

Rising action involves the event, lack of understanding, or change of heart that leads to conflict. *Falling action* is the event, understanding, or change of heart that solves the problem or resolves the conflict. How the loose ends are tied together, or how

(continued)

(continued from previous page)

the characters respond to the resolution is shown in the *denouement*. The problem is resolved in *closed endings*; in *open endings*, the problem is not resolved, leaving the reader to wonder what happens next and speculate on the future. An author uses *stream of consciousness* when a sequence of thoughts, perceptions, or feelings is used to narrate a story rather than having a narrator merely relate events; stream of consciousness uses psychological time instead of "real" time.

Narration: Who is telling the story, a nameless, faceless narrator, a character in the story, a "character" who is telling what he or she heard? Does the narrator's identity matter?

If the story is told in the first-person point of view, the narrator uses *I*; third-person point of view uses *he, she,* and *they*. When the narrator knows everything about the characters, including their unexpressed thoughts and feelings, the point of view is called omniscient or limited omniscient.

Theme: What lesson does the reader learn from the story? Is it different from the lesson learned by the characters (irony)?

Verbalizing the theme of a literary work can sometimes be done in a word (mutability), but at other times a complete sentence is required (Crime doesn't pay.). An author may indirectly argue from a particular position in fiction. A work of fiction, or any other work of art, may be created for the purpose of making an argumentative statement. Interpretative fiction that increases our understanding of life and human nature does so in a particular direction that may be clearly intended by the author.

Tone: What is the author's attitude toward the subject? Is it serious, lighthearted, angry, amused, sad, happy, ironic?

Mood: What is the emotional atmosphere of the story? Is it sympathetic, hostile? Is it different from the tone (irony)?

Usually tone and mood are so closely related that it is difficult to distinguish between the two, but in some works the contrast is the heart of the story. In Eudora Welty's "Why I Live at the P.O.," for example, the author is amused by the main character, who maintains an attitude of self-righteous anger throughout the story. Much of the humor in this story is based on that irony.

Imagery: Does the author create a world the reader can see, hear, touch, smell, taste? Does the author use straight description or figurative language to create the world? Is there a relationship between the imagery and figurative language and the theme?

(continued)

(continued from previous page)

A strong relationship between imagery and theme often results in symbolism: The ivy on the wall dies as the main character dies. The broken-down house becomes an outward and visible sign of the decay of a once-great family. At times, the imagery is used simply to create a believable world, a backdrop for action.

Style: Does the writer use mainly long, complicated sentences, short simple sentences, or a combination of both? Does the writer use much imagery? Does the author use special words frequently, like words in a different language or words not commonly used? Does the author return to some subject or plot pattern in each work? Does the author use formal or informal language, vernacular dialogue, jargon, or so forth?

The Portable Phonograph
Walter Van Tilburg Clark

Clark's story is set in the aftermath of war when the pleasure of art is rationed and guarded.

1   The red sunset with narrow, black cloud strips like threads across it, lay on the curved horizon of the prairie. The air was still and cold, and in it settled the mute darkness and greater cold of night. High in the air there was wind, for through the veil of the dusk the clouds could be seen gliding rapidly south and changing shapes. A queer sensation of torment, of two-sided, unpredictable nature, arose from the stillness of the earth air beneath the violence of the upper air. Out of the sunset, through the dead, matted grass and isolated weed stalks of the prairie, crept the narrow and deeply rutted remains of a road. In the road, in places, there were crusts of shallow, brittle ice. There were little islands of an old oiled pavement of the road too, but most of it was mud, now frozen rigid. The frozen mud still bore the toothed impress of great tanks, and a wanderer on the neighboring undulations might have stumbled, in this light, into large, partially filled-in and weed-grown cavities, their banks channeled and beginning to spread into badlands. These pits were such as might have been made by falling meteors, but they were not. They were the scars of gigantic bombs, their rawness already made a little natural by rain, seed, and time. Along

the road, there were rakish remnants of fence. There was also, just visible, one portion of tangled and multiple barbed wire still erect, behind which was a shelving ditch with small caves, now very quiet and empty, at intervals in its back wall. Otherwise there was no structure or remnant of a structure visible over the dome of the darkling earth, but only, in sheltered hollows, the darker shadows of young trees trying again.

2   Under the withering arch of the high wind a V of wild geese fled south. The rush of their pinions sounded briefly, and the faint, plaintive notes of their expeditionary talk. Then they left a still greater vacancy. There was the smell and expectation of snow, as there is likely to be when the wild geese fly south. From the remote distance, towards the red sky, came faintly the protracted howl and quick yap-yap of a prairie wolf.

3   North of the road, perhaps a hundred yards, lay the parallel and deeply entrenched course of a small creek, lined with leafless alders and willows. The creek was already silent under ice. Into the bank above it was dug a sort of cell, with a single opening, like the mouth of a mine tunnel. Within the cell there was a little red of fire, which showed dully through the opening, like a reflection or a deception of the imagination. The light came from the chary burning of four blocks of poorly aged peat, which gave off a petty warmth and much acrid smoke. But the precious remnants of wood, old fence posts and timbers from the long-deserted dugouts, had to be saved for the real cold, for the time when a man's breath blew white, the moisture in his nostrils stiffened at once when he stepped out, and the expansive blizzards paraded for days over the vast open, swirling and settling and thickening, till the dawn of the cleared day when the sky was thin blue-green and the terrible cold, in which a man could not live for three hours unwarmed, lay over the uniformly drifted swell of the plain.

4   Around the smoldering peat, four men were seated cross-legged. Behind them, traversed by their shadows, was the earth bench, with two old and dirty army blankets, where the owner of the cell slept. In a niche in the opposite wall were a few tin utensils which caught the glint of the coals. The host was rewrapping in a piece of daubed burlap four fine, leather-bound books. He worked slowly and very carefully, and at last tied the bundle securely with a piece of grass-woven cord. The other three looked intently upon the process, as if a great significance lay in it. As the host tied the cord, he spoke. He was an old man, his long, matted beard and hair gray to nearly white. The shadows made his brows and cheekbones appear gnarled, his eyes and cheeks deeply sunken. His big hands, rough with frost and swollen by rheumatism, were awkward but gentle at their task. He was like a prehistoric priest performing a fateful ceremonial rite. Also his voice had in it a suitable quality of deep, reverent despair, yet perhaps at the moment, a sharpness of selfish satisfaction.

5   "When I perceived what was happening," he said, "I told myself, 'It is the end. I cannot take much; I will take these.'"

6   "Perhaps I was impractical," he continued. "But for myself, I do not regret, and what do we know of those who will come after us? We are the doddering remnant of a race of mechanical fools. I have saved what I love; the soul

of what was good in us is here; perhaps the new ones will make a strong enough beginning not to fall behind when they become clever."

7   He rose with slow pain and placed the wrapped volumes in the niche with his utensils. The others watched him with the same ritualistic gaze.

8   "Shakespeare, the Bible, *Moby Dick,* the *Divine Comedy,*" one of them said softly. "You might have done worse, much worse."

9   "You will have a little soul left until you die," said another harshly. "That is more than is true of us. My brain becomes thick, like my hands." He held the big, battered hands, with their black nails, in the glow to be seen.

10   "I want paper to write on," he said. "And there is none."

11   The fourth man said nothing. He sat in the shadow farthest from the fire, and sometimes his body jerked in its rags from the cold. Although he was still young, he was sick and coughed often. Writing implied a greater future than he now felt able to consider.

12   The old man seated himself laboriously, and reached out, groaning at the movement, to put another block of peat on the fire. With bowed heads and averted eyes, his three guests acknowledged his magnanimity.

13   "We thank you, Doctor Jenkins, for the reading," said the man who had named the books.

14   They seemed then to be waiting for something. Doctor Jenkins understood, but was loath to comply. In an ordinary moment he would have said nothing. But the words of *The Tempest,* which he had been reading, and the religious attention of the three made this an unusual occasion.

15   "You wish to hear the phonograph," he said grudgingly.

16   The two middle-aged men stared into the fire, unable to formulate and expose the enormity of their desire.

17   The young man, however, said anxiously, between suppressed coughs, "Oh, please," like an excited child.

18   The old man rose again in his difficult way, and went to the back of the cell. He returned and placed tenderly upon the packed floor, where the firelight might fall upon it, an old portable phonograph in a black case. He smoothed the top with his hand, and then opened it. The lovely green-felt-covered disk became visible.

19   "I have been using thorns as needles," he said. "But tonight, because we have a musician among us"—he bent his head to the young man, almost invisible in the shadow—"I will use a steel needle. There are only three left."

20   The two middle-aged men stared at him in speechless adoration. The one with the big hands, who wanted to write, moved his lips, but the whisper was not audible.

21   "Oh, don't!" cried the young man, as if he were hurt. "The thorns will do beautifully."

22   "No," the old man said. "I have become accustomed to the thorns, but they are not really good. For you, my young friend, we will have good music tonight."

23   "After all," he added generously, and beginning to wind the phonograph, which creaked, "they can't last forever."

24   "No, nor we," the man who needed to write said harshly. "The needle, by all means."

25   "Oh, thanks," said the young man. "Thanks," he said again in a low, excited voice, and then stifled his coughing with a bowed head.

26   "The records, though," said the old man when he had finished winding, "are a different matter. Already they are very worn. I do not play them more than once a week. One, once a week, that is what I allow myself."

27   "More than a week I cannot stand it; not to hear them," he apologized.

28   "No, how could you?" cried the young man. "And with them here like this."

29   "A man can stand anything," said the man who wanted to write, in his harsh, antagonistic voice.

30   "Please, the music," said the young man.

31   "Only the one," said the old man. "In the long run, we will remember more that way."

32   He had a dozen records with luxuriant gold and red seals. Even in that light the others could see that the threads of the records were becoming worn. Slowly he read out the titles and the tremendous, dead names of the composers and the artists and the orchestras. The three worked upon the names in their minds, carefully. It was difficult to select from such a wealth what they would at once most like to remember. Finally, the man who wanted to write named Gershwin's "New York."

33   "Oh, no," cried the sick young man, and then could say nothing more because he had to cough. The others understood him, and the harsh man withdrew his selection and waited for the musician to choose.

34   The musician begged Doctor Jenkins to read the titles again, very slowly, so that he could remember the sounds. While they were read, he lay back against the wall, his eyes closed, his thin, horny hand pulling at his light beard, and listened to the voices and orchestras and the single instruments in his mind.

35   When the reading was done he spoke despairingly, "I have forgotten," he complained; "I cannot hear them clearly."

36   "There are things missing," he explained.

37   "I know," said Doctor Jenkins. "I thought that I knew all of Shelley by heart. I should have brought Shelley."

38   "That's more soul than we can use," said the harsh man. *"Moby Dick* is better."

39   "By God, we can understand that," he emphasized.

40   The Doctor nodded.

41   "Still," said the man who had admired the books, "we need the absolute if we are to keep a grasp on anything."

42   "Anything but these sticks and peat clods and rabbit snares," he said bitterly.

43   "Shelley desired an ultimate absolute," said the harsh man. "It's too much," he said. "It's no good; no earthly good."

44   The musician selected a Debussy nocturne. The others considered and approved. They rose to their knees to watch the Doctor prepare for the playing,

so that they appeared to be actually in an attitude of worship. The peat glow showed the thinness of their bearded faces, and the deep lines in them, and revealed the condition of their garments. The other two continued to kneel as the old man carefully lowered the needle onto the spinning disk, but the musician suddenly drew back against the wall again, with his knees up, and buried his face in his hands.

45   At the first notes of the piano the listeners were startled. They stared at each other. Even the musician lifted his head in amazement, but then quickly bowed it again, strainingly, as if he were suffering from a pain he might not be able to endure. They were all listening deeply, without movement. The wet, blue-green notes tingled forth from the old machine, and were individual, delectable presences in the cell. The individual, delectable presences swept into a sudden tide of unbearably beautiful dissonance, and then continued fully the swelling and ebbing of that tide, the dissonant inpourings, and the resolutions, and the diminishments, and the little, quiet wavelets of interlude lapping between. Every sound was piercing and singularly sweet. In all the men except the musician, there occurred rapid sequences of tragically heightened recollection. He heard nothing but what was there. At the final, whispering disappearance, but moving quietly so that the others would not hear him and look at him, he let his head fall back in agony, as if it were drawn there by the hair, and clenched the fingers of one hand over his teeth. He sat that way while the others were silent, and until they began to breathe again normally. His drawn-up legs were trembling violently.

46   Quickly Doctor Jenkins lifted the needle off, to save it and not to spoil the recollection with scraping. When he had stopped the whirling of the sacred disk, he courteously left the phonograph open and by the fire, in sight.

47   The others, however, understood. The musician rose last, but then abruptly, and went quickly out at the door without saying anything. The others stopped at the door and gave their thanks in low voices. The Doctor nodded magnificently.

48   "Come again," he invited, "in a week. We will have the 'New York.'"

49   When the two had gone together, out towards the rimed road, he stood in the entrance, peering and listening. At first, there was only the resonant boom of the wind overhead, and then far over the dome of the dead, dark plain, the wolf cry lamenting. In the rifts of clouds the Doctor saw four stars flying. It impressed the Doctor that one of them had just been obscured by the beginning of a flying cloud at the very moment he heard what he had been listening for, a sound of suppressed coughing. It was not nearby, however. He believed that down against the pale alders he could see the moving shadow.

50   With nervous hands he lowered the piece of canvas which served as his door, and pegged it at the bottom. Then quickly and quietly, looking at the piece of canvas frequently, he slipped the records into the case, snapped the lid shut, and carried the phonograph to his couch. There, pausing often to stare at the canvas and listen, he dug earth from the wall and disclosed a piece of board. Behind this there was a deep hole in the wall, into which he put the phonograph.

After a moment's consideration, he went over and reached down his bundle of books and inserted it also. Then, guardedly, he once more sealed up the hole with the board and the earth. He also changed his blankets, and the grass-stuffed sack which served as a pillow, so that he could lie facing the entrance. After carefully placing two more blocks of peat upon the fire, he stood for a long time watching the stretched canvas, but it seemed to billow naturally with the first gusts of a lowering wind. At last he prayed, and got in under his blankets, and closed his smoke-smarting eyes. On the inside of the bed, next to the wall, he could feel with his hand the comfortable piece of lead pipe.

For Writing and Discussion

1. What is your reaction to the story? Could you see the setting of Clark's story in your mind's eye? Briefly describe the setting. What words does Clark use to create an ominous mood? Did you feel the intensity of emotion as the men experienced the pleasure of music? Describe how you felt as you read the description of the young man's agony, or pleasure.

2. What do you think Clark was saying in the story about art? About fear (when Doctor Jenkins hides the phonograph and goes to bed with his lead pipe)? About war? What argument is inherent in his story?

3. Think about things you would take if you had only a few minutes to flee from an impending disaster that would destroy your home and civilization as you know it. List five items and think about why you value each item.

4. Aristotle saw art as an expression of the possible and probable, rather than the actual, or real. What is the value of exploring the possible, but sometimes improbable, as science fiction writers do?

5. Enjoying science fiction requires a "willing suspension of disbelief." How does good science fiction, either in prose or visual form, help the reader or viewer acquire a "willing suspension of disbelief"?

Once Upon a Time
Nadine Gordimer

Gordimer's story explores the chilling effects of apartheid in South Africa.

1   Someone has written to ask me to contribute to an anthology of stories for children. I reply that I don't write children's stories; and he writes back that at a recent congress/book/seminar a certain novelist said every writer ought to

write at least one story for children. I think of sending a postcard saying I don't accept that I 'ought' to write anything.

2   And then last night I woke up—or rather was wakened without knowing what had roused me.

3   A voice in the echo-chamber of the subconscious?

4   A sound.

5   A creaking of the kind made by the weight carried by one foot after another along a wooden floor. I listen. I felt the apertures of my ears distend with concentration. Again: the creaking. I was waiting for it; waiting to hear if it indicated that feet were moving from room to room, coming up the passage—to my door. I have no burglar bars, no gun under the pillow, but I have the same fears as people who do take these precautions, and my windowpanes are thin as rime, could shatter like a wineglass. A woman was murdered (how do they put it) in broad daylight in a house two blocks away, last year, and the fierce dogs who guarded an old widower and his collection of antique clocks were strangled before he was knifed by a casual labourer he had dismissed without pay.

6   I was staring at the door, making it out in my mind rather than seeing it, in the dark. I lay quite still—a victim already—but the arrhythmia of my heart was fleeing, knocking this way and that against its bodycage. How finely tuned the senses are, just out of rest, sleep! I could never listen intently as that in the distractions of the day; I was reading every faintest sound, identifying and classifying its possible threat.

7   But I learned that I was to be neither threatened nor spared. There was no human weight pressing on the boards, the creaking was a buckling, an epicentre of stress. I was in it. The house that surrounds me while I sleep is built on undermined ground; far beneath my bed, the floor, the house's foundations, the stopes and passages of gold mines have hollowed the rock, and when some face trembles, detaches and falls, three thousand feet below, the whole house shifts slightly, bringing uneasy strain to the balance and counterbalance of brick, cement, wood and glass that hold it as a structure around me. The misbeats of my heart tailed off like the last muffled flourishes on one of the wooden xylophones made by the Chopi and Tsonga migrant miners who might have been down there, under me in the earth at that moment. The stope where the fall was could have been disused, dripping water from its ruptured veins; or men might now be interred there in the most profound of tombs.

8   I couldn't find a position in which my mind would let go of my body— release me to sleep again. So I began to tell myself a story; a bedtime story.

9   In a house, in a suburb, in a city, there were a man and his wife who loved each other very much and were living happily ever after. They had a little boy, and they loved him very much. They had a cat and a dog that the little boy loved very much. They had a car and a caravan trailer for holidays, and a swimming-pool which was fenced so that the little boy and his playmates would not fall in and drown. They had a housemaid who was absolutely trustworthy and an itinerant gardener who was highly recommended by the neighbours. For

when they began to live happily ever after they were warned, by that wise old witch, the husband's mother, not to take on anyone off the street. They were inscribed in a medical benefit society, their pet dog was licensed, they were insured against fire, flood damage and theft, and subscribed to the local Neighbourhood Watch, which supplied them with a plaque for their gates lettered YOU HAVE BEEN WARNED over the silhouette of a would-be intruder. He was masked; it could not be said if he was black or white, and therefore proved the property owner was no racist.

10   It was not possible to insure the house, the swimming pool or the car against riot damage. There were riots, but these were outside the city, where people of another colour were quartered. These people were not allowed into the suburb except as reliable housemaids and gardeners, so there was nothing to fear, the husband told the wife. Yet she was afraid that some day such people might come up the street and tear off the plague YOU HAVE BEEN WARNED and open the gates and stream in . . . Nonsense, my dear, said the husband, there are police and soldiers and tear-gas and guns to keep them away. But to please her—for he loved her very much and buses were being burned, cars stoned, and schoolchildren shot by the police in those quarters out of sight and hearing of the suburb—he had electronically-controlled gates fitted. Anyone who pulled off the sign YOU HAVE BEEN WARNED and tried to open the gates would have to announce his intentions by pressing a button and speaking into a receiver relayed to the house. The little boy was fascinated by the device and used it as a walkie-talkie in cops and robbers play with his small friends.

11   The riots were suppressed, but there were many burglaries in the suburb and somebody's trusted housemaid was tied up and shut in a cupboard by thieves while she was in charge of her employers' house. The trusted housemaid of the man and wife and little boy was so upset by this misfortune befalling a friend left, as she herself often was, with responsibility for the possessions of the man and his wife and the little boy that she implored her employers to have burglar bars attached to the doors and windows of the house, and an alarm system installed. The wife said, She is right, let us take heed of her advice. So from every window and door in the house where they were living happily ever after they now saw the trees and the sky through bars, and when the little boy's cat tried to climb in by the fanlight to keep him company in his little bed at night, as it customarily had done, it set off the alarm keening through the house.

12   The alarm was often answered—it seemed—by other burglar alarms, in other houses, that had been triggered by pet cats or nibbling mice. The alarms called to one another across the gardens in shrills and bleats and wails that everyone soon became accustomed to, so that the din roused the inhabitants of the suburb no more than the croak of frogs and musical grating of cicadas' legs. Under cover of the electronic harpies' discourse intruders sawed the iron bars and broke into homes, taking away hi-fi equipment, television sets, cassette players, cameras and radios, jewelry and clothing, and sometimes were hungry enough to devour everything in the refrigerator or paused audaciously to drink

the whisky in the cabinets or patio bars. Insurance companies paid no compensation for single malt, a loss made keener by the property owner's knowledge that the thieves wouldn't ever have been able to appreciate what it was they were drinking.

13   Then the time came when many of the people who were not trusted housemaids and gardeners hung about the suburb because they were unemployed. Some importuned for a job: weeding or painting a roof; anything, *baas*, madam. But the man and his wife remembered the warning about taking on anyone off the street. Some drank liquer and fouled the street with discarded bottles. Some begged, waiting for the man and his wife to drive the car out of the electronically-operated gates. They sat about with their feet in the gutters, under the jacaranda trees that made a green tunnel of the street—for it was a beautiful suburb, spoilt only by their presence—and sometimes they fell asleep lying right before the gates in the midday sun. The wife could never see anyone go hungry. She sent the trusted housemaid out with bread and tea, but the trusted housemaid said these were loafers and *tsotsis*, who would come and tie her up and shut her in a cupboard. The husband said, She's right. Take heed of her advice. You only encourage them with your bread and tea. They are looking for their chance . . . And he brought the little boy's tricycle from the garden into the house every night, because if the house was surely secure, once locked and with the alarm set, someone might still be able to climb over the wall or the electronically-closed gates into the garden.

14   You are right, said the wife, then the wall should be higher. And the wise old witch, the husband's mother, paid for the extra bricks as her Christmas present to her son and his wife—the little boy got a Space Man outfit and a book of fairy tales.

15   But every week there were more reports of intrusion: in broad daylight and the dead of night, in the early hours of the morning, and even in the lovely summer twilight—a certain family was at dinner while the bedrooms were being ransacked upstairs. The man and his wife, talking of the latest armed robbery in the suburb, were distracted by the sight of the little boy's pet cat effortlessly arriving over the seven-foot wall, descending first with a rapid bracing of extended forepaws down on the sheer vertical surface, and then a graceful launch, landing with swishing tail within the property. The whitewashed wall was marked with the cat's comings and goings; and on the street side of the wall there were larger red-earth smudges that could have been made by the kind of broken running shoes, seen on the feet of unemployed loiterers, that had no innocent destination.

16   When the man and wife and little boy took the pet dog for its walk round the neighbourhood streets they no longer paused to admire this show of roses or that perfect lawn; these were hidden behind an array of different varieties of security fences, walls and devices. The man, wife, little boy and dog passed a remarkable choice: there was the low-cost option of broken glass embedded in cement along the top of walls, there were iron grilles ending in lance-points, there were attempts at reconciling the aesthetics of prison architecture with the

Spanish Villa style (spikes painted pink) and with the plaster urns of neo-classical facades (twelve-inch pikes finned like zigzags of lightning and painted pure white). Some walls had a small board affixed, giving the name and telephone number of the firm responsible for the installation of the devices. While the little boy and the pet dog raced ahead, the husband and wife found themselves comparing the possible effectiveness of each style against its appearance; and after several weeks when they paused before this barricade or that without needing to speak, both came out with the conclusion that only one was worth considering. It was the ugliest but the most honest in its suggestion of the pure concentration-camp style, no frills, all evident efficacy. Placed the length of walls, it consisted of a continuous coil of stiff and shining metal serrated into jagged blades, so that there would be no way of climbing over it and no way through its tunnel without getting entangled in its fangs. There would be no way out, only a struggle getting bloodier and bloodier, a deeper and sharper hooking and tearing of flesh. The wife shuddered to look at it. You're right, said the husband, anyone would think twice . . . And they took heed of the advice on a small board fixed to the wall: Consult DRAGON'S TEETH The People For Total Security.

17   Next day a gang of workmen came and stretched the razor-bladed coils all around the walls of the house where the husband and wife and little boy and pet dog and cat were living happily ever after. The sunlight flashed and slashed, off the serrations, the cornice of razor thorns encircled the home, shining. The husband said, Never mind. It will weather. The wife said, You're wrong. They guarantee it's rust-proof. And she waited until the little boy had run off to play before she said, I hope the cat will take heed . . . The husband said, Don't worry, my dear, cats always look before they leap. And it was true that from that day on the cat slept in the little boy's bed and kept to the garden, never risking a try at breaching security.

18   One evening, the mother read the little boy to sleep with a fairy story from the book the wise old witch had given him at Christmas. Next day he pretended to be the Prince who braves the terrible thicket of thorns to enter the palace and kiss the Sleeping Beauty back to life: he dragged a ladder to the wall, the shining coiled tunnel was just wide enough for his little body to creep in, and with the first fixing of its razor-teeth in his knees and hands and head he screamed and struggled deeper into its tangle. The trusted housemaid and the itinerant gardener, whose 'day' it was, came running, the first to see and to scream with him, and the itinerant gardener tore his hands trying to get at the little boy. Then the man and his wife burst wildly into the garden and for some reason (the car, probably) the alarm set up wailing against the screams while the bleeding mass of the little boy was hacked out of the security coil with saws, wire-cutters, choppers, and they carried it—the man, the wife, the hysterical trusted housemaid and the weeping gardener—into the house.

For Writing and Discussion

1. What argument is inherent in Gordimer's story? In what way does the story-within-a-story beginning set up the argument?

2. What does Gordimer's story say about fear? about walls? about communities?

3. Gordimer's story has the tone of a parable. What moral lesson does the story teach?

The Story of an Hour
Kate Chopin

1 **K**nowing that Mrs. Mallard was afflicted with a heart trouble, great care was taken to break to her as gently as possible the news of her husband's death.

2 It was her sister Josephine who told her, in broken sentences; veiled hints that revealed in half concealing. Her husband's friend Richards was there, too, near her. It was he who had been in the newspaper office when intelligence of the railroad disaster was received, with Brently Mallard's name leading the list of "killed." He had only taken the time to assure himself of its truth by a second telegram, and had hastened to forestall any less careful, less tender friend in bearing the sad message.

3 She did not hear the story as many women have heard the same, with a paralyzed inability to accept its significance. She wept at once, with sudden, wild abandonment, in her sister's arms. When the storm of grief had spent itself she went away to her room alone. She would have no one follow her.

4 There stood, facing the open window, a comfortable, roomy armchair. Into this she sank, pressed down by a physical exhaustion that haunted her body and seemed to reach into her soul.

5 She could see in the open square before her house the tops of trees that were all aquiver with the new spring life. The delicious breath of rain was in the air. In the street below a peddler was crying his wares. The notes of a distant song which some one was singing reached her faintly, and countless sparrows were twittering in the eaves.

6 There were patches of blue sky showing here and there through the clouds that had met and piled one above the other in the west facing her window.

7 She sat with her head thrown back upon the cushion of the chair, quite motionless, except when a sob came up into her throat and shook her, as a child who has cried itself to sleep continues to sob in its dreams.

8 She was young, with a fair, calm face, whose lines bespoke repression and even a certain strength. But now there was a dull stare in her eyes, whose gaze

was fixed away off yonder on one of those patches of blue sky. It was not a glance of reflection, but rather indicated a suspension of intelligent thought.

9   There was something coming to her and she was waiting for it, fearfully. What was it? She did not know; it was too subtle and elusive to name. But she felt it, creeping out of the sky, reaching toward her through the sounds, the scents, the color that filled the air.

10   Now her bosom rose and fell tumultuously. She was beginning to recognize this thing that was approaching to possess her, and she was striving to beat it back with her will—as powerless as her two white slender hands would have been.

11   When she abandoned herself a little whispered word escaped her slightly parted lips. She said it over and over under her breath: "free, free, free?" The vacant stare and the look of terror that had followed it went from her eyes. They stayed keen and bright. Her pulses beat fast, and the coursing blood warmed and relaxed every inch of her body.

12   She did not stop to ask if it were or were not a monstrous joy that held her. A clear and exalted perception enabled her to dismiss the suggestion as trivial.

13   She knew that she would weep again when she saw the kind, tender hands folded in death; the fact that had never looked save with love upon her, fixed and gray and dead. But she saw beyond that bitter moment a long procession of years to come that would belong to her absolutely. And she opened and spread her arms out to them in welcome.

14   There would be no one to live for during those coming years; she would live for herself. There would be no powerful will bending hers in that blind persistence with which men and women believe they have a right to impose a private will upon a fellow creature. A kind intention or a cruel intention made the act seem no less a crime as she looked upon it in that brief moment of illumination.

15   And yet she had loved him—sometimes. Often she had not. What did it matter! What could love, the unsolved mystery, count for in face of this possession of self-assertion which she suddenly recognized as the strongest impulse of her being!

16   "Free! Body and soul free!" she kept whispering.

17   Josephine was kneeling before the closed door with her lips to the keyhole, imploring for admission. "Louise, open the door! I beg; open the door—you will make yourself ill. What are you doing, Louise? For heaven's sake open the door."

18   "Go away. I am not making myself ill." No; she was drinking in a very elixir of life through that open window.

19   Her fancy was running riot along those days ahead of her. Spring days, and summer days, and all sorts of days that would be her own. She breathed a quick prayer that life might be long. It was only yesterday she had thought with a shudder that life might be long.

20   She arose at length and opened the door to her sister's importunities. There was a feverish triumph in her eyes, and she carried herself unwittingly

like a goddess of Victory. She clasped her sister's waist, and together they descended the stairs. Richards stood waiting for them at the bottom.

21   Someone was opening the front door with a latchkey. It was Brently Mallard who entered, a little travel-stained, composedly carrying his grip-sack and umbrella. He had been far from the scene of accident, and did not even know there had been one. He stood amazed at Josephine's piercing cry; at Richards' quick motion to screen him from the view of his wife.

22   But Richards was too late.

23   When the doctors came they said she had died of heart disease—of joy that kills.

For Writing and Discussion

1. What does this story say about the relationship between emotions and the physical body? Relate Louise's joy prior to seeing her husband to the loss of identity some people feel in a relationship.

2. What is the irony in the doctors' assessment of the cause of death?

Practice: Comparing and Evaluating Styles

Using several of the elements of prose fiction listed on pages 383–385, compare stylistic elements of two stories. Look at how characters are revealed, the author's use of the elements of fiction, the use of descriptive modifiers to paint word pictures, the kinds of sentences and level of language, and so forth, and decide which style you prefer and why. Evaluate the role style of writing plays in the overall effectiveness of each story. The following questions may help guide your analysis:

1. Is the story written in first-person, third-person, or omniscient point of view?
2. Why did the author mention _____ ? (Relate a specific incident to overall purpose)
3. Discuss transitions in time, including flashbacks and foreshadowing.
4. Discuss word choices and levels of language.
5. Identify sentence structures and the effects.
6. Discuss meaning and effectiveness of figurative language.
7. Discuss your reactions to the stories and why.
8. How does straight description and figurative language work together to create imagery?
9. What is the author's attitude toward the subject (tone)? What is the mood of the story? Are mood and tone complementary or contrasting?
10. What kind of person is the protagonist (stereotypical, atypical in a certain way)?

Practice: Reporting on Literary Criticism

Reading the evaluations of literary works can enhance our understanding. Critics, through careful study of a literary work, may make discoveries about the meaning or elements of a work that escape other readers. Exploring literary criticism can lead to still more ideas and insight. Using on-line or printed library sources, find at least one article of literary criticism about the works of your favorite author. Prepare a brief written or oral report on your findings. (See Part Ten for information on finding, using, and documenting sources.)

Chapter 21

ART AND COMMUNITY

The Instinct to Beautify . . .
Kamaladevi Chattopadhyay

1   In both ancient and modern times, tribal people have sought to bring beauty into their everyday lives. Not content with merely providing for the creature comforts, these people began to ornament articles that they used every day, along with their garments, the places they lived, and their own bodies. The walls of their huts became canvases on which pictures blossomed. A strategic item like a bow or arrow was embellished with decorations, water pots took on pleasing shapes, and designs were invented for mundane cookware. The legacy of this instinct to beautify not only gives us today countless creative traditions, but also provides modern generations with a link to their past.

2   It seems obvious that this urge to transform functional items into works of aesthetic value emerged as part of a community's close intimacy with nature, with its changing rhythms of the day and night, seasons, and the life cycles.

3   Each community lived an integrated pattern that responded to the joys and burdens of life, taking them in its flow. Crafts exhibited an intuitive sense of going with, rather than against, the grain of daily existence. Craftmanship was an activity that involved the entire person, bringing together the mind and the material for a specific purpose. There was no professional class of craftsmen or craftswomen. Each person was a creator.

4   Human beings developed a sense of aesthetics from the pleasure of a job well done. They satisfied—unconsciously maybe, but with the right instinct— all the conditions later associated with master craftsmanship. This was not determined merely by the outer appearance of an object. The act of creating the object had to be a human activity that fulfilled a definite function. It had to have a place in a social pattern, for each human being is part of a social milieu.

5   Tribal people decorate themselves and almost everything around them. Throughout my homeland of India, boards on the front of tribal people's houses feature human figures. Similarly, they elaborately and intricately decorate doors, the eaves of the roofs, musical instruments, couches on which the dead are laid out, graves of famous warriors, and items of household use such as mugs, plates,

pipes for smoking, and combs. The textile designs range from the most subtly simple to the most elaborate manifestation of complex techniques. The basketry is exquisite, with incredibly refined weaving and a wealth of beautiful shapes and designs. The wood carvings are startlingly alive.

6   In fact, all their products vibrate with life, as though the makers infused something of themselves into their artistic creations. By looking at nature, tribal peoples learn how to understand artistic concepts such as size, shape, and proportion and then are able to integrate what they have learned into their art. This is how the great artistic and craft traditions must have been molded and history made.

7   So why is it important that these traditions get passed down each generation to new practitioners? Because the arts and crafts created by previous generations inspire the next by showing that every human being is endowed with some creative talent and can find appropriate expression through stimulated and disciplined guidance.

8   Yet it is important that the tradition never get fossilized into rigidity, for the crafts have to reflect the common experiences of the community. Changes have to reflect the flow and movements of life as well as shifts in psychology and taste. When something new shoots up it should reflect an immediate experience. To be meaningful, tradition has to be a live force, unlike the copying of styles that is now so much a part of modern civilization.

9   Traditional crafts reflect the landscape, the seasons, the moods of the day. Into the crafts are woven the epics, the legends, the romantic heroic tales of the countryside. They heighten the big events in human life: the wonder of birth, the joy of marriage, the mystery of death. In each event the crafts play a special role, for they live and grow and have their being in everyday life.

10   When we wander away from creation and fill it with sheer mechanics, we get out of our depth. The answer is creativity, not in the isolation of the poet in the ivory tower, but as part of a living community with a dynamic tradition. This is what the traditional crafts represent and bring home to us.

11   Humankind is a union of almost infinite diversity. Each person receives some gift from the past and has a gift of new hope to give to the future. The challenge of our time is to offer one another the opportunity to create traditions that will be passed down to future generations.

Does Serious Art Need to Be Ugly?
Jon Spayde

A new debate rages about the meaning of truth and beauty.

1 Rows and rows of trumpet and tuba mouthpieces stick out of a wall, accompanied by a photo showing a pair of black lips and a newspaper clipping quoting former L.A. mayor Tom Bradley on urban fear (Lorna Simpson's *Hypothetical*). A sketchy painting of a female face, every orifice assaulted by penises (Sue Williams's *Try to Be More Accommodating*).

2 Whether it's enigmatic or easy to read, the art filling cutting-edge galleries and definitive exhibitions like New York's Whitney Biennial these days is likely to mount a soapbox and make sexual-political-polycultural points with the help of any number of explanations on the wall or in the catalog. What it is not likely to be is particularly appealing to the eye, and even if it is, its comeliness doesn't seem to matter to critics.

3 This state of affairs has some thoughtful and far-from-conservative critics concerned. "There is a rumble in the art world," writes Laurie Hogin in an issue of *New Art Examiner* (April 1994) given over to the question of beauty. "People are wondering why the question of whether or not a work of art is beautiful and well-crafted is excluded from discussions of its relevance to cultural production."

4 Anti-aestheticism in the art world is the legacy of many trends: the cerebral play of French dadaist Marcel Duchamp (who considered fragmentary notes he wrote to himself, and even the chess games he played, as part of his body of artwork); the brutally simple forms made by the minimalist painters and sculptors of the '60s and '70s; and the conceptual art of the same era, in which texts proposing art projects sometimes stood in for the projects themselves.

5 Even more important, though, are academic trends that have worked their way from comparative literature departments into the art schools: sophisticated feminism, French critiques of the organization of thought, and postcolonial theory, which analyzes expression against the backdrop of the white West's struggle to rule the world.

6 In short, theory, which once commented on art, is now integral to its making—and that's one good reason why beauty is often a stranger in the studio. For theory-sharp feminist artists like Laura Cottingham, another contributor to the same special issue of *New Art Examiner*, the trouble with beauty is not just its association with toxic ideals of the female form; its seductions lull critical thought itself to sleep. "Since beauty is summoned from a idea of perfection," she writes, "it must maintain its purity through either the elimination or naturalization of conflicts." Hogin lauds anti-aesthetic art as "the speech of change, convulsive and urgent."

7   But what sort of speech is coming from the political art of the present moment? For some, it's hectoring and holier-than-thou. "People just get annoyed at being instructed and deprived of anything to look at," complains Dave Hickey, another *New Art Examiner* contributor. "I really don't need some 20-year-old lecturing me on virtue. I'm more interested in vision and desire." A few pages further on, Howard Risatti offers a diagnosis: "Many who now believe that art (and the artist) has lost its position of importance in society . . . believe that art must engage what is perceived to be 'important' and 'relevant' subject matter. In a literal sense, subject matter is now being used to 'stand in' for the aesthetic."

8   Cottingham appears to agree that contemporary political art isn't self-confident about its relationship with the body politic: "Nothing is more obvious," she asserts, "than the fact that there is absolutely no agreement as to what we as a society and as individuals expect from visual culture."

9   Alexander Melamid would probably agree too, mournfully. The Russian émigré artist and his partner Vitaly Komar hired a public opinion pollster to ask a sample of Americans about their tastes in art. The results were published in *The Nation* (March 14, 1994), and Komar and Melamid actually painted the painting America said it wanted—a beautiful one, with lots of blue, some animals, and curvy lines. In a fascinating accompanying interview, Melamid professes a genuine, unjokey desire to connect with his public, telling moving stories of his admiration for ordinary folks in his Bayonne, New Jersey, neighborhood—while sounding a different note at other moments: "Stop playing the game that we're freewheeling artists. We're not! We're slaves of this society," and "I feel myself, as an artist and as a citizen, just totally obsolete. I don't know why I am here."

10   Clearly, the beauty debate easily turns into a richly political tussle over what artists owe their audiences. While the B-word probably is too fraught with sexist baggage to return as an ideal, wrestling with what beauty does for a viewer, what beauty means when it is not toxic, can help artist and viewer refresh their relationship.

11   Dave Hickey, the champion of "vision and desire," sketches a compelling alternative ideal for political art, in which beautiful images of disturbing things (he cites the late Robert Mapplethorpe's gorgeous photographs of outrageous gay sexuality) honor the viewer by giving her or him pleasure—while also, in Hickey's words, "persuading the beholder of other ideas and attitudes."

12   But what if the very idea of the artist as persuader is the problem? Theory in many fields shows us how all areas of life are saturated with political meaning and how the model of politics as nothing more than public argument has become outmoded. "Art must be more than a site of opinion," writes Richard Bolton in an earlier issue of *New Art Examiner* (November 1993). "It must be a place where audiences can experience complex feelings, questions, doubt, and hope." A world, then, of both visual and intellectual richness, *and* a kind of utopia.

13   For Bolton, all art is utopian, simply by virtue of implying, or somehow referring to, a world in which desires (the artist's, the audience's) are fulfilled. For some artists, that is a better-looking world; for others, a more just one. Surely there is beauty in both visions, and Bolton dares to combine them. As he ringingly puts it, "[A new art practice] will, I believe, arrive at a new understanding of beauty, redefined as the quality that lies at the very heart of social transformation."

For Writing and Discussion

1. Suzanne Langer, in "The Cultural Importance of Art," defines art as "the epitome of human life, the truest record of insight and feeling" that "objectify[s] feeling so that we can contemplate and understand it." Relate Langer's definition to Chattopadhyay's ideas about art. Does Langer's definition suggest that the need for expression through art is innate, or instinctual, as Chattopadhyay claims? What is the artist's function in society?

2. What "record of insight and feeling" is depicted in the "ugly" art described by Jon Spayde? Is "ugly" art a true reflection of society or merely commercialization by a few of its members?

3. Ralph Waldo Emerson wrote in "Wealth," "Art is a jealous mistress, and if a man ha[s] a genius for painting, poetry, music, architecture, or philosophy, he makes a bad husband and an ill provider, and should be wise in season and not fetter himself with duties which will embitter his days and spoil him for his proper work." Goethe said, "Talent develops itself in solitude; character in the stream of life." Relate Emerson's and Goethe's statements to both men and women, argue for or against their claims.

4. Robert Kennedy once said, "Some people see things as they are and ask 'Why?' I see things as they could be and ask 'Why not?'" How do Kennedy's words apply to the artist?

5. What role do you believe art can (or should) play in a community? List ways that art can be fostered in the community.

6. List ways that you can develop your own creativity, and explain the role art plays in your life. How important do you think creativity is to personal happiness?

THE POWER OF STYLE: REALISM AND IMPRESSIONISM

Style in art is related to the historical period and culture in which it is produced. For instance, the style of painting that seeks to represent reality is colored by the cultural perceptions and feelings of the artist, what the artist *knows* and *means*, or intends. David Parrish's painting of a Yamaha motorcycle is hard to distinguish from a photograph, yet the camera's eye and the artist's eye more often see things differently.

The Impressionist seeks to record on canvas sensations of light and color and form rather than what he sees. Van Gogh's *Starry Night* depicts the feeling of the "vastness of the universe filled with whirling and exploding stars and galaxies of stars, beneath which the earth and men's habitations huddle in anticipation of cosmic disaster" (Gardner's *Art through the Ages*).

Practice: Seeing and Feeling

Study a painting, perhaps one that is hung in the foyer of a campus or office building. What elements of the painting seem to depict what the artist *saw?* What the artist *felt?* What is the focal point of the painting (where are your eyes drawn first)? How do color and form work together to create an atmosphere, or mood? What do you feel as you look at the painting? What thoughts come to your mind as you look at the painting? How is the content treated? Do you think the painting makes a purposeful statement? If so, what?

CHAPTER SUMMARY

In Chapters 19–21, you have had opportunities to explore different kinds of art and how art may make a statement and entice the listener or reader or viewer to reach a new understanding about life and the natural world. The artist uses *pathos* to persuade us to open our eyes, our minds, to new possibilities or to have new feelings about the familiar. You have looked at the role *ethos* plays in creation and how *logos*, purposeful arguments, can be involved in music, literature, and art. In Part Eight, you will have an opportunity to read literature that argues with satire.

Chapter 22

WRITING CHALLENGE

Choose a movie, novel or story, a piece of fine art, or a piece of music that you enjoy (or enjoyed), and write an evaluation of the work of art or music movement. Your audience will be your classmates. Assume they will decide whether to spend money and time on the work of art, based on the power of your evaluation. Remember that evaluation arguments contain a series of substantiation arguments; your interpretations and assessments are supported with evidence from the work. The Guide to Writing will help you with your analysis. See the student papers in Chapters 15 and 18 for examples of evaluations.

Alternative Assignment   Write a piece of prose fiction that contains an indirect argument, perhaps in the form of a futuristic journal entry similar to the student paper ("New Year's Eve, 2012") on page 412.

Journal Topic Suggestions

- How different kinds of art can enrich your life
- What life might be like without art
- How you can increase your enjoyment of art
- What the lyrics of a particular song mean to you
- How you felt after you read a particular story

GUIDE TO WRITING

Open evaluations are devoted to answering such questions as "What makes a good movie?" This type of argument attempts to establish a standard, and substantiation arguments are created to establish the relevance of each trait of a movie. Closed evaluations apply standards to a given example. Each trait of the example is examined in light of the standard. For this assignment, apply standards in the evaluation of a work of art and substantiate your assessment of how well the work meets those standards.

Planning and Prewriting

In choosing your topic, you will want to consider your personal interests and your resources. If you are an artist, for instance, and interested in American

Impressionism, it could be to your advantage to research the topic thoroughly and bring your personal feelings and opinions about the movement into your evaluation. Similarly, if you are knowledgeable about a kind of music (its major artists, its origins, and so forth) and would like to know more, you might enjoy the research involved in analyzing a music movement. If, however, you have limited interest in or knowledge about such a topic, you can limit your need for resources by choosing a movie or book.

Still, you will need to do a thorough analysis of the book or movie, which will involve watching the movie or reading the book several times. Before you choose, you may want to read through the Questions for Evaluating . . . on pages 406–408.

Doing a focused freewriting about what you already know and believe about the topic will help you get started. You can probably use some of the ideas you generate in the paper. Also, after each reading or viewing of your source, write your responses and reactions.

To guide your analysis, read and respond to the following questions about your topic. Organize your findings into an informal outline to guide your writing. Remember to write down page numbers where you found examples or direct quotations in books. If you are using a movie, you may want to set the counter on the VCR so that you can note the location of particular scenes that you want to study further.

QUESTIONS FOR EVALUATING A MUSIC MOVEMENT

1.   What are the accepted standards that apply to music movements?
2.   How can you support your definition of the standards?
3.   What are the historical roots of the movement?
4.   Who are the major artists or groups associated with the movement? What are their contributions?
5.   Does the movement reflect a reaction against other kinds of music? If so, how?
6.   What are the most significant elements of the music? Significant or prominent instruments?
7.   What is the most outstanding characteristic of the lyrics (if applicable)?
8.   Do the clothes of the musicians contribute to mood or meaning during live concerts or in videos?
9.   Are stage props used during live concerts or in videos? If so, what is their significance?
10.   In what ways is the music in this movement different from or superior to works involving other techniques?
11.   What elements make the music powerful and moving?
12.   What is the social context for the movement, and how is that context reflected in the music?
13.   How does that reflection of social context supply meaning?

QUESTIONS FOR EVALUATING PROSE FICTION

1. What standards will you apply?
2. What is the theme of the story? Do you notice familiar literary motifs? How do they relate to the theme?
3. What elements does the author use to involve the reader in the work (plot, setting, narration, dialogue, satire, and so forth)?
4. What are the most significant characteristics of the author's style? (Look at sentence structure, level of language, kind of language, and so forth.)
5. Discuss the effectiveness of the elements and their relation to theme.
6. Describe the imagery and/or patterns of words in the work. Is it used strictly to set the scene? Create a world? Is it used to describe (reveal) characters' attitudes, conflicts, contradictions, situations? Does it move toward or become symbolism?
7. Describe and analyze the author's use of symbolism. Show how symbolism is used to create or support the theme.
8. Does the narration of the work use the stream-of-consciousness technique? If so, what is its significance or effect?
9. How do flashbacks and foreshadowing contribute to the work?
10. What role does the work's setting play?
11. How do the characters in the work contribute to the theme? Were you able to visualize fully the characters and scenes in the book? If so, what elements helped you?
12. Analyze the conflict(s) in the work. What type or types of conflict exist (human against human, human against self, human against nature)? What is the relationship between conflict, resolution of conflict, and theme?
13. Discuss the work's significance to you and why. What does your own experience bring to your interpretation of the work?
14. Does the story have special significance for an age or ethnic group, religious movement, or gender? In what way?

QUESTIONS FOR EVALUATING A MOVIE

1. What standards will you apply?
2. What is the theme of the movie?
3. What elements does the director use to involve the audience in the work (action, setting, special effects, the abstract and the concrete, and so forth)? What is the significance of major elements, and how do they relate to theme?
4. Evaluate the dialogue. Do the lines of each character ring true, or do they sometimes seem forced and phoney?
5. How do the characters contribute to the film? Do you think the actors were appropriately cast?

6. How do the actors' paralanguage, gestures, and body language contribute to characterization?
7. Does the costuming have special significance? Technical aspects such as lighting? If so, how?
8. Discuss the soundtrack and its effectiveness in creating mood.
9. Describe the visual imagery in the film. Is it used strictly to set the scene? create a world? Is it used to describe (reveal) characters' attitudes, conflicts, situations? Does it move toward or become symbolism?
10. Are there patterns of words or images? Familiar motifs? Overriding metaphors? If so, how do they relate to theme?
11. How would you characterize the film in terms of romanticism (emphasis on feeling, originality, or depicting life as we might like it to be) or realism (depicts life as it is; often shows the harsher side of life and base side of human nature)? What is the significance?
12. Describe and analyze the film's use of symbolism. Show how symbolism is used to create or support the theme.
13. How do flashbacks and foreshadowing contribute to the film?
14. Analyze the conflict(s) in the film. What type or types of conflict exist (human against human, human against self, human against nature)? What is the relationship between conflict, resolution of conflict, and theme?
15. Discuss the movie's significance to you and why. What does your own experience bring to your interpretation of the film?
16. Does the movie have special significance for an age or ethnic group, religious movement, or gender? In what way?

QUESTIONS FOR EVALUATING AN ART MOVEMENT

1. What are the accepted standards related to art movements?
2. What are the major characteristics of the movement?
3. Who are the major artists associated with the movement? What are their individual contributions?
4. Does the movement reflect a reaction against traditional forms and movements? If so, how?
5. How does the movement treat the natural world? Give examples.
6. What major techniques are used in this school, or movement?
7. In what ways is the art in this movement different from or superior to works involving other techniques?
8. What elements make the art powerful and moving?
9. What is the social context for the movement, and how is that context reflected in the art?
10. How does that reflection of social context supply meaning?

Organizing and Drafting

Evaluation arguments may be arranged in either of the following formats:

> Announce and defend standards of evaluation in the first section and then apply the standards in the second section.
>
> A series of single standards, or standard traits, are announced, defended, and applied one at a time.

You will probably recognize the choices of arrangement above as the "whole-to-whole" and "part-to-part" arrangement of comparison and contrast essays. In fact, that is precisely what you will be doing—comparing your example to a standard.

In a third possible arrangement, the standard is not defined or defended because it is assumed to be known and accepted by the audience. For book reviews, for instance, the reviewer assumes the audience knows and accepts a certain standard of quality. However, this standard may vary from publication to publication, and a reviewer must know the predisposition of the publication's audience.

By the time you begin writing, you will have more than enough ideas for your paper. Before you write, arrange your material in logical order so that you can focus on one section at a time. You will probably want to prepare an informal outline or list details and examples under headings related to the elements you want to focus on. Reread your freewritings and any source material. As you write, keep in mind the following precautions:

- Do not write a summary. Although your paper may include a summary of some element of work, your paper should go beyond merely telling what happened.
- Include statements of evaluation about elements of your topic, and support your opinions with details, examples, or reasons.
- Detailed information should include direct quotations or vivid descriptions (art) from the work(s). Clearly indicate in your first draft any passages that are from an outside source.

Evaluating and Revising

PARTNER EVALUATION

Read your partner's essay through to get a general impression. Jot down your initial response to the essay. Was it interesting? Did you learn something from reading it? Was it logically organized? Now read the essay again, this time slowly, evaluating each item in the following list as you read.

1. Is there a clear pattern of organization?
2. Is the standard clearly defined and defended?

3. Did your partner include relevant information about the art form in the introduction? Is the introduction clearly written? Does it make you want to read more? How can the introduction be improved?

4. Is each claim about the work of art or art movement supported with details, examples, and quotations? If not, what claims need more support?

5. Does each paragraph contain a clear focus? Do any of the paragraphs contain information or ideas that are unrelated to the rest of the paragraph? If so, which paragraphs?

6. Are transitions provided to guide the reader through the analysis? If not, where are transitions needed?

7. Do you have questions about any of the ideas or information? Do any of the ideas or judgments need clarifying? If so, note where your partner might add information.

8. What information or ideas are especially interesting? Note the positive aspects of the paper.

9. Are any of the sentences unclear or awkward? Put brackets around sentences that might be improved. Did your partner use a variety of sentence structures?

10. Does the ending adequately conclude the essay, or does the essay just stop? How might the ending be improved?

11. What other ideas for improving the paper can you suggest?

Before revising, reread your paper, jotting down additional ideas and marking sentences that interrupt the logical order. Read your partner's evaluation of your paper, carefully considering each suggested change. Decide what revisions you want to make and mark your draft to include the changes.

Editing and Proofreading

The following checklist will guide you in editing.

1. Can any groups of sentences be combined? Are there awkward or overloaded sentences that can be separated into clear, concise sentences?

2. Should any words or phrases be replaced with words or phrases that more accurately or vividly describe? (Look at verbs and common nouns.)

3. Are all pronoun references clear, and do they agree in number with their antecedents?

4. Are first-person pronouns limited and relevant when used? (Phrases such as "I think" and "In my opinion" can be deleted. All opinions and judgments should be yours unless clearly noted.)

5. Do all verbs agree with their subjects in number?

6. Should any passive constructions be changed to active? (Look for forms of *be*.)

7. Are direct quotations correctly introduced?

Proofread your paper carefully to eliminate typos, misspellings, and faulty punctuation. Check to make sure that all words are spelled correctly, each sentence is punctuated correctly, each sentence is punctuated correctly, there are no sentence fragments or run-on sentences, and direct quotations are included in quotation marks. Be sure your final draft is neat and in manuscript form (see Part Ten).

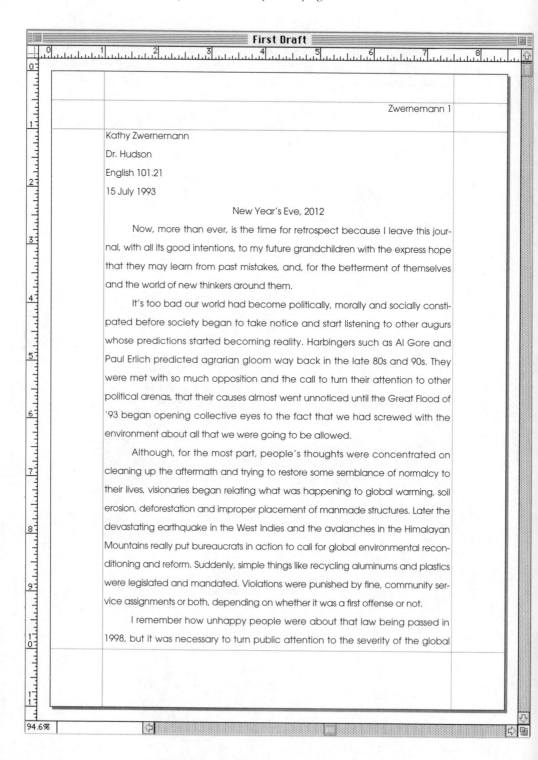

First Draft

Zwernemann 1

Kathy Zwernemann

Dr. Hudson

English 101.21

15 July 1993

New Year's Eve, 2012

Now, more than ever, is the time for retrospect because I leave this journal, with all its good intentions, to my future grandchildren with the express hope
that they may learn from past mistakes, and, for the betterment of themselves
and the world of new thinkers around them.

It's too bad our world had become politically, morally and socially consti-
pated before society began to take notice and start listening to other augurs
whose predictions started becoming reality. Harbingers such as Al Gore and
Paul Erlich predicted agrarian gloom way back in the late 80s and 90s. They
were met with so much opposition and the call to turn their attention to other
political arenas, that their causes almost went unnoticed until the Great Flood of
'93 began opening collective eyes to the fact that we had screwed with the
environment about all that we were going to be allowed.

Although, for the most part, people's thoughts were concentrated on
cleaning up the aftermath and trying to restore some semblance of normalcy to
their lives, visionaries began relating what was happening to global warming, soil
erosion, deforestation and improper placement of manmade structures. Later the
devastating earthquake in the West Indies and the avalanches in the Himalayan
Mountains really put bureaucrats in action to call for global environmental recon-
ditioning and reform. Suddenly, simple things like recycling aluminums and plastics
were legislated and mandated. Violations were punished by fine, community service assignments or both, depending on whether it was a first offense or not.

I remember how unhappy people were about that law being passed in
1998, but it was necessary to turn public attention to the severity of the global

94.6%

═══════════════ **First Draft** ═══════════════

crisis. Manufacturers were closely observed for CO_2 emissions and fined for first offense violations. If they did not conform, they were forced to close, and the government usually came in and took over operations. Of course, these actions had devastating economic and political impacts.

Unemployment soared because of the unstable relations between government and multinational conglomerates. Farmers all over the world lost precious fertile land to soil erosion and river silt and moved their families to urban areas where they were met with shortages of employment and housing, and an increase in crime and hunger.

Because of the migration to the cities, literacy rates dropped. Education was a luxury afforded only to the children of those who were specialized in a field and reasonably job secure. The gap between rich and poor continued to grow wider.

I suppose that is when the trend towards a new world government began. Heads of State met at the 1999 World Restoration Summit. The world was going up in a haze of UVB and a burgeoning sect of its civilization was so hungry for nourishment, self-respect and a sense of equilibrium that it was paralyzed. Even though the desire to reach a higher quality of living and the chutzpah were there, the knowledge and planning were lacking.

A great deal was accomplished during the Summit's nine months. While the restrictions imposed on industry trickled down and were felt by everyone from the globalcrats to the landfill workers, it was the beginning of a new beginning, like lancing a boil to get it to heal.

Automobile travel was limited to emergency vehicles. Private vehicles were seized and stored. The average person could apply for a requisition and check out their mopedmobiles, but they were allowed to travel only 1,000 miles per year. The use of natural gas replaced the burning of fossil fuels, which helped the environment some.

94.6%

Zwernemann 3

Talks stirred for a while about banning the use of electric lights during daylight hours, but instead we were subjected to brown-outs. After a few weeks, most people just automatically began to conserve. If someone saw a neighbor's light on in the daytime, that neighbor was subject to some pretty cruel looks. I'm sure they would have lynched someone who strung Christmas lights to burn all through the month of December like we did until 1996. That was a nice memory. I guess it didn't really seem like Christmas anyway since the winters had gotten so warm. Snow was a rare commodity. The little that fell resembled soot and smelled like sulfur and burned the skin.

World Government, headed by a panel of "First World" leaders agreed to subsidize agriculturists and assign them areas of restoration where farmers were paid to redevelop and nurture farmland back to fertile states. If they stayed with the project for seven years, the land was theirs. It was a long-term payoff and a tedious process that was not without setbacks. But the agrarians soon caught on. I guess it was about 2010 when the payoff began with bumper crops in everything from wheat to catfish.

Before the crisis occurred, I took the position as Economics Editor at Quantum Magazine, a leading advocate of social, economic and political reform. A year later, when things started reaching epidemic proportions, I was commissioned by Poligress to be its conscience of sorts, to be a watchdog of the legislative and economic restoration committees. It was during my own field study that I saw the smudged faces of children who were pilfering through the putric stench of landfills for just a morsel of usable food or a remnant to wear. I looked into the empty eyes of mothers who had forgotten how to nurture in their quest to keep their children *alive*.

My mind won't let go of the too hardened, pregnant 13-year-old sitting on the roadside near a chain of cardboard shelters on the way to Dublin, patting her swollen abdomen with one hand and holding a worn book of Emily

94.6%

Zwernemann 4

Dickinson's poetry with the other. She explained how she wished she had lived during that time, when the moors were rich with heather and clouds of pure white floated aimlessly by. I was chilled with the thought that she had never seen a pastoral setting that I took for granted at her age during a time when a young girl didn't have to think of what she could bargain away of herself to avoid starving. When I asked her if she preferred a baby boy or girl, she said blankly that it really didn't matter and asked, "Do coffins come in pink and blue?" We both knew she would probably never be able to feed the child she was carrying.

The haunting expression of her hopelessness stayed with me all the way back to New Mexico. On the shuttle home, I thought how blessed I was to have escaped the blight and enjoy a comfortable lifestyle. I tried to squeeze the lingering image from my mind. What could I do? I couldn't take all the children who needed mothering, I told myself. Two weeks later, I networked with a few friends and associates to organize a parenting institute for teen mothers, who were usually the children of teen mothers themselves, in an effort to educate and break the cycle.

It was supported primarily through private funds, by people who found themselves on the greenest side of the fence dividing the haves and the have-nots. Because currency had become global, most transactions took place by computer. <u>Quantum</u> was distributed worldwide through Computer Read, so we reported the horrors we had seen and asked for donations. We thought that if we could save the children, we could eventually save the world. Soon, we had established 217 institutes globally, from Sydney to Hong Kong. After two years, 10,000 children were processed.

They were given food and medical attention immediately. That was followed by a three-week nurturing session to re-introduce some of the kids and initiate others to the concepts of compassion and concern. Qualified and visionary teachers were recruited. Training programs followed, focusing on

94.6%

First Draft

Zwernemann 5

mind expansion. We wanted to teach these kids to shape the future without obliterating the past.

By 2007, we had turned out 15,000 visionary scholars in medicine, economic planning, agriculture, sociology, global politics, and education. While each student had a specialty, each had a broad scope of knowledge and understanding. They had inherited greenhouse gases, depleted water systems, and landfills in an overpopulated world. The institute gave them the wisdom to know how to cope and how to make the world better for generations to come.

We armed students with the intellectual tools to fight for the survival of civilization, and they are succeeding. In the past five years, our students' influence has lowered population growth. (Traditionally, the lower the literacy rate, the higher the birth rate.) As they are hired by multinationals in poorer countries, they go out and spread the wisdom among the different cultures.

On the whole, with moms and dads back working the farms and multinational companies offering competitive prices for goods, the World Government and Poligress are regulating trade and offering incentives such as low taxes and free child care. The next generation may just lead us to a Utopian-like society. Sure there are miles to go, but you know what they say about the longest journey.

It's funny how every year at this time, I close my eyes to think about what was important enough to register in this special annual entry. In my retrospect, I always see the face of the little woman-child in Dublin. I even named her Maggie, because our brief conversation excluded introductions. I always wonder what happened to her and the baby, but this is the first time I've codified her existence and given her credit for inspiring the Parenting Institute that brought so much light to so many.

The Power of Satire

I-Feel-Like-I'm-Fixin'-To-Die Rag
Joe McDonald

When McDonald wrote the song that became the anthem of the anti-war move-
ment, he was only slightly older than the average 19-year-old G.I. in Vietnam.

Come on all of you big, strong men;
Uncle Sam needs your help again.
He's got himself in a terrible jam
Way down yonder in Vietnam.
5 So put down your books and pick up a gun.
We're gonna have a whole lot of fun.
   [Refrain]
   And it's one, two, three,
   What are we fighting for?
   Don't ask me; I don't give a damn.
10   Next stop is Vietnam.
   And it's five, six, seven,
   Open up the Pearly Gates.
   Well, there ain't no time to wonder why.
   Whoopee! We're all gonna die.
15 Well, come on generals, let's move fast;
   Your big time has come at last.

Gotta go out and get those Reds.
The only good Commie is one that's dead.
And you know the peace can only be won
20 When we blow 'em all to kingdom come.
          [Refrain]
Come on Wall Street, don't be slow;
Why man, it's war a go-go.
There's plenty good money to be made
Supplying the army with the tools of the trade.
25 Just hope and pray that when they drop the bomb,
They drop it on the Viet Cong.
          [Refrain]
Well, come on mothers throughout the land,
Pack your boys off to Vietnam.
Come on fathers, don't hesitate,
30 Send them off before it's too late.
Be the first one on your block
To have your boy come home in a box.
          [Refrain]

Chapter 23

━━━━━━━━━━━━●━━━━━━━━━━━━

SATIRE

In "I-Feel-Like-I'm-Fixin'-To-Die Rag," McDonald's verse form and crude irony reflect the classical satiric form which originated in Rome more than two thousand years ago. The iambic pentameter or quadrameter verses, usually in couplets, were rude and coarse and spoken directly. Centuries later, satire became a popular English form when verse was written according to strict conventions that were borrowed, however inaccurately, from Greek and Latin form.

Although there was experimentation with form during the eighteenth and nineteenth centuries, critics still drew a distinction between humorists and satirists. The satirist was "full of bile," or at least indignant, and his aim was to persuade through humor or wit—to promote change in humanity or humanity's institutions. In fact, masterful rhetoric (in the classical sense, argumentation) is the mark of great satire.

Satire in America Modern satire is most often prose instead of verse and is usually indirect. (Contemporary exceptions include Mark Russell's and *Saturday Night Live*'s political lyrics and social commentary.) The crushing blow of the satirist is often softened by, in addition to humor or wit, one or several devices. Anger is controlled; the attack is indirect so as not to alienate the audience with unrestrained and offensive anger. The writer may also distance him or herself by speaking through a narrator.

It is not surprising that American satire followed British satire in form, and it is also not surprising that a favorite topic has been politics. During the period of the American revolution, satire was popular (Trumbull's *M'Fingal,* Freneau's *The British Prison Ship*, and so on). During the late 1800s political satirist Finley Peter Dunne, "Mr. Dooley," kept a watchful eye on Washington, and Mark Twain began a period in which he prodigiously wrote social satire, although much of it he refrained from publishing. Still, when satire is mentioned, Twain is on the tip of the tongue; when book jackets advertise satire, it is often lauded as being "in the tradition of Swift and Twain."

A Salutation Speech

From the Nineteenth Century to the Twentieth, taken down in shorthand by Mark Twain
Mark Twain

Twain hesitated to speak out directly about political issues until after 1900 when he was encouraged by the public response to "A Salutation Speech," published in the New York Herald *on December 30, 1900.*

I bring you the stately matron named Christendom,
returning bedraggled, besmirched, and dishonored from
pirate-raids in Kiao-Chou, Manchuria, South Africa and
the Philippines, with her soul full of meanness,
5   her pocket full of boodle and her mouth full
of pious hypocrisies. Give her soap and a towel,
but hide the looking-glass.

The War Prayer
Mark Twain

Like McDonald, Twain protests war in "The War Prayer," a piece that he insisted could not be published until after his death, saying, "I have told the truth in that, and only dead men can tell the truth in this world."

1   It was a time of great and exalting excitement. The country was up in arms, the war was on, in every breast burned the holy fire of patriotism; the drums were beating, the bands playing, the toy pistols popping, the bunched firecrackers hissing and spluttering; on every hand and far down the receding and fading spread of roofs and balconies a fluttering wilderness of flags flashed in the sun; daily the young volunteers marched down the wide avenue gay and fine in their new uniforms, the proud fathers and mothers and sisters and sweethearts cheering them with voices choked with happy emotion as they swung by; nightly the packed meetings listened, panting, to patriot oratory which stirred the deepest deeps of their hearts, and which they interrupted at briefest intervals with cyclones of applause, the tears running down the cheeks the while; in the

churches the pastors preached devotion to flag and country, and invoked the God of Battles, beseeching His aid in our good cause in outpouring of fervid eloquence which moved every listener. It was indeed a glad and gracious time, and the half dozen rash spirits that ventured to disapprove of the war and cast a doubt upon its righteousness straightway got such a stern and angry warning that for their personal safety's sake they quickly shrank out of sight and offended no more in that way.

2   Sunday morning came—next day the battalions would leave for the front; the church was filled; the volunteers were there, their young faces alight with martial dreams—visions of the stern advance, the gathering momentum, the rushing charge, the flashing sabers, the flight of the foe, the tumult, the enveloping smoke, the fierce pursuit, the surrender!—then home from the war, bronzed heroes, welcomed, adored, submerged in golden seas of glory! With the volunteers sat their dear ones, proud, happy, and envied by the neighbors and friends who had no sons and brothers to send forth to the field of honor, there to win for the flag, or, failing, die the noblest of noble deaths. The service proceeded; a war chapter from the Old Testament was read; the first prayer was said; it was followed by an organ burst that shook the building, and with one impulse the house rose, with glowing eyes and beating hearts, and poured out that tremendous invocation—

God the all-terrible! Thou who ordainest,
Thunder thy clarion and lightning thy sword!

3   Then came the "long" prayer. None could remember the like of it for passionate pleading and moving and beautiful language. The burden of its supplication was, that an ever-merciful and benignant Father of us all would watch over our noble young soldiers, and aid, comfort, and encourage them in their patriotic work; bless them, shield them in the day of battle and the hour of peril, bear them in His mighty hand, make them strong and confident, invincible in the bloody onset; help them to crush the foe, grant to them and to their flag and country imperishable honor and glory—

4   An aged stranger entered and moved with slow and noiseless step up the main aisle, his eyes fixed upon the minister, his long body clothed in a robe that reached to his feet, his head bare, his white hair descending in a frothy cataract to his shoulders, his seamy face unnaturally pale, pale even to ghastliness. With all eyes following him and wondering, he made his silent way; without pausing, he ascended to the preacher's side and stood there, waiting. With shut lids the preacher, unconscious of his presence, continued his moving prayer, and at last finished it with the words, uttered in fervent appeal, "Bless our arms, grant us the victory, O Lord our God, Father and Protector of our land and flag!"

5   The stranger touched his arm, motioned him to step aside—which the startled minister did—and took his place. During some moments he surveyed the spellbound audience with solemn eyes, in which burned an uncanny light; then in a deep voice he said:

6   "I come from the Throne—bearing a message from Almighty God!" The words smote the house with a shock; if the stranger perceived it he gave no attention. "He has heard the prayer of His servant your shepherd, and will grant it if such shall be your desire after I, His messenger, shall have explained to you its import—that is to say, its full import. For it is like unto many of the prayers of men, in that it asks for more than he who utters it is aware of—except he pause and think.

7   "God's servant and yours has prayed his prayer. Has he paused and taken thought? Is it one prayer? No, it is two—one uttered, the other not. Both have reached the ear of Him who heareth all supplications, the spoken and the unspoken. Ponder this—keep it in mind. If you would beseech a blessing upon yourself, beware! lest without intent you invoke a curse upon a neighbor at the same time. If you pray for the blessing of rain upon your crop which needs it, by that act you are possibly praying for a curse upon some neighbor's crop which may not need rain and can be injured by it.

8   "You have heard your servant's prayer—the uttered part of it. I am commissioned of God to put into words the other part of it—that part which the pastor—and also you in your hearts—fervently prayed silently. And ignorantly and unthinkingly? God grant that it was so! You heard these words: 'Grant us the victory, O Lord our God!' That is sufficient. The *whole* of the uttered prayer is compact into those pregnant words. Elaborations were not necessary. When you have prayed for victory you have prayed for many unmentioned results which follow victory—must follow it, cannot help but follow it. Upon the listening spirit of God the Father fell also the unspoken part of the prayer. He commandeth me to put it into words. Listen!

9   "O Lord our Father, our young patriots, idols of our hearts, go forth to battle—be Thou near them! With them—in spirit—we also go forth from the sweet peace of our beloved firesides to smite the foe. O Lord our God, help us to tear their soldiers to bloody shreds with our shells; help us to cover their smiling fields with the pale forms of their patriot dead; help us to drown the thunder of the guns with the shrieks of their wounded, writhing in pain; help us to lay waste their humble homes with a hurricane of fire; help us to wring the hearts of their unoffending widows with unavailing grief; help us to turn them out roofless with their little children to wander unfriended the wastes of their desolated land in rags and hunger and thirst, sports of the sun flames of summer and the icy winds of winter, broken in spirit, worn with travail, imploring Thee for the refuge of the grave and denied it—for our sakes who adore Thee, Lord, blast their hopes, blight their lives, protract their bitter pilgrimage, make heavy their steps, water their way with their tears, stain the white snow with the blood of their wounded feet! We ask it, in the spirit of love, of Him who is the Source of Love, and who is the ever-faithful refuge and friend of all that are sore beset and seek His aid with humble and contrite hearts: Amen."

10   (After a pause.) "Ye have prayed it; if ye still desire it, speak! The messenger of the Most High waits."

11   It was believed afterward that the man was a lunatic, because there was no sense in what he said.

For Writing and Discussion

1. In the salutation to the twentieth century, Twain refers to the Western countries as *Christendom*. To what countries might Twain refer? Some Americans were opposed to expansionism, or imperialism as some called it. In "Conquest of the U.S. by Spain," William Graham Sumner argues that expansionism of U.S. interests into other countries is detrimental to the country. What position does Twain express in "A Salutation Speech"?

2. When Twain read "The War Prayer" to his daughter Jean and others, they cautioned him not to publish it because the public would think it sacrilege. Why do you think the public might have thought it sacrilegious then? Do you think the piece would have the same effect on a general readership today?

3. Twain often donned a mask, or persona, for his controversial writings. Who is his persona in this piece? Do you think his use of a persona and a fictive setting is more effective than a straight editorial would have been? Why or why not?

4. Critics of Twain's late works accuse him of being bitter, cynical, and misanthropic, of actually hating humankind. Others argue that it was Twain's love of humans and sensitivity toward their suffering that prompted writings such this piece. What do you think?

5. Compare and contrast Twain's "War Prayer" with McDonald's "I-Feel-Like-I'm-Fixin'-to-Die Rag."

Practice: Search and Evaluate

In Twain's work we find satire that played a part in helping to stop the suffering of millions of people under the sadistic rule of King Leopold of the Belgium Congo. In a collection of Twain's work, find and read *King Leopold's Soliloquy*. In other sources, find information about the British group of activists that asked Twain to write the piece and about the part President Roosevelt played in removing King Leopold from the Belgium Congo. Evaluate Twain's role in the affair and generalize about the potential for celebrity artists to be activists.

THE POWER OF STYLE: THE FACES OF SATIRE

Satire may be presented in prose, in poetry, in drama, and in visual arts. Below are some of the many faces of satire.

Burlesque: Comedy characterized by ridiculous exaggeration. Burlesque in its highest form can be satire. David Worcester notes that burlesque first makes us laugh, then "the critical or corrective laughter of satire enters when the story is recognized as a mirror in which the actions or conditions of men are purposely distorted."

Comedy: Light and humorous literature. Although satire might be light (see Horatian satire) and humorous, comedy and satire differ in intent. Comedy might treat, for instance, several social issues as generally unrelated topics with an intent of entertaining; satire is intended to persuade or, in some cases, parody, but it is always sustained.

Formal satire: Direct as opposed to using a narrator. May be Horatian (gentle, meant to right wrongs through sympathetic laughter) or Juvenalian (angry, contemptuous of wrong).

Invective: Abusive, severe censure, oral or written. Although some satire may include an invective element, it rises above common invective through the author's distancing his anger and softening his abuse with humor and wit and often high-flown verbosity. (i.e., "She is a louse" is invective; "She is an insect, capturable with a fine-toothed comb" [Twain] is satirical.)

Indirect satire: Uses narratives, characters. Sometimes in Menippean form, which may be a dialogue, or colloquy, dealing more with mental attitudes or ideas than with characters. Twain's "What Is Man?" is an example.

Irony: Discrepancy between the expected and the unexpected, the appropriate and the inappropriate, either verbal, situational, or dramatic.

Sarcasm: Irony, under the pretext of praise, that is bitter and personal.

I Want a Wife
Judy Syfers

In this classic feminist satire, Syfers points an accusing finger at the traditional "wife" role, a role that for many women is repressive.

1   I belong to that classification of people known as wives. I am A Wife. And, not altogether incidentally, I am a mother.

2   Not too long ago a male friend of mine appeared on the scene fresh from a recent divorce. He had one child, who is, of course, with his ex-wife. He is looking for another wife. As I thought about him while I was ironing one evening, it suddenly occurred to me that I, too, would like to have a wife. Why do I want a wife?

3   I would like to go back to school so that I can become economically independent, support myself, and, if need be, support those dependent upon me. I want a wife who will work and send me to school. And while I am going to school I want a wife to take care of my children. I want a wife to keep track of the children's doctor and dentist appointments. And to keep track of mine, too. I want a wife to make sure my children eat properly and are kept clean. I want a wife who is a good nurturant attendant to my children, who arranges for their schooling, makes sure that they have an adequate social life with their peers, takes them to the park, the zoo, etc. I want a wife who takes care of the children when they are sick, a wife who arranges to be around when the children need special care, because, of course, I cannot miss classes at school. My wife must arrange to lose time at work and not lose the job. It may mean a small cut in my wife's income from time to time, but I guess I can tolerate that. Needless to say, my wife will arrange and pay for the care of the children while my wife is working.

4   I want a wife who will take care of *my* physical needs. I want a wife who will keep my house clean. A wife who will pick up after my children, a wife who will pick up after me. I want a wife who will keep my clothes clean, ironed, mended, replaced when need be, and who will see to it that my personal things are kept in their proper place so that I can find what I need the minute I need it. I want a wife who cooks the meals, a wife who is a *good* cook. I want a wife who will plan the menus, do the necessary grocery shopping, prepare the meals, serve them pleasantly, and then do the cleaning up while I do my studying. I want a wife who will care for me when I am sick and sympathize with my pain and loss of time from school. I want a wife to go along when our family takes a vacation so that someone can continue to care for me and my children when I need a rest and change of scene.

5   I want a wife who will not bother me with rambling complaints about a wife's duties. But I want a wife who will listen to me when I feel the need to

explain a rather difficult point I have come across in my course of studies. And I want a wife who will type my papers for me when I have written them.

6   I want a wife who will take care of the details of my social life. When my wife and I are invited out by my friends, I want a wife who will take care of the babysitting arrangements. When I meet people at school that I like and want to entertain, I want a wife who will have the house clean, will prepare a special meal, serve it to me and my friends, and not interrupt when I talk about things that interest me and my friends. I want a wife who will have arranged that the children are fed and ready for bed before my guests arrive so that the children do not bother us. I want a wife who takes care of the needs of my guests so that they feel comfortable, who makes sure that they have an ashtray, that they are passed the hors d'oeuvres, that they are offered a second helping of the food, that their wine glasses are replenished when necessary, that their coffee is served to them as they like it. And I want a wife who knows that sometimes I need a night out by myself.

7   I want a wife who is sensitive to my sexual needs, a wife who makes love passionately and eagerly when I feel like it, a wife who makes sure that I am satisfied. And, of course, I want a wife who will not demand sexual attention when I am not in the mood for it. I want a wife who assumes the complete responsibility for birth control, because I do not want more children. I want a wife who will remain sexually faithful to me so that I do not have to clutter up my intellectual life with jealousies. And I want a wife who understands that *my* sexual needs may entail more than strict adherence to monogamy. I must, after all, be able to relate to people as fully as possible.

8   If, by chance, I find another person more suitable as a wife than the wife I already have, I want the liberty to replace my present wife with another one. Naturally, I will expect a fresh, new life; my wife will take the children and be solely responsible for them so that I am left free.

9   When I am through with school and have a job, I want my wife to quit working and remain at home so that my wife can more fully and completely take care of a wife's duties.

10   My God, who *wouldn't* want a wife?

For Writing and Discussion

1. Do you think the picture Syfers paints for married women is the same today as it was in 1971 when Syfers wrote this essay? Why or why not?

2. What do you think is the most common problem for women today? What do you think can be done about it?

3.   Do you think pointing out the inequities as Syfers does in this essay can make a difference? What effect do you think this essay has had on the millions of women who have read it? on men?

4. Look back at the "Maxine!" cartoon in Chapter 1 (page 10), and compare the themes of the cartoon and Syfer's piece.

Practice: Writing Satire

Write a satirical argument, perhaps using one of the pieces in this chapter as a model. To choose a topic, think of something you feel strongly about. Share your piece with a small group or with the class. Reading the paper aloud to yourself before reading it to others will help you eliminate problems beforehand.

How to Drive Fast
P. J. O'Rourke

1   **W**hen it comes to taking chances, some people like to play poker or shoot dice; other people prefer to parachute-jump, go rhino hunting, or climb ice floes, while still others engage in crime or marriage. But I like to get drunk and drive like a fool. Name me, if you can, a better feeling than the one you get when you're half a bottle of Chivas in the bag with a gram of coke up your nose and a teenage lovely pulling off her tube top in the next seat over while you're going a hundred miles an hour down a suburban side street. You'd have to watch the entire Mexican air force crash-land in a liquid petroleum gas storage facility to match this kind of thrill. If you ever have much more fun than that, you'll die of pure sensory overload, I'm here to tell you.

2   But wait. Let's pause and analyze *why* this particular matrix of activities is perceived as so highly enjoyable. I mean, aside from the teenage lovely pulling off her tube top in the next seat over. Ignoring that for a moment, let's look at the psychological factors conducive to placing positive emotional values on the sensory-end product of experientially produced excitation of the central nervous system and smacking into a lamppost. Is that any way to have fun? How would your mother feel if she knew you were doing this? She'd cry. She really would. And that's how you know it's fun. Anything that makes your mother cry is fun. Sigmund Freud wrote all about this. It's a well-known fact.

3   Of course, it's a shame to waste young lives behaving this way—speeding around all tanked up with your feet hooked in the steering wheel while your date crawls around on the floor mats opening zippers with her teeth and pounding on the accelerator with an empty liquor bottle. But it wouldn't be taking a chance if you weren't risking *something*. And even if it is a shame to

waste young lives behaving this way, it is definitely cooler than risking *old* lives behaving this way. I mean, so what if some fifty-eight-year-old butt-head gets a load on and starts playing Death Race 2000 in the rush-hour traffic jam? What kind of chance is he taking? He's just waiting around to see what kind of cancer he gets anyway. But if young, talented *you,* with all of life's possibilities at your fingertips, you and the future Cheryl Tiegs there, so fresh, so beautiful—if the two of *you* stake your handsome heads on a single roll of the dice in life's game of stop-the-semi—now *that's* taking chances! Which is why old people rarely risk their lives. It's not because they're chicken—they just have too much dignity to play for small stakes.

4   Now a lot of people say to me, "Hey, P.J., you like to drive fast. Why not join a responsible organization, such as the Sports Car Club of America, and enjoy participation in sports car racing? That way you could drive as fast as you wish while still engaging in a well-regulated spectator sport that is becoming more popular each year." No thanks. In the first place, if you ask me, those guys are a bunch of tweedy old barf mats who like to talk about things like what necktie they wore to Alberto Ascari's funeral. And in the second place, they won't let me drive drunk. They expect me to go out there and smash into things and roll over on the roof and catch fire and burn to death when I'm sober. They must think I'm crazy. That stuff scares me. I have to get completely shit-faced to even think about driving fast. How can you have a lot of exciting thrills when you're so terrified that you wet yourself all the time? That's not fun. It's just *not fun* to have exciting thrills when you're scared. Take the heroes of the *Iliad,* for instance—they really had some exciting thrills, and were they scared? No. They were drunk. Every chance they could get. And so am I, and I'm not going out there and have a horrible car wreck until somebody brings me a cocktail.

5   Also, it's important to be drunk because being drunk keeps your body all loose, and that way, if you have an accident or anything, you'll sort of roll with the punches and not get banged up so bad. For example, there was this guy I heard about who was really drunk and was driving through the Adirondacks. He got sideswiped by a bus and went head-on into another car, which knocked him off a bridge, and he plummeted 150 feet into a ravine. I mean, it killed him and everything, but if he hadn't been so drunk and loose, his body probably would have been banged up a lot worse—and you can imagine how much more upset his wife would have been when she went down to the morgue to identify him.

For Writing and Discussion

1. Is "How to Drive Fast" more effective than a straight lecture on the risks of drinking and driving? Why?

2. What phrases or structures in O'Rourke's writing are characteristic of spoken dialogue?

3. The word *satire* literally means "a dish filled with mixed fruits." Explain the appropriateness of the word *satire* to identify the genre of literature.

4. Benjamin Franklin expressed surprise that anyone who was clever enough to write satires was foolish enough to publish them. The fact that there are relatively few pieces of satire published may speak to both aspects of Franklin's statement. But it is generally agreed among critics that writing satire takes great skill—that it is an art. What elements of satire make it difficult to write?

Practice: Search and Evaluate

P. J. O'Rourke is masterful at using humor in prose to make a point about serious subjects. Other satirists use cartoons to make us laugh and encourage us to reflect. Find an example of a satiric cartoon, and explain the point the cartoonist makes with humor.

A Modest Proposal
Jonathan Swift

A master of satire, Swift used his pen to protest the horrid living conditions in his native Ireland.

For Preventing the Children of Poor Parents in Ireland
from Being a Burden to Their Parents or Country,
and for Making Them Beneficial to the Public

1   It is a melancholy object to those who walk through this great town or travel in the country, when they see the streets, the roads, and cabin doors, crowded with beggars of the female sex, followed by three, four, or six children, all in rags and importuning every passenger for an alms. These mothers, instead of being able to work for their honest livelihood, are forced to employ all their time in strolling to beg sustenance for their helpless infants, who, as they grow up, either turn thieves for want of work, or leave their dear native country to fight for the Pretender in Spain, or sell themselves to the Barbados.

2   I think it is agreed by all parties that this prodigious number of children in the arms, or on the backs, or at the heels of their mothers, and frequently of their fathers, is in the present deplorable state of the kingdom a very great additional grievance; and therefore whoever could find out a fair, cheap, and easy

method of making these children sound, useful members of the commonwealth would deserve so well of the public as to have his statue set up for a preserver of the nation.

3   But my intention is very far from being confined to provide only for the children of professed beggars; it is of a much greater extent, and shall take in the whole number of infants at a certain age who are born of parents in effect as little able to support them as those who demand our charity in the streets.

4   As to my own part, having turned my thoughts for many years upon this important subject, and maturely weighed the several schemes of other projectors, I have always found them grossly mistaken in their computation. It is true, a child just dropped from its dam may be supported by her milk for a solar year, with little other nourishment; at most not above the value in scraps, by her lawful occupation of begging; and it is exactly at one year old that I propose to provide for them in such a manner as instead of being a charge upon their parents or the parish, or wanting food and raiment for the rest of their lives, they shall on the contrary contribute to the feeding, and partly to the clothing, of many thousands.

5   There is likewise another great advantage in my scheme, that it will prevent those voluntary abortions, and that horrid practice of women murdering their bastard children, alas, too frequent among us, sacrificing the poor innocent babes, I doubt, more to avoid the expense than the shame, which would move tears and pity in the most savage and inhuman breast.

6   The number of souls in this kingdom being usually reckoned one million and a half, of these I calculate there may be about two hundred thousand couples whose wives are breeders; from which number I subtract thirty thousand couples who are able to maintain their own children, although I apprehend there cannot be so many under the present distress of the kingdom; but this being granted, there will remain an hundred and seventy thousand breeders. I again subtract fifty thousand for those women who miscarry, or whose children die by accident or disease within the year. There only remain any hundred and twenty thousand children of poor parents annually born. The question therefore is, how this number shall be reared and provided for, which, as I have already said, under the present situation of affairs, is utterly impossible by all the methods hitherto proposed. For we can neither employ them in handicraft nor agriculture; we neither build houses (I mean in the country) nor cultivate land. They can very seldom pick up a livelihood by stealing till they arrive at six years old, except where they are of towardly parts; although I confess they learn the rudiments much earlier, during which time they can however be looked upon only as probationers, as I have been informed by a principal gentleman in the country of Cavan, who protested to me that he never knew above one or two instances under the age of six, even in a part of the kingdom so renowned for the quickest proficiency in that art.

7   I am assured by our merchants that a boy or a girl before twelve years old is no salable commodity; and even when they come to this age, they will not yield above three pounds, or three pounds and half a crown at most on the

Exchange; which cannot turn to account either to the parents or the kingdom, the charge of nutriment and rags having been at least four times that value.

8   I shall now therefore humbly propose my own thoughts, which I hope will not be liable to the least objection.

9   I have been assured by a very knowing American of my acquaintance in London, that a young healthy child well nursed is at a year old a most delicious, nourishing, and wholesome food, whether stewed, roasted, baked, or boiled; and I make no doubt that it will equally serve in a fricassee or a ragout.

10   I do therefore humbly offer it to public consideration that of the hundred and twenty thousand children, already computed, twenty thousand may be reserved for breed, whereof only one fourth part to be males, which is more than we allow to sheep, black cattle, or swine; and my reason is that these children are seldom the fruits of marriage, a circumstance not much regarded by our savages, therefore one male will be sufficient to serve four females. That the remaining hundred thousand may at a year old be offered in sale to the persons of quality and fortune through the kingdom, always advising the mother to let them suck plentifully in the last month, so as to render them plump and fat for a good table. A child will make two dishes at an entertainment for friends; and when the family dines alone, the fore or hind quarter will make a reasonable dish, and seasoned with a little pepper or salt will be very good boiled on the fourth day, especially in winter.

11   I have reckoned upon a medium that a child just born will weigh twelve pounds, and in a solar year if tolerably nursed increaseth to twenty-eight pounds.

12   I grant this food will be somewhat dear, and therefore very proper for landlords, who, as they have already devoured most of the parents, seem to have the best title to the children.

13   Infant's flesh will be in season throughout the year, but more plentiful in March, and a little before and after. For we are told by a grave author, an eminent French physician, that fish being a prolific diet, there are more children born in Roman Catholic countries about nine months after Lent, than at any other season; therefore, reckoning a year after Lent, the markets will be more glutted than usual, because the number of popish infants is at least three to one in this kingdom; and therefore it will have one other collateral advantage, by lessening the number of Papists among us.

14   I have already computed the charge of nursing a beggar's child (in which list I reckon all cottagers, laborers, and four-fifths of the farmers) to be about two shillings per annum, rags included; and I believe no gentleman would repine to give ten shillings for the carcass of a good fat child, which, as I have said, will make four dishes of excellent nutritive meat, when he hath only some particular friend or his own family to dine with him. Thus the squire will learn to be a good landlord, and grow popular among the tenants; the mother will have eight shillings net profit, and be fit for work till she produces another child.

15   Those who are more thrifty (as I must confess the times require) may flay the carcass; the skin of which artificially dressed will make admirable gloves for ladies, and summer boots for fine gentlemen.

16   As to our city of Dublin, shambles may be appointed for this purpose in the most convenient parts of it, and butchers we may be assured will not be wanting; although I rather recommend buying the children alive, and dressing them hot from the knife as we do roasting pigs.

17   A very worthy person, a true lover of his country, and whose virtues I highly esteem, was lately pleased in discoursing on this matter to offer a refinement upon my scheme. He said that many gentlemen of his kingdom, having of late destroyed their deer, he conceived that the want of venison might be well supplied by the bodies of young lads and maidens, not exceeding fourteen years of age nor under twelve, so great a number of both sexes in every country being now ready to starve for want to work and service; and these to be disposed of by their parents, if alive, or otherwise by their nearest relations. But with due deference to so excellent a friend and so deserving a patriot, I cannot be altogether in his sentiments; for as to the males, my American acquaintance assured me from frequent experience that their flesh was generally tough and lean, like that of our schoolboys, by continual exercise, and their taste disagreeable; and to fatten them would not answer the charge. Then as to the females, it would, I think with humble submission, be a loss to the public, because they soon would become breeders themselves; and besides, it is not improbable that some scrupulous people might be apt to censure such a practice (although indeed very unjustly) as a little bordering upon cruelty; which, I confess, hath always been with me the strongest objection against any project, how well soever intended.

18   But in order to justify my friend, he confessed that this expedient was put into his head by the famous Psalmanazar, a native of the island Formosa, who came from thence to London above twenty years ago, and in conversation told my friend that in his country when any young person happened to be put to death, the executioner sold the carcass to the persons of quality as a prime dainty; and that in his time the body of a plump girl of fifteen, who was crucified for an attempt to poison the emperor, was sold to his Imperial Majesty's prime minister of state, and other great mandarins of the court, in joints from the gibbet, at four hundred crowns. Neither indeed can I deny that if the same use were made of several plump young girls in this town, who without one single groat to their fortunes cannot stir abroad without a chair, and appear at the playhouse and assemblies in foreign fineries which they never will pay for, the kingdom would not be the worse.

19   Some persons of a desponding spirit are in great concern about that vast number of poor people who, are aged, diseased, or maimed, and I have been desired to employ my thoughts what course may be taken to ease the nation of so grievous an encumbrance. But I am not in the least pain upon that matter, because it is very well known that they are every day dying and rotting by cold and famine, and filth and vermin, as fast as can be reasonably expected. And as to the younger laborers, they are now in almost as hopeful a condition. They cannot get work, and consequently pine away for want of nourishment to a degree that if any time they are accidentally hired to common labor, they have

not strength to perform it; and thus the country and themselves are happily delivered from the evils to come.

20   I have too long digressed, and therefore shall return to my subject. I think the advantages by the proposal which I have made are obvious and many, as well as of the highest importance.

21   For first, as I have already observed, it would greatly lessen the number of Papists, with whom we are yearly overrun, being the principal breeders of the nation as well as our most dangerous enemies; and who stay at home on purpose to deliver the kingdom to the Pretender, hoping to take their advantage by the absence of so many good Protestants, who have chosen rather to leave their country than to stay at home and pay tithes against their conscience to an Episcopal curate.

22   Secondly, the poorer tenants will have something valuable of their own, which by law may be made liable to distress, and help to pay their landlord's rent, their corn and cattle being already seized and money a thing unknown.

23   Thirdly, whereas the maintenance of an hundred thousand children, from two years old and upwards, cannot be computed at less than ten shillings a piece per annum, the nation's stock will be thereby increased fifty thousand pounds per annum, besides the profit of a new dish introduced to the tables of all gentlemen of fortune in the kingdom who have any refinement in taste. And the money will circulate among ourselves, the goods being entirely of our own growth and manufacture.

24   Fourthly, the constant breeders, besides the gain of eight shillings sterling per annum by the sale of their children, will be rid of the charge for maintaining them after the first year.

25   Fifthly, this food would likewise bring great custom to taverns, where the vintners will certainly be so prudent as to procure the best recipes for dressing it to perfection, and consequently have their houses frequented by all the fine gentlemen, who justly value themselves upon their knowledge in good eating; and a skillful cook, who understands how to oblige his guests, will contrive to make it as expensive as they please.

26   Sixthly, this would be a great inducement to marriage, which all wise nations have either encouraged by rewards or enforced by laws and penalties. It would increase the care and tenderness of mothers toward their children, when they were sure of a settlement for life to the poor babes, provided in some sort by the public, to their annual profit instead of expense. We should see an honest emulation among the married women, which of them could bring the fattest child to the market. Men would become as fond of their wives during the time of their pregnancy as they are now of their mares in foal, their cows in calf, or sows when they are ready to farrow; nor offer to beat or kick them (as is too frequent a practice) for fear of a miscarriage.

27   Many other advantages might be enumerated. For instance, the addition of some thousand carcasses in our exportation of barreled beef, the propagation of swine's flesh, and improvements in the art of making good bacon, so much wanted among us by the great destruction of pigs, too frequent at our tables,

which are no way comparable in taste or magnificence to a well-grown, fat, yearling child, which roasted whole will make a considerable figure at a lord mayor's feast or any other public entertainment. But this and many others I omit, being studious of brevity.

28   Supposing that one thousand families in this city would be constant customers for infants' flesh, besides others who might have it at merry meetings, particularly weddings and christenings, I compute that Dublin would take off annually about twenty thousand carcasses, and the rest of the kingdom (where probably they will be sold somewhat cheaper) the remaining eighty thousand.

29   I can think of no one objection that will possibly be raised against this proposal, unless it should be urged that the number of people will be thereby much lessened in the kingdom. This I freely own, and it was indeed one principal design in offering it to the world. I desire the reader will observe, that I calculate my remedy for this one individual kingdom of Ireland and for no other that ever was, is, or I think ever can be upon earth. Therefore, let no man talk to me of other expedients: of taxing our absentees at five shillings a pound: of using neither clothes nor household furniture except what is of our own growth and manufacturer: of utterly rejecting the materials and instruments that promote foreign luxury: of curing the expensiveness of pride, vanity, idleness, and gaming in our women: of introducing a vein of parsimony, prudence, and temperance: of learning to love our country, in the want of which we differ even from Laplanders and the inhabitants of Topinamboo: of quitting our animosities and factions, nor acting any longer like the Jews, who were murdering one another at the very moment their city was taken: of being a little cautious not to sell our country and conscience for nothing: of teaching landlords to have at least one degree of mercy toward their tenants: lastly, of putting a spirit of honesty, industry, and skill into our shopkeepers; who, if a resolution could now be taken to buy only our native goods, would immediately unite to cheat and exact upon us in the price, the measure, and the goodness, nor could ever yet be brought to make one fair proposal of just dealing, though often and earnestly invited to it.

30   Therefore, I repeat, let no man talk to me of these and the like expedients, till he hath at least some glimpse of hope that there will ever be some hearty and sincere attempt to put them in practice.

31   But as to myself, having been wearied out for many years with offering vain, idle, visionary thoughts, and at length utterly despairing of success, I fortunately fell upon this proposal, which, as it is wholly new, so it hath something solid and real, of no expense and little trouble, full in our own power, and whereby we can incur no danger in disobliging England. For this kind of commodity will not bear exportation, the flesh being of too tender a consistence to admit a long continuance in salt, although perhaps I could name a country which would be glad to eat up our whole nation without it.

32   After all, I am not so violently bent upon my own opinion as to reject any offer proposed by wise men, which shall be found equally innocent, cheap, easy, and effectual. But before something of that kind shall be advanced in

contradiction to my scheme, and offering a better, I desire the author or authors will be pleased maturely to consider two points. First, as things now stand, how they will be able to find food and raiment for an hundred thousand useless mouths and backs. And secondly, there being a round million of creatures in human figure throughout this kingdom, whose sole subsistence put into a common stock would leave them in debt two millions of pounds sterling, adding those who are beggars by profession to the bulk of farmers, cottagers, and laborers, with their wives and children who are beggars in effect; I desire those politicians who dislike my overture, and may perhaps be so bold to attempt an answer, that they will first ask the parents of these mortals whether they would not at this day think it a great happiness to have been sold for food at a year old in this manner I prescribe, and thereby have avoided such a perpetual scene of misfortunes as they have since gone through by the oppression of landlords, the impossibility of paying rent without money or trade, the want of common sustenance, with neither house nor clothes to cover them from the inclemencies of the weather, and the most inevitable prospect of entailing the like or greater miseries upon their breed forever.

33   I profess, in the sincerity of my heart, that I have not the least personal interest in endeavoring to promote this necessary work, having no other motive than the public good of my country, by advancing our trade, providing for infants, relieving the poor, and giving some pleasure to the rich. I have no children by which I can propose to get a single penny; the youngest being nine years old, and my wife past childbearing.

For Writing and Discussion

1. What was your response to this essay? Did you find it shocking? Had you already guessed what the narrator was about to propose before he proposed it?

2. To whom is Swift writing? What kind of person do you think he visualized as he wrote?

3. Characterize Swift's persona. What is his tone? What devices does the persona use to attempt to build the *ethos?* What is the effect?

4. David Shields writes in *A Handbook for Drowning,* "I wrote so many satires about capital punishment for my high school newspaper that students who didn't read carefully started calling me 'The Beheader.'" Why does satire require careful reading? How might a careless reader interpret McDonald's lyrics? Twain's "The War Prayer"? O'Rourke's "How to Drive Fast"? Swift's "A Modest Proposal"?

5. Some people argue that satire is only meant to entertain, not to persuade. Argue that satire is or is not used as a persuasive device. Cite specific examples to support your position.

THE POWER OF STYLE: A CLOSER LOOK

What makes "A Modest Proposal" so memorable? Is it the idea itself? Is it Swift's style, and, if so, what are the elements that make the piece memorable? Or, is it a combination of content and style? To analyze Swift's essay, Edward P. J. Corbett looks closely at each aspect of the rhetorical situation: the *writer* (What was the writer trying to accomplish? Why did he write the piece in the first place?), the *reader* (Who is the audience? What reaction can be expected from the reader?), and the *work* (What does it mean? How is that meaning created? What stylistic elements are at work to make the piece "good," or memorable?) Corbett's analysis of Swift provides an excellent model for stylistic analysis. Although the piece he analyzes is long and complex, the elements of stylistic analysis are relatively simple. As you read Corbett's analysis, try jotting down the basic elements of analysis.

Analysis of "A Modest Proposal"
Edward P. J. Corbett

1   I might begin this stylistic analysis by defining what kind of discourse *A Modest Proposal* is, since genre makes its own demands on the kind of style that an author will employ. With reference to the literary genres, *A Modest Proposal* can be classified as satire, and with reference to the four forms of discourse, satire must be classified as argumentation. If we were using the classical rhetorician's three kinds of persuasive discourse to further specify what type of argumentation we have here, we would classify *A Modest Proposal* as an instance of "deliberative" discourse, since Jonathan Swift is bent on changing the attitude of the propertied class toward the Irish poor and ultimately on moving this class to take some action that would remedy the lot of the poor.

2   In 1728, a year before *A Modest Proposal* was published, there had been a devastating famine in Ireland caused by three successive failures of the harvest. This famine had aggravated the misery of a people that had already been reduced to abject poverty by years of heavy taxation, repressive laws, and absentee landlordism. As Louis A. Landa has pointed out, Swift hoped to expose

the contradiction between a favorite maxim of the mercantilist economic writers—namely, that people are the riches of a nation—and the practice of reducing the majority of subjects to a condition of grinding poverty. The prevalence of the poverty was plain to see, and there had been no lack of proposals, from the political economists, of ways to remedy the condition of the poor. But the ruling class and the absentee landlords were not listening; fattening on the revenues from the land, they were not much concerned about the condition of the peasants who were producing their wealth. Swift was determined to get their ear. He would shock them into attention. And he would shock them into attention with a monstrous proposal presented by means of two of his favorite satiric techniques—using a mask and using irony.

3   To make his use of the mask or *persona* effective, Swift must create a character who is consistent, credible, and authoritative. This must be a character who, in a sense, "sneaks up" on the reader, a character who lulls the reader into expecting a sensible, practical solution of the Irish problem and who, even after he has dropped his bombshell, maintains his pose and his poise. This character will exert a curious kind of ethical appeal—a man who at the beginning of the essay gives the impression of being serious, expert, and well-meaning but who gradually reveals himself to be shockingly inhuman and naive. The character that eventually emerges is that of a fool whose insanity becomes, as Martin Price puts it, "a metaphor for the guilt of responsible men."

4   One of the consequences of this use of a *persona* is that the style of the essay will not be Swift's style; rather it will be a style appropriate to the character that Swift has created. True, some of the characteristics of Swift's style will be present; no author can entirely submerge his own style, except perhaps when he is engaged in writing a parody of another author's style. But if Swift does his job properly, the message of the essay will be conveyed to us in a style that differs, at least in some respect, from the style that Swift displays when he is speaking in his own voice.

5   One of the respects in which the style of *A Modest Proposal* differs noticeably from Swift's usual style is the sentence-length. The average sentence-length in this essay is 56.9 words per sentence. And we note some remarkable variations above and below that average. Although 46 percent of his sentences are composed of less than 47 words, almost 30 percent of his sentences are longer than 67 words (see Appendix for additional statistics on sentence-length). It is interesting to compare this sentence-length with that in two other works where Swift used a *persona*. In studying 200 paragraphs of *Gulliver's Travels* and 100 paragraphs of *A Tale of a Tub*, Edwin Herbert Lewis discovered the average sentence-length to be 40.7 words—almost 50 percent shorter than the average sentence in *A Modest Proposal*. What has happened to the "conciseness" that Herbert Davis says is the most distinctive quality of Swift's style? What has happened of course is that in *A Modest Proposal* we are listening to a man who is so filled with his subject, so careful about qualifying his statements and computations, so infatuated with the sound of his own words, that he rambles on at inordinate length.

6   We note this same tendency to qualify and ramify his thoughts in other characteristics of the proposer's sentence structure. We note this, for one thing, in his frequent use of parenthesis. Sometimes the parenthetical matter throws in a gratuitous aside—"(as I must confess the times require)"; or editorializes—"(although indeed very unjustly)"; or qualifies a statement—"(I mean in the country)"; or insinuates an abrupt note of ethical appeal—"(it would, I think with humble submission, be a loss to the public)." Interpolated gestures like these, especially when they are as frequent as they are in this essay, betray a man who is unusually concerned for the accuracy of his statements and for the image he is projecting to his audience.

7   Something of the same tendency is evident in the many absolute constructions in the essay. Most of these occur at the end of fairly long sentences—e.g. "the charge of nutriment and rags having been at least four times that value" (par. 7); "their corn and cattle being seized and money a thing unknown" (par. 22). These trailing-off phrases create the effect of a thought suddenly remembered and desperately thrown in. What is clever, though, about Swift's use of these trailing-off phrases, placed as they are in an emphatic position, is that in many cases they carry the real sting of the sentence. Here is that topsy-turviness of values that constitutes one of the main strategies of the essay—important things couched in ironical terms or hidden away in weak structures.

8   This tendency to ramify, qualify, or refine statements is evident too in the proposer's habit of compounding elements. I am referring not so much to the common eighteenth-century practice of using doublets and triplets, of which there are a conspicuous number in *A Modest Proposal,* as to the proposer's habit of stringing out words and phrases beyond the common triad, so that we get the effect almost of an exhaustive cataloguing of details or qualifiers. I am referring to instances like these:

> stewed, roasted, baked, or boiled (par. 9)
> of curing the expensiveness of pride, vanity, idleness, and gaming in our women (par. 29)
> equally innocent, cheap, easy, and effectual (par. 32)
> by advancing our trade, providing for infants, relieving the poor, and giving pleasure to the rich (par. 33)

What is observable about the proposer's amplifications is that his epithets are rarely just synonymous variations, such as the displays of *copia* that were common in Anglo-Saxon poetry and Euphuistic prose. In a phrase like "innocent, cheap, easy, and effectual," each adjective adds a distinct idea to the predication.

9   Along with this heavy compounding, Swift occasionally uses the scheme of polysyndeton—e.g. "in the arms or on the back or at the heels" (par. 2); "dying and rotting by cold and famine and filth and vermin" (par. 19). Multiplying conjunctions like this has the effect of further stringing out the list. Swift sometimes adds to the compounded elements the scheme of alliteration, as in the just-quoted "famine and filth and vermin" or in the triplet "parsimony, prudence, and temperance" (par. 29). In these examples, we get the impression of

a man who is beginning to play with words. In the only other conspicuous use of alliteration, "in joints from the gibbet" (par. 18), our impulse to laugh at this sporting with words is suddenly restrained by our realization of the horror of the image. At other times, Swift will reinforce the compounding with the scheme of climax, as in the two or three examples in the first paragraph of the essay, or with the scheme of anticlimax, as in the example quoted above from paragraph 33.

10   Although all of this compounding is done within the framework of parallelism, parallelism is not a characteristic of the proposer's style or of Swift's style in general. But Swift demonstrates that he knows how and when to use parallel structure. In paragraph 29, the key paragraph of the essay, he lays out his long enumeration of "other expedients" on a frame of parallel structure. The list is long, the list is important, and Swift wants to make sure that his readers do not get lost in this maze of coordinate proposals.

11   Another thing that the long rambling sentences and the frequent compounding might suggest is a "spoken" style. If one compares spoken style with written style, one notes that spoken style tends to be paratactic—a stitching together of coordinate units. We have just observed this kind of rhapsodic structure in the word and phrase units of *A Modest Proposal*, but when we look at the kinds of grammatical sentences (see Appendix), we observe a marked predominance of the subordinate structures that typify a sophisticated written style. Over half of the sentences are complex, and almost a third of the sentences are compound-complex. Although there are five simple sentences in the essay, there is not a single compound sentence, which is the commonest structure in extemporaneous spoken discourse. So although the essay may give the impression of a certain colloquial ease, this impression is not being produced by the syntax of the sentences.

12   Further evidence of a calculated literary style is found in the proposer's inclination to periodic structure. As Walter J. Ong said in a recent article on prose style, "Oral composition or grammatical structure is typically nonperiodic, proceeding in the 'adding' style; literary composition tends more to the periodic." We see this periodic structure exemplified in a sentence like the first one of paragraph 4: "As to my own part, having turned my thoughts, for many years, upon this important subject, and maturely weighed the several schemes of other projectors, I have always found them grossly mistaken in their computations." No one *speaks* a sentence like that; sentences like that are produced by someone who has time to plot his sentences.

13   This tendency to delay the main predication of the sentence is most pronounced within another structural pattern that is so common in the essay as to be a mannerism. I refer to the proposer's habit of putting the main idea of the sentence into a noun clause following the verb of the main clause. These noun clauses follow either personal structures like "I am assured by our merchants that . . . ," "I have reckoned that . . . ," "he confessed that . . ." or impersonal structures like "it is not improbable that . . ." and "it is very well known that. . . ." There are at least nineteen instances like these, where the main idea of the

sentence is contained in the noun clause. And frequently the proposer further delays the main idea by making us read almost to the end of the noun clause before he gives us the main predication. A prime example of this is the final sentence of paragraph 18;

> Neither indeed can I deny, that if the same use were made of several plump young girls in this town, who, without one single groat to their fortunes, cannot stir abroad without a chair, and appear at the playhouse and assemblies in foreign fineries, which they will never pay for, the kingdom would not be the worse.

Reading a sentence like this, we wonder whether the man will ever get to the point, and in this case, when the point is finally reached, we find that it is deflatingly anti-climactic.

14   This tendency toward periodic structure is evidence not only of a deliberate written style but of a habit of the *persona* that suits Swift's rhetorical purpose. I suggested earlier that part of Swift's rhetorical strategy is to create a character who will, as it were, "sneak up" on the reader. The frequent use of periodic structure is one of the ways in which the proposer "sneaks up" on the reader.

15   And we see this same tactic in the early paragraphs of the essay. In the first two paragraphs we see the long, leisurely, meandering sentences in which the proposer, in a matter-of-fact tone, describes the present condition of the poor. There is further dawdling in paragraph 4, where in two rambling sentences he seeks to establish his credentials with his audience. Then in paragraph 6, the second longest paragraph of the essay, we are subjected to a litany of cold, hard figures of "computations." In the short paragraph 9, we hear the disturbing sputter of a lighted fuse as the proposer retails the testimony of his American acquaintance about what a delicacy a year-old child is. Then in paragraph 10, after the expenditure of almost a thousand words on preliminaries (almost a third of the essay), the proposer drops his bombshell. Nor does his pace become any more frenetic from this point on. He continues to "lead out" information, testimony, and arguments.

16   The noticeable periodic structure of many of the sentences, then, is part of Swift's strategy of sneaking up on the audience, of disarming the reader in order to render him more sensitive to the blow that will be delivered to the solar plexus. The proposer tells us in paragraph 27 that he is "studious of brevity." But he is not brief at all; he takes his own good time about dealing out what he has to say to his audience. This is not the curt Senecan amble; this is the rambling Ciceronian cadence. The Circeronian cadence does not fit Jonathan Swift, of course, but it does fit the character he has created and does contribute to the rhetorical effectiveness of the essay.

17   We could pursue this discussion of sentences and schemes, but let us move on to a consideration of the diction of the essay. Let us see what a study of the diction tells us about Swift's strategies and about the proposer's style.

18   To begin with, we might advert briefly to the words and idioms that mark the essay as a product of the eighteenth century. One of the things that has often been remarked of Swift's style is that it is strikingly modern. As one of my students said to me, "When I'm reading Swift, I have the feeling that I'm reading George Orwell all over again." One of the reasons certainly for this impression of modernity is the diction and idiom. Swift uses very few words and idioms that are outdated. But he does use just enough dated words and expressions to prevent our getting the impression that we are reading the morning newspaper. I counted about a dozen idioms which were peculiar to the eighteenth century or were still current in the eighteenth century but are no longer current—expressions like "of towardly parts" (par. 6), "no gentleman would *repine* to give ten shillings" (par. 14), "I cannot be altogether *in* his sentiments" (par. 17) (see Appendix for additional examples). If one were attempting to date this piece from internal evidence, probably the two words that would be the best index of the period in which this essay was written would be *shambles* (par. 16) and the *chair* (par. 18) in which the plump young girls ride about town. The *OED* would tell us that in the eighteenth century *shambles* meant "a place where meat is sold," "a slaughter house" and that *chair* designated a means of transportation. Expressions like these give the essay its Augustan flavor, but aside from these, the diction and idiom are remarkably modern.

19   The Appendix carries a note about the monosyllabism of the essay. Only about one-third of the nouns in the first ten paragraphs are monosyllabic, and I suspect that there is a much higher percentage of polysyllabic, Latinate diction in *A Modest Proposal* than we will find in most of Swift's other prose works, especially in that prose where he is speaking in his own voice. This polysyllabic diction is appropriate of course for the kind of pedantic character that Swift has created in *A Modest Proposal.* The proposer wants to pass himself off on his audience as a man who has indulged in a great deal of scientific, scholarly study of the problem, so as to enhance his authority—"having turned my thoughts, for many years, upon this important subject, and maturely weighed the several schemes of other projectors" (par. 4).

20   The mathematical and mercantile terminology is also contributing to the image of the dedicated investigator and the political arithmetician. Besides the many figures cited, there are repeated uses of words like "compute," "reckon," "calculate," "shillings," "pounds," "sterling," "accounts," "stock," "commodity," "*per annum.*" By putting jargon like this in the mouth of his proposer, Swift is making him talk the language of the other political economists who had turned their attention to the problem. We might say of the cold-bloodedness with which the proposer delivers himself of these terms that it represents his disinterested endeavor to propagate the worst that is known and thought about the problem in the Anglo-Irish world.

21   The most notable of the lexical means that Swift uses to achieve his purpose is the series of animal metaphors (see the Appendix). Charles Beaumont has pointed out that Swift is here employing the ancient rhetorical device of

diminution, the opposite effect of amplification. Swift first reduces his human beings to the status of animals and then to the status of food furnished to the table when these animals are slaughtered. So we pass from animal images like "dropped from its dam" and "reserved for breed" to such slaughtered-animal images as "the carcass," "the fore or hind quarters," and "the skin of which, artificially dressed." We feel the impact of these metaphors when we realize that .Swift is suggesting that the Anglo-Irish landlords were treating human beings no better than they treated their domestic animals. The proposer points up this inhuman treatment when he says, in paragraph 26, that if his proposal were adopted, "men would become as fond of their wives, during the time of pregnancy, as they are now of their mares in foal, their cows in calf, or sows when they are ready to farrow."

22   Another trope that Swift uses to achieve diminution is litotes—the opposite trope to hyperbole. Here are four prominent examples of litotes or understatement. In paragraph 2, the proposer refers to the burden of the prodigious number of beggar children as "a very great additional grievance." In paragraph 17, he speaks of the practice of substituting the bodies of young lads and maidens for venison as "a little bordering on cruelty." At the end of the periodic sentence in paragraph 18, he says that "the kingdom would not be the worse" if the bodies of plump young girls were sold as a delicacy for the table. The most notable example of litotes in the essay—and the one that serves as the chief tip-off to the irony of the essay—is found in the first sentence of the key paragraph 29: "I can think of no one objection that will possibly be raised against this proposal, unless it should be urged that the number of people will be thereby much lessened in this kingdom." The frequent use of litotes fits in well with the proposer's tendency to underplay everything.

23   The proposer not only underplays his proposal (note "a modest proposal") and his arguments to justify the proposal but also underplays his emotions. One has a hard time of it finding emotionally freighted words in the essay. Only in paragraphs 1 and 5 do I find conspicuous clusters of what I. A. Richards calls "emotive words":

> paragraph 1: Melancholy, all in rags, helpless infants, dear native country, crowded

> paragraph 5: abortions, horrid practice, murdering their bastard children, alas, tears and pity, poor innocent babes, savage and inhuman breast

The only other place in the essay where I sense the proposer losing a tight rein on his emotions is in his outburst in paragraph 18 against the plump young girls of the town, and in this instance, the anger simmering under these words is, I suspect, the emotional reaction of the clergyman Swift rather than the worldly proposer. And this is the one place in the essay where I feel that Swift momentarily drops the mask and speaks in his own voice.

24   Swift considerably enhances the emotional impact of his message by this underplaying. And the other trope that is responsible for the emotional power

of the essay is irony. As I remarked before, irony is an over-arching device for the entire essay: the proposer means what he says, but Swift does not. Irony, however, is a prevalent device within the essay too. I counted at least fifteen instances of words being used ironically. Rather than weary you with the entire catalogue, let me quote a few representative examples (the ironical words are italicized):

> will make two dishes at an *entertainment* for friends (par. 10)
>
> the fore and hind quarters will make a *reasonable* dish (par. 10)
>
> will make admirable gloves for *ladies* and summer boots for *fine gentlemen* (par. 15)
>
> some *scrupulous* people might be apt to censure (par. 17)

The horror of this irony hits us all the harder when we realize that the proposer, in his naivete, intends his words to be taken literally. These are the places where I can almost see Swift grinning through the lines of print.

25   Swift does something with words in this essay that I had not noticed him doing in any of his other prose works. He repeats key words so that they almost become motifs in the essay. The Appendix lists some of these repeated words and records the frequency of repetition. Note particularly the repetitions and variations of the words *child* and *parent*. Swift realizes that the proposal violates one of the most fundamental of human relations—the parent-child relation. When this violation of the normal child-parent relation is joined with a suggestion of cannibalism, a practice that almost universally offends the sensibilities of mankind, we get a proposal of the utmost monstrosity. And if Swift can get his audience to react violently enough to the revolting proposal, there is hope that they will resort to some of the "other expedients" for a solution to the problem of poverty. Basically that is his main rhetorical strategy in the essay.

26   I cannot wholly account for the rhetorical function of the repetition of the kingdom-country-nation diction. Swift may be seeking to emphasize that the poverty of the people is a problem of national scope, one in which the welfare of the entire nation is crucially involved. Hasn't this been the theme that President Johnson has been urging in his efforts to promote his Poverty Program? Another explanation may be that Swift is suggesting that just as, on the domestic level, the normal child-parent relationships have broken down, the kingdom-citizen relationships have broken down on the national level.

27   This kind of repetition of key words and phrases is a device that we have come to associate with Matthew Arnold's style. Anyone who has read Arnold's prose extensively knows how effective this tactic can be for purposes of exposition. Although repetition is not a mannerism of Swift's style in general, we can appreciate the emotional effect that Swift achieves in this argumentative piece with these drumbeat repetitions. These insistent repetitions keep bringing us back to the full implications of the modest proposal. . . .

28   This analysis has revealed, I hope, that there is considerable stylistic artifice in *A Modest Proposal*, but hasn't this essay become memorable mainly

because of the monstrousness of the proposal and the cleverness of the ironical form? As a matter of historical fact, Swift did *not* succeed in persuading his audience to do something about a lamentable situation. But he did succeed in producing a great piece of literature.

APPENDIX

SOME STATISTICS ON SWIFT'S "A MODEST PROPOSAL"

3474 words

33 paragraphs

61 sentences (For this study, a sentence is defined as a group of words beginning with a capital letter and ending with some mark of terminal punctuation.)

Average number of words per paragraph   105.2

Average number of sentences per paragraph   1.84

18 one-sentence paragraphs

7 two-sentence paragraphs

4 three-sentence paragraphs

3 four-sentence paragraphs

1 five-sentence paragraph (#29)

Shortest paragraph #8 (20 words)—a transitional paragraph (other transitional paragraph, #20, is 34 words long)

Longest paragraph #29 (289 words)—"other expedients" (a key paragraph)

Average number of words per sentence   56.9

Number of sentences 10 words or more *above* average   18

Percentage of sentences above average   29.5%

Number of sentences 10 words or more *below* average   28

Percentage of sentences below average   45.9%

Longest sentence   179 words (par. 32)

Other long sentences: 164 words (par. 6); 141 words (par. 29); 119 words (par. 18); 109 words (par. 4); 102 words (par. 13)

Shortest sentence   11 words (last sentence of par. 27)

(other short sentence: first sentence of transitional paragraph #20)

34 Complex sentences

18 Compound-complex sentences

5 Simple sentences (paragraphs 4, 19, 20, 27)

4 Elliptical or incomplete sentences (paragraph 10, 29 (two), 31)

REPEATED WORDS

child (children)	25		kingdom	13	
infants	6	33	country	9	27
babes	2		nation	5	
			the year	6	
mother	6		one year old	1	
parents	7	20	annually	3	16
breed (breeders)	7		solar year	2	
			per annum	4	
number	7		food	7	
compute	5	15	flesh	4	19
reckon	2		carcass	5	
calculate	1		plump	3	
propose	5	9	gentlemen	5	
proposal	4		persons of quality	2	12
			beggars	5	

DICTION OR IDIOM PECULIARLY EIGHTEENTH-CENTURY
(The number in parentheses refers to the paragraph in which the expression occurs.)

(6) of *towardly* parts

(10) increas*eth* to twenty-eight pounds

(13) fish being a *prolific* diet

(14) no gentlemen would *repine* to give ten shillings

(16) *shambles* may be appointed

(16) dressing them hot from the knife

(17) the *want* of venison . . . for *want* of work and service

(17) I cannot be altogether *in* his sentiments

(18) who came from *thence, above* twenty years ago

(18) without a *chair*

(19) and I have been desired to employ my thoughts what course may be taken

(19) But I am not *in the least pain upon* that matter

(19) and thus the country and themselves are *in a fair way* of being delivered from the evils to come

(25) bring great *custom* to taverns where the *vintners* will certainly be so prudent

(26) emulation among the married women, *which* of them could bring

(32)   to reject any offer, proposed by wise men, *who* [which?] shall be found equally innocent, cheap, easy, and effectual

ANIMAL IMAGERY

(3)   at the *heels* of their mother

(4)   a child just *dropped* from its *dam*

(10)   reserved for breed

(10)   more than we allow to sheep, black-cattle, or swine

(10)   therefore one *male* will be sufficient *to serve* four *females*

(10)   to let them *suck* plentifully . . . to render them plump and fat for a good table

(10)   the fore or hind quarter

(14)   for the *carcass* of a good fat child

(15)   flay the *carcass* . . . the skin of which, artificially *dressed*

(16)   as we do roasting pigs

(26)   men would become as fond of their wives, during the time of their pregnancy, as they are now of their mares in foal, their cows in calf, or sows when they are ready to farrow

(27)   propagation of swine's flesh

(27)   the great destruction of pigs

(27)   fat *yearling* child

MONOSYLLABISM

29   In the first ten paragraphs of the essay, there are 1127 words; of these, 685 (60%) are monosyllabic. But since a good many of these monosyllabic words are pronouns, prepositions, conjunctions, or auxiliary verbs, we get an unreliable estimate of Swift's diction. If we look at the nouns only, we get a different picture. In these same ten paragraphs, there are 204 nouns. Of these, 73 are monosyllabic (36%), 131 are polysyllabic. If we regard only the substantive words in these paragraphs, we get, for Swift, an unusually high number of polysyllabic words.

Practice: Analyzing Style

Using elements from Corbett's model, analyze one of your own essays. In addition to sentences, you may want to analyze your use of modifiers. (Computer programs are available to analyze many elements of style.)

CHAPTER SUMMARY

In this chapter, you have read pieces that were entertaining and others that were shocking. You have seen that satire can be dark and shocking or light and humorous, but it usually prompts reflection. Persuasive satire, at its best, knocks the reader out of complacency, even though the awakening might come some time after the piece is read. The best satire is so memorable that it stays in the back of the mind and surfaces, perhaps at strange times, to prompt further reflection.

You have also looked closely at the elements of satire, the devices used to create the power of satire. The skills you apply to your analysis of satire will serve you in analyzing and developing your own writing style.

Chapter 24

WRITING CHALLENGE

Write an analysis of one of the pieces of satire in Chapter 23 or another piece that your instructor approves. In your paper, deal with aspects of the work such as meaning, purpose, and how the elements come together to make an effective piece. Use Corbett's analysis of "A Modest Proposal" and the "Guide to Analyzing Satire" to help you in your analysis. You will probably want to choose a shorter piece and focus on fewer elements than Corbett did in "Analysis of 'A Modest Proposal.'" (See student evaluations on pages 300, 303, and 354 for help with documenting a single-source paper.)

Journal Topic Suggestions

- Your reaction to one of the pieces in Chapter 23
- The kind of humor that makes you laugh
- The time you laughed until you cried
- How a good laugh makes you feel afterward
- Something that comes to your mind often and why you think about it
- The tears of a clown

GUIDE TO ANALYZING SATIRE

Satirists often use a backdoor approach to persuading the reader. Swift's ghoulish proposal to market and consume babies is meant, first, to shock the reader into thinking about Irish poverty and, next, to persuade the reader to propose his or her own solutions to the problem and, finally, to take action to implement a solution. As a straightforward editorial, Swift might have said, "Listen, folks. The terrible poverty in Ireland cannot go on. Parents who work hard and still cannot buy enough food to keep their children from starving need help. Economists have proposed solutions, but these solutions have not been workable. Furthermore, no one has taken the necessary steps to implement even bad solutions. Those who can do something about the poverty seem to be ignoring the problem. We need action—now!"

Such a plea, earnest as it might have been, could have been easily forgotten. Or Swift could have used the invective, attacking his readers directly with something such as, "You fat cats sit back on your haunches and live off the flesh of the poor just as though you were actually eating them. Your high status and stuffy speech only masks the reality—you are despicable, slimy creatures, driven by greed and unfit to inhabit the planet." Such an attack would certainly have caused the reader to become defensive and to regard the accusations as simple slander, ignoring the truths in the message and responding with, "The guy is a nut case. Who's he referring to, anyway? *I'm* not slimy. It's not *my* fault that everyone doesn't have caviar three times a day."

But Swift used the power of satire to create a proposal that could not be forgotten. In fact, even distanced by time and circumstance from the problem itself, it is unlikely that a reader will ever forget the gist of Swift's piece.

Planning and Prewriting

Much of the work involved in writing a stylistic analysis is slow and tedious. Yet the discoveries you make as you go will make your work rewarding. Begin by reading the essay quickly and writing down your first reaction. You will probably want to read the essay through several times before you begin your analysis of the stylistic elements of the essay.

PURPOSE AND AUDIENCE

The following questions can be used in your analysis of the writer's purpose and intended audience.

1. What is the main point or theme of the essay?
2. How did the essay effect you?
3. Did it make you think about the topic in a new way?
4. Did you learn something you did not know before while reading the essay?
5. Was there a specific occasion or event that prompted the essay? If so, do you want to know more about the event? Is it relevant to your analysis?
6. What is the author's tone, or attitude, toward the subject (serious, lighthearted, angry, amused, sad, happy, ironic)?
7. Do you detect an underlying emotion while reading the essay? If so, what is that emotion, and how does the author expose it?
8. What is the author's purpose in writing the essay? What reaction do you think the author would like you to have to the piece? Is the piece effective; did you, in fact, have that expected reaction?
9. Who is the author's audience? Is the piece directed at a particular age group, people in a particular profession, or to a particular gender? What are the clues that suggest the particular audience?
10. Does the author attempt to establish himself or herself as an authority? If so, how?

ORGANIZATION

1. Is organization important to the development of the argument in the essay?
2. Can you isolate paragraphs that contain mostly description? narration? causal relationships? process analysis? comparison and contrast? narration?
3. What is the organization of the essay? Is it organized by chronology (time order of events)? by importance of elements (from the least to the most important or vice versa)? spatially (from closest to most distant)?

DEVICES

1. Does the author use a persona, or mask? If so, what is the effect of the persona? Is the mask sustained throughout the essay?
2. Is there humor in the essay? If so, is it created mainly with irony or other figurative devices such as plays on words? with anecdotes? What is the effect?
3. Does the author use sensory images to involve the reader?
4. Does the author use hyperbole (exaggeration) or litotes (understatement)? What is the effect?
5. Does the author directly attack anyone or anything in the piece? What indirect attacks does the author make?
6. Does the author use repetition of words or ideas? What is the effect?

DICTION

As you read the essay slowly, what kind of words strike you? You might highlight with different colored markers sensory language, formal or informal language, words that are related to a common topic, and so on. Edward P. J. Corbett claims that many discoveries can be made by actually copying in long hand a passage from the essay. An in-depth analysis of diction involves actually counting mono- and polysyllabic words and words that fall into specific categories (modifiers, epithets, emotive words, and so on) and identifying the function of the words, or the effect created through diction. (See "Analysis of *A Modest Proposal,*" page 436.) A less thorough analysis might involve randomly chosen passages, rather than an entire work. These questions can help you analyze an author's diction.

1. What is the author's level of language? Do you notice many words that you seldom hear in everyday conversation, or are most of the words common? Are most of the words short, containing only one or two syllables, or do many of the words contain several syllables? Are there slang words in the essay? Are there words that are not in common use today?

2. Is there an abundance of words that have something in common—perhaps words that have emotional connotations, words that are related to a particular topic (crime, family, diet, and so on) or field (science, law, electronics, and so on)?

3. What do you notice about the verbs in the piece? Are most of them active, or are there many state-of-being verbs (passive)? Are they mostly general or specific?

4. Do most of the nouns have a concrete meaning, or are there many words dealing with abstract concepts? Are there many modifiers?

5. Do any of the words give you clues about the author's interests, time period, bias, or education?

6. Does the author create a world we can see, hear, touch, smell, taste? Does he use straight description or figurative language to create the world? Is there a relationship between the imagery or figurative language and the theme?

SENTENCES

A thorough analysis of sentence structure involves counting words in sentences, types of sentences, number of sentences per paragraph. You will probably want to closely analyze at least a 100-word passage from the essay. Look for specifics as suggested by the following guidelines:

1. Is your impression that the author has a straightforward, readable style or is the writing rather dense and somewhat difficult to read? Does the work seem to have characteristics of speech, or does it seem to be a "written" style, characterized by many delayed predications because of introductory clauses?

2. Are most of the sentences simple and compound, or are there many complex and compound-complex sentences?

3. Is there a variety of sentence lengths in the essay, including very short sentences? What is the effect?

4. Does the author use polysyndenton (compounding with conjunctions—"We had bacon and eggs and toast and orange juice and coffee for breakfast")? If so, what is the effect?

5. Do you detect a certain rhythm in the writing? If so, how is it created? What is the effect?

Organizing and Drafting

Writing the first draft may prove to be the easiest part of the process. If you have done a thorough analysis, your brain is saturated with ideas about the piece; you have knowledge that is ready to spill onto the page. You have made your writing task easy.

To make the writing task even easier, make an informal outline of the material you have gathered. Your outline may have headings for each of the aspects under "Planning and Prewriting." Write your discoveries under each heading. As you plan your essay, assume that your audience has read the essay. This assumption will help you avoid the pitfall of summarizing the essay for your reader.

As you begin writing your analysis, remember to provide adequate support for any claims you make about the author's style. You will need to paraphrase, summarize, and use direct quotations from the essay. (See The Power of Style on page 230.)

Evaluating and Revising

PARTNER EVALUATION

Read your partner's analysis through to get a general impression. Jot down your initial response to the essay. Was it interesting? Did you learn something from reading it? Was it logically organized? Then read the essay again, this time slowly, evaluating each item in the following list as you read.

1. Did the writer include the author and title of the essay in the introduction? Is the introduction clearly written? Does it make you want to read more? How can the introduction be improved?
2. Is each claim about the essay supported with details and quotations from the essay? If not, what claims need more support?
3. Does each paragraph contain a clear focus? Do any of the paragraphs contain information or ideas that are unrelated to the rest of the paragraph? If so, which paragraphs?
4. Are transitions provided to guide the reader through the analysis? If not, where are transitions needed?
5. Do you have questions about any of the ideas or information? Do any of the ideas need clarifying? If so, note where the author might add information.
6. What information or ideas are especially interesting? Note the positive aspects of the paper.
7. Are any of the sentences unclear or awkward? Put brackets around sentences that might be improved. Did the writer use a variety of sentence structures?
8. Does the ending adequately conclude the essay, or does the essay just stop? How might the ending be improved?
9. What other ideas for improving the analysis can you suggest?

REVISING

Before revising, reread your analysis, jotting down additional ideas and marking sentences that interrupt the logical order. Read your partner's evaluation, carefully considering each suggested change. Decide what revisions you want to make and mark your draft to include the changes.

Editing and Proofreading

The following checklist will guide you in editing.

1. Can any groups of sentences be combined? Are there awkward or overloaded sentences that can be separated into clear, concise sentences?
2. Should any words or phrases be replaced with words or phrases that more accurately or vividly describe? (Look at verbs and common nouns.)
3. Are all pronoun references clear, and do they agree in number with their antecedents?
4. Do all verbs agree with their subjects in number?
5. Should any passive constructions be changed to active? (Look for forms of *be*.)
6. Are direct quotations correctly introduced?

   Before submitting your final draft, proofread each sentence, moving your lips or saying the words aloud. Remember to check for punctuation and spelling errors.

Proposing Solutions

Americans have always assumed, subconsciously, that all problems can be solved; that every story has a happy ending; that the application of enough energy and good will can make everything come out right. In view of our history, this assumption is natural enough. As a people, we have never encountered any obstacle that we could not overcome.

Adlai E. Stevenson, *Call to Greatness*

Chapter 25

PROBLEM SOLVING

Proposals for solutions to problems may not be the most common type of writing, yet proposals are heard every day in conversation. How often have you heard someone say, "Well, she should just dump him" or "Congress should (do this or that)" or "The solution is so simple. I can't believe those bozos can't see it"?

Solutions to the nation's problems are offered daily around family dinner tables and over coffee cups. A solution may seem simple when only the near-sighted perspective of the speaker is considered, overlooking the views of 250 million citizens, the problems involved in making the solution work, and the possible consequences. But addressing audience, implementation, and consequences are all part of the process involved in getting to "Yes!" in persuading an audience to accept and, furthermore, to act on, a proposed solution.

In this chapter, we first look at problem-solving as a simple, individual process—something you do many times every day. Covering your nakedness in the morning, for instance, may involve complications, but ultimately you dress for the day, making your own choice about what to wear. You have the luxury (or responsibility) of solving some problems on your own; however, many of the problems you attempt to solve involve other people.

This chapter provides an opportunity to problem-solve with a group and hear the different perspectives and ideas that your classmates bring to the problem-solving process. After working with a group to solve a problem, you will have the opportunity to read two proposals for reducing crime, a problem many Americans view as the nation's most serious. You may not agree with either of the solutions, but the ideas and perspectives of others offer at least a starting point for discussion.

You will then be asked to write your own proposal. Recalling the dynamics of the group and the diverse points of view will help you address your audience and possible opposition as you write. The Guide to Writing will help you work through the process of writing a proposal.

THE PROCESS OF PROBLEM SOLVING

Our lives are full of problems, complications, options, and solutions or ways to reach goals. In fact, the most direct route to starting the problem-solving process is to turn the problem into a goal—covering your nakedness/dressing appropriately for the day, for instance. The simple task of dressing in the mornings involves the same steps of logical reasoning that can be used to solve even the most complicated problems. Often the first decision we make each day is deciding what to wear, and making a decision is part of the problem-solving process, a process that is often, like the writing process, recursive.

> *State the problem/goal*
>   Naked/Dressing appropriately for the day's activities
>
> *Review relevant information*
>   Outside temperature/season of the year
>   Day's activities (school, work, leisure activities, church, travel, and so on)
>   Who you might see and what kind of impression you want to make
>
> *Consider alternatives*
>   What is clean and pressed?
>   What is comfortable?
>
> *Consider future consequences*
>   What might you want to save to wear for a future activity?
>   (Return to "Review relevant information.")

Make a decision about what to wear (solve the problem/make a plan), based on what you know (planned activities) and the alternatives (different outfits) available.

To carry the model further, you would next implement the plan/solution by dressing in the clothes you have chosen. This part involves a step-by-step process in itself, your personal routine for dressing yourself.

Evaluate the solution

At some point you might decide the choice was a good one—perhaps you meet someone that makes you glad you wore your best shirt. Or you might decide that the choice was not good. Perhaps you needed warmer clothes and decide to put the outfit you chose away until next spring.

People use a process to solve simple problems daily, often without even realizing that the same process can be used to solve even the most complicated personal problems, family problems, business problems, community problems, and national problems. But when the process of solving problems breaks down, we are left with faulty solutions or none at all.

HOW PROBLEM SOLVING BREAKS DOWN

When you solve a problem and make a decision as an individual, you are in control. Even so, a breakdown at any point in the process may cause you to reach a faulty conclusion. Suppose, for instance, that you choose to ignore relevant information and make a decision based solely on an emotional preference that we'll call the Human Factor; the situation may still turn out okay. Either way, you have chosen, and you either enjoy or suffer through the results of your decision.

But when even one other person is added to the decision-making process, the process becomes more complicated. Each person has emotional preferences, value judgments, and life experiences that become relevant information; the Human Factor has just been doubled, not to mention the myriad of logical reasons that may have some merit. And when groups of people or communities or nations work at solving problems—the possibilities are endless. So, we defer much decision-making to governmental bodies of elected representatives and spend a lot of time discussing what those representatives do. Often, the solutions are faulty because some part of the process has broken down.

Reasons for Problem-Solving Breakdowns

The problem-solving process can break down for any number of reasons. Some of the most common are

- failing to define the problem or correctly identify its causes,
- failing to state the problem as a realistic goal,
- ignoring relevant information such as the Human Factor,
- failing to see the problem as a part of a complex system,
- failing to consider alternatives,
- failing to predict accurately possible consequences,
- choosing a solution that is impossible or too costly to implement, and
- failing to take responsibility for implementing a plan.

Examples of these breakdowns can be seen as headlines in newspapers and the lead stories on evening newscasts. The debate over abortion, for example, has broken down into two camps. Word wars have gotten out of control, and strong-arm methods have become common. It is unlikely that the two extremes will kiss and make-up. You can say that neither side will change the other's minds. Faith and morals are involved. Passion runs deep on both sides, and some groups are more likely to attack each other than sit down for a rational discussion. So, what can be done? Do we want our presidents and representatives elected solely on their stands on abortion, stands that might be based on public opinion polls in the first place?

While some pro-lifers use the term *pro-abortionists* to define those who advocate the right to choose abortion, actually no one is saying "Yea, abortion!" What both sides have in common may be a desire to eliminate the need for abortion by eliminating unwanted pregnancies. So, the breakdown comes from not agreeing on and working toward a common goal, the beginning of a solution for both sides.

Problem solving can go awry when future consequences are not considered or are not accurately predicted. The decision to stop institutionalizing the mentally ill for long-term care seemed like a good idea a generation ago: The mentally ill should be mainstreamed, and, of course, the states would save money. Some of those who were formerly institutionalized did become self-sufficient. Others, however, now live in jails or on the street and would benefit from long-term care in an institution.

At other times the breakdown comes from failure to search out relevant factors. Consider, for instance, the fact that the United States has the highest infant mortality rate of any industrialized nation and the rate is going up. Defining the problem is easy; the statistical analysis tells us that we have a problem, and we know that this is not good and that the goal is to reduce the infant mortality rate. As soon as the report was released, a cause was identified (lack of and quality of health care) and a solution was offered (make health care more widely available and increase the quality). Certainly, health care is important, but is lack of and quality of health care really the cause? In answering that question, we must consider all relevant factors.

If the infant mortality rate has gone up over the past thirty years, is there a corresponding decline in the availability and quality of health care?

If the answer is "no," we must look elsewhere for the causes of an increasing rate of infant mortality. We know that more small and unhealthy babies are kept alive than were thirty years ago because of increased technology. Although prenatal care is often lacking, public hospitals are still required by law to accept patients whether or not they can pay for services.

So, what has happened over the past thirty years that might account for the higher infant mortality rate?

We might consider the following factors:

- More U.S. babies are born to teenage mothers, and teen mothers have babies with lower than average birth weights and more than average complications.
- More babies today are born to drug-addicted mothers than were 30 years ago, and drug-addicted mothers have babies with lower than average birth weights and more than average complications.
- Today, almost one-third of births are illegitimate, so there is no traditional family structure for the mother during pregnancy. The mother's pregnancy is likely to be filled with turmoil and uncertainty, and research indicates that an unborn child can be affected by the mother's emotional state.

With statistics to compare to those of other industrialized countries, we can create an argument. Still, there are other factors (environmental pollution, diet and nutrition, and so on) to explore before we can say with reasonable certainty that we have found *the* cause and can, therefore, be sure that we know the solution. And a solution that seems perfect for one area of the country might not work for another area.

However, the fact that we don't know all the possible relevant factors and cannot be absolutely sure of the solution does not mean we must sit back and wait until we have the answers to all the questions. We know that several different systems (medical, family, social, economic) are involved, so we can examine each system to look for starting points. And we can try, through pilot projects, to study the problem and find answers. For instance, a program to reduce teen pregnancy in a specific area of the country might result in a reduction in infant deaths. Although that would not necessarily be the only relevant factor, at least we would have some data to feed into the problem-solving process.

HURRICANE MADNESS

After hurricane Andrew destroyed tens of thousands of homes in southern Florida, the army was sent in to build tent cities to house temporarily the more than 200,000 who were left homeless by the storm.

Let us outline a problem-solving process.

Problem/goal
A major hurricane leaves thousands of people homeless/Provide shelter for the homeless hurricane victims

Relevant information
Rebuilding or repairing their homes will take time.
The people need shelter now.

Considering alternatives
What's the fastest way to provide shelters?
    Information: Build temporary shelters
What resources already exist for temporary shelters?
    Information: The military has tents available
Who is already trained to erect tents quickly?
    Information: The military
How can they provide the most shelters in the shortest period of time?
    Information: Build them in close proximity

Proposed solution
Send in the army to erect tent cities

However, once the tents were erected more than one week after the storm, the people didn't want to move in. Soldiers reportedly ordered people to move into them, but the people refused. The bureaucratic decision-making process had erred; the bureaucrats had failed to consider some important factors.

Factor: During the week after the storm, people were not simply standing out in the weather waiting for roofs over their heads. Many had already turned to friends and relatives for comfort and shelter.

Factor: After the storm, those who had salvageable homes and belongings quickly went to work to protect what they had. They were afraid that if they left their belongings to move into a tent city, they would lose what they had left to looters.

What the people needed most were supplies for and help in rebuilding. Perhaps if the Army had disbursed the tents in neighborhoods immediately after the storm, the people could have used them for shelter while staying close to the remains of their homes. At any rate, the problem-solving process had produced a faulty solution because relevant factors had been ignored.

But even the best laid plans go awry when they are not properly implemented. When making decisions, the problems inherent in implementing the solution must be considered. How much money will it cost? How much time will it take? How much work will be involved? How will it be managed? What design or method will be used? What materials will be needed? All of these questions must be considered in proposing a solution. The ideal solution is worthless if it cannot be implemented.

And history is full of examples of failure to look ahead to consider the consequences of a plan of action. Supporting Sadaam Hussein was once seen as a solution to the problem with Iran: If we help Iraq win its war against Iran, Iran will no longer be a Middle East threat. Well, you know the rest of the story.

Practice: Problem Solving in Groups

There are no easy answers to complicated problems, but as citizens you will be charged with policy decisions—either directly as legislators and policy makers or indirectly as voters who study each candidate's platform on major issues. In the business world, you will solve problems daily. Unless you are a sole proprietor of a business and don't really care what your employees think, you will work with many different people who have a variety of perspectives about how things should be done.

In small groups derive a solution for one of the problems below (public education, welfare, allocating medical resources, or the federal budget) that might be acceptable to both liberal and conservative thinkers. Decide whether the plan should be implemented as a pilot project or as national policy. Each group should elect a recorder to write down points and a leader to keep the discussion moving and on track. (Refer to the information on group dynamics and etiquette on page 87 if necessary.) Report your solutions to the class in group written reports or oral presentations.

PROBLEM: PUBLIC EDUCATION

Most people agree there is a problem with our public school system, and certainly most agree there is a need for quality education, and that the future of our society depends on it. While the country is in desperate need of a solution to the problem of a poor public education system (by standards of other developed nations), our government leaders seem to be locked into a debate about money. Public argument has grown stale and often breaks down into two sides—usually classifiable as liberal and conservative.

Liberal	Conservative
We need more money for education.	Throwing money at the problem won't solve it.
Students in urban schools don't compare well with students in suburban areas, and urban schools are generally poorer.	Many of the great people in past generations were educated in one-room schools with a teacher who was paid starvation wages.
We owe it to our kids to give them the best that money can buy.	You can't *give* anyone an education. If students want it, they will *take* it. Mark Twain attended school only until age twelve, but he spent his life educating himself. Students have to take responsibility for their own learning.
The best teachers don't want to teach in urban schools.	Maybe they want to reach retirement without getting stabbed by a pre-penitentiary student.
Urban schools don't have money for computers and other things that suburban schools have.	You don't need a computer to learn to read and write. That's part of the problem—spending too much time in front of a screen. Students need to read. Students *must* read to become educated and able to compete in society.
We need more programs to help the poor so they will be able to learn when they are in school.	How can you learn when you are afraid for your life, when you are ducking the bullets of your classmates? Build more prisons, not programs.
School children face crime in school because of joblessness. And you can hardly expect them to do well in school when they don't know whether they will get a job when they graduate. We need more money for job programs.	What do you want to do—guarantee them $100,000 salaries? That's what it would take to compete with the illegal drug industry. Kids have to start at the bottom like their parents did.
We need more money for programs to prepare graduates to do college work. How can they go to college if they aren't prepared in the public school system? By the way, we need more money for college grants, too.	So, a student can goof off for twelve years of public school at taxpayers' expense and then have four more free years to goof off? A student who wants an education should be willing to work for it. That's the only way it means anything.

Liberal (continued)

At any cost, we should ensure that each child gets a quality education. Education is what separates the lower class from the middle and upper classes, regardless of gender, race, or creed.
It's society's fault.
It's the government's responsibility.

Conservative (continued)

We can agree on the last part. But throwing more money at education will not ensure that each child gets a quality education. You're dreaming if you think it will. It's been tried, and it didn't work.

It's the student's fault.
It's the parent's responsibility.

Problem: The public education system is not working to provide quality education for all.
Goal: Find a solution that is workable and acceptable to both sides.

PROBLEM: THE "WELFARE" SYSTEM

Many people are concerned that the welfare system, or the Aid to Families with Dependent Children (AFDC) program, is not working as it was intended. The program was first designed to be a temporary solution for people who, for a variety of reasons, could not support their families for a short period of time. Today, it has become a lifestyle for many—a lifestyle that imprisons in poverty. There is a shared view that the welfare program is bad. Almost no one argues that welfare is good. People on welfare need to rise above poverty in order to live better lives. In a coffee shop, you might hear an easy solution: Welfare should be eliminated, and those currently receiving welfare should go to work.

Let's explore that solution by looking at possible advantages and possible consequences.

Advantages

Save tax dollars that go to AFDC and Medicaid
Break the "Welfare Cycle"

Possible Consequences/Disadvantages

With unemployment rates of 11% or higher for some areas, even qualified applicants have a tough time finding work, and many welfare parents lack education and job skills. Hundreds of thousands of children would be at risk of malnutrition and even starvation.
Since there is some relationship between crime and poverty, some increase in crime could be expected. That increase would cost taxpayers.
Since many parents would be unable to feed their children, some would be forced to give up custody to state institutions, resulting in increased spending for institutional care.
Without Medicaid benefits, county hospitals would pick up the tab for more uninsured patients; hospitals would pass on costs to paying patients.

So, this "easy" solution might actually result in increased cost to taxpayers, not to mention the effects on children—effects that would not be tolerated by even the most calloused. But we certainly do need a solution that addresses this very complex problem. Find a solution that might be acceptable to two factions that have differing opinions on the issue.

The questions and information below might be used to prompt group discussion.

1. What is the purpose of the welfare program?
2. Has it served its purpose well?
3. How can long-term welfare be reduced while preserving help for those in temporary need?
4. How do you ensure that the children will not suffer?
5. How do you ensure that food stamps and money intended to feed and cloth children will not be used by addict mothers or fathers to purchase drugs?
6. What kind of training programs would motivate welfare mothers and fathers to better themselves?
7. How can you ensure that welfare recipients who finish training programs will actually receive jobs that will support a family?
8. Is it right to discourage welfare recipients from having more children?
9. How do you balance a welfare recipient's right to bear children against the taxpayers' right not to have to support them?
10. What conclusions can be drawn from the information below?
    - One half of all welfare recipients were teen moms.
    - Thirty percent of all babies born today are born to single moms.
    - Most single-parent households live below the poverty level.
    - Although the stereotypical welfare mother is often depicted as African-American, there are more white mothers on AFDC than black mothers (but not a bigger percentage of the population group).
11. From the chart below and the chart on page 464, what conclusions can you draw?

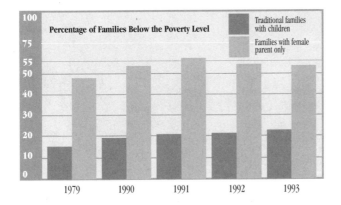

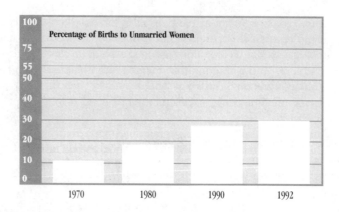

PROBLEM: ALLOCATING MEDICAL RESOURCES

The APACHE computer system uses a data bank of more than 17,000 cases to compute a critically ill person's chance of survival. This technology can be used to determine who will get scarce medical resources and who will not. At a cost of more than $2,000 a day for a critically ill person, pulling the plug on hopeless cases and giving treatment to someone who has a better chance of survival will probably be the harsh reality of the future. As medical technology advances to the point that people can be kept alive indefinitely at a cost that mortgages the resources of future generations, decisions must be made about how that technology will be used and how resources will be allocated.

Work out a compromise proposal that specifies how medical resources should be allocated and who should make the decisions after you have discussed different perspectives on the following case.

Case: A seventy-five-year-old, critically ill patient needs medical treatment.

Estimated cost: $500,000

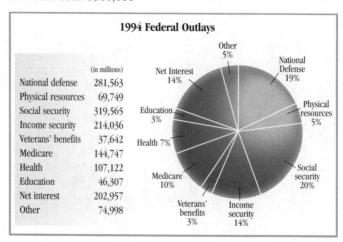

APACHE prognosis:
  0% chance of survival without the treatment
  25% chance of survival with the treatment

What position might the following people be likely to take and why:
  The patient's family
  The patient's doctor
  Medicare authorities
  Parents of a child who needs medical treatment the family cannot afford
  A party-line Democrat who does not know the family
  A party-line Republican who does not know the family

PROBLEM: THE FEDERAL BUDGET

Most citizens are aware that they cannot spend more than their income, that good financial management requires a balanced budget. However, the federal government continues to operate in the red. Although there is general agreement in Congress that a problem exists, there is little agreement on how to solve the problem. Below is a federal budget. Decide how to cut the budget by 10% to save money that can be applied to the national debt. Consider the consequences of each cut you recommend and calculate costs for new programs.

The questions below can be used to prompt discussion.

1. What new programs are needed to deal with the rising crime rate? Prevention programs? Increased law enforcement spending? New prisons?
2. What will the consequences be of declining defense spending (base closings, personnel reductions, and so on)?
3. What conclusions can you draw from the chart below? How will the shift affect the tax base and entitlement spending?

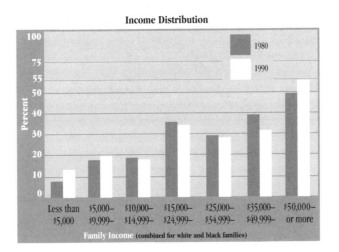

4. What conclusions can you draw from the chart above? How will changing demographics affect the tax base and entitlement spending?

Practice: Search and Evaluate

Dr. Willard Galen, medical ethicist, claims that medical technology can bankrupt our country in the future. He argues that what is available to use in treatment is so costly that in a few years, when the baby-boomer generation has retired and is dependent on Medicare, the working young people will be unable to pay the health care cost of 69 million retired Americans.

One solution to the problem of rising health care costs was offered by the state of Oregon. The Oregon Plan proposed to provide everyone with certain kinds of medical services. Other expenses, such as spending $1,000,000 in an effort to keep a one-pound baby alive, would not be paid.

Find a newspaper or magazine article outlining the Oregon Plan or another proposed health care plan. Write out possible objections, from whom the objections might come, and how those objections might be addressed.

Practice: Business and Community

For this activity, you are the president of a company that manufactures baseballs. The company is located in a small town, and many of the residents in the town

Problem		Goal	
The company is at risk of bankruptcy		To save the company	
Solutions	Cost		Possible Consequences/ Disadvantages
Plan			
Budget			

depend on the company in some way for their livelihoods, either directly or indirectly. Global competition has driven down profit margins to the point that you worry about possible bankruptcy in the future. Your major expense is the cost of labor. Prior to the passage of the North American Free Trade Agreement, you had considered moving your company to Mexico but decided not to. Since the NAFTA agreement, you are reconsidering your options.

Write a brief proposal to the citizens of the town outlining your decision about how to best save your company. Begin by outlining the problems, potential solutions, and possible future consequences. You may want to use a graphic organizer similar to the one shown on page 466.

OPPOSING VIEWS

Less Bang-Bang for the Buck:
The Market Approach to Crime Control
Reuben M. Greenberg

Greenberg, a police chief since 1982, proposes by example a solution that was implemented in Charleston, South Carolina. Greenberg outlines the program fully in his book Let's Take Back Our Streets.

1   The past two decades have seen a dramatic increase in crime in most American cities. Drug trafficking, and the violence that accompanies it, have paralyzed many urban areas, making them practically unlivable. The situation seems to worsen daily. In Charleston, South Carolina, we are reversing the national trend. During 1989, we had the lowest number of burglaries in the city since 1958. We also had the fewest armed robberies in a quarter century, the lowest number of auto thefts in 27 years, and the lowest number of larcenies in 22 years. Not only did the crime rate fall by 40 percent from 1982 to 1989; the actual number of armed robberies and burglaries went down, even as the population rate in Charleston was rising.

2   In Charleston, 8 percent of our population lives in public housing. Yet public housing residents and their visitors are responsible for only 1.8 percent of all armed robbery, rape, homicide, assault, larceny, arson, and auto theft crimes, and 2.6 percent of the minor offenses. In the past seven years, we have had only one person killed in the projects, and in 1990 we made only six drug arrests in public housing. Public housing is now one of the safest places in Charleston to live in.

3   We were able to decrease crime and make our neighborhoods safe with little expense and relatively few arrests by just paying attention to one simple principle: a market-based approach to law enforcement.

STANDARD LAW ENFORCEMENT DOESN'T WORK

4   The first target in our war on crime was street-level drug dealing—for two reasons. First, open-air dealing was causing citizens, and even the police, to abandon entire sections of the city to the criminal element. These areas, which had been prosperous for decades, began to decline and businesses began to falter through no fault of their own. We wanted to reclaim these areas from the criminals. We wanted to eliminate or diminish the drive-by shootings, the fights and the knifings, the arguments, and the aggravated assaults that took place on the street—the mushroom effect whereby an innocent bystander is injured or killed in a turf dispute between dealers. Second, we felt that at the street level a municipality could have the most impact with the least amount of assistance from state or federal agencies.

5   At first we followed standard law enforcement procedure and concentrated on simply arresting dealers. We quickly discovered that this wasn't going to work. Within four hours—sometimes even less time than that—these dealers would be released on bond or bail and just go back out on the street with their alternate stash, selling drugs as openly as ever. It was obvious to us and to the law-abiding people of the neighborhood that we, the police, were impotent, completely unable to handle the situation. We would go out, make buys from the dealers again—which was very easy—arrest them, and they would be back on the street again within four hours. Many of these dealers had 10 or 12 different cases pending at the same time. In one case a dealer had been arrested on 20 separate occasions for possession or sale of narcotics, but not even his first case had made it through the criminal justice system.

6   It didn't take us long to realize that merely arresting dealers would not stop the street-level drug dealing. Even if we were lucky enough to have a dealer go to jail, bond out after about four hours, step off the curb at the county jail and get run over by a Mack truck, we would still be in no better position than we had been before. The location where he had been selling the drugs was just too profitable. Once he was out of the way, some other person would take his place. Even if a dealer were given the death penalty, we would be no better off than before, because the location itself was the key, and some other drug dealer would move in to take up the slack. It soon became clear to us that the solution was not to go after the dealer but to go after his market and to make it unprofitable.

FLASHING OUR WEAPONS

7   First, we identified 31 locations where drugs were sold in Charleston, about 17 of which were major open-air markets. This time, instead of using four or five officers in an undercover operation with a sophisticated intelligence van, we tried something simple, very economical, and as it turned out, very effective. We assigned one uniformed officer to stand with the drug dealer at his corner.

8   The officer stood about 40 feet away—I think that is the distance that even the American Civil Liberties Union would say that you can be away from drug dealers and not hear their conversations or otherwise deny their right to privacy. We weren't interested in whatever conversation they may have had, or in speaking to

them at all—anything they may have said to us would be a lie. We were there to put a crimp on their business by scaring off their customers.

9   These drug dealers had been arrested many, many times. They were not afraid of us; they understood how the system worked. But most of their customers had not been arrested, did not really understand how the criminal justice system worked, and did not want to learn.

10   Our program had an immediate impact. With a uniformed police officer stationed 40 feet away, no one came near the drug dealer, even to say hello. All of the automobiles that came to the area would drive by the first time, come around a second time, and leave. In order to assist us, we added a weapon to our arsenal: a Polaroid™ camera with a flash. When these drivers would come by the second time we would take their photograph. And that would be the last that we saw of that particular customer. (It turns out, to the dismay of some super-libertarian groups, that it is not against the rights to take a photograph in public. There is no expectation of privacy when you are walking down the street, for example, and are photographed or captured by the lens of a news camera.)

RETAIL ECONOMICS

11   Critics of our strategy argued that the drug dealers would simply go someplace else, and, in fact, they did; they went a block up or down the street. But, we found that they operated on the same basis as any other retail business, even though their business was illegal. They could not move too far from their established base of operation because they had no way of communicating their new location to their customers. Most of the people we arrested for buying drugs did not know the name of their dealer. They just knew they went to a certain location at a certain time of day when the dealer was there, and exchanged money for the drugs. But they didn't know his name, and he certainly didn't know theirs. So he couldn't go 10 blocks away or across town as critics had said he would. The dealer was really captured within an area of about two blocks.

12   Not only were there good business reasons why the drug dealers couldn't move, there was another very important reason as well. As one drug dealer told us, "You can get killed trying to move someplace else." After all, that's what turf wars are all about.

13   The naysayers also told us that we were going to have to cover these 31 drug markets 24 hours a day, seven days a week. Because we didn't have the resources to do anything even close to that, we initially zeroed in on five very carefully selected locations, each to be patrolled by one officer. We learned very quickly that we didn't have to cover these areas seven days a week. We would cover them on those days the drug dealers made the greatest profit—Wednesday through Saturday. On Sunday, Monday, and Tuesday we would let them rest, or if you will, sell as many drugs as they wanted. We could afford to. There just isn't the demand there is the rest of the week. About 70 percent to 80 percent of the drug sales took place Wednesday through Saturday to recreational drug users.

14   Not only did we not have to cover these areas seven days a week, we didn't have to cover them 24 hours a day. All we had to do to really have an impact on

their business was to cover them from about 6:00 in the evening until about 2:00 in the morning in most places.

15   After two or three weeks—which was much sooner than we originally thought—these dealers left. They could no longer make a living selling drugs at that location. At the retail drug level, volume is very important. Street-level drug sales typically range from $5 to as much as $50 today—particularly for cocaine, marijuana, and amphetamines. Drug dealers must sell a large volume in order to make their business viable. We denied them their volume by ruining the most profitable hours of the day on the most profitable days of the week, simply by posting a police officer, in uniform, 40 feet away.

16   After a very short period of time we found that we could reduce dramatically the resources that we applied in the areas, although we could not altogether leave these five locations. After four to five weeks, just one officer could cover three or four locations, freeing the other officers to go elsewhere. We could never abandon the areas we took, but we could drastically reduce our efforts in those areas.

POLICE GRAFFITI

17   As we were driving the drug dealers out of business, we did other things to reinvigorate the neighborhoods, and to make the officers' job of standing alongside the drug dealers more pleasant. We spruced up the area. We began this project because we were a little selfish; the officers didn't want to stand among a lot of debris, paper, trash, flies, food, dead animals, and so forth, that had not been removed from the roadway.

18   The clean-up of the area was very important. If you are going to convince people—merchants, citizens, shoppers—that an area is safe, it has to look safe. And they are not going to be convinced that it is safe if there is gang graffiti and profanity on the walls and debris in the roadways. The clean-up was essential, and unfortunately, we had to do it ourselves. The public works people and the sanitation department had their own priorities, and they didn't coincide with ours. So we used our own resources.

19   We got prisoners out of the jail to pick up trash. By chance, some of them had been in prison for street-level drug dealing, and, also by chance, some had been dealing in those very same areas to which they were now taken to clean up. It was interesting to see the reactions of the people in the neighborhood to seeing these dealers, who weeks or months before were loaded down with gold chains and all kinds of apparent wealth, now wearing orange jumpsuits that said "County Jail" on them.

20   We even developed our own graffiti—big squares we painted over existing graffiti, because we could not afford to match the paint of the surrounding areas. The black, green, or beige paint against a white background was much more attractive, I can tell you, than some of the words that it blocked out. These squares said, in effect, "This is police turf."

21   Within days, when people came around to buy drugs, the area looked a lot different; it looked like somebody cared about it. Paper, trash, and debris had been removed, not on a one-time basis, but every day. The first time it took us four or

five days to clean up the various areas. But once we finished the initial clean-up, we were able to stay ahead of the problem. Subsequent clean-ups often took less than an hour.

22   We discovered that we only had to maintain our resources in each area until the word was out on the street that "this is no longer a place where you can buy drugs." As we liberated each of these original areas from drugs and crime, we would go to another area, and then another. Today, we probably have only one part-time open-air drug market.

DOMINO'S THEORY

23   Now, where did these drug dealers go? About 30 percent went out of the drug-selling business altogether. Not as many as we had hoped, but if you can drive 30 percent of all street-level drug dealers out of business with an expenditure of almost nothing—no additional personnel, no additional resources—that's pretty good. Especially if you are not overcrowding the jails and creating paperwork in the process. And no one else is going to come to that same spot to sell drugs when that dealer leaves, because he can't make a living selling drugs in that location either.

24   Some people expected that the drug dealers who were driven out of business on the street would merely continue selling drugs by using beepers. Rather than establishing a street location, beeper dealers have a paging number and deliver drugs to their call-in customers. But at the street-level, it is virtually impossible to make a living with beeper deliveries.

25   It was very easy for us to see the economic model when we put it on the blackboard and substituted the word "drugs" for "pizza." As you well know, you can have a pizza delivered to your home for $10 or $11, but the pizza company will do everything that it can to get you to buy a second pizza. There is a very good reason for that; the real profit is made in the second pizza. All of the overhead—the wear and tear of the vehicle, the insurance, and the salaries—is basically absorbed by the cost of the first pizza. The second pizza involves just a few more ingredients, and virtually no more labor, transportation, or insurance costs. Therefore, even if the second pizza only costs $5, the pizza maker still makes more actual profit on it than he does on the first one.

26   The point is, the dealers couldn't make a living simply by delivering at $10 or $15 an item to a customer who had called in on the phone. The few who seemed to be doing so against the odds had one thing in common: they were juveniles who lived at home. In other words, their overhead was taken care of. So reducing the street-level dealing did not cause an increase in phone-order drug deliveries.

SAFETY IN THE PROJECTS

27   After concentrating on ridding our streets of open-air drug markets, we turned our attention to Charleston's public housing. Like most cities, Charleston's public housing was rife with crime. And because 8 percent of all Charlestonians live in public housing, we decided it was worth our while to examine what made public housing fundamentally different from other types of housing. We found

that the people living in public housing were more often the victims of criminal activity than the perpetrators of it. Criminals concentrated in those areas because our forces did not patrol heavily in public housing projects, leaving residents an easy target.

28   We resolved that we would no longer abandon these areas to the criminal element; we would establish ourselves as the dominant force. We added foot patrols and other kinds of patrols, and they were modestly effective. But finally we came upon the real solution. And that was to develop a kind of public housing that would be fundamentally different than public housing anywhere else, and at the same time similar to much of the private housing that exists in our country.

29   First we went to the ACLU and to the neighborhood legal systems to explain to them what the problem was as we saw it and how we wanted to go about dealing with it. People suggested that we would not get cooperation from the ACLU or from neighborhood assistance programs. Some predicted that not even the housing authority would cooperate. They were wrong. All three groups were at least as eager as we were that law enforcement people would take the initiative.

SCREENING FELONS

30   We decided to screen people who went into public housing, in much the same way that any other landlord screens a tenant. First come, first serve would no longer be enough. Public housing officials already screened applicants regarding their financial status (whether they made a certain amount of money or were employed, or what kind of bank account they had) but allowed convicted felons (armed robbers, burglars, child molesters, arsonists, and rapists) access to public housing with no restrictions whatsoever. The only place in our city where people had to live with convicted criminals was public housing. Nobody else had to do that. Other landlords could keep them out.

31   We weren't interested particularly in keeping out anyone who had been arrested for driving while under the influence of alcohol; we didn't feel that they would endanger the quality of life within a public housing environment to the extent that it was necessary to exclude them. The same was true for shoplifters. We did exclude people who were recently convicted—and I want to stress convicted—of armed robbery, burglary, sexual assault, arson, or child molestation.

32   We also decided to evict anyone who was engaging in illegal activities. In this case, we did not require that the perpetrator be convicted in a criminal court; we simply went after him in a civil court. After all, that's what an eviction is; it is a civil action, where the individual has violated the terms of his or her lease. All we had to do, for example, was to prove that we had found cocaine in the dresser drawer in the second bedroom during the execution of a search warrant. No one yet has been able to convince any of the judges that he had a good reason to have cocaine or other illegal drugs in his apartment.

SECTION 8 COUNTRY CLUB

33   The naysayers said that this program was not going to succeed, because out of the 8,000 residents, we would have to evict 3,000 to 4,000 people to make the

neighborhood "safe." We were prepared to do that, but we didn't think it was necessary, and we were correct. We have had to evict only about 80 individuals or families from public housing in Charleston over a six-year period.

34   We didn't have to evict nearly as many people as originally thought, because public housing tenants did some interesting things. They stopped engaging in criminal activity. And it was for a very simple reason. Whereas arrests had not prevented them from committing crimes—after all, they could be out of jail within four hours—not having a place to sleep or live had a tremendous impact. Screening also encouraged some people to come forward and turn in family members who were involved in prostitution, illegal drugs, illegal liquor, and various other violations, because the entire household was placed at risk of being evicted from public housing.

35   We also decided to treat people in public housing as if they lived in the country club or an upscale apartment house. No outsider can enter a fancy apartment house unless a tenant gives permission to the doorman. Well, at 7:00 on Saturday nights, we set up a roadblock just like the gate at a country club in front of a Section 8 housing project called Bayside, where there was a serious drug problem. Nobody was allowed into the complex without permission from the tenant he had come to visit. An officer would call the tenant on a cellular phone; if there was no phone in the apartment, the officer would escort the visitor to the tenant's door.

36   We discovered several things in doing this. First, many of the tenants we called claimed they had never heard of the person who had come to visit them. At least they didn't want to let the police know they knew them. Second, we found that the vast majority of people who came to Bayside at night were non-residents. They were criminal predators who came to sell drugs or engage in other illegal activities. By eliminating their presence, we eliminated much of the crime in our Section 8 housing. Third, it turned out that some of the visitors to Bayside were people we had been looking for. As one officer called the person the visitor had come to see, another would check his license plate number in our computer system. We arrested a murderer, burglars, drunk drivers, and many drug dealers. We ended up killing a lot of birds with one well-placed stone.

37   In almost no time criminal activities at Bayside dropped off dramatically. Our checkpoints became less frequent because criminals got the message that they were not welcome there. We still act as doormen about once a month, just to make our point. For the most part, though, our crime problem at Bayside has been solved.

FRINGE BENEFITS

38   Our efforts to improve public housing and to close down open-air drug markets have yielded unintended benefits for Charleston in the last year. As the success of our crime-reduction strategies has become more widely known in South Carolina, areas around Charleston have petitioned to become part of our city. In the past two years we have gained more than 26 square miles of territory, much of which is used for commercial purposes. The owners of the 500 stores that have recently become part of Charleston know that, while our city taxes are a little

higher than those they were paying before, the superior police protection they receive makes the move a good choice. The money these businesses pay into city coffers in turn helps keep taxes for citizens in Charleston down, while giving a boost to the city economy. On the negative side, Charleston's rapid growth caused our crime rate to rise in 1990 and 1991. Because these crimes are, for the most part, taking place in the city's newly acquired territories, however, we suspect that this increase in illegal activity is temporary. We know that we have a winning formula to combat a temporary increase in crime.

39   In Charleston, South Carolina, we found that simply by targeting specific neighborhoods we could have an immediate and lasting reduction of street-level drug dealing and the victimization associated with it. We also proved that it was possible over time to reduce significantly the incidence of crime in public housing. Moreover, we accomplished this without massive increases in manpower, money, or other resources, and without overburdening the jails or other parts of the criminal justice system. All we had to do was look at street crime and drug dealing as a business, and fight it by reducing the profit margin until the business was no longer worthwhile to operate. Criminals, just like everyone else, respond to market forces. We just needed to show them that, literally, crime doesn't pay.

THE POWER OF STYLE: USING NARRATION

Reuben Greenberg tells the story of the Charleston, South Carolina police department's success in reducing crime to propose that other cities do the same. Narration is a powerful argumentative tool. In telling a story, the writer turns from theory to practice and uses a specific example to make a point. Narratives are easy for the reader to follow because they are organized chronologically.

Narratives usually begin with a "set up," or background information telling about the circumstances leading to the events. Greenberg begins by explaining the extent of the problem, tells what doesn't work, proceeds to tell the story of how the problem was solved in Charleston, and ends by suggesting that the Charleston model is one that can be emulated in other cities to curb drug-related crimes.

Revolving-Door Justice: Plague on America
Robert James Bidinotto

Dangerous criminals are being hustled out the back door of our prisons as fast as cops, prosecutors and judges put them in.

1   The career of Morris Bud Vroman is a stark testament to why Americans no longer feel safe. This Michigan native had a long criminal record—including assault, larceny and weapons charges—when he was convicted of breaking and entering in 1983 and sentenced to six to 15 years. In prison, he amassed dozens of major violations for habitually disobeying orders, refusing to work, threatening to kill a guard and fighting with other inmates.

2   When Vroman's case came before the parole board in 1988, he was turned down. Notes from the proceeding described him as "a wild-eyed guy" whose behavior while incarcerated had been "frankly downhill."

3   Then Vroman took classes in "impulse control," and a prison report noted "a positive change in his behavior." After three state declarations of prison "overcrowding emergencies," Vroman was paroled to a Detroit halfway house in February 1989.

4   He was employed briefly but was fired for fighting. After that he lasted only two days in job-training sessions, then refused to take part in a mental-health program. Finally, he stopped reporting to his parole officer altogether and disappeared.

5   Vroman surfaced over a year and a half later. Spotting a 16-year-old Detroit girl waiting for a bus to school, he forced her into a vacant building, repeatedly assaulted her sexually, then tried to strangle her. He was arrested for criminal sexual conduct and larceny.

6   At his trial, Vroman sat sketching bullets blasting through the prosecutor's head. When the jury pronounced him guilty, the parolee glared at his victim and said, "You're dead, bitch."

7   Dangerous Compromises. In recent years, states have enacted some of the stiffest criminal sentences in the world, yet we are losing the war against crime. One key reason is that tough penalties aimed at hardened criminals are being systematically undermined. Plea bargains permit criminals to escape punishment for the crimes they actually commit. And because there is not enough space to house them, convicts are hustled out of prisons as fast as harried cops, prosecutors and judges shove them in. Parole is granted to individuals who should never receive it; parole violations are ignored. "Good behavior" credits shave months, even years, off time served.

8   Virginia's parole-board chairman, Clarence L. Jackson, acknowledges that many convicts in his state serve as little as one-sixth of their sentence. In Massachusetts, ten years may actually mean an inmate must do only 12 months.

9   National figures reveal an astonishing fact: the time prisoners spend behind bars has been *declining*. In 1960, according to the federal Bureau of Justice Statistics (BJS), the mean time served in prison for all offenses was 28 months; by 1990, it had fallen to just 22. Violent offenders will do, on average, less than four years. The mean time served by murderers released in 1990 was only 7 1/2 years.

10   **Hidden Crimes.** The undermining of public safety begins with plea bargaining. This practice allows prosecutors to recommend a lighter sentence if a defendant will plead guilty to a lesser charge. This "bargain" spares everyone the bother of a trial.

11   Because criminals often don't get charged with their most serious crimes, plea bargaining lets them evade serious punishment. In a recent investigation, *The Record* newspaper in Hackensack, N.J., also exposed how plea bargaining can make a criminal seem much less dangerous than he really is.

12   Conrad Jeffrey was arrested in 1985 for kidnapping and attempted aggravated sexual assault on a 12-year-old boy in Newark. The initial charges of kidnapping, terroristic threats, child endangering and attempted aggravated sexual assault were reduced through a plea bargain to attempted kidnapping. He was sentenced to five years and paroled in less than two.

13   Next Jeffrey was charged with aggravated assault, auto theft, resisting arrest, drunken driving, leaving the scene of an accident and eluding the police. He was able to plead the charges down to burglary of a motor vehicle and aggravated assault. Jeffrey was given concurrent sentences of four years for the two charges, but was paroled again. Then he pulled a knife on a 14-year-old Hackensack girl.

14   Jeffrey could have gone to prison for a long time under New Jersey's habitual-offender law. But partly because a pre-sentencing report was vague about the circumstances of his earlier record, he was allowed once more to plead guilty to reduced charges.

15   Jeffrey spent the mandatory minimum 2 1/2 years in prison before he was again released in March 1993. Two weeks later, he was arrested for threatening a man in Newark. His parole was not revoked.

16   On May 5, 1993, seven-year-old Divina Genao was abducted from the courtyard of her Passaic apartment building. An informant's tip sent police to a boardinghouse. Hearing screams in a room, they kicked in the door. According to pending charges, Conrad Jeffrey lunged out at them. Inside, little Divina's body was on the bed. Jeffrey has been indicted for her murder.

17   **Worthless Pledges.** "Parole" originally meant "word"—in the sense of "giving one's word." It is the conditional early release of an inmate from confinement, on his pledge that he will behave himself. In theory, a parolee is still under state supervision. If he commits a crime or violates parole, he can be "flopped," or sent back to prison to serve the remainder of his sentence.

18   The reality is very different. "Parole has become a population valve to control prison overcrowding," explains Kenneth Babick, a parole and probation officer in Mulnomah County, Oregon. "It bears little relation to behavior behind bars or on the outside."

19   Michigan's lax parole system was further highlighted by a series of articles in the Detroit *Free Press* in the wake of the chilling case of Leslie Allen Williams.

20   Williams was first paroled in 1972 after serving one year of a one- to five-year sentence for breaking into a store in Novi, Mich. A plea bargain had reduced the charge to attempted breaking and entering. On parole, he broke into a home in Wixom where a 15-year-old girl was sleeping and tried to choke her. Charged with breaking and entering, and assault with intent to commit great bodily harm, he was once again allowed to plea bargain—this time to breaking and entering.

21   Since Williams was on parole, he should have been returned to prison for the remainder of his previous five-year sentence. Instead, he got a sentence of 18 months to ten years.

22   After two years he was paroled in July 1975, and within weeks he abducted a teen-ager at gunpoint and raped her. Williams was sentenced for this crime to a reassuring 14 to 25 years. Yet he was paroled *again* in January 1983.

23   Two weeks after his release, Williams kidnapped a woman and threatened her with a screwdriver. He had once again broken parole, and he had up to 18 years left on the meter for his previous crime. He received a new sentence of seven to 30 years.

24   Williams was out on the streets a fourth time in 1990. "Your granting a parole so swiftly, your belief in my efforts and progress has been an inspiration," he wrote to the parole-board member who had urged his release.

25   In 1991, he went on a rampage. Kidnapping Kami Villanueva, 18, from her South Lyon, Mich., home, he raped and then strangled her. When he encountered sisters Michelle and Melissa Urbin—teen-age honor students out for a walk—they, too, were murdered.

26   A few months later, he attacked Cynthia Marie Jones, 15, and her boyfriend in a Milford park. After tying the young man to a tree at knifepoint, Williams raped the girl, then stabbed her to death. Meanwhile, his parole officer reported that Williams was having "no problems."

27   The reign of terror finally ended in May 1992. Williams was captured after kidnapping a woman at gunpoint as she placed flowers on her mother's grave. He is now serving multiple life sentences.

28   Murray Burley denounced the parole system that had freed the killer of his granddaughter, Cynthia Marie Jones. "I am more frightened of that system and the people who operate it than I am of Williams," he told reporters. "We don't know how many Williamses they have let out."

29   In fact, parole horror stories are anything but unusual. One federal study that tracked 109,000 former prisoners found that 63 percent of them were re-arrested for serious crimes—including 2300 homicides, 3900 forcible sex crimes, 17,000 robberies and 23,000 assaults. Today, well over half a million convicts are out on parole.

30   A study by the National Council on Crime and Delinquency discovered that half of all the new prison admissions in California in 1987 were parole violators. And BJS statistics reveal that 32 percent of all the murders solved by police are committed by criminals out on bail, probation or parole. . . .

31   As was recently noted by the *Washington Post*, citizens must "have confidence that punishment will bear some reasonable relationship to the severity of the crime." Here is how we can ensure that it does.

32   **1. Build more prisons.** Overcrowding is universally acknowledged to be a driving force behind the early release of dangerous convicts. Constructing more cells to isolate such criminals from society should be a top priority.

33   "Most of our predatory violence is committed by chronic offenders who are cycled in and out of corrections facilities," notes former U.S. Attorney General William Barr, who now heads the First Freedom Coalition, a nationwide organization to strengthen the criminal-justice system. "If you put additional police on the street with no prison space behind them, all you're going to do is spin the revolving door faster."

34   Prisons more than pay for themselves. Several investigations have confirmed that the crimes committed by the average offender cost society at least twice as much as their cells do.

35   **2. Restrict plea bargaining.** Many officials protest that without plea bargaining, courts would become hopelessly clogged. But Oakland County, Michigan, has virtually eliminated plea bargaining without the predicted problems.

36   "Actually, our court dockets and waiting time are getting shorter because of our no-plea-bargain policy," says Oakland prosecutor Richard Thompson. "Once you say you're ready to deal, defense attorneys stall, waiting for the most lenient deal. Here, they know they're not going to manipulate the system."

37   **3. Truth in sentencing.** Public safety demands that current parole and good-behavior systems be tightened dramatically.
"At a minimum, parole violators should be sent back to prison to serve their full terms," declares George Ward, chief assistant prosecutor in Wayne County, Michigan. More than a dozen states and the federal government have gone even further, abolishing parole entirely.

38   Other states are tightening up the "good time" system. Arizona limits good-time credits to no more than 15 percent of an inmate's sentence. Says Steve Twist, the state's former chief assistant attorney general, "The public needs to know that a sentence means what it says."

IT'S UP TO YOU

39   Many argue that you can't fight crime with stiff sentences because building more prisons is too costly. "We're going broke," an opponent of more incarceration declares. We can't "build our way out" of the crime problem, one corrections official has complained.

40   Figures compiled by the Census Bureau and the Bureau of Justice Statistics reveal a different story. Only a small fraction of direct state government expenditures go to building and operating prisons, even in the ten states that spend the most on correctional institutions: California, 2.9 cents out of every budget dollar; New York, 2.5 cents; Florida, 3.3 cents; Michigan, 2.9 cents; Texas, 2.5 cents; Massachusetts, 2.7 cents; Illinois, 2.2 cents; New Jersey, 2.2 cents; Georgia, 3.1 cents; Ohio, 1.5 cents.

41   If elected state officials refuse to act in the face of the crime threat, are citizens powerless to respond? Not necessarily. Citizen initiatives offer an opportunity to bypass political bottlenecks. In Washington state, for example, a bill to put away for life criminals convicted of three serious felonies was buried in the legislature. But a statewide signature drive put the measure, called "Three Strikes and You're Out," on the ballot. Voters in this traditionally liberal state approved it last November by a three-to-one margin.

42   Seventeen other states provide for such initiatives, and all states ought to give their citizens similar power to enact legislation in this way. When they can speak directly on the issue, people are willing to pay the price for public safety. In Texas last fall, a $1-billion bond issue to build thousands of new state cells went before the voters. They approved it by a landslide.

For Writing and Discussion

1. What is Reuben Greenberg's solution to street crime? What kind of support does he use in "Less Bang-Bang for the Buck"? How does Greenberg create *ethos?*

2. What different systems were involved in Greenberg's solution? Do you think his program would work in all cities? Why or why not? What specific elements of his proposal do you think are most effective?

3. Contrast Greenberg's solution with Robert James Bidinotto's in "Revolving-Door Justice." If Greenberg and Bidinotto represent two factions of thought about crime, what compromise might address the ideas and concerns of both?

4. Murray Rothbard, in "Coping with Street Crime," presents this solution to the problem of street crime:

> . . . First, permit and encourage every citizen to be armed to the teeth and ready to defend himself with maximum and not minimum force. Right now, in our cities, victims have been effectively disarmed. Gun and other weapons control have deprived the average citizen of the right to defend himself adequately. In New York City, the happy hunting ground of street crime, people are not only deprived of guns, but they cannot even carry Mace, and women are not allowed to carry hat pins in their purses for self-defense. . . .
>
> Next to ending all weapons control, the most important step is to unleash the police and encourage them to administer instant punishment of street criminals. Only instant punishment can be understood by high-time preference criminals. During the 1930's, New York City, despite the poverty and unemployment of the Depression, was virtually free of street crime. Why? Because the police engaged in instant beating and clobbering of the perpetrator, either on the spot or inside the station house. And, more importantly, everyone knew it.

Do you believe society is moving toward Rothbard's solution? (Consider the fact that vigilantes are often hailed as heroes and that several states have passed

laws allowing citizens to carry concealed weapons.) What are possible consequences of Rothbard's proposal?

Relate Rothbard's solution to Aristotle's assessment of the criminal mind in
"Why People Commit Crimes" (page 307). Do you believe the delay in punishment is a decisive factor for most criminals? Why or why not?

5. Some people see as a major contributor to the problem of crime the fact that
criminals are often seen as heroes and that criminal behavior is sometimes
applauded rather than condemned. This perception of some criminals is not
new: Bonnie and Clyde and other gangsters of the 1930s were considered heroes
by many poor and working class people. How do you explain this phenomenon?

6. Some social scientists are concerned about today's growing number of
sociopaths, or people who do not have social consciences (little voices inside that
differentiate right from wrong). Many people are concerned about increasing
incidents of sociopathic behavior among teenagers, and even children, who can
take a human life without remorse "for the fun of it" or for a pair of athletic
shoes. One explanation is that the focus on building self-esteem in children has
obliterated the concepts of shame and guilt. What is your explanation for the
increase in sociopathic behavior? What might help reverse the current trend?

THE POWER OF STYLE: ACTIVISM

Loyalty to petrified opinion never broke a chain or freed a human soul.

Mark Twain

Activism is the natural result of problem solving. Once a solution is
born, the next step is to take action to implement the solution. The definition of the word *activist* often relies on whether a particular activist's
cause is one that is favorable to the definer.

Depending on how one viewed the situation, for instance, the Boston
tea partiers were either patriots or rabble-rousers. Many people will
speak out only when they believe they or those they love have been
directly violated. Even then, some people believe the "powers that be"
will manage fine without interference from Mr. and Ms. Average Citizen,
and they are likely to regard citizen activists with the suspicion that
some kind of personal gain must be the underlying motive for the
(continued)

(continued from previous page)

Activist

Denotation	Connotation	Connotation
(dictionary definition)	(positive—when cause is favorable)	(negative—when cause is unfavorable)
someone who takes action to further a social or political cause	courageous person; mover and shaker; freedom fighter; patriot	rabble-rouser; troublemaker; hell-raiser; loudmouth

activism or that they are lunatics. At times, the combination of frustration and passion moves activists to a shrillness that seems to validate the accusation of lunacy. Activism is not the norm of human behavior.

Research studies conducted in the 1970s suggest that conformity and obedience are the norm, that going along with the crowd and keeping the status quo is a part of human nature. In one study, a group that included several people who were involved in the experiment and one innocent research subject were asked to make a judgment about which of three lines matched a standard. With members of the research group deliberately giving a wrong answer after a period of giving correct answers, one-by-one seventy percent of the research subjects gave in and agreed with the group's obviously wrong answers. Less than thirty percent had the courage to speak out, to express the truth they saw with their own eyes.[1]

In another study conducted by Stanley Milgram to try to determine whether blind obedience was a part of human nature and accountable for many of the Nazi war atrocities, research subjects gave what they believed were electric shocks to people (who pretended to be in great pain) because they were told that the shocks were used as a teaching method. A majority of the research subjects obeyed authority figures without question.

Activism may be as simple and low-risk as writing a letter to a legislator or a parole board, or it may involve taking an unpopular position and speaking out when others are apathetic. The greater the commitment to a cause and the greater the activism, the more likely the activist will pay a price. An activist can expect opposition; it may range from ridicule to a car bomb. As James Russell Lowell noted, "Not a change for the better in our human housekeeping has ever taken place that wise and good men have not opposed it—have not prophesied that the world would wake up to find its throat cut in consequence."[2]

---

[1] Solomon Asch's conformity experiments.
[2] From "On Democracy," a speech delivered in England in 1884.

(continued)

(continued from previous page)

To the activists we owe a great debt. Walt Whitman wrote in *Democratic Vistas,* "The eager and often inconsiderate appeals of reformers and revolutionaries are indispensable, to counterbalance the inertness and fossilism making so large a part of human institutions." But change is frightening to many, even when the change is desirable and necessary. So, an activist must take the risks involved in going against the crowd, and the reward of results may be slow in coming.

However, an individual's efforts can effect change. Think of Candace Lightner's efforts to organize Mothers Against Drunk Driving after her 13-year-old daughter was killed by a drunk driver. MADD has been a powerful lobby for tougher laws against driving while intoxicated.

As a result of Henry Young's trial, the dungeons of Alcatraz were closed in the early 1960s. In the 1980s, Nancy Conn was attacked and left for dead at the same time her cousin was killed by a stranger. The man escaped from prison and tried again to kill Conn. One year after his escape, the Alabama parole board released the man. Nancy Conn's activism resulted in legislation that allowed a victim to be present and speak at an attacker's parole hearing.

After Megan Kanka was killed by a neighbor who her parents didn't know was a convicted sex offender, activism resulted in legislation in New Jersey that requires that the public be notified when convicted sex offenders are released in a community. (If you are thinking that it makes sense to inform parents when a child molester is near their children, keep in mind that many people believe the legislation violates the rights of the child molester and plan to fight all the way to the Supreme Court.)

Practice: Search and Speak Out

Find the address of a state or national representative, and write a letter expressing your opinion about a state or federal issue and proposing or supporting new legislation.

R E M I N D E R

Letters to legislators have a better chance of being read if they are brief and a better chance of being taken seriously if they are in formal language and contain succinct arguments. Use your knowledge of *ethos, pathos,* and *logos* to create a persuasive letter.

CHAPTER SUMMARY

In this chapter you have had opportunities to practice the process of problem-solving and explore the relationships among effective problem-solving and addressing attitudes, perceptions, systems, and future consequences. The readings in this chapter provided different perspectives on the solution to crime, and the Writing Challenge in Chapter 26 asks you to write your own proposal for a solution to a problem.

Chapter 26

WRITING CHALLENGE

Policy recommendations, or proposals for solutions, include the kinds of arguments you have already written—substantiation and evaluation. Policy recommendations call for a clear definition or explanation of the problem just as substantiation arguments call for a clear definition of the issue. An argument for or against gun control involves definition, explanation, and substantiation in the form of reasons, anecdotes, examples, statistics, and so forth. The writer says, "This is my stand, and I'll tell you why. I hope to persuade you to agree with me." A policy recommendation includes the same kinds of arguments.

Policy recommendations, however, go beyond merely persuading the audience, the reader, to agree. Policy recommendations include evaluations of existing policies and alternative proposals. And policy recommendations ask the audience to act.

Write a paper in which you recommend a solution to a problem or a change in policy that will solve a campus, community, or social problem. Make sure your solution can be implemented, briefly summarize how it will be done, and tell who will do it. Make clear whether your audience is the general citizenry or people who are empowered to make changes. Focusing on a smaller problem and solution that is easily implemented will make your writing task easier. (See the student paper on page 471. The proposal was sent to the owner of a restaurant.)

Journal Topic Suggestions

- A simple solution to a major problem
- The role ego plays in problem solving and decision making
- The role ego played in making a particular decision
- How minimizing the role of ego affects decision making
- Why you do or do not want to play a role in solving community problems
- An example of problem solving for the "common good"
- How solving an environmental problem plays today against tomorrow
- An example of problem solving with future generations in mind
- Causes for which you would be willing to take an active role
- How you can use problem-solving methods to make your life better

GUIDE TO WRITING A PROPOSAL

Planning and Prewriting

CHOOSING A TOPIC

To find a topic, recall the things you have discussed recently with friends. Is there a school issue for which you believe you know the solution? Do you recall an incident on campus that made you think, "That rule should be changed" or "That should never happen again"? Are you concerned about a community issue that seems to have a reasonable solution? Do you believe you know the solution to a social problem facing the country, or can you support the need for and recommend a pilot project that may yield more data about solving the problem?

PRIMING THE BRAIN

Remember that great minds have sought solutions to many of our social problems. There are no easy answers. If a solution seems too easy to be true, it probably is. Look harder for possible negative consequences and consider whether enough people would agree to implement your recommendation to make it a realistic possibility.

To prepare yourself for this assignment, find at least one newspaper article and two magazine articles on the topic. Ideally, the two magazines should represent differing perspectives. The liberal-slanted *The New Republic* and the conservative *National Review* are possibilities.

If you choose a school or community problem, you might have a difficult time finding related articles, but you could substitute interviews with people who disagree on related issues. Write at least three questions that you hope to have answered through your reading or interviews.

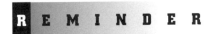

R E M I N D E R

You may also want to explore personal feelings and possible reasons for those feelings in your journal.

EXPLORING THE TOPIC

You can use the following lists of questions to explore a problem and possible solutions.

Questions for Substantiating the Problem

1. What is wrong with the present way of doing or handling (something)?
2. What policies, procedures, laws, customs, or traditions are involved in (something)?

3. Who suffers from (something)?
4. What is the cost of (something) in terms of money, time, and human suffering?
5. How will (something) be affected by predicted changes (increasing costs, population, social trends)?
6. Who is my audience? Citizens? Policy makers?
7. What does my audience already know?
8. Will my audience understand what I mean by (something)?
9. How can I convince my audience that I'm a credible source?
10. Will my audience have different perspectives or experiences that I should acknowledge?
11. What logical arguments will appeal to my audience?
12. How can I appeal to my audience's emotions in a fair way?
13. What policies, procedures, or laws are related to the problem?
14. What customs and traditions are related to the problem?
15. What facts or statistics are related to the problem?
16. What examples and anecdotes illustrate the problem?

Questions for Evaluating Alternative Solutions

1. What are alternative proposals or views on how (something) should be done?
2. What are the merits of those proposals or views?
3. Is my audience likely to favor alternative proposals?
4. If so, how can I show that I respect opposing views?
5. What are the disadvantages of those proposals or views?
6. What do the advocates of those proposals fail to consider?
7. How costly are the alternative proposals?
8. How difficult would it be to implement the alternative proposals?

Questions for Substantiating and Evaluating My Solution

ADVANTAGES

1. Why is my solution better?
2. Why is it more likely to work than other solutions?
3. How does the cost compare to the cost of other solutions?
4. What logical appeals will convince my audience?

DISADVANTAGES

1. What barriers would have to be overcome to implement my solution?
2. How can I convince my audience that these barriers *can* be overcome?
3. Have I thought of all possible consequences?

PLAN FOR IMPLEMENTING

1. What actions must be taken to implement my solution?

2. Who must take these actions and when?
3. Why is it worth the effort to take action?

CONCLUSION AND BENEFITS TO AUDIENCE

1. What benefits will my audience realize?
2. Will the benefits be immediate or long-term?
3. What are the consequences of not taking action?
4. How can I pull my solution together with a clincher that leaves the audience willing and ready to act?

Organizing and Drafting

Practice: Analyzing Scope and Organization

Recall the proposals you read in this chapter. You may want to scan over them to determine the percentage of space devoted to each area of the proposal. After determining the amount of space devoted to each area of the proposal, you can see that establishing the fact that your problem is, in fact, a serious problem is important.

R E M I N D E R

Formal proposals in the business world have a standard form that includes headings such as Scope, Need, Plan, Budget, and Personnel, and differs from the essay form of this paper. However, you may want to include headings as you organize and draft your paper and omit them in the final draft.

	Proposal 1 % of space	Proposal 2 % of space
Proving the problem is a problem (includes definitions, facts, examples, and so forth)		
Discussing alternative solutions/status quo (includes advantages and disadvantages; refuting the claims of opposition)		
Stating the proposed solution (includes telling audience what action should be taken)		

After exploring your topic fully, you will be saturated with information and bursting with conviction. You may find that you have written several pages more than your reader needs or wants to read. In fact, you may find that you need to cut out some material before you offer it to a partner for evaluation.

Evaluating and Revising

EVALUATING APPEALS

After you have finished a draft of your paper, read it over to evaluate your use of the three modes of persuasion.

Logos   Did you structure your arguments well, defining and establishing the problem and addressing alternative solutions? Did you use recent, reliable, and relevant evidence to support your claim that a change should be made in the way things are now done?

Pathos   The reader must feel the urgency of the problem and sympathize with those who suffer because of the problem and realize the consequences of not taking action now. Will a concerned reader become emotionally involved in your issue?

Ethos   Have you demonstrated your good sense, good will, and good moral character in your paper? Do you reveal in your paper that your are sincere and knowledgeable, reasonable, free from bias and special interest, and sensitive to the feelings of your audience?

PARTNER EVALUATION

Read your partner's paper through carefully, making check marks beside passages that are unclear or that you suspect have some other kind of problem. Write out your initial response to the paper, noting positive aspects (Was it interesting? Did you learn something?) and possible problems (Was any part of it confusing?). Next, respond to each of the questions below on a separate sheet of paper. On your partner's paper, bracket any sentences that are unclear or that you believe contain errors in usage or mechanics.

Evaluation checklist

1. Was the problem clearly stated and explained in the introduction? What is the problem?
2. Did the writer include sufficient support to convince you that the problem is indeed a problem that needs attention? Are you confused about any of the support? If so, ask the writer to clarify it.

3. Do you have questions about some of the information, perhaps whether it is up-to-date or credible? If so, write your questions.

4. Is any of the information unnecessary? Suggest information that the writer might consider cutting.

5. Is the information logically organized? Can you suggest another organization? If so, write down the change of sequence.

6. Is the writer's attitude toward and treatment of the subject consistent? If not, point out changes in the writer's tone.

7. Do you "buy" the writer's solution? If you could, would you act on this proposal?

REVISING

When cutting, look for excessive examples or extended anecdotes. Ask yourself, "Have I told more of a story than I need to make my point? Will two examples illustrate my point well enough? Can cut the third point?"

R E M I N D E R

Check each paragraph by turning the topic sentence into a question. Be sure each sentence in the paragraph answers the question. If the paragraph contains an anecdote that supports your proposal, make sure you have given adequate details but haven't gotten carried away with the story itself.

REVISION CHECKLIST

1. Have I given proper credit to others for the use of their ideas?
2. Have I given adequate details to support each claim?
3. Have I cut out unnecessary material that may bore or irritate my reader?
4. Are my emotional appeals fair and valid?
5. Does my support contain informal fallacies? (See pages 204–219.)

Editing and Proofreading

THE POWER OF STYLE: ELIMINATING WORDINESS

Trying to impress readers with the seriousness of ideas opens the temptation to use wordy phrases that may seem pompous or irritating to the audience. You may have felt the need to use such phrases in an effort to stretch 400 words of good ideas into a 500-word essay. However, busy readers appreciate writing that is to-the-point.

Practice: Eliminating Wordiness

Revise the following sentences, replacing or eliminating wordy and redundant phrases.

1. I see no reason at this point in time why we should not rely, as has often been the case in the past, on the generation of ideas through brainstorming.
2. I am of the opinion that, in regard to overall production, the indications are that a substantial increase of ideas will be realized through brainstorming.
3. The new modern, up-to-date computer system contains state-of-the-art technology.
4. In view of the fact that the weather is unseasonably warm, we can take into consideration measures to conserve energy.

EDITING/PROOFREADING CHECKLIST

1. Have I eliminated wordy or redundant phrases?

2. What is my attitude toward my audience? Have I talked down to the reader?

3. What is my style? Is it conversational or formal? Have I used clichés or slang that is inappropriate?

4. What tone do I reveal in my writing? Serious? Sarcastic? Humorous? Is any humor or sarcasm appropriate?

5. Is my final draft in manuscript form?

6. Have I proofread each sentence from the last to the first to eliminate mechanical errors?

First Draft

To: (name of restaurant owner)

From: Sha'nin Hollar

Date: 15 November 1995

Re: Handicapped accessibility

All people should have access to places they want to go. This includes people with different kinds of mobilit--those in wheelchairs and using walkers. It concerns me as a citizen that the Blue Boat restaurant is not accessible for handicapped people.

Having a physical disability in such a structurally complicated world can become very difficult for people confined to wheelchairs or using walkers. For example, there are many physical objects or structures such as stairs, hills, and narrow passageways that disabled people have to be aware of when traveling from place to place. The <u>Americans with Disabilities Act</u> states in Title III, section 504(b) that business owners must "ensure that buildings and facilities are accessible, in terms of architecture and design . . . and communication, to individuals with disabilities."

There is, however, a problem concerning the structure of the Blue Boat in correspondence with the law. There are no available accesses to the building to accommodate handicapped people.

There are two entrances, one at the front of the building and one at the back. Both entrances have steps that people have to climb in order to get into the building. Therefore, it is impossible for people confined to wheelchairs or using walkers to get inside the restaurant without having someone physically carry them up the steps. For handicapped people, having to be physically carried up steps can be degrading to their self-esteem.

College students often socialize in groups in public places. Socializing to college students, disabled or not, is a major part of their present life. Having a restaurant in a college town can be very profitable. Yet it is important to take

94.6%

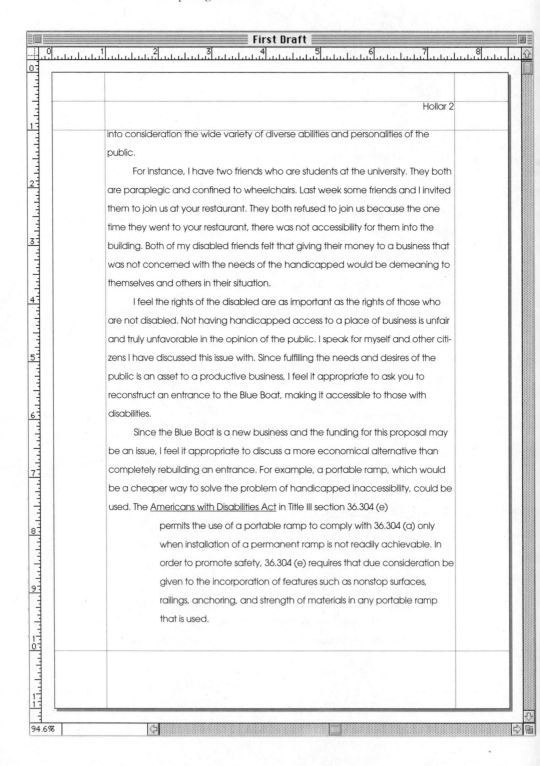

into consideration the wide variety of diverse abilities and personalities of the public.

For instance, I have two friends who are students at the university. They both are paraplegic and confined to wheelchairs. Last week some friends and I invited them to join us at your restaurant. They both refused to join us because the one time they went to your restaurant, there was not accessibility for them into the building. Both of my disabled friends felt that giving their money to a business that was not concerned with the needs of the handicapped would be demeaning to themselves and others in their situation.

I feel the rights of the disabled are as important as the rights of those who are not disabled. Not having handicapped access to a place of business is unfair and truly unfavorable in the opinion of the public. I speak for myself and other citizens I have discussed this issue with. Since fulfilling the needs and desires of the public is an asset to a productive business, I feel it appropriate to ask you to reconstruct an entrance to the Blue Boat, making it accessible to those with disabilities.

Since the Blue Boat is a new business and the funding for this proposal may be an issue, I feel it appropriate to discuss a more economical alternative than completely rebuilding an entrance. For example, a portable ramp, which would be a cheaper way to solve the problem of handicapped inaccessibility, could be used. The <u>Americans with Disabilities Act</u> in Title III section 36.304 (e)

permits the use of a portable ramp to comply with 36.304 (a) only when installation of a permanent ramp is not readily achievable. In order to promote safety, 36.304 (e) requires that due consideration be given to the incorporation of features such as nonstop surfaces, railings, anchoring, and strength of materials in any portable ramp that is used.

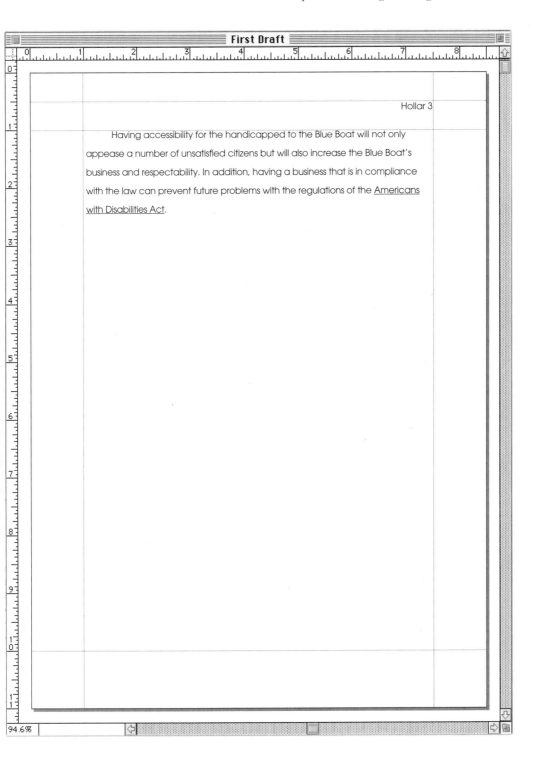

First Draft

Hollar 3

Having accessibility for the handicapped to the Blue Boat will not only appease a number of unsatisfied citizens but will also increase the Blue Boat's business and respectability. In addition, having a business that is in compliance with the law can prevent future problems with the regulations of the <u>Americans with Disabilities Act</u>.

The Research Process and Paper

I search. That's the truth of any inquiry. Re-search doesn't say it, rather implies complete detachment, absolute objectivity. Time to clear the miasma and admit that the best searchers act both subjectively and objectively and write so that professionals and the public can understand their searches and profit from them. Time to get down to the basics, which are not footnotes, but curiosity, need, rigor in judging one's findings and the opinions of experts and helping others test the validity of the search.

Ken Macrorie

Chapter 27

RESEARCHING

WHY?

As you prepare for the research paper assignment, you may be asking, "Why? Who writes term papers in the real world? Is this busy work, or what?" Here is a response to those legitimate questions.

The U.S. Department of Labor created a task force to determine what students should learn in school to prepare them for the real world of work. Thousands of businesses and industries were surveyed by the Secretary's Commission on Achieving Necessary Skills (SCANS) task force to determine what employers believed every employee should know to succeed in jobs at all levels. The information was compiled into a list of five competencies and three foundation skills. Foundation knowledge, or basic skills necessary to function well in the workplace (and the world), was divided into three categories.

FOUNDATION

Basic Skills—ability to read, write, compute, speak, and listen

Thinking Skills—ability to think creatively, make decisions, solve problems, visualize things in the mind's eye, learn and relearn, and reason

Personal Qualities—responsibility, self-esteem, sociability, self-management, and integrity

You probably can look through the Foundation list and feel confident that you have mastered many of those skills. The SCANS Competencies, however, may be more challenging.

COMPETENCIES

Resources—allocating time, money, materials, space and staff

Information—acquiring and evaluating data, organizing and maintaining files, interpreting and communicating, and using computers to process information

Systems—understanding social, organizational, and technological systems, monitoring and correcting performance, and designing or improving systems

Technology—selecting equipment and tools, applying technology to specific tasks, and maintaining and troubleshooting technologies

Interpersonal Skills—working with teams, teaching others, serving customers, leading, negotiating, and working well with people from culturally
diverse backgrounds

Today's real world demands an array of new skills, and the need for these
skills will certainly increase. So, here is the answer to the question at the beginning of this chapter: Completing a research project and paper provides practice in
and development of skills you will need to succeed in the workplace of the
future. While it is true that few people in the real world write academic research
papers, everyone in the real world needs to know how to use resources and
technology, to acquire and use information, and to understand systems. You
have already used these skills and competencies in completing assignments in
this text. Now you have an opportunity to assimilate and demonstrate your
knowledge in at least four of the five SCANS competencies as you complete your
research project and paper. What you learn in the process may be far more
important to your future than your final product, the paper itself.

Also important is to think of other ways to use the information you acquire
during your search. After you have completed the research process and paper,
you will be more informed than most other people about your topic, or issue.
Think about how you can use the information in a letter to your representative or
to a newspaper, in a political flyer or brochure that informs and persuades others,
in a political speech, in a formal proposal for change, or in a discussion forum on
the Internet.

WHAT?

The Writing Challenge in this chapter calls for an argumentative research paper.
You will write a longer, more detailed version of the kind of argumentative
papers you wrote for earlier chapters. You will find sources related to your topic
and incorporate information from those sources to build your own convincing
argument.

The assignment requires careful attention to documentation and the use of
MLA (Modern Language Association) or APA (American Psychological Association)
style. You will paraphrase, summarize, and quote the words of others, give credit
to those sources in parenthetical documentation, and prepare a Works Cited or
References page to help your reader locate the information you have cited.

HOW?

At the risk of sounding like someone's grandparent who "walked five miles to
school in knee-deep snow (barefooted)," let me remind you that you live in a
wonderful time. If you had ever typed a single page five or six times to eliminate
errors or to leave the correct space for a footnote, you might be tempted to kiss
your computer each time you turn it on. Making a correction is a simple and
quick action now, not a career.

The same goes for the research process. In the not-so-good-ol' days, research involved hours of copying by hand lengthy notes from books that couldn't be taken from the library. Today, dust collects on the old indexes as students use computers to slash research time by plugging in key words, perusing computer data banks, accessing government statistics and magazine and newspaper articles, and pushing print buttons to get hard copies to take home and mark up with highlighters. This chapter provides information on CD-ROM data banks and on-line searches in addition to information on traditional research tools. You will also find information on how to document sources found on the Internet and in CD-ROM data banks.

WRITING CHALLENGE

Write a paper in which you support an assertion with information from outside sources and properly document those sources. Review Part Three for help with creating arguments.

PLANNING AND PREWRITING

Creating an Arguable Thesis

Choose a topic that is important to you. As a starting point, think of your general interests. Reviewing your journal writings would be a good place to begin if you don't already have a topic in mind. There are arguable issues related to almost any topic. From a general topic, explore the different related issues to find an arguable thesis—one that you can support.

R E M I N D E R

Although there are often more than two sides to an issue, we must have *at least* two sides for an arguable topic.

Your thesis statement will be an assertion that you will support with reasons. Although a purpose statement is not the same as a thesis statement, a purpose statement can be used in prewriting to develop a thesis statement.

The purpose of my paper is to convince my audience that street crime can be significantly reduced by legalizing drugs and providing drugs in controlled settings for addicts.

After you have formulated a purpose statement, discard the first part of the sentence; the independent clause that follows the word *that* will be your thesis statement.

Street crime can be significantly reduced by legalizing drugs and providing drugs in controlled settings for addicts.

To check your thesis statement, turn it into a question.

Why will legalizing drugs and providing them in controlled settings to addicts reduce street crime?

Every reason, anecdote, and detail should answer some part of that question.

Statistics reveal that the percentage of street crime that is directly related to drug use is . . .
An indirect relationship exists in . . . Legalizing drugs will . . .
Providing drugs to addicts is necessary because . . .
The controlled setting is necessary because . . .
To illustrate . . . , consider . . . , in many ways typical of addicts across the country.
Street crime will be reduced because . . .
Experimental studies in other countries indicate . . .
Opponents of the legal use of street drugs contend that . . . ; however, . . .

(For more help with creating a thesis statement, see page 164.)

Debriefing

To determine what you already know about your topic and where you might go to find additional information as you write, begin by asking more questions. Also analyze your audience and keep its characteristics in mind while researching your topic. Use the following lists of questions to guide your planning.

CURRENT KNOWLEDGE

What is my definition of the topic?
How is it distinguished from related topics?
What facts do I know about my topic?

What is my opinion about the topic?

What are some related issues? (List several issues related to the topic.)

What is my stance on related issues?

Who or what influenced my opinion?

Is my opinion secondhand, or do I have personal experiences that contribute to my feelings about the topic?

Are there causes and results related to my topic?

What examples or anecdotes can I cite?

LOOKING FOR ANSWERS

What do I need to know about my topic? (List several questions related to the topic.)

Do I know someone who has an expert opinion or information on the topic? What questions would I ask that person in an interview?

What subject headings might I use to start my search on the CD-ROM indexes, the Internet, or the card catalog and print indexes?

What kind of source material do I need to focus on?

Is the topic related to other current issues? If so, how can I find the most current information? (List possible current sources such as magazines or newspapers.)

What kind of books and journals might contain the information I need? (List possible books or journal articles that might contain background information.)

AUDIENCE

Who is my audience?

What do my readers already know?

What information do my readers need?

How do others feel about my topic?

Is the topic related to political issues that might have liberal and conservative views? If so, what might the liberal and conservative positions be?

List groups or factions that may have opposing opinions and what those opinions might be. (See page 91.)

What opposing opinions do I need to address?

What kinds of arguments would be most convincing to the opposition?

How can I establish credibility with my audience?

T I P

Go through your prewriting for possible subject headings and write them on separate index cards or pages of a notebook that you can take to the library. This will become your working bibliography. As you start your search, write down call numbers of books, titles, and authors; titles of magazine articles, dates of publication, and page numbers; and journal articles, volume numbers, and page numbers under the subject headings.

Spelunking

Although we are not talking about exploring caves here, certain comparisons can be drawn. You may find yourself in unknown territory as you search through cyberspace to find current statistics or original research, the nooks and crannies of the library to find a book, or dungeons of microfilm to find a newspaper article. If you are new to your school and have not explored the library, find out about the guided tours most libraries offer. That will be the quickest way to familiarize yourself with the options available and where they are located. You may also be told how to use any computer data banks and where to find instructions for on-line searches. Librarians are there to help and are happy to answer questions; however, you will want to know enough about the library to find basic sources independently.

R E M I N D E R

Your need for the library will not end with this course. During your college career and, in fact, for the rest of your life, you will find yourself needing information for solving problems, writing reports, preparing presentations, and so forth. Everything you learn now will make your task easier later.

PERUSING POSSIBILITIES

THE INTERNET

The Internet is a network of networks through which information can be sent and retrieved from computer to computer. What was once used mainly by scientific and academic communities for international communication has evolved into a department-store-like assembly of search tools, gateways to information data banks, and newsgroups housed under the World Wide Web. While it is true that you may not find the information you need on the Internet, you can at least find additional sources to check in the library or order through the interlibrary loan service. Learning how to use on-line sources will be the easy part; learning about available databanks will take time.

Start with your school computer lab or library to find information about campus services which allow you to set up your user address and start browsing for information sources. The quickest way to learn is to take off, using instructions provided for the particular system at your school. However, some preparation will expedite on-line searches. If you have a list, for instance, of information you need and possible key words, you can avoid down time or giving up a computer to someone else just before you remember an important search item.

If you have a personal computer, you may already be on-line through one of the commercial services that provide user-friendly interfaces to the Internet. Some services provide student research help. For instance, America On-Line provides help in reducing research time through the Academic Research Service. You can also post questions on bulletin boards, but remember that most of the information on the Internet is provided by volunteers. You could get inaccurate information, so always double-check facts. Also, the Internet is dynamic, constantly changing. Addresses change, information is updated, and sources come and go, so remember to include the date you retrieved the information on your Works Cited page (see page 513).

Practice: On-Line Searches

In a recent newspaper, find information about a new research study that is related to your topic. Use your school's on-line system to search the Internet for the original research study. Download and print the study.

PERIODICAL INDEXES

CD-ROM Databases   CD-ROM searches are faster and more efficient than searching print sources for periodicals related to your topic. Instead of looking at several different bound indexes that each contain only one year's index and looking under several different identifiers to find information, you can simply type in key words for a topic title search covering several years' publications.

Computer indexes include the *Magazine Index*, the *National Newspaper Index*, *NewsBank*, and *Info Trac*, which indexes articles from both magazines and newspapers. The *MLA International Bibliography*, which indexes literary criticism, is also available on CD-ROM.

Practice: Finding Sources in CD-ROM Data Banks

To see for yourself the importance of choosing key words, search a general topic (crime, trade, or education) and note the number of entries (possibly more than one thousand). Browse through a few of the entries, then try another search with a second identifier (juvenile crime, international trade, elementary education). The search will take less time, and you will see fewer entries. Next, add another identifier or choose more specific key words (drugs/juveniles; U.S. trade/Japan; elementary education/ESL).

Printed Indexes Printed indexes in a variety of fields include the *Art Index, The Philosopher's Index,* the *Humanities Index,* the *Business Periodicals Index,* the *Education Index,* the *General Science Index,* the *Index to Legal Periodicals,* and the *Social Sciences Index.* Other indexes are more general and cover newspapers and magazines.

The *National Newspaper Index* contains stories and articles from major newspapers in the United States, and the *Canadian News Index* lists stories and articles in major newspapers in Canada.

The *Readers' Guide to Periodical Literature* is available now on computer discs in some libraries; however, this guide is available in most libraries in its book form. Articles from more than 200 magazines are indexed in the *Readers' Guide* by year. Updates for the current year are contained in booklets and compiled at the end of the year. You may need to check subject headings in several yearly editions. You will find the abbreviated form used for the different magazines listed in the front of the book or booklet. Remember, however, that although there are some reputable sources listed, other sources may not be so trustworthy. And since the publication is for the general public, many of the best sources (medical journals, for instance) are not listed. Also keep in mind that many magazines have formats or political agendas that result in the omission of valuable information. Try to find articles on your topic in several different types of magazines.

GOVERNMENT DOCUMENTS

Most university libraries contain separate sections for the thousands of published reports that are produced by government agencies. The person in charge of cataloging the reports and helping students with viewing microfilm will know what is available or at least can steer you in the right direction. You will find statistical information, research reports, and public service pamphlets that may be helpful. The *Monthly Index to the United States Government Publications* indexes this material. (Government documents may also be retrieved from on-line sources.)

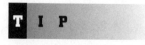

Before you begin your search for source material, read through the
section on MLA style to make sure you know what information is

required for proper documentation. Not doing so can be disastrous. Suppose, for instance, that you copy a section of a book and the title page for later study and then realize at the midnight hour that you don't have the publication year for your Works Cited page. It's okay to cry, but before you turn in your paper, you must go back to the library. (Looking up the book in the card catalog will save a trek through the stacks.) <u>Shortcut:</u> If you are copying pages from a magazine, check to see whether the date and name of the publication is at the bottom of facing pages. If so, you will not need to write it on the top of the first page.

THE CARD CATALOG: PRINT AND COMPUTER FILES

Whether on 3 × 5-inch cards or in a computer, a card catalog contains three kinds of "cards": author, title, and subject. (Works of fiction are listed only by author and title.) Some small libraries combine the author and title cards, but your search, whether on a computer or through index cards, will involve having a starting point (a subject, a name, or a title) and knowing the alphabet. You should find operating instructions near a computer card catalog, but most will require keying in simple choices (A for author, T for title, S for subject, KT for key term).

If you search through a subject index for your topic and do not find anything, try other possibilities. For instance, if you are looking for sources on the effects of television violence on children, you may first try *television,* then *violence,* then *children.* Your next option is to use the *Library of Congress Subject Headings* guide to find the headings used in cataloging books. For instance, if you are looking for information on *unidentified flying objects* (UFOs), the *Subject Headings* guide will direct you to use the heading *flying saucers* to find the information you want.

After you have located a book, you can use the index to find quickly the information that is relevant to your topic and use any bibliographies in the book to find additional sources. Working through the following exercise will serve as practice in using the parts of a book to find information.

T I P

Write down the complete call number, title, and author for possible sources. You may think you can remember the information for as long as it takes to reach the stacks, but any distraction on the way can wipe it out of your short-term memory. Just memorizing the first line of the call number doesn't work either. You may find that there are dozens of books with that classification.

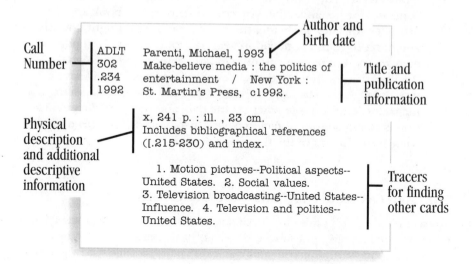

Call Number — ADLT 302 .234 1992

Author and birth date

Parenti, Michael, 1993

Make-believe media : the politics of entertainment / New York : St. Martin's Press, c1992.

Title and publication information

Physical description and additional descriptive information

x, 241 p. : ill. , 23 cm.
Includes bibliographical references ([.215-230) and index.

1. Motion pictures--Political aspects-- United States. 2. Social values. 3. Television broadcasting--United States-- Influence. 4. Television and politics-- United States.

Tracers for finding other cards

An Entry from a Computer Catalog

```
--------------------------------AFPL Library Catalog---------
----------------------------
AUTHOR (s):     Parenti, Michael, 1993-
TITLES (s):     Make-believe media : the politics of entertainment /
                Michael Parenti

                New York : St. Martin's Press, c1992.
                x, 214 p. : ill. ; 23 cm.
                Includes bibliographical references  (p.215-230) and
                index.

OTHER ENTRIES:  Motion pictures Political aspects United States.
                Social values.
                Television broadcasting      United States Influence.
                Television and politics      United States

Format:         BOOK

LOCN:  SO FUL ADLT      STATUS: Not Checked Out--
CALL#: 302.234 PARENTI
```

R E M I N D E R

**Eliminate the article (*a, an, the*) when searching for a title and also
when alphabetizing your Works Cited entries. Entries that have
abbreviations or numbers as the first word will be alphabetized as
though they were spelled out. Look under "Mac" for "Mc," "Mister"
for "Mr.," "Nineteen" for the book *1984.***

ENCYCLOPEDIAS

You may want to consult an encyclopedia for background reading on a topic, but
remember that the information may be dated. General encyclopedias such as the
Encyclopaedia Britannica and *Compton's Encyclopedia* on CD-ROM contain
alphabetized articles on thousands of subjects. The brief bibliographies listed
after an article might offer help in finding primary sources.

Specialized encyclopedias in a variety of fields (education, advertising, science and technology, social work, human behavior) offer valuable overviews. For
instance, for background reading on the effects of television violence on children
you might read an article on the developmental stages of children in the *Encyclopedia of Human Behavior: Psychology* and an article on violent behavior in the
International Encyclopedia of the Social Sciences before searching for books or
magazine and journal articles on research studies.

Priming the Brain

After you have collected your source material, you will want to spend plenty of
time reading before you actually begin writing your paper. Think about how
much easier it is to give a speech on a topic you know about. The same applies
to writing a research paper. Once you have saturated your brain with information
and ideas about your topic, the process of writing will be easy. In fact, paring
down the material you want to include may be the hardest part. Refer to your
responses to the debriefing exercise on page 498 to guide your reading.

R E M I N D E R

**To organize material as you read, make a master list using codes or
colors, and identify sections of the material that you plan to use in
your paper. When you begin work on each section of your first
draft, reread the material coded to that section; work in appropriate ideas by summarizing, paraphrasing, or quoting; and include
parenthetical documentation.**

Evaluating Sources

In evaluating sources, keep the three R's of testing sources in mind. Ask of each source

Is it *RECENT?*

Is it *RELIABLE?*

Is it *RELEVANT?*

Is It RECENT?   Is the publication current enough to include the latest knowledge on a certain topic? "Facts" change as new information is learned. An accepted fact of the past is that one way humans are distinguished from animals is that humans use tools; animals do not. Later, other characteristics were chosen: the ability to reason, the capacity for altruism, the ability to plan ahead, etc. "Facts" change as more is learned about animals.

Is It RELIABLE?   If you didn't already know, you learned in Part Four that just because something is in print does not make it so. Analyze each possible source for reliability. Is the publication respectable and known for its truthful treatment of issues? Does the author seem to have an ax to grind, a reason to omit information that does not support his thesis?

Is It RELEVANT?   If you turn your thesis statement into a question, does the information in the source answer the question or in a vital way contribute to an answer to the question? If not, get rid of it. (Yes, cutting is painful after you went through the process of finding the information. The payoff is a better grade.)

R E M I N D E R

Consider your audience as you collect information for your paper: Who is my audience? How can I establish credibility with my audience? What information will interest my readers? What information do my readers need? What do my readers already know? Do I need to define any terms? How can I hold my reader's attention?

Changing Your Thesis

As you read, you may change the thesis of your paper or even the general focus. You may, for instance, begin your reading with the idea that locking up criminals and throwing away the key is the solution to the crime problem but realize as you read that a solution is much more complex. Say you find out as you read that there is a direct correlation among teen pregnancy, poverty, and crime. Perhaps you decide that you want to argue for a certain type of prevention program, such as a program to offer at-risk teenage girls cash incentives to go on birth control and stay in school.

BACK TO THE TRENCHES

If you change the focus or the thesis of your paper, you may want to go back to the library and search for information under new subject headings. In the process of doing so, you will be learning more about a valuable tool—the research process itself—in addition to adding information to the data bank that is in your head. After you have made notes from your sources, see page 168 for help with incorporating your source material into your own writing and page 527 for help with MLA documentation.

Some computer programs are fussy about changing margins for a final draft. To avoid trouble, check the section on MLA Manuscript Form on page 533 and set your margins and heading space before you begin.

Chapter 28

Planning and Writing

Organizing and Drafting

Your thesis will be an assertion, and you will provide information to support that assertion. After you have formulated a thesis, let it guide you in preparing an outline. A helpful outline may be a simple list of main points or a more structured outline. If you do take the time to write a fairly complete, even if informal, outline, your paper will be much easier to write. The following rough outline on sexist language in contemporary advertising would make the drafting part of the writing process the easiest part.

THESIS:
Although the general public and media have become sensitive to sexist language, advertisers still use sexist language to appeal to men, women, and even children in ways that promote the old standards and send messages that should not be tolerated.

I. Introduction
 A. Thesis
 B. Definition of "sexist language"
 C. Changes over past decade
 D. Subtle effect of sexist language
  1. Quotations from psychologists
  2. General information about findings

II. Sexist language in ads directed at men
 A. Television ads
  1. Examples
  2. Messages that are sent with language
  3. Possible effects of messages
 B. Magazine ads
  1. Advertising language contrasted with general media language
  2. Message that is sent to target populations
  3. Possible effects of language

III. Sexist language in ads directed at women
    A. Television ads
        1. Examples
        2. Messages that are sent with language
        3. Possible effects of messages
    B. Magazine ads
        1. Advertising language contrasted with general media language
        2. Message that is sent to target populations
        3. Possible effects of language

IV. Sexist language in ads directed at children
    A. Examples
        1. Television ads
        2. Ads on toys and cereal boxes
    B. Advertising language contrasted with language in other media
    C. Message sent
    D. Possible effects
        1. Quotations from psychologists
        2. Data on average viewing

V. Conclusion
    A. Summary of findings
    B. Argumentative conclusion

R E M I N D E R

Caution: Do not overuse long direct quotations. Summarize or paraphrase information unless you have a good reason for quoting directly. See the sections on summarizing, paraphrasing, and quoting in Part Four for help.

Documenting Your Sources

WHY BOTHER?

There are two very good reasons to document sources.

1. To avoid plagiarism by giving proper credit for others' ideas and information. Everyone knows that turning in a paper copied from someone else is plagiarism, but failure to document sources properly can carry the same penalties.

2. To give the information your reader needs to locate the sources you
    have used in order to study them further or to verify your interpretation.
    Using the conventions of a particular style of documentation helps your
    reader find quickly the information required to locate the source.

R E M I N D E R

**Failure to document sources properly constitutes plagiarism. See
page 223 for more on plagiarism.**

The Modern Language Association (MLA) provides the style, or conventions, for documenting sources in papers for most humanities classes and publications in most related fields. (Linguists use LSA style.) Other "style sheets"
include the American Psychological Association (APA) style, which is used in
most social sciences, and the number system, which is used in applied sciences.
What these style sheets have in common is the kind of information required for
documentation and a strict adherence to convention—consistency. They differ in
the treatment (form, punctuation, order) of the information.

MLA style is the favored style for humanities courses and publications.
However, if you plan to major in one of the social sciences, you may be required
to use one of the other style sheets for papers in other classes. If so, your instructor may allow you to use the APA style (see page 535) for this research paper.

You may be required to buy the *MLA Handbook for Writers of Research
Papers,* the *Publication Manual of the American Psychological Association,* or
another publication that contains complete guidelines. You will find the basics of
using MLA style for documenting a research paper in Chapter 29 and for using
APA style in Chapter 30. The student research paper on page 513 uses MLA style.

T I P

**Few people memorize anything but the basics of MLA or APA style
because there are so many variations. Remember to look up each
variation. Guesswork won't do.**

EVALUATING AND REVISING

Partner Evaluation

Read your partner's paper through carefully, making check marks beside passages that are unclear or that you suspect have some other kind of problem.

Write out your initial response to the paper, noting positive aspects (Was it interesting? Did you learn something?) and possible problems (Was any part of it confusing?). Next, respond to each of the questions on the evaluation checklist on a separate sheet of paper. Finally, bracket on your partner's paper any sentences that are unclear or that you believe contain errors in usage or mechanics.

Evaluation Checklist

1. Was the writer's thesis clear in the introduction? What is the writer's main point?
2. Did the writer include sufficient information about the subject? Is any of the information confusing? If so, ask the writer to clarify it. Do you have questions about some of the information, perhaps whether it is up-to-date or credible? If so, write your questions.
3. Is any of the information unnecessary? Suggest information that the writer might consider cutting.
4. Is the information logically organized? Can you suggest another organization? If so, write down the change of sequence.
5. Do transitions guide you from one idea to the next and from one group of ideas (paragraph) to the next? If not, note the problem area.
6. Is the writer's attitude toward and treatment of the subject consistent? If not, point out changes in the writer's tone.

EDITING AND PROOFREADING

After you have considered your partner's comments and written as many revisions as necessary to produce a final draft, make sure your paper conforms to the manuscript conventions of MLA or APA style. (See page 533 for MLA manuscript form and page 538 for APA manuscript form.)

T I P

Many of the errors that might occur in recopying a paper (e.g., omitting words or lines) can be eliminated by using a word processor. However, tangled sentences and repetitions might occur when a revision is made and old sentences or phrases are not deleted. Proofread the final hard copy again, even if you proofread revisions on the computer.

RESEARCH PAPER CHECKLIST

Use the following checklist as you prepare your final draft.

1. Is the manuscript complete and arranged in proper order with correct pagination and margins?
2. Are all references properly documented according to MLA style?
3. Is every quoted passage faithful to the original and accurately punctuated?
4. Does every quotation smoothly fit the grammatical structure and context of my writing?
5. Is every statement backed by evidence or examples?
6. Are there any spelling errors or typographical mistakes?
7. Are all pronoun references clear? (Check *it, this, that, these, he/she, they, who, whom, which*)
8. Are all verbs in the proper tense and in agreement with their subjects?
9. Are any sentences passive which could be active? (Check *be* verbs: *is, are, was, were, being, be, been*)
10. Are the transitions between paragraphs and between ideas clear?
11. Does each paragraph contain a unifying main idea and support?
12. Are my words and phrases clear, correct, and at a level appropriate to the overall tone of my paper? (Check for colloquialisms, clichés, and slang)

R E M I N D E R

Proofread your final manuscript before handing it in. Remember that reading your paper aloud, or at least moving your mouth for every word, is a good proofreading technique.

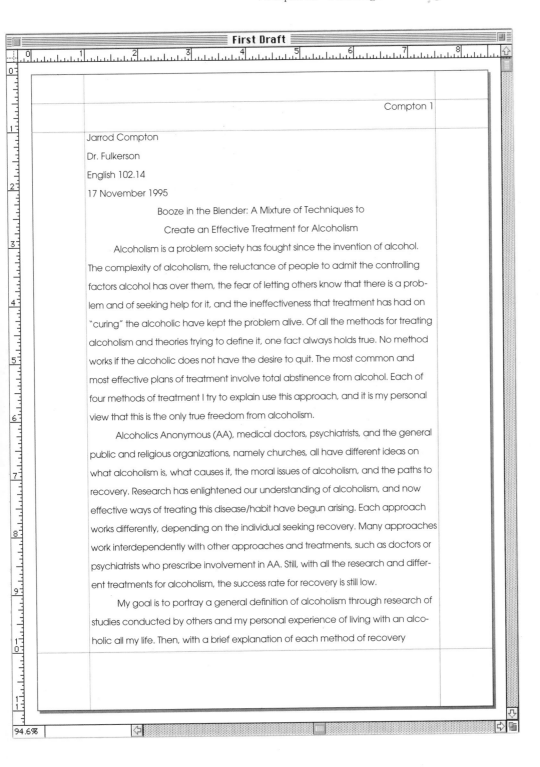

First Draft

Compton 1

Jarrod Compton

Dr. Fulkerson

English 102.14

17 November 1995

Booze in the Blender: A Mixture of Techniques to

Create an Effective Treatment for Alcoholism

Alcoholism is a problem society has fought since the invention of alcohol. The complexity of alcoholism, the reluctance of people to admit the controlling factors alcohol has over them, the fear of letting others know that there is a problem and of seeking help for it, and the ineffectiveness that treatment has had on "curing" the alcoholic have kept the problem alive. Of all the methods for treating alcoholism and theories trying to define it, one fact always holds true. No method works if the alcoholic does not have the desire to quit. The most common and most effective plans of treatment involve total abstinence from alcohol. Each of four methods of treatment I try to explain use this approach, and it is my personal view that this is the only true freedom from alcoholism.

Alcoholics Anonymous (AA), medical doctors, psychiatrists, and the general public and religious organizations, namely churches, all have different ideas on what alcoholism is, what causes it, the moral issues of alcoholism, and the paths to recovery. Research has enlightened our understanding of alcoholism, and now effective ways of treating this disease/habit have begun arising. Each approach works differently, depending on the individual seeking recovery. Many approaches work interdependently with other approaches and treatments, such as doctors or psychiatrists who prescribe involvement in AA. Still, with all the research and different treatments for alcoholism, the success rate for recovery is still low.

My goal is to portray a general definition of alcoholism through research of studies conducted by others and my personal experience of living with an alcoholic all my life. Then, with a brief explanation of each method of recovery

94.6%

First Draft

Compton 2

I'll show how each intertwine to help alcoholics on the path to mental, physical, and spiritual well-being.

Before one can draw an accurate picture of an alcoholic if he is not one himself, a basic understanding of what alcoholism is must be drawn. This is a very difficult task, however. There are four main definitions of what alcoholism is and what causes it. Each definition stems out to more specific sub-definitions, but the basics are enough to understand why it is a condition so difficult and complex to treat. Table 1 is a summary of points of agreement and divergence among the four main institutions of definition of what alcoholism is, what causes it, the moral issues concerning alcoholism, and the types of recovery recommended by each.

Table 1

	AA	Disease	Moral	Personality
What causes alcoholism?				
Moral/spiritual factors	Yes	No	Yes	No
Biological factors	Yes	Yes	No	No
Psychological factors	Yes	No	No	Yes
Social/environmental factors	Yes	No	No	Yes
Primary casual emphasis	Spiritual	Physiological	Volitional	Developmental
What is alcoholism?				
Disease/illness	Yes	Yes	No	Yes
Unitary entity	No position	Yes	No	Yes
Personality	Character flaws	Irrelevant	Weak will	Immature traits
Moral issues				
Choice about drinking	Earlier, not later	No	Yes	Yes
Responsibility for past	Yes	No	Yes	Yes
Responsibility to recover	Don't drink; work the steps	Accept treatment	Behave	Accept treatment
Acceptability of coercion	No	Yes	Yes	Yes
Recovery				
Source of healing	God	Medical	Morality	Psychotherapy
Helping style	Empathic	Expert	Exhortation	Confrontation
Attitude toward moderation	Skeptical	Prohibitive	Permissive	Variable

(Miller and Kurtz 164)

94.6%

===== **First Draft** =====

Compton 3

Alcoholics Anonymous is one the largest programs for recovery of alcoholism and drug abuse in the United States and Canada with approximately 900,000 members as of 1989(Blum and Payne 35). AA describes alcoholism as a spiritual disease affected by many other outside factors.

The disease model drawn mainly by scientists and physicians defines alcoholism as a physiological disease caused by hereditary genes. There are four core assumptions that define the disease model.

1. Alcoholism is a unitary disease entity that is qualitatively distinct and discontinuous from normality. . . . . (T)here are no gray areas; one either is or is not alcoholic.

2. The causes of alcoholism are solely biological, rooted in heredity and physiology. Behavioral, family, and personality disturbances are merely symptoms of the underlying physical abnormality in how the body reacts to alcohol.

3. The definitive symptom of developed alcoholism is an inability to control consumption after the first drink. This is an inexorable reaction to the chemical ethanol, resulting from the physical abnormality.

4. This condition is irreversible and cannot be cured, only palliated. (Miller and Kurtz 160)

This is the traditional disease model, although, the book I will cite the most does not take entirely to this, as I will explain later on.

The moral model of alcoholism is the one viewed mostly by churches and the non-alcoholic society. "If adherents to this model advert to any 'loss of control' on the part of chronic drinkers, it may be interpreted as further evidence that drunkards are generally of weak and depraved character" (Miller and Kurtz 160) is a statement that very accurately defines the view of many with the assumption of the moral model. It is also the stand usually taken when someone

94.6%

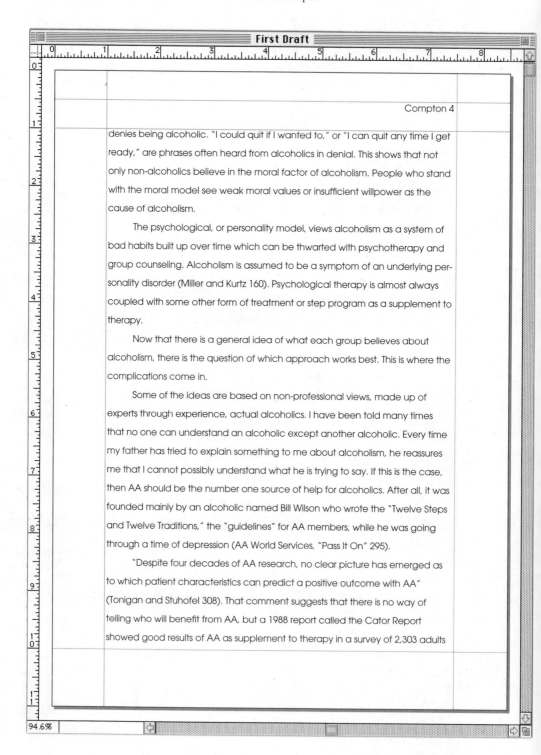

Compton 4

denies being alcoholic. "I could quit if I wanted to," or "I can quit any time I get ready," are phrases often heard from alcoholics in denial. This shows that not only non-alcoholics believe in the moral factor of alcoholism. People who stand with the moral model see weak moral values or insufficient willpower as the cause of alcoholism.

The psychological, or personality model, views alcoholism as a system of bad habits built up over time which can be thwarted with psychotherapy and group counseling. Alcoholism is assumed to be a symptom of an underlying per-sonality disorder (Miller and Kurtz 160). Psychological therapy is almost always coupled with some other form of treatment or step program as a supplement to therapy.

Now that there is a general idea of what each group believes about alcoholism, there is the question of which approach works best. This is where the complications come in.

Some of the ideas are based on non-professional views, made up of experts through experience, actual alcoholics. I have been told many times that no one can understand an alcoholic except another alcoholic. Every time my father has tried to explain something to me about alcoholism, he reassures me that I cannot possibly understand what he is trying to say. If this is the case, then AA should be the number one source of help for alcoholics. After all, it was founded mainly by an alcoholic named Bill Wilson who wrote the "Twelve Steps and Twelve Traditions," the "guidelines" for AA members, while he was going through a time of depression (AA World Services, "Pass It On" 295).

"Despite four decades of AA research, no clear picture has emerged as to which patient characteristics can predict a positive outcome with AA" (Tonigan and Stuhofel 308). That comment suggests that there is no way of telling who will benefit from AA, but a 1988 report called the Cator Report showed good results of AA as supplement to therapy in a survey of 2,303 adults

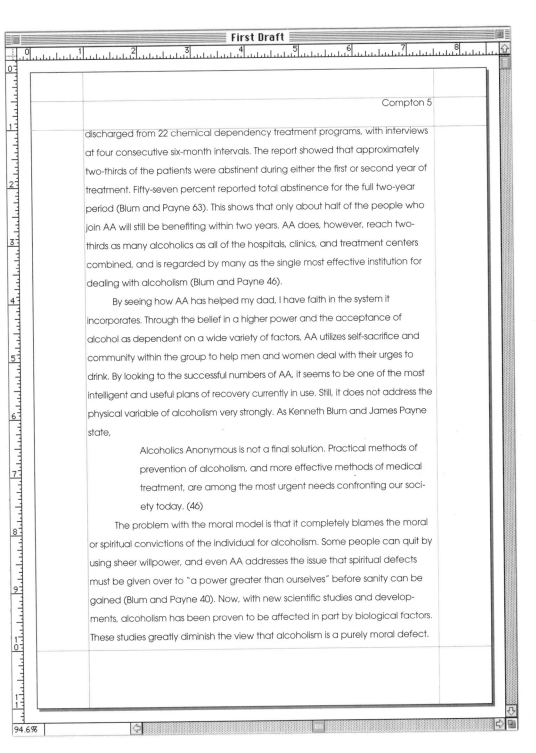

First Draft

Compton 5

discharged from 22 chemical dependency treatment programs, with interviews at four consecutive six-month intervals. The report showed that approximately two-thirds of the patients were abstinent during either the first or second year of treatment. Fifty-seven percent reported total abstinence for the full two-year period (Blum and Payne 63). This shows that only about half of the people who join AA will still be benefiting within two years. AA does, however, reach two-thirds as many alcoholics as all of the hospitals, clinics, and treatment centers combined, and is regarded by many as the single most effective institution for dealing with alcoholism (Blum and Payne 46).

By seeing how AA has helped my dad, I have faith in the system it incorporates. Through the belief in a higher power and the acceptance of alcohol as dependent on a wide variety of factors, AA utilizes self-sacrifice and community within the group to help men and women deal with their urges to drink. By looking to the successful numbers of AA, it seems to be one of the most intelligent and useful plans of recovery currently in use. Still, it does not address the physical variable of alcoholism very strongly. As Kenneth Blum and James Payne state,

> Alcoholics Anonymous is not a final solution. Practical methods of prevention of alcoholism, and more effective methods of medical treatment, are among the most urgent needs confronting our society today. (46)

The problem with the moral model is that it completely blames the moral or spiritual convictions of the individual for alcoholism. Some people can quit by using sheer willpower, and even AA addresses the issue that spiritual defects must be given over to "a power greater than ourselves" before sanity can be gained (Blum and Payne 40). Now, with new scientific studies and developments, alcoholism has been proven to be affected in part by biological factors. These studies greatly diminish the view that alcoholism is a purely moral defect.

94.6%

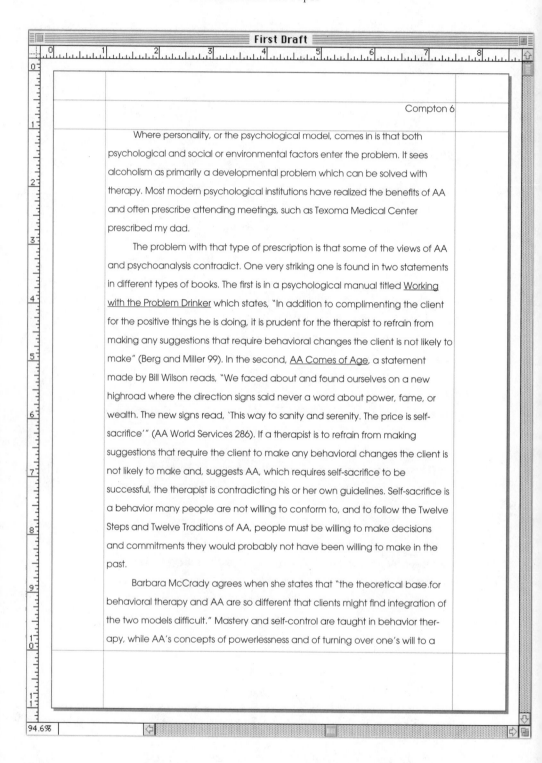

Compton 6

Where personality, or the psychological model, comes in is that both psychological and social or environmental factors enter the problem. It sees alcoholism as primarily a developmental problem which can be solved with therapy. Most modern psychological institutions have realized the benefits of AA and often prescribe attending meetings, such as Texoma Medical Center prescribed my dad.

The problem with that type of prescription is that some of the views of AA and psychoanalysis contradict. One very striking one is found in two statements in different types of books. The first is in a psychological manual titled <u>Working with the Problem Drinker</u> which states, "In addition to complimenting the client for the positive things he is doing, it is prudent for the therapist to refrain from making any suggestions that require behavioral changes the client is not likely to make" (Berg and Miller 99). In the second, <u>AA Comes of Age</u>, a statement made by Bill Wilson reads, "We faced about and found ourselves on a new highroad where the direction signs said never a word about power, fame, or wealth. The new signs read, 'This way to sanity and serenity. The price is self-sacrifice'" (AA World Services 286). If a therapist is to refrain from making suggestions that require the client to make any behavioral changes the client is not likely to make and, suggests AA, which requires self-sacrifice to be successful, the therapist is contradicting his or her own guidelines. Self-sacrifice is a behavior many people are not willing to conform to, and to follow the Twelve Steps and Twelve Traditions of AA, people must be willing to make decisions and commitments they would probably not have been willing to make in the past.

Barbara McCrady agrees when she states that "the theoretical base for behavioral therapy and AA are so different that clients might find integration of the two models difficult." Mastery and self-control are taught in behavior therapy, while AA's concepts of powerlessness and of turning over one's will to a

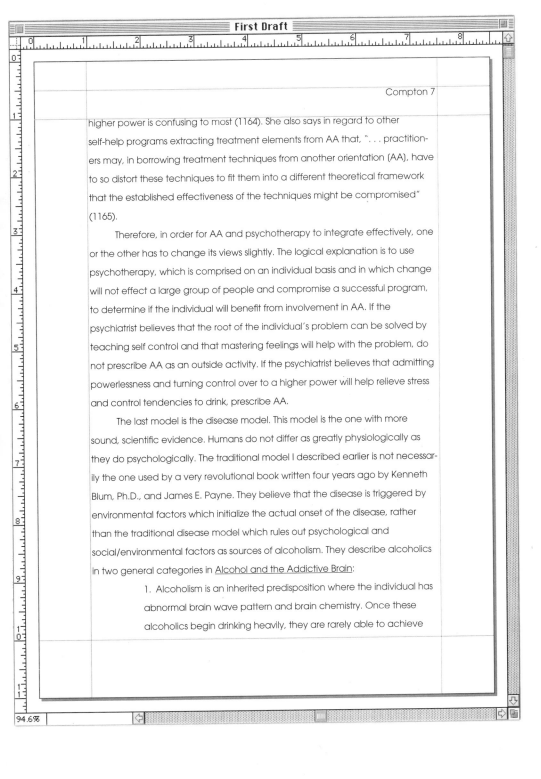

Compton 7

higher power is confusing to most (1164). She also says in regard to other self-help programs extracting treatment elements from AA that, ". . . practitioners may, in borrowing treatment techniques from another orientation (AA), have to so distort these techniques to fit them into a different theoretical framework that the established effectiveness of the techniques might be compromised" (1165).

Therefore, in order for AA and psychotherapy to integrate effectively, one or the other has to change its views slightly. The logical explanation is to use psychotherapy, which is comprised on an individual basis and in which change will not effect a large group of people and compromise a successful program, to determine if the individual will benefit from involvement in AA. If the psychiatrist believes that the root of the individual's problem can be solved by teaching self control and that mastering feelings will help with the problem, do not prescribe AA as an outside activity. If the psychiatrist believes that admitting powerlessness and turning control over to a higher power will help relieve stress and control tendencies to drink, prescribe AA.

The last model is the disease model. This model is the one with more sound, scientific evidence. Humans do not differ as greatly physiologically as they do psychologically. The traditional model I described earlier is not necessarily the one used by a very revolutionary book written four years ago by Kenneth Blum, Ph.D., and James E. Payne. They believe that the disease is triggered by environmental factors which initialize the actual onset of the disease, rather than the traditional disease model which rules out psychological and social/environmental factors as sources of alcoholism. They describe alcoholics in two general categories in <u>Alcohol and the Addictive Brain</u>:

1. Alcoholism is an inherited predisposition where the individual has abnormal brain wave pattern and brain chemistry. Once these alcoholics begin drinking heavily, they are rarely able to achieve

94.6%

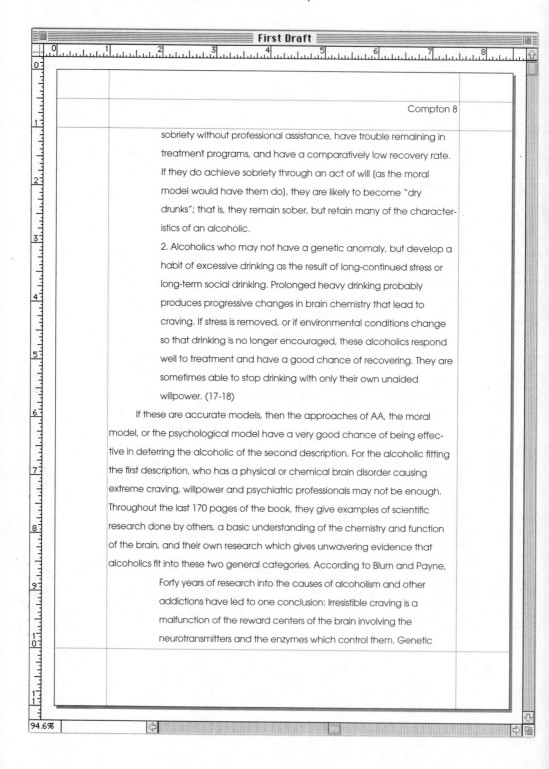

First Draft

Compton 8

sobriety without professional assistance, have trouble remaining in

treatment programs, and have a comparatively low recovery rate.

If they do achieve sobriety through an act of will (as the moral

model would have them do), they are likely to become "dry

drunks"; that is, they remain sober, but retain many of the character-

istics of an alcoholic.

2. Alcoholics who may not have a genetic anomaly, but develop a

habit of excessive drinking as the result of long-continued stress or

long-term social drinking. Prolonged heavy drinking probably

produces progressive changes in brain chemistry that lead to

craving. If stress is removed, or if environmental conditions change

so that drinking is no longer encouraged, these alcoholics respond

well to treatment and have a good chance of recovering. They are

sometimes able to stop drinking with only their own unaided

willpower. (17-18)

    If these are accurate models, then the approaches of AA, the moral

model, or the psychological model have a very good chance of being effec-

tive in deterring the alcoholic of the second description. For the alcoholic fitting

the first description, who has a physical or chemical brain disorder causing

extreme craving, willpower and psychiatric professionals may not be enough.

Throughout the last 170 pages of the book, they give examples of scientific

research done by others, a basic understanding of the chemistry and function

of the brain, and their own research which gives unwavering evidence that

alcoholics fit into these two general categories. According to Blum and Payne,

    Forty years of research into the causes of alcoholism and other

    addictions have led to one conclusion: Irresistible craving is a

    malfunction of the reward centers of the brain involving the

    neurotransmitters and the enzymes which control them. Genetic

94.6%

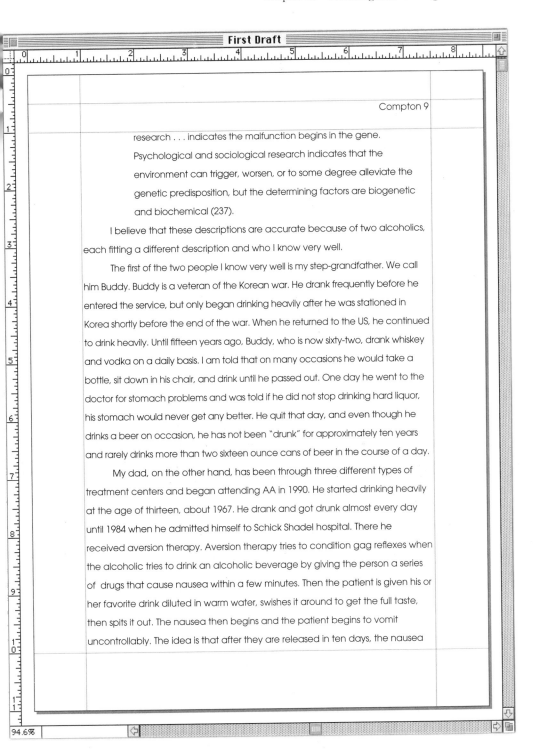

First Draft

Compton 9

research . . . indicates the malfunction begins in the gene. Psychological and sociological research indicates that the environment can trigger, worsen, or to some degree alleviate the genetic predisposition, but the determining factors are biogenetic and biochemical (237).

I believe that these descriptions are accurate because of two alcoholics, each fitting a different description and who I know very well.

The first of the two people I know very well is my step-grandfather. We call him Buddy. Buddy is a veteran of the Korean war. He drank frequently before he entered the service, but only began drinking heavily after he was stationed in Korea shortly before the end of the war. When he returned to the US, he continued to drink heavily. Until fifteen years ago, Buddy, who is now sixty-two, drank whiskey and vodka on a daily basis. I am told that on many occasions he would take a bottle, sit down in his chair, and drink until he passed out. One day he went to the doctor for stomach problems and was told if he did not stop drinking hard liquor, his stomach would never get any better. He quit that day, and even though he drinks a beer on occasion, he has not been "drunk" for approximately ten years and rarely drinks more than two sixteen ounce cans of beer in the course of a day.

My dad, on the other hand, has been through three different types of treatment centers and began attending AA in 1990. He started drinking heavily at the age of thirteen, about 1967. He drank and got drunk almost every day until 1984 when he admitted himself to Schick Shadel hospital. There he received aversion therapy. Aversion therapy tries to condition gag reflexes when the alcoholic tries to drink an alcoholic beverage by giving the person a series of drugs that cause nausea within a few minutes. Then the patient is given his or her favorite drink diluted in warm water, swishes it around to get the full taste, then spits it out. The nausea then begins and the patient begins to vomit uncontrollably. The idea is that after they are released in ten days, the nausea

94.6%

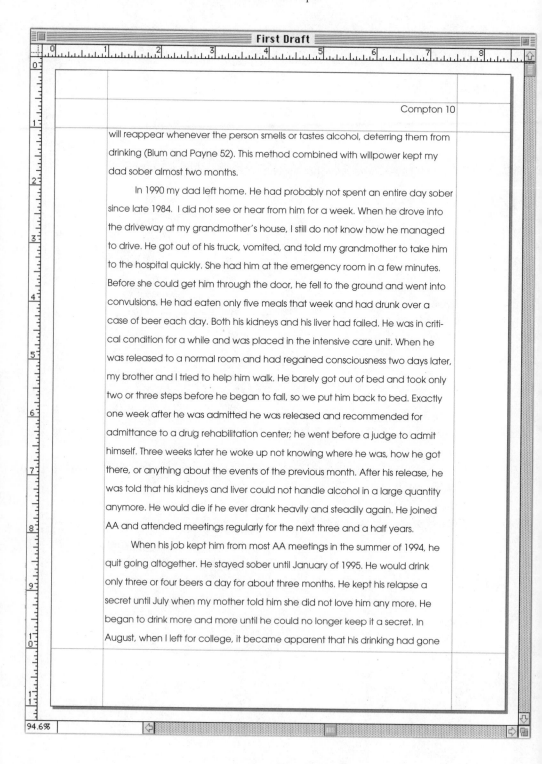

First Draft

Compton 10

will reappear whenever the person smells or tastes alcohol, deterring them from drinking (Blum and Payne 52). This method combined with willpower kept my dad sober almost two months.

In 1990 my dad left home. He had probably not spent an entire day sober since late 1984. I did not see or hear from him for a week. When he drove into the driveway at my grandmother's house, I still do not know how he managed to drive. He got out of his truck, vomited, and told my grandmother to take him to the hospital quickly. She had him at the emergency room in a few minutes. Before she could get him through the door, he fell to the ground and went into convulsions. He had eaten only five meals that week and had drunk over a case of beer each day. Both his kidneys and his liver had failed. He was in critical condition for a while and was placed in the intensive care unit. When he was released to a normal room and had regained consciousness two days later, my brother and I tried to help him walk. He barely got out of bed and took only two or three steps before he began to fall, so we put him back to bed. Exactly one week after he was admitted he was released and recommended for admittance to a drug rehabilitation center; he went before a judge to admit himself. Three weeks later he woke up not knowing where he was, how he got there, or anything about the events of the previous month. After his release, he was told that his kidneys and liver could not handle alcohol in a large quantity anymore. He would die if he ever drank heavily and steadily again. He joined AA and attended meetings regularly for the next three and a half years.

When his job kept him from most AA meetings in the summer of 1994, he quit going altogether. He stayed sober until January of 1995. He would drink only three or four beers a day for about three months. He kept his relapse a secret until July when my mother told him she did not love him any more. He began to drink more and more until he could no longer keep it a secret. In August, when I left for college, it became apparent that his drinking had gone

94.6%

First Draft

Compton 11

out of control. He called me one night, less than a week after I moved away. He was crying and began telling me, with extremely slurred speech, how lonely and depressed he was now that I had left him. It scared me. First, I knew what too much alcohol could do to his liver and kidneys, and second, he talked with a suicidal tone. I talked to him for almost four hours and finally convinced him to let my grandmother come get him and take him to the hospital. He admitted himself to a psychiatric hospital the next morning. There he was given anti-depressant medication until he went through a detoxification period of five days. Now he attends a psychotherapy session once a week and frequently goes to AA meetings. He says he feels better than he ever has now that he is dealing with the causes of his alcoholism, mainly depression, rather than just refraining from drinking. He says that his loneliness is helped by the sense of belonging he gets from AA meetings, and psychoanalysis has helped him deal with his depression. He feels more confident about staying sober this time than he has in his previous attempts to stop drinking.

The purpose of these long examples is to show how one person can quit drinking with little stimulation using only his own willpower, while another cannot refrain even when the consequence is very likely to be death. It also shows how some alcoholics do not benefit from only one type of treatment, but are more successful when more than one is incorporated to deal with the different factors which can drive him or her back to drinking. A treatment center alone helped my dad for only one month, but going through a treatment center and attending AA regularly lasted nearly four years. For some that would have been enough to stay sober indefinitely. My dad, however, shows many of the signs of an alcoholic with a genetic defect which causes a craving that is temporarily satisfied with alcohol, the "born" alcoholic (Blum and Payne 134). Stubbornness, ill-humor, irritability, anger, rage, depression, and self-destructiveness all fit my dad, but there are many other symptoms which apply to different people (Blum and Payne 17). Buddy fits

94.6%

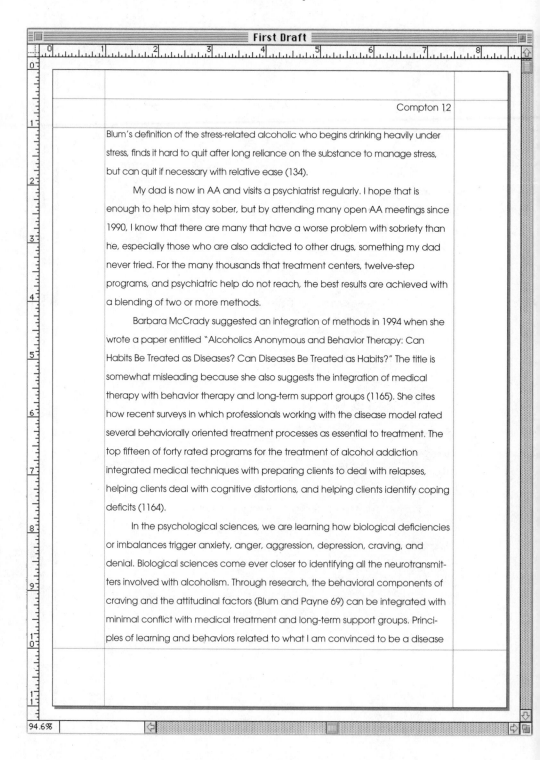

Blum's definition of the stress-related alcoholic who begins drinking heavily under stress, finds it hard to quit after long reliance on the substance to manage stress, but can quit if necessary with relative ease (134).

 My dad is now in AA and visits a psychiatrist regularly. I hope that is enough to help him stay sober, but by attending many open AA meetings since 1990, I know that there are many that have a worse problem with sobriety than he, especially those who are also addicted to other drugs, something my dad never tried. For the many thousands that treatment centers, twelve-step programs, and psychiatric help do not reach, the best results are achieved with a blending of two or more methods.

 Barbara McCrady suggested an integration of methods in 1994 when she wrote a paper entitled "Alcoholics Anonymous and Behavior Therapy: Can Habits Be Treated as Diseases? Can Diseases Be Treated as Habits?" The title is somewhat misleading because she also suggests the integration of medical therapy with behavior therapy and long-term support groups (1165). She cites how recent surveys in which professionals working with the disease model rated several behaviorally oriented treatment processes as essential to treatment. The top fifteen of forty rated programs for the treatment of alcohol addiction integrated medical techniques with preparing clients to deal with relapses, helping clients deal with cognitive distortions, and helping clients identify coping deficits (1164).

 In the psychological sciences, we are learning how biological deficiencies or imbalances trigger anxiety, anger, aggression, depression, craving, and denial. Biological sciences come ever closer to identifying all the neurotransmitters involved with alcoholism. Through research, the behavioral components of craving and the attitudinal factors (Blum and Payne 69) can be integrated with minimal conflict with medical treatment and long-term support groups. Principles of learning and behaviors related to what I am convinced to be a disease

First Draft

brought on by mental, physical, and sociological problems, and behavior change techniques could be applied to enhance change. Treatment could be delivered within a framework "that labels alcoholism as a chronic, relapsing disease, and long-term support groups such as AA would remain an integral component of treatment" (McCrady 1165).

It should be known that AA is not the only form of support group, since 51% of the people who leave AA do so because of spiritual aspects of the program (McCrady 1165), but it is my personal favorite because it has a higher success rate than other programs (Blum and Payne 35) and because of the success my dad has had while in the program.

Kenneth Blum and James Payne, in their conclusion, envision an almost utopian future in which

> (T)he chemical and electrical function of the brain chemistry is understood; pharmaceutical and nutritional intervention as an adjunct to Twelve-Step programs and professional treatment is precise and effective; and the technique of defective-gene (replacement has been perfected, enabling us to break the genetic chain of inherited addiction. In this world, each individual will be able to enjoy the inborn legacy of reward and pleasure without having the need for addictive substances, without having to pay the price of addiction and pain. (249)

With medical and psychological research, and a cooperation between the two and other programs to help and understand each alcoholic as an individual with different problems requiring different solutions, the vision will hopefully become a reality in the near future.

94.6%

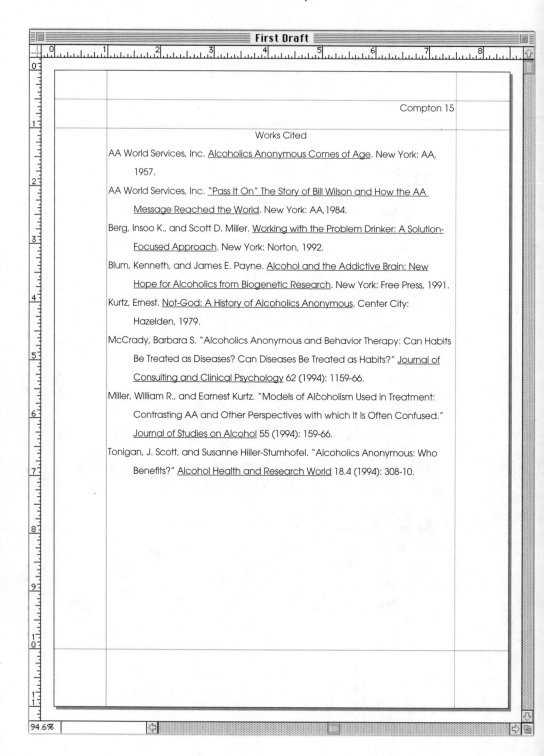

Compton 15

Works Cited

AA World Services, Inc. <u>Alcoholics Anonymous Comes of Age</u>. New York: AA,
    1957.

AA World Services, Inc. <u>"Pass It On" The Story of Bill Wilson and How the AA
    Message Reached the World</u>. New York: AA,1984.

Berg, Insoo K., and Scott D. Miller. <u>Working with the Problem Drinker: A Solution-
    Focused Approach</u>. New York: Norton, 1992.

Blum, Kenneth, and James E. Payne. <u>Alcohol and the Addictive Brain: New
    Hope for Alcoholics from Biogenetic Research</u>. New York: Free Press, 1991.

Kurtz, Ernest. <u>Not-God: A History of Alcoholics Anonymous</u>. Center City:
    Hazelden, 1979.

McCrady, Barbara S. "Alcoholics Anonymous and Behavior Therapy: Can Habits
    Be Treated as Diseases? Can Diseases Be Treated as Habits?" <u>Journal of
    Consulting and Clinical Psychology</u> 62 (1994): 1159-66.

Miller, William R., and Earnest Kurtz. "Models of Alcoholism Used in Treatment:
    Contrasting AA and Other Perspectives with which It Is Often Confused."
    <u>Journal of Studies on Alcohol</u> 55 (1994): 159-66.

Tonigan, J. Scott, and Susanne Hiller-Stumhofel. "Alcoholics Anonymous: Who
    Benefits?" <u>Alcohol Health and Research World</u> 18.4 (1994): 308-10.

Chapter 29

MLA Documentation Style

Citing Sources in Your Text

Since 1984, MLA style has used parenthetical citations instead of the old system of using little numbers correlated to footnotes (or endnotes). This welcome change makes the writer's task much easier. And instead of using *bibliography* to identify the list of books used as sources, MLA now uses *works cited,* a term that more accurately describes the books, articles, and even nonprint sources that might be cited in a paper.

Basic MLA citation format

Parenthetical citations include the author's name and the page number where the information can be found. The reader can then use the author's name to look up the full reference to the source on the Works Cited page.

Parenthetical citation

> One of the main changes in the television industry over the past decade is that the control of "monopolistic networks is crumbling" (MacDonald 264).

> MacDonald notes that over the past decade the "hard control of the (television) industry exercised by monopolistic networks is crumbling" (264).

Works Cited entry

> MacDonald, J. Fred. <u>One Nation under Television: The Rise and Decline of Network TV</u>. New York: Pantheon, 1990.

A direct quotation of four or more lines is indented one inch or ten spaces from the left-hand margin. Quotation marks are omitted.

Parenthetical citation

David Rieff, in "Victims, All?" claims that the country has become a nation of emotional cripples, a nation in which everyone has, for one or another reason, victim status:

> Imagine a country in which millions of apparently successful people nonetheless have come to believe fervently that they are really lost souls--a country where countless adults allude matter-of-factly to their "inner children," who, they say, lie wounded and in desperate need of relief within the wreckage of their grown-up selves. (49)

Note: The author's name is given in the text, so only the page number is necessary in the citation. Notice that the period goes *before* the parenthetical citation for indented quotations.

Works Cited entry

Rieff, David. "Victims, All?" Harper's October 1991: 49-56.

R E M I N D E R

Keep long quotations to a minimum; summarize or paraphrase instead.

Using more than one work by the same author

Mark Twain noted that our opinions are products of outside influences; he refers to these second-hand opinions as "corn-pone opinions" ("Corn-Pone" 1400).

Works Cited entries

Twain, Mark. "Corn-Pone Opinions." The Family Mark Twain. New York: Dorset, 1988. 1400-1403.

---. "Hellfire Hotchkiss." Mark Twain's Satires and Burlesques. Ed. Franklin R. Rogers. Berkley: U of California P, 1967. 172-74.

Using a source that is quoted in another source

> The <u>Washington Post</u> was embarrassed to find that a novel it had praised as "achingly familiar and breathtakingly new" was plagiarized from a 40-year-old book that was considered unworthy of praise at the time it was first published (qtd. in Pappas 24).

Works Cited entry

> Pappas, Theodore. "All Such Filthy Cheats." <u>Chronicles</u>. September 1994:
> 23-25.

PREPARING A WORKS CITED PAGE

The final page of your paper should be a Works Cited page on which the sources you have cited are arranged in alphabetical order. Below are some examples of MLA style. Refer to the *MLA Handbook for Writers of Research Papers* for additional examples. (See page 526 for a sample Works Cited page.)

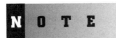

If you have used MLA style before, you probably used two spaces after periods in Works Cited entries. The 1995 edition of the *MLA Handbook for Writers of Research Papers* eliminates the two-space feature of past editions (and eliminates the problem of trying to remember to include two spaces).

Books

Book by one author

> Ehrlich, J. W. <u>The Lost Art of Cross Examination</u>. New York: Dorset, 1970.

Book by two authors

> Huff, Roland, and Charles R. Kline, Jr. <u>The Contemporary Writing
> Curriculum: Rehearsing, Composing, and Valuing</u>. New York:
> Teachers CP, 1987.

Book by three authors

> Moore, W. Edgar, Hugh McCann, and Janet McCann. <u>Creative and Critical Thinking</u>. 2nd ed. Boston: Houghton, 1974.

Note: If more than three authors are listed, use the name of the first author and "et al." (Smith, John, et al.)

Corporate authorship

> U.S. Department of Labor. <u>Report of the Secretary's Commission on Achieving Necessary Skills</u>. Washington, D.C.: Dept. of Labor, 1988.

Named editor(s)

> Levine, Mark L., and Eugene Rachlis, eds. <u>The Complete Book of Bible Quotations</u>. New York: Pocket, 1986.

Author and editor

> Twain, Mark. <u>The Autobiography of Mark Twain</u>. Ed. Charles Neider. 1966. New York: Harper, 1990.

Note: The year listed prior to current publishing information indicates the book is a reprint of an earlier work.

Edition after the first

> Perrine, Laurence. <u>Literature: Structure, Sound, and Sense</u>. 5th ed. San Diego: Harcourt, 1988.

Anthology

> Breton, Marcela, ed. <u>Hot and Cool: Jazz Short Stories</u>. New York: Plume, 1990.

Work in an anthology

> Baldwin, James. "Sonny's Blues." <u>Hot and Cool: Jazz Short Stories</u>. Ed.
> Marcela Breton. New York: Plume, 1990. 92-130.

Note: If the work is by the editor of the anthology, type *In her* (or *his*) before the title of the work. (In her <u>Hot and Cool: Jazz Short Stories</u>.)

Two or more volumes

> Paine, Albert Bigelow. <u>Mark Twain</u>. 3 vols. New York: Chelsea, 1980.

Encyclopedia

> "Coriolis effect." <u>The Concise Columbia Encyclopedia</u>. 1983 ed.

Translation

> Rousseau, Jean-Jacques. <u>The Social Contract</u>. Trans. Maurice Cranston.
> New York: Penguin, 1968.

Articles and Interviews

Article in a scholarly journal

> Dutton, Sandra, and Holly fils-Aime. "Bringing the Literary Magazine into
> the Classroom." <u>College Composition and Communication</u>.
> 44.1 (1993): 84-85.

Note: If the journal has continuous pagination, omit the issue number (.1) that follows the volume number.

Article in a magazine

> Koelbl, Susanne. "Access Denied." <u>National Review</u>. 29 Aug. 1994: 29-33.

Note: The date is used before the month instead of the volume and issue number that is used for journals.

Article in a newspaper

> Collins, Glenn. "Single-Father Survey Finds Adjustment a Problem." <u>New York Times</u> 21 Nov. 1983, late ed.: B17.

Note: If the article does not have a by-line, use the title of the article in the first position.

Book review

> Rodman, Peter. "How the West Was Won." Rev. of <u>Victory: The Reagan Administration's Secret Strategy that Caused the Collapse of the Soviet Union</u>, by Peter Schweizer. <u>National Review</u> 29 Aug. 1994: 60-61.

Published interview

> Julia Roberts. "Julia Makes Trouble." By David Rensin. <u>Rolling Stone</u>. 14 July 1994: 56-65.

Note: If the interview is untitled, use the word *Interview* without quotation marks.

Unpublished interview

> Smith, Jane. Personal interview. 23 June 1994.

Nonprint Sources

CD-ROM database

> Taylor, Jack A. "The Evolution and Future of Cognitive Research in Music." <u>Arts Education Policy Review</u>. 94.6 (1993): 35-41. <u>Magazine Article Summaries</u>. CD-ROM. EBSCO. Apr. 1996.

Note: In addition to original publication information, include the name of the database, the publication medium (CD-ROM), the name of the vendor, and the electronic publication date. If the material was not previously published in print, include the author, title, date, title of database, medium, vendor, and electronic publication date.

Internet source

U. S. Department of Education. <u>America 2000: An Education Strategy,</u>

<u>1991</u>. Online. Tenet. 30 Apr. 1996.

Note: The word *Online*, the name of the computer service, and the date of access are included in addition to publication information.

Television program

"Hezbollah." <u>60 Minutes</u>. Mike Wallace and Bob Simon. CBS. WRAL,

Raleigh. 27 Apr. 1996.

Movie

<u>Schindler's List</u>. Dir. Steven Speilberg. Perf. Liam Neeson. Universal, 1994.

Note: If focusing on Speilberg's direction of the film, list his name first and follow with *dir.* (Speilberg, Steven, dir.)

Record album or tape

Carnes, Kim. <u>Light House</u>. EMI America, 1986.

Note: If a song from the album is mentioned, place the title in quotation marks before the name of the album.

Computer program

Thiesmeyer, Elaine C., and John E. Thiesmeyer. <u>Editor</u>. Computer

software. MLA, 1990.

MLA MANUSCRIPT FORM

To prepare a manuscript or classroom assignment in MLA style, use one side of standard, 20-pound paper. Double-space all lines; left, right, top and bottom margins should be one inch. (Some instructors require wider margins in which to write comments and corrections.)

Each page (including the first) should have your last name and a page number, separated with a space but no comma, in the upper-right corner, outside the top margin, one-half inch from the top of the page. MLA style does not

require a title page; instead a heading that includes your name, course information, and date is double-spaced on the upper, left-hand side of the first page
(shown on page 513). If you are required to submit a title page or an outline,
follow your instructor's guidelines.

Chapter 30

APA DOCUMENTATION STYLE

Although there are other styles (American Sociological Association: ASA) used in the social sciences, the APA (American Psychological Association) style is the most common and the one requested by many professors.

CITING SOURCES IN YOUR TEXT

Parenthetical citations include the author's name, year of the publication, and page number. The reader can then use the author's name to look up the full reference to the source on the References page.

Parenthetical citation

> One of the main changes in the television industry over the past decade is that the control of "monopolistic networks is crumbling" (MacDonald, 1990, p. 264).

> MacDonald (1990, p. 264) notes that over the past decade the "hard control of the (television) industry exercised by monopolistic networks is crumbling."

References entry

> MacDonald, J. F. (1990). <u>One nation under television: The rise and decline of network TV</u>. New York: Pantheon.

A direct quotation of more than forty words is indented five spaces from the left-hand margin. Quotation marks are omitted.

Parenthetical citation

David Rieff (1991), in "Victims, All?" claims that the country has become a nation of emotional cripples, a nation in which everyone has, for one or another reason, victim status:

> Imagine a country in which millions of apparently successful people nonetheless have come to believe fervently that they are really lost souls—a country where countless adults allude matter-of-factly to their "inner children," who, they say, lie wounded and in desperate need of relief within the wreckage of their grown-up selves. (p. 49)

Note: The author's name is given in the text, followed by the publication date. Therefore, only the page number is necessary in the citation. Notice that the period goes *before* the parenthetical citation for indented quotations.

Note: Put in brackets any changes or additions that are necessary for clarity.

References entry

Rieff, D. (1991, October). Victims, all? <u>Harper's</u>, 49-56.

PREPARING A REFERENCES PAGE

The final page of your paper should be a page titled "References," on which the sources you have cited are arranged in alphabetical order. Initials only are given for authors' first and middle names. Only the first word of the title of an article is capitalized, and titles of articles are not placed in quotation marks. For book references, the first word in the main title and in the subtitle are capitalized; all the other words in the title begin with lowercase letters.

Books

Book by one author

Ehrlich, J. W. (1970). <u>The lost art of cross examination</u>. New York: Dorset.

Book by two authors

Huff, R., & Kline, C. R., Jr. (1987). <u>The contemporary writing curriculum: Rehearsing, composing, and valuing</u>. New York: Teachers CP.

Book by three authors

> Moore, W. E., McCann, H., & McCann, J. (1974). <u>Creative and critical thinking</u> (2nd ed.). Boston: Houghton.

Corporate authorship

> U.S. Department of Labor. (1988). <u>Report of the secretary's commission on achieving necessary skills</u>. Washington, D.C.: Author.

Note: When the author and publisher are identical, use the word *Author* as the name of the publisher.

Named editor(s)

> Levine, M. L., & Rachlis, E. (Eds.). (1986). <u>The complete book of bible quotations</u>. New York: Pocket.

Edition after the first

> Perrine, L. (1988). <u>Literature: Structure, sound, and sense</u> (5th ed.). San Diego: Harcourt.

Two or more volumes

> Paine, A. B. (1980). <u>Mark Twain</u> (Vols. 1-3). New York: Chelsea.

Articles and Interviews

Article in scholarly journal

> Dutton, S., & Fils-Aime, H. (1993). Bringing the literary magazine into the classroom. <u>College Composition and Communication</u> 44(1), 84-85.

Article in a magazine

> Koelbl, S. (1994, August 29) Access denied. <u>National Review</u>, 29-33.

Article in a newspaper

> Collins, G. (1983, November 21). Single-father survey finds adjustment a
> problem. <u>New York Times</u>, p. B17.

Note: If the article does not have a by-line, use the word *Staff* in the author
position.

Interview

> Rensin, D. (1994, July 14) Julia makes trouble. (Interview with Julia
> Roberts). <u>Rolling Stone</u>, 56-65.

Note: Because they do not provide recoverable data, personal and unpub-
lished interviews are not cited in the reference list. They are, however, cited in
the text.

APA MANUSCRIPT FORM

APA style maintains margins of at least one inch for all sides. A shortened form
of the title and page number is located on each page outside the top margin.

A title page includes the shortened title, and page number in the right-
hand corner; the title, author's name, and school is double-spaced in the center
of the page. Another line typed is immediately after the page number, beginning on the left margin, says "Running head," followed by a colon and the
shortened title. (This information is mainly for articles to be published and may
be omitted by your instructor.)

Sources are listed on a new page titled References. Entries are double-
spaced, with first lines beginning at the left margin and additional lines
indented five to seven spaces (the same amount as a paragraph). For additional guidelines, see the *Publication Manual of the American Psychological
Association,* 4th ed.

CREDITS

PART THREE

PART FOUR

PART FIVE

PART SIX

PART SEVEN

PART EIGHT

PART NINE

INDEX

STUDENT PAPERS

THE POWER OF STYLE